On behalf of the
Polish Studies Center
I take great pleasure in
presenting you this book.

Constitution and Reform in Eighteenth-Century Poland

The Constitution of 3 May 1791

USTAWA
RZĄDOWA.

~~~~~~

PRAWO UCHWALONE.

Dnia 3. Maia, Roku 1791:

~~~~~~~~~~~~~~~~~~~~~~

w WARSZAWIE,
w Drukarni Uprzywileiowaney M. GRÖLLA,
Księgarza Nadwornego J. K. Mci.

The title page of one of the first editions of the Constitution of 3 May 1791. Ustawa Rządowa, Prawo Uchwalone. Dnia 3 Maia, Roku 1791. W Warszawie, w Drukarni Uprzywileiowaney, M. Grölla...(1791).

Constitution and Reform in Eighteenth-Century Poland

The Constitution of 3 May 1791

Edited by
Samuel Fiszman

Indiana University Polish Studies Center

Indiana University Press - Bloomington and Indianapolis

Manufactured in the United States of America.

Printed on acid-free paper.

Library of Congress Cataloging-in-Publication Data

Constitution and reform in eighteenth-century Poland / edited by Samuel Fiszman.
    p.   cm.
  ISBN 0-253-33317-2 (cl : alk. paper)
  1. Poland--Politics and government--1763–1796. 2. Constitutional history--Poland. I. Fiszman, Samuel.

DK4329.5.C66 1997
943.8'025--dc21
                                   97-6877

1 2 3 4 5 02 01 00 99 98 97

Table of Contents

The ornaments in this book are taken from 18th century Polish publications

Acknowledgments

The publication of this book was made possible through generous grants from:

The Fund for Central and East European Book Projects, Amsterdam.
The Kościuszko Foundation, New York.
The American Institute of Polish Culture, Miami.
The Rosenstiel Foundation, New York.

Nine of the studies that comprise this volume were presented in their initial form at the conference "The Bicentennial of the Polish Constitution of 3 May, 1791 and the Tradition of Polish Democracy" held at Indiana University October 7-8, 1991 under the auspices of the academic exchange program between Indiana University and Warsaw University. The conference was organized under the direction of Samuel Fiszman, Professor in the Department of Slavic Languages and Literatures, with assistance from the Indiana University Polish Studies Center, the Department of Slavic Languages and Literatures, and the Warsaw University American Studies Center.

The conference was sponsored by: The International Research and Exchange Board (IREX), Polish Airlines (LOT), Stefan Batory Foundation (Warsaw), Sigma Lambda Scholars Fund, Legion of Young Polish Women (Chicago), Polish Century Club Incorporated of Indianapolis, Polish Cultural Society of Indiana, Inc. Funding was generously provided by a number of programs at Indiana University: the Multidisciplinary Ventures Fund, the Polish Studies Center, the Department of Slavic Languages and Literatures, Research and University Graduate School, the School of Law, the Russian and East European Institute, International Programs, the Political Science Department and the History Department.

In conjunction with the conference Professor Samuel Fiszman organized an exhibition at Indiana University's Lilly Library and published a catalogue of rare publications concerning 18th century Poland and the Constitution of 3 May 1791. An additional exhibition of posters, portraits, documents and secondary works was on display at the Indiana University Main Library. Also in conjunction with the conference and in celebration of the Bicentennial of the 3 May Constitution, Professor of Voice Teresa Kubiak organized and performed together with faculty and students a concert of Polish music from the Baroque to the 20th century at the Indiana University School of Music.

The conference opened with greetings and remarks by Professor Kenneth R. R. Gros Louis, Vice President and Chancellor, Indiana University; Professor Timothy Wiles, Director of the Polish Studies Center at Indiana University; Kazimierz Dziewanowski, Ambassador of the Republic of Poland; and John R. Davis, former American Ambassador to Poland.

The organization of the conference was accomplished with the assistance of Mrs. Lois Plew, the program assistant of the Polish Studies Center and Mrs. Eleanor Valentine-Jakubiak, Associate Director of the Russian and East European Institute at that time, and Professor Michał Rozbicki, Assistant Director of the Polish Studies Center at that time.

Preparations for publication of the essays that comprise this volume would have been impossible without the considerable financial assistance generously bestowed by the Office of the Vice-President and Chancellor, Indiana University's Research and the University Graduate School, the Office of International Programs and the Russian and East European Institute.

Translators from Polish and German texts which were sent in after the conference are: Dr. Janusz Duzinkiewicz, University of Iowa, Dr. Jerzy Kołodziej and Mary Helen Ayres, Indiana University, Dr. George Makowski, University of North Alabama, Dr. Philip Pajakowski, Saint Anselm College, and Beata Pawlikowska, Indiana University.

The editorial work on the volume was done with the help of the resources and cooperation of many libraries. These include the Indiana University Main Library and the Lilly Library, The Library of Congress, Washington D.C. and the following libraries and museums in Poland. In Warsaw: Biblioteka Uniwersytecka, Biblioteka Narodowa, Biblioteka Sejmowa, Muzeum Narodowe, Muzeum Historyczne; in Cracow: Biblioteka Czartoryskich, Muzeum Narodowe, Fundacja Książąt Czartoryskich przy Muzeum Narodowym; and in Kórnik: Biblioteka Polskiej Akademii Nauk. In France: Bibliothèque Polonaise, Paris.

This volume benefited greatly from the advice and help of Dr. Łukasz Kądziela at the Historical Institute of Warsaw University. In the course of the volume's preparation he looked after the affairs of its realization, enriching its contents with suggestions, contacting individual contributors in Warsaw, and assisting in securing indispensable materials in libraries and museums. Without Dr. Kądziela's help the present volume would not have come into existence. Valuable suggestions regarding problematic issues were given by Professor Piotr S. Wandycz and Dr. Andrzej Ciechanowiecki. Professor Zofia Zielińska and Dr. Łukasz Kądziela assisted in supplementing the notes. Assistance regarding the accuracy of texts was given by Professors Rett R. Ludwikowski, William B. Edgerton, Timothy Wiles who helped in various ways in the publication of the volume, Dr. Jerzy Kołodziej, my son-in-law Dr. George O'Brien, Dr. Bill Johnston and Nathaniel Wood. Additional translations and the final editing were provided by Dr. Jerzy Kołodziej and Mary Helen Ayres.

The volume was prepared for printing on computer by Mrs. Lois Plew, program assistant of the Polish Studies Center. Administration of funds was supervised by Mrs. Mollie Duckett, administrative assistant in the Department of Slavic Languages and Literatures.

In the course of organizing the conference and later in the preparation of the texts for print my wife Alicja Zadroźna-Fiszman gave unstintingly of her considerable help, advice and encouragement.

A fragment of the so called Baryczka's Panorama of Warsaw 1775-1780 by an unknown artist (Muzeum Historyczne w Warszawie). Photo W. Wolny.

Introduction

Eastern Europe, except for Poland, at this time meant the Russian, Austrian, and Prussian monarchies. In none of them with exceptions for Hungary, was there any elected parliamentary body with powers like those now contemplated for the Polish diet. All of them were lands of peasant serfdom, and while the Polish constitution did nothing to emancipate the peasants, it was in part the work of men, like Kollontay, whose thoughts moved in this direction. In none of the three monarchies did towns enjoy such self-government as was envisaged for Poland. Even in the West, even in England, there were few towns where each property-owner could actually cast a vote for councilman or mayor. In neither Russia, Prussia, nor the Hapsburg empire were burghers as free to acquire rural land as under the new Polish laws. Nor could they so readily rise into the gentry.

Robert R. Palmer[1]

In the late 18th century, along with the United States and France, the Polish-Lithuanian Commonwealth was one of the three countries in which a constitution was adopted, and the document was acknowledged as a milestone by republican thinkers in Europe and America. This volume constitutes the first attempt in English to present 18th century Poland at a time of political and social reform and cultural revival. The progressive currents in a number of fields which led to the adoption of a constitution are surveyed across the entire 18th century in Poland, and set in the context of the Enlightenment. The main subject of this book is the Constitution of 3 May 1791 seen from various angles as the most important realization of the movement toward reform in 18th century Poland. These essays also reexamine the tradition of Polish parliamentarism in the previous centuries, and the connection between the American, Polish and French ideas of a democratic state at the end of the 18th century.

This reexamination begins in this volume with an article by Norman Davies in which the Constitution of 3 May 1791, "a classic product of European Enlightenment," is discussed in the context of the history of the Polish-Lithuanian Commonwealth and its democratic traditions, with an emphasis on its limitations and its achievements, particularly in the field of religious tolerance. Countering the argument launched by the powers which partitioned the Commonwealth–that it had been destroyed because it was "ungovernable"– Davies states: "The fact is, it was destroyed exactly because the Constitution of 3 May had made it governable."

The next two studies trace the origin and development of the parliamentary system in Poland before the 18th century. Anna Sucheni-Grabowska presents the circumstances under which the Polish parliamentary system was formed and explains the reason for its steady growth in the 16th and 17th centuries. She sheds light on the manner in which the Senate, the Chamber of Deputies and particularly the regional dietines worked, and she examines the relations between the dietines and the Diet; the role of the king; the functioning of the Diet, including the struggle over the "execution of the laws;" the principle of unanimity in adopting laws in the Diet; and the circumstances under which diets were dissolved. In connection with the latter, she delves into the problem of the *liberum veto*.

Wenceslas J. Wagner describes the constitutional system of the Commonwealth as a system based "on a government of law rather than of men." He argues that the introduction of democratic institutions in the Commonwealth was not "a groundless extortion of concessions from the king," not a simple accumulation of privileges, but the recognition of fundamental rights which "set up modern solutions to the problem of the relations between the government and the governed." Turning from a "positive evaluation of Polish public life in old times" to "some abuses in the application of civic freedoms," Wagner examines the historical premises on which the ill-reputed *liberum veto* was based and compares the principles of unanimity in the Diet with an approach toward the veto and unanimity in other countries as well as in contemporary international organizations.

Both Sucheni-Grabowska and Wagner's studies serve not only as an introduction to the traditions of the Polish parliamentary system, they are also an explanation of the aims and the character of reforms in the 18th century, including those of the Constitution of 3 May.

The numerous attempts at reform in the 18th century Polish-Lithuanian Commonwealth are presented in the study by Józef Andrzej Gierowski. The author surveys the reforms and proposals for reform which were initiated in the period between the Dumb Diet in 1717 and the Four-Year Diet of 1788-92. The Constitution of 3 May, "an important step on the road to a modern state," is viewed by the author as resulting from a long quest for reform, both political and social. Gierowski then proceeds to trace the numerous steps in this process which included Stanisław Dunin Karwicki's plan for political reform in the beginning of the century; plans for military and financial reforms initiated by the Czartoryskis and the Potockis in the 1740s as well as the changes in education by Konarski, also in the 1740s; King Stanisław Leszczyński's program of political and social reforms in 1749; Stanisław Konarski's proposal for improvements in the parliamentary system in the years 1760-63; the creation of the Commission for National Education in 1773; Andrzej Zamoyski's project to codify the laws in 1778; and ending with the proposals for reform which can be found in the profound works of the main thinkers of the Polish Enlightenment, Stanisław Staszic and Hugo Kołłątaj, which were published before and during the Four-Year Diet. Gierowski's overview of the numerous reform programs and reforms in 18th century Poland is proof that it is justified to label this period in Polish history also as a century of reform.

Gierowski mentions in his article the interference of Russia and Prussia in many of the attempts at reform in the Commonwealth. The main thesis of the article by Zofia Zielińska is that the internal weakness of the Commonwealth, above all the shortcomings in its social system throughout the entire 18th century, was directly caused by the loss of its sovereignty to Russia. The turning point was in 1715-1720 when Peter I, in mediating the conflict between the nobility and August II, managed to establish in Poland a strong Russian party and a lasting Russian influence which blocked any attempt at reform. The Treaty of Potsdam in 1720 between Russia and Prussia, a treaty renewed numerous times until 1792, foresaw that mutual cooperation was a means of preventing the strengthening of the Commonwealth through reforms. Zielińska presents examples of the inner mechanism of Russian and Prussian policies which by the use of provocation, bribery and armed intervention, and by their support of the two pillars of the gentry's "golden freedom"– the *liberum veto* and the free election of the king–were able to keep the Commonwealth in a state of inertia and subjugation. In spite of such obstacles, it was possible to carry out some reforms prior to the Four-Year Diet. However, a fundamental modernization of the state took place only during the Four-Year Diet when Poland, taking advantage of a momentary weakness in the wardship of Russia and Prussia, was able to carry out a fundamental modernization of the state.

The proclamation of the Constitution of 3 May, etching by Józef Lerski acc. to a drawing by Jean Pierre Norblin 1792 (Muzeum Narodowe w Warszawie).

One of the most important and far reaching achievements of the reform movement in the Commonwealth before the promulgation of the Constitution was undoubtedly the reform in education. Kamilla Mrozowska's study deals with the close connections in this area between Polish ideas on education and those of the Enlightenment in England and France. In Poland the preparatory steps in this reform were changes introduced in the curriculum of the Piarist schools by Stanisław Konarski, the founding by him of the Collegium Nobilium, and the creation by King Stanisław August of a secular, state-run Cadets Corps. The crowning achievement of Polish educational reform was the establishment of the Commission for National Education, justly called the first ministry of education in Europe. Its work related to all educational establishments from elementary schools to universities and it had a hand in the new curriculum which it instituted and the new textbooks it published. It should further be noted that the work of the Commission for National Education had wide resonance in other countries of Europe and that it influenced the Russian school reform of 1803.[2]

Together with a program of national education, the idea of nation, of national consciousness, forms a central theme of the Polish Enlightenment. In his study Andrzej Walicki focuses on questions which are especially important "for a proper understanding of the specific contributions of the epoch of the Enlightenment to the birth of modern nationhood in Poland." Examining the concept of nationhood in the Polish-Lithuanian Commonwealth, he emphasizes its political aspects and thereby opposes the widely accepted notion which attributes ethnic nationalism to Central and Eastern Europe. Walicki analyzes "the specificity of the idea of national sovereignty" as developed by the thinkers of Polish Enlightenment, particularly by Hugo Kołłątaj and Stanisław Staszic and concludes that the Constitution of 3 May, which saw property ownership as the basis of political rights, was not the final product of the political ideology of the Polish Enlightenment. Its final transformation into the concept of a "nation of the people" is only found in the Proclamations of Tadeusz Kościuszko during the uprising.

Political and social writing during the Four-Year Diet is the topic of Anna Grześkowiak-Krwawicz's article. The author stresses that while political writing constitutes an important element in Poland's entire history, it flourished especially during the Four-Year Diet. Debates about the reform of the state took place not only in the Diet; it also became the subject of numerous large treatises, polemical articles, letters and even sermons. Grześkowiak-Krwawicz analyzes both the stylistic merits and the content of the most important published political and social works in which foreign models were utilized, particularly those from England and the United States.

Along with educational, political and social spheres, changes in other areas of Polish culture also produced a remarkable renaissance. Adam Zamoyski in his article "The Art of the Possible" examines the special role played by Stanisław August in the area of literature and the arts. An overview of the literature, drama and music of the time is followed by an analysis of the King's political, personal and artistic aims as revealed in his patronage of the arts; in his efforts to build collections of paintings, medals, and engravings; by inviting foreign and native artists; in his commissions of a multitude of architectural projects; and in his attempts to encourage others to follow his example. Although the King's grandiose plans were ultimately curtailed by the grim external situation faced by his country, he accomplished a great deal in a brief time and thanks mainly to his activity "an artistic and intellectual environment of great brilliance and sophistication had come into being in Poland."

The impact of the American Constitution on Polish political opinion before and during the Four-Year Diet is discussed by Zofia Libiszowska. America's war for independence, the Articles of Confederation and the American Constitution "met with great interest and approval in Poland" as illustrated by numerous articles and reprints in the press. During the Four-Year Diet both sides in the constitutional debate, the so-called "Republicans" and the party of reform, the "Patriots," used the American Constitution for different purposes and reached different conclusions. Most often references to the American Revolution were "rhetorical ornaments" which "nevertheless influenced the climate of the discussion and awakened social and political consciousness even if they did not offer actual models and solutions suited to Polish problems."

Although the Constitution of 3 May is present in many articles in this volume it constitutes the main subject of analysis in articles by Jerzy Michalski and Zbigniew Szcząska. Michalski, after a short presentation of Poland's international situation before and during the Four-Year Diet, focuses his attention on the preparatory stages in the writing of the draft and the final text of the Constitution; on an evaluation of the two laws passed before its adoption, the Law of the Dietines and the Law of the Cities ("the most significant social reform of the Four-Year Diet"); and, finally, on the circumstances surrounding the passage of the Constitution, where he analyzes its basic ideas and its achievements "in the realm of theory and phraseology and in its concrete norms." The last part of Michalski's article is devoted to the legislative process after May 3 and plans for future reforms which Kołłątaj termed "economic" and "moral" constitutions. Future Polish generations living in bondage, states Michalski, perceived the Constitution as the country's "great moment of rebirth, a great social turning point" and as "a symbol of patriotism and an uncompromising aspiration for independence."

Zbigniew Szcząska analyzes the articles of the Constitution and their implementation in the impressive number of laws produced during the one year when the Constitution was in force. The author shows that despite the absence in the Constitution of an explicitly formulated bill of rights and despite the fact that it preserves the division between the estates, certain statements included in the Constitution as well as regulations and laws passed after its adoption, when taken together, constitute "a kind of Polish bill of rights." Both Szcząska and Michalski emphasize that many provisions in the Constitution and in other laws passed by the Diet "indicate an attempt to gradually depart from estate division" and envision that in the future all the estates will "comprise the Polish nation." Szcząska devotes a large part of his discussion to an examination of the political system created by the Constitution and to the activities of the many newly elected bodies.

A comparison between the first three written constitutions, the American, the Polish and the French, all briefly alluded to in the previous papers, is the subject of Rett R. Ludwikowski's study. Despite the differences in tradition which existed in each of the three countries and despite the variety of local circumstances that occasioned the adoption of each constitution, the author finds far greater similarities, particularly those concerning the manner of the adoption of the constitution, the principle of the division of powers, and the establishment of an independent judiciary. An examination of the three constitutions, the author concludes, reveals an intensive interaction of ideas between the three countries. "It also shows remarkable similarities in the intellectual background of the framers of the constitutions and textual similarities in the constitutional texts."

Some of the important laws and projects briefly analyzed or only mentioned in preceding studies are more closely examined in articles that follow. The Law on Cities, which formed an integral part of the Constitution, as well as reform proposals concerning the legal status of the Jewish population are discussed by Krystyna Zienkowska who traces the differences in the situation of the Christian and the Jewish urban population before the Four-Year Diet. The Law on Cities granted the burghers most of their demands, but it did not fulfill their requirements concerning the number and the level of their participation in the Diet. The Law was applicable only to inhabitants of royal cities, nevertheless, it included some provisions that "opened a possibility that private towns also could obtain such rights." The Law on Cities was applicable only to the Christian residents of the royal cities. Economic competition, cultural differences, and the conviction that the Jewish community constituted a separate estate are among the factors which contributed to the reasons for this clause in the Law. On the other hand, the basic ideas of the Enlightenment, financial considerations, an awareness that the status of a large Jewish population must be regulated, were all reasons why the Diet undertook to reform the legal status of the Jews. The author discusses the various drafts of the reform proposals and details the provisions of the final version. Accepted by the Diet Deputation at the end of May, 1792, these provisions came too late to be passed into law by the Diet, the work of which was interrupted by the Russian invasion. Together with granting new privileges, the main idea which permeated this proposed reform was tolerance, the "acceptance of religious and cultural differences."[3]

Juliusz Bardach argues in his study that the omission in the Constitution of 3 May of the problem of mutual relations between the two components of the Polish-Lithuanian state resulted from a lack of agreement on this sensitive matter between the side which tended toward centralization and unification of the state and those with more moderate views concerning the character of the future federated state. The intention of protecting the separate rights of Lithuania found its full expression only in the law entitled the Mutual Guarantee of the Two Nations, passed unanimously by the Diet on October 20, 1791. It included provisions that guaranteed "equal representation of the Grand Duchy in the central administration and the preservation of certain institutional differences." While confirming the political rights of the Grand Duchy, it also stressed "the dual character of the state." The Law of Mutual Guarantee, as a fundamental statute, was recognized as having the same importance as the provisions of the 'Union of Lublin.'"

The Four-Year Diet's initiative aimed at modernizing Polish local government is considered to be one of the Diet's most important reforms. Łukasz Kądziela explains in rich detail that the circumstances under which the system of local government was established determined its obligations to serve both the army and civilian needs. The Civilian-Military Commissions of Order, which operated under different statutes in Poland and Lithuania, and which were elected every two years by the so-called electoral dietines, had broad powers. They were to function as "organs of local self-government and the central governments' local agents." The long catalog of tasks given to the Commissions includes, among others, the collection of annual census information, the collection of taxes, the maintenance of local roads, and the filing of reports to

The acclamation of the Constitution of 3 May. Copperplate by Daniel Chodowiecki 1791. (Muzeum Narodowe w Warszawie). Photo H. Romanowski.

An allegory of the promulgation of the Constitution of 3 May, etching by Johann Hieronimus Loeschenkohl 1791. (Muzeum Narodowe w Warszawie). Photo Anna Pietrzak.

the Central Treasury Commission and the Police Commission about the economic condition of their territory. More importantly, they were to supervise freedom of the press, primary education in elementary and parish schools, and to serve as local courts.

Among plans to reform the judiciary, the Constitution of 3 May also envisioned the appointment of "a Committee for the formation of a civil and criminal code of laws." Adam Lityński examines reforms in criminal law during the Four-Year Diet against the background of the ideas and postulates of the humanitarian movement in criminal law. According to the author, the "democratic tradition of the Polish political and legal culture" made Poland "particularly receptive to trends moderating the system of criminal law." Hence the ideas of the humanitarians fell on fertile ground in Poland and activated native efforts. The author presents the state of criminal law in the Polish Commonwealth before the Four-Year Diet and the changes discussed and adopted during the Diet, accentuating the fact that the direction of such changes "aimed at the transformation of legal procedure from privilege to universal principle in court proceedings." Main attention in the study is given to the preparatory work for the codification of law in the Polish-Lithuanian Commonwealth, subsequently called the Code of Stanisław August, and to an analysis of the proposals submitted by the two Commissions, one for Poland and one for Lithuania. Lityński emphasizes that the principle of personal equality before the law was enforced during the Kościuszko uprising and states: "The introduction of laws and legal practices in the spirit of humanitarianism in such unfavorable conditions is one of most fulfilling moments in the annals of European criminal law in the decisive Enlightenment period."

Jörg K. Hoensch's article constitutes a kind of recapitulation of the reform movement in 18th century Poland, but from a different angle, namely in the light of Polish-French relations and mutual influences. Hoensch underlines the significance of "the penetration of the *citoyen* concept of the encyclopedists"into Poland where the concept of noble citizenship had a long tradition, and the importance of the transference, through Rousseau, of Polish civic-patriotic mentality into prerevolutionary France. He focuses specifically on the influence of the French Revolution and constitutional discussions and of the American debates of 1787-89 on the framers of the Polish Constitution and discusses the essential role played by the Polish Constitution in the creation of "the ultimate draft of the French revolutionary Constitution of September 3 and 13, 1791." Like Davies in the first essay in the volume, Hoensch concludes that the demise of Poland was "an indication not of its powerlessness, but rather a discovery of its internal strength which had become frightening to the Russian Empire."

The sessions of the Four-Year Diet and particularly the adoption of the Constitution of 3 May aroused great attention and were followed by the press both in Europe and the United States. Samuel Fiszman in his presentation of the great international importance of the Constitution states that "it would be hard to find a serious journal or newspaper in Europe or the United States which did not discuss, sometimes at length, the significance of the Polish Constitution." The prominent newspaper, *Gazette de Leyde*, characterized the Constitution as "*une Pièce aussi essentielle, soit pour l'histoire de l'époque présente, soit pour le connaissance du Droit Public.*" In France the most reputable gazette, the *Moniteur,* included frequent and detailed coverage of events in Poland. In the revolutionary press the Constitution caused an immediate and heated polemic. In England Edmund Burke acclaimed the Polish peaceful revolution of 1791, contrasting it with the French. In the United States George Washington wrote: "Poland, by the public papers, appears to have made large and unexpected strides towards liberty."

The attitude of the Kościuszko Insurrection toward the resolutions of the Four-Year Diet and the Constitution of 3 May is analyzed by Jerzy Kowecki. According to the author "the Insurrection of 1794 did not grant to the legislation of the Four-Year Diet the power of binding law, but created its own system of law and government. However, this does not mean that it opposed the Diet. In various areas one can easily see references to it as well as a continuation, but a continuation which as a rule greatly radicalized solutions previously achieved." This radicalization is most clearly visible in social changes, whereby the civil rights of the burghers and their participation in government were increased, and particularly in the introduction of "comprehensive and profound changes" in the situation of the peasants. The framers of the Constitution of 3 May considered their work as a first step in the direction of reform; the Kościuszko Insurrection made a further step in "modernizing the social structure of the nation" by its "departure from a class oriented society." The Insurrection failed, but its war against the invaders and its social reforms strengthened the will of the nation to endure the partition and to continue its struggle for national independence.

After World War I, when Poland was reborn as a democratic state, the Marshal of the Legislative Diet in his speech inaugurating constitutional deliberations paid tribute to the Constitution of 3 May. The preamble to the adopted Constitution of 1921 also made a direct reference to the "glorious traditions of the historic Constitution of 3 May." Andrzej Ajnenkiel examines the role the Constitution played in the debates surrounding the creation of the 1921 Constitution. Although it came into play during the discussions about the new Constitution, the 18th century document provided only the format and some ideas and specific language rather then structural solutions for the new state. The Constitution of 3 May was also utilized in debates before the Constitution of 1935.

The last study in the volume is Piotr S. Wandycz's comparison between the circumstances which led to two revolutions in Poland, the first, the work of the Four-Year Diet between 1788 and 1792 and its culmination in the Constitution of 3 May, the second, the battle of the trade union *Solidarność* in 1980 and its victory over the Communist government in Poland in 1990. Bloodless and restrained, both revolutions brought about deep changes and international attention to Poland. The two revolutions occurred "in vastly different conditions," yet there are in both "some features which, if not analogous, permit drawing interesting parallels" as for example: "the notion of compromise and non-violence," "the concept of civil society," the notion of "returning to Europe," and "the international context of the two revolutions." Wandycz treats both in the context of the sweep of Polish history, exploring the conflicts and problems for which each was an answer.

The brief comments above should not be taken as a summary of the articles' rich content; they serve rather, to demonstrate the fact that the present volume forms a coherent whole in which individual texts complement and supplement one another.

An attempt was made to clarify in context specifically Polish terms used in individual essays, but two most frequently encountered terms require further elaboration. The first is the name of the Polish state. While the term *res publica* in reference to Poland appears in the deliberations of scholars in Cracow already at the beginning of the fifteenth century, the term *regnum* was in regular use and Jan Długosz entitled his work written in the years 1455-80 as *Annales seu Cronicae incliti Regni Poloniae*. A change in terminology came about in the next century, which saw the flowering of the Renaissance, with its ties to the classical tradition, and the flowering of Polish parliamentarism. Andrzej Frycz Modrzewski called his work, an incomplete edition of which first appeared in Cracow in 1551, and which treated reforms in the Polish state and society, *Commentariorum de Republica emendanda*, employing a term used for several decades in Polish common political parlance. As Claude Backvis writes: "A new conception of nation and society becomes crystallized around the notion of the term *Rzeczpospolita* (Republic), ...one which strives for the common weal" and one which supplanted the word *państwo* (nation) in common usage as the term referring to Poland.[4] Thus one encounters in the present volume such terms as Respublica, Commonwealth, and, after the union with Lithuania, Respublica or The Commonwealth of Two Nations, as well as the less frequently used terms (for formal differentiation), The Polish Crown and The Grand Duchy of Lithuania and their shorter versions, The Crown and Lithuania. Quite often the shortest term Poland is also used.

The other term which needs clarification is the reference to the Polish parliament, the *Sejm*, which was at times termed in Latin documents as *Dieta* and which is translated here as Diet following the example of the first English translation of the 3 May Constitution of 1791. The *Sejm*, from the moment of its final formation at the end of the fifteenth century, consisted of the Senate, appointed by the king, and the House of Representatives, which was elected. The preeminence of one or the other chamber in this period can be demonstrated in numerical terms. At this time the Senate consisted of 81 members and the House about 40. In measure with the growth in importance of the House, and in the following centuries its dominance, the numerical proportions given above also underwent changes to the advantage of the House. In the middle of the sixteenth century there were 140 senators and approximately 160 deputies, and in the middle of the seventeenth the ratio was 148 to 175.[5] According to the Law on Diets passed on May 16, 1791, the Senate was to number 132 members and the House of Representatives, 204. In the text of the 3 May Constitution the House of Representatives is designated as the primary body, "as a manifestation and repository of supreme national authority" and "a temple of legislation." A reading of the articles in the present volume indicates that even though the Constitution took the term *Sejm* to mean a conjoining of both chambers of the parliament, in actual fact the term *Sejm* was even earlier and more and more frequently understood as a synonym for the House of Representatives. In time the meaning of the term evolved and after World War I, when the Polish parliament was reestablished, as well as in the present day, it refers unambiguously to the House of Representatives.

The present work contains a few repetitions, especially in articles which examine the central issues of the book. Such repetition, while shedding light on the main theme from a variety of mutually complementary points of view, is unavoidable since it would be impossible to bring proofs to an argument without reference to specific points in the Constitution.

There was no attempt to unify the articles which comprise the book, neither from the point of view of style nor more importantly, from the point of view of reconciling opinions which differ but do not contradict one another.

A commemorative poster, printed in Chicago in 1891 on the one hundredth anniversary of the Constitution of 3 May. Copperplate by S.F. Czapliński and Pelania Majewska (Library of Congress). Reprinted from W.S. Kuniczak. *My Name is Million* (New York: Doubleday and Company, 1978). Credit: Bantam Doubleday Dell Publishing Group, Inc.

It is easy in reading a book of this nature to point to important questions dealing with Polish parliamentarism, reforms in the 18th century, the Four-Year Diet, or the Constitution of 3 May, which were barely touched on, or even omitted altogether. In this regard it is hoped that the extensive footnotes, which refer the reader to the literature on the subject matter at hand, will serve as partial recompense.

A different fate awaited each of the first three published constitutions, lawful documents which emerged from the ideas of the Enlightenment and which laid the foundations of modern constitutionalism. The 1787 Constitution of the United States, revered and honored as the basis of the American political system, is still in force, though revised and supplemented by later amendments. The French Constitution of 1791 lasted until 1793, when the Jacobean Convention passed a new Constitution. The Polish Constitution was formally binding for only fourteen months at which time it was abolished as a result of armed intervention by Russia. Even though it could not serve as a binding legal document, it has survived to this day as a symbol of values which foreign might was incapable of destroying. Unable to function as a guarantor of national sovereignty and the freedom of its citizenry, the Constitution was a guardian of the nation's memory of espoused social and political reforms and of aspirations for national independence during the long night of bondage when Poland was not only crossed off the map of Europe, but attempts were made to eradicate all memory of its existence. Playing a momentous role in its immediate effect, which began a transformation both of the society and of the state, the Constitution also played a significant role in its long-term effects as a vibrant factor present in the life of the nation. The polemics which accompanied its creation continued when its provisions were given greater precision by inclusion in specific statutes. These polemics already began to change their character during the Kościuszko Insurrection and underwent fundamental changes after the fall of the state, when the Constitution became the point of departure for differences of opinion regarding, in equal measure, the reasons for the loss of independence and the form that the reborn nation would assume.

The controversy surrounding the manner in which the Constitution was viewed gathered strength after the defeat of the November Uprising in 1830. The Literary Society, established in Paris in 1832 under the leadership of Prince Adam Czartoryski, in its yearly celebrations on the anniversary of the Constitution declared itself to be the faithful continuator of ideas contained in the 3 May Constitution. This tradition was opposed by the emigree Polish

Democratic Society, among others, who sharply criticized the limited nature of social reforms contained in the Constitution. In different form, such arguments found their continuation in the debates of various political parties in the 19th and 20th centuries, in independent Poland after World War I, and in the altered situation of post World War II Poland.

During the period of the November 1830 and January 1863 uprisings differences in interpreting the Constitution found expression mainly in the programs of political parties or in the pronouncements of those representing a variety of ideological orientations, both historians and writers like Joachim Lelewel and Adam Mickiewicz. In the second half of the 19th century, the polarization of positions regarding the Four-Year Diet and the Constitution of 3 May is evident in extensive historical studies where contending attitudes toward the Constitution formed a part of the controversy between two schools in Polish historiography, the so-called Cracovian and Varsovian. Thus, the Constitution played a significant role in the most important debates about the fate of the nation's past and future. It came to play yet another role in moments especially threatening to the nation's existence, as Stefan Kieniewicz points out in his discussion of national uprisings in the 19th century: "In moments of a national crisis when it becomes necessary to rouse the masses to repel the invader, arguments about the past fall silent and 3 May is incorporated into a patriotic stream which unites all classes of the population under one banner."[6] Such an assertion can be applied with equal justification to later times: the period of World War I; the German occupation and the Warsaw uprising during World War II; and the enslavement of Poland after the war. The Constitution served as a catalyst for national accord not only in exceptional moments, but, unfailingly it played its role in the daily life of the people and in the public opinion of many generations, where the Constitution is not simply an exemplar of legal norms, but rises to the level of a historical symbol of patriotism and becomes a personification of the nation's indestructible spiritual strength.

The three constitutions--the American, Polish, and French--the most significant expression of constitutionalism of the Enlightenment, played an important role in the history of their nations, but it fell to the Polish Constitution to play a role not required of the other two: that of a symbol guiding the efforts of future generations in their struggle to preserve the Polish Nation and re-establish the Polish State. As Stanisław Staszic declared: "Even a great nation may fall, but only a contemptible one can perish." The memory of 3 May 1791, a day which confirmed Poland's sovereignty, helped the nation to survive. To quote Robert Howard Lord:

> The work of the Four Years' Diet, the lofty character of its leaders, the generous enthusiasm and high hopes of the period, the Constitution of the Third of May, the effort of the Polish army in 1792, and the new struggle for liberty under Kościuszko in 1794--these things brought at least this inestimable advantage that they furnished the nation with a treasure of spiritual goods upon which it could live and maintain its faith in itself and its future after the loss of its independence. From these tragic but ennobling experiences later generations could convince themselves and the unprejudiced outside world that this nation had not deserved to perish. And so, we think, the Patriots of 1788 deserved well of their country. They did not succeed in saving the Polish state--perhaps no one could have done that; but they did succeed in saving Polish nationality and the spiritual life of their people, which was, after all, more important.[7]

Notes

1. Robert R. Palmer, *The Age of the Democratic Revolution.* v.1 (Princeton, Princeton U.P. 1959), pp. 433-34.

2. For a more detailed discussion concerning the influence of the work of the Commission for National Education on the Russian school reform of 1803, see: Nicholas Hans, *History of Russian Educational Policy (1701-1917)* (London: P.S. King, 1931), pp. 35-41; Stefan Truchim, *Współpraca polsko-rosyjska nad organizacją szkolnictwa rosyjskiego w początkach XIX wieku* (Polish-Russian cooperation in the organization of the Russian school system at the beginning of the 19th century) (Wrocław: Ossolineum, 1960); Jerzy Skowronek, "Udział A.J. Czartoryskiego w pracach nad reformami wewnętrznymi w Rosji, 1801-1807" (A.J. Czartoryski's participation in the works of the internal reforms in Russia, 1801-1807) *Przegląd Historyczny* 3 (1967) 471-73; Daniel Beauvois, *Lumières et Société en Europe de l'Est: l'Université de Vilna et les écoles polonaises de l'Empire russe (1803-1832)* (Paris: Champion, 1977) Vol. 2, passim; W.H. Zawadzki. *A Man of Honour, Adam Czartoryski as a Statesman of Russia and Poland 1795-1831* (Oxford: Clarendon Press, 1993), pp. 52-58.

3. According to Daniel Beauvois: "It is beyond question that it is to Polish influence (notably that of Prince A.J. Czartoryski) on the young Tsar Alexander I that the statute for the Jews of the Empire of 9 December 1804 owes its relative liberalism...Czartoryski, then the most influential of the Emperor's familiars, was himself inspired, as to the Jewish question, by Polish Enlightenment thought which

had been manifested in the Four Year Diet's lengthy discussion of social reforms...There is no doubt that the prince was acquainted with the projects aimed at introducing equal rights for the Jews, proposed during the Polish Four Year Diet." in: Chimen Abramsky, Maciej Jachimczyk, Antony Polonsky, eds. *The Jews in Poland* (Oxford: Basil Blackwell, 1986) p. 81; Jerzy Skowronek, Udział A.J. Czartoryskiego, 473-74; W.H. Zawadzki, *A Man of Honour*, p. 81.

4. Władysław Czapliński, *Dzieje sejmu polskiego do roku 1939* (The history of the Polish Parliament until 1939) (Kraków: Wyd. Literackie, 1994), pp. 26-27, 48.

5. Claude Backvis, "Les Thèmes majeurs de la pensée politique polonaise au XVI siècle." *L'Annuaire de l'Institut de Philologie et d'Histoire Orientales et Slaves*, 14 (1957): particularly part 2.

6. Stefan Kieniewicz, "Tradycja Trzeciego Maja w latach powstań narodowych (1830-1864)." (The tradition of 3 May in the years of national uprisings (1830-1864) in *Sejm Czteroletni i jego tradycje*, ed. Jerzy Kowecki (Warszawa: PWN, 1991), p. 236. A history of this tradition in the 19th and 20th centuries occupies one half of this volume. This tradition is also the main subject of a large volume *Konstytucja 3 Maja w tradycji i kulturze polskiej* (The Constitution of 3 May in Polish tradition and culture) ed. Alina Barszczewska-Krupa (Łódź: Wyd. Łódzkie, 1991). This subject is also discussed in a number of articles in *Pierwsza w Europie. 200 rocznica Konstytucji 3 Maja 1791-1991* (The first in Europe. The 200th anniversary of the Constitution of 3 May 1791-1991), ed. Henryk Kocój (Katowice: Uniwersytet Śląski, 1989) as well as in the following publications: Stanisław Dzięciołowski, *Konstytucja 3 Maja w tradycji polskiej* (The Constitution of 3 May in Polish tradition) (Warszawa: Epoka, 1991); Jan Ziołek, *Konstytucja 3 Maja. Kościelno-narodowa tradycja święta* (The Constitution of 3 May. The holiday in the church-national tradition) (Lublin: Katolicki Uniwersytet Lubelski, 1991); Andrzej Wierzbicki, *Konstytucja 3 Maja w historiografii polskiej* (The Constitution of 3 May in Polish historiography) (Warszawa: Wyd. Sejmowe, 1993); *Konstytucja 3 Maja, 200-lecie tradycji* (The Constitution of 3 May, 200th anniversary of the tradition), ed. Barbara Grochulska (Warszawa: Wyd. Sejmowe, 1994); *Konstytucja 3 Maja i jej tradycje* (The Constitution of 3 May and its traditions) (Wrocław: Ossolineum, 1992); *Konstytucja 3 Maja prawo-polityka-symbol* (The Constitution of 3 May, law-politics-symbol), ed. Anna Grześkowiak-Krwawicz (Warszawa: Polskie Towarzystwo Hitoryczne, 1992).

7. Robert Howard Lord. *The Second Partition of Poland. A Study in Diplomatic History.* (Cambridge: Harvard Univ. Press, 1915), p. 491.

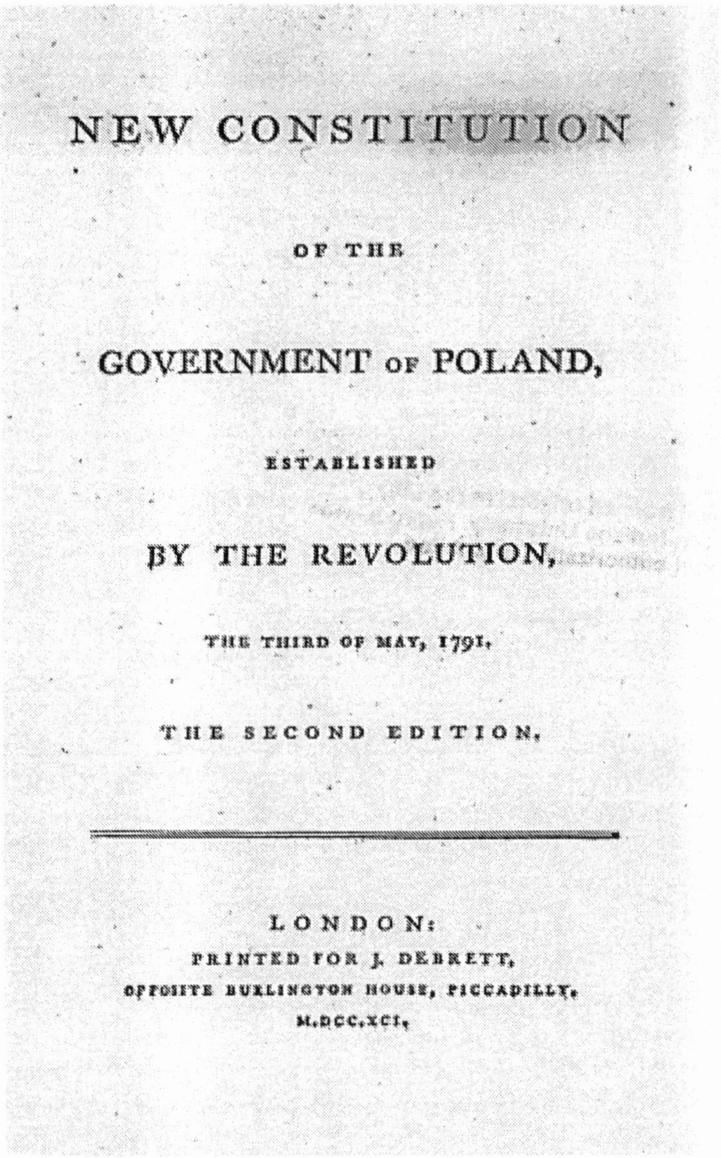

NEW CONSTITUTION

OF THE

GOVERNMENT OF POLAND,

ESTABLISHED

BY THE REVOLUTION,

THE THIRD OF MAY, 1791,

THE SECOND EDITION,

LONDON:

PRINTED FOR J. DEBRETT,

OPPOSITE BURLINGTON HOUSE, PICCADILLY,

M.DCC.XCI.

New Constitution of the Government of Poland established by the Revolution the Third of May 1791. The second edition. London: J. Debrett, 1791. Translated by Franciszek Bukaty the Polish Minister Resident in London, it also included the Declaration of the States Assembled, the Law on Dietines and Law on Cities. The title page. (Indiana University Lilly Library).

1

The Third of May 1791

Norman Davies

Compared to the events in the USA or in France, the Polish Revolution was rather mundane. The scene in the Senate Chamber of the Royal Castle in Warsaw on 3rd May 1791, was tense enough but not in itself specially dramatic. Some two hundred members of Parliament were meeting on the second day after the Easter recess, and a noisy crowd, twenty or thirty thousand strong, was listening expectantly in the gallery and beneath the windows. They were witnessing a sort of peaceful, parliamentary *coup d'état*. The parliamentary agenda had been changed without notice, and, in the absence of many potential opponents, a bill for the radical reform of the country's government was being pushed through. The bill's promoters, who included the King, the Speaker and self-styled "Patriotic Party," had been preparing in ill-kept secrecy. Its opponents, who had met the previous night in the Russian Ambassador's residence to discuss armed intervention, had been caught off balance. When they raised points of order against the breach of parliamentary procedures, the Speaker told them: "This is a day of revolution, and all formalities must be suspended." The King (who was to prove the last king of Poland) was present with an armed retinue. When his throne was mobbed by supporters, eager for the royal assent, he swore an oath proffered by the Bishop of Cracow, then spoke the words, *Juravi Domino, non me poenitebit. "Przysięgałem Bogu, żałować tego nie będę."* (I have sworn to God; I shall not regret it.) The company then trooped out to the cathedral for the new Constitution to receive the Church's blessing. At the same time, a

1

group of oppositionists headed for the Warsaw courthouse to lodge a legal protest. It was the sort of controversial day which might have taken place in any of the few countries which possessed a parliamentary system at the time. It would probably not be so well remembered if it had not led first to war with Russia, and within four years to the destruction of the entire State. For the Constitution sparked a crisis which was to cut short Poland's independent political history until the twentieth century.

The Constitution of 3 May was the culmination of the work of the Great Parliament which had been in almost constant session for the past three years. The extensive reform programme of that Parliament had been conceived by the King as a corollary to his intended revision of the Republic's humiliating relationship with its neighbors. Ever since the disaster of the First Partition of 1772, he had been hoping to re-establish an independent position in foreign affairs, and, after the death of Frederick the Great in 1786, and the succession of a more sympathetic Prussian King, he had felt things moving his way. In 1787, when he met the Empress Catherine at a galley on the Dnieper at Kaniów, he had urged the Russians to accept Poland-Lithuania as a genuine partner and ally. He had hoped to put an end to the decades of chaos and resentment resulting from Russia's constant interference in the Republic's affairs. At Kaniów, however, he had received a rude shock. The Empress turned him down flat - indicating that she had no interest either in a reformed Poland or in a Polish alliance. She wanted Poland-Lithuania to remain a Russian protectorate. But the parliamentary reform programme went ahead regardless. From the start, therefore, the work of the reformers proceeded in defiance of Russia's wishes, and was seen by all concerned as a process designed to shake off Russian domination of Poland. The recovery of independence, desired by the King and reformers, but opposed by a clique of pro-Russian magnates, lay at the center of the operation.

At the same time the Great Parliament had been turned into a confederation, so that it could operate by majority voting. This procedure was aimed at defeating the *liberum veto*, the nefarious practice retained at Russian insistence ever since 1717, and regularly used by St. Petersburg's Polish agents to block unwelcome changes. The *liberum veto* was cynically recalled by Russian and Prussian propaganda as evidence of Poland's unfitness to govern itself. In reality, it had only survived thanks to the treaties of guarantee which had held the Republic in subjection for seventy years.

Logically enough, the first celebration of the Constitution took place on the first anniversary, that is on 3 May 1792. The streets of Warsaw were lined with troops in gala uniforms. The bands and banners of the city guilds supplied the music and the decorations. A procession to the Church of the Holy Cross was headed by ministers, senators, and by delegations from distant towns and palatinates. Amidst the ringing of bells, and shouts of *Vivat rex*, and patriotic songs, the King arrived in a crystal coach to deliver his speech: "*Prawdziwy i jedyny cel utworzenia nowej formy rządu nie był inny, tylko żeby, ile po ludzku być może, wszyscy narodu polskiego współziomkowie równie byli uczestnikami udziału wolności i ubezpieczenia własności swoich...*" (The real and exclusive aim of this new form of government was none other than to ensure, as far as is humanly possible, that all fellow-citizens of the Polish nation should in equal measure share in the common liberties and the security of their property.)

After a solemn Mass, the King laid the foundation stone of the Church of Divine Providence (which was destined never to be built). For even as they celebrated in Warsaw, a Russian Army was preparing to invade, and to crush the Constitution and all it stood for. Less than two weeks later, the Russians crossed the frontier, accompanied by a group of Polish collaborators. That invasion began the cycle of events which was to destroy the Polish-Lithuanian state.

Three May 1792 proved to be the last occasion for many years when the Constitution could be openly celebrated. For most of the nineteenth and twentieth-century Warsaw has been ruled by alien powers - by Prussians, Tsars, Nazis, or Communists, none of whom were eager to permit the anniversary to be publicly remembered. In the last 200 years, the anniversary celebrations of 3 May have been permitted on less than one quarter of the possible occasions. It is a fair barometer of Poland's subjugation. In our century, they took place, interestingly enough in 1916, 1917 and 1918 under German Occupation, from 1919-1939 during Poland's brief inter-war independence; and for a couple of years after the Second World War. After that, they were totally suppressed by the Communist Government until revived, under pressure from Solidarity, in 1981.

So, one is dealing with a Constitution that never really took off, that was suppressed almost as soon as it was enacted. It was an infant strangled in its cradle. That is why it raised such emotions, why it has become one of the prime symbols amidst all of Poland's other terrible oppressions.

The Constitution of 3 May needs to be discussed in the context of the country which produced it. The Commonwealth, of Poland-Lithuania - the *Rzeczpospolita* - was a very different country from the Poland of today. Like the United Kingdom of England and Scotland, it was a dual state which had passed from a personal union of crowns to a voluntary constitutional union. In 1791, the Kingdom of Poland and the Grand Duchy of Lithuania had been joined together for more than four hundred years, that is longer than England and Scotland. It was no passing aberration, no *Saisonstaat* as the Prussians were apt to say. Indeed, it was much older, and better established than the neighboring Kingdom of Prussia.

The Polish Commonwealth was also very large. Suffice it to say, that its population of 11 million was twice that of Great Britain, and its territory of roughly 1 million km² was similar to that of France or of Texas. Prior to the rise of Muscovy, it had been absolutely the largest state in Europe.

More importantly, Poland-Lithuania was not a democracy of the modern type, but a democracy nonetheless, with ancient roots and strong principles. It was a democracy of nobles, who elected their King and who undertook their deliberations both in provincial assemblies and in the central Diet or Parliament. Contrary to what its enemies said, it was a democracy which worked - at least till the era of its terminal decline. If it resembled any of its neighbors, it was less like the great Russian Republic of Novgorod, destroyed by the Muscovites, and more like the Holy Roman Empire on the other side in Germany. Its noble citizens enjoyed far-reaching liberties which included the Principle of Unanimity and the Right of Resistance. The former invalidated any law that was not guaranteed by all. The latter laid down that any ruler who broke the laws could be legally opposed. The fundamental privileges of the nobles, their *Magna Charta,* dated from 1374, their freedom from arrest, their *Habeas Corpus,* from 1425. Their statute from 1454 conceded that no new tax would be levied, and no army raised without the consent of the dietines. Their constitution of *Nihil Novi* dated from 1505 ruled that no new laws could be introduced without the consent of both chambers of the Parliament. The final Act of Union between Poland and Lithuania took place at Lublin in 1569.

One would like to add some nuances to this abbreviated, not to say rose-tinted picture, but one has also to say that even the basic facts do not always find their way into general textbooks. To those who point out, quite correctly that these noble democrats of Poland-Lithuania were serf-owners, and few historians would deny them the title of democrat for that. Serfdom in east and central Europe like slavery in the southern states, repulsive though it is to modern ideas, was a fact of life which Poland shared with all its neighbors - Germany, Austria, Russia. One thing looks slightly odd. Among all those thousands of American historians working on their early constitutional period, hardly anyone has noticed the very obvious similarities between the USA and Poland-Lithuania.

Old Poland was a multinational, multidenominational and multicultural society. Multiculturalism is a common term in modern politics; and one cannot suggest that Poland-Lithuania was somehow a forerunner of diversification. It is not entirely irrelevant to enquire how a pre-modern state sought to cope with the numerous national, religious and linguistic groups in its midst. It did so in ways, which for their day, were rare, if not exceptional.

At a time when most countries in Europe were intent on creating a modern, centralized and bureaucratic state, Poland-Lithuania persisted in maintaining its traditions of local and communal autonomy. At a time when most of Europe was racked by murderous religious wars, Poland-Lithuania succeeded in practicing a far-reaching, though by no means perfect degree of religious toleration.

The various communities involved make a long list. The vernacular languages were, in order of their frequency: Polish, Ruthenian (that is, in modern parlance, Ukrainian and Byelorussian), Yiddish, Lithuanian, German, Tatar, Armenian.

The official languages in order of importance, were: in the Kingdom of Poland, Latin, Polish, and with time an inimitable blend of Latin and Polish known as *macaroni*: in the Grand Duchy of Lithuania to 1600, *ruski* (that is, Old Byelorussian), later, as in the Kingdom, Latin and Polish: and finally, in the cities of Royal Prussia, German and Latin.

The main religious communities included the following: Roman Catholicism (which was the religion of state), Calvinist Protestant (which attracted a large sector of the nobility in the late sixteenth century), Lutheran Protestant (in the German cities), the unitarian Polish Brethren, Greek Catholics or Uniates (who appeared in force in the Ruthenian population after 1596), Orthodox Christians including refugee Old Believers from Russia, Armenian Christians, Moslems, Orthodox rabbinical Judaism, Chassidid Judaism (which began life in Poland, in the 1730s), Karaite Judaism, and lastly Jewish Frankism, which appeared in the 1750s. As a result, the sacred languages which were in circulation, and which were taught in the religious schools, included: Church Latin, Old Church Slavonic, Armenian, Arabic and Hebrew. What present-day Poles do not always realize: in those earlier centuries, the link between Polishness and Roman Catholicism was not so close as it became in later times, also, that Polish-speaking Roman Catholics formed barely 50% of the total inhabitants - it is impossible to say exactly because there was no census prior to the partitions.

Communal autonomy was one of the pillars of this complicated society. There were autonomous jurisdictions on the social plane where nobles, clergy, and burghers each governed their own affairs in their own assemblies, under their own privileges, and in their own law courts. And there were autonomous jurisdictions of different sorts relating to particular regions, cities, or religious groups. A couple of examples must suffice - the city of Gdańsk-Danzig, and Polish Jewry.

Danzig, which was the chief port and the largest city of the *Rzeczpospolita*, enjoyed greater autonomy than any other comparable city in northern Europe. Having begged for incorporation into the Kingdom of Poland in the mid fifteenth century, it was granted extensive charter and liberties in 1585 by Poland's great King, Stefan Batory who thereby ensured its loyalty for the rest of the Commonwealth's existence. The citizens of Danzig were solidly German by language and culture, to the point where Polish visitors to the city were habitually reduced to conversing there in Latin. Yet these German Danzigers were fiercely proud of being Polish. The one person the Danzigers loved to hate was the German King of Prussia and hence Germany. That is why, when Danzig was so annexed in 1793, without their consent, they promptly rebelled.

The Jewish community of Poland-Lithuania also enjoyed far reaching autonomy. It was protected by royal charters going back to the thirteenth century, and frequently renewed. The Jews had the unconditional right to practice their religion without harassment. They governed themselves in a self-regulating *kahal* or "commune" in most Polish cities. They collected their own taxes; and for two hundred years, until 1764, they legislated and debated in their own parliament, the Council of the Four Lands. In an age when Jews were barred from practically every major country of Europe, most notably from Germany and Russia, Poland-Lithuania provided the one large safe haven where Jewry could survive and, generally speaking, flourish. It was the great "place of refuge," and should not be forgotten. At least 80 per cent of all Jews alive today can trace their family origins to somewhere in Poland-Lithuania.

Of course, the old slogan "Paradise for the noble, purgatory for the Jews, and hell for the peasants" requires a detailed gloss. The realia are complicated enough.

The statutes *De non tolerandis Judaeis* for example, deserve mention. Several Polish cities, including the capital, Warsaw, passed legislation against Jews residing and trading within the city walls: and that legislation is sometimes cited to suggest that Warsaw was guilty of discriminating against Jews. On the other hand, one has to recognize that the Jews were in a similar position to several other groups, such as nobles and peasants, who were also barred from residing in the city. Indeed, the great mass of the population who were serfs *ad terram adscripti*, tended to think of the Jews as over privileged. What is important, is to see what actually happened. In the case of Warsaw, the Jews, who were barred from the city, joined forces with the Polish nobles, who were

Die neue Polnische Constitution
La nouvelle Constitution Polonnoise

An allegory of the Constitution of 3 May. Stanisław August extending his protection to peasants, tradesmen, as well as to the arts and justice. Copperplate by Daniel Chodowiecki in "Goettinger Taschen Calender für das Jahre 1793" (Muzeum Narodowe w Warszawie). Photo H. Romanowski.

also barred from the city, and set up a series of commercial and residential districts in the immediate vicinity of the city walls. The Noble-Jewish alliance was one of the dominant features of old Polish society. Without it, there is no way of explaining how the city of Warsaw, whilst trying to enforce a policy of not tolerating Jews, was also the center of absolutely the largest Jewish community in the world.

On the wider question of religious toleration, Poland-Lithuania had no equal. It was the only major state of early modern Europe to have a statute of universal toleration built into its fundamental laws. The act of the Confederation of Warsaw, first enacted in 1573 and many times renewed, required the King and all the nobles to settle religious differences without resorting to force. The only small group to be specifically excluded, on the insistence of the Calvinists, were the Polish Brethren, who, as unitarians were regarded as less than Christian by the main Christian denominations. And even they were able to escape any effective persecution through the sympathy of various protective cities or magnates. It has to be said that the principle of toleration was sometimes observed in the breach; and that in the eighteenth century, the Roman Catholic Church grew more militant, more exclusive. Even so, in Poland-Lithuania there was no St. Barthelemy's Eve, and no wars of religion. Compared with countries like Great Britain which did not fully emancipate its Catholics until 1829 and its Jews until 1860, the Polish record was impressive.

In all these questions of autonomy and toleration, there was one obvious and damaging gap - namely in Rus', that is, in today's Ukraine. Ukraine spent four to five centuries of its formative development first in Lithuania then in Poland- and it is that long experience which made it so very different from its fellow East Slav neighbor, Russia. It had a rich cultural identity, immense economic potential and great strategic significance. One might have expected that the supposedly democratic, and tolerant Republic would have paid attention to its interests. Yet, for a whole gamut of reasons, Ukraine was not granted the liberties which others enjoyed. The Orthodox Church of the East was never on an equal footing with Roman Catholicism, and for four decades in the early seventeenth century was actually suspended. The Uniate Greek Catholic Church to which most Ukrainians belonged after 1596, was not admitted to the episcopal benches of the Senate. The Dnieper Cossacks, who supplied the principal military force of the eastern palatinates were denied both the full autonomy and status of nobility which they much desired. As a result, after several bloody revolts, the Cossacks under Bohdan Chmielnicki launched the Rising to end all Risings in 1648. The stirring and tragic events of those years are known to all literate Poles through the historical novels of Henryk Sienkiewicz. Ten years after 1648, when a proposal emerged for the creation of a tripartite Republic, i.e. Poland-Lithuania-Ukraine, the proposal was no longer politically viable. The greater part of Ukraine, including Kiev, jumped straight from the Polish frying pan into the Russian fire, from which it is extricating itself only now. By 1791, twenty years after the First Partition, when Lwów and much of Galicia had passed to Austria, most of the Republic's Ukrainians had long since passed under Russian control.

But to return to the Constitution. There are three salient points in its make-up that need to be borne in mind.

Firstly, one has to remember that the once great Commonwealth of Poland-Lithuania had fallen on hard times. Ever since the Cossack and Swedish wars, which killed more than a quarter of the entire population, it had been in severe economic regression. And for seventy years before 1791, it had been run as a form of Russian protectorate - reminiscent in many striking ways to the puppet states set up in eastern Europe by the Soviet Union after 1945. In 1772, it had been subjected to the first of three Partitions that dismembered it piece by piece. It had its own King and its own government, but ever since the time of Peter the Great it had been disarmed and subject to constant Russian interference and intimidation. It was in a state of anarchy that Russian policy deliberately maintained. The main aim of the new Constitution was to shake off this Russian control, and to recover genuine independence. (It was pushed through in a brief interval when the Russian Army was preoccupied in a Turkish War.)

Secondly, the Constitution was formulated in the full flood of the Enlightenment. It introduced an enlightened, limited monarchy of the British type - that is, a hereditary but constitutional monarchy: the division of powers, a Parliament representing both halves of the state (Poland and Lithuania), a suffrage extended to both gentry and bourgeoisie. Associated legislation had brought in a strong standing army for defending it against Poland's militaristic neighbors, and an effective civil service. To modern ears, this sounds rather unexciting. But for the time, and the place, it was well worthy of note. True enough, Poland's Constitution had its shortcomings, especially in the social sphere. Unlike its French counterpart, it did not abolish serfdom at a stroke. In that sphere, it confined itself to bringing the serfs within the scope of the law. This was, in fact, a significant step forward. Indeed the Polish Constitution's preference for evolutionary as opposed to revolutionary change, was one of the qualities which attracted the approval of many contemporaries. The enthusiasm of Edmund Burke, for example, whose criticism of the excesses of the French Revolution is generally taken to be the starting-point of modern conservatism, was unbounded. Burke's approval of the Polish Revolution ought to be as well known as his disapproval of the French one. Of the Third of May, he wrote:

> The means were as striking to the imagination, as satisfactory to the reason, and soothing to the moral sentiments... Humanity has everything to rejoice and to glory in—nothing to be ashamed of, nothing to suffer. So far as it has gone, it probably is the most pure...public good which ever has been conferred on mankind... Everything was kept in its place and order, but in that place and order everything was bettered. To add to this happy wonder this unheard-of conjunction of wisdom and fortune, not one drop of blood was spilled, no treachery, no outrage...
> Happy people if they know to proceed as they have begun.

At a later date, Karl Marx expressed a similarly fulsome opinion.

To my mind, the Constitution of 3 May is a classic product of the European Enlightenment. In political matters, the *philosophes* looked above all to British sources, both in the theories of John Locke and to the practices of the Westminster system; and the Polish reformers followed their lead. The pre-eminent Polish scholar of the subject, the late Emanuel Rostworowski, has described the Constitution as a compromise between the wishes of a lifelong Anglophile King, and the republican leanings of the "Patriot" leaders, who looked more to the example of the United States. This blend of British and American influences is not so common in eastern Europe to say the least. What is depressing, is that so little such information finds its way into general circulation. How often, in surveys of the European Enlightenment, can one look in vain for any mention of the Polish Constitution! How much space is given to Poland's neighbors the so-called Enlightened Despots, such as Frederick or Catherine the Great, who were so very much more despotic than enlightened.

Thirdly, one has to keep track of the revolutionary context in Europe as a whole. Western Europe was transfixed by the extraordinary torrent of changes in France. Prussia and Austria, though not entirely hostile to Poland's renaissance, were preparing for a French War. In eastern Europe, therefore, Russia was left virtually a free hand. The Russian Empress, Catherine the Great, had opposed the King's schemes from the start, and in 1787, at the meeting mentioned earlier at Kaniów (near Czernobyl), she had rejected all suggestions of a Russo-Polish relationship of equal terms. What she wanted was a Poland permanently disarmed and permanently accessible to any manipulations that suited St. Petersburg's purpose. As a result, she regarded the demarche of the Polish Parliament as a calculated insult to herself and a breach of the treaties of guarantee. From there, it was a simple step for her to denounce the Constitutionalists as Jacobins (which they expressly were not), to treat her own Polish partisans as the only legitimate group (which they were not), and to resort to force. The Russo-Polish War of 1792-3: the Second Partition, the National Rising of Tadeusz Kościuszko and the final act of vivisection of 1795, all flowed from that decision. In the preamble to the treaties of partitions, the partitioners took care to emphasize that Poland-Lithuania had been destroyed reluctantly by the will of God and for the good of mankind, because it was ungovernable.

The events of the late eighteenth century no doubt seem pretty distant from contemporary affairs. Yet there are good reasons for keeping the past in mind when considering the extraordinary collapse of the Soviet Block in Europe in recent years, and the subsequent disintegration of the Soviet Union itself. Poland's loss of its Constitution had repercussions which are still being felt today. It provided the empires of eastern and central Europe with an unnatural political monopoly which lasted throughout the nineteenth century, and which in the twentieth century, provided the focus not only European, but of world conflict.

The destruction of Poland-Lithuania was a necessary precondition for the rise of Prussia and for the expansion of Russia-in-Europe. Without the partitions, it is hard to conceive either of a Germany dominated and united by Prussia, or of the German-Russian rivalry which provided the central issue of two world wars.

By turning against the Constitution of 3 May, Catherine the Great was setting the course which underlay much of modern European history. A strong Prussia, and a bloated Russia, with a common frontier running through the heart of historic Poland, were essential elements both of the nineteenth-century peace, and of the twentieth century's wars.

By the same token, the crushing of the Constitution denied all the nations of Poland-Lithuania any chance of political evolution within the democratic framework which an undefeated Commonwealth might have provided. One cannot say how the *Rzeczpospolita* might have fared in the age of Nationalism. It may well have suffered the fate of Austro-Hungary. For Poles, Lithuanians, Byelorussians and Ukrainians and Jews, however, no alternative destiny can hardly have matched the miseries which awaited them under the partitions.

By losing their statehood, the former citizens of the Republic also lost their voice, their ability to state their case in the world with authority. The world fawns on success, and the empires, who in their day were mighty successful, were able to spread their propaganda with impunity. Most historians in the West get no further than simply repeating the partitioners' own alibis. They simply repeat that official story about the Republic being destroyed because it was "ungovernable." The fact is, it was destroyed exactly because the Constitution of 3 May had made it governable.

> An abbreviated version of a paper presented to the Department of History, Harvard University on May 15, 1991 as the August Zaleski Memorial Lecture.

Onstitucye Seymu Wal-
nego Koronacyey Krolewskiey 1576.

2

The Origin and Development of the Polish Parliamentary System through the End of the Seventeenth Century

Anna Sucheni-Grabowska

I. From Direct Participation *(sejm virtim)* to a Representative Parliament.

The transformation of patrimonial monarchies into estate monarchies and the associated decentralization of the ruler's power in Europe was generally connected to the emancipation of the estates. The estates were allowed a voice in public affairs whenever their help, especially financial help, was needed, in agreement with the Roman principle of *quod omnes tangit ab omnibus comprobari debet* (what concerns all should be approved by all). Communication between rulers and ruled required an appropriate forum. This was provided by national and provincial assemblies of the estates. The oldest of these appeared in the Iberian peninsula (the *Cortes*). Later they arose in England, Hungary, and France (the Estates General). The varied paths of historical development followed by individual countries had an obvious effect on their growing medieval parliamentary structures. Similarly, Poland, which consisted of local princedoms from 1138 to 1320, showed some of the general traits of parliamentary development as well as specific national characteristics.

Poland's traditional assembly was the *wiec,*[1] known in thirteenth-century sources as *colloquium generale* or *solemne.* The *wiec* worked on the following lines: the prince and the highest dignitaries of the princedom, and sometimes urban notables, met to decide matters of concern; the decisions made by this select group were then announced and approved by a mass meeting of the local populace called for that purpose. During the thirteenth century, these assemblies were replaced by assemblies of princes together with court and local officials. The decline of the primacy of the oldest Piast in residence in Cracow over the other Piast princes increased the importance of the assemblies of those principalities. The prince expected that a *wiec* should approve his decisions on matters of war and peace. He granted privileges to the gentry, the church, and to the cities, as well as land grants, the assessment of taxes, and other obligations. Each *wiec* also administered justice.

The unification of the Kingdom under Władysław the Short (1320-1333) and Kazimierz the Great (1333-1370) brought a decrease in the frequency at which the traditional assemblies met. The kings called them sporadically and used them to pass new laws, to put existing laws in order, and in connection with the negotiations concerning the return of the Pomorze and Kujawy from the Teutonic Knights. Kazimierz, who had no male progeny, also used the assemblies in his attempt to establish the succession to the throne in Poland in favor of his nephew Louis of Anjou, King of Hungary. It is most likely that the negotiations that the King and Polish notables attended in Hungary were preceded by a *wiec* in Poland. When King Kazimierz fell seriously ill at the camp near Lublin (1351), Louis of Anjou was declared successor to the Polish throne in case of his uncle's death. In 1355 in Buda, Louis guaranteed "all the estates of the Polish Kingdom" their accustomed rights, including a promise not to impose taxes and to pay indemnities for foreign military expeditions. The privilege granted by Louis at Košice in 1374 in exchange for recognition of the right of one of his daughters to the Polish succession limited knights' taxes to two *grosze* per acre, assured the integrity of Poland's borders, reaffirmed lifelong tenure of local gentry offices, and promised that the most important royal offices would be given to Poles.[2]

In France and in the German speaking lands the main reason for calling parliamentary assemblies was taxation.[3] In Poland, however, the activity of the estates centered not only on issues of taxation but also on the complicated Polish succession and its evolution in the direction of elective kingship under Louis of Anjou and the first Jagiellons (1370-1434). This gave a public and legal character to meetings of the estates that revealed itself during the long interregnum (1382-84) that followed Louis' death. At that time, the estates organized regional, provincial and national assemblies, which declared in favor of the succession of Princess Jadwiga, Louis daughter, who was crowned in Cracow in 1384, and swore to defend Poland against foreign attack and to keep the peace at home.

In general there exist two points of view concerning the beginning of the Polish Parliament. According to the "evolutionary" point of view the above regional and provincial assemblies inaugurated a native parliamentary system, and the national assemblies were the starting point for the later General Diet (*sejm walny*).[4] This opinion challenges the other interpretation, which found the Diet's origin in a much later period by applying institutional criteria.[5] According to the "institutionalists," representation is what makes a parliament. Representation, however, evolved slowly as one of the forms of estate assemblies and is itself a term that has many meanings. A representative assembly may also be one of local notables and officials who were not selected by the citizens, but who act rather *ex officio* in the name of a region's people, creating a mixed system where direct participation (*virtim*) was combined with some means to represent those who were not present. Such a mixed system existed in the Grand Duchy of Lithuania under Zygmunt I (and it is possible that the Jagiellons introduced this fifteenth-century Polish practice to Lithuania).[6]

Under the first Jagiellonian Kings, three types of assemblies came into being. They were: the General Diet (*sejm walny, conventio generalis totius Regni, dieta, parlamentum generale),* the regional assemblies, dietines (*sejmik, conventio particularis, or terrestris*), and the provincial diets, one each for Małopolska and Wielkopolska. At first, the diets were attended by members of the royal council, crown officials, delegates from the cities, the bishops' chapters, and the nobility participating directly. The provincial diets were probably instrumental in the introduction of deputies – representatives from local areas, since mass participation in a provincial diet was probably rare and would be the result of a meeting of exceptional importance.[7]

The General Diet did not, at first, have to be uniform in its composition. It could combine direct participation and representation. For a long time the representatives themselves were not chosen according to fixed, permanent rules. In France selection of delegates to the Estates General was only formalized at the end of the fifteenth century, though the Estates began meeting in 1302. The Iberian *Cortes* were established during the twelfth and thirteenth century, but delegates were chosen only starting in the last half of the fourteenth century. Selection of delegates proved complicated because the kings, despite protests, insisted on using the administrative structures they controlled to choose representatives. It was the Hungarian assembly that introduced representation, as properly understood, in the middle of the fifteenth century. A considerable period of time separated the establishment of estate assemblies, and the selection of representatives to them in England, Bohemia, and the German lands.[8] Similarly in Poland, although the formation of the first representative Diet took place at the end of the fifteenth century, in the fourteenth century the evolutionary process which led to the establishment of the future General Diet had already started. There is, therefore, no reason to depart from the practice of scholars of parliamentary institutions in other countries and date the establishment of the Polish Parliament from the formation of Poland's first representative Diet. Parliamentary representation is at present linked with the existence of democratic political structures, but, during the rise of estate monarchies, societies at first appealed to age-old traditions of direct democracy.

Due to the complications which arose when Jagiełło, the Grand Duke of Lithuania, assumed the throne, the gentry was able to oppose him at various assemblies throughout his reign.[9] In 1386, Jagiełło was baptized as Władysław and upon marrying Jadwiga, was acclaimed King of Poland by the gentry assembled at Lublin. The gentry participated in large numbers in the assemblies at which the new King swore allegiance to the laws of Poland (Cracow and Korczyn 1386, Piotrków 1388). Jadwiga's childless death in 1399 made her husband's continued exercise of power problematic, while his subsequent marriages raised troubling questions about the right of succession. In this situation the need for the consent of the governed was again recognized in 1399. A whole series of assemblies was held around Poland as part of the disagreements over the succession of Prince Władysław, Jagiełło's son by the Lithuanian-Ruthenian Princess Sonka of Holszany. The court wanted a guarantee of the Prince's succession. In return for their acknowledgment the subjects wanted an assurance from the King that before ascending the throne the Prince would swear to recognize and uphold all existing laws. Of special interest to the gentry were the limitations upon the judicial powers in criminal matters of the King's officers (*starosta*), separation of the *starosta's* powers from those of the elected territorial judges *(obieralny sędzia ziemski)*, and the inviolability of gentry property. After several years of quarreling the King agreed to their demands. At the 1430 General Diet in Jedlnia secular and clerical notables, knights and nobles, the cities, and "the whole of the Kingdom of Poland" unanimously approved the succession of one of the King's sons, whichever one the estates would deem most fit to rule. The document drawn up by the Diet gave the succession to the Jagiellonian dynasty but at the same time gave the Diet the right to chose which son would inherit, establishing in this way the rule of an elected monarch that was restricted to the dynasty of the Jagiellons. Jagiełło on his part ensured that his successor would agree to uphold the "rights and freedoms" enjoyed by all the estates prior to his coronation. The most important right gained from the monarchy in 1425 (and secured in 1430 and 1433) was the *Neminem captivabimus nisi iure*

The Royal Castle on the Wawel Hill in Cracow. Part of the panorama of Cracow by Matthaus Merian the Elder, Amsterdam 1619 (Muzeum Narodowe w Krakowie, Fundacja XX Czartoryskich).

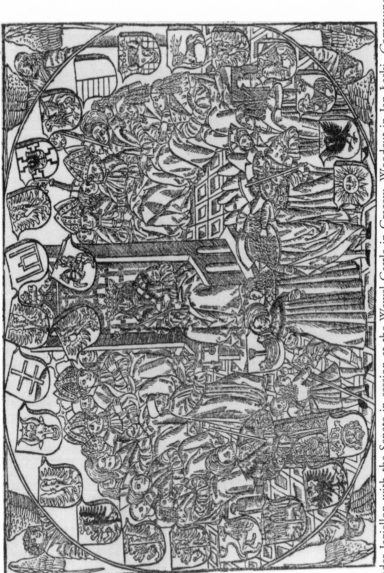

King Aleksander Jagiellon with the Senate in session at the Wawel Castle in Cracow. Woodcut in Jan Łaski, *Commune incliti Poloniae Regni privilegium*, Cracoviae, 1506. (Biblioteka Uniwersytecka w Warszawie). Photo A. Bodytko.

victum, which guaranteed that no nobleman who owned land, even the smallest piece, could be arrested without a court order unless he was caught committing a crime.[10] The English act of *Habeas Corpus* came years later in 1679.

The youth of Władysław III, and later the dramatic end of his short rule in the Battle of Varna in 1444, Kazimierz Jagiellon's (who ruled Lithuania from 1440) three-year delay in taking power in Poland, and his tardiness in recognizing the privileges of the estates, all roused Polish society and resulted in frequent assemblies. Among these assemblies the General Diet gradually took on characteristics of a regular assembly. The frequency of General Diet meetings during Kazimierz Jagiellon's long reign (1447-1492) was notable. The preferred meeting place was Piotrków on the border of Małopolska and Wielkopolska. These facts produced a Diet with full, or at least partial, representation from local regions probably by about the mid-fifteenth century. In any case, in 1468 there was a clear system of representation. Two deputies from each regional dietine *(sejmik ziemski)* were called to the Diet at Piotrków.[11]

During the reign of Kazimierz Jagiellon the main concern of the Polish gentry estate turned from taxation and succession to problems of public life and social and political affairs. In contrast, the cities which had been enjoying many privileges and which actively backed Jagiełło and Sonka for the succession, fell silent and were unable to develop strong forms of cooperation. The prosperity of the cities was not accompanied by their participation in the legislative process and in the political life of the country. Also, the royal court did not attempt to include the cities in political struggles. The gentry struck at the cities at the Diet of 1496, prohibiting them from obtaining land and limiting their access to bishops' chapters.

The gentry gained an enormously important privilege that opened the doors to its political emancipation in 1454. According to the Statutes of Nieszawa, the king could neither introduce new taxes nor summon a general levy *(pospolite ruszenie)* without the consent of the dietines. The latter provision gave the gentry influence over matters of war and peace. Further, this act limited the king's ability to pawn crown lands and included gentry demands against the oligarchy elite aimed at strengthening the egalitarianism of the whole gentry estate.[12]

Thanks to the rights the gentry received in 1454 the internal organization of Parliament could be set up rapidly. The powerful voice gained by the gentry could best be heard at the General Diet. It also became easiest for the monarch to settle in the Diet those matters that were within the competence of the estates. The main role of the dietines was the election of deputies and transmitting the voice of the electorate to the Diet.

At first cities took part in diets and dietines by sending delegations. But later this took a different direction. Dietines evolved into gatherings of local landowners, gentry and magnates. Cities, towns, and villages always belonged to the owners of the land on which they stood, that is, to the crown, churches, monasteries, or the nobility. It was tacitly understood that the dietines, representing territorial units, provided for the cities and villages because the landowners who owned them participated in these assemblies. The same principle was later applied to Diet deputies as representatives of a region joined in a single dietine. The situation of the clergy was similar. Poland's Parliament was unlike those of other European states in that the clergy were not included in the Diet. Only bishops became part of the Parliament as members of the Senate. The exclusion of the clergy did not prevent clerics from attending diets and dietines as observers or petitioners on their own behalf or for the townspeople. The Diet included only delegates from Cracow, the capital, and later also from Wilno.[13]

II. The Parliament in the Sixteenth and Seventeenth Centuries.[14]

1. Calling the Diet, the Diet's powers

The Jagiellonian kings strictly adhered to the idea that calling the Diet was an exclusive prerogative of the monarch, and they rejected noble demands for yearly Diet sessions. An obligation on the part of the king to call the Diet was introduced only in 1573. The Henrician Articles enacted in that year, which were submitted for acceptance to Henry of Valois, Poland's first "free elected" King following the extinction of the Jagiellonian dynasty, were a reaffirmation of the gentry's acquired privileges and rights, and required the king to call an ordinary Diet every two years and extraordinary sessions in case of "sudden need." In practice the Henrician Articles did not make the sessions of the Diet more frequent. From 1493 to 1572, the end of the Jagiellonian dynasty, there were seventy two diets, an average of 1.11 per year. In the one hundred twenty three years between 1573 and 1696, one hundred fourteen diets met, an average of 1.07 per year.[15] The averages smooth out variations in how often diets met. There were times when no Diet met for a few years and times when two Diets met in a single year. Nonetheless, the frequency with which the Polish Diet assembled is striking in a period when, in most European states, there was a tendency to limit the activity of estate assemblies or to eliminate them from public life.[16]

The frequent meetings of the Commonwealth's Diet were the result of the Parliament's broad competency. The traditional responsibilities of the Diet were like those of other European parliaments—approving taxes and administering justice. This was a continuation of the medieval relationship between ruler and ruled wherein the ruler provided "Schutz und Schirm," in the German formula, and the subjects gave "Rat und Hilfe." In the modern period, this relationship was in fact no more than the estates bearing the tax burden for the ruler.[17]

In Poland, however, the competency of the Parliament was greater. The nobility, because it was the "knightly estate," was free from direct taxation as it was in other countries.[18] But the king was not free to tax the commoners, a right that belonged to kings in France, for example. Taxation of the towns and villages included in the land exemption of estate owners required an act of the Diet in Poland.

The Nieszawa Statutes of 1454 gave the dietines the right to look into pending legislation, into decisions on new taxes and to summon the general levy. The transformation at the end of the fifteenth century of the General Diet into a two-chambered Parliament with elected deputies required the legal recognition of participation by deputies. Such legislation was included in the constitution *Nihil Novi*, adopted by the Diet in 1505. (A bill adopted by the Parliament was referred to as "constitution.") That constitution stated that the monarch could not issue new laws that affected "common rights" *(pospolite prawa)* or "anyone's rights" without the joint consent of the senators and deputies.[19]

Polish legislation did not define the Diet's authority in the area of domestic policy or the area of royal administration. Nevertheless, the Diet exerted some influence in both areas and gradually increased it. It alaready exercised some power through its directives concerning how laws should be carried out. Such instructions were numerous at the provincial and general diets under Kazimierz Jagiellon (1447-1492). During the sixteenth century, Diet requests to the king for more executive power were common. In the next century, this desire was expressed in the so called exorbitancies *(egzorbitancje)*, Diet complaints about royal and official violations of the law, known as *gravamina* in the Hungarian Parliament. These documents typically claimed that royal power was being extended at the expense of the law. Protected by this legalistic shield, the authors of such complaints voiced their discontent with the haphazard workings of the royal administration or with officials in high offices. Concepts of the structure of executive power were still fluid. Habit often caused each complaint made about executive or judicial affairs to become a species of law.

2. Dietines and the Diet

Depending on the reason they were called to assemble, the dietines are traditionally divided into pre-diet dietines to elect deputies to the Diet, electoral ones to elect territorial judges, others to elect deputies to the Crown Tribunal, and still others, the reporting dietines, to render an account of the diets' resolutions. The assemblies were then called for some single reason, but once together the participants tried to take care of other business characteristic of self-government, including matters of finances, taxes, and public safety.[20]

From the point of view of the political life of the state most important were the pre-diet dietines, where deputies to the Diet were elected. After the king agreed with the senators by sending them letters, so-called *litterae deliberatoriae,* on the time and agenda for a session of the Diet, the royal chancellery sent a circular letter to the king's officers (*starosta)* announcing the dates for the dietines, provincial diets and for the General Diet. In each region the *starosta* was responsible for publicizing the circular in places where people congregated.

The king dispatched a representative to each dietine with a royal message. This emissary could be secular or clerical. Sometimes secretaries of the chancellery, or even local officials spoke for the king. The king's message explained the state's affairs, described the overall condition of foreign affairs and threats to Poland. Most often it raised the issue of taxes needed for defense and asked that wise deputies be elected to the Diet and be given broad mandates by the electors.

After the royal representative spoke, he was ceremonially led out of the place where the dietine met so that his presence would not constrain those assembled in their discussions. A marshal presided over the deliberations. Dietines usually met in churches. The members of the dietines held their discussions in two ways. They either all met together or the local potentates met separately as a "knights' circle" (*rycerskie koło*). This was meant to prevent high clerics or great landowners from pressuring the middle gentry. But very often the division of the dietines did not stop elite influence over other members of the dietines, especially over the poor dependent gentry in the service of members of the elite. Some dietines had a large group of senators, like the dietines of Kalisz and Poznań, which met together in the town of Środa. If all attended, a meeting of these combined dietines included the voivode of each, the Archbishop of Gniezno, the Bishop of Poznań, and thirteen castellans. The Sandomierz dietine held at Opatów included the voivode, the church hierarchs whose benefices lay in Sandomierz, and eight castellans. The Mazowsze voivodeship had ten dietines following the customs of the old Piast Princedom, a vassal of Poland until 1526. These assemblies followed the

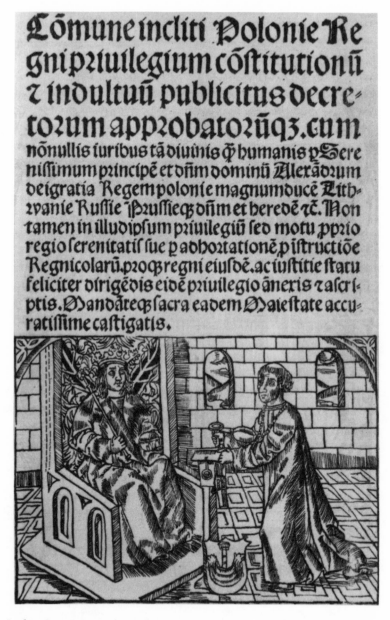

Cõmune incliti Polonie Regni priuilegium cõstitutionũ z indultuũ publicitus decretoꝛum appꝛobatoꝛũ̄qʒ.cum nõnullis iuribus tã diuinis ꝗ̃ humanis p̃Serenissimum pꝛincipẽ et dñm dominũ Alexãdꝛum dei gratia Regem polonie magnum ducẽ Lithꝛvanie Ruffie iPꝛuffiecʒ dñm et heredẽ zc̃. Mon tamen in illud ipsum pꝛiuilegiũ sed motu pꝛoꝑio regio serenitatis sue p adhoꝛtationẽ p istructiõe Regnicolarũ.pꝛoꝗʒregni eiusdẽ.ac iustitie statu feliciter dirigẽdis eidẽ pꝛiuilegio ãneris z ascriptis.Mandãtecʒ sacra eadem Maiestate accuratissime castigatis.

Jan Łaski, *Commune incliti Poloniae Regni privilegium*, Cracoviae, 1506. Title page with the woodcut: Chancellor Jan Łaski presenting King Aleksander Jagiellon with the collection of statutes of Polish public and judicial laws which were drawn up on the initiative of the Diet in Radom (1505) and the king's recommendation. (Biblioteka Uniwersytecka w Warszawie). Photo A. Bodytko.

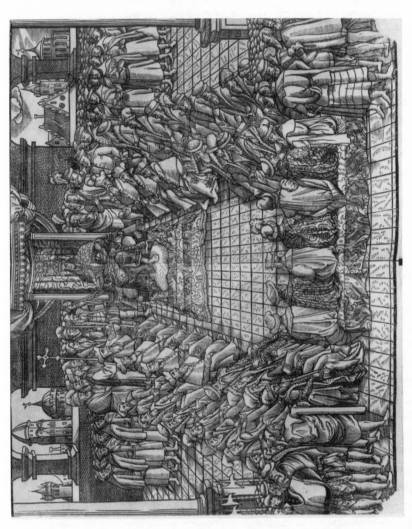

The Polish Diet with King Zygmunt II August in session at the Wawel Castle in Cracow. Woodcut in Jan Herburt, *Statuta y przywileie koronne*, w Krakowie, 1570. (Biblioteka Uniwersytecka w Warszawie). Photo A. Bodytko.

traditional division by "lands" (*ziemie*). Each of Mazowsze's dietines were to have been attended by one castellan, and, theoretically, the Bishop of Płock was to have attended all of them, which proved to be impossible.

The constitutions of 1510 and 1565 required all senators, secular or clerical, to attend the dietines of their region and threatened significant fines for failure to attend.[21] Deputies to the Diet often complained about senators failing to appear at the dietines. They wanted to gain support from these dignitaries for the instructions the dietines issued to the Diet. Other royal officials, not senators, more frequently participated in the dietines, as required by law. County officials of different ranks also attended.

Before the Union of Lublin (the Union with Lithuania concluded at the Lublin Diet in 1569) Poland had twenty-eight dietines. Twelve covered voivodeships (in two cases two voivodeships shared a dietine), and sixteen dietines served lands following the division in the previous duchies. (Ten of these were in the Mazowsze, two in Rawa, and two in Wielkopolska.) Research completed to date indicates significant independence on the part of the middle gentry in the dietines of Sandomierz, Sieradz, Poznań-Kalisz, and of the small dietines of Mazowsze. The Mazowsze dietines were very rarely dissolved prematurely. The Mazowsze voivodeship dietines were the first, in 1598, to introduce majority voting in elections of deputies to the Diet, of deputies to the Crown Tribunal, and of court officials. The Diet confirmed this principle by passing the necessary legislation. The dietines of the Grand Duchy of Lithuania, following the example of other dietines, adopted majority voting in 1613.

The distribution of dietines after the Union of Lublin in 1569 kept changing. This was due to the Union itself, which increased the number of dietines, to the consolidation of Royal Prussia's differing parliamentary system with Poland's Diet, to the gain and loss of territory, and to occasional splits of one dietine into two. We can provisionally estimate that sixty-eight dietines existed in the Commonwealth at this time. The number of dietines in Poland proper was increased by the dietines of Royal Prussia, Polesie, Volhynia and the Ukraine. A dietine was established in Livonia. Under Zygmunt August there were twenty-one dietines in the Grand Duchy of Lithuania. There were twenty-four in the seventeenth century. The Second Lithuanian Statute of 1566 set the number of deputies from each district at two.[22] It is notable that the Lithuanian Statute allowed only landed gentry to participate in the dietines while in Poland the right of nobles without land to participate in dietines varied.

For the individuals assembled at a dietine the most important matter to be decided was the contents of the instructions to the delegates elected to the Diet, the "articles." These contained the dietine's responses to the king's message and other points of general character or of local concern. Special requests for the king and additions to the text appeared at the end of such documents as petitions *(petita)*. Instructions and resolutions written by the dietines were often typical. But under the layers of repetition and requests to the king couched in Baroque expressions, were also wise observations and evidence of true civic concern that reached beyond local interests. The instructions interwove rational plans to reform the regulations and proceedings of the Diet together with demands that the privileges gained by the estates should not be diminished in the least. The instructions given the deputies were varied and many times set firm limits on their actions as legislators. Still their actions became freer when decisions were made that in general agreed with the political desires of the majority of the gentry. Limits on the freedom of action of elected representatives were widely known and were a true indication of the contractual relationship between the estates' electorates and those they elected. They existed in the Iberian *Cortes*, the English and Hungarian Parliaments, and in the French Estates General. Limits served to protect the estates from the pressure of the monarch.

3. The functioning of the Parliament

In accordance with tradition, until 1569 regular sessions of the Parliament were held in Piotrków and coronation sessions in Cracow. In 1569 the Parliament was moved to Warsaw to make it easier for senators and deputies from the Grand Duchy of Lithuania to attend. For the same reason it was decided in 1676 to hold every third session in Grodno.

The doctrine of the "three estates in council"–the King, the Senate and the Chamber of Deputies–dominated the Polish parliamentary system and guaranteed the primacy of law in the Commonwealth. The Parliament as a legislative body fulfilled this principle, and the large role the king played in the Parliament made him a participant in ruling the state. The political writer Łukasz Górnicki articulated this principle quite clearly when he spoke of the joint rule of the state by the King, by his council (the Senate) and by the deputies.[23] This understanding of the Polish system originated in the late fifteenth century and paved the way for the later notion of the combined monarchy (*monarchia mixta*).

The most important political events of the Commonwealth occurred in the Parliament. The kings were surrounded by senators, that is, members of the royal council, an institution with a long genealogy. After the Union of Lublin in 1569, the Senate consisted of one hundred thirteen senators from Poland--thirteen bishops, twenty two voivodes, seventy three castellans and five ministers (Crown Grand Marshal, Chancellor, Vice-Chancellor, Treasurer and Marshal of the Court)--and twenty seven from Lithuania, among them two bishops, nine voivodes, ten castellans and five ministers (Lithuanian Grand Marshal, etc.). The 1569 Lublin Diet regulated also the legal status of Royal Prussia and eight senators (two bishops, three voivodes and three castellans) were admitted to the Senate. The hetmans, who were extremely influential during the seventeenth century, were not counted as ministers, but they usually belonged to the Senate by virtue of the multiple offices they held as castellans or voivodes. In 1598, Livonia's legal status was reorganized to match the rest of the Commonwealth, and three Livonian castellans and voivodes entered the Senate, in addition to the bishop previously admitted.

The Chamber of Deputies numbered nearly one hundred seventy five in the 1630s when the Commonwealth was at its largest size. As a rule two from each dietine were elected. The oldest voivodeships of Małopolska and Wielkopolska sent six deputies each. The number of deputies from Royal Prussia varied and was sometimes quite large. After 1598, Livonia sent six deputies to the Diet.

The balance of political power changed in the Commonwealth and, reflecting these political shifts, the relationships between the three parliamentary "estates" changed, producing both temporary and permanent alterations in the workings of the Parliament. The formal agenda of the sessions remained almost unchanged for the entire period under consideration, until the reforms of the eighteenth century.[24] Each session began with a solemn mass dedicated to the Holy Spirit, which usually included a special sermon. Next, the deputies gathered in their hall. Beginning in the late sixteenth century, deputies' credentials were verified, which could result in the exclusion of deputies from participation in the Diet and sometimes caused lengthy disagreements. The office of the speaker, the Marshal of the Chamber of Deputies, developed in the 1550s, and after the Union of Lublin a Lithuanian deputy was elected Marshal every third term. The Marshal's powers, long based on custom, were defined by law only in 1669 and then written into the constitution of 1678. The Marshal's oath recorded in the 1678 constitution contains his promise not to sign the constitution of a Diet session unless the assembled estates expressed their approval of the document.

The Marshal welcomed the king at a joint meeting of the Chamber and Senate and gave a keynote speech in the name of the deputies. Then, the deputies filed past the king, each kissing his right hand. When the delegates had demonstrated their fealty, the Chancellor or Vice-Chancellor presented the "proposition" from the throne. It was generally similar to the king's message to the dietines. In the sixteenth century, the senators followed with their own statements, called *vota*. In the seventeenth century, the senators' statements were preceded by the reading of nominations for vacant offices, of the *pacta conventa* (conditions renewed at every accession to the Polish throne, starting with the election of Henry of Valois in 1573, under which the future king could rule), of the *senatus consulta* (decisions taken by resident senators—an advisory council to the king during the intervals between sessions of the Diet), and also of the complaints about violations of the law. The senators' statements, usually made by those holding the highest ranks, expressed their opinions of the king's platform; no vote was taken, however. At that point the Parliament separated into its two houses. The Senate deliberated with the king or alone. The Chamber of Deputies worked on drafting legislation. If necessary the two houses met together or communicated through their representatives. Before the end of a session, the houses jointly debated the final approval of legislation, the conclusion *(konkluzja)*. All three parliamentary "estates" had to agree on a draft before it could become law. The king had the right to veto legislation, as did the two houses of the Parliament. The king's veto was logical because, into the eighteenth century, the new laws adopted were issued exclusively in his name. The session ended with the selection of resident senators and of other special appointees. The Marshal made an oration bidding farewell to the king, and the deputies took leave of the king, each again kissing his hand.

In the seventeenth century, there were frequent so-called sessions of nations, i.e., separate Polish and Lithuanian sessions, which shortened the general debates at the Diet. During Diet sessions, numerous commissions met to handle special business, such as auditing the treasury accounts. The Diet was also the highest court. The king sat as judge advised by the senators. In 1578 the Polish Tribunal was established, followed by the Lithuanian Tribunal in 1581, to serve as the highest legal forum. Certain cases, however, remained in the purview of the king's court in the Diet, such as those cases that concerned the monarch or the state (insults to the monarch, treason, government finances, discipline of royal officials, the life and honor of noblemen).

It should be emphasized in discussions about sixteenth and seventeenth-century Polish parliamentarism that new laws were rarely written. Generally, older laws were reinterpreted or their scope broadened. Changed political conditions gave these legal acts some variation, but their spirit was in fact drawn from the legal registers of the fifteenth century, and their actual form was shaped by a broad program advanced during the years of the last two

Jagiellon kings, which for the reasons given above defined its goal as the "execution of the laws."

The reaffirmation or updating of old laws was most often undertaken as a result of their violation by the rulers. This was, therefore, law-making as a form of retaliation, and this must be taken into account. It sometimes happened that a new legal act limited the power of the king or the Senate. Thus it is worth knowing the deputies' motivation for taking such action.

The struggle over the "execution of the laws" was fought in the Diet first under the two kings Zygmunt I and II (until 1562), and then until the enactment of the executionist reforms during the following seven years.[25] The executionist platform struck at the dynastic policy of the Jagiellons and at the property and political position of the elite gathered in the Senate. The kings opposed the Chamber of Deputies' desire for a closer integration of Poland and Lithuania. They preferred the existing system of personal union under which two separate states were joined in the person of the monarch. The Grand Duchy offered the descendants of Giedymin who sat on the Polish throne dynastic titles and great power. Lithuania was then a beneficial political alternative to Poland.

The executionist camp, which included many religious dissenters, wanted freedom of religion and an end to the authority of church courts over laymen in matters of faith and tithes. These desires obviously caused conflict between the Chamber of Deputies and the bishops of the Senate. Until that time the secular courts carried out the rulings of the ecclesiastical courts. The secular courts were freed of this responsibility as part of the executionist reforms which paved the way for the act of religious tolerance, the Act of the Confederation of Warsaw of 1573.

The Chamber of Deputies in those years fought bitter battles with the dignitaries of the Senate. The senators gathered multiple high offices in their hands, violating laws passed in 1454 and 1504, and received life-long rights to incomes from crown lands for free. The deputies loyal to the executionist movement demanded the dignitaries give up their multiple offices. This was also a fight over reorganizing the law courts and administration. Those who held the position of the king's officer (*starosta*) played an important role in this affair, because they were responsible for criminal courts and keeping order in the territories entrusted to them. They rarely performed their duties personally, though they received rich crown lands as a reward for holding their office. Often holding the post of *starosta* concurrently with appointments as voivodes and castellans, they sat in the Senate and were decided opponents of the executionist movement.

Because of the points of conflict listed above, the king supported the Senate. During the 1550s, the king authoritatively declared that the lower house could only make decisions about taxes and that it was subordinate to the Senate. The political strength of the landed gentry, however, proved too strong to break. Leaders of the executionist movement and experienced parliamentarians were able to expand the role of the Chamber of Deputies.[26] In 1559, the Chamber of Deputies made tax legislation dependent on the acceptance of its demands by the king and the Senate.

King Zygmunt II August reacted by trying to rule without Parliament. He refused to assemble the Diet for nearly four years and stayed in Lithuania. The correspondence carried on at this time by politicians, both senators and spokesmen for the executionist movement, show the enormous value they placed on the parliamentary system. They all asked the King to call the Diet as soon as possible, believing that a Diet would provide the only chance of reaching an understanding between the parties.

Meanwhile, Tsar Ivan IV brutally invaded Livonia, which had been negotiating an agreement that would place it under the protection of Zygmunt II August. The eastern borders of Lithuania were seriously threatened. In September 1562, the mass levy of Lithuanian and Rus gentry assembled near Vitebsk and demanded that the King call a joint session of the Polish and Lithuanian Diets and ask for military aid from Poland. Hidden behind these demands was the idea of union.

The mood in Lithuania, fear of an attack by Ivan IV, open conflict with his Polish subjects, and lack of money for arms all acted to convince Zygmunt II August to call the Diet at the end of 1562 and allow it to undertake executionist reforms. The diets of 1562-1569 returned part of the crown lands to the treasury and ensured the defense of the southern frontiers against Tatar raiding with a quarter of the revenue from those lands, which enabled them to establish a standing army called Quarter Troops *(wojsko kwarciane)*. The diets revived and extended restrictions on holding multiple offices, and assured the abolition of ecclesiastical jurisdiction over matters of faith. The Union of Lublin in 1569 which included three nations–the Polish, Lithuanian, and Rus–was finally achieved. Zygmunt August gave this Union, of which he became a passionate supporter, a federative character, recognizing the political differences of the Grand Duchy. These decisions were not reached without conflict. Lithuanian dignitaries opposed the Union. They saw in it a threat to their domination of the Grand Duchy and feared common diets with Poland and the effect they would have on the political emancipation of the Lithuanian and Rus gentry.

FIDEM SERVAVI: IN RELIQVO,
REPOSITA EST MIHI CORONA.

PIERWSZA POWIN-
NOSC KROLEWSKA, AL-
bo Artykuł przyśięgi iego.

Wierze iego polećią rrad Seymowy, Práwá Korun-
né, Wolnośći, rozdawánie vrzędów, Sćitośłw, &c.

*Da obiáśnienia tego artykułu, że tytuły náléży rzędem poła-
noni, i ich obiáśnienia statuty należą.*

O SEYMIECH,

O powaznośći vstaw Seymowych:
á iże Seym reprźesentuie ciáło v-
szytkiégo Kroleśtwá.

Oycz Jan Olbrycht / z łáski Bożey Krol Polski / za spólnym y
błogim posádzeniem z Prełaty / Pány / Vrzędniki stanie / y z
Posłami ziemskiemi / y poddánemi nászémi wszytkiemi: Ducho-
wnemi y świeckiemi, którzysmy się ta do Piotrkowá zgromá-
dzili, y ktorzy tu reprezentuiemy ciáło tegoż Kroleśtwá z dostá-
C 4

Jan
Olbrycht
1496.

Stanisław Sarnicki, *Statuta y metrika przywileiów koronnych*, Kraków, 1594 (Statutes and register of Crown Privileges). A page including the resolutions passed by the Diet in Piotrków in 1496 concerning the obligations of the king and the rights of the Diet which "represents the body of the whole Kingdom." The reaffirmation of old laws was the main aim of the "execution of the laws'" movement. (Biblioteka Sejmowa, Warszawa).

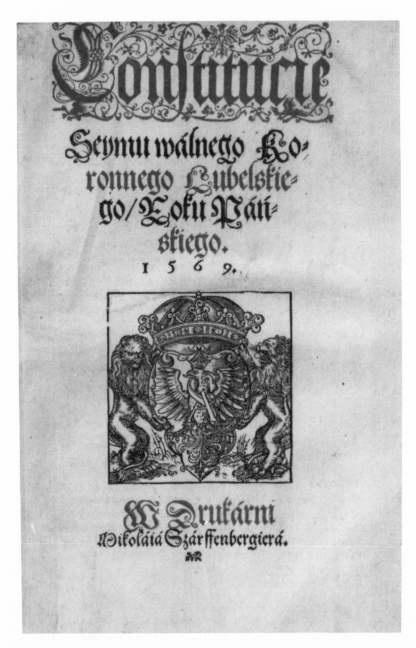

Constitucie Seymu walnego Koronnego Lubelskiego, Roku Pańskiego 1569.
(Constitutions of the General Diet in Lublin. In the year of our Lord 1569). Title
page of the resolutions passed by the Diet in Lublin in 1569, including the act of the
Union between Poland and Lithuania. (Biblioteka Sejmowa, Warszawa).

The struggle waged by the executionist camp created possibilities for improving the operation of the Parliament. Parliamentary reforms were made possible by the conjuncture of the King's positions with those of several consecutive diets in the 1560s. Although the monarch was not a legislator or deciding voice in the Diet, he was nevertheless considered the authoritative interpreter of the law *(legis interpretator)*. However, Zygmunt II August proved to be a conservative in the Jagiellonian tradition and as such avoided precise definition of Diet procedures. Such procedures needed the approval of the Diet, which could place limitations on the King's power. The King, as a result, was ambivalent about legislative procedure. He maneuvered between the Senate and the Chamber of Deputies, attempting to maintain an advantageous middle position. The King's vacillations were also caused by his fear of the Chamber of Deputies' power and of the mass of gentry dietine participants that stood behind it. Thanks to the support of the King, the Senate was several times able to force the reexamination and rejection of measures already approved by the Chamber of Deputies. In another case, Zygmunt II August asserted that the king and deputies were the deciding participants in passing legislation and that the presence of the senators was unnecessary for making laws. During the arguments about the "execution of the laws," he stated that he would always approve the decisions agreed on by the Senate and the Chamber of Deputies. These examples show the fluidity of parliamentary procedure in the often unprecedented situations encountered during the dynamic diets of the executionist period. Such circumstances created a climate that was especially conducive to reform, and, in fact, several proposals were made in such a fundamental area as the introduction of majority voting, but they proved to be unsuccessful.

Parliament's procedural heritage was not all of a piece at the end of the Jagiellonian dynasty. The Golden Age left behind a positive model of the Diet's workings, thanks to the highly developed political culture of the monarchs and the estates. Above all the political sense of the deputies was well developed, and they frequently were more attuned to the country's needs than the senators were.

The right to initiate legislation was fairly clearly defined. It belonged to the king, first of all, by virtue of his position. The king exercised his power in this area through consultations by special letters with senators before he called a session of the Diet, through messages and representatives he sent to the dietines, and through "propositions" from the throne announced before Diet deliberations began. The Senate took part in the monarch's decision to initiate legislation by responding to royal letters and through statements *(vota)* it issued at the opening of the Parliament, the agenda of which could go beyond that of the king's original messages. The notion to deny the Chamber of Deputies' their right to initiate legislation made by Chancellor Jan Ocieski during the stormy arguments over the "execution of the laws" at the 1555 Diet, had little basis in reality. The Chamber of Deputies' right to initiate legislation had its roots in the very beginnings of parliamentary organization, in petitions placed before the monarch. Under Zygmunt I these petitions no longer were contained in separate documents that accompanied the dietines' instructions to their deputies, but gradually became part of the dietines' instructions themselves, the so-called "articles." Petitions were later restricted to dietines' requests on behalf of private individuals. In the 1540s, royal acceptance of dietine "articles" or instructions became a condition for approval of the king's initiatives, especially on taxes, and this marked the establishment of the Chamber of Deputies' right to initiate legislation as called for by the executionist movement. This right was often ignored, but the Chamber of Deputies successfully pressed its case. Sometimes the king aided the Chamber of Deputies by asking it to present legislative proposals. After 1562, this happened at a number of diets in connection with the introduction of executionist reforms. Finally, at the end of the Jagiellonian period, all three of the parliamentary "estates" had attained the right to initiate legislation. The "estate" that introduced a piece of legislation prepared a preliminary text (*terminacja*). The other "estates" examined the draft. Each house first discussed the draft separately with the aim of reaching agreement on its final form. Agreement could be expressed in two ways—as *jednozgodność*, meaning no dissent was expressed, which was an acceptable conclusion, or by unanimity, *jednomyślność*, when all expressed consent, which was preferred. In practice, debates, which were sometimes quite heated, would conclude when there was no final expression of opposition. Historians are inclined to consider this a type of majority voting. It was, at most, like majority voting only in its result. The ease with which common decisions were reached at this time was the result of a consensus on the executionist reform. The dietines' instruction to the delegates did, however, have a strong influence. In some cases, these instructions made agreement in the lower house impossible.

As was already mentioned, a draft agreed upon in the Chamber of Deputies, or presented to the Chamber by the Chancellor in the name of the king or by the Senate and amended in the Chamber, was then presented to the king and senators by all the deputies, usually represented by the Marshal. After the draft was discussed, a common decision was made to submit the draft to the king for final approval, the *konkluzja*. The king formally "concluded" legislation.

The great statesman of the period, Primate Stanisław Karnkowski, wrote about the process of adopting legislation, stating that "the truth is that His Majesty retains the right of final approval, but *non ex iudicio eius proprio, sed ex sententia omnium ordinum Regni,* that is, it should be the right of the Senate and the knights' circle (Chamber of Deputies)." He added that the decisions reached by the three estates might not be the same, but that in such an event the duty of the Diet was to bring together different positions and produce a single acceptable version of legislation. That task should be made easier by the wisdom and uprightness (*prawość*) of the King and the Senate.[27]

Starting in 1563, the deputies and senators gained the right to send representatives to the royal chancellery to participate in drafting laws. This new custom was not recorded in the Diet constitutions, but was accepted in practice as the records for the Diets of 1562-63, 1565, and 1569 show. It was only in 1588, perhaps after the frequent bad experiences under Stefan Batory (1576-1586), that the drafts by representatives of both houses had to be read aloud in their and the king's presence. The sealing of the text became possible only after it received the approval of the king, Senate, and the Chamber of Deputies.[28]

Although these changes in procedure were approved, Zygmunt III altered the final versions of legislation more than once. Indirect protest against such actions was expressed in the 1633 constitution: "Conclusion of the Diet."[29] The 1633 constitution also introduced new rules for the lower house. The Marshal could present to the joint chambers only drafts approved by the house. He had to present drafts at least five days before the end of a session (an ordinary Diet was limited to six weeks by the Henrician Articles of 1573). Both restrictions on the Chamber of Deputies apparently helped it operate more efficiently by cutting down on extended, sterile haggling.[30] The legislators did not, however, anticipate that limits on the length of Diet sessions would be abused in the case of the first *liberum veto* (1652). They probably thought that the importance of matters under consideration would allow a session to be prolonged in exceptional circumstances. Evidence of the growing power of the Chamber of Deputies was the recognition by the 1633 constitution of its long held and exercised right to initiate legislation along with the other two parliamentary estates. The constitution of 1633 was renewed in 1678 and 1690.

The struggle over the "execution of the laws" became a struggle of the Chamber of Deputies to gain control over the high offices of the Senate. The executionists did not win legal restrictions on the arbitrariness of these officials appointed for life. The appointment of the previously mentioned resident senators during the intervals between the sessions of the Diet contained a warning that the king together with these senators should not make decisions on matters that were the responsibility of the Chamber of Deputies. The constitution of 1588 renewed that warning and declared such improper decisions void. The statute of 1607 on "The Residence of Senators" recommended that the resolutions from the king's deliberations with the resident senators and officials concerning public matters of state should be written down and presented to the next Diet. The Vasa Kings did not carry out these and subsequent laws. Władysław IV fought a long battle in the diets over these issues. In 1641 he gave in and agreed to the statute "*De reddenda ratione Senatus consultorum.*"[31] The points of concern were "the dignity" of the king, and the agreement of the resolutions with accepted law. It is hard to deny that this requirement limited the monarchs' freedom of political action. But the gentry deputies felt called on to participate in the main affairs of government and to control the executive branch. The Commonwealth's system of government did not, however, clearly divide legislative and executive power, nor did the governments of other contemporary states. The government of the Commonwealth followed the overly complicated structure of the office of the king. The king remained the "majesty," *Sacra Regia Maiestas* in official chancellery documents, holding the highest personal authority. As head of the state he was subject to supervision by the Parliament, the sovereign body of the Commonwealth. At the same time, he was part of the Parliament.

The position of the king in the Parliament remained prominent. He maintained his important role in forming the law, and without his approval bills could not be passed; he had the right to originate legislation, although he shared it with both houses. Despite the limits placed on the monarch by the Commonwealth's system, the facts indicate significant political activity and independence of action by the kings.

4. Diets without resolutions

Diets that dissolved without passing any resolutions occurred from the very beginning of the Polish parliamentary system. Such an outcome resulted from the interruption of Diet proceedings in a variety of ways, and requires some explanation. Diets at which conflicts between the estates were aired sometimes ended without an agreement being reached. For example, the king may have rejected a draft from the lower house and the lower house in turn rejected taxes proposed by the king.

The principles of "agreement" or "unanimity" meant that sessions of the Diet were subject to dissolution because of the opposition of a group of deputies or even by a single deputy (senators were rarely involved). A session could be dissolved in different ways. The gentlest way was to suspend the Diet's work (*sisto activitatem*). In this case the Diet continued to debate, but could not vote on legislation. During these debates, efforts were made to reach an agreement with the group in opposition, and these efforts sometimes succeeded. However, dissolving the Diet was irreversible. This was first done by the deputy from the Lithuanian town of Upita, Władysław Siciński in 1652, as a protest against the continuing of a Diet session past the statutory six weeks. A number of historians do not, therefore, regard this as a typical *liberum veto* (free right to veto) and claim the first dissolution by *liberum veto* for the 1669 Diet. In that year, the coronation Diet of Michał Korybut Wiśniowiecki was dissolved just as it began by Kiev deputy Jan Olizar.[32] During the eighteenth century, "spoiling" the Diet became more frequent by using the formula *"liberum rumpo"* (the right to break up the assembly).

Since there are no works that differentiate all the circumstances under which diets were dissolved without adopting resolutions we will treat all such cases identically. Let us add that the absence of such a work often leads to simplified and distorted conclusions. One of these is that diets that ended without producing legislation were characteristic of the seventeenth century and did not occur, or were very rare, under the Jagiellonians, therefore showing the marked degeneration of the Diet in the later period. Here is a summary table of the diets that ended without passing legislation in the period under study.

Polish Diets 1493-1696
Including convocational and electoral diets

Period	No. yrs.	Diets Called	Diets Failed	Percent Failed
1493-1572	80	72	14	19.44
1573-1648	75	70	12	17.14
1648-1696	48	44	17	38.63
total	203	186	43	23.11

The table requires some commentary that takes into account shorter periods of time whose examination will give us a more precise knowledge of the Diet. Under Jan Olbracht and Alexander the Jagiellons (1492-1501, 1501-1506) two diets of thirteen passed no resolutions (15.4 percent). Out of forty two diets held by Zygmunt I (1506-1548), six passed no laws (14.3 percent), five of them in the years 1542-1548. Zygmunt II August (1548-1572) called seventeen Diets, of which six passed no laws (35.3 percent). At some of these six diets, royal documents were read, but these were not laws passed by the estates.

Fourteen diets assembled during Henry Valois' and Stefan Batory's reign (1573-1586) and three failed to produce laws (21.4 percent). Under Zygmunt III (1587-1632), six of thirty nine diets were unproductive (15.4 percent). Three of Władysław IV's (1632-1648), seventeen diets dissolved prematurely (17.6 percent). In the second half of the seventeenth century, the diets that did not produce legislation were distributed as follows: Jan Kazimierz (1648-1668), seven of twenty two (31.8 percent); Michał Korybut Wiśniowiecki (1669-1673), four or eight (50 percent); Jan III (1674-1696), six of fourteen (42.8 percent).

It is noteworthy that in the first decade after Siciński broke up the 1652 Diet, traditionally regarded as the first *liberum veto*, only one of nine diets (1654) failed to adopt legislation successfully.

Examination of this matter over the entire period under study indicates that diets failed to produce legislation when historical events predetermined such outcomes. Thus the series of diets that did not produce legislation under both Zygmunt I and II can be viewed as a form of obstructionism or a blow aimed at the monarchs for their refusal to adopt the executionist program. These diets, especially those held under Zygmunt II August, played an important role as an all-Polish forum for discussion of the "execution of the laws" whose realization they prepared. The Diet of 1572 was cut short by the King's illness and sudden death.

The dates of Zygmunt III's failed diets provide an especially good illustration. Five of them took place during the controversial early part of his reign, from the "Inquisitional Diet" of 1592, which investigated the King's supposed plan to reach an agreement with the Habsburgs about the Polish crown in exchange for regaining the Swedish throne, to the Sandomierz Rebellion of 1606. Eleven diets were called in those years. It seems surprising, therefore, that in the later years of his reign, of twenty-two diets called between 1607 and 1632, only one diet broke up without a result, the Diet of 1615. These were years during which Zygmunt III stabilized his position in the Commonwealth.

Jan Herburt z Fulsztyna, *Statuta y przywileie koronne*, w Krakowie, 1570. Title page of Jan Herburt's Crown Statutes and Privileges which constitutes a codification of Polish Law and is Herburt's own Polish version of his *Statuta Regni Poloniae in ordinem alphabeti digesta*, Cracoviae, 1563. Published after the Union of Lublin, it shows the coats of arms of Poland and Lithuania. (Biblioteka Uniwersytecka w Warszawie). Photo A. Bodytko.

The fruitless diets of Jan Kazimierz in the years 1664-1668 (during which only one of six diets was able to pass a constitution) were caused by contemporary events, i.e., the battle between the royal court and the gentry over the election of Duke d'Enghien to the Polish throne during the king's lifetime, and the Lubomirski Rebellion in 1565-6. A similar cluster of events interrupted the diets of Korybut's reign, and show the effects on Parliament of the confederations of Gołąb and Szczebrzeszyn. Analogously, the unsuccessful domestic policies of Jan III Sobieski at the end of his reign caused frequent dissolutions of the diets after 1688.[33]

The above observations suggest that even when the principle of unanimity was practiced, and even after the first *liberum veto*, over 75 percent of Polish diets concluded successfully through the end of the seventeenth century. Nevertheless the possible harmfulness of this principle has been many times emphasized by contemporaries.

The decided majority of historians base their negative assessment of the *liberum veto* on the assumption that its application was closely connected to the theory of unanimity.[34] Contemporaries, however, did not take such a strict view of the conjuncture of these two elements. Most of the kings and senators who supported a strong monarchy opposed unanimity, though there were exceptions. According to one argument, majority voting was in the interest of the king, since he had so many ways to influence deputies (rights to intestate property without heirs, rights to crown lands, grants of privilege, appointments, money).

Voices that spoke for perfecting the parliamentary system were heard even before the *liberum veto* was used in the Diet. Later in the reigns of Zygmunt III and Władysław IV the principle of unanimity met many times with sharp criticism, mainly by senators who supported the principle of powerful kings. In the reign of Zygmunt III, these critics of unanimity included Zbigniew Ossoliński, voivode of Polesie,[35] and the two senators from Chełm, Jan Kuczborski, bishop, and Jan Weiher, voivode. They spoke in favor of majority voting in matters of national defense and retaining unanimity in voting that affected fundamental rights.[36] Under Władysław IV, supporters of majority voting included Mikołaj Spytek Ligęza, castellan of Sandomierz, Kasper Denhoff, voivode of Sieradz, and Aleksander Sokołowski, bishop of Kiev.[37]

Most important in the analysis of this question is the actual attitude of the nobility, that is of the dietines and the Diet. Protests against individual delegates dissolving a Diet session without justifiable cause were especially loud when the Diet of 1615 ended without producing any legislation. At the dietines that preceded the next Diet, that of 1616, almost all demanded that the system of voting in the Diet be reformed and the lower house took the same position when it met.[38] Some dietines' instructions to their deputies took a sharp tone on the issues demanding legal action, and accused the magnates of pressuring the deputies and of causing the disruption of the Diet.[39]

The dissolution of the 1652 Diet when the *liberum veto* was used for the first time (an action severely criticized by contemporaries) and Poland's situation after the destructive wars of the seventeenth century, would seem to have provided fertile ground for parliamentary reform. Between 1658 and 1660, the court, and senators allied with it, prepared a number of reform plans.[40] The plan for majority voting presented to the Diet of 1661 was not approved. The deciding factor in the plan's rejection was that it was presented to the Diet at the same time as a royal scheme to have the Duke d'Enghien elected King while Jan Kazimierz was still alive *(vivente rege)*, although there were grave popular reservations about the election.[41] The gentry understood that the first result of their agreement to majority voting in the Diet would be a guarantee of the Polish throne to the French prince.

Voices in favor of rationalizing the Parliament's decision-making process continued to be heard from time to time, most often as a reaction to the disruption of the Diet or to proposed changes in Diet procedure, but for different reasons they failed to win approval. [42]

Why was the principle of unanimity upheld for so long, despite frequent criticism of the Diets workings under it? Why did an enlightened gentry, conscious of the demands of political life and well acquainted with the procedures of the dietines and Diet, treat that principle as unalterable?[43] As has been stated above, contemporaries did not equate the theory of unanimity with the ease with which diets could be dissolved. It would be a mistake to claim that there was a cult of interrupting the Diet among the deputies. Quite the opposite, they felt that dissolving the Diet showed their failure to carry out their commissions as deputies. Sometimes they saw it as treason, a frivolous abuse of the principle of unanimity to stop debate and cut short a Diet session without passing legislation.[44] They did not see the solution to the problem in breaking with the tradition of unanimity, but in preventing abuses of it. They believed that through persuasion, debate, and mutual concessions the "estates" assembled in council could reach a consensus after a lengthy "wearing down" of each other's positions without violating the medieval maxim *quod omnes tangit ab omnibus comprobari debet.*"[45] In theory they could reach unanimous agreement. According to Józef Siemieński, an "absence of ill will" or of clear active opposition (*nemine contradicente)* was enough for legislation to be enacted.[46]

Working from the principle of unanimity there was no need to count votes, since, according to the favorite saying of the gentry, "truth is not counted, it is proved." Andrzej Wyczański summed up the real meaning of the effort put into achieving unanimity in diets by quoting the lapidary phrase quoted above.[47] Claude Backvis remarked that the institution of unanimity "served to bring forth authentic debate and built up the skills needed for reaching healthy compromises."[48] Zbigniew Ogonowski undertook a defense of the *liberum veto* and tried to penetrate the mentality of old Polish legislators as deeply as possible.[49]

The harmful effects of the principle of unanimity became clear only in the eighteenth century when the situation of the Commonwealth drastically changed, when the power of its neighbors–the absolutist monarchies of Russia, Prussia and Austria–increased to the point that by bribery and every other possible means, they were able to use unanimity and especially *liberum veto* as a tool to break up the diets and to cause the decline of Poland's political system.

In this way the institution of unanimity, which Polish contemporaries considered a symbol of traditional freedom, gradually grew to serve foreign interests and to pose a mortal threat to the Commonwealth.

This threat did not seem real to the generations of Poles living in the sixteenth and seventeenth centuries, since they could not know the future and since the spirit of territorial expansion by military force was alien to their historical tradition. For the supporters of Polish democracy the real threats to the foundations of the state were not all foreign. They considered the establishment of a hereditary absolute monarchy in Poland a threat as well. And, in fact, absolutism was the dominant political form in the Europe of their day.

Finally, turning to a more general historical question: was absolutism capable of producing the best type of modern state, or did the path to "modernization" lie in constitutional monarchy, practiced in Poland and England? Stanisław Russocki has addressed this question.[50] He recalled the ideas advanced by Gotthold Rhode: that absolutism is not the only indicator of modernity and that scholars' conclusions on the subject will differ, depending on whether they believe that the criteria of modernity are the growth of state power and the creation of a standing army, or the formation of parliamentary structures so that progress is expressed in guaranteed civil rights and citizens' participation in political life. If one uses the latter criteria for analysis, said Rhode, "then the gentry democracy of the Commonwealth was, until 1688, more 'modern' than early absolutism."[51] Let us add that this was so despite the faulty medieval parliamentary idea of unanimity.

Notes

1. Works concerning the origins of the Polish Parliament include: Claude Backvis, "L'origine de la Diète'viritim'pour l'élection du roi en Pologne" *Annuaire de l'Institut de Philologie et d'Histoire Orientales et Slaves* 20 (1973): 45-128; Juliusz Bardach, *Historia państwa i prawa Polski* (The history of the Polish state and Polish law) (Warszawa: PWN, 1964), pp. 249-251; "La formation des assemblées polonaises au XVe siècle et la taxation" *Anciens Pays et Assemblées d'États* 70 (1977): 251-295; Michał Bobrzyński, "Sejmy polskie za Olbrachta i Aleksandra" (Polish diets in the reigns of Olbracht and Aleksander) in *Szkice i studia historyczne* (Kraków, 1922), vol. 1 pp. 184-257; Henryk Chodynicki, *Sejmiki ziem ruskich w wieku XV* (The dietines of the Rus lands in the 15th century) (Lwów: 1906); Karol Górski, *Communitas-Princeps-Corona Regni. Studia selecta* (Warszawa: PWN, 1976); Stanisław Kutrzeba, *Historia ustroju Polski w zarysie* (An outline of Polish political history) (Lwów: 1921), vol 2, *Litwa*, pp. 93-106; Wacław Odyniec, *Dzieje Prus Królewskich 1454-1772* (The history of Royal Prussia 1454-1772) (Warszawa: PWN, 1972), pp. 28-58; Adolf Pawiński, *Sejmiki ziemskie. Początek ich i rozwój...* (Dietines: their origins and development) (Warszawa: 1895); Franciszek Piekosiński, *Wiece, sejmiki, sejmy i przywileje ziemskie w Polsce wieków średnich* ("Wiece," dietines, diets and noble privileges in medieval Poland) (Kraków: Akademia Umiejętności, 1900); Antoni Prochaska, *Geneza i rozwój parlamentaryzmu za pierwszych Jagiellonów* (The origins and development of parliamentary government under the first Jagiellons) (Kraków: 1898); Stanisław Roman, *Przywileje nieszawskie* (The Nieszawa privileges) (Wrocław: Ossolineum, 1957); Stanisław Russocki, "Narodziny zgromadzeń stanowych" (The birth of estate assemblies), *Przegląd Historyczny* 59, 2 (1968): 214-226; "Les assemblées représentatives en Europe Centrale. Préliminaire d'une analyse comparative," *Acta Poloniae Historica* 30 (1974): 33-52; Józef Siemieński, "Od sejmików do sejmu (1454-1505" (From dietines to the diet, 1454-1505), in *Studia historyczne ku czci Stanisława Kutrzeby* (Kraków, 1938) vol. 1, pp. 445-460; Bogdan Sobol, *Sejm i sejmiki ziemskie na Mazowszu Książęcym* (The diet and the dietines in the Princedom of Mazowsze) (Warszawa: PWN, 1968); Jerzy Włodarczyk, "Sejmiki Łęczyckie do początku XVI wieku" (The dietines of Łęczyca until the beginning of the sixteenth century) *Czasopismo Prawno-Historyczne* 12,1 (1960): 9-46; Zygmunt Wojciechowski, *Państwo polskie w wiekach średnich. Dzieje ustroju* (Poland in the Middle Ages: The political system) (Poznań: Księgarnia Akademicka, 1945); *L'État polonais au Moyen Age. Histoire des institutions* (Paris: 1949).

2. Jerzy Wyrozumski, *Kazimierz Wielki* (Kazimierz the Great) (Wrocław: Ossolineum, 1986), pp. 60-63, 90, 157, 202-209; *Volumina legum. Prawa, konstytucye y przywileie Królestwa Polskiego, Wielkiego Xięstwa Litewskiego y wszystkich Prowincyi należących...* (hereafter referred to as *VL*) (The laws, constitutions and privileges of the Kingdom of Poland, the Grand Duchy of Lithuania and all Provinces...), 8 vols. (Warszawa: 1733-1782), vol. 1, pp. 55-58; Piekosiński, *Wiece...*, p. 18; Bardach, *Historia państwa...*, pp. 422-426.

3. François Dumont, ed., *Études sur l'histoire des Assemblées d'États* (Paris: Presses Universitaires de France, 1966), pp. 95-222; Günther Burkert, *Ferdinand I und die Steirischen Stände* (Graz: 1976), pp. 26-27; Klaus Köhle, *Landesherr und Landstände in der Oberpfalz von 1400-1583* (München: Neue Schriftenreihe des Stadtarchives München, 1969), pp. 94-97, 99-101, 110-111; Nico Sapper, *Die schwäbisch-österreichischen Landstände und Landtage im 16. Jahrhundert* (Stuttgart: Müller und Gräft, 1965) pp. 125, 132, 134-139.

4. Bardach, "Początki sejmu" (The origins of the diet) in *Historia sejmu polskiego*, vol. 1, ed. Jerzy Michalski (Warszawa: PWN, 1984), pp. 10-15, 24-27.

5. Stanisław Kutrzeba, *Sejm walny dawnej Rzeczypospolitej polskiej* (The general Diet in the old Polish Commonwealth) (Warszawa: 1923), pp. 41-72.

6. For more on the Lithuanian Diet in the sixteenth century, see: Oskar Halecki, *Dzieje unii jagiellońskiej* (The history of the Jagiellonian union), vol. 2 (Kraków: Akademia Umiejętności, 1920).

7. Bardach, "Początki sejmu" in *Historia sejmu polskiego* pp. 35-36.

8. Claude Soule, "Les États Généraux de France (1302-1789)", in *Études présentées à la Commission Internationale pour l'Histoire des Assemblées d'États,* vol. 35 (Heule, 1968), pp. 58-63; Charles Eszlary, *Histoire des institutions publiques hongroises*, vol. 2 (Paris: 1963), p. 86-88; Stanisław Russocki, *Protoparlamentaryzm Czech do początku XV wieku* (Czech protoparliamentarianism to the beginning of the 15th century) (Warszawa: Uniwersytet Warszawski, 1973), pp. 105-107; Köhle, *Landesherr und Landstände* pp. 94-100.

9. Tadeusz Silnicki, *Prawo elekcji królów w dobie jagiellońskiej* (Royal electoral law under the Jagiellonians) (Lwów: 1913).

10. For a discussion of privileges and laws before 1505, see: Piekosiński, *Wiece.*

11. Prochaska, *Geneza*, p.43.

12. Roman, *Przywileje;* Bardach "Początki sejmu," in *Historia sejmu polskiego*, pp. 32-35.

13. Henryk Karbownik, "Udział przedstawicieli kapituł w sejmach i sejmikach dawnej Rzeczypospolitej (w XV-XVIII wieku)" (The participation of clerical representatives in the diets and dietines of the old Polish Commonwealth from the 15th to the 18th century), *Czasopismo Prawno-Historyczne*, 22 (1970): 169-176; Marian J. Mika, "Udział Poznania w sejmach Rzeczypospolitej od końca XV w. do 1791 r." (The participation of Poznań in the diets of the Commonwealth from the end of the 15th century to 1791), *Studia i Materiały do Dziejów Wielkopolski i Pomorza* 6, 2 (1961): 257-302; Jerzy Reder, "Posłowie miasta Lublina na sejmy dawnej Rzeczypospolitej" (Deputies from the city of Lublin at the diets of the old Polish Commonwealth), *Czasopismo Prawno-Historyczne*, 6, 2 (1954): 253-286; Leon Ryman, "Udział Krakowa w sejmach i sejmikach Rzeczypospolitej" (The participation of Kraków in the diets and dietines of the Commonwealth), *Rocznik Krakowski* 7 (1895): 187-

258; Władysław Kowalenko, "Geneza udziału stołecznego miasta Wilna w sejmach Rzeczypospolitej" (The origin of participation by the capital city of Wilno in the diets of the Commonwealth), *Ateneum Wileńskie* 4, 12 (1927): 79-137.

14. On the Polish Parliament during the sixteenth and seventeenth centuries, see: *The Polish Parliament at the Summit of Its Development (16th-17th Centuries)* ed. Władysław Czapliński (Wrocław: Ossolineum 1985); Czapliński, "Sejm w latach 1587-1696" (The Diet in the years 1587-1696) in *Historia sejmu polskiego*, pp. 217-299; Jan Dzięgielewski *Izba poselska w systemie władzy Rzeczypospolitej w czasach Władysława IV* (The significance of the house of deputies in the Commonwealth under Władysław IV) (Warszawa: Wydawnictwo Sejmowe, 1992); Konstanty Grzybowski, *Teoria reprezentacji w Polsce epoki Odrodzenia* (The theory of parliamentary representation in Renaissance Poland) (Warszawa: PWN, 1959); Władysław Konopczyński, *Le Liberum Veto. Étude sur le développement du principe majoritaire* (Paris: Institut d'Études Slaves de l'Université de Paris, 1930); *Liberum veto. Studium historyczno-porównawcze* (Liberum veto. Historical-comparative study) (Kraków, 1918); Stanisław Kutrzeba, *Sejm walny...*; Henryk Olszewski, *Sejm Rzeczypospolitej epoki oligarchii 1652-1763* (The Diet of the Commonwealth during the era of oligarchy, 1652-1763) (Poznań: Uniwersytet A. Mickiewicza, 1966); Anna Sucheni-Grabowska, "Badania nad elitą władzy w latach 1551-1562" (A study of the power elite in the years 1551-1562) in *Społeczeństwo Staropolskie*, ed. Andrzej Wyczański (Warszawa: PWN, 1976), vol. 1, pp. 57-119; "Sejm w latach 1540-1586" (The Diet in the years 1540-1586) in *Historia sejmu polskiego*, pp. 114-216; *Spory królów ze szlachtą w złotym wieku* (Conflict between the kings and the gentry during the Golden Age) (Kraków: Krajowa Agencja Wydawnicza, 1988); *Tradycje polityczne dawnej Polski* (The political tradition of old Poland) eds. Anna Sucheni-Grabowska, Anna Dybkowska (Warszawa: Spotkania, 1993); Wacław Uruszczak, *Sejm walny koronny w latach 1506-1540* (The general Diet of Poland in the years 1506-1540) (Warszawa: PWN, 1980). For further works on the Polish Parliament see : *Historia sejmu polskiego*, pp. 420-428.

15. *Historia sejmu polskiego*, pp. 179-180, 239; Władysław Konopczyński, *Chronologia sejmów polskich 1493-1793* (A chronology of Polish diets 1493-1793) (Kraków: PAU, 1948). For the Lithuanian diets held before 1569, see note 6.

16. After the controversial session of 1484, the Estates General were called in 1560, 1561, 1576, 1588, 1614, and 1789. The English Parliament met every three to four years during the 16th century. Charles I ruled without Parliament between 1619 and 1640. The importance of the English Parliament was finally established at the end of the 17th century. In the German lands the practice of calling parliaments varied. Saxony and Bavaria had regular meetings of their assemblies in the 16th century, but they grew less frequent in the 17th century. The significance of the *Cortes* declined, repeatedly undercut by the Habsburgs, until the *Cortes* disappeared around 1665. Many similarities existed between the Polish and Hungarian parliaments. In Hungary the Parliament was lively before the Turkish invasion of 1541 and operated in a

limited way in the diminished territory of Transylvania and in the Habsburg lands. Ferdinand I Habsburg, though he called 28 sessions of the Parliament in the years 1526-1563, tried to reduce its influence. Compare to d'Eszlary, *Histoire*, vol. 2, p. 95, vol. 3, pp. 81-83.

17. Compare to the saying common in Austrian Schwaben "Landtag ist Geldtag" and the unwillingness to take part in popular assemblies in which the cost of travel played a role. In effect a form of political passivity was developing. See: Sapper, *Die...Landstände*, pp. 126-128. Developments were similar in most south German states, such as the Upper Palatinate. See: Köhle, *Landesherr*, pp. 48-51, 102-103, 110-111.

18. The exemption of nobles from taxation was guaranteed by the privilege of 1374, confirmed by later rulers, and extended in the statutes of 1454. The nobility as an estate was released from taxation in most countries because of their contribution to the defense of the state. Compare to Marcel Marion, *Dictionnaire des institutions de la France aux XVIIe et XVIIIe siècles* (Paris: Picard, 1969), pp. 526-532.

19. Uruszczak, *Sejm walny*, pp. 128-135.

20. Works on the dietines include: Bardach, "Députés à la diète en Pologne d'Ancien Régime", *Acta Poloniae Historica*, 39 (1979): 143-185; "Formes des Assemblées Représentatives de Grand Duché de Lituanie après l'Union de Lublin (1569)" in *Études présentées à la Commission Internationale pour l'histoire des Assemblées d'États*, vol. 48 (Warszawa: Editions de l Université de Varsovie, 1975), pp. 159-184; Józef A. Gierowski, *Sejmik Generalny Księstwa mazowieckiego na tle ustroju sejmikowego Mazowsza* (The general dietine of the Princedom of Mazowsze in the context of the Mazowsze dietine system) (Wrocław: Ossolineum, 1948); Wojciech Kriegseisen, *Samorząd szlachecki w Małopolsce w l. 1669-1717* (Gentry self-rule in Małopolska, 1669-1717) (Warszawa: PWN, 1989); *Sejmiki Rzeczypospolitej szlacheckiej w XVII i XVIII w.* (The 17th and 18th-century dietines of the gentry Commonwealth) (Warszawa: Wydawnictwo Sejmowe, 1991); Adam Lityński, *Szlachecki samorząd gospodarczy w Małopolsce (1606-1717)* (Gentry economic self-rule in Małopolska, 1606-1717) (Katowice: Uniwersytet Śląski, 1974); Edward Opaliński, *Elita władzy w województwie poznańskim i kaliskim za Zygmunta III* (The power elite of the Poznań and Kalisz voivodeships under Zygmunt III) (Poznań : Wydawnictwo Poznańskie, 1981); Adolf Pawiński, *Rządy sejmikowe w Polsce 1572-1795. Na tle stosunków województw kujawskiech* (Rule by the dietines in Poland, 1572-1795. Based on conditions in the voivodeships of Kujawy) (Warszawa: PIW, 1978); Stanisław Płaza, *Sejmiki i zjazdy szlacheckie województwa poznańskiego i kaliskiego. Ustrój i funkcjonowanie (1572-1632)* (The dietines and gentry assemblies of the Poznań and Kalisz voivodeships, their structure and operation, 1572-1632) (Kraków: PWN, 1984); *Sejmiki i zjazdy szlacheckie województwa sieradzkiego. Ustrój i funkcjonowanie (1572-1632)* (The dietines and gentry assemblies of the Sieradz voivodeships, their structure and operation 1572-1632) (Kraków: PWN, 1987); Józef Siemieński, *Organizacja sejmiku ziemi dobrzyńskiej* (The organization of the Dobrzyń

dietine) (Kraków: Akademia Umiejętności, 1906); Wiesław Śladkowski, *Skład społeczny, wyznaniowy i ideologia sejmiku lubelskiego w 1. 1572-1648* (The social and denominational composition and the ideology of the Lublin dietine, 1572-1648) Annales Universitatis Mariae Curie-Skłodowska, vol. 12 (Lublin: 1947), pp. 129-156; Stanisław Śreniowski, *Organizacja sejmiku halickiego* (The organization of the Halicz dietine) (Lwów: 1938); Zofia Trawicka, *Sejmik województwa sandomierskiego w latach 1572-1696* (The Sandomierz dietine, 1572-1696) (Kielce: WSP im. J. Kochanowskiego, 1985); Wacław Urban, "Skład społeczny i ideologia sejmiku krakowskiego w 1. 1572-1606" (The social composition and ideology of the Kraków dietine, 1572-1606) *Przegląd Historyczny* XL.3 (1953): 309-333; Jerzy Włodarczyk, *Sejmiki łęczyckie* (The dietines of Łęczyce) (Łódź: Uniwersytet Łódzki, 1973). For additional works on dietines see: Kriegseisen, *Sejmiki Rzeczypospolitej,* pp. 281-3.

21. *VL,* vol. 1, p. 372 (1510), vol. 2, p. 676 (1565).

22. The 1566 Statute: "Statutum Lituanicum Alterius Editionis," *Archiwum Komisji Prawniczej Akademii Umiejętności,* vol, 7 (Kraków, 1900), pp. 45-46, 70-73.

23. Łukasz Górnicki, "Droga do zupełnej wolności" (The road to complete freedom) in Łukasz Górnicki, *Pisma,* ed. Roman Pollak, vol. 2 (Warszawa: PIW, 1961), p. 483.

24. Gotfryd Lengnich's description of the 1742 diet's procedures bears witness to this. Gotfryd Lengnich, *Prawo pospolite Królewstwa Polskiego* (The general law of the Polish Kingdom) (Kraków: 1836), pp. 341-377. See also: Uruszczak, *Sejm walny,* pp. 148-190; Olszewski, *Sejm Rzeczypospolitej,* pp. 168-358; Dzięgielewski, *Izba poselska,* pp. 48-68.

25. See Anna Dembińska, *Polityczna walka o egzekucję dóbr królewskich w latach 1559-64* (The political battle over the administration of Crown property, 1559-1564) (Warszawa: Towarzystwo Naukowe Warszawskie, 1935); Zygmunt Wojciechowski, *Zygmunt Stary 1506-1548* (Zygmunt I, the Old) (Warszawa: S. Act, 1946); "Les débuts du programme du l'exécution des lois en Pologne au début du XVIe siècle," *Revue Historique de Droit Français et Etranger* 2 (1951): 173-192; Irena Kaniewska, *Małopolska reprezentacja sejmowa za czasów Zygmunta Augusta 1548-1572* (Małopolska Diet representation under Zygmunt August 1548-1572), Zeszyty Naukowe Uniwersytetu Jagiellońskiego, vol. 351 (Kraków: (1974); Sucheni-Grabowska, *Monarchia dwu ostatnich Jagiellonów a ruch egzekucyjny. Geneza egzekucji dóbr* (The reigns of the last two Jagiellons and the executionist movement) (Wrocław: Ossolineum, 1974); "Społeczność szlachecka a państwo" (Gentry society and the state) in *Polska w epoce Odrodzenia,* ed. Andrzej Wyczański (Warszawa: Wiedza Powszechna, 1986), pp. 13-107. On the Lithuanian union and the executionist movement see Bardach, "Krewo i Lublin" (Krewo and Lublin), *Kwartalnik Historyczny* 3 (1969): 583-619; "Związek Polski z Litwą" (The Polish-Lithuanian Union) in *Polska w epoce Odrodzenia,* pp. 108-161.

26. Stanisław Grzybowski, *Mikołaj Sienicki. Demostenes sejmów polskich* (Mikołaj Sienicki, The Demosthenes of the Polish diets) Odrodzenie i Reformacja w Polsce, vol.2 (Wrocław, 1957), pp. 91-132.

27. Stanisław Karnkowski, "Obyczaj i porządek odpraw sejmowych" (The customs and order of diet meetings) in *Pisma ks. Stanisława Karnkowskiego*, ed. Kazimierz J. Turowski (Kraków, 1859), pp. 5-21.

28. *VL*, vol. 2, p. 1209.

29. *VL*, vol. 3, p. 786.

30. Czapliński, "Sejm w latach 1587-1696" in *Historia sejmu* polskiego, p. 264.

31. *VL*, vol. 2, p. 1598; vol. 4. pp. 3-4; see also Olszewski, *Sejm Rzeczypospolitej*, pp. 234-236; Czapliński "Z problematyki sejmu polskiego w I połowie XVII w." (On the Polish diet of the first half of the 17th century) *Kwartalnik Historyczny*, 77, 1 (1970): 36-37; Dzięgielewski, *Izba poselska*, p. 97.

32. Konopczyński compiled the names of delegates who dissolved the diet in the years 1652-1764. Of the 73 individuals recorded, 9 were from Małopolska, 7 from Wielkopolska, 5 from the voivodeships of Rawa and Płock. By comparison, 24 delegates from the territories of Kiev, Bełz, Bracław, Wołyń, Podole, and Halicz dissolved the Diet. Lithuanian delegates did so 28 times. In sum delegates from Lithuania and the eastern lands of the Commonwealth dissolved the Diet 52 of 73 times. Konopczyński, *Le Liberum Veto*, p. 218.

33. Zbigniew Wójcik, *Jan Sobieski 1629-1696* (Warszawa: PIW, 1983), pp. 443-510.

34. It is impossible to list all these historians here, from Józef Szujski and Michał Bobrzyński to the present. The most recent sharp critic of the principle of unanimity is Zbigniew Wójcik, *Liberum Veto* (Kraków: Krajowa Agencja Wydawnicza, 1992).

35. Czapliński, "Sejm w latach 1587-1696" in *Historia sejmu polskiego*, pp. 275-6, 278. Czapliński quotes Ossoliński at the Diet of 1606: "It is a great dishonor to the Commonwealth to have such a government where one person, for a trifle or out of stubbornness, might cause its fall."

36. Stefania Ochmann, *Sejmy lat 1661-1662. Przegrana batalia o reformę ustroju Rzeczypospolitej* (The diets of 1661-1662: The lost battle for political reform of the Commonwealth) (Wrocław: Ossolineum, 1977), p. 143; Jan Seredyka, *Sejm z 1618 roku* (The Diet of 1618) (Opole: WSP im. Powstańców Śląskich, 1988); Andrzej Opaliński, Bishop of Poznań, made a similar statement. Seredyka also includes information about a draft plan presented at the Diet of 1613 by Marcin Szyszkowski, Bishop of Kraków, to change Diet procedures, pp. 58, 135.

37. Olszewski, *Sejm Rzeczypospolitej*, pp. 58, 327.

38. Ochmann, *Sejmy z lat 1615-1616* (The diets of 1615-1616), (Wrocław: Ossolineum, 1970) pp. 142-143, 175.

39. Teki Pawińskiego, 20, p.32 (Rożan, 1616). (Unpublished files of A. Pawiński), Ms. The Library of PAU, Kraków. Teki Pawińskiego 33, p. 62 verso (Wizna, 1616). The dietine of Rożan plainly demanded that "*pluralitas votorum* be applied to closing the Diet." Anna Filipczak-Kocur, *Sejmik sieradzki za Wazów* (The Sieradz dietine under the Vasa Kings) (Opole: 1989), p. 58.

40. The most complete plan for the reform of diet procedure appears in a document from about 1660. See, Stefania Ochmann-Staniszewska, *Pisma polityczne z czasów panowania Jana Kazimierza Wazy 1648-1668* (Political works from the reign of Jan Kazimierz Vasa, 1648-1668), vol. 1, 1648-1660 (Wrocław: Instytut Historii PAN, 1989), pp. 236-243. See also Ochmann "Plans for Parliamentary Reform in the Commonwealth in the Middle of the 17th Century" in *The Polish Parliament at the Summit of its Development*, pp. 163-187.

41. Ochmann, *Sejmy lat 1661-1662*, pp. 94-95, passim. See also Jan Pasek, *Pamiętniki* (Memoirs), ed. Władysław Czapliński (Wrocław: Ossolineum, (1952), p. 351.

42. Krystyn Matwijowski, *Pierwsze sejmy z czasów Jana III Sobieskiego* (The first diets of Jan Sobieski III) (Wrocław: Ossolineum, 1976), p. 76; Olszewski, *Sejm Rzeczypospolitej*, pp. 328-331.

43. For further discussion of this question, see: Czapliński, "The principle of unanimity in the Polish Parliament" in *The Polish Parliament at the Summit of Its Development*, pp. 112-119, and in *Historia sejmu polskiego*, pp. 274-283.

44. The dietine of Liw demanded in its instructions of 7 February 1667 that delegates who "departed the house of deputies in protest that is not based in law, and not *bonum publicum* or *iniuriam publicam* but *privatam concerneret*, should be judged by the entire house and *documentis convictus* as a person *perduellis* and *hostis patriae*" and that the absence of such delegates from the Diet should "as *praeiudiciosa* to the Commonwealth not be allowed to obstruct the *cursum consiliorum publicorum*."

45. The voluntary surrender by society of rights that protected it from the eventuality of future abuses by monarchical governments was impossible where the voice of society was in fact taken into account. See: Sucheni-Grabowska, "Sejm w latach 1540-1587" in *Historia sejmu polskiego*, pp. 198-200. Teki Pawińskiego 5, p. 99 verso 100.

46. Józef Siemieński, "O jednomyślności w parlamentaryzmie polskim w XVI wieku" (On unanimity in Polish parliamentary practice in the 16th century) *Sprawozdania z posiedzeń TNW*, Wydział II Nauk Historycznych, Społecznych i Filozoficznych, 42 (1949): 32-46.

47. Andrzej Wyczański, *Polska Rzeczą Pospolitą Szlachecką* (Poland, a Commonwealth of the gentry) (Warszawa: PWN, 1991), pp. 223, 324-326.

48. Claude Backvis, "Wymóg jednomyślności a 'wola ogółu'" (The requirement of unanimity and 'the will of the whole'), *Czasopismo Prawno-Historyczne*, 27, 2 (1975): 161-173; "L'exigence de l'unanimité dans la décision et ses effets sur l'esprit et les

méthodes de la délibération parlementaire", *Bulletin de la Classe des Lettres et des Sciences Morales et Politiques* (Académie Royale de Belgique) 5 série, 67 (1981-4): 152-171.

49. Zbigniew Ogonowski, "W obronie liberum veto. Nad pismami Andrzeja Maksymiliana Fredry," (In defense of the *liberum veto*. On the works of Andrzej Maksymilian Fredro) in *Filozofia polityczna w Polsce XVII wieku i tradycje demokracji europejskiej* (Warszawa: Instytut Filozofii i Socjologii PAN, 1992), p. 41.

50. Stanisław Russocki, "Probleme frühmoderner Staatlichkeit in Polen und in den deutschen Ländern" in *Polen und Deutschland im europäischen Staatensystem vom späten Mittelalter bis zur Mitte des 19.* Jahrhunderts (Braunschweig: Gemeinsame Deutsch-Polnische Schulbuchkommission, 1992), pp. 58-60.

51. Gotthold Rhode, *Handbuch der europäischen Geschichte* (Stuttgart: Th. Schieder, 1971), vol. 3, p. 1008.

Translated by George Makowski

CONSTITVCIE
Seymu Walnego Warsaw-
skiego/ Roku/ M.D.CXXXj.

3

Some Comments on Old "Privileges" and the "Liberum Veto"

Wenceslas J. Wagner

The very idea of a constitutional system suggests that the basic public relations in the state in question are regulated rather than left to the whim of the ruling emperor, king, prince, dictator or clique; in other words, the strong presumption is that the rule of law obtains and there is no room for arbitrary decisions of the government which, along with all citizens, must abide by the main principles accepted by the society. The government is one "of law" rather than "of men."

Traditionally, these principles were developing little by little and were not written down in a single document. Even at the present time, England does not have a constitution adopted as a single enactment. The country is recognized as a model modern democracy, but its life is based on many laws elaborated by the Parliament, judicial decisions, customs and usages. The road to the present respect of human rights and the nation's participation in the government was long and difficult. The *Magna Carta Libertatum*, granted by King John Lackland in 1215 to his barons was not to be applied to all the citizens, and besides, it remained a dead letter for a few centuries to come. It was necessary to have the Cromwell revolution to steer the nation towards a more liberal future.

In most other countries the situation was much worse. In France, King Louis XIV used to say: "*L'état c'est moi!*" and exercised uncontrolled power over his nation. Again, a revolution, which began in 1789, was necessary to stop the abuses of the monarchy.

Compared to all the more important countries of the world, Polish history was unusually quiet as far as internal relations were concerned. No devastating revolutions, no bloody religious wars, no king-killing by the citizens. The troubles were externally generated by invasions and aggressions on the part of belligerent and greedy nations. But even in the field of relations with other nations, Poland's past was unusual: she integrated into one powerful union a few of the neighboring nations, and particularly Lithuania with which she was associated for four centuries, until the downfall of the Polish-Lithuanian Commonwealth partitioned by Prussia, Russia and Austria in 1795. Even after the partitions, brotherhood and unity were felt between the two nations. Liberty movements and insurrections, originating in Poland spread to Lithuania.

While in other important countries of the world (with the possible exception of England) the power of the ruler was not checked by anything, the Polish-Lithuanian Commonwealth developed a parliamentary system. Its final form was embodied in the 1505 constitution *Nihil Novi*, by virtue of which the King was not to enact any new law without the consent of the Parliament.

After Poland lost her independence in 1795, her history was written mostly by historians of the partitioning powers, particularly the Prussians and the Russians.[1] It is well known that one of their main theories was that the downfall of Poland was caused by the Poles themselves. Their governmental system was said to be anarchistic; their democratic institutions - to be a result of the predominant position of one social class: the nobility; and their religious freedom and tolerance of anyone's opinions - to constitute a weakness which has led the country to a disaster. Besides foreign commentators, some Polish historians, particularly from the so-called "Cracow school," went far in the direction of strong criticism of Poland's past.[2] Along with the "scholars" from the ranks of Poland's enemies, they used to repeat stereotypes accusing the Poles of lacking political sense, of making it impossible for the government to exercise its power and of giving their own private interests precedence over the public good.

Such theories found easy acceptance in the West, for which it was the easiest thing to forget about the Polish question and to accept the facts brought about by Poland's partitions which, in their general outlines, have not been changed either by Napoleon or the Congress of Vienna. It is true that from time to time there were some statements in the press or even in parliaments which were a proof that there was sympathy for the Polish nation, and the exclamation to the Tsar, visiting France: "Long live Poland Sir!" made history, but the words not less known: "Order has been established in Warsaw" were the

The Royal Castle in Warsaw in 1656. Part of a copperplate panorama of Warsaw by Nicolas Perelle based on Erik J. Dahlberg's drawing, included in Samuel Pufendorf *De Rebus a Carolo Gustavo Sveciae Rege gestis*...Norimbergae, 1696. (Muzeum Narodowe w Warszawie).

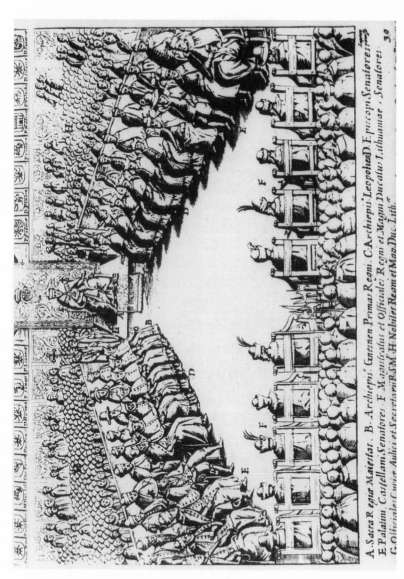

A. Sacra Regia Maiestas. B. Archiepi: Gnetnen Primas Regni. C. Archiepis: Leopolien D. Episcopi Senatores
E. Palatini, Castellani, Senatores. F. Magistratus et Officiale: Regni et Magni Ducalus Lithuaniae. Senatores:
G. Officiales Curiae Aulici et Secretarii R.F.M. H. Nobiles Regni et Mag: Duc: Lith.

The Diet with King Zygmunt III in session at the Royal Castle in Warsaw. Copperplate by Giacomo Lauro, 1622 (Biblioteka Sejmowa, Warszawa) reflections of the prevailing trend to stability in Europe and to the maintenance of peace at any price.

The situation in Poland became especially tragic after the downfall of the January uprising of 1863. After the collapse of the "Spring of Nations" and the short period of the Crimean War, the diplomacy of the great powers established a world system in which small nations did not have anything to say and movements towards freedom did not have much chance to be successful. The defeat of France in the war with Prussia and the downfall of Napoleon III did not exert a strong influence on the developments in other countries. During the last decades of the XIX century the partitioning powers could do anything they pleased in Poland (and in Lithuania) without incurring any danger of reaction (and frequently, even without raising much interest) on the part of Western states.

In such circumstances, it is not surprising that historical ideas in various countries, including Poland, began to be oriented in the direction set by the partitioning powers. This approach became embedded so deeply that it was not discarded by historical research even after the recovery of independence, although it was challenged by a number of scholars. One of these approaches is the belief that Polish nobility, moved by its own interests, was able to wrestle from the king ever more concessions, usually called "privileges." Relevant acts of the king are known in history under this term.

However, everything should be understood in the light of the era in which the historical event took place. According to the standards of today, the introduction of democratic institutions in Poland did not have the character of privileges. A permission to keep a hat on the head in the presence of the king could be called a privilege - but the historical Polish "privileges" were simply dealing with the recognition of fundamental human rights while securing the respect of human dignity and curbing the arbitrariness of the ruler.

At present, in all democratic and law respecting nations, the principles introduced by the old Polish "privileges" are recognized as basic elements of the life of the society. The king's promise of 1425, *Neminem captivabimus nisi iure victum* (nobody will be arrested without a court's order), preceded by two and a half centuries the *Habeas Corpus Act* in England. At the present time, it is recognized as elementary in democratic systems in the true meaning of this word, but at the beginning of the XV century it was revolutionary. The Polish approach could not be welcomed by tyrants and absolutists and their theoreticians like Bodin,[3] and could easily be treated as "anarchy" because it limited the arbitrariness of the rulers.

Another example, taken from still older times: the Privilege of Košice of 1374. More than six centuries ago the Polish king gave up the possibility of imposing new taxes without the consent of the nobility. In our own era it is well established that taxes must be imposed by the parliament as the representative of the whole nation. But in old times the citizen did not have anything to say in this matter - indeed, in no other matters as well. As the Supreme Court of the United States observed - the power to tax is a power to destroy.

Fiscal oppression, so frequently exercised by state authorities and feudal lords resulted - at the last stage - in the difficult situation of the peasants. Financial questions were also responsible to a larger extent for the American Declaration of Independence and the Great French Revolution. By virtue of the Constitution of the United States, the initiative to establish taxes, contrary to other problems, must originate in the lower house as more representative than the Senate.

From among other well known examples one could also mention the Privilege of Czerwińsk of 1422 which guaranteed that the king would not take over private property without a court order. A similar provision found its place in the 5th Amendment to the American Constitution (1791) and was recognized, three and a half centuries after the acceptance of this principle in Poland, as a great democratic achievement.

The Statutes of Nieszawa (1454) and the constitution *Nihil Novi* (1505), established that the legislative powers belong to the Parliament and that the king himself will not make new laws. The term "constitution" did not have the same meaning attached to it as it does today. Although it was an act having an important significance for the state, it did not regulate all politico-legal relations of the society. It was a broad statute which laid down the principles of one of the main problems of collective life.

Irrespective of terms used with reference to the old basic Polish sources of democratic institutions, we should remember that they constituted rules which introduced order into the governmental system and set up modern solutions to the problem of the relations between the government and the governed, rather than - as is sometimes represented - groundless extortion of concessions from the king, which made it impossible for the authorities to properly exercise their functions and which led to anarchy.

Again, frequently an old Polish saying is cited that "Poland is based on the lack of government." This notion should be corrected at every occasion. It is an unfair mutilation of old Polish generations' conviction that "Poland is based not on the government but on virtue," in other words, that the main

Stanisław Kożuchowski, *Constytucye, statuta y przywileie koronne y W.X.Lit. na Walnych Seymach uchwalone od roku Pańskiego 1550 aż do roku 1726...Mokrzyk, 1732.* (Constitutions, Statutes and Privileges of the Crown and the Grand Duchy of Lithuania by General Diets from the year of our Lord 1550 to the year 1726). The drawing on the vignette symbolizes the Polish-Lithuanian Commonwealth as a state governed by law. (Biblioteka Sejmowa, Warszawa) Photo: A. Wełnicki.

foundations of state life are the precepts of morality rather than this or that exercise of governmental powers. It could be compared to a well established American approach to public affairs, which requires a maximal limitation of state powers and a broad recourse to private initiative. This idea was clearly reflected by Jefferson's statement to the effect that the best government is the one which governs the least. To some extent, its Polish parallel is the old saying that the king should reign rather than govern.

Historical facts which are uncontested warrant a positive evaluation of the Polish public life in old times, and an enthusiastic recognition of Poland's contribution to the development of democratic principles and respect of human rights. This, however, should not make us oblivious of some abuses in the application of the principle of civic freedoms which were detrimental to the political system of the country and undermined its development. In the first place we should mention the famous, ill-reputed and repeatedly criticized institution of *liberum veto*.

In spite of the fact that the consequences of the use of the veto before the middle of the 17th century were limited, some voices were heard at that time advancing reform. In the second half of the 17th century the *liberum veto* started to alter its character from expressing a protest against one resolution to entirely dissolving the Diet session. But only in the 18th century, with the degeneration of the Polish political thought, the *liberum veto* changed into *liberum rumpo,* voluntarily causing the dissolution of the Diet and the annihilation of all its decisions, making its deliberation fruitless.[4]

It is difficult to be its defender, but negative comments about it were so frequently uttered and are so widely known that it seems unnecessary to restate them. Rather, it would-be proper to consider whether there were no historical or reasonable premises on which the veto was based. Was it an idea having no justification whatsoever - or did it grow from old beliefs, did it have roots in recognized traditions?

Liberum veto was based on the principle of unanimity which was the accepted rule in the Polish Parliament and remained in force despite many times voiced criticism. One of the reasons for this reluctance - as Władysław Czapliński puts it:

> was the belief, rather general at that time, that old customs should be maintained, that lightly no changes should be introduced into the existing system. True, unanimity was not established by some particular statute, but was based on tradition. As a senator stated at the Diet of 1611: "sometimes, an example is stronger than law."[5]

The Polish system was leading to a strong support of the established legal order. Of course, the application of the principle of veto could have a negative impact on problems which were not connected with changes of the law but were dealing with decisions concerning current affairs. However, history shows that for many long years there was no abuse of the veto in Poland. For the first time the representative from Upita, Siciński used the veto in 1652, and two years later it was used by deputy Białobłocki. Until then - and in many instances also afterwards - the deputy who had an opinion different from the others was giving up his point of view if he knew that he was isolated and his approach was contrary to that of the others - and did not use his right to the veto.

In many instances, isolated separate opinions of the deputies were ignored, and up to the middle of the XVII century it was necessary to have a numerous group of oppositionists to prevent the Diet from functioning. Usually it happened when such a group intended to force the king to satisfy some of its demands under the threat of obstructing the procedure of adopting resolutions. But there were cases where opposition of even a considerable number of deputies did not result in the developments they hoped for. Thus, in 1590, in spite of the fact that out of 136 deputies, 30 left the deliberations, "the Diet continued to work and its decisions were not questioned."[6]

In some instances the minority, voicing an opinion different from the majority, felt obligated to explain its stand. Thus:

after the Seym of 1578 the Cracow nobility answered that its deputies objected to the resolutions of other districts "not because they undertook to be stubborn, but as they had authority given by us, they did not dare to do anything else, as good Poles, respecting the laws and the freedom of the nobility, and as good deputies, abiding by instructions of their brothers; they had to behave as they did."[7]

It can be added that on "confederated" Diets there was no veto. Considering that confederations were created rather frequently, this principle severely limited the use of the veto.

One must remember that a deputy was speaking in the Diet not only for himself but for the whole province which elected him. He had to defend its interests which were frequently in conflict with those of other provinces, and at the dietines he was getting instructions on what stand he should take with respect to various problems. He could not lightheartedly disregard the wishes of his electors, the more so that on the "reporting dietines" he had to submit reports about what happened in the Diet and how he performed his functions. Frequently, he believed that he could not consent to a Diet's resolution without consulting his "provincial faction." At the 1627 Diet the deputies from the district of Cracow did not want to disregard their instructions. They met with the comment that "all should not perish because of the stubbornness of one province;" however, their position met with respect. Frequently, the opponent of a resolution would give up, with regret.[8]

In order to avoid unpleasant situations, the Mazovian dietines, and also some others, would recommend to their deputies to consult with the others "from the whole Kingdom" before taking the final stand, which broadened their freedom of action and "emphasized the all-Polish, central character of the functioning of the parliamentary representation."[9]

A strict connection of the elected representatives with the electorate was, or still is, the rule in many countries. In the United States those elected to the Congress consider themselves, first of all, as representatives of their electoral district, or of their state, on the national forum, and endeavor to promote decisions favorable to it. The situation was similar in England, at least down to the XVII century, and in other European countries.[10]

Claude Backvis rightfully pointed out that the old approach was transformed in England into a system which is still stronger, but instead of local instructions the representatives have to follow the instructions of the party to which they belong, and to vote in conformity with them, irrespective of what the parliamentary discussions reveal:

> In reality, a minister in the British parliament pretends that he addresses the　opposition representatives, and these in turn pretend that they speak to the government and to their colleagues who are in the majority - and all this with full awareness that the whole wealth of their arguments has no influence whatever on the outcome of the voting which is forthcoming.[11]

The general philosophical foundation of *liberum veto* was the conviction that what has been established and perpetuated in the course of centuries should be changed only if the whole nation rather than its part recognizes that some new approach is necessary.

> ...it was felt that the adoption of new laws demanded the consensus of the entire gentry and their full commitment... One cherished this general consensus which was achieved, as Krzysztof Radziwiłł used to say, "by a brotherly demand" rather than by shouting, pressing or using material arguments.[12]

Therefore, it should be stated that *liberum veto* was not a result of the tendency to anarchy, but grew out of "the spirit of class solidarity."

Various kinds of veto have been and are used in parliaments and institutions. By virtue of Art. I, Sec. 3 of the Constitution of the United States, every state, great or small (and the differences are tremendous, both with respect to the

EFFATA REGUM POLONIÆ
usque ad IOANNEM CASIMIRUM
à
Nicolao de Chwalkowo Chwalkowski CELSISSIMI IN LIVONIA CURLANDIE et SEMGALLIÆ DUCIS
Capitaneo Schrundensi et ad AVLAM REGIAM POLONAM Residente collecta

The Diet with King Jan III Sobieski in session in the Chamber of Senators at the Royal Castle in Warsaw, Copperplate by Charles de la Haye before 1694. Included in Mikołaj Chwałkowski, *Effata regnum Poloniae usque ad Ioannem Casimirum...*, Varsovia, Typis Collegiis Scholarum Piarum, 1694 (Biblioteka Sejmowa, Warszawa). Photo A. Wełnicki.

number of the inhabitants and the area) has an equal representation in the
Senate: two senators; and "no state, without its consent, shall be deprived of
its equal suffrage in the Senate" (Art. V). This is a kind of veto in interstate
relations.

A similar principle was introduced into international life in the current
century. In the Council of the League of Nations, unanimity of all its members
was necessary for the validity of its resolutions; in other words, every country
which was a member of the Council had a right to veto.

The same approach was accepted for the Security Council of the United
Nations Organization, with an important limitation: the five great powers
alone were granted this right: China, France, Great Britain, the United States
and the USSR. All resolutions concerning aggression, threat of war, military
operations, infringement of neutrality, etc. may be annihilated by the use of
the veto on the level of relations between the nations.

By the way, it is right to state that without the right to the veto the UNO
would not be established, anyhow in the form it has been called into life. The
great powers would not consent to a procedure which could make it possible
for the small countries to outvote them in vital matters.

The American "filibuster" performs a similar function, in internal relations
of the United States, as the *liberum veto*, and is available to the individual
members of Congress. By virtue of this institution, the speakers may speak as
long as they wish. They are not bound to abide by the subject matter of the
discussion. They may bring any book, written on any possible topic, and read
it to those present, without being subjected to any limitation of time. The
only problem is the perseverance of the speaker - how long his physical strength
will permit him to continue.

Of course, this kind of obstructing the decision-making process is much
easier if instead of one opponent there are two. In this case they may alternate
on the rostrum, and each of them can rest after each appearance. Yes, there is
a possibility of terminating the filibuster by voting a "cloture" by the majority
of two thirds, but this is an unpopular measure, applied rarely and reluctantly
because it is contrary to the tradition and the principle of freedom of speech.
Practically, one person can make it impossible to adopt a resolution he does
not like.

In the majority of the countries the development of the parliamentary system
was slow, tedious, and interrupted by struggles aiming at the increase of the
rights of the nation with respect to the rulers. This process is still in progress in
some states. It is well known that some societies were unable, until now, to
establish a legislative system based on the principle of freely elected

representatives of the people. Even if it exists in theory, it is sometimes a complete fiction in practice.

In Poland, it was different for centuries. One of the important features testifying to the Polish dedication to civil liberties was the freedom of association. The Poles could always organize, discuss public affairs express their ideas, profess the religion they believed in, and participate in solving the problems of public life. In old Poland, at least with respect to those social classes which counted: the nobility and the clergy, democratic principles were applied, and sometimes they were pushed too far. The shortcomings of the old Polish institutions including the *liberum veto* have been to a large degree eliminated by the Constitution of 3 May.

Notes

1. For a detailed discussion on this subject see: Marian Henryk Serejski, *Europa a rozbiory Polski* (Europe and the partitions of Poland) (Warszawa: PWN, 1970).

2. For a critical view on the "Cracow school" see: Władysław Smoleński, *Szkoły historyczne w Polsce* (Historical schools in Poland) (Warszawa: 1898), pp. 123-166); Andrzej Wyczański, *Polska Rzeczą Pospolitą Szlachecką* (Poland a Commonwealth of the gentry) (Warszawa: PWN, 1991), pp. 9-10.

3. See: Waldemar Voisé, "Deux républiques opposées - Fricius et Bodin" in *Europolonica* (Wrocław: Ossolineum, 1981), pp. 22-29.

4. Władysław Czapliński, "Sejm w latach 1587-1696" (The Diet in the years 1587-1696) in *Historia sejmu polskiego*, vol. 1 ed. Jerzy Michalski (Warszawa: PWN, 1984), p. 282.

5. Czapliński, *Sejm w latach*, p. 275.

6. Czapliński, *Sejm w latach*, p. 278.

7. Anna Sucheni-Grabowska, "Sejm w latach 1540-1586" (The Diet in the years 1540-1586) in *Historia Sejmu Polskiego*, vol.1, ed. Jerzy Michalski (Warszawa: PWN, 1984).

8. Czapliński, *Sejm w latach*, p. 277.

9. Sucheni-Grabowska, *Sejm w latach*, p. 146.

10. Sucheni-Grabowska, *Sejm w latach*, p. 147-148.

11. Claude Backvis, "Wymóg jednomyślności a `wola ogółu'" (The requirement of unanimity and `the will of the whole'), *Czasopismo Prawno-Historyczne*, 27, 2(1975), p. 167; "L'exigence de l'unanimité dans la décision et ses effets sur l'esprit et les méthodes de la délibération parlementaire," *Bulletin de la Classe des Lettres et des Sciences Morales et Politiques* (Académie Royale de Belgique) 5 série, 67 (1981-4), p. 164.

12. Czapliński, *Sejm w latach*, p. 275, 276.

LEGES,
STATUTA,
CONSTITUTIONES
PRIVILEGIA,
REGNI POLONIÆ
Magni Ducatus Lithvaniæ.

Omniumq; Provinciarum Annexarum,

à Comitiis Visliciæ Anno 1347. celebratis
...usq̃ ad ultima Regni Comitia:

In Typographia S. R. M. & Reipublicæ Collegij
Varsaviensis *Scholarum Piarum*, in UNUM OPUS
Absolutissimum, Collegij ejusdem Operâ, PRIMÙM
COLLECTA, & Sumptibus Publicis REIMPRESSA.
Anno Salutis Humanæ 1732.

Leges, Statuta, Constitutiones Privilegia, Regni Poloniae, Magni Ducatus Lithuaniae... in Typographia S.R.M. & Reipublicae Collegii Varsaviensis Scholarum Piarum...1732. The title page of the first volume. (Biblioteka Narodowa, Warszawa). A fundamental code of laws known as *Volumina Legum* published by Warsaw Piarist on the initiative of and under the editorship of Stanisław Konarski, who wrote the general introduction, and Józef Andrzej Załuski. Six volumes appeared in the years 1732-39. In 1782 volumes 7 and 8 appeared, volume 9 in 1889 and 10 in 1952,

4

Reforms in Poland after the "Dumb Diet" (1717)

Józef Andrzej Gierowski

The Constitution of 3 May 1791 included provisions leading to the modification of the Polish state into a modern constitutional monarchy, a political system very much commended by many representatives of the Enlightenment. Certainly the social and political theories advanced by French thinkers as well as English and American models had a decided influence on the preparation of the Government Statute. Nonetheless, ultimately the Constitution was the final product of Polish political thought, applied to the political needs and circumstances of the late eighteenth century. Although the Constitution did not change the nature of the state, in which the nobility still played the leading role, it nevertheless opened up opportunities for further reforms. Thanks to the compromise between the nobility and the rich burghers, the Constitution, considered to be a "gentle revolution" by contemporaries, became for Poland an important step on the road to a modern state.

The Constitution of 3 May showed that this road did not have to pass through the stage of absolute monarchy. Efficiency in government and social reform did not have to be imposed from above by an absolute ruler and his close advisors. Rather it could be introduced by that part of the nobility, which, influenced by economic change, the ideology of the Enlightenment, and a growing feeling that the country was threatened by the hostile absolutism of its neighbors, realized the necessity for these steps. Tendencies toward reform by the nobility had appeared in Poland a considerable time earlier, but they became particularly strong in the early eighteenth century. A crescendo of voices demanded reform of the Diet and its transformation into an effective organ of central power, the appointment of a standing council, which would manage the affairs of state, and fiscal and military measures to ensure the independence of the country. In time new demands were voiced for state intervention in economic affairs, for protection of trade and industry, and for protection of the peasants against their lords, creating conditions in which they would be able to increase production on their farms.[1]

The organization of the Commonwealth changed as a result of these demands, slowly transforming the state which was close to anarchy into a state of a modern type. The central government's power was still far from being fully effective, but nonetheless the foundation for a modern state had been solidly laid.

In the early eighteenth century, both the majority of the magnates and wide masses of the nobility remained deeply convinced, in spite of all experience to the contrary, that the government of the Commonwealth was perfect and that any change could only bring ruinous results. Behind this idealization of the old Commonwealth was the conviction that if Poland were deprived of a strong government, disarmed and pacified, she would no longer arouse the interest of her neighbors. After many years of exhausting wars this desire for peace at any price, even at the risk of self-annihilation, prevailed over all political common sense. The nobility simultaneously believed in weak government and in their own ability to stand together at the critical moment of danger to prevent disaster. According to their conviction, changes in the political system would bring the threat of royal absolutist ambitions. Among the causes of the general inertia was Poland's Saxon connection, the Polish-Saxon personal union. Poland's Wettin ruler was a foreign monarch who neither knew nor understood the mechanism of the Commonwealth. It was a paradox that such an adherent of absolutist government as August II was compelled to rule a Commonwealth based on the principles of the nobility's freedoms.

The accounts of foreign diplomats, who had the opportunity of candid conversations with August II, leave us no doubt that the King was unhappy with the *status quo* and aspired to sovereign rule free from interference by the estates. Achievement of that goal required a hereditary succession, to free the monarch from his dependence on noble electors, and subordination of the Diet to the king.

But the introduction of these conditions was not easy. Saxony and her financial and military power was not able to force a strong monarchy on Poland. The nobility of the Commonwealth regarded the right to elect the king as their fundamental privilege, the source of most of their other political rights.

Nevertheless, August II worked throughout his reign to bring his son Frederick August to the Polish throne either by avoiding free elections or by limiting their scope. Later, August III engaged in similar maneuvers.[2]

Hereditary succession had very limited support in Poland. Even though, as one of the most able Polish politicians of the day, Bishop Konstanty Szaniawski admitted to the Prussian envoy in 1717, "free elections have become a pure chimera. Poland would be better off under hereditary kings and could still call herself a free nation,"[3] no one had the nerve to present such arguments to the assembled nobility. Still, hereditary succession remained a political choice and in 1791 the Wettin dynasty received hereditary rights to the Polish throne.

Subordination of the Diet to the crown was also fraught with difficulties. At first there were attempts to discover a substitute for the Diet. One choice was to adopt the institution of confederated diets that could pass legislation by majority vote. When this idea met with the decided opposition of the nobility, there was an attempt to create a "standing Diet". It would deliberate in the same composition longer than the statutory six weeks, and reconvene periodically using the provisions of the so-called *limita*, that is, adjournments. This would require a restriction of the *liberum veto*. On a number of occasions the Diet was adjourned, which provoked noble indignation and accusations that the King wanted to turn the Diet into an English Parliament. In 1726 the Diet abolished the King's power to adjourn its sessions. The King was defeated in his struggle to master the Diet.[4] Nevertheless, the Diet, despite its victory, slipped into a state of crisis which lasted for the next forty years.

The idea of having some kind of permanent council at the king's side to transact important business between sessions of the Diet or of a secret council similar to the secret cabinet in Saxony found no support in Poland during the first half of the eighteenth century. However, this notion influenced reform of the Commonwealth during the second half.[5]

During the reign of August II and his son, the ambitions of the Saxon Wettins harmed all serious plans for reform. The nobility learned to detect the hidden menace of absolutism in every plan for constitutional change, which made it all the harder to convince the nobility of the necessity of modernizing the government later in the century. Yet not everybody was happy with this state of affairs. Some nobles, seeing no way to improve Polish government, retired from public life. Others embarked on an arduous struggle to remove the degenerate forms which had appeared in the body politic and were now eating away like a cancer at the organism of the Commonwealth. These men wished to improve and modernize the state without doing violence to the principles on which it had originally been founded.

The first really serious examination of the possibilities for political reform came from the pen of a wealthy member of the middle nobility, Stanisław Dunin Karwicki. A seasoned parliamentarian, who frequently represented his region at the Diet or in the confederations, and a Calvinist esteemed and respected by the Catholic nobility, he had thorough knowledge of the deficiencies of the Commonwealth. When the Swedes invaded Poland in the first years of the Great Northern War, he wrote a treatise entitled *De ordinanda Republica seu de corrigendis defectibus in statu Reipublicae Poloniae.* Although it was not printed, it survives in many copies, a testimony to its popularity and significance.

Karwicki saw the fundamental weakness of the Commonwealth in the impossibility of reconciling the king's power with the freedom of the nation. He proposed to leave "the kings with all their preeminence, but circumscribing their power, so as to remove all fear of their authority and in this way calm the anxieties to which such apprehensions give rise." The power of the Diet should be augmented and conditions should be created under which it could function efficiently. Above all, it should be a "prompt" or "standing Diet," with a restricted *liberum veto.* The Diet should be divided into three great commissions, one for regional matters, a second for foreign policy and the third for financial and military affairs. The royal estates were to be transferred to the treasury to support a small but modernized army. The directors of the central government's departments were to be elected by the Diet. Karwicki also proposed a fundamental reform in how the king was elected.[6]

Karwicki presented the first such comprehensive and consistent plan for reform of the Commonwealth since the sixteenth century. The experience of the preceding century showed that Polish parliamentary institutions needed the most changes. Karwicki proposed neither restriction nor abolition of Parliament, which the Saxon kings wanted, but Parliament's rationalization, so that the Diet would exercise the highest authority in the land as a fully sovereign body. Not all of Karwicki's proposals were timely, but virtually all later eighteenth-century reformers turned to his ideas about Polish governmental reorganization.

Only a few of Karwicki's reforms were adopted in 1717 by the Dumb Diet, so-called because the deputies surrounded by Russian troops were not allowed to speak, and were forced to approve the treaty of Warsaw, signed on November 3, 1716, which was concluded with Russian mediation. The Dumb Diet ended the Confederation of Tarnogród, which fought against the presence of the Saxon army in the Commonwealth. The Confederation brought no spectacular successes but managed to bring about a compromise agreement

Stanisław Leszczyński. Copperplate by D. Collin after a drawing by Girardet, 1758. (Fundacja XX Czartoryskich, Muzeum Narodowe w Krakowie). Photo M. Wesołowska.

GŁOS WOLNY

WOLNOŚĆ

UBESPIECZAIĄCY.

ROKU PANSKIEGO
M. DCC. XXXIII.

(Stanisław Leszczyński), *Głos wolny wolność ubespieczaiący* (A free voice in defense of freedom), Roku Pańskiego M.DCC.XXXIII (Nancy: 1749). Title page. (Fundacja XX Czartoryskich, Muzeum Narodowe w Krakowie).

with August II. By the Treaty of Warsaw relations between the Commonwealth and Saxony were settled on the basis of an exclusively personal union. The representatives of the King and of the Confederation adopted a partial reform of government, the first in the eighteenth century.

The financial and military reform of 1716 fixed the size of the standing army at 24,000 men, which in view of the need to pay officers' salaries in effect reduced the army to about 18,000, a very low figure compared to Poland's neighbors. A positive aspect of the reform was the introduction of permanent taxation on royal, ecclesiastical, and noble estates. This did not mean taxation of the nobility, only of their serfs. However, it was a step forward from the situation at the turn of the seventeenth and eighteenth centuries. After 1716, the Commonwealth's budget went from four to about ten million Polish zlotys per year. Although specially constituted treasury tribunals were established to supervise systematic payments to the troops, the army did not receive central financial support and was expected instead to support itself by collecting from crown estates. Furthermore, attempts were also made to define the obligations and the rights of high government officials, above all the hetmans. In addition, the rights of the dietines (*sejmiki*) in matters of taxation were restricted, and there were attempts to ban confederations and to restrict the Senate to its lawful obligations. Not all these decisions proved to have equal value; ultimately the decentralization of the treasury and the reduction in the size of the army proved disastrous.[7]

These reforms appeared to be only the beginning of larger changes, or so it seemed in light of the King's proclamations to subsequent Diets, which foretold continued financial-military reform and the adoption of a mercantilist economic policy. The nobility added its demands for new regulations concerning relations between church and state to the royal plans. After the struggle between the court and the hetmans, the Commonwealth returned to the question of government reform at the Diets of 1724 and 1726. A special commission was set up for the conduct of foreign affairs. Also, the Diet reformed the tribunal.[8] But Karwicki's most important proposition on rationalizing the Diet was ignored and the *liberum veto* was restored. This paralyzed the Diet until 1764.

In such a political stalemate the ideology of the Enlightenment became a new and powerful stimulus toward ending the decline of the state and restoring its strength. The acceptance of the new ideology in Poland was associated with the struggle to emerge from political, economic, and cultural stagnation. The influence of the Enlightenment on society in the Commonwealth was also linked to changes in early eighteenth-century social attitudes and to the acceptance of new economic ideas, of new patterns in government and politics,

and of the principles of rationalist thought. However the formation of new
social attitudes is a prolonged and cumulative process and changes began with
the activity of inspiring individuals and small groups that slowly gained
influence in society.

The spread of Enlightenment ideas was helped by changes in education.
Of crucial importance was Piarist Stanisław Konarski's establishment of the
Collegium Nobilium in Warsaw in 1740. The college became the model for
other new colleges, first of the Piarist, and then of the Jesuit order. This was
the beginning of educational reform, one of the most important achievements
of the Polish Enlightenment. A further step toward the modernization of
education was the creation of the Commission for National Education in 1773
dedicated to reforming the whole educational system.[9]

The intellectual revival of the early Enlightenment added a new dimension
to the struggles between the camps of two rival magnate families - the
Czartoryskis (popularly referred to as "the family") and the Potockis. At first
they competed for important government appointments for themselves and
their clients. Then they adopted political slogans, thereby turning their factional
strife into a struggle over the nature of reform and in this manner enriching
the program of reforms.

The events of the War of the Polish Succession after the death of August II
again impressed on the nobility the illusory nature of any political ideas not
backed up with sufficient force. As a result, financial and military reforms
were seen as urgent tasks. More than one political writer demanded an army
of a hundred thousand men and the funds to support them. In theory, all
agreed on this. Yet, when the great commission was set up to prepare the
necessary proposals at the Diet of 1736, opponents soon found sufficient reasons
to put off the matter until the next Diet. However, later Diets during the
reign of August III were disrupted and no decisions were made.

The issues of military and financial reforms were raised again on the eve of
the Diet of 1744 when the international situation was particularly favorable
for the Commonwealth. Both warring magnate factions therefore put forward
their projects for reform. Stanisław Poniatowski, the father of the future King,
expressed "the family's" point of view in his *List ziemianina do pewnego
przyjaciela z innego województwa*, 1744 (Letter from a landowner to a certain
friend from another province) in which he explored means of increasing the
army's strength. He proposed a reform of the tax system based on a national
mercantilist policy, industrialization, and economic protection of the burghers.
He also proposed restricting the right to disrupt debates at the dietines or the
Diet.

At the same time, Antoni Potocki circulated his own letter to the dietines. He came out in support of financial military reform and a more efficient operation of the Diet. He put forward a project for the appointment of a standing commission as the King's privy council. Its membership would include not only senators and nobles appointed at sessions of the Diet, but burghers as well. He wanted to recognize the burghers as a separate estate with rights to representation in the Diet. Unfortunately Potocki helped dissolve the Diet in the interests of Frederick the Great, thus wrecking the most important attempt since 1717 to reform the Commonwealth. The Potockis were also responsible for the breakup of the Diets in 1746 and 1748, when efforts were being made to reform the Polish government.[10]

The question of how to bring order to the Commonwealth continued to be a subject of lively debate and was frequently discussed by the nobility at the dietines. Publicists also engaged in polemics on the topic, writing pamphlets and leaflets that were sometimes printed but far more often copied by hand. The *status quo* did not lack defenders, but there were also mature reformist voices. Unlike the reformers of the first quarter of the century, the writers of the 1740s did not confine themselves to the question of how to put the political system in order. They stressed that reform of the government could only bring the results expected if it were associated with a change in social relations. By this they meant improved status for the peasants and broader rights for the burghers.

The fullest program of reforms in this sense is found in the work *Głos wolny wolność ubezpieczający* 1733 (1749) (A free voice in defense of freedom), probably written by King Stanisław Leszczyński and later included in his collection entitled *Oeuvres du Philosophe Bienfaisant* (Paris, 1763). Leszczyński's point of departure for his observations is close to that of Karwicki. He emphasized the need to restrict the power of the monarchy, to transfer royal estates to the treasury, and, following the English example, to make ministers responsible to the Diet for all actions taken in the name of the king. He recommended restricting the *liberum veto*, abolishing the Senate's status as a separate institution and its incorporation into the Diet, and reorganizing the ministries into collegiate bodies. Kings would be elected by a special Diet. For the security of the Commonwealth there would be an army of fifty thousand in time of peace, and one hundred thousand men in time of war.

Leszczyński's social proposals form the most important part of his discussion. He criticized the clergy for their devotion to material possessions and demanded the transfer of excess clerical income to the state. He derided the nobility for their demagogic democracy and demanded the removal from the dietines of military officers and nobles without land – the magnates' chief political backers. Above all he defended the oppressed peasants and the burghers. He spoke out against the manorial system, against the limitation of peasants' personal freedom, against the lords' power of life and death over their serfs. He also appealed for increased protection of commerce and industry, which would improve conditions for the burghers.[11]

Głos wolny remained influential to the end of the Commonwealth. The reforms of the Great Diet and the Constitution of 3 May had their roots in Leszczyński's political tract.

The next period of reform activity began in the 1760's. It was then that Stanisław Konarski published his greatest work, *O skutecznym rad sposobie*, 1760-63 (On effective counsel). He was the first to reject the *liberum veto* in an uncompromising manner, a step he considered a necessary condition for any improvement in the Polish parliamentary system. A reformed Diet, wrote Konarski, would have full legislative authority and would organize the executive. The Diet would be elected for a term of two years by the property owning nobility. Royal power was to be restricted, though Konarski did not reject the introduction of hereditary succession. Konarski proposed that a standing council of residents made up of the ministers, the Primate, senators nominated by the king, and deputies nominated by the Diet would exercise executive power. Altogether Konarski's system had strong connections to Karwicki's earlier plans.

Konarski's work had a great influence on the political life in Poland. During the interregnum of 1763-4 after the death of August III, "the Family" adopted many of Konarski's ideas in its reform program. Chancellor Andrzej Zamoyski presented the Czartoryski program at the Convocation Diet in 1764, before the election of the new King. He demanded that the Diet be made more efficient by the introduction of majority voting, that an executive council be set up, and that the collegial system be introduced in government departments. These ideas could not be fully realized because of opposition to them by Frederick the Great and Catherine II. Changes were limited to a partial improvement in the functioning of the Diet by the introduction of new rules of procedure, and by allowing majority voting in financial and economic affairs. These improvements were effective – henceforth not a single Diet was dissolved. The competence of the highest military and financial offices was reduced and taken over by commissions, elected by the Diet. The Convocation Diet also initiated a new policy towards the burghers. So began the transformation of the state into an orderly "enlightened" Commonwealth.

Stanisław Konarski by an unknown painter. (Muzeum Narodowe w Warszawie) Photo
S. Sobkowicz.

O SKUTECZNYM
RAD SPOSOBIE
ALBO
O UTRZYMYWANIU
ORDYNARYINYCH
SEYMOW.

Nemo eſt tam Inimicus cauſæ huic, qui nos
malos Cives, ſut homines improbos,
dicere audeat. *Cicero ad Cæc.*

w WARSZAWIE

w Drukarni J. K Mći y Rzpltey
u XX. *Scholarum Piarum,*
Roku MDCCLX.

Stanisław Konarski, *O skutecznym rad sposobie albo o utrzymaniu ordynaryinych seymów*, v. 1-4 (On effective counsel or on the preservation of ordinary Diets) w Warszawie w Drukarni J.K.Mci y Rzpltey u XX. Scholarum Piarum, 1760-1763. Title page. (Biblioteka Narodowa, Warszawa).

The new King, Stanisław August Poniatowski, favored reform. As a substitute for a permanent executive body he assembled his so-called Conference of King and Ministers to serve as a cabinet. A special commission undertook the regulation of the coinage. The King also appointed Commissions "of good order" for the towns.[12]

The reforms soon stopped, blocked by the conservative opposition that was supported by St. Petersburg and Berlin. Also the Confederation of Bar, which took up arms in 1768 against the Russian intervention in Poland, proclaimed the defense of the independence of the Commonwealth, but in its traditional form. After the First Partition, Russian interference made serious reform impossible. This did not stop the flow of reform plans. Among others the former leader of the Confederation of Bar, Bishop Adam Krasiński, in his memorandum on the reform of law and the government, proposed a hereditary monarchy, the introduction of a standing council, an effective reform of the Diet, and some social reform. At the same time, the Piarist lawyer and historian, Wincenty Skrzetuski defended the principle of national sovereignty, declaring his support for a hereditary monarchy that would put an end to the abuses of free elections, and emphasized economic policies that would strengthen the Commonwealth.[13]

The Diet of 1773-1775, convened after the First Partition of Poland, introduced only limited reforms. A Permanent Council was set up as an instrument by which the Russian Ambassador exercised his control over the King. It was composed of thirty-six councilors from the Senate and the house of deputies. It limited some of the royal prerogatives and imposed some restrictions on the power of the magnate-ministers. It was divided into five departments responsible to the most important ministers: foreign affairs, police, war, justice, and the treasury. There was also a limited military-financial reform. The crown lands came under the control of the treasury, which was to rent them out on fifty-year leases. The most notable achievement of this Diet was its establishment of the Commission for National Education.

Thus the third attempt at political reform since 1717 resulted in half measures. What was worse, the Diet, under the pressure of the Russian Ambassador Stackelberg, hampered the possibility of further basic reforms. The Diet had to assure the exercise of traditional fundamental rights: free election of the king, the right to refuse obedience to the crown, the principle of unanimity (with some exceptions), etc. These rights were guaranteed by Russia, Prussia and Austria. In the newly formed institutions, and particularly in the Permanent Council, positions of importance were held by individuals whose chief concern was their own questionable self-interest, or who served as lackeys of the foreign powers.[14]

It should be emphasized, however, that even in these dramatic circumstances new steps had been taken towards modernizing the state. Without the Commission for National Education, the radical change in attitude which took place in the next period would have run a much more sluggish course. The Permanent Council also proved a useful institution, solving many problems of internal policy and facilitating changes in economic and social life.

In the next few years, significant weaknesses (both in terms of external interference and internal opposition) were revealed in connection with Andrzej Zamoyski's Code of Laws entitled *Zbiór praw sądowych*, 1778 (The collection of judicial laws). The need for a new codification of the law was a matter which had been raised some time before. The Diet of 1776 entrusted preparation of a new collection of laws to a commission directed by Andrzej Zamoyski. Zamoyski, with the agreement of the King, decided to go beyond the narrow instructions he received from the Diet and compiled a Code of laws intended to standardize the laws in use in the Commonwealth, and to bring them in line with the ideas of the Enlightenment, plotting the direction of further social change. There was a propaganda campaign, designed to secure favorable reception of the Code by the nobility. The wisest pronouncement concerning the codification project came from the political writer, Józef Wybicki. In his *Listy patriotyczne do Jaśnie Wielmożnego eks-kanclerza Zamoyskiego prawa układającego pisane*, 1777-78 (Patriotic letters to His Honor Ex-Chancellor Zamoyski compiling a code of law), Wybicki primarily dealt with basic problems of social life, advocating better conditions for the peasants and improvements in the rights of the burghers. The draft Code presented in 1778 did not diminish noble privilege but it increased the rights of burghers and mitigated the harsh legal disabilities of the serfs. Large towns received the right to send representatives to the Diet, a measure in line with earlier enactments. The Code also contained provisions allowing burghers to acquire land and facilitating their ennoblement. It also defined the manner in which burghers and nobles could form commercial companies together. A new view of peasants found eloquent expression in the sections of the Code that separated serfs bound to the soil with manorial obligations from free peasants whose settlement was governed by contract. Zamoyski preferred leniency toward serfs and wanted to restrict the pursuit of runaways. He also brought back regulations dating from 1496 that allowed a serf's second and fourth children to move to a town and take up a trade.

Andrzej Zamoyski, Grand Chancellor of the Crown, 1764-67, engraving by an unknown artist. (Biblioteka Uniwersytecka w Warszawie, Gabinet Rycin).

ZBIOR
PRAW SĄDOWYCH
NA MOCY KONSTYTUCYI
ROKU 1776.

PRZEZ

J. W. *Andrzeia Zamoyskiego*,

EX-KANCLERZA KORONNEGO, KAWALERA ORDERU ORŁA BIAŁEGO,

UŁOZONY,

Y NA SEYM ROKU 1778.

PODANY.

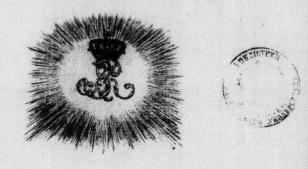

w WARSZAWIE. ROKU 1778.

NAKŁADEM J. W. *ZAMOYSKIEGO*,

w DRUKARNI J. K. MCI. GRÖLLOWSKIEY.

Andrzej Zamoyski, *Zbiór praw sądowych* (A collection of judicial laws) w Warszawie, M. Gröll, 1778. Title page. (Biblioteka Uniwersytecka w Warszawie).

Zamoyski was not allowed to propose laws that changed the highest institutions of government. However, he included regulations concerning the obligations of the Jewish population, the loss of noble privileges by nobles who did not own property, and on the relationship between church and state. Zamoyski's Code of Laws was not perfect; nonetheless, it was an attempt to put Polish law in order and to bring it into line with the needs of an "enlightened" Commonwealth.

When the draft Code was laid before the public for discussion it met with objections from foreign interests and from the conservative nobility. The papal nuncio G. A. Archetti, deeply perturbed by the Code, which, in his opinion, violated the rights of the church in Poland, embarked on energetic action against it. He won the support of the magnates and also of the Russian ambassador Stackelberg, who feared that the introduction of the Code might lead to far-reaching political changes. At the final debate of the Diet of 1780 the deputies rejected the Code categorically as prejudicial to noble rights and privileges. Though rejected by the Diet, the work done by Zamoyski's commission was later used during the Great Diet and in the Constitution of 3 May.[15]

From the defeat of Zamoyski's Code of Laws to the summoning of the Great Diet in 1788, political life in the Commonwealth followed a sluggish and murky course. It was a time of a parting of the ways between the young magnates, like Adam Czartoryski or Stanisław and Ignacy Potocki and the old conservatives. New political programs were written that caused a realignment of political parties. Not unexpectedly, it was during this time that the most profound works by thinkers of the Polish Enlightenment appeared. Most prominent among them were the books of Stanisław Staszic. At first, Staszic did not play an active part in political life, though he deeply felt the shortcomings of the Polish system of government. This led him to write two books that had an unusually powerful effect on public opinion in Poland. These were his *Uwagi nad życiem Jana Zamoyskiego*, 1787 (Remarks on the life of Jan Zamoyski) and *Przestrogi dla Polski*, 1790 (Warnings for Poland). Staszic endowed his pronouncements with an extraordinary power of suggestion. Although he was a confirmed republican, he recognized that conditions in the Commonwealth made it essential to bolster the power of the monarch by abolishing free elections of the king and introducing a hereditary monarchy. The Diet would have to undergo thorough reform, including the introduction of the majority principle and the creation of a common chamber of burghers and nobles, in which both estates would have an equal number of votes. Staszic also attached great importance to the expansion and modernization of the army.

Staszic believed that simultaneous changes in economic and social policy were of fundamental importance. He demanded a protective policy for Polish trade and crafts, equalization of burgher and noble rights, and improved conditions for the peasants, whose miserable state was depicted by him as exceptionally shocking. He regarded peasant poverty and subjugation as the chief cause for the weakness of the Commonwealth. Sharing the views of the physiocrats, Staszic saw the farmer's labor as the basis of society's welfare, emphasizing that he meant the labor of the peasant. On the other hand, Staszic attacked the magnates harshly as the chief instigators of Poland's downfall.[16]

Hugo Kołłątaj was a theorist of reform like Staszic, but was much more active politically. He influenced the decisions of the Great Diet and affected the attitudes of its deputies and public opinion with his propaganda. He recruited a group of able publicists and men of letters who formed what came to be known as "Kołłątaj's Forge," the most powerful center of political propaganda that ever existed in the old Commonwealth.

Kołłątaj frequently took up his pen to join in numerous debates. Starting in 1788 he published his most important work in the form of letters to Stanisław Małachowski, Marshal of the Great Diet. *Do Stanisława Małachowskiego Anonima listów kilka,* 1788-89 (To Stanisław Małachowski several letters by an anonymous author). He included in these letters his most important ideas on the state of the Commonwealth and the possibility of its reform, many of which he shared with Staszic. Kołłątaj, however, was guided to a greater extent by the possibilities of the moment. The demands of political tactics were uppermost in his thoughts. As a result we find contradictions in Kołłątaj's works that make it hard to ascertain his doctrine.

Like Staszic, Kołłątaj recognized social change as fundamental to successful reform, insisting, for example, that burghers should have the same rights as nobles. All social and political reforms had to assure the more efficient functioning of government. A reformed Diet would play the leading role in government. It would be permanent and operate on the majority principle. Executive power would also originate in the Diet, although Kołłątaj declared himself in favor of the separation of powers. He also supported hereditary succession to the Polish throne.

Kołłątaj's views were of particular significance for constitutional reform, for he was soon to participate in drafting the most important document of the Great Diet. He was one of the authors of the Constitution of 3 May, together with Stanisław August, Ignacy Potocki, Stanisław Małachowski and Scipione

Piattoli. Kołłątaj personified the application of theory to practice. He worked to transform his ideas and those of his predecessors into real constitutional change.[17]

The Constitution of 3 May was a "gentle revolution," as Kołłątaj called it. It had its roots in the ideas of Karwicki and his successors, in the attempts at reform from the Dumb Diet to Zamoyski's codification, and even in the absolutist dreams of August II. The Constitution of 3 May is naturally associated with the Great Diet, but while it was a product of discussions of the deputies and senators, it was also a result of a long search for reform in the Commonwealth that began early in the eighteenth century. Ultimately the Constitution proved to be a great achievement in the sense that it showed the Polish way to the formation of a modern state.

Notes

(Notes prepared by the editorial staff)

1. Władysław Konopczyński, *Polscy pisarze polityczni XVIIIw. (do Sejmu Czteroletniego)* (Polish political writers of the 18th century (up to the Four-Year Diet)) (Warszawa, PWN, 1966). See also: Jörg K. Hoensch, *Sozialverfassug und Politische Reform. Polen im vorrevolutionären Zeitalter.* (Köln: Böhlau, 1973); Jerzy Lukowski, *Liberty's Folly. The Polish-Lithuanian Commonwealth in the Eighteenth Century, 1697-1795* (London: Routledge, 1991).

2. Józef Gierowski, "Polska, Saksonia i plany absolutystyczne Augusta II" (Poland, Saxony... and the absolutist plans of August II) in *Polska w epoce Oświecenia*, ed. Bogusław Leśnodorski (Warszawa: Wiedza Powszechna, 1971), pp. 60-105.

3. Józef Gierowski, "Personal - oder Realunion?" in *Um die polnische Krone*, eds. Johannes Kalisch and Józef Gierowski (Berlin: Rutten und Loening, 1962), p. 290.

4. Władysław Konopczyński, *Le liberum veto* (Paris: H. Champion - Gebethner i Wolff, 1930); Józef Gierowski, *Między saskim absolutyzmem a złotą wolnością* (Between Saxon absolutism and golden freedom) (Wrocław: Ossolineum, 1953); Henryk Olszewski, *Sejm Rzeczypospolitej epoki oligarchii 1652-1763* (Polish Diet in the oligarchy epoch 1652-1763) (Poznań: Wyd. Uniw. A. Mickiewicza, 1966); Jerzy Michalski, "Sejm w czasach saskich" (The Diet in the Saxon times) in *Historia sejmu polskiego*, vol. 1, ed. Jerzy Michalski (Warszawa: PWN, 1984), pp. 300-349.

5. Władysław Konopczyński, *Geneza i ustanowienie Rady Nieustającej* (The genesis and the establishment of the Permanent Council) (Kraków: Akademia Umiejętności - Gebethner i Wolff, 1917).

6. Stanisław Dunin Karwicki, *Dzieła polityczne z początku XVIII wieku* (Political works at the beginning of the 18th century), eds. Adam Przyboś and Kazimierz Przyboś (Wrocław: Ossolineum, 1992).

7. Michał Nycz, *Geneza reform skarbowych sejmu niemego* (The genesis of the fiscal reforms of the Dumb Diet) (Poznań: Poznańskie Towarzystwo Przyjaciół Nauk, 1938).

8. In addition to the works quoted in note 4 see: Jerzy Michalski, *Studia nad reformą sądownictwa i prawa sądowego w XVIII wieku* (On the reform of the judicial system and judicial law in the 18th century) (Wrocław: Ossolineum, 1958).

9. Władysław Konopczyński, *Stanisław Konarski* (Warszawa: Wyd. Kasy im. Mianowskiego, 1926); William John Rose, *Stanislas Konarski: Reformer of Education in XVIII-century Poland* (London, 1929); Ambroise Jobert, *La Commission d'Education Nationale en Pologne* (1773-1794) (Paris: Librairie Droz, 1941).

10. Michael G. Müler, *Polen zwischen Preussen und Russland* (Berlin: Colloquium Verlag, 1983); Zofia Zielińska, *Walka "Familii" o reformę Rzeczypospolitej 1743-1752* (The struggle of "the Family" for reform of the Commonwealth) (Warszawa: PWN, 1983).

11. Józef Feldman, *Stanisław Leszczyński* (Wrocław-Warszawa: Książnica-Atlas, 1948); Emanuel Rostworowski, "Czy Stanisław Leszczyński jest autorem 'Głosu wolnego'" (Is Stanisław Leszczyński the author of the "Free Voice?") in Emanuel Rostworowski *Legendy i fakty XVIII w.* (Warszawa: PWN, 1963).

12. Władysław T. Kisielewski, *Reforma książąt Czartoryskich na sejmie konwokacyjnym r. 1764* (The reform of the princes Czartoryski at the Convocation Diet 1764) (Sambor: J. Czaiński, 1880); Bogusław Leśnodorski, "Mowy Andrzeja Zamoyskiego na konwokacji 1764 r." (Andrzej Zamoyski's addresses at the Convocation Diet 1764) in *Księga pamiątkowa 150-lecia Archiwum Głównego Akt Dawnych w Warszawie* (Warszawa: PWN, 1958), pp. 338-339; Jerzy Michalski, "Reforma sądownictwa na sejmie konwokacyjnym" (Reform of the judiciary at the Convocation Diet) in *Między wielką polityką a szlacheckim partykularyzmem. Studia z dziejów nowożytnej Polski i Europy ku czci Profesora Jacka Staszewskiego* (Toruń : Wyd. Uniwersytetu Mikołaja Kopernika, 1993), pp. 295-313.

13. Aleksander Kraushar, *Książę Repnin i Polska* (Prince Repnin and Poland) (Warszawa: Gebethner i Wolff, 1900), 2 vols.; Kazimierz Rudnicki, *Biskup Kajetan Sołtyk* (Kraków: W.L. Anczyc, 1906); Władysław Konopczyński, *Konfederacja barska* (Confederation of Bar) (Warszawa: 1936-38), 2 vols; "Biskupa Adama Krasińskiego traktat o naprawie Rzeczypospolitej" (Bishop Adam Krasiński's treatise on the reform of the State) ed. Władysław Konopczyński, *Przegląd Narodowy* 6, 4 (1913): 344-359, 5 (1913): 492-515; Jerzy Michalski, "Propaganda konserwatywna w walce z reformą w początkach panowania Stanisława Augusta" (Conservative propaganda and its struggle against reform at the beginning of Stanisław August's reign) *Przegląd Historyczny* 42, 3-4 (1951): 536-562; George T. Łukowski, *The Szlachta and the Confederacy of Radom 1764-1767/68: A Study of the Polish Nobility* (Romae: Institutum Historicum Polonicum Romae, 1977).

14. Jerzy Michalski, "Sprawa chłopska na sejmie 1773-1775" (The peasant problem at the 773-1775 Diet), *Przegląd Historyczny* 45 (1954): 3-13; "Problem *ius agratiandi* i kary śmierci w Polsce w latach siedemdziesiątych XVIII w." (The issue of *ius agratiandi* and the death penalty in Poland in the 1770's), *Czasopismo Prawno-Historyczne* 10, 2 (1958): 175-196; "Rejtan et les dilemmes des Polonais au temps du premier demembrement," *Acta Poloniae Historica* 63/64 (1991): 27-88; Daniel Stone, *Polish Politics and National Reform 1775-1788.* (New York: Boulder, Colorado U. Press, 1976).

15. Ewa Borkowska-Bagieńska, *"Zbiór praw sądowych" Andrzeja Zamoyskiego* (Collection of judicial laws by Andrzej Zamoyski) (Poznań: Wyd. Uniw. im. A. Mickiewicza, 1986); Emanuel Rostworowski, "Myśli polityczne" Józefa Wybickiego czyli droga od konfederacji barskiej do obiadów czwartkowych" ("The political thoughts" of Józef Wybicki, or the road from the Confederation of Bar to the Thursday dinners) in *Józef Wybicki Księga zbiorowa*, ed. Andrzej Bukowski (Gdańsk: Ossolineum, 1975), pp. 11-34.

16. Czesław Leśniewski, *Stanisław Staszic, jego życie i ideologia w dobie Polski Niepodległej* (1755-1795) (Stanisław Staszic, his life and ideology in the era of independent Poland (1755-1795)) (Warszawa: Gebethner i Wolff, 1926); Władysław Konopczyński, "Polscy pisarze polityczni XVIII wieku (Czasy Sejmu Czteroletniego)" (Polish political writers of the 18th century (the period of the Four-Year Diet)), MS. Jagiellonian Library, BJ, no. 52/61.

17. Hugo Kołłątaj, *Listy Anonima i Prawo polityczne narodu polskiego* (Anonymous letters and Political law of the Polish nation), eds. Bogusław Leśnodorski and Helena Wereszycka (Warszawa: PWN, 1954), 2 vols; *Kołłątaj i inni. Z publicystyki doby Sejmu Czteroletniego* (Kołłątaj and others. From the political literature of the time of the Four-Year Diet) ed. Łukasz Kądziela (Warszawa: Wyd. Szkolne i Pedagogiczne, 1991); Zofia Zielińska, *Kołłątaj i orientacja pruska u progu Sejmu Czteroletniego* (Kołłątaj and the Prussian orientation on the eve of the Four-Year Diet) (Warszawa: PAX, 1991); Emanuel Rostworowski, "Marzenie dobrego obywatela czyli królewski projekt konstytucji" (The dream of a good citizen or the king's project of the constitution) in Rostworowski, *Legendy i fakty*; Maria Pasztor, *Hugo Kołłątaj na Sejmie Wielkim w latach 1791-1792* (Hugo Kołłątaj at the Great Diet in the years 1791-1792) (Warszawa: Wyd. Sejmowe, 1991); Andrzej Walicki, *The Enlightenment and the Birth of Modern Nationhood: Political Thought from Noble Republicanism to Tadeusz Kościuszko* (Notre Dame: Univ. of Notre Dame Press, 1990).

Załuski Library in Warsaw. Copperplate by I.F. Milius. 1752. (Biblioteka Uniwersytetu Warszawskiego, Gabinet Rycin). The Library, founded in 1747 by the brothers Załuski, Andrzej Stanisław Bishop of Cracow and Józef Andrzej Bishop of Kiev, was the first Polish public library.

5

Poland between Prussia and Russia in the Eighteenth Century

1. The Effects of the Great Northern War: The Commonwealth as a Russian Protectorate

The essential change that the first years of the Great Northern War brought in the international position of the Polish Commonwealth lay in the fact that Peter I gained a lasting influence in the Polish Republic. Remaining with his army on Polish soil after the abdication of August II under the terms of the 1706 Treaty of Altranstadt, the Tsar had time to become acquainted with the leaders of the pro-Saxon Confederation of Sandomierz and to attach many of them, including the most influential hetmans, to himself. Peter I established his influence among the Polish magnates after the victory at Poltava, among other things forcing August II–in return for Peter's agreement that August II be reinstated to the throne in 1709–to appoint people connected to Russia to a number of important positions. Symbolic of the new elite was the completely immoral Ludwik Pociej, who owed to Peter his elevation to the most important Lithuanian post, the Grand Hetman of Lithuania.

During his stay in Poland, the Tsar gained a good understanding of the country's power structure. He recognized the predominance of the magnates who, under cover of the gentry's notion of democracy, attained hegemony in the state in the second half of the seventeenth century. He was also able to perceive the egoism of many representatives of this wealthiest part of the noble estate. In practice this knowledge implied the possibility of playing the magnates against the Polish king whenever the latter undertook attempts at reform intended to strengthen the state and royal authority.

The Russians' watchful attention to maintaining the Commonwealth in the weakened state in which it found itself at the beginning of the eighteenth century were facilitated by certain antiquated features in the existing form of government. Historians regard the most important weakness to have been the requirement of unanimity in passing laws in the Polish Diet. The practice of the second half of the seventeenth century established unanimity to mean that if even one deputy raised an objection (*liberum veto*) to any proposed legislation, the Diet was regarded as dissolved, which meant that even measures enacted before the veto was cast lost their validity.

The destructive activity of those who would dissolve the Diet was made possible by certain aspects of the prevailing social psychology, the most important of which was the deep distrust of the nobility for the king. The nobles regarded the democratic political system, which they referred to as their "liberty," as the highest value, and they saw the monarch as a potential enemy of liberty since he was thought to have an essential tendency toward absolutism. From the conviction that the king presented a natural threat to liberty sprang a series of institutional safeguards that were intended by their creators to protect democracy from assault by the monarch. The *liberum veto* was regarded as the most important of these safeguards because it allowed any minority to resist the initiatives of the majority that the king could have bribed.

And indeed, the history of Europe of the sixteenth and seventeenth centuries provided many examples that justified fears of royal absolutism. But the measures undertaken to protect liberty in the Commonwealth contained their own serious threats. Thus, a few collaborating deputies bribed with thirty pieces of silver and silently backed by magnates and foreign powers who hid behind them, could guarantee the failure of all attempts to reform and strengthen the state by protesting against the rest of the Diet. Besides the Diet no one had the right to make the most important decisions in the Commonwealth.

In addition to the *liberum veto,* the free election of the king was regarded as a second pillar of liberty. Elected for life, the king concluded a sort of contract with the electors, by which he confirmed the constitutional principles of liberty and made a further, more explicit pledge, the *Pacta Conventa.* In case the king infringed on the democratic constitution, and thus broke the electoral contract, noble society had the right to refuse obedience to his authority and resort to the ultimate weapon, rebellion.

Concentration of attention on the preservation of liberty against seemingly constant threats also had repercussions on the external activities of the state. This caused a reluctance to form an active foreign policy that was elevated to the level of a pacifist principle. The history of modern Europe provides numerous examples of monarchs who, strengthened by foreign alliances and with armies gathered for war at their disposal, successfully carried out absolutist rule. In eighteenth-century Poland, however, fear of a strong monarchy carried a certain serious risk: protecting its liberty against political danger from the monarch, the country was not provided with indispensable alliances, resulting in the isolation of the Commonwealth in the international arena.

One more remark must be added to the above. The approach inspired by the republican ideology, presented here in an abbreviated form, preferred defensive activity in relation to the king and passivity in foreign affairs; it did not stimulate positive, reformist activity, which by strengthening the state would simultaneously strengthen the monarch.

It was Poland's tragedy that the reign of August II, from 1697 to 1733, fully justified the republican biases sketched above. Throughout his reign, aspiring to strengthen and consolidate his authority as well as to subordinate the Commonwealth to Saxony, August II could not bring himself either to attain a deeper understanding of the constitutional principles of his Polish subjects or to formulate appropriate aims and methods of political activity. Even when he planned beneficial reforms such as the liquidation of the *liberum veto,* the introduction of a hereditary monarchy, or the limitation of the hetmans' privileges, his means of proceeding, such as the illegal actions of the Saxon army, the undisguised tendencies toward absolutism, and attempts to subordinate the Commonwealth to Saxony, alienated not only the magnates, who were jealous of their privileges, but also the nobles, who were committed to democracy and the independence of the Commonwealth. In the skillful hands of Peter I, the intensification of the conflict between the King and nobles– *inter maiestatem ac libertatem*–became the main instrument of blocking the internal consolidation of the Commonwealth.

It is doubtful that even a monarch who was more far-sighted and had more insight into Poland's problems than August II could have achieved anything given the fact that August after his restoration to the throne found a strong Russian party that the Tsar had established in Poland before Poltava. It was certain, however, that August II's discounting of the biases and sentiments of his Polish subjects facilitated the machinations of the Tsar, whose goal was to block reforms that would strengthen Poland. The crucial moment in Peter I's efforts came in the years 1715 to 1720.

When in the general Confederation of Tarnogród of 1715 the nobility rebelled against the King (not without Russian inspiration) because of the illegal presence of the Saxon army in Poland, Peter I intervened to mediate the conflict but did not allow an immediate agreement between the rebels and

August II. Peter I brought Russian armies into Poland and supported the rebellious nobility when August II's camp gained the upper hand; he supported the King, when the latter was threatened with dethronement. Through his representative in the Commonwealth, Grigory Dolgoruky, the Tsar constrained the two sides to negotiate a settlement that gave neither a clear advantage. In the course of the struggle the Tsar also strongly defended the hetmans, who were loyal to him and who behaved in an equivocal manner, and he did not allow the nobility to break their power. The one-day "Dumb Diet," which ended the conflict on February 1, 1717, not only approved the results of Russian mediation (the so-called Treaty of Warsaw), but also introduced measures that permanently weakened the military potential of the Commonwealth.[1]

Peter I's triumph heightened the vigilance not only of the frustrated August II but also of other rulers. Emperor Charles VI and the King of England and Elector of Hanover, George I, feared that the imperial aims of the Tsar would extend to Mecklenburg and the Baltic Sea. The treaty arranged between the three monarchs in Vienna on January 5, 1719, foresaw, among other things, that Peter would be compelled to withdraw his army from the Commonwealth and that Russian influence would be removed from that state. The realization of these plans depended on Poland entering the alliance, a step which rested on the decision of the Diet. Never before in the reign of August II had the convergence of the aims of the monarch and the Commonwealth been so plain or the prospects for foreign support for Polish vindication so real. Nevertheless, two successive Diets–the first in 1719-1720, the second in the fall of 1720–were broken up. In both instances the deputies who cast the *veto* were inspired by the four hetmans of the Commonwealth. Among them Ludwik Pociej played the most important role, acting in agreement with the Russian representative and the Prussian resident.

The argument that according to Polish law the command over armies comprising foreign contingents belonged not to the hetmans but to the Saxon Minister Jakob Heinrich Flemming (who had been granted Polish nobility) served as a pretext for rupturing the Diet. This innovation, intended to ensure August II's control over the Polish army and proclaimed by the agitators for the hetmans, the Russians, and the Prussians, as the road to Saxon *absolutum dominium* touched a nerve in republican sensibilities. A second factor played on by anti-Diet propaganda was the pacifism of Polish society, intensified by fresh memories of the sixteen-year devastation of the Great Northern War and the Confederation of Tarnogród.

The acquiescence shown by the majority of noble society to the wreckers of the Diets of 1720, and thereby the failure to appreciate the opportunity offered the Commonwealth by the Treaty of Vienna, displays an aspect of perhaps the

Portraits of European rulers, participants in the Great Northern War 1716 (Fundacja XX Czartoryskich, Muzeum Narodowe w Krakowie).

Constytucye na zakończeniu Konfederacyi Tarnogrodzkiey, y innych Konfederacyi Prowincyalnych y Partykularnych do niey referujacych się, tak Szlacheckich iako y Woyskowych Koronnych y W.X.L...R.P. MDCCXVII Miesiąca Lutego, dnia pierwszego w Warszawie postanowione. (Constitutions ending the Confederation of Tarnogród...in 1717 A.D. in Warsaw, adopted the first of February). (Biblioteka Narodowa, Warszawa). Title page of the pacificatory one-day Diet, the so-called Dumb Diet which, without any discussion, approved the Warsaw treaty in 1716, signed under Russian mediation between August II and the confederated gentry.

deepest political and cultural crisis. The hostile actions undertaken by the Commonwealth's neighboring state, in cooperation with the hetman oligarches, worked hand in hand with the profound disorientation of the nobility, which, extremely distrustful of its own monarch, did not recognize the magnitude of the external danger that confronted the state.

In the face of the threat that the Treaty of Vienna and August II's efforts to emancipate himself presented to Russian dominance in Poland, Peter I allied himself on February 17, 1720, with the ruler of Prussia, Frederick William I. The Treaty of Potsdam signed by the two states foresaw mutual cooperation to maintain in Poland an elective monarchy as well as the existing form of government with all its faults.

The interests of Russia and Prussia in the Commonwealth were not identical. The ruler of relatively small Prussia dreamed of annexing Polish territory. The Russian tsar stood in the way of this; in the interests of maintaining Russian hegemony over the entire Commonwealth, he had repeatedly rejected Prussian proposals in this regard in the years before the Treaty of Potsdam. A precondition of this hegemony, however, was the blocking of the internal strengthening of Poland, of its renewal through reforms. The same goal guided the Prussians; for them ever to expect an opportunity for partition, Poland must remain in a state of weakness. Despite long-term differences in their goals, the immediate interests of Russia and Prussia in regard to Poland were the same and rested on the prevention of its revitalization. This commonality of aims determined the longevity of the Prussian-Russian alliance against the revival of Poland in the eighteenth century. Initiated in 1720 in Potsdam, the alliance was renewed in 1726, 1729, 1730, 1740, 1743, 1764, 1769, 1772, 1777, and 1792; in addition, from 1730, the principle of upholding elective monarchy and disallowing the king "to curb liberties" was reinforced by an article extending the protection to Polish dissidents and dissenters by both powers. This was one more means of interfering in the affairs of the Commonwealth.[2]

2. The Reign of August III: St. Petersburg and Berlin
As the Guardians of Impotence

The narrowness of the political horizons of the nobility was an essential factor allowing the egotistic magnates and the powers opposed to the renewal of Poland to hold the Commonwealth in a state of weakness. Nevertheless signs of renewal appeared in the 1720s. A political faction arose that elaborated a complete reform program and with the support of the Saxon court (especially

Minister Jakob Heinrich Flemming) attempted to attain the most important offices in the state. This party or, "family," was composed of two brothers, Michał Fryderyk and August Aleksander Czartoryski, as well as their sister's husband, Stanisław Poniatowski. Attempts to place Poniatowski or others connected to the "family" in key positions in the state, previously held by the hetmans but now vacant, were the cause of sharp political conflicts in the Diets during the last years of August II's reign. The struggle revealed, on the one hand, the determination of the "family," supported by the court, to attain their goals and, on the other, the recalcitrance and self-interest of their rivals, the Potocki party. Acting in concert with neighboring powers, for whom relative balance between the opposing camps in Poland became a convenient means of maintaining the weakness of the Commonwealth, the leaders of the Potocki camp, who also aspired to the hetmans' positions, induced a rupture of every Diet from 1729 to the death of August II (February 1, 1733) when new circumstances emerged.

The tumultuous events of the penultimate royal election (1733-1735) and the first years of the reign of August III brought a reversal for the Czartoryskis when the Potockis and their adherents gained the hetmans' posts. Nonetheless, the antagonism between the "family" and the Potocki camp did not die out and remained at the core of internal political divisions in Poland throughout the reign of August III (1733-1763).

The Czartoryskis did not relinquish the reformist intentions that had remained unrealized under August II. Recovering from the electoral defeat, the princes, particularly in the second half of the 1730s, undertook concerted and successful efforts to establish lasting, solid support among the nobility. The political orientation of the "family" also changed. From an anti-Russian position under August II, the "family" shifted to a pro-Russian stance under his successor. This shift resulted from the realization that Poland was in no position to resist Russian might, as well as from misperceptions regarding St. Petersburg's intentions toward the Commonwealth.

The leaders of the "family" realistically interpreted the annexationist intentions of Prussia toward Poland and correctly judged that, in consideration of the weaknesses of the country, Russia provided the only safeguard against Prussian aggression. Ignorant of secret clauses of the Russo-Prussian treaties that were lethal for Poland, the Czartoryskis assumed that powerful Russia, capable of fielding an army of 200,000 men, would not oppose an increase of the Polish military to 30,000. This illusion on the part of the leaders of the "family" intensified after Frederick II's attack on Silesia (1740). Believing (as we now know, falsely) that the Prussian conquest of Silesia was unwelcome to

Russia, the Czartoryskis calculated that the year 1740 would bring a new, and for Poland more favorable, international situation. Its essence was to be a war between Russia and Prussia, in which Warsaw would become a welcome ally to St. Petersburg. Further, this would mean new opportunities for Polish reforms, since Russia would be interested not only in tolerating but in supporting them. Reality was to reveal the illusionary nature of such calculations.

It seems that the circumstances of the penultimate royal election brought a turning point in the political consciousness among the broad masses of the nobility. Despite the greatest electoral participation in the history of the Commonwealth, in which 13,500 electors proclaimed Stanisław Leszczyński king, August III was imposed by Russia as the ruler of Poland. The intervention of a Russian corps of 30,000 men sufficed to subdue the nobles' levy in mass of the Confederation of Dzików in defense of Leszczyński's kingship. After this experience military recruitment became a general reform postulate. The Pacification Diet of 1736, the first Diet under August III to enact legislation, did not resolve to enlarge the army but it did establish a commission to elaborate a plan for recruitment, preceded by a review of earnings to find out the real financial means of the state. This financial-military reform never came about, for all successive Diets under August III, from 1738 to 1762, were ruptured. Closer consideration of the fate of one of them, the Grodno Diet of 1744, will allow a look at the mechanism of disaster.

The special opportunities for the Diet of 1744 rested on the momentary convergence of the interests of Poland and Saxony in the international arena. Dresden, allied with the anti-Prussian coalition in this phase of the Silesian Wars, was interested in Polish military expansion and the participation of the Commonwealth in the war against Berlin. In view of August III's normally slight involvement in Polish affairs, this turn of events provided encouraging circumstances for reform. We know that, besides the enlargement of the army and Poland's entry into the anti-Prussian coalition, the Czartoryskis and the Minister Heinrich Brühl, de facto in charge of Saxon policy, planned to restrict the *liberum veto*, reform the central organs of state administration, and to open the way to an inherited throne.

In preparation for the Diet the court sought to gain the support of Russia for its plans and offered in return an alliance of the Commonwealth with its eastern neighbor. This request did not meet with a positive reception from Empress Elizabeth. Her answer, that the reforms were a matter not for Russia but for the king and the Commonwealth, amounted to a refusal of support.

Despite the extraordinary efforts of the court and the "family," the Diet of 1744 (like the two previous Diets) was broken up. Prussia and its ally France remunerated the obstructors, who came from the Potocki party and made use of the proven means of the *liberum veto*.[3] If it is true that the Potocki camp, which opposed the court and resented the "family," had its own reform plan with priority given to military enhancement, the rupture of the Diet by the agents of this party demonstrated that its magnate leaders preferred to negate an increase in the army that was imperative for the state rather than to allow parliamentary victories to strengthen their rivals, the Czartoryskis and Poniatowskis. It is difficult not to judge this a subordination of state interest to the private interests of the magnate oligarches.

The failure of the Diet of 1744 convinced the leaders of the "family" that as long as the *liberum veto* existed even the union of their strength with that of the court would not suffice to restrain the obstructionists in the Diet. At this point they could only turn to extraordinary means. Polish law allowed for an expression of such means in the confederation Diet, which could not be broken up by "free opposition."

The text of the proclamation calling for a confederation Diet was already prepared when a threatening declaration by Empress Elizabeth arrived in Warsaw from St. Petersburg in December 1744. The sovereign of Russia warned that she would not allow "any confederation, any disturbances, or any innovations that might be directed either against the sacred person of the king or against the liberties and prerogatives of the Commonwealth, regardless of by whom or under what pretext they were raised." In case such warnings were ignored, the declaration promised to strike those behind such undertakings with full force.

The text from St. Petersburg was not an empty threat; it was directed as much against Prussia, which threatened August III with a rebellion by his opponents, as against Brühl and the Czartoryskis, who were said to be planning an assault on "liberty." With this, the fate of the confederation Diet was sealed; having withdrawn the proclamation of the Diet, August III left for Dresden.

The scenario tested in 1744 for preventing a confederation Diet from meeting was repeated by St. Petersburg four years and again six years later, after the Potockis had broken up the Diets of 1748 and 1750. Before the Diet of 1750, Empress Elizabeth further warned August III against excessive favoritism towards one party, that is, the "family," in appointment to offices. Just as in the time of Peter I, a relative balance between the competing parties guaranteed Russia that none would be in a position to subordinate its opponent and bring about a reformist coup.[4]

Constitutiones Comitiorum Pacificationis Extraordinariorum, oder: Pohlnische
Reichs - Verfassungen, welche auf dem, Zwey Wochen hindurch, in Warschau
gehaltenen, und zur Herstellung des allgemeinen Ruhe - Standes in Pohlen, den 25
Tag des Monats Junii im Jahr des Herrn 1736 ausserordentlich angesetztem
Pacifications Reichs-Tage errichtet... Dressden (Biblioteka Sejmowa, Warszawa).
(Photo A. Wełnicki). Title page of the German translation of the extraordinary
Pacification Diet in Warsaw, 1736.

DYARYUSZ

SEYMU *CONVOCATIONIS*

Siedmio - Niedzielnego

WARSZAWSKIEGO

Zdania, Mowy, Projekta y Manife-
sta w sobie zawieraiący,
przez Sessye

ZEBRANY.

R. P. 1764.

w WARSZAWIE
W Drukarni J.K. MCI y Rzeczypospolitey
Societatis JESU.

Dyaryusz Seymu Convocationis Siedmio-Niedzielnego Warszawskiego Zdania,
Mowy, Projekta y Manifesta w sobie zawieraiący przez Sessye zebrany. R.P. 1764.
(Diary of the seven week Convocation Diet in Warsaw... 1764 A.D.) Title page. The
Diet which deliberated during the interregnum after the death of August III, although
held under Russian control and restrictions, nevertheless partially carried out
Czartoryski's reform program concerning the administration and the economy.
(Biblioteka Sejmowa, Warszawa).

The loosening in the late 1740s of the alliance that had bound St. Petersburg and Berlin since 1720, and ultimately led to war between the two courts (1756-1762), did not imply new chances for reform in the Commonwealth. The conflict between Prussia and Russia did not result in a change in either state's relation to the question of strengthening Poland; both remained hostile to such efforts.

The thirteen successive wasted Diets during the reign of August III bore witness not only to the hostile activities of Russia and Prussia but also to the deep decline of the nobility from among whom, after all, the obstructionists and their magnate supporters were drawn. General calls for strengthening the military after 1736 were accompanied by an almost superstitious dread among parts of the nobility of *absolutum dominium*, by a perception of the *liberum veto* as the essence of liberty, and by a fear of active participation in international affairs. The changes initiated by the educational reforms of 1740 (Stanisław Konarski's Collegium Nobilium and the reform of the Jesuit schools in the 1750s) could not bear fruit quickly. The last years of the reign of August III represented a period of great political stagnation. Denied favor from the King and Brühl, the Czartoryskis owed their survival on the surface of political life above all to Russian protection, on which they placed their hopes for the coming interregnum. On the other hand, Jerzy Mniszech's "camarilla" concentrated its activity at the court and constituted a new incarnation of the Potocki party, which brought together magnate careerists who lacked any deeper understanding of the needs of the state or any reformist concepts. Their company suited August III and Brühl, who undertook no further reform attempts after their separation from the "family" in 1752.[5]

3. The Reforms of the "Family" and Repnin's Reaction

The power structure in Central Europe that was established by the Seven Years' War predetermined that whoever sought the Polish crown after the death of August III (October 5, 1763), could attain it only with the acceptance of the Empress of Russia, Catherine II.

The appropriation of the crown to Stanisław Poniatowski the younger (the son of the cofounder of the "family," who died in 1762) resulted from a double calculation of the Empress. First, she judged that she knew her former lover well enough to be certain of his absolute subservience to the demands of St. Petersburg. Second, because the new King belonged to no European dynasty he lacked even the weak support that the Wettins had derived from their family connections in many royal houses. This was to guarantee the Polish king's complete dependence on Russia.

In response to the Polish election St. Petersburg returned to the alliance with Berlin as the foundation of its foreign policy. The treaty, signed on April 11, 1764, included–besides immediate electoral obligations–the usual issues: maintenance of free elections and constitutional "liberties" in the Commonwealth and the restoration of the rights of religious dissenters.

As under Peter I, the dominant party in the alliance–especially after Frederick II's recent difficulties in the Seven Years' War–was Russia. Accordingly, Berlin's role in the Commonwealth was to be limited to buttressing the policy of St. Petersburg. One should not, however, underestimate the influence of Prussia's anti-Polish prompting, constantly warning Russia of the threat posed by Polish emancipationist and reformist plans. Frederick II's denunciations, of which the *Politische Correspondenz* provides eloquent testimony, resulted not only from the belief that not even the slightest constitutional improvement should be allowed in Poland, but also from the divergent aims of St. Petersburg and Berlin in Warsaw. Whereas for Russia the inertia of the Commonwealth watched over by the Russian ambassador in Warsaw, represented an ideal state of affairs, from the point of view of Berlin, St. Petersburg's undisturbed domination of Poland removed any chance of partition. Such chances could only arise if the Polish political situation became stormy. Only then could Frederick calculate that Catherine–discouraged by a lack of stability in a Poland dominated exclusively by Russia–would wish to divide Poland, thereby buying quieter rule in the portion allotted to her.

The "family," with the support of tens of thousands of Russian soldiers, completely dominated the country during the interregnum, and vehemently undertook reform at the Convocation Diet (May-June, 1764). The unlimited power of the hetmans was restricted by the creation of a collegial Military Commission, while the authority of the treasurer was checked by the establishment of a Treasury Commission. The Russian ambassador blocked the most important reform, the abolition of the *liberum veto*. "Free opposition" was to be only partially limited by the introduction of majority voting on financial and economic matters. After the election of Stanisław August (September 7, 1764), the Czartoryskis had taken practically full control of Polish politics and did not allow the representatives of the Potockis, whom they had defeated with the aid of the Russian army, to regain their previous importance.

Catherine's decision to depart from the principle of maintaining a rough balance between the opposing factions in Poland resulted from her conviction that both the older leaders of the "family" and the young King would be completely submissive to St. Petersburg's demands. Of these demands, which

Russia revealed only after the election, the most important were the acceptance by the Commonwealth of a Russian guarantee of the Polish constitution, including, above all, the *liberum veto* and elective monarchy, as well as the restoration of full rights to the religious dissenters, of whom Catherine made herself the official advocate.

Against the expectations of the Empress and Nikita Panin, the principal architect of Russian foreign policy, neither the King nor the Czartoryskis showed any readiness to accept these demands. Catherine II clearly did not appreciate the reformist zeal that motivated Stanisław August. Regarding the raising of the country from the stagnation of the Saxon period as his historical mission, the King was aware that the petrification of the *liberum veto* and the subjection of constitutional changes to Russian approval (and this was the significance of the Russian guarantee) contradicted this mission. The King saw less danger in the Russian demands regarding dissenters, but he, as well as the Czartoryskis, had to reckon with the petulance of the nobility on this question.

The refusal of the Coronation Diet to ratify the Russian postulates after its deliberations in Warsaw in November and December, 1764, provoked surprise and disappointment in St. Petersburg. Prussia played a special role in deepening these unfavorable feelings toward Poland. Although Frederick II did not favor full equality for dissenters in Poland because he feared this would encourage the immigration of skilled Protestants from Prussia to the Commonwealth, the exasperation of the Empress with the King and the Czartoryskis suited his purposes. Earlier than Catherine II, the Hohenzollern recognized the reformist aspirations of Stanisław August and intensively sought means to create a permanent barrier for him in St. Petersburg. Playing on Catherine's jealous self-love and fanning Russian distrust of Polish reform efforts, the Prussian ambassador to Russia also made repeated protestations regarding dissenters in 1765-1766, a fact which also played an essential role in shaping the demands that St. Petersburg finally placed on the Poles.

The price for the refusal of the Diet of 1766 to conform to the demands of Russia and Prussia, who jointly demanded legislative confirmation of political equality for Protestants and the Orthodox, was the definitive disfavor of St. Petersburg toward the Czartoryskis. This meant the disappearance of the old princes from the political scene. Stanisław August also met defeat at this Diet in his attempt to force further legislative restriction on the *liberum veto* despite Russia's explicit opposition. Finally capitulating before superior force, the King remained on the throne, but the conditions under which he exercised authority underwent fundamental changes.

In combating the reformist efforts of the Polish King, the Russian ambassador, Nikolai Repnin, found allies among the members of Mniszek's "camarilla," which had been defeated at the royal election. Lured by the hope of repealing the reforms introduced by the Czartoryskis and of dethroning Stanisław August, the Potockis and their allies, under the close supervision of Repnin, who brought additional Russian soldiers to Poland, first organized the Confederation of Radom in June, 1767, and then gathered in Warsaw for a confederated Diet in October. Terrorized by the ambassador's abduction of opposing senators, the Diet accepted the Russian guarantee of the Polish political system, granted equal rights to Protestants and Orthodox, and finally, accepted the "eternal and invariable" cardinal laws, with the *liberum veto* and elected monarchy as the most prominent among them. The spectacular reconciliation that Repnin staged between the Radom confederates and Stanisław August demonstrates that St. Petersburg had retained the preelectoral variant of holding a tight rein on Polish political life by setting the court and the republican opposition against one another.[6]

It does not appear that the Prussian insinuations mentioned above played a decisive role in the transformation of the problem of religious dissenters into a fundamental instrument of Russia's political pressure on Poland. Interesting are the changes which this matter underwent in Petersburg. In the years 1766-67 it was turned into a question of principle in Polish-Russian relations: relevant legislation was forced on Poland which was later rescinded for the most part during the Diet after the First Partition. It is, therefore, quite possible that the confusion sewn by Russia on the Polish political scene by the demands concerning the dissenters was intended not only to put an end to the reformationist activity of Stanisław August and the Czartoryskis, but that it had deeper intentions. Namely, starting with 1763 the religious issue became a tool consistently and forcefully used by the influential Chernyshev coterie to annex to Russia a large part of Polish territory. Proposing such a goal, the vice-director of the Military Council, Zakhar Chernyshev, stated that the general chaos and the large number of Russian troops in Poland argued for its success. The problem of dissenters, the forceful resolution of which required the presence of additional tens of thousands of Russian Troops, provided an excellent pretext for achieving this goal, not yet realized in 1763-1764.[7] Such an interpretation would explain why Russia, having completed the partition and interested at that time in a lasting pacification of its protectorate, would rescind a significant portion of pro-dissenter legislation which it had backed earlier.

4. The Road to the First Partition

The beginning of military activities by the Bar Confederation in February, 1768 made clear that hopes for the pacification of the Commonwealth through the Confederation of Radom were an illusion. The Mniszek "camarilla," which had enacted the measures to protect dissenters only under pressure, felt itselves further cheated by Stanisław August's retention of the throne as well as by Repnin's retention of some of the Czartoryskis' legislation. The outbreak of the Bar Confederation directed against Russia, the King, the "family," dissenters, and reformers—that is, "in defense of faith and liberty"—had serious international consequences, for it convinced the Ottoman Empire to declare war against Russia.

In conjunction with the war, the four-year struggle of the tsarist army with the constantly shifting eruptions of the Bar partisans provided Prussia with a great opportunity. While ostensibly favoring the confederates and simultaneously renewing proposals for partition in St. Petersburg, Frederick finally received a positive response from Catherine II in January 1771. The final decision was made on the Neva in June of that year, after which for nearly a year St. Petersburg and Berlin sought to convince Vienna to join in the partition. This was essential for the stability of the new "system" which was to be created on the foundation of the partition: an alliance of the three black eagles, which was to replace Panin's "northern system," based on the Russo-Prussian alliance.[8]

The Diet of 1773-1775, called under Russian pressure to ratify the treaty of partition signed in St. Petersburg on August 5, 1772, extended the guarantee of the Polish political system to the three partitioning states. This was only a formal innovation, however, for the real helmsman in diminished Poland remained Russia. Its ambassador after 1773, Otto Stackelberg, never left Stanisław August's side and intervened in the smallest details of government.

The fact that Stackelberg did not even need to resort to breaking up the Diet to block innovations that St. Petersburg objected to demonstrated the degree to which Poland was overshadowed by Russia during the "Stackelberg proconsulate" that lasted to 1788. In 1776, proceeding under a scenario closely arranged with the ambassador, the first Confederation Diet after the partition finished working out the form of the Permanent Council imposed by Russia; after this, five successive general Diets were held. The sterility of their legislation, limited to accepting reports and choosing members of executive organs, was attributable to Stackelberg's extensive control over the appointment of deputies as well to the magnate opposition, which remained at the ambassador's disposal to be let loose when it was necessary to restrict the excessive independence of the King. The principle of opposing the influence of the monarch to that of the magnate opposition continued to be an effective instrument of political control over Poland in these years.[9]

In discussing the role of Prussia and Russia in exploiting the weakness of the Commonwealth in the eighteenth century, we have almost completely neglected Poland's relations with other European countries. This is due to the fact that the Commonwealth had no chance to gain support against the lethal tendencies of its two neighbors.

The direct interests of England–Europe's greatest power–did not extend on the Continent beyond the eastern border of the Holy Roman Empire. Moreover, except for a few, exceptional moments, England did not regard the growth of the power of Russia (and later Prussia), with which it had lively relations, as a threat. France, in turn, which would have gladly regarded Poland as a barrier to Russia, the ally of Austria, proved irresolute when it became engaged in Polish affairs (as it did in 1733) and quickly withdrew when faced with opposition. In the second half of the eighteenth century, the financial ruin of France gradually worsened and after its last intervention in support of the Bar Confederation, the Bourbon monarchy avoided further political activity in the Commonwealth.

Austria, which, especially after the loss of Silesia, regarded Prussia as its greatest enemy, set its hopes for regaining the lost province on Russia. The price that Vienna was ready to pay St. Petersburg for help against Berlin included, among others, full respect of Russian sovereignty in its Polish protectorate. Moreover, on the eve of the election of 1764, despite the awareness that the Prussian threat linked them to Poland, Austria–like Russia and Prussia– recognized as vital the principle of upholding in Poland the system of liberties, including all of its degenerated features. Finally, Vienna's participation in the partition clearly demonstrated that Poland could expect no real help from its southern neighbor.

A similar conclusion applies to Sweden in view of its dependence on Russia; the Ottoman Empire was similarly weakened and, like Poland, subject to Russian aggression in the eighteenth century. Moreover, the Ottoman Empire, like Austria, had adopted the principle of the maintaining Polish "liberties" as its reason of state in 1764.[10]

In the face of hostile intentions on the part of Russia and Prussia, the weak Commonwealth could expect no help from the five European powers. This meant that, after August II's capitulation at Altranstädt and as a result of the unfavorable turn of events in the first phase of the Great Northern War for

Poland, the attempt to revive the state through reforms had no chance. All that remained was the struggle for the revival of the nation–a condition of its very survival.

5. The Great Reform and the Aggression of the Neighboring States: The Final Partition of Poland

After repeated fruitless attempts to gain foreign support in the years1765-1766 and again in 1773, Stanisław August realized that Poland could not rely on foreign aid against the dictates of the hostile neighboring powers. There remained only the option of governing under the existing conditions or of abdicating, which, at the end of 1766 meant ceding the state to the Mniszek party and, in 1773, risking the complete partition of Poland. Poniatowski remained on the throne, and, to his credit, throughout his reign, he did not cease to seek opportunities to achieve what was attainable for the country in the existing circumstances. The best-known examples of this activity are the Commission for National Education, appointed during the Partition Diet of 1773, as well as seeking out active and competent people among the middle gentry and facilitating their advancement in the state service, Such a step bore fruit on the eve of the Four-Year Diet in the appearance of a new element on the political scene: a group that was bound to the monarch and freed from the tutelage of the great lords. Their support was to eventually provide a counterweight to the magnate opposition.[11]

Thanks to the great educational reforms, a generation was brought up that deeply understood the need for fundamental constitutional reform and with difficulty accepted the national humiliation of Stanisław August's dependence on Stackelberg. Daily experiencing the ambassador's lordship over Poland, this generation dreamed of the opportunity to strike a blow for independence. They pinned their hopes primarily on the Russo-Turkish war.

The outbreak of the war in August, 1787, provoked enormous animation in Poland. It was assumed that the fighting would be protracted and would cause Russia considerable difficulties. This meant that the Diet opening in October, 1788, would be presented with an exceptional opportunity: engaged in war, the Empress would be prepared to make concessions to secure peace in Poland.

After the experience of the First Partition, Stanisław August above all feared to anger Russia. Thus, although he also regarded this war as an opportunity for reforms, he sought to carry them out with Catherine's agreement. Having this in mind he traveled to Kaniów in the spring of 1787 to meet the Empress and win her approval for his program. The program comprised an increase in the size of the army, the taxes that this entailed, and a confederation Diet. In order not to arouse Catherine's distrust, the King in addition proposed an alliance of the Commonwealth with Russia. Both states would guarantee their territorial integrity (this would ensure Poland against a new partition), and part of the new Polish army would be committed to the common struggle with the Ottoman Empire. The return of Poland to active participation in the international arena would be in itself an important achievement.

The project went against the dominant mood of dislike and even hatred of Russia among the gentry. The mood was further nourished by the apparently rising dissonance between St. Petersburg and Berlin. From the beginning of the 1780s, the increasing anti-Turkish activity of Russia determined that St. Petersburg drew closer to Vienna and loosened its ties to Berlin. A symptom of this was Catherine II's refusal to extend the Russo-Prussian treaty of alliance, which expired in March 1788. Some Polish politicians drew the conclusion that sooner or later Berlin would recognize Warsaw as a useful ally against St. Petersburg and therefore support Polish reformist efforts. Until September 1788, when news of the proposed Polish-Russian alliance reached the Spree, Berlin did nothing to confirm the calculations of the Polish Prussophiles.

Although the Prussian stance greatly disturbed Stanisław August, the King, while awaiting a response to the Kaniów proposals, was forced to remain passive. Russia delayed taking a position as long as possible in order to hamper the King in preparing reforms. A final decision was reached on the Neva in June 1788. The Empress permitted a confederation Diet and small-scale military recruitment and taxation; further, she agreed to an alliance, but in a form that perverted Stanisław August's intentions. The purpose of the changes was clear: to ensure that Poland would not become a full-fledged member of the international community. Even this alliance proved to be impossible, however, for Prussia cast a veto against it.

The news of the proposed alliance caused Frederick William II to take action to upset the Kaniów project. Notifying St. Petersburg of his objections to a Polish-Russian alliance, the Hohenzollern almost simultaneously sent to Warsaw a declaration courting the Diet at its opening. He assured Poland of his friendly intentions, warned against the harmful Kaniów alliance project, and finally hinted at the possibility of a defensive alliance of Prussia with the Commonwealth, protecting it against Russia.

The lack of elementary diplomatic experience among the deputies, caused by decades of Polish passivity in the international arena, bore the fruit Berlin expected. The pleasant words and treatment of the Commonwealth as a partner, instead of a vassal, made an impression on the inexperienced deputies, who misread Frederick William II's real intentions. By gaining influence on the Diet, the Prussian king sought to evoke decidedly anti-Russian pronouncements from it. This would undercut Stanisław August's policy and cause Russia to withdraw its approval of the alliance and reforms. Then, Berlin could drop its friendly tone toward the Diet and reach an agreement with St. Petersburg on a new partition.

The Prussian provocation achieved complete success. Regarding Frederick William II's declaration as proof that Poland had emerged from isolation, had found support in Berlin against St. Petersburg, and could undertake bold reformist measures, the Diet, in its first month of deliberations, enacted the recruitment of 100,000 soldiers and presently dissolved the Permanent Council. This meant a definitive break with Russia. Stanisław August, who did not share the enthusiasm for Prussia and fathomed the intentions of the Hohenzollern, lost his majority in the Diet and was powerless against the collapse of his political plan.

Catherine II, who closely watched the developments in Warsaw, had already decided to settle matters with the Poles. She sought, however, to postpone this until the conclusion of the war with the Ottoman Empire. To lull Warsaw's vigilance until that time, the Empress decided to feign indifference to what took place there. In this way the Great Diet gained the time for four years of unhampered legislative activity. This activity soon overstepped the boundaries that Frederick William II wished to set. Forced to pretend goodwill toward Poland, the Prussians could not brake the reformist momentum of the Diet, and international circumstances even induced them to conclude an alliance with the Commonwealth in March 1790.

This alliance, undertaken by Berlin with the thought of a future war with Austria in which Polish territory and the Polish army could prove useful, was also intended to secure the acquisitions of territory the Prussians longed for in Poland. They could realize them in one of two ways. Russia, for whom an alliance of Berlin with Warsaw was unacceptable, could act to disrupt it by returning to an alliance with Prussia and agreeing to a new partition. Under the second variation Berlin, would extort the cession from the Poles directly; this was to be the payment for the Prussian alliance.[12]

The Prusso-Austrian agreement at Reichenbach (July, 1790) made clear that there would be no war between the two states. With this, the Polish alliance lost its value for Berlin. When, in addition, the Commonwealth thwarted Prussian hopes for a voluntary cession of territory, the alliance of March, 1790, ceased to make sense. The passage of the Constitution of 3 May, 1791, further strengthened Prussia's negative attitude toward its Polish ally.

When, in April, 1791 the stance taken by England definitely frustrated plans to form a coalition for war against Russia, Prussia drew closer to Vienna. The pacification of Europe required a new alliance system. Vienna and Berlin shared an interest in intervening in revolutionary France. Their differences, however, touched on their relations to Poland. Whereas Austria sought to avoid a new partition (for this would dangerously strengthen the Hohenzollern state) and therefore sought to gain Catherine II's tolerance for the post-May realities in Poland, Prussia hoped that Russia's rejection of the Constitution of 3 May would open the possibility of further dividing Polish territory. Recognizing that the Empress would not accept the changes in Poland, Vienna decided at the beginning of 1792 to take part in the next partition. At the same time (February, 1792) Berlin signaled St. Petersburg that it would not move to support its Polish ally in the event of Russian intervention in the Commonwealth. This implied a readiness to accept an offer of partition.

When the Empress undertook military intervention in Poland (May, 1792), Prussia in fact refused to aid the Commonwealth and waited for compensation from Russia. Events on the French front determined that proposals for partition reached Berlin only later. Catherine II used them to press Prussia to strengthen its engagement in France. The history of the intervention on the Seine also determined that Austria was eliminated from the partitioning powers, and the treaty signed in St. Petersburg in January, 1793, for the Second Partition foresaw the participation only of Russia and Prussia.[13]

Both the extent of the partition and the provocative behavior of the Russian dignitaries toward the truncated Commonwealth indicated that St. Petersburg inclined toward the complete liquidation of the Polish state. The outbreak of the Kościuszko Insurrection in March, 1794, accelerated this decision. In July, 1794, Catherine II invited Austria and Prussia to negotiate a further partition. Bargaining between Vienna and St. Petersburg over the extent of their gains delayed the final decision. Russia and Austria signed a treaty only in January, 1795; in October of that year Prussia reached a corresponding agreement with St. Petersburg and Vienna.[14]

As a result of the configuration of power in Central Europe that took shape already at the beginning of the Great Northern War, the Polish state had no chance to survive as an independent country in the eighteenth century. There remained only the struggle for the preservation of the nation. The enactment of the Constitution of 3 May made certain that that struggle would be victorious.

Notes

1. Józef Feldman, "Geneza konfederacji tarnogrodzkiej" (The genesis of the Confederation of Tarnogród), *Kwartalnik Historyczny* 42 (1928); Józef Andrzej Gierowski, *Między saskim absolutyzmem a złotą wolnością* (Between Saxon absolutism and golden liberty) (Wrocław: Ossolineum, 1953); *W cieniu Ligi Północnej* (In the shadow of the Northern League) (Wrocław: Ossolineum, 1971); Andrzej Kamiński, *Konfederacja sandomierska wobec Rosji w okresie poaltransztadzkim 1706-1709* (The Confederation of Sandomierz in relation to Russia after the Treaty of Altranstädt) (Wrocław: Ossolineum, 1969); Władysław Konopczyński, *Le liberum veto* (Paris: 1930); Michał Nycz, *Geneza reform skarbowych sejmu niemego* (The genesis of the financial reforms of the Dumb Diet) (Poznań: Poznańskie Towarzystwo Przyjaciół Nauk, 1983).

2. Józef Andrzej Gierowski, "Polityka pruska wobec Rzeczypospolitej po traktacie utrechckim" (Prussian policy toward the Commonwealth after the Treaty of Utrecht), in Gierowski, *W cieniu Ligi Północnej;* Kazimierz Jarochowski, "Próba emancypacyjnej polityki Augustowej i intryga Posadowskiego, rezydenta pruskiego w Warszawie roku 1720" (August's attempt at political emancipation and the intrigue of Posadowski, the Prussian resident in Warsaw in 1720), in Kazimierz Jarochowski, *Nowe opowiadania i studia historyczne* (Warszawa: 1882); L.R. Lewitter, "Poland, Russia, and the Treaty of Vienna of 5th January 1719," *Historical Journal* 13 (1970); Fiodor Martens, ed., *Sobraniie traktatov i konventsii zakliuchennich Rossiiu s inostrannimi derzhavami* (Collected treaties and conventions concluded by Russia with foreign powers), vols. 4-5 (St. Petersburg: 1880-1883); Klaus Zernack, "Negative Polenpolitik als Grundlage deutsch-russischer Diplomatie in der Mächtepolitik des 18 Jahrhunderts," in Uwe Liszkowski, ed., *Russland und Deutschland* (Stuttgart: E. Klett, 1974).

3. Counting on gaining the Polish throne after the death of August III, Paris meanwhile opposed reforms that could have ensured the succession of the Wettins.

4. Szymon Askenazy, "Fryderyk II i August III" (Frederick II and August III), in Szymon Askenazy, *Dwa stulecia* , vol. 1 (Warszawa: 1903); Klemens Kantecki, *Stanisław Poniatowski,* vols. 1-2 (Poznań: 1880); Walter Mediger, *Moskauer Weg nach Europa* (Braunschweig: 1952); Michael Müller, *Polen zwischen Preussen und Russland* (Berlin: Colloquium, 1983); Emanuel Rostworowski, *O polską koronę. Polityka Francji w latach 1725-1733* (Struggle for the Polish crown: French policy in the years 1725 to 1733) (Wrocław: Ossolineum, 1958); Mieczysław Skibiński, *Europa a Polska w dobie wojny o sukcesję austriacką* (Europe and Poland in the period of the War of the Austrian Succession), vols. 1-2 (Kraków: 1912-1913); Zofia Zielińska, *Walka "familii" o reformę Rzeczypospolitej 1743-1752* (The struggle of "the family" for reform of the Commonwealth 1743-1752) (Warszawa: PWN, 1983).

5. Stanisław Bednarski, *Upadek i odrodzenie szkół jezuickich w Polsce* (The decline and renewal of Jesuit schools in Poland) (Kraków: 1933); Władysław Konopczyński, *Mrok i świt* (Darkness and dawn) (Warszawa: 1911); *Polska w dobie wojny siedmioletniej* (Poland in the period of the Seven Years' War), vols. 1-2 (Warszawa: 1909-1911); *Stanisław Konarski* (Warszawa: 1926).

6. Szymon Askenazy, *Die letzte polnische Königswahl* (Göttingen: 1894); Jürgen Hoensch, "Der Streit um den polnischen Generalzoll 1764-1766," *Jahrbücher für Geschichte Osteuropas* 18 (1970); Władysław Kisielewski, *Reforma książąt Czartoryskich na sejmie konwokacyjnym r. 1764* (The reforms of the Princes Czartoyski at the Convocation Diet of 1764) (Sambor: 1880); Aleksander Kraushar, *Książę Repnin i Polska* (Prince Repnin and Poland), vol. 1-2 (Warszawa: 1900); Maria Cecylia Łubieńska, *Sprawa dysydencka 1764-1766* (The problem of the Dissidents, 1764-1766) (Warszawa: 1911); George Tadeusz Łukowski, *The Szlachta and the Confederacy of Radom, 1764-1767/8* (Rome: Institutum Historicum Polonicum Romae, 1977); Jerzy Michalski, "Problematyka aliansu polsko-rosyjskiego w czasach Stanisława Augusta, Lata 1764-1766" (Problems of a Polish-Russian alliance in the age of Stanisław August, 1764-1766), *Przegląd Historyczny* 75 (1984); Julian Nieć, *Młodość ostatniego elekta* (The youth of the last king) (Kraków: 1935); Emanuel Rostworowski, "Edukacja ostatniego króla" (The education of the last king), in Emanuel Rostworowski, *Popioły i korzenie* (Kraków: Znak, 1985).

7. An unusually interesting hypothesis about the decisive role played by Zakhar Chernyshev in advocating the demands concerning the dissenters was put forward by the Russian historian Boris Nosov at the Polish-German-Russian Conference on the Partitions of Poland which took place in Moscow in June, 1994. He argued the necessity of paying greater attention than had hitherto been the case to the annexationist policies of Petersburg toward Poland beginning in the 1760's. Further previously unknown arguments about Zakhar Chernyshev's role in the realization of Russian annexationist plans in Poland were presented by Zofia Zielińska at the Polish-German conference in Torun in May, 1995. Chernyshev's plan in 1763 was discussed by Sergei Soloviev *Istoria Rossii s drevneishikh vremen* (History of Russia from its earliest period), (Moskva: 1881), p. 302; U.L. Lehtonen, *Die Polnischen Provinzen Russlands unter Katharina II in den Jahren 1772-1782*, (Berlin, 1907), p. 174-175; see also Herbert H. Kaplan, *The First Partition of Poland* (New York: Columbia U. P. 1962) p. 28.

8. Adolf Beer, *Die erste Teilung Polens*, vols. 1-3 (Wien: 1873); Tadeusz Cegielski, *Das alte Reich und die erste Teilung Polens* (Stuttgart: 1988); David Bayne Horn, *British Public Opinion and the First Partition of Poland* (Edinburgh: Oliver and Boyd, 1945); Kaplan, *The First Partition of Poland*; Władysław Konopczyński, *Konfederacja barska* (The Bar Confederation), vol. 1-2 (Warszawa: Volumen, 1991); Emanuel Rostworowski, "Gra trzech czarnych orłów" (The game of the three black eagles), in *Popioły i korzenie;* "Na drodze do pierwszego rozbioru" (The road to the First Partition), *Roczniki Historyczne* 18 (1949); Albert Sorel, *La question d'orient* (Paris: 1902).

9. Aleksander Czaja, *Między tronem, buławą, a dworem petersburskim* (Between the throne, the Hetman's baton, and the court of St. Petersburg) (Warszawa: PWN, 1986); Władysław Konopczyński, *Geneza i ustanowienie Rady Nieustającej* (The genesis and establishment of the Permanent Council) (Kraków: 1917); Stanisław Kościałkowski, *Antoni Tyzenhauz*, vols. 1-2 (Londyn: Wydawnictwo Społeczności Akademickiej Uniwersytetu Stefana Batorego w Londynie, 1970-1971); Jerzy Michalski, *Polska w dobie wojny o sukcesję bawarską* (Poland in the period of the War of the Bavarian Succession) (Wrocław: Ossolineum, 1964); Kazimierz Marian Morawski, *Ignacy Potocki* (Kraków: 1911); Stanislas-Auguste, *Mémoires*, edited by Sergiej Gorianow, vols. 1-2 (St.Peterbourg-Leningrad: 1914-1924).

10. Józef Feldman, *Na przełomie stosunków polsko-francuskich 1774-1787* (At the turning point in Polish-French relations, 1774-1787) (Kraków: 1935); Władysław Konopczyński, "Anglia a Polska w XVIII w." (England and Poland in the eighteenth century), *Pamiętniki Biblioteki Kórnickiej* 4 (1947); *Fryderyk Wielki a Polska* (Frederick the Great and Poland) (Poznań: Instytut Zachodni, 1947); *Polska a Szwecja* (Poland and Sweden) (Warszawa: 1924); *Polska a Turcja* (Poland and Turkey) (Warszawa: 1936); W. F. Reddaway, "Great Britain and Poland, 1762-1772," *Cambridge Historical Journal* 4 (1934); Emanuel Rostworowski, "Polska w układzie sił politycznych Europy XVIII w." (Poland in the European power structure of the eighteenth century), in Bogusław Leśnodorski, ed., *Polska w epoce Oświecenia* (Warszawa: Wiedza Powszechna, 1971).

11. Jean Fabre, *Stanislas-Auguste et l'Europe des Lumières* (Paris: Les belles lettres, 1952); Ambroise Jobert, *La Commission d'Education Nationale en Pologne* (Paris: Librairie Droz, 1941).

12. Bronisław Dembiński, *Polska na przełomie* (Poland at the turning point) (Warszawa: 1913); Walerian Kalinka, *Sejm Czteroletni* (The Four-Year Diet), vols. 1-2, (Warszawa: Volumen, 1991); Emanuel Rostworowski, *Legendy i fakty XVIII w.* (Legends and facts of the eighteenth century) (Warszawa: PWN, 1963); *Ostatni król Rzeczypospolitej* (The last king of the Commonwealth) (Warszawa: Wiedza Powszechna, 1966); *Sprawa aukcji wojska na tle sytuacji politycznej przed Sejmem Czteroletnim* (The problem of military recruitment against the background of the political situation before the Four-Year Diet) (Warszawa: PWN, 1957).

13. Bronisław Dembiński, "Ignatius Potocki's Mission to Berlin, 1792," in *Baltic and Scandinavian Countries* 3, 1 (1937); Robert Howard Lord, *The Second Partition of Poland* (Cambridge: Harvard Univ. Press,1915).

14. Zbigniew Góralski, *Austria a trzeci rozbiór Polski* (Austria and the third partition of Poland) (Warszawa: PWN, 1979); R. H. Lord, "The Third Partition of Poland," *Slavonic Review* 3 (1924-1925); Michael Georg Müller, *Die Teilungen Polens 1772, 1793, 1795* (München: 1984).

Translated by Philip Pajakowski

XIĄŻKA

O

EDUKACYI DZIECI

z Francuzkiego na Polski język

PRZEŁOŻONA.

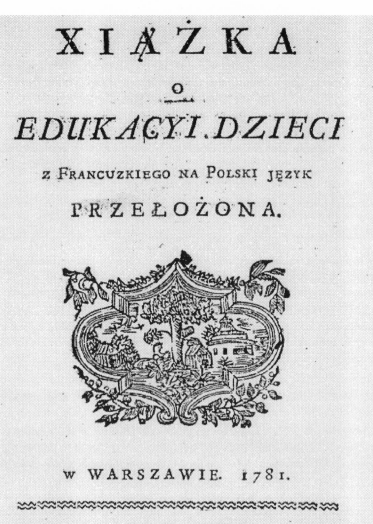

w WARSZAWIE. 1781.

w Drukarni J. K. Mci y Rzeczypospolitey
u XX Scholarum Piarum.

Xiążka o edukacyi dzieci z francuzkiego na polski język przełożona, w Warszawie, w Drukarni J.K.Mci y Rzeczypospolitey u XX Scholarum Piarum, 1781. Title page of the Polish translation of John Locke's, *Some Thoughts on Education* (Biblioteka Uniwersytecka w Warszawie).

6

Educational Reform in Poland during the Enlightenment

Kamilla Mrozowska

Polish ideas about education late in the eighteenth and early in the nineteenth century were strongly influenced by the new trends in European philosophy that dated from the middle 1700s. Chief among the thinkers who affected education was René Descartes. His *Discours de la méthode* was not only the foundation of a rational understanding of natural phenomena, providing new rules for the pursuit of knowledge, but it also influenced a search for new methods of conveying knowledge. John Locke recognized the role of sense experience as the source of knowledge and reflection in his *Essay Concerning Human Understanding* (Polish translation 1784) and so directed the further course of educational ideas. His 1693 work, *Some Thoughts on Education* (Polish translation 1781), was not organized as an educational piece, but contained all the important pedagogical tendencies that were later worked out in theory and practice during the eighteenth century. Though Locke favored individual home tutoring, many of his ideas were applied to the classroom in England and elsewhere. Locke's *Some Thoughts on Education* was like a manifesto calling for a connection between education and life's demands and included valuable suggestions about how education might become more in touch with life.

The main ideas of Enlightenment education–rationalism, empiricism, and utilitarianism–originated in England and France. Natural law and its derived economic doctrine, physiocracy, propounded in France by François Quesnay, dominated the formation of new curricula, the definition of educational goals,

113

and the writing of new educational plans. The encroachment of law and economics into the area of education was both the cause and result of stronger ties between educational change and economic and political reforms than had existed in previous centuries. This was particularly true in Poland.

Polish Enlightenment educational thought took shape slowly. New ideas reached Poland from France, England, Italy, and Germany. Enlightenment pedagogy developed later in Poland than in Western Europe, which does not, however, mean that Polish ideas were simply derivative. Polish educational thought was, to a large degree, defined by domestic social and political conditions and the need for basic reforms.

Gentry democracy in its increasingly decadent forms created different circumstances for the development of educational ideas as compared to the West. On the one hand, the number of enlightened individuals who knew educational literature, who were active in education, and who had broad intellectual horizons and bold ideas was much smaller in eighteenth-century Poland than in the enlightened monarchies, because of Poland's growing economic and social backwardness, the degeneration of the political system, and the resulting cultural stagnation. On the other hand, the political system allowed for greater freedom of expression, for bolder thought linking education to political, economic, and social reforms. Thus, educational problems discussed in Poland were different from those discussed in the West.

Among the first issues raised in Poland was civic education, predating French concern in that area. Civic education was a paramount concern in Polish reform initiatives and statements on education during the Enlightenment. Civic education in ever richer forms became the principle that guided Polish approaches to the national system of education and even to home tutoring.

Polish educational reformers were convinced that to change the *status quo* they must change the social and political consciousness of the gentry. Therefore, shaping political opinion through education became the most important part of Polish educational thought. Only education in a school community according to a carefully planned curriculum could guarantee that ideas of citizenship would be reshaped. It is not surprising that an individual who was as much a statesman as he was an educator was first to push for educational reform. Stanisław Konarski was educated by the Piarist Order and became one of its members.[1] He began his career as a teacher at one of the well known Piarist colleges. From 1725-1729 he supplemented his education and teaching experience at the Collegium Nazarenum in Rome, which influenced his later reform work. He also studied in Paris for a short time, and he acquainted himself with the schools of Venice and the German states. Konarski supported

Stanisław Leszczyński and worked for his election to the Polish throne after the death of August II, thus gaining a fuller knowledge of political affairs. Konarski's political activity and his work codifying Polish law (*Volumina legum,* vols. 1-6, 1732-39) deepened his conviction that only thoroughgoing reform could save Poland from collapse. He was convinced that reform could not succeed unless a new generation was educated to understand the necessity of reform and its substance.

In 1740 the Collegium Nobilium founded by Konarski opened its doors in Warsaw. It was an elite boarding school for children of the magnate class. The new school was modeled on the Collegium Nazarenum and on western European noble academies. Unlike those schools, the Collegium Nobilium had a carefully defined character-building curriculum. The most important and longest lasting of Konarski's contributions to education was his formulation of an ideal of character-building directed towards patriotism and citizenship.[2] It is worth remarking that Konarski's ideas on civic education preceded the appearance of this term in French educational literature in the works of La Chalotais and Rolland d'Erceville by over a decade.[3] Konarski frequently presented his ideas on education in many of his works. He made his most important and best- known statement in 1754 in a speech at the dedication of the new building for the Collegium Nobilium. He addressed the assembled notables, clergy, and gentry on "shaping an honest person and a good citizen" *(De viro honesto et bono cive ab ineunte aetate formando).* A good citizen should, above all, be faithful throughout his life to a "supreme love of the fatherland" even if it meant sacrificing his personal interests and ambitions. Young people, said Konarski, should be constantly imbued with a respect for existing laws, for the king, the government, and with the necessity of obeying them. But, one cannot be a good citizen unless one is a good person. A good person is deeply religious, yet is not a religious bigot. He loves justice. He is honest, open, modest, and tolerates other views and customs.[4]

Konarski had a greater appreciation for the character-building role of subject-teaching than his contemporary pedagogues. In the lower grades of the Collegium the emphasis in the curriculum was on languages. Readings from ancient authors were, however, chosen to give the boys examples of courage, self-sacrifice, and justice. In the upper grades, boys studied old Polish authors, Polish history and geography. Thus the students learned about their own country and how to properly express themselves in Polish. Though Latin came first, Konarski made sure modern languages were also taught.

Rhetoric was the most important subject at the Collegium, as it was around Europe. At the Collegium, however, and later at all the Piarist schools, the content of rhetoric lessons went far beyond the treatment of the subject generally accepted at that time. Training in effective and pleasing speaking was also used as civic training. The topics chosen for presentations related to politics, social issues, economics, and education. They were meant to introduce students to new ideas, to make them critical of prevailing customs, to lead students to seek ways to change their society for the better.

For the higher grades the culmination of work and a test of achievement in Latin rhetoric were the school dietines (*sejmiki*) or debates. Traditionally school dietines were true reflections of gentry assemblies with arguments, noise, and fights. At the Collegium, however, a serious atmosphere prevailed during the school dietines. One after another students presented their positions gravely discussing the "improvement of Polish customs" and "how to make our fatherland a happier place."[5]

Because the Collegium Nobilium was an elite school it provided virtually luxury accommodations for its students. At the same time, students were cut off from their families while at school in order to distance the boys from the social faults that Konarski hoped to eliminate in the younger generation.

Many enlightened citizens who went on to hold high government offices received their educations at the Collegium Nobilium. Among the school's famous students were Ignacy and Stanisław Potocki. Ignacy was a member of the Commission for National Education and an author and defender of the Constitution of 3 May. Stanisław was a statesman in the Duchy of Warsaw and Congress Kingdom of Poland. In the Congress Kingdom he was a leading education official and worked to further education in Poland.

Konarski's educational work went beyond the Collegium Nobilium. He correctly understood that it was not enough to patiently reeducate the social elite. It was necessary to educate wider circles of gentry and bourgeois youth, those boys who attended the Piarist Order's schools. The Piarists were second only to the Jesuits in the number of schools they operated in the Kingdom and Lithuania. There were twenty-eight Piarist colleges and fifty-seven Jesuit colleges before the First Partition. Most of the schools of both orders were three to five year colleges whose curricula emphasized languages and grammar.

After overcoming many difficulties and defeating the opposition of senior members of his order, Konarski received papal permission to reform the Piarist schools in Poland. New rules were drawn up between 1753 and 1756 that redefined the Piarist schools. The reformed Piarist colleges differed from the Collegium Nobilium. Polish was more widely used and Latin instruction was simplified. In the upper grades mathematics and laboratory physics were introduced–subjects that had application in everyday life. More subjects were included as themes for assignments in rhetoric.

Collegium Nobilium, copperplate, from the rim of a Plan of Warsaw by Pierre Ricaud de Tirregaille, 1762 (Muzeum Narodowe w Warszawie). Reprinted from Władysław Konopczyński, *Stanisław Konarski* (Warszawa, 1926).

Medal with the inscription *Sapere auso* (To him who dared to be wise) struck in 1765 by King Stanisław August in honor of Stanisław Konarski. (Medalier Johann F. Holzhaeusser). Reprinted from Władysław Konopczyński, *Stanisław Konarski*, (Warszawa, 1926).

More intelligent teachers were sent abroad to improve their teaching methods and broaden their knowledge. Many enlightened Piarists joined the reform camp and worked to raise the level of Polish intellectual life. Among them were the first supporters of physiocratic economic ideas in Poland (for example Antoni Popławski), ideas which later influenced the introduction of new subjects into the school curriculum.

The Piarist drive to modernize their schools caught the attention of the Jesuits, who saw the new Piarist colleges as dangerous competitors to their own schools. After 1762 the Polish Jesuit schools benefitted from the arrival of members of the order expelled from France. The French Jesuits were generally better educated and they understood the necessity of adapting curricula to the new trends in education. Polish Jesuits also began to study outside of Poland more often. A result of these wider contacts was that certain larger Jesuit colleges became centers for the teaching of physics, mathematics, and astronomy. Laboratories were equipped and observatories set up, notably in Lwów, Poznań and Warsaw.

Another influential new circle that played an important role in Polish cultural and political life was established in Warsaw during the 1760s. It was centered in the Knight's School (*SzkołaRycerska*) established by King Stanisław August Poniatowski in 1765.[6] The school, also called the Cadets' Corps of His Royal Majesty and the Republic *(Korpus Kadetów Jego Królewskiej Mości i Rzeczpospolitej)*, was founded less than a year after Stanisław August's coronation and began work at the beginning of 1766. For two more years, efforts continued to ensure the school a solid financial base, to find suitable teachers, and to find an appropriate place for the school. It was only in 1768 that the school's organizational statute and curriculum were finally decided on. The Cadets' Corps had a dual system of organization. It was military, as shown by the division of the School into brigades, the numerous officers, and military training. At the same time, for instructional purposes, students were divided by grades and their education was also meant to prepare them to hold civilian posts. The Cadets' Corps had a seven-year curriculum. In grades one thru four the emphasis was on general knowledge: languages, history, geography, mathematics, physics, geometry, and drafting. In the upper grades, the concentration was on military engineering in grades five and seven and on basic law in grade six.

The clearly stated curriculum influenced the selection of teachers and military officers to serve at the Cadets' Corps. The school's staff was chosen for their professional preparation and knowledge of the subjects to be taught, which were more important than nationality, religious confession, or estate. This distinguished the Cadets' Corps from the Collegium Nobilium. There were also other differences. The Cadets' Corps was Poland's first state school. It was supervised by the King and supported by the Polish and Lithuanian treasuries (2/3 and 1/3 respectively) and cadets enrolled from each province in the same proportion. Because the King was head of the school, he had overall control over it and informally supervised all its activities. Many gifted students of limited means owed their education to the King, including Tadeusz Kościuszko, who fought in the American War of Independence (1775-1783) and led the Polish uprising of 1794.

Responsibility for the finances and yearly inspection of the Cadets' Corps was in the hands of the Diet's Military Commission *(Komisja wojskowa)*. The Cadets' Corps' exclusive ties to government institutions fixed its secular character. Most of the administrators and staff were not in holy orders, though the clergy was not excluded. When the Corps was first established, there were not enough properly prepared officers and teachers in Poland to staff the school, and most of the staff was foreign, frequently Lutheran or Calvinist by religion. Over time the numbers of foreigners decreased. The shift was most apparent among the junior officers who directly and constantly supervised the cadets and had the greatest character-building influence on them. These junior officers were mostly Poles and, after a time, only Poles were recruited for those positions.

Foreigners were very important as senior officers and administrators. Beginning in 1768, the Cadets' Corps worked according to the Royal Statutes (*Ustawy Królewskie)*, which were closely connected to the *Règlement Général*. Englishman John Lind, director of instruction, and Adam Louis Bos Roger

(Bosroger), an experienced French officer, probably collaborated in drawing up both of these sets of regulations. Although Bos Roger was only at the school during the years 1766-1768, he left a lasting mark. He introduced military engineering, cartography, and drafting plans for fortifications into the curriculum. It is worth mentioning that historians believe that it was Kościuszko's skills in these very areas that gained him such recognition during his service in America, and Kościuszko was one of Bos Roger's students.

The Cadets' Corps owed its course and method of teaching strategy and tactics to another foreign officer, Prussian Lieutenant-Colonel Anton Leopold Oelsnitz (at the Corps 1767-1776?). Oelsnitz used his experience in the well organized Prussian army to shape his teaching. The valuable lessons that could be learned from the French and Prussian military were skillfully used to educate Polish officers thanks to the personal care of the Corps' commandant, Prince Adam Kazimierz Czartoryski, the wise support of the King, and the primacy of civic and patriotic elements in the Corp's educational program. The careers of many former cadets showed that this educational combination yielded the desired results.

The cosmopolitan make-up of the Corps' staff required attitudes of tolerance and respect. At a time when religious prejudices were visible, the tolerant climate at this special school had an enormous character-building influence. Despite the cosmopolitan character of the faculty, the main school goal was teaching patriotic and civic values. In this respect the Cadets' Corps followed the course laid down by Konarski twenty-five years before. The school's lapidary definition of its character-building aims as *"à former un bon citoyen et un homme sociable"* faithfully repeated these ideas. In the Corps' 1768 statutes, we find a point reminiscent of Konarski's 1754 speech. *"Chaque Cadet doit avoir tojours la droiture dans son coeur, la justesse dans son esprit et la vérité sur les lèvres."*[7] This admonition was made to the cadets in various forms at every possible occasion.

The curriculum, teaching methods, ideas of character-building, and conduct regulations for cadets were all developed in their general form between 1768 and 1771. John Lind, from England, played a significant part in drawing up these basic policies. As director of instruction (1767-1772), he was responsible for the teaching program of the institution including standards of teaching and supervision of the examinations. Lind felt that there was a self-evident connection between subject-teaching and character-building. He put heavy emphasis on the use of Polish in teaching and therefore on his teachers to learn Polish. In the Cadets' Corps curriculum more time was allotted to the study of history, geography, literature, and Polish law than in the Piarist colleges. Lind directed that teachers should appeal more often to students' reason than to their rote memory and that experience and observation should be used to help students understand their subjects. This approach clearly shows the influence of John Locke and of the best English schools. School discipline, believed Lind, should work through students' feelings of ambition, honor, and self-worth, not through fear. Honor and a sense of self-worth were two traits that should distinguish the graduates of the Cadets' Corps.

Lind's years in Warsaw and his close cooperation with Stanisław August left him with strong ties to Poland. After Lind returned to England he kept up his contacts with the King. Lind also became an unofficial spokesman for Poland. In his writings he condemned the First Partition and tried to draw the attention of English statesmen and English public opinion to Poland's plight.

Christian Pfleiderer, a Wurttemberger, was the next director of instruction. He followed the direction set by Lind. Pfleiderer was at the Cadets' Corps from 1766 to1782, first as a professor of mathematics, then as director of instruction. His main contribution to the school was his thorough attention to teaching methods. Much of his teaching methodology could still be used today, especially those about the relationships between teachers and students and realistic evaluation of students' work and their effort. Pfleiderer was one of that group of foreigners who played a meaningful role in putting reform ideas in Poland into action, at the Cadets' Corps and elsewhere.

The same may be said for the last director of instruction, Michał Hube. Hube was a native of Toruń who knew German and Latin better than Polish, but considered himself a Pole. He proved his Polish allegiance through many years of service, especially in the most difficult period, 1792-1795.

First place among those who not only influenced the growth of the Cadets' Corps but who played a leading role in Polish Enlightenment culture belongs to the commandant of the Corps, Adam Kazimierz Czartoryski. He was the King's closest co-worker during the difficult early period when the form of the school was worked out. Czartoryski's frequent and direct contacts with young people at that time made him aware of the obstacles to achieving the King's educational plans.

Thanks to Czartoryski, a number of textbooks were written or translated that proved useful to the cadets and other students. His great contribution was in writing *Katechizm moralny,* 1774 (Moral catechism). Often called *Katechizm rycerski* (Knight's catechism), this short clear work used the easily accessible form of questions and answers to explain ideas like truth, honor, self-worth, obedience, and love of the fatherland. The work appealed to students' reason, feelings, and ambitions. It is not surprising that the Catechism became a textbook used by a wide circle of young people in many schools. The topics discussed in the Catechism received further development in *Definicje różne przez pytania i odpowiedzi*, 1774 (Various definitions made through questions and answers) written for a more mature audience. Both works were reprinted many times and were important tools of character building.

Character building at the Cadets' Corps proceeded from different premises than at the reformed Piarist schools, where religion remained the foundation of civic training. At the Cadets' Corps the emphasis was on shaping an independently thinking person. That did not mean, however, that the school countenanced intellectual libertinism. Religion continued to play a role in students' lives. The cadets attended compulsory religious services and heard Sunday sermons. The school, however, provided no religious instruction.

In accord with the King's intentions for the Cadets' Corps most of its students were sons of the middle or impoverished nobility. Unlike the Collegium Nobilium, which educated the social elite, the Corps was, in a sense, a democratic school that educated the military and intellectual elite. Though early plans provided for two-hundred cadets, in the end about sixty boys attended the school yearly. The cadets received their tuition, room and board, uniforms, and instructional materials. It is worth noting that the Corps' specialized library was one of the largest and best of its type in Europe.

Alongside those cadets with full scholarships, a certain number of students were admitted who paid a small sum for their education in the Corps. There were also day students who lived with the professors or with their families. By these means the number of cadets increased significantly. Lack of documentation about the numbers of paying students makes it impossible to say how many there were. A reasonable estimate is that about 1500 students of all categories attended the Cadets' Corps over the thirty years of its existence. Not all of them completed their course of study. We can, however, say that even those students who attended for only two or three years acquired an understanding of those values that the school tried to teach. Students came to the Corps from many parts of Poland and Lithuania, often traveling long distances to attend the school. Many Poles who studied at the Cadets' Corps left their mark on Polish history. Tadeusz Kościuszko was one of the Corps' first students. His later adjutant, Julian Ursyn Niemcewicz, a statesman, publicist, poet in his own right, as well as a deputy to the Four-Year Diet, was a student from 1770-1776. He spent the years 1797-1807 in the United States. Available statistics show that the Cadets' Corps produced some 120 military officers who took part in the 1794 uprising, later serving in Napoleon's army and Dąbrowski's legion. Some of them participated in the November Uprising

The Kazimierzowski Palace in Warsaw, the seat of the Cadets' Corps, watercolor by Zygmunt Vogel, 1785. (Muzeum Narodowe w Warszawie). Photo H. Romanowski.

King Stanisław August in the uniform of the Cadets' Corps, by Marcello Bacciarelli (Zamek Królewski w Warszawie). Reprinted from *Powstanie Kościuszkowskie* (Zamek Królewski, Warszawa, 1994).

of 1830. Former cadets served in the Four-Year Diet and supported the Constitution of 3 May. Roughly sixty served in important civil posts in the Duchy of Warsaw and in Congress Poland. The majority of former cadets followed the spirit of the times and joined masonic lodges.

The Cadets' Corps played a meaningful role in the educational reforms of the Enlightenment in Poland. The contribution to Polish reform made by the Corps was an unquestionable achievement of Stanisław August Poniatowski.

The crowning achievement of Polish educational reformers was the establishment of the Commission for National Education *(Komisja Edukacji Narodowej)*, Europe's first national school authority.[8] The Commission was established as a result of the disbanding of the Jesuit Order. News of Pope Clement XIV's *breve* of 21 July 1773 dissolving the Order reached Warsaw in early September. It caused an uproar among the delegates to the Diet and among the nobility in general who had unlimited trust in the Jesuits. Much opposition had to be overcome before the papal *breve* could be executed. At the same time quarrels arose over the fate of Jesuit property, which was claimed by the church, the nobility, and by some former Jesuits.

After numerous talks, consultations, and negotiations, the decision was reached that, in principle, the property should be used for educational purposes. First, however, the value and income of the property had to be assessed. Two commissions were set up to do this—one for Poland and one for Lithuania. Each commission selected auditors to determine the value of the Jesuit "inheritance". It was also decided that a separate commission would take over the Jesuit schools. Thus it happened that the same Diet on which fell the dishonor of approving the First Partition also established the Commission for National Education which was to play such a large part in shaping younger generations. As Cracow deputy Felix Oraczewski put it, "to make people Poles, and make Poles citizens, will be the source of all desired national achievements."[9]

The Commission for National Education was established 14 October 1773. The act that founded it gave the Commission authority over all schools that educated the nobility "without exception."[10] That meant the Commission's supervision extended to the former Jesuit schools, to schools run by other religious orders, and to both academies, Cracow and Wilno. The Commission also intended to take over parish schools. There was one exception, however: the Cadets' Corps remained under the King's directorship.

The Commission for National Education was to remain "under the protection" of Stanisław August. He exercised his protection through a benevolent concern for its affairs and by helping the Commission during its most difficult times. The King chose the Commission's members, at least formally. The Commission received broad freedom of action. It was only answerable to the Diet for its budget. Eight members, four Diet deputies and four senators made up the Commission. In 1776, the number of members was raised to twelve. But the hardest work and greatest responsibility fell to the Commission's first members.

The four members from the Senate were: Ignacy Massalski, Bishop of Wilno and head of the Commission, 1773-1776; Michał Poniatowski, Bishop of Płock, the King's brother, head from 1776; August Sułkowski, voivode of Gniezno; and Joachim Chreptowicz, Vice-Chancellor of Lithuania. The Commission members from the lower house were: Ignacy Potocki, Adam Kazimierz Czartoryski, Andrzej Zamoyski, and Antoni Poniński. All of the commissioners, except Poniński, who contributed nothing to the Commission, were enlightened individuals of high intellect, though their moral standards were not always equal to their intellectual achievements.

The act that established the Commission also called for plans for school reorganization and for new curricula. The response was considerable for the time. The plans submitted contained interesting ideas and suggestions. The Commission used some of these, asking the authors to cooperate with the Commission in its work. Letters arrived from enlightened citizens from the Commonwealth and abroad. Unfortunately, few have survived to the present day. First to respond to the Commission's call for plans and ideas was Franciszek Bieliński. His first letters written at the end of 1773 and the beginning of 1774 caught the commissioners' attention and they urged him to keep working on his educational plans. Bieliński's educational views were probably influenced by his encounter with French works on the subject during his 1763 sojourn in Paris. At the same time, Antoni Popławski, a Piarist and colleague of Konarski, was studying in France. He became a strong advocate of physiocracy. His 1774 school reform plan played an important role in the later work of the Commission. Pierre Samuel Dupont de Nemours had a short and dynamic period of work with the Commission. Well known at the time as a theoretician and supporter of the physiocrats, he arrived in Warsaw in early 1774 and became the Commission's secretary for "foreign affairs." He intended to stay in Poland for several years, but returned to France in three months when summoned by Turgot. While in Warsaw, he worked out plans for parish schools, military education, and for the overall organization of the educational system.[11] Not all the plans have survived. It is hard to tell to what extent his ideas on educational organization affected the final form of the system developed by the Commission. Dupont did not forget his time in Poland after he returned to France. He corresponded with the King and later defended the King's good name, taking a public stand as a friend of Poland and the Poles.

When they started their work, the members of the Commission for National Education tried to find out about the state of the former Jesuit schools and about the possibilities of using ex-Jesuits in the schools. In order to gather this information, the commissioners divided the Commonwealth into districts and inspected the schools either personally or through their representatives. What they found was not encouraging. Many school buildings were rapidly deteriorating. Other buildings necessary for the operation of the schools were also suffering neglect. Estates owned by the schools were falling apart. Former Jesuits, unsure of their futures, were abandoning the schools, often taking school property with them. The number of students had fallen seriously. The situation called for quick corrective measures, but reorganization of former Jesuit finances was delayed.

The auditing commissions that were to protect and assess Jesuit property acted slowly. Numerous abuses occurred, which diminished the income from the order's lands and caused once rich income producing holdings to deteriorate. When the Diet tried to audit the Commission in 1776 it found it impossible. The account books were full of gaps and falsifications.

That same Diet put all former Jesuit property under the direct authority of the Commission for National Education. Historians' estimates of the value of that property are varied and cannot be ascertained. It is generally accepted that over 30 percent was lost in the breakup of the order. For many years after the dissolution of the Jesuits, Commission accountants worked to solve problems caused by previous abuses. After 1776, however, the financial affairs of the Commission were properly administered. The Commission's account keeping was praised by a number of Diet delegations that audited government finances. Setting the Commission's finances in order and keeping them that way was the work of commissioners Andrzej Zamoyski and Franciszek Bieliński (member 1776-1782) and of the Commission's scrupulous treasurer Karol Lelewel.

Nonetheless, the Commission had to give up its early plans to build up education at all levels and was even forced to limit the number of schools maintained by Commission funds. Emphasis was put on secondary schools. Despite the many obstacles and difficulties that went along with organizing a new system of schools the Commission gave much attention to the internal organization of schools, to working out new curricula, and to school rules. These matters drew in most of all those commissioners who already had experience in education, for example, Adam Kazimierz Czartoryski and Ignacy

Potocki (a onetime student of the Collegium Nazarenum). In the spring of
1775, a Society for Elementary Books *(Towarzystwo do Ksiąg Elementarnych)*
was established with Ignacy Potocki as president. The secretary was Grzegorz
Piramowicz, a former Jesuit, an experienced educator, and a dedicated and
knowledgeable school reformer. For twelve years Piramowicz was in charge of
all the Society's work. The first intention was that the Society would prepare
textbooks for the new curricula. Actually, the Society became the instructional
department of the Commission for National Education, taking upon itself the
full burden of work associated with organizing and operating the new school
system.

The Society had ten, then later twelve members. Members were nominated
from among the most experienced educators in Poland: Piarists, former Jesuits,
and the directors of instruction of the Cadets' Corps worked with the Society.
All of the members were individuals with broad intellectual horizons, mostly
educated abroad, and were acquainted with new trends in education and other
fields. From the beginning its work proceeded in several directions. New
curricula were written and edited. The Society worked to assure a supply of
new textbooks by the best authors through commissioning books and holding
contests for textbooks. Almost all the members of the Society worked to inform
the mostly conservative nobility about the new curricula and ideas about
education and to win them over to the new ways. The members also tried to
attract European intellectuals to their cause, hoping for their help and support.
To gain European involvement in its effort, the Society sent out curricula and
textbook outlines to learned journals *(Journal de Bouillon, Nova Acta
Eruditorum,* etc.). Jean Henri Samuel Formey, secretary of the Prussian
Academy of Sciences in Berlin, sent his laudatory comments and informed
Piramowicz that he had turned over the educational plan he received to the
Academy.[12] Formey also wrote that German journals would publish notes on
the plan edited by him. The renowned physician Jean Philippe de Limbourg,
member of the Royal Society in London and of the Physicians' Society in
Paris, replied in a similar vein.[13] From Mannheim the secretary of the local
Academy of Sciences, André Lamey, wrote the Society for Elementary Books
that he had made the Polish educational plan known.[14] The text of the outlines
together with critical comments appeared in *Nova Acta Eruditorum Lipsensis,
Anni,* 1774.[15] The Society also sent out the textbook outlines to France to the
honorary member of the Commission, Pierre Samuel Dupont de Nemours
and to the physiocrat economist Nicolas Baudeau, who translated the text
into French and published it in Paris in 1775. Baudeau visited Poland in
1769 on the invitation of Bishop Massalski and later published two works

Adam Kazimierz Czartoryski, mezzotint by Josef A. Kappeller acc. to Josef Grassi
(Biblioteka Uniwersytecka w Warszawie, Gabinet Rycin).

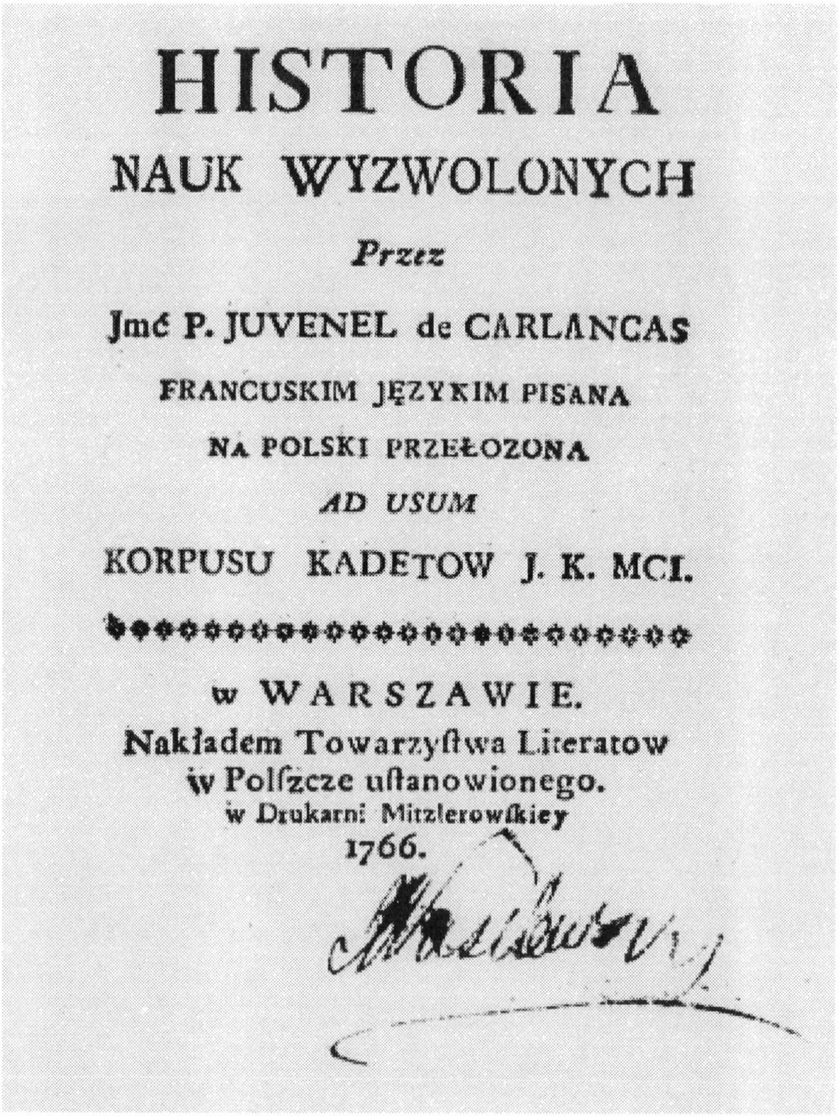

HISTORIA
NAUK WYZWOLONYCH

Przez

Jmć P. JUVENEL de CARLANCAS

FRANCUSKIM JĘZYKIM PISANA

NA POLSKI PRZEŁOZONA

AD USUM

KORPUSU KADETOW J. K. MCI.

❧◆❀◆❀◆❀◆❀◆❀◆❀◆❀◆❀◆❀◆❀◆❀◆❀◆❀◆❀

w WARSZAWIE.
Nakładem Towarzystwa Literatow
w Polszcze ustanowionego.
w Drukarni Mitzlerowskiey
1766.

Félix de Juvenel de Carlencas, *Historia nauk wyzwolonych...*, na polski przełożona *ad usum* Korpusu Kadetów J.K. Mci. (The History of liberal arts...translated into Polish for the use of the Cadets' Corps of His Majesty the King) w Warszawie, W. Mitzler, 1766. Title page. (Biblioteka Uniwersytecka w Warszawie). Carlencas' work *Essais sur l'histoire des belles lettres, des sciences et des arts*, Lyon, 1740, twice reprinted and translated into English, was one of many textbooks on various subjects published for the use of the Cadets' Corps. The translation was supplemented with information about Polish literature, and with an introduction by Adam K. Czartoryski.

containing his commentary on the country's situation. A translation of the outlines appeared in 1778 in the *Journal Encyclopédique*.[16] Commission and Society members' travels abroad also gave them a chance to spread Polish ideas and compare them to the achievements of others. "In Turin I found learning in good condition," wrote Piramowicz to I. Potocki on 29 June 1780, "the provisions for public education surpass those of any other Italian state.... An excellent educational program, but ours is broader in how it encompasses the entire goal and in that it is directed to that one goal. I described some of the points of our plan to them... They praised it highly, as they did our elementary textbook plans."[17]

Of course the Commission for National Education's work attracted the attention of foreigners living in Warsaw. These included a professor of history and natural history at the Cadets' Corps, Jean Baptiste Dubois. This young, extremely gifted Frenchman with wide ranging interests gave many proofs of his interest in Polish culture.[18] In 1777, Dubois, working with Italian geologist and mineralogist Jean-Philippe Carosi, outlined a textbook for the Commission's schools.[19] But it turned out that neither of the authors had sufficient knowledge of Poland's natural life and resources for their outline to be accepted. Still, both men served Poland well. Dubois published many articles concerning Poland in *Esprit des Journaux* and in *Journal Encyclopédique de Bouillon*. Carosi contributed his geological and mineralogical studies of the Polish southwest provinces.

About this same time, 1776, the Society for Elementary Books received an interesting *"Plan de réformation des études élémentaires"* from Frenchman Jean Alexis Borrelly, a member of the Prussian academy.[20] Elementary education was, however, put aside as part of the long term goals of the Society at this time, and Borrelly's plan shared the fate of other unused proposals.

Designing the new secondary schools took almost five years (1774-1779). The reformed schools were to impart useful knowledge and shape civic attitudes according to ideas of social cooperation and tolerance. One of the means to raise patriotic consciousness was to make the schools "national," that is, to make Polish the language of instruction at all levels. In the two lower grades the course of general studies covered arithmetic along with Latin and Polish grammar. In the upper grades arithmetic gave way to algebra and geometry. Starting in the third grade boys learned Latin rhetoric, history, and geography. The first place among all the subjects went to moral instruction based on natural law, which was taught in all grades, and was meant to shape students' values. In the lower grades students learned about ideas like truth, responsibility, and moral duty through examples drawn from everyday life. The pupils were taught that their chief duty was to their families, those closest to them, their subordinates, and to their fellow citizens. An individual's rights should depend on how well he performs his civic duties. In the upper grades these ideas were to be taught through instruction in law and in political economy.

Practical knowledge was to come from the study of physics, natural history (botany and zoology), horticulture, agriculture, and health. The curriculum had a broadly practical character. There was a visible physiocratic influence and in the methods used – empiricism and rationalism. The students were to recognize the practical application of the theoretical material they had learned in various forms and situations. For this reason instructional aids and practical exercises like surveying and working school gardens were recommended. Rote learning was to be limited and independent thought and rational analysis substituted. Logic, taught in the graduating year, was also to strengthen the influence of rationalism.

The wide reaching and varied curriculum required a change from the old system of a single teacher for each grade. Single teachers taught all subjects in the first two grades under the new system. Starting in the third grade the curriculum was divided into four thematic units, each taught by a different teacher in all the upper grades. There were four subject teachers, one each in rhetoric, mathematics, physics, and law.

The Society for Elementary Books also worked to obtain textbooks that fit the new course˜of study. Competitions only partly satisfied the Society's expectations. In some cases the Society decided to commission textbooks from selected authors for subjects to which it attached special importance. Antoni Popławski, for example, was commissioned to write textbooks for the program of moral instruction, and he completed books for the first three grades. Etienne de Condillac was asked to write a logic textbook. He delivered the manuscript in 1778. Ignacy Potocki translated its first part but the whole work in a new translation was published only in 1802. The original text, published in France in 1780, was used as a textbook in the schools. Editorial work on all the textbooks progressed very slowly because of the high standards of the Society's members, the need for translations into Polish, and diversion of the Society's attention by other matters. Despite Society efforts, textbooks were not written for all the subjects in the curriculum. A number of textbooks appeared too late to be of real help to teachers and students. Overall, from 1775 to 1792 seventeen textbooks and six exercise and reference books (selections from Latin authors, dictionaries, logarithmic tables), and six teachers' manuals appeared as a result of the Society's work. The teachers' manuals contained notes to textbooks and often included a significant body of suggestions on teaching methods and explanations to help with preparing lessons. This information was an invaluable aid to those who wanted and knew how to use it. The teachers' manuals were something completely new in educational literature. The idea of "textbooks of teaching methods" was used in Poland into the twentieth century.

Many of the textbooks and teachers' manuals published by the Society were remarkable for the modern treatment of their subjects and their inclusion of the newest scientific findings. These works are well thought of by today's educators, historians of education, and academics (for example the textbooks on mathematics by the Swiss mathematician, Simon L' Huillier, and *Wstęp do fizyki* (Introduction to physics) by Michał Hube).[21] The production of these books in Polish also helped develop Polish scientific language.

The first decade for the Commission for National Education, 1773-1783, was a time of organizational work aimed at laying the foundation of a new system of education. The school inspections carried out at this time allowed the Commission to see the real state of the schools, their needs, and the quality of the teaching staff. Financial difficulties caused significant changes in the educational system. In Poland, the Commission turned over nine of the twenty-four former Jesuit colleges to other religious orders. Among others, the Piarists received three, giving them a total of thirteen secondary schools. The Basilians, a Greek rite order, received three schools, giving them eight schools altogether in the south. The network of schools included the two so-called "academic colonies". These were schools established at the end of the sixteenth century under the auspices of the Cracow Academy. By the end of the seventeenth century they numbered about thirty. Later, some disappeared while others became parish schools. The Commission for National Education took over the oldest, the Collegium Nowodworscianum (founded in 1588 and reformed by Kołłątaj) and a small school in Pińczów. In Lithuania the Jesuits had seventeen colleges before the disbanding of their order, the Piarists eight, and the Basilians two. The Commission took over the Jesuit schools and founded an additional three schools. The Commission was less generous with the former Jesuit schools in Lithuania than it had been in Poland. Only the Dominicans benefited there, receiving one school. The Dominicans opened two schools themselves. The Basilians opened three new schools of their own. The ex-Jesuit schools and so-called "academic colonies," financed by and under the direct supervision of the Commission, received the status of state schools. The religious schools were to conform to the curriculum of the Society for Elementary Books and were subject to government inspection. The Commission, however, did not influence the choice of teachers or administrators.

Starting in 1780, the final division of the country into school districts was made. The departments were replaced by districts – five in Poland, four in Lithuania. The desire of the Piarists in Poland to keep their schools separate is visible in the designation of Piarist schools as part of a special "district" wherever they might be located.

At this same time, a hierarchical scheme of school administration was established within the educational system. The new organizational scheme was not a novelty in Poland. It was similar to a late sixteenth-century plan in which the Cracow Academy set up a system of districts (so called "colonies") with secondary and primary schools under their control. Antoni Popławski adapted this French idea, which Bartholémy Rolland d'Erceville (referred to earlier) promoted from 1763-1768, and which had initially been introduced to the Commission for National Education by its first secretary, the physiocrat Samuel Dupont de Nemours. At the head stood the Commission. The former Academies of Cracow and Wilno (now called Main Schools) were directly responsible to the Commission. The Main Schools supervised the district schools, that is, upper level secondary schools. The rector of district schools controlled the subdistrict schools within their districts. All schools operated by religious orders were rated as subdistrict schools except the Piarist schools in Warsaw. The prorector of subdistrict schools supervised the lowest level of schooling, the parish schools.

Parish schools were designated for peasant children, townspeople, and the impoverished gentry. The parish schools were the weakest part of the Commission's system. Though there was a lively interest in elementary education when the Commission began its work, mainly under the influence of physiocratic ideas, neither the money available nor the social order prevailing permitted radical changes in primary education. Parish schools depended on local priests and the philanthropy of noble estate owners. They were often ephemeral. They used whatever teachers could be found and suffered from low standards and poor material conditions. There were not enough parish schools to satisfy society's needs. Only a few parish schools maintained by members of the Commission met the Commission's expectations. Both of the Commission's presidents took direct action to increase the number of parish schools. Massalski funded a teachers' seminary in Wilno. Poniatowski set up teachers' seminaries in Łowicz and Kielce. They did not produce lasting results. There were not enough funds to develop the primary schools and the nobility did not understand the need for them.

While it was a solitary achievement, the only significant result of the Society for Elementary Books' concern with parish schools was the publication of

USTAWY

KOMMISSYI EDUKACYI NARODOWEY

D L A

STANU AKADEMICKIEGO

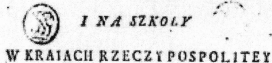

I NA SZKOŁY

W KRAIACH RZECZYPOSPOLITEY

PRZEPISANE

w WARSZAWIE

ROKU 1783.

Ustawy Kommissyi Edukacyi Narodowey dla Stanu Akademickiego i na szkoły w Kraiach Rzeczypospolitey przepisane, (Statutes of the Commission for National Education established for the Academic Estate and for the schools in the lands of the Commonwealth) w Warszawie, 1783. Title page. (Biblioteka Uniwersytecka w Warszawie).

Design for the Academy of Sciences by Dominik Merlini 1774-76 (Biblioteka Uniwersytecka w Warszawie, Gabinet Rycin). The most ardent promoter of the idea of organizing an association of scholars and subsequently an Academy of Sciences was Józef A. Załuski. On the order of the King, Merlini prepared this magnificent project, which unfortunately, was never realized.

Elementarz dla szkół parafialnych, 1785 (Primer for parish schools), produced cooperatively by its members, and Grzegorz Piramowicz's *Powinności nauczyciela,* 1787 (The teacher's duties). Piramowicz's short work was meant for teachers. It contained a wealth of pedagogical knowledge and practical suggestions. Unappreciated by contemporaries, it appeared in numerous editions in the nineteenth and twentieth centuries.

In 1780, the decision was made to collect all the previously issued educational directives, recommendations, and instructions into a single corpus. All the members of the Commission and the Society worked on this project. Grzegorz Piramowicz was the editor. A draft of the collected "statutes" was sent to the rectors of the Main Schools and the district schools to elicit their remarks and ideas. The outcome of these consultations was a large number of changes in various chapters of the collection. The Commission finally approved the "Statutes of the Commission for National Education for the Academic Estate" *(Ustawy Komisji Edukacji Narodowej dla stanu akademickiego)* which became unconditionally binding within the Commission's jurisdiction at the beginning of the 1783-1784 academic year.[22]

Under the Statutes the academic estate became a separate social group with a specific legal status defined by education and employment without regard for estate of birth. The academic estate included all those who worked in academic schools, members of the Main Schools, and members of the Commission and of the Society for Elementary Books. The Statutes were the first code of school regulations to define precisely the organizational basis of the school system, the internal organization of schools, the goals, curricula, tasks and methods of teaching, and the rights and responsibilities of teachers and students. In terms of their scope and the rich variety of questions they addressed, the Statutes constitute an example of innovation in educational thought of importance not only for Poland.

The goals of character-building were expressed in almost every chapter, in the main, repeating the ideas of Stanisław Konarski. The methods to achieve the goals enjoined by the Statutes were like those used at the Cadets' Corps. Old traditions from the religious schools (regulations for the daily lives of teachers) were combined with a movement towards secularizing the academic schools by promoting an ideal of civic education. Moral instruction was to play an especially important role in the process of education. Religious instruction was provided only in the first two grades; however, great importance was attached to the students' religious services. Finally, the Commission tried slowly to enlarge the number of secular teachers. Although most of the Statutes were concerned with secondary schools (district and subdistrict schools), they also included chapters detailing the organization and tasks of the Main Schools.

The Commission was somewhat delayed in undertaking the reform of the two Academies. This was because of embryonic plans to establish new universities. When financial limitations forced the abandonment of those ambitious plans, the commissioners decided to take advantage of an earlier offer by the Cracow Academy and begin university reforms. The real author of the reform plan for the Cracow Academy was Hugo Kołłątaj. His ideas, as they were put into practice, also influenced the organization of the Wilno Academy.

Kołłątaj came from an impoverished gentry family. For a short time he studied at the Cracow Academy and then went on to study in Vienna and Italy. His time at Italian universities allowed him to deepen his knowledge of natural law and political economy, acquainted him with the doctrines of the physiocrats, and awakened his interest in natural sciences. He returned to Poland in 1775. Accepted as a member of the Society for Elementary Books, he attracted the attention of Michał Poniatowski, who accurately assessed his intelligence, energy, and initiative. Kołłątaj was sent to Cracow where he was to inform himself about the actual state of the Academy. His mission was a complete success. It is likely that he already had an idea for reforms that would return the university to its former stature. Kołłątaj said that he found a "gothic" system of organization that was neither conducive to the development of knowledge nor responsive to demands of pedagogy. Of the university's four schools, only the school of philosophy, which had been reformed some ten years earlier, approached his concept of what the university should be. The school of medicine was practically non-existent. At the school of law the only department that attracted students was natural law. The school of theology was the richest and largest of the four schools and dominated the university. After his return to Warsaw, the young inspector submitted his report about the state of the Cracow Academy and then a plan *O wprowadzeniu dobrych nauk do Akademii i o założeniu seminarium dla nauczycieli szkół wojewódzkich* (For the introduction of good learning at the Academy and the establishment of pedagogical schools for teachers of provincial schools).[23] Poniatowski received the plan positively, thanks to which Kołłątaj was able to move on to developing further plans. The introduction of "good learning" meant further changes in the school of philosophy, including funding a series of new departments: physics, natural history, higher mathematics, history, and literature. Kołłątaj also envisioned an expanded medical school similar to those at other European universities and a larger law school, but he wanted to trim the school of theology.

ELEMENTARZ

DLA SZKÓL PARAFIIALNYCH NARODOWYCH,

ZAWIERAIĄCY

I. NAUKĘ PISANIA i CZYTANIA.

II. KATECHIZM.

III. NAUKĘ OBYCZAIOWĄ,

IV. NAUKĘ RACHUNKÓW.

Piérwszy ráz wydany.

Bez oprawy gri 27.

w KRAKOWIE 1785.

w Drukarni Szkoły Głowney Koronney.

Elementarz dla szkół parafialnych narodowych (Primer for national parish schools) w Krakowie, w Drukarni Szkoły Główney Koronney, 1785. Title page. (Biblioteka Uniwersytecka w Warszawie).

POWINNOSCI
NAUCZYCIELA

MIANOWICIE ZAS w SZKOŁACH
PARAFIALNYCH
I SPOSOBY ICH DOPEŁNIENIA.

Dzieło użyteczne Pasterzom, Panom i ich
Namieśnikom o dobro Ludu troskliwym,
Rodzicom i wszystkim Edukacyą bawią-
cym się.

w WARSZAWIE

w Drukarni Nadworney J. K. Mci.
i P. Kom: E. Naro: Roku 1787.

(Grzegorz Piramowicz) *Powinności nauczyciela mianowicie zaś w szkołach parafialnych i sposoby ich dopełnienia* (The teacher's duties in the parish schools, and the manner of their implementation) w Warszawie, w Drukarni Nadworney J.K. Mci. i P. Kom. E. Naro. Roku 1787. Title page. (Biblioteka Uniwersytecka w Warszawie).

His plans went much farther towards creating a center of learning in Cracow. Again, lack of money as well as of the necessary professors influenced the eventual course of change.

In the area of teacher training, Kołłątaj wanted to return to old traditions, to the time when the Cracow Academy supplied teachers for many Polish schools. He believed that now the Academy should educate teachers for the reformed schools. An opponent of education by religious orders, he wanted secular teachers to staff the academic schools. According to Kołłątaj, clerical teachers could quickly be replaced by secular teachers. Education at the academic schools should be free of religious prejudice and the students' lives should not be subject to excessive regulation. On the point of religion in education, Kołłątaj's plans stood in opposition to the ideas expressed earlier by Antoni Popławski. Popławski paid special attention to teacher training in his ideas on reforming the Piarist schools. He saw the teachers' seminary as a closed institution where a limited number of students studied according to a set curriculum and in which everyday life was regulated by detailed rules. Similarly teachers working in the schools, preferably clergymen, should conform to strict rules and should be under the close supervision of a rector or prorector.

In their final form, the reformed Main Schools discarded the old division into four schools, replacing it with a separation into two colleges, the physical and moral. The physical college covered mathematical and physical sciences and natural history (including zoology, botany and mineralogy). Chemistry lectures used the latest theories in the field. Medicine was also part of the physical college and the number of chairs of medicine was systematically increased. The new professors of medicine were educated at Italian, German, and French universities.

The moral college covered law, theology, and literature. Despite opposition from the theologians, the number of chairs of theology was cut and funding decreased. This caused Kołłątaj much unpleasantness, for he was accused of acting against the best interests of the Main School. The number of chairs in the school of law increased. The new chairs included one of canon law and, finally in 1790, a chair of Polish law. Antoni Popławski's lectures in natural law and political economy enjoyed unflagging success.

The reorganization of the Main Schools proved very productive, especially in Cracow. In the decade 1783-1793, the number of chairs increased and the quality of the lectures improved. At the physical college useful organizational changes and modernized teaching methods were observable. A botanical garden was laid out and an astronomical observatory built on its grounds. A new building went up housing lecture halls and laboratories for physics, mechanics, chemistry, mineralogy, and biology. The medical department received an anatomy laboratory, a small clinic and later a hospital. Kołłątaj wanted to ground his reforms in the cooperation of well-educated young people and so worked to send the most intelligent teachers abroad to study. Thanks to Kołłątaj's work and the concern of the Commission for National Education, the Main School in Cracow obtained many bright, dedicated professors full of reforming zeal. The most eminent among them was undoubtedly Jan Śniadecki, a professor of mathematics and astronomy, a scholar with broad intellectual horizons and enormous organizational talent. He became secretary of the Main School and Kołłątaj's right hand during Kołłątaj's tenure as rector (1782-1786). Śniadecki's enormous correspondence bears witness not only to his influence on various of Kołłątaj's actions, but also to his ability to gain students' confidence, especially that of graduates who were already working as teachers. They sent him letters telling him about their work, their difficulties, and even their personal problems.[24]

Those studying to be teachers did not have an easy time of it. The Commission for National Education, probably in expectation of the nobles' reluctance, gave up on Kołłątaj's ideas on teacher training and entrusted the organization and direction of the pedagogical schools to Popławski. He, however, left that post after three years, and there followed a period of frequent changes. The number of students was limited and their course of study was never clearly defined. In spite of these weaknesses, the academic schools received a slow flow of secular teachers and, towards the end of the Commission's existence, they were a decided majority of the academic estate. Dedicated to their Alma Mater, they supported school reform, and usually brought new ideas and useful knowledge to their schools. Many of them remained faithful to the heritage of the Commission for National Education in their later work.

The reform of the Wilno Academy took a different course. Founded by the Jesuits in 1579, the school never developed into a full university and had only two schools – philosophy and theology. The abolition of the Jesuit Order was a blow to the Wilno Academy. Many professors retired as a result. Those who remained found it hard to work under the new school authorities. If the Academy did not collapse completely it was owing to its president (from 1780), former Jesuit Marcin Poczobut, an internationally known astronomer. He was loyal to the Commission for National Education, but he did not have the energy and zeal for reform that marked Kołłątaj. Poczobut faced greater difficulties than Kołłątaj in organizing a physical college. He took a different approach than the Cracow reformer in finding appropriate professors. He tried to recruit foreign scholars. Wilno, however, was too far from the centers of

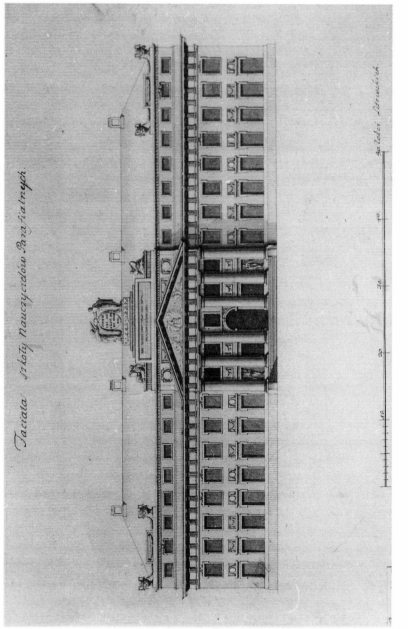

Design for a parish pedagogical school by M. Knackfus, 1776. (Biblioteka Uniwersytecka w Warszawie, Gabinet Rycin).

O
EDUKACYI
FIZYCZNEY I MORALNEY
PŁCI ŻENSKIEY
WYKŁAD
z FRANCUZKIEGO.

w WARSZAWIE.
w Drukarni P. Düfour Konfyl: Nad: Druk: J.K.
Mci i Rzpltey, Dyrektora Druk: Korp: Kad:

M.DCC. LXXXIX.

(Ludwika Byszewska) *O edukacyi fizyczney i moralney płci żenskiey*, wykład z francuzkiego. (On the physical and moral education of women, translated from French) w Warszawie, P. Düfour. 1789. The title page. (Biblioteka Z.N.im. Ossolińskich, Wrocław). The education of young women was one of many issues discussed by the Commission for National Education. It became the subject of many opinions, proposals, publications and also the Commission's set of rules, prepared by Adam K. Czartoryski, regulating private boarding schools.

European culture and the working conditions too primitive to be attractive. A period of frequent turnover of professors' chairs followed and some chairs were vacant for a long time. Despite orders to conduct instruction in Polish most lectures were in Latin, French or German. Only the astronomical observatory established under Poczobut's direction was a meaningful achievement in the development of the Main School of Lithuania at this time. The moral college was more successful. More of the professors had an education the quality of which guaranteed a high standard of teaching. While in Cracow there was no department of history, and the teaching of literature was limited to lectures on ancient authors, in Wilno work in both history and literature was closer to Kołłątaj's original plans. Piarist father Hieronim Stroynowski taught natural law and political economy. He was also the first Polish author of a textbook in political economy.

Generally speaking the Main School of Lithuania lagged behind Cracow during the life of the Commission for National Education. The University of Wilno had its period of excellence in the early nineteenth century. There is no doubt that, though change was slow at Wilno, the university reform, often called the Kołłątaj reform, reshaped both universities and started them on the road to further growth. Kołłątaj's attempts to develop a wide-scale research program at the universities were, nonetheless, unsuccessful. Although the gaps between learning in Poland and in the West rapidly started to narrow, there were many obstacles to a more accelerated development of learning in Poland. These included: Poland's backwardness caused by the state of politics and the economy at the turn of the seventeenth and eighteenth centuries, Michał Poniatowski's disinclination to take measures that did not give quick and practical results, slow growth of support for learning, and the many responsibilities that the Main Schools had as institutions which supervised lower-level schools.

Required yearly inspections of lower schools took two professors at Cracow away from their regular duties for several months. Time-consuming meetings were held to discuss inspection reports, to prepare reports and recommendations for the Commission, and to discuss matters of concern. The exhausting and detailed correspondence of the Main Schools with the Commission and the lower schools fell mostly to the secretaries, but it often involved other professors as well.

The nobility did not accept the Commission's reforms readily. Nobles reacted with distrust to the new curriculum, and they disliked secular teachers. It was with difficulty that the propaganda work of the Society for Elementary Books broke down that distrust. One way that the public gained a closer look at the new schools was through public school performances organized at the end of the academic year to the assembled parents and local citizens. Teachers gave speeches on current social, political, and economic problems. Similarly the Main Schools held public lectures on special occasions to popularize the new directions in learning or to acquaint the public with important individuals at the university.

Proof that the nobles' distrust was breaking down came in the form of letters to the Commission, thanking its members for the useful knowledge imparted to young people and for the responsible care taken with them. Slowly, the number of students increased. But it was not easy to overcome old habits and prejudices. One must remember that the Statutes only took full effect in 1783 and one can only speak of the reform being put into action after that date. There was, therefore, not enough time to change the mentality of the nobility. Further, the numbers of students educated at the Commission's schools, the Cadets' Corps, and loyal religious schools were too small to bring about a real change in attitudes.

The time of trial came during the Four-Year Diet. On the one hand, the conservative movement mobilized. A longing for the Jesuits reappeared and criticism of the Commission increased. On the other hand, the academic estate was united in support of the reform movement and of Kołłątaj, with whom many former colleagues and students of the Main School kept up friendly relations. Direct contact between Cracow and Warsaw increased. Under these conditions it became apparent that Kołłątaj had built for himself a strong backing during his inspection and reform of the Cracow Academy. His work at Cracow had allowed him to become familiar with the Main School and with the environment that other schools operated in and thus with the mood and ideas of the broad masses of the gentry. When he became leader of "The Forge," a club of radical reformers, the people he worked with included members of the academic estate. Professors of law from Wilno and Warsaw took part in work on the so-called Code of Stanisław August.

The ratification of the Constitution of 3 May was widely acclaimed at the schools and the celebrations they organized included many regular citizens. This was a successful way to promote the new Constitution. The Constitution's first anniversary was greeted in similar style. When the war with Russia began in 1792, school directors complained that their older students wanted to leave to join the army.

Later, there was defeat. The government formed by the Confederation of Targowica ruled. The Commission was split in two, one for Poland, the other for Lithuania. Though it was later reunited, it never regained its former spirit.

ARYTMETYKA

DLA

SZKOŁ NARODOWYCH

w WARSZAWIE

w Drukarni Nadworney J. K. Mci,
Roku 1778.

Simon L'Huillier, *Arytmetyka dla szkół narodowych* (Mathematics for National Schools) w Warszawie, w Drukarni Nadworney J.K. Mci, 1778. Title page. (Biblioteka Uniwersytecka w Warszawie). The Society for Elementary Books published 31 textbooks, among them L'Huillier's three textbooks on mathematics, geometry and algebra. In 1777 L'Huillier, a Swiss mathematician, won the international competition for textbooks sponsored by the Society. In 1783 he was elected member of the Society.

UKŁAD
GRAMMATYKI

DLÁ

SZKÓŁ NARODOWYCH

z Dziéła iuż fkonczonego

WYCIĄGNIONY.

Za pozwoléniém Zwiérzchnośći Edukacyyney.

w WARSZAWIE 178ſ.

w Drukarni Michała Grölla, Xięgárza Nadwor-
négo J. K. Mći.

Onufry Kopczyński, *Układ grammatyki dla szkół narodowych* (A grammar for
National Schools) w Warszawie, Michal Gröll, 1785. Title page. (Biblioteka
Uniwersytecka w Warszawie).

The Second Partition and the Kościuszko uprising shook the Commonwealth. The Commission's real work ended in 1792; even though it still held school inspections in 1793, in the rump of Polish territory these had no meaning. At the time of the Kościuszko uprising, the Commission for National Education was replaced by the Department of National Instruction. The Department failed to become active in the broad sphere the Commission had worked in and can hardly be acknowledged to have continued the Commission's work. Kościuszko's defeat resulted in the Third Partition, which wiped Poland off the map of Europe. The uprising was defeated, but not the nation.

The Commission for National Education had carried on its work for twenty years. It began life in a dramatic time, after the First Partition, and ended its existence in the year of Kościuszko's uprising. The first decade was a time of putting finances in order, of assessing the state of the Jesuit colleges, of developing projects and plans, and of issuing the first directives that laid the foundation for school reform. At the end of that period, the idea arose of creating a unified educational system based on connecting schools at all levels and establishing a hierarchy intended to guarantee the unity of the entire educational system in terms of both instructional curricula and character building.

The whole body of questions about the workings of the system of education was addressed in the Statutes for the Academic Estate, the first European school code to take such a modern and universal approach. For the first time, educational plans based on Enlightenment ideas, including both the thoughts of western philosophers and valuable Polish traditions, were to be brought to life under the leadership and supervision of a central school authority responsible to the Diet in financial matters and informally responsible to the king in matters of educational policy.

The second decade was the time when the Statutes of 1783 were put into effect. It was a period during which theoretical assumptions, plans, and goals worked out collectively during the first decade were implemented.

The university reform completed in Cracow in 1783 entirely reorganized that institution. In introducing a modern curriculum the reformers tried to adapt to d'Alembert's and Diderot's classification of science. These attempts were not entirely successful. Nonetheless, the university's internal organization changed completely. Thanks to young professors, who were largely educated abroad, there was enormous progress in the content and method of instruction. New centers of learning that later developed fully in the nineteenth century were established at this time. Thanks to Kołłątaj's reform the Jagiellonian University was able to survive the most difficult times of 1800-1870.

Full implementation of the new educational system required much longer than the less than twenty years the Commission existed. During that time it had to change the organization of school administration, fight for money, work out the legal basis for its actions, write, publish, and distribute new textbooks, train teachers, and do battle with the conservative opposition. The complicated history of the Polish nation between 1795-1918 points to the nation's will to live and its stubborn striving to regain independence. It is reasonable to ask to what degree those attitudes on the part of Polish society were the result of Konarski's dogged struggle for civic education, the influence of the educators from the Cadets' Corps, and the work of the mass of teachers supervised by the Commission for National Education. Gaps in the documentary record do not allow even an approximation of what proportion of society received an education appropriate to the ambitions of the Polish Enlightenment in the late eighteenth century. Judging, however, by the longevity of the Commission's educational heritage during the partition period, the role of the Commission for National Education, and of institutions that acted in the same spirit, was enormous.

The Statutes for the Academic Estate remained a model for the following generations even when many of its provisions became obvious anachronisms. School organizers in the Grand Duchy of Warsaw and the Congress Kingdom referred to the Statutes, though the school systems set up under those governments differed from the organizational principles of the Commission for National Education.

The Commission for National Education had an incontrovertible influence on the Russian school reform of 1803.[25] The Russian system introduced at that time was modeled on the Polish Commission's system in the areas of school administration, including the role of the universities, and to a degree in the curricula. It is, therefore, not surprising that the growth of education was most successful in the western provinces of the Russian empire, those parts of the Polish-Lithuanian Commonwealth taken by Russia in the Second and Third Partitions. Simultaneously, during the first two decades of the nineteenth century, the University of Wilno flourished, led by Jan Śniadecki (1807-1815). Overall supervision of the university, and of the whole school system, was in the hands of the curator, Prince Adam Jerzy Czartoryski, supported by the advice of his father Prince Adam Kazimierz, a former member of the Commission. The cooperation between Hugo Kołłątaj and Tadeusz Czacki, organizer of the gymnasium, later a liceum, in Krzemieniec, also bears witness to the continuity of the Commission's educational heritage and to the work of educators associated with the Commission.

At that time, the University of Wilno and the schools in Wilno's educational region produced many individuals who became famous for their work in a number of fields. The generation educated in those years largely determined the future course of Polish and not only Polish culture. The seed sown by the Commission for National Education yielded an exceptionally rich harvest.

Notes

1. Stanisław Konarski, *Pisma wybrane* (Selected works), ed. Juliusz Nowak-Dłużewski, intr. Zdzisław Libera (Warszawa: PIW, 1955), 2 vols; *Ustawy szkolne dla polskiej prowincji pijarów* (School statutes for the Polish province of the Piarists), ed. Jan Czubek, intr. Stanisław Kot (Kraków, M. Aret, 1925); Hugo Kołłątaj, *Stan oświecenia w Polsce w ostatnich latach panowania Augusta III (1750-1764)* (The state of education in Poland in the last years of the reign of August III (1750-1764)), ed. Jan Hulewicz (Wrocław: Ossolineum, 1953); Władysław Konopczyński, *Stanisław Konarski* (Warszawa, 1926); Łukasz Kurdybacha, *Działalność pedagogiczna Stanisława Konarskiego* (Pedagogical work of Stanisław Konarski) (Wrocław: Ossolineum, 1957); William John Rose, *Stanislas Konarski. Reformer of Education in XVIIIth Century Poland* (London, 1929).

2. Ambroise Jobert, *La Commission d'Éducation Nationale en Pologne (1773-1794. Son œuvre d'instruction civique* (Paris; Librairie Droz, 1941), pp. 81-118.

3. Louis-René Chalotais Carduc de la, *Essai d'éducation nationale, ou plan d'études pour la jeunesse,* par...(Gènève, 1763); *Compte rendu aux chambres assamblées par M. Rolland, des différentes mémoires envoyées par les universités sises dans ressort de la cour... relativement au plan d'étude à suivre dans les collèges non dépendants des universités et à la correspondance à établir entre les collèges et les universités. Du 13 mai 1768.* (Paris, 1768).

4. Konarski, *Pisma wybrane,* vol. 2, pp. 123, 130 passim.

5. Konarski, Pisma wybrane, pp. 317-379.

6. Jobert, *La Commission...*, pp.119-154; Adam Czartoryski, *Katechizm rycerski* (Knight's catechism), ed. Henryk Mościcki (Warszawa, 1925); Jean Fabre, "La propagande des idées philosophiques en Pologne sous Stanislas-Auguste et l'École varsovienne des Cadets", *Revue de Littérature Comparée* (1935): 643-693; Mieczysława Miterzanka, *Działalność pedagogiczna Adama ks. Czartoryskiego, generała ziem podolskich* (The pedagogical work of Prince Adam Czartoryski, General of Podolia) (Kraków, 1931); Kamilla Mrozowska, *Szkoła Rycerska Stanisława Augusta Poniatowskiego (1765-1794)* (The Knights' School of Stanisław August Poniatowski 1765-1794) (Wrocław: Ossolineum, 1961).

7. "Règlement pour les Cadets", item 11, see Mrozowska, *Szkoła Rycerska...*, p. 121.

8. Jobert, *La Commission*..., pp. 155-480 including a bibliography of sources and publications pp. 1-24. The bibliography is supplemented with works published in the years 1938-1978 in the Polish translation of Jobert's work: *Komisja Edukacji Narodowej*, tr. Mieczysława Chamcówna (Wrocław: Ossolineum, 1979), pp.236-305; Ambroise Jobert, *Magnats polonais et physiocrates français* (1767-1774) (Paris: Librairie Droz, 1941); Łukasz Kurdybacha, "The Commission for National Education in Poland 1773-1794", *History of Education 2 (1973)*: 133-146; *Komisja Edukacji Narodowej)* (The Commission for National Education), ed. Stanisław Tync (Wrocław: Ossolineum, 1954), see pp. 565-723 for Statute of 1783; Józef Lewicki, *Ustawodawstwo szkolne za czasów Komisji Edukacji Narodowej* (Educational legislation of the Commission for National Education) (Kraków, 1925); *Pisma i projekty pedagogiczne doby Komisji Edukacji Narodowej* (Works and educational plans in the time of the Commission for National Education), ed. Kamilla Mrozowska (Wrocław: Ossolineum, 1973); *Protokóły posiedzeń Komisji Edukacji Narodoweji 1773-1785* (Minutes of the meetings of the Commission for National Education's meetings 1773-1785), ed. Mieczysława Mitera-Dobrowolska (Wrocław: Ossolineum, 1973); *Protokóły posiedzeń...1786-1794* (Minutes...1786-1794), ed. Tadeusz Mizia (Wrocław: Ossolineum, 1969); *Raporty generalnych wizytatorów szkół Komisji Edukacji Narodowej w Wielkim Księstwie Litewskim (1782-1792)* (The reports of the inspectors general of the Commission for National Education in the Grand Duchy of Lithuania (1782-1792), eds. Kalina Bartnicka and Irena Szybiak (Wrocław: Ossolineum, 1974); *Raporty Szkoły Głównej Koronnej o generalnych wizytach szkół Komisji Edukacji Narodowej* (The reports of the Main Crown School on the general inspection of the schools of the Commission for National Education), eds. Kamilla Mrozowska and Anna Zielińska (Wrocław: Ossolineum, 1981); *Działalność edukacyjna Jana Śniadeckiego* (The educational work of Jan Śniadecki) (Wrocław: Ossolineum, 1980); Kalina Bartnicka, *Wychowanie patriotyczne w szkołach Komisji Edukacji Narodowej* (Patriotic education in the schools of the Commission for National Education) (Wrocław: Ossolineum, 1973); Mirosława Chamcówna, *Uniwersytet Jagielloński w dobie Komisji Edukacji Narodowej... 1777-1786* (The Jagiellonian University in the time of the Commission for National Education...1777-1786) (Wrocław: Ossolineum, 1957); Mirosława Chamcówna, *Uniwersytet Jagielloński... w latach 1786-1795* (The Jagiellonian University...1786-1795) (Wrocław: Ossolineum, 1959); Władysław Maria Grabski, *U podstaw wielkiej reformy* (At the foundations of the great reform) (Łódz: Wydawn. łódzkie, 1984); Jan Hulewicz, "Opinia publiczna wobec Komisji Edukacji Narodowej" (The Commission for National Education and the public opinion) in *Studia z dziejów kultury polskiej* (Warszawa: Gebethner i Wolf, 1949); Ambroise Jobert, "Une correspondance polonaise de Condillac", *Revue d'Histoire Moderne*, 11 (1936): 414-433; Janina Lubieniecka and Czesław Majorek, *Książki szkolne Komisji Edukacji Narodowej* (Schoolbooks of the Commission for National Education) (Warszawa, 1975); Kamilla Mrozowska, *Walka o nauczycieli świeckich w dobie Komisji Edukacji Narodowej na*

terenie Korony (The struggle over secular teachers in Poland in the time of the Commission for National Education) (Wrocław: Ossolineum, 1956); Kamilla Mrozowska, *Funkcjonowanie systemu szkolnego Komisji Edukacji Narodowej na terenie Korony w latach 1783-1793* (The functioning of the school system of the Commission for National Education in Poland 1783-1793) (Wrocław: Ossolineum, 1985); Hanna Pohoska, *Wizytatorowie generalni Komisji Edukacji Narodowej. Monografia z dziejów administracji szkolnej* (The inspectors general of the Commission for National Education. A study of the school administration) (Lublin, 1957); Jan Poplatek, *Komisja Edukacji Narodowej. Udział byłych jezuitów w pracach Komisji Edukacji Narodowej* (The Commission for National Education. The participation of former Jesuits in the work of the Commission for National Education) (Kraków, 1973); Irena Szybiak, *Nauczyciele szkół średnich Komisji Edukacji Narodowej* (Secondary school teachers of the Commission for National Education) (Wrocław: Ossolineum, 1980); Irena Szybiak, *Szkolnictwo Komisji Edukacji Narodowej w Wielkim Księstwie Litewskim* (The schools of the Commission for National Education in the Grand Duchy of Lithuania) (Wrocław: Ossolineum, 1973); Stanisław Salmonowicz, "Podstawy prawne funkcjonowania Komisji Edukacji Narodowej" (The legal bases for the operation of the Commission for National Education), in *Rozprawy z Dziejów Oświaty,* 23 (1980): 37-63; Stanisław Tync, *Nauka moralna w szkołach Komisji Edukacji Narodowej* (Moral education in the schools of the Commission for National Education) (Kraków, 1922).

9. "Mowa J. W. Imci P. Oraczewskiego z d. 29 kwietnia 1773 r." (Speech of P. Oraczewski, 29 April 1773) in *Komisja Edukacji Narodowej,* ed. Stanisław Tync, p. 18.

10. "Uniwersał Komisji z 24 października 1773 r." (Proclamation of the Commission of 24 October 1773), in *Komisjia...* ed Tync, pp.24-30.

11. "Vues Générales. Moyens d établir des écoles paroissiales," MS, Archives of the Polish Academy of Sciences, Kraków, no. 2200; "Principes de l éducation politique," MS, Czartoryski Library, Kraków, no. 818.

12. *Pisma i projekty pedagogiczne...,* ed. Kamilla Mrozowska, pp. 175-176.

13. *Pisma i projekty...,* ed. Mrozowska, pp. 177-179.

14. *Pisma i projekty...,* ed. Mrozowska, p. 179.

15. *Pisma i projekty...,* ed. Mrozowska. For the remarks of Jan Albertrandi and Kazimierz Narbutt about this criticism, see pp. 180-188.

16. Protokóły posiedzeń Komisji Edukacji Narodowej 1773-1785. (Minutes of the meetings of the Commission for National Education 1773-1785) Mieczysława Mitera-Dobrowolska ed. (Wrocław: Ossolinem, 1973) p.64.

17. Grzegorz Piramowicz, Powinności nauczyciela..., pp. 131-132.

18. Jean-Baptiste Dubois de Jancigny was at the Cadets' Corps from 1774 to 1779. He studied Polish intensively and among his publications are *Essai sur l'histoire littéraire de Pologne*, 1778 and a piece, *Casimir le Grand*, 1775, both dedicated to King Stanisław August Poniatowski. In 1779 he was made an honorary member of the Society for Elementary Books, but he left Poland that same year because of poor health. He maintained a correspondence with Ignacy Potocki and the King and published articles about Poland in various periodicals.

19. Jean-Philippe Carosi was curator of Stanisław August's natural history collection. In 1787 he prepared a catalog of Poland's natural resources for G.L. Buffon, which earned him Buffon's special thanks.

20. Published in the Hague in 1775.

21. Simon L'Huillier, a Genevan mathematician, was the winner of the international competition announced by the Society for Elementary Books for a mathematics primer. He became a member of the Society and spent 10 years in Poland and published a textbook on mathematics in 1778, on geometry in 1780-1781, and on algebra in 1782. Later he became a professor at the University of Geneva and published an enlarged version of the algebra textbook in German and French. See Jobert, La Commission.... pp. 287-289.

22. Certain corrections were made in the Statutes in 1790 and again in 1793.

23. Łukasz Kurdybacha, *Kuria rzymska wobec Komisji Edukacji Narodowej w latach 1773-1783* (The Roman Curia's attitudes toward the Commission for National Education 1773-1783) (Kraków, 1949). Kołłątaj's text appears on pp. 68-87.

24. The archive of the Jagiellonian University MS 274 contains numerous letters from directors of district schools, teachers, and inspectors written to Jan Śniadecki in his capacity as secretary of the Main School in Kraków.

25. Daniel Beauvois, *Lumières et Société en Europe de l'Est. L'Université de Vilna et les écoles polonaises de l Empire russe 1803-1832* (Paris: Champion, 1977), 2 vols, passim.

Translated by George Makowski

(w Drukarni Nadwor: JKMci i P.K.E.N.)

7

The Idea of Nation in the Main Currents of Political Thought of the Polish Enlightenment

Andrzej Walicki

The ideas of nation, national consciousness, national education and so forth belonged to the central themes of the Polish Enlightenment. All intellectual currents of the epoch were correlated with different views on "the national question" and their developments can, as a rule, be described as reflecting the transition from the old "nation of the gentry," with its conservative-republican ideology, to a new, more comprehensive notion of nation with a corresponding programme of modern nation-building.[1] Hence this topic should entail a reconstruction of the main controversies which belonged to the intellectual life of the epoch. I shall concentrate on a brief, selective presentation of a few topics, especially important, in my view, for a proper understanding of the specific contributions of the epoch of Enlightenment to the birth of modern nationhood in Poland. In spite of this emphasis on specificity, I shall also try to show that the case of the Polish-Lithuanian Commonwealth, which was after all the largest state in the East-Central Europe, completely refutes the so-called "Hans Kohn dichotomy," that is a widely accepted theory claiming that nationalism in Europe was divided from its very beginnings into two diametrically opposed types: Western nationalism and the nationalism of Central and Eastern Europe.[2] According to this theory, Western nationalism was a product of the Enlightenment, a rationalist ideology, centered around the notions of political legitimacy and active citizenship, while its Eastern counterpart was a romantic collectivism, centered around the irrational, pre-civilized folk-concept. The example of Poland-Lithuania shows however that the concept of nationhood had there a distinctively political content, referring to citizenship, and not ethnicity, and that the major thinkers of the Polish Enlightenment, before the final downfall of the Polish state, developed this notion in a "Western" manner, in accordance with the so-called "French model of the nation."

Our first topic must be, of course, the relationship between modern nationhood and the legacy of the "democracy of the gentry." We have been accustomed to thinking of the Polish Enlightenment as a movement of ideas committed to the strengthening of the executive power and therefore strongly opposed to the "republicanism" of the conservative, "Sarmatian" gentry. In fact, however, there was also an "enlightened" version of "Sarmatianism" and its contribution to the general ideological output of the Polish Enlightenment should not be neglected. Michał Wielhorski, the main ideologist of the Confederation of Bar, defended the republican institutions of Polish-Lithuanian Commonwealth by quoting from John Locke.[3] His republicanism could not be reduced to the defense of the feudal liberties of the gentry–it was modern and "enlightened" enough to inspire Rousseau to write his *Considérations sur le gouvernement de Pologne*, a treatise warmly sympathizing with the "gentry republic." The difference between the "feudal" republicanism of the Polish gentry and the "bourgeois" republicanism of the West was, obviously, not as absolute as the Marxist historians would have us believe, while their essential similarity, namely the common devotion to political freedom, was clearly perceived. Owing to this Polish conservatives rejoiced at the successes of the American Revolution and one of the leaders of the Confederation of Bar, Kazimierz Pułaski, even became an American national hero. Even more paradoxical, though not illogical, was the fact that Hetman Seweryn Rzewuski, one of the most reactionary of Polish magnates, was an enthusiastic admirer not only of Franklin and Washington but also of the French revolution. He rejoiced at the seizure of the Bastille and wanted the French to show the world that free nations could dispense with kings.[4]

For the gentry republicans "nation" was a political and legal concept, deprived of linguistic or ethic connotations: it was conceived as a body politic, embracing all active citizens, i.e. all members of the gentry, irrespective of their native language or ethnic background. In other words, it was perfectly possible to be "*gente Ruthenus, natione Polonus.*" But this indifference towards ethnicity should not be presented as anticipating the

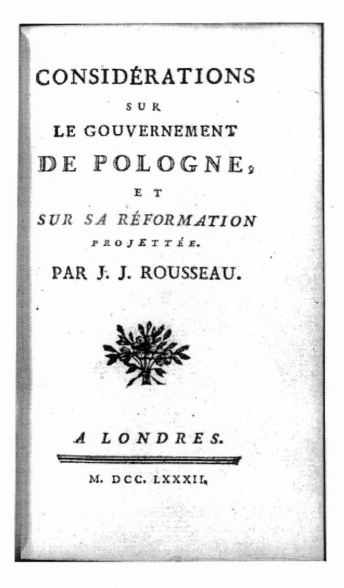

CONSIDÉRATIONS

SUR

LE GOUVERNEMENT

DE POLOGNE,

ET

SUR SA RÉFORMATION

PROJETTÉE.

PAR J. J. ROUSSEAU.

A LONDRES.

M. DCC. LXXXII.

Jean-Jacques Rousseau, *Considérations sur le gouvernement de Pologne, et sur sa réformation projettée*, Londres, 1782. Title page. (Indiana University, Lilly Library).

Hieronim Stroynowski, *Nauka prawa przyrodzonego, politycznego, ekonomiki polityczney i prawa narodów* (The study of natural and political law, political economy, and the law of nations), Wilno, Drukarnia Królewska przy Akademii, 1785. Title page. (Biblioteka Uniwersyteka w Warszawie).

modern notion of "multi-culturalism." The gentry republicans of the old Commonwealth described themselves as "Sarmatians" and the term "Sarmatianism" referred, as is known, to a distinctive culture common to all of them, remarkably homogeneous and deliberately created as a unifying bond. The nation of the gentry was still multi-lingual but not multi-cultural; it took great care to cultivate and develop its cultural unity, which finally led also to linguistic polonization of its non-Polish members.

The central element in the republican view of the nation was the idea of popular sovereignty. They defined the nation as the collective subject of the sovereign political will, that is as the opposite of a population subject to a monarch. From this point of view "nation" and absolute monarchy were, of course, mutually exclusive, while participatory republic was the only form of mature nationhood; even England did not deserve to be called a nation because its political freedom was too limited.[5] Many theorists of gentry republicanism concluded from this that Poland-Lithuania was the only true nation in Europe. Interestingly, the most enlightened among them, for instance Michał Wielhorski (already mentioned), or the castellan of Vitebsk, Adam Rzewuski, did not try to defend the view that nation should be restricted to one estate only; on the contrary, they insisted that this was a transient phenomenon, caused by special historical circumstances, and declared their willingness to see the rights of active citizenship made universal, related to the entire population of the country. Adam Rzewuski wrote: "O, how ardently I want that no privileged class would exist and that burghers and peasants become simply humans and Poles."[6]

The sincerity of these words should not be questioned. They harmonized with the inner logic of the idea of popular sovereignty, so dear to Rzewuski. This idea made him, as well as Wielhorski and many other gentry republicans, an ardent admirer and disciple of Rousseau. To be a "gentry republican" in eighteenth-century Poland did not necessarily entail being socially conservative. Adam Rzewuski was not alone in criticizing the Constitution of 3 May not only for the introduction of hereditary monarchy but also for inadequately improving the situation of the peasantry.[7] This inner logic of the republican conception of the nation explains the possibility of an easy transition from the "old republicanism" of the Sarmatian gentry to the "new republicanism," free from the retrospective ideals of "Sarmatian" ideology and unequivocally committed to progressive ideas of the radical Enlightenment. A good illustration of this is Wojciech Turski who began his political career in the ranks of the "old-republican" opponents of progressive reforms but soon became a radical Jacobin, or an "enlightened republican,"[8] and an advocate of a revolutionary alliance between Jacobin France and Poland, as two bastions of republican freedom.[9]

Another consequence of the republican conception of the nation was the deep conviction that members of the nation had an inalienable right to both internal and external sovereignty. Hence the adherents of the republican conception, although defining the nation in purely political terms, could see themselves as a nation even after the final disappearance of their state. Subjects of one monarchy can become loyal subjects of another, but sovereignty embodied in the nation, not in the monarch, involves a legitimate right to self-mastery which is with us "as long as we live" (to quote from the Polish national anthem).[10] Owing to this, the partitions of Poland transformed the conservative republicanism of the gentry into a revolutionary force, setting against the legitimist principles of the Holy Alliance a new principle of political legitimacy: the principle of national self-determination.[11] This was not yet the modern principle of national self-determination, based upon a linguistic, monoethnic conception of nation. But precisely because of this it was more in tune with the prevailing political views of the epoch and more convincing in its logic, especially in its invocation of historical rights, even for the monarchs themselves.

The second question which I want to raise is the specificity of the idea of national sovereignty as developed by the thinkers of the Polish Enlightenment. To put it briefly, in Poland the idea of external national sovereignty had its main source in the conception of the internal sovereignty of the nation of the gentry in its relation to the king, while in the West the concept of sovereignty was developed by the theorists of absolutism (Jean Bodin), as a concept pertaining to the state making it the highest legal authority, the highest arbiter in human affairs. Hence in the Western political tradition the conception of sovereignty sanctioned the practice of power politics in the name of *raison d'état* while in Poland it was invoked, as a rule, to defend the legitimate rights of nations, even stateless ones, and to limit the excessive ambitions of the states by subordinating them to the principles of a supranational law of nations. Because of this the Polish Enlightenment gave birth to a rich theoretical literature dealing with these problems. A physiocrat, Hieronim Stroynowski, put forward a theory that every nation had four natural rights: (1) the right to free and independent existence, (2) the right to defend itself by force, (3) the right to the certainty that international agreement would not be violated and, finally, (4) the right to demand help from other nations.[12] Similar ideas were developed by many other Polish jurists and political thinkers of the age.[13] It should be stressed that the right to self-determination was never restricted, explicitly or implicitly, to European peoples: Polish public opinion did not sympathize with colonialism and took the side of the distant colonized peoples.[14]

The tendency to see international legal order as a safeguard of national sovereignty, and not something incompatible with it, proved to be very durable in Poland. After the partitions Stanisław Staszic came to the conclusion that the only means of introducing the rule of law into international relations was to organize a universal Association of Nations.[15] Hugo Kołłątaj, who became an admirer of Napoleon, dreamt of securing the rights of nations in a restored "Western Empire" while young Adam Czartoryski, as the Russian minister of foreign affairs, wrote in 1803 an extensive memorandum about the need to foster the creation of a "Society of States" which would put an end to the state of nature in relations between nations.[16] In later years similar ideas were taken up and developed, in the language of speculative philosophy or religious messianism, by the leading thinkers of Polish Romanticism, including Adam Mickiewicz and the greatest Polish philosopher of the romantic epoch, August Cieszkowski.[17] The transition between the Enlightenment idea of the "society of nations" and the Romantic vision of the regenerated humankind is exemplified by Czartoryski's *Essai sur la diplomatie* (Paris-Marseille, 1830). This splendid work was inspired by the Enlightenment views on the law of nations but, at the same time, abandoned the Enlightenment concept of the nation-state, setting against it the Romantic concept of the nation as a "divine creation," contrasted with the state as an artificial, human creation. The reasons for this remarkable continuity of thought were complicated and numerous, but one of them was undoubtedly that in the Polish political tradition, shaped by the best features of the democracy of the gentry, sovereignty was seen as an attribute of the nation rather then of the state; that it had always been conceived as decentralized sovereignty and, therefore, did not imply an undivided monopoly on power. Another feature of this tradition—the somewhat archaic inability to distinguish clearly between politics and morality, combined with the awareness of one's own weakness, was, of course, a powerful stimulus for seeking national salvation by limiting the sovereignty of the states for the sake of international justice.

Let us proceed now to a few remarks on the two greatest thinkers of the "Party of Reform:" Hugo Kołłątaj, the main architect of the Constitution of 3 May, and Stanisław Staszic. I shall concentrate mainly on their different attitudes towards the legacy of the gentry democracy and their different proposals for the future. Kołłątaj's views on passing from the "nation of the gentry" to the "new nation" can be summarized in three points.

First, he remained faithful to the republican view that sovereignty should belong not to the king but to the nation. He stressed that the reformed Poland would not become a monarchy, in spite of the introduction of the principle of heredity. The Polish king would become head of a Commonwealth, and not a monarch.[18] The "golden freedom" of the gentry was to be limited, but the republican ethos of active citizenship, active participation in political life, was to be strengthened. To achieve this aim, the Parliament was to be made a permanently active ruling body, holding both the legislative and the executive power.

Second, the "nation of the gentry" was to become a "nation of proprietors", that is, active citizenship was to become dependent on property qualifications. The landless gentry were seen by Kołłątaj as clients of big magnates and, therefore, representing not their own will but the will of their patrons.[19] Following the French physiocratic ideas, Kołłątaj wanted to entrust the fates of the nation to the owners of land since the landed property was in his eyes a guarantee of having a stake in one's country and, therefore, a precondition of rational, enlightened patriotism. The Great Diet implemented these ideas by giving political rights to the landowning burghers while depriving the landless gentry of their right to vote.

Third, the peoples of a nation should become homogeneous, speaking the same language and living under the same laws.[20] This view was a conscious attempt to apply to the Polish-Lithuanian Commonwealth the so-called Jacobin conception of the nation, keenly suspicious of regional and cultural differences as incompatible with national unity and social modernization.[21] In the Polish conditions it meant the unification of laws, the recognition of the Polish language as a unifying force for all the provinces of the state, as the language of the court, government offices, and schools, with the exception of religious matters, which were to be taught in the language of the rite.[22] The rights of religious minorities were to be respected but only in strictly religious matters. Thus, for instance, Jews were to be deprived of their autonomy, subject to Polish jurisdiction, forced to attend Polish schools and dress like other Poles.[23]

It should be stressed that these ideas had nothing in common with the so-called "cultural nationalism," characteristic, according to Hans Kohn, of Germany and East-Central Europe. Kołłątaj was concerned with the political unity of the nation and showed no interest in the irrational social ties, including the mystique of national culture. His conception of nation was political, rationalist, consciously modeled on revolutionary France.

Stanisław Staszic by Louis Marteau. Reprinted from Piotr Chmielowski, *Historia literatury polskiej,* Lwów, 1914.

U W A G I
NAD ŻYCIEM
JANA ZAMOYSKIEGO
KANCLERZA i HETMANA·W. K.

Do dzisieyszego stanu Rzeczypospolitey Polskiey przystosowane. ——

Stanisław Staszic, *Uwagi nad życiem Jana Zamoyskiego Kanclerza i Hetmana W.K. Do dzisieyszego stanu Rzeczypospolitey Polskiey przystosowane* (Remarks on the life of Jan Zamoyski, Chancellor and Great Hetman of the Crown, applied to the current state of the Polish Commonwealth) n.p., n.d. (1787?). Title page. (Biblioteka Narodowa, Warszawa).

The other leading theorist, Stanisław Staszic, was a burgher and propagated another variant of the "French model of nation"–a variant stressing the positive historical role of royal absolutism and extremely critical of the entire "republican" tradition of the gentry. The decisive element in his conception of nation was not internal sovereignty, i.e. political freedom, but the abolition of feudal estates, i.e. social integration based upon equality before the law. As to sovereignty, he repeatedly emphasized the priority of external politics, that is, the necessity of putting the interests of the state in relations to its neighbors above the civic and political freedom of the citizens: a country surrounded by absolute monarchies, he argued, cannot afford to allow its citizens to exercise internal freedom at the cost of external security.[24] In his *Przestrogi dla Polski,* 1790 (Warnings for Poland) he pretended to have changed his monarchical leanings and presented himself as a believer in direct transition from feudal anarchy to an "orderly republic"; this, however, was merely a tactical move, expressing his awareness of the fact that an open attack on the Polish republican tradition would immediately alienate the overwhelming majority of the Great Diet. In fact he treated "the gentry democracy" as a truly disastrous form of government. Even the word "freedom" was suspicious to him as too often concealing the interests of the privileged classes.[25]

Like Kołłątaj, Staszic supported the conception of the "nation of proprietors," i.e. of depriving non-proprietors of political influence. But he rejected the privileged treatment of the landed property and demanded for the burghers one half of all seats in the Diet. Staszic agreed with Rousseau, that education should shape the souls of the citizen in a national pattern and clearly paraphrasing Rousseau he wrote: "on opening its eyes for the first time, a child should see nothing beyond the fatherland, for which alone it will one day have the duty of closing them."[26] Although he sometimes used the word "nation" in its purely political sense, as a body of citizens, he was more and more inclined to give it another meaning: to define it in ethnic, cultural and linguistic terms, as a community of people formed by a common history but once created, capable of existing even without a state of its own. He also made a distinction between "inborn" and "acquired" nationality, the first comprising blood-ties, language and some specific features of national culture, the second finding expression in forms of government, laws and civilization. While the "inborn" nationality should be preserved intact, the "acquired" one should keep pace with universal progress.[27]

After the partitions Staszic finally abandoned the republican view of nation as a body of free citizens and made a long step towards the ethnolinguistic conception of nation. This new, "tribal" conception of nation turned his attention to the Slavic traits, common to Poles and Russians and thus provided him with arguments for a Panslavic program.[28]

The gradual replacement of the political definition of nation by the ethnic-cultural conception was certainly one of the most important shifts in the Polish political thought of the late Enlightenment. It was fostered mainly by two phenomena: the growing radicalism of certain progressive writers and the downfall of the Polish state. Franciszek Jezierski, representing the radical wing of the group calling itself "Kołłątaj's Forge," pointed out that there could be nations deprived of statehood (Italy), or of national unity (Germany), but held together by common culture; he did so with the intention of distinguishing between the nation and its ruling class, including the "proprietors," and stressing the nation-building role of the "common folk," as creators of both the national idiom and the distinctively national customs.[29] After the final partition these ideas became popular among patriots of all political persuasions, including the outspoken conservatives. "The nation is constituted by its language,"[30] said Julian Ursyn Niemcewicz, and the ex-Jacobin, Samuel Bogumił Linde, started to work on his monumental Dictionary of the Polish language. Both of them, as well as Kołłątaj and Staszic, belonged to the newly created Warsaw Society of the Friends of Learning, whose declared aim was to study national language, culture and history in order to help their compatriots to exist as a stateless nation. Of course, to define the Polish nation in ethnic-cultural terms was by then not an easy task. The domination of the Polish culture in the vast territories of the Grand Duchy of Lithuania and in the Ukraine, as well as the underdevelopment of the Ukrainian and Belorussian as literary languages, created a widespread illusion that Poland-Lithuania could, in principle, be transformed into a linguistically and culturally homogeneous nation in the same way in which it was being done in revolutionary France. It would be quite anachronistic to explain this view in terms of some kind of Polish "imperialism." It was rather a logical consequence of the fact that the Enlightenment conception of the Polish nation defined nationality in terms of citizenship and political loyalty, not in terms of ethnolinguistic differentiation. Like the French Jacobins, Polish patriots of the Enlighten-ment period (with few exceptions, mentioned above) considered ethnic differences to be immaterial in defining nationality. For them, the peasantry

Hugo Kołłątaj by Józef Peszka. (Muzeum Narodowe w Warszawie).

Do
STANISŁAWA
MAŁACHOWSKIEGO
REFERENDARZA KORONNEGO.
MARSZALKA SEYMOWEGO
i
Konfederacyi Generalney.
A N O N Y M A
Listów kilka.

CZĘŚĆ II.

o Poprawie Rzeczypospolitey.

Stat casus renovare omnes, eandemque reverti
Per Trojam, & rursus Caput objestare periclis.
VIRG. ÆNEID. L. II.

1788.
Od dnia 7. Paźdź. do dnia 7. List.

Hugo Kołłątaj *Do Stanisława Małachowskiego Referendarza Koronnego, Marszałka Seymowego i Konfederacyi Generalney Anonyma listów kilka.* Część 11. O Poprawie Rzeczypospolitey. (To Stanisław Małachowski, Crown Referendary, the Marshal of the Diet and the General Confederation, several letters from an anonymous author. Part 2, On the Reform of the Commonwealth), n.p., 1788. Title page. (Biblioteka Uniwersyteka w Warszawie).

of the Commonwealth was one whole mass which still had to be aroused to Polish national consciousness through the abolition of serfdom, grants of property rights, and general civil enfranchisement. They could see that this would be more difficult in the case of the Orthodox Ukrainian peasantry then in that of the ethnically Polish peasantry, or, for example, the Catholic peasantry of Lithuania. But they did not believe that it was impossible: they thought it was only necessary to develop Polish education in the ethnically non-Polish territories and to introduce true equality of Roman Catholics, Uniates and the Orthodox before the law. From their viewpoint it was the duty of Polish patriots to carry out this task–their duty not only to themselves, but also, and indeed above all, to all potential Poles, even if as yet they spoke a language other than Polish.

It should be stressed that this viewpoint was shared by Tadeusz Kościuszko who was more radical in social matters, and more tolerant of ethnic differences, than Hugo Kołłątaj. Kościuszko used the words "Pole" and "Polish" in two senses: a narrower sense, referring to people who spoke Polish and practiced the Roman Catholic faith, and a broader sense which embraced all "fellow countrymen," thus including the Uniates who spoke Ukrainian or Belorussian, and even the Orthodox clergy who came under the authority of the Russian Metropolitan in Kiev. In the first sense, the adjective "Polish" corresponded significantly with the word "English," while in the second sense, it covered all the inhabitants of the Commonwealth and was thus the equivalent of the word "British." Kościuszko was aware of Moscow's successes in exploiting the anti-Polish resentments of the Orthodox population of the Commonwealth and reacted to this by stressing that the Polish Orthodox Ruthenians had the same fatherland as the ethnic Poles and deserved to be included in the Polish nation on equal terms with Catholics. But, on the other hand, he shared the "Jacobin" belief that the development of a Polish education system in the eastern territories would lead to the linguistic polonization of the Orthodox population, putting an end to their separatist tendencies and thus paving the way for a politically unified, although religiously differentiated, Polish nation.

No doubt, these views were hardly compatible with the idea of a multicultural national community, which would encourage manifestations of ethnic diversity and renounce all efforts to achieve cultural homogeneity. But whatever we think about it, we must realize that the ideologists of the Polish Enlightenment could not afford to ignore the centralizing tendency of European progress. The unifying tendency was inherent in the very nature of nationalism as an undermining ideology. Ernest Gellner in his

Nations and Nationalism defines nationalism as a species of patriotism which favors cultural homogeneity.[31] Polish nationalism of the Age of Enlightenment, exactly like its French counterpart, provides an important corroboration of this thesis. We can say, using Gellner's words, that it was "based on a culture striving to be a high (literate) culture" and that this was the reason why it could not recognize separate national identities of the Lithuanian, Ukrainian, and Belorussian peasants. The later exuberance of romantic idealizations of the cultural diversity of the old Sarmatian Commonwealth should not obscure this important fact.

The Enlightenment concept of the Polish nation indicates that in the eighteenth century the process of forming a modern Polish nation was taking place in Poland along the lines similar to those followed in the countries of Western Europe. The course of this process changed under the pressure of external circumstances: the partitions of Poland. From the moment when Poland was placed under the yoke of foreign powers, the identification of citizenship and nationality ceased to be possible, for it would have meant that Poles were to turn into Germans or Russians. This was unthinkable for a nation with a high level of national consciousness and it thus became necessary to abandon the political concept of the nation. This, however, entailed consequences which the Poles had not foreseen, and which for a long period they did not wish to accept, for it accelerated and in its own way validated the process of "ethnic awakening" of the stateless nations, including the non-Polish population of the former Commonwealth. In this way Polish nationalist aspirations came to be an important factor in the general "national awakening" in East-Central Europe. This, in turn, had to come into conflict with the historic claims of the Polish patriots.

Thus, Lord Acton seems to have been right in stressing that the partitions of Poland undermined the hitherto existing system of political legitimacy and paved the way for "the theory of nationality" as an entirely new legitimizing device, with all its consequences for "the ancient European system."[32] It seems perfectly arguable that if pre-partition Poland had survived within the existing, or slightly reduced, state boundaries, and if the Enlightenment reforms, which also covered the integration of Lithuania and the linguistic homogenization of the state on the French model, had been crowned with success, the whole process of favoring modern nationalities in the area of Central and Eastern Europe would have proceeded differently.[33] The Constitution of 3 May, together with the entire legislative work of the Great Diet, is often seen as the best summary of the progressive legacy of the Polish Enlightenment. However, for the sake of historical accuracy, it is necessary to qualify this widespread opinion. We must be aware of some specific features of the Constitution. First of all, it must be stressed that the Constitution did not reflect the radical tendency in the Enlightenment reform program. On the contrary, it was a product of an uneasy compromise between two moderate wings of the reform movement: the westernizing constitutional monarchists and the "enlightened Sarmatians" whose ideology remained linked to the republican values of the socially conservative and ardently Catholic Bar Confederation. Its main concession to the first group was its espousal of hereditary monarchy, a system foreign to the native tradition of the democracy of the gentry. Its concessions to the second group included the solemn endorsement of all the privileges of the noble estate (with the exclusion of the landless gentry) and, also, endowing the Roman Catholic faith with the status of "the dominant national religion." This was a tribute to the conservatives and a far cry from the standpoint of the most progressive thinkers of the Polish Enlightenment. The views of the latter were adequately expressed in the following words of Tadeusz Kościuszko: "The nation should be the lord and master of its own fate, and its rights should therefore be superior to those of the church; no religion could contravene them by appealing to divine law, but on the contrary, every religion should be obedient to the laws established by a given nation."[34]

The overall, moderately modernizing spirit of the Great Diet found expression, above all, in an idea which reflected an important phase in the evolution of nation-building ideologies in Poland but was not allowed, nonetheless, to take strong roots in the Polish soil: the idea of a "nation of property-owners." The architects of the Constitution saw it as a means of saving the status of the landed nobility while, at the same time, not exposing the government, which they willed to be strong, to the anarchic leanings of the landless gentry. It is obvious, however, that the inner logic of the Enlightenment concept of the nation, in conjunction with the republican principle of the sovereignty of the people, had to lead the most progressive thinkers of the Polish Enlightenment to a different conception, radically opposed to both the estate-exclusiveness of the "noble nation" and the property-qualifications, as envisaged by the Great Diet. This was, of course, the conception of the "nation of the people," set forth by F.S. Jezierski (who stressed the role of the "commonality in the national community") and embraced by other Polish "Jacobins" from the "Kołłątaj's Forge." It is important to remember that this conception was loudly proclaimed by

Tadeusz Kościuszko who categorically refused to fight for the privileged alone, and whose idea of the Polish nation embraced all inhabitants of the Commonwealth, irrespective of their estate, property, religion, or ethnic origin. Thus, it is fair to say that the last will of independent Poland is to be found in the proclamations of Kościuszko's uprising, and not in the legislative acts of the Great Diet.

Notes

1. For a more detailed study of these problems see my book *The Enlightenment and the Birth of Modern Nationhood. Polish Political Thought from Noble Republicanism to Tadeusz Kościuszko*. (Notre Dame: University of Notre Dame Press, 1989).

2. For a systematization of Kohn's ideas see Louis L. Snyder, *The Meaning of Nationalism*. Foreword by Hans Kohn. (New Brunswick, N.J.: Rutgers University Press, 1954). Cf. also Aira Kemilainen, *Nationalism: Problems Concerning the Word. The Concept and Classification* (Jyväskylä: Jyväskylän Kasvatusopillinen Korkeakoulu, 1964).

3. See Michał Wielhorski, *O przywróceniu dawnego rządu według pierwiastkowych Rzeczypospolitej ustaw* (On the restoration of the ancient government in accordance with the fundamental laws of the Republic) (n.p., 1775).

4. Seweryn Rzewuski, *O sukcesyi tronu w Polszcze rzecz krótka* (A short essay on succession to the throne in Poland) (Warszawa, 1789), pp. 25, 45. On the Polish perception of American revolution see Zofia Libiszowska, *Opinia polska wobec rewolucji amerykańskiej w XVIII wieku* (The Polish opinion of the American Revolution in the 18th century) (Łódź-Wrocław: Ossolineum, 1962).

5. Adam Wawrzyniec Rzewuski, *O formie rządu republikańskiego myśli* (Thoughts on the republican form of government) (Warszawa, 1790), pp. 73-4.

6. Rzewuski, *O formie rządu*, p. 168.

7. In a private letter written one month after the passing of the Constitution he wrote: "I find the rights of the peasants included in the new constitution insufficiently clear and an inadequate assurance of the freedom and property of the poor yokel against the proud covetousness which will bring his undoing." Quoted in Adam Próchnik, *Demokracja Kościuszkowska* (Kościuszko democracy) (Warszawa: "Wiedza," 1946), p. 37.

8. This was his own term. See Wojciech Turski, *Myśli o królach, o sukcesyi, o przeszłym i przyszłym rządzie* (Reflections on kings, on succession, on the past and future government) (Warszawa, 1790), p. 10.

9. See Próchnik, *Demokracja*, p. 66.

10. This has been stressed by Janusz Maciejewski in his "Pojęcie narodu w myśli republikantów 1767-1775," (The concept of nation in the thought of republicans,

1767-1775) in Janusz Gockowski and Andrzej Walicki, eds., *Idee i koncepcje narodu w polskiej myśli politycznej czasów porozbiorowych* (Warszawa: PWN, 1977), p. 34.

11. Cf. Janusz Tazbir, *Kultura szlachecka w Polsce* (Gentry culture in Poland) (Warszawa: Wiedza Powszechna, 1978), pp. 71-2.

12. Hieronim Stroynowski, *Nauka prawa przyrodzonego, politycznego, ekonomiki politycznej i prawa narodów* (The study of natural and political law, political economy, and the law of nations) (Wilno, 1785), part 4, paragraph 5.

13. Cf. Stanisław Hubert, *Pogląd na prawo narodów w Polsce czasów Oświecenia* (View on the law of nations in Poland during the Enlightenment) (Wrocław: Ossolineum, 1960).

14. Cf. Janusz Tazbir, *Rzeczpospolita szlachecka wobec wielkich odkryć* (The gentry republic in relation to the great discoveries) (Warszawa: Wiedza Powszechna, 1973), p. 203.

15. See the last canto of his historiosophical poem *Ród ludzki* (The Human race). Cf. Walicki, *The Enlightenment*, pp. 61-2.

16. See Józef Ujejski, *Dzieje polskiego mesjanizmu do powstania listopadowego włącznie* (The history of Polish messianism up to and including the November Uprising) (Lwów: Ossolineum, 1931), and Jerzy Skowronek, *Antynapoleońskie koncepcje Czartoryskiego* (Czartoryski's anti-Napoleon concepts) (Warszawa: PWN, 1969), pp. 48-53.

17. For a detailed presentation of their ideas see Andrzej Walicki, *Philosophy and Romantic Nationalism: The Case of Poland.* (Oxford: Clarendon Press, 1982).

18. Hugo Kołłątaj, *Listy Anonima i Prawo polityczne narodu polskiego* (Anonymous letters and Political law of the Polish nation). Ed. Bogusław Leśnodorski and Helena Wereszycka (Warszawa: PWN, 1954), vol. 2, pp. 47-8.

19. Kołłątaj, *Listy Anonima.*, vol. 1, pp. 292-6.

20. Kołłątaj, *Listy Anonima.*, vol 1, pp. 367-70.

21. The French Jacobins conducted their great Gallicization campaign under the banner of the struggle against counterrevolution. The deputy Barère put it as follows: "Federalism and superstition speak Breton; emigrés and hatred for the republic speak German; the counterrevolution speaks Italian; favoritism speaks Basque. Let us destroy these dangerous tools of error." (Quoted from Hans Kohn, *Prelude to Nation States: The French and German Experience. 1789-1815* (Princeton: Princeton University Press, 1967), p. 91.

22. Kołłątaj, *Listy Anonima*, vol. 1, p. 370, and vol. 2, p. 246.

23. Kołłątaj, *Listy Anonima.*, vol. 2, p. 329.

24. See Stanisław Staszic, *Pisma filozoficzne i społeczne* (Philosophical and social works), ed. Bogdan Suchodolski (Warszawa: PWN, 1954), vol. 1, p. 165.

25. Cf. Stanisław Staszic, *Ród ludzki. Wersja brulionowa.* (The human race: Draft version) ed. Zbigniew Daszkowski (Warszawa: PWN, 1959), vol. 3, pp. 270-1.

26. "The newly born infant," wrote Rousseau, "upon first opening his eyes, must gaze upon the fatherland, and until his dying should behold nothing else." Jean-Jacques Rousseau, *The Government of Poland.* Trans. Willmore Kendall (Indianapolis and New York: Bobbs-Merrill, 1972), p. 19. Cf. Staszic, *Pisma*, vol. 1, p. 20.

27. Staszic, *Pisma*, vol. 2, pp. 276-8.

28. See his *Myśli o równowadze politycznej w Europie* (Reflections on the Political Balance in Europe). *Pisma*, vol. 2, pp. 301-321.

29. Cf. Franciszek Salezy Jezierski, *Wybór pism* (Selected works) ed. Zdzisław Skwarczyński (Warszawa: PWN, 1952), pp. 217-8 and 244.

30. Quoted from Andrzej Feliks Grabski, *Myśl historyczna polskiego Oświecenia* (Historical thought of the Polish Enlightenment) (Warszawa: PWN, 1976), p. 391.

31. See Ernest Gellner, *Nations and Nationalism* (Ithaca: Cornell University Press, 1983), p. 138.

32. See his essay "Nationality," in John Emerich Edward Dalbert-Acton, *History of Freedom and Other Essays* (Freeport, N.Y., 1907), p. 276.

33. Cf. Roman Szporluk, "Poland and the Rise of the Theory and Practice of Modern Nationality," *Dialectics and Humanism*, Warszawa 2 (1990): 43-64.

34. Tadeusz Kościuszko, "Memoriał do A. J. Czartoryskiego" (Address to A. J. Czartoryski), *Kwartalnik Historyczny* 4 (1965): 899.

8

Political and Social Literature during the Four-Year Diet

Anna Grześkowiak-Krwawicz

Political literature played a distinctive role in the political life of the Polish Republic throughout its entire existence. It accompanied all the most important events such as wars, confederations and elections. In journals and pamphlets current events were commented upon, the goals and actions of friendly political groups were promoted, while those of political adversaries were attacked. Apart from these, but much more rarely, larger treatises would appear, which commented on the political system as such, its advantages, or, especially in the second half of the eighteenth century, its flaws and the necessity to correct them.

Political literature not only permanently injected itself into Polish political practice but it also arose from it. With obligatory unanimity in the Diet and in dietines, all decisions were the result of compromise, often achieved after laborious and stormy negotiations among the interested parties. In such a situation, the art of convincingly representing a position was important and necessary. Therefore, elocution was regarded as one of the main skills to be mastered by the citizens of the Republic. Persuasion of fellow citizens was conducted not only in oral debate but also in print. Freedom of expression in Poland was conducive to this. The nobility regarded freedom of expression as one of the pillars of Polish liberty. In practice, there were no forbidden topics whose mention could have invited repression. This principle applied not only to the spoken but also to the printed word in the eighteenth century, in

175

particularly to the second half; as late as the 1760s and even during the early years of Stanisław August's reign, a large part of the polemics on current political matters were conducted with the help of handwritten works circulated hand to hand and diligently copied into nobles' annals and diaries.[1] Foremost among the printed works which appeared at that time were political treatises on general topics. With a growing interest in the printed word and an expanding number of publishers, authors began to appreciate the possibilities of extending their circle of readers through print. As a result, during the Four-Year Diet most of the political literature and all the more ambitious propaganda treatises appeared in print. To be sure, so-called "written gazettes" continued to circulate in the country providing information and rumors about the most interesting events. In addition, the sharpest political lampoons aimed at specific individuals and short satirical verses also circulated in manuscript form, but, in comparison to printed works, their importance was rather insignificant.[2] Poland was free from censorship and complete freedom of the printed word reigned. Debates on political topics could be published with complete liberty as attested to by the pronouncement of authors of widely differing viewpoints ranging from the ultraconservative defenders of the old system who suggested in no uncertain terms that Stanisław August was aiming at despotism to those fewer in number, but no less fervent, advocates of strengthened royal powers. As stated by Bogusław Leśnodorski, in Europe only England and Holland equaled the liberty of discussion and intellectual freedom which existed in Poland.[3]

In such a favorable environment and amidst a political enlivening that was intense even for Poland, the political literature of the Four-Year Diet represented to a great degree the crowning of a long tradition. Its role in those years is best described by Roman Pilat, the researcher who was the first to deal with this phenomenon, when he writes that: "it created almost a second diet alongside the real one."[4]

This assessment applies not only to the importance of the publicistic discussion but also to the background of its participants. Just as the Diet was noble, it can be said, allowing for some simplification, that political literature was created by the nobility for the nobility.[5] This was completely natural in Polish circumstances since it was the nobility that held power in the state and felt responsible for its politics. Other estates, and actually one can only speak here of the townspeople, were only seeking political (and also civil) rights and hence were less interested in the process of national politics, which they did not influence. Moreover, even writers of bourgeois extraction, the most famous of whom was Staszic, realized that their audience consisted primarily of nobles, and this left a mark on the way they presented their arguments. Writers from the middle and lower nobility predominated. All were educated and at times their education had been quite complete. Some of them were still the typical "dietine (and diet) political writers" who practiced their printed polemics on the margins of their political activities in the Diet, the dietines, the tribunals, or in the quiet of country life. Increasingly, however, there appeared those authors who mixed their writing with other forms of public activity, especially priests, educators in the schools of the Commission for National Education, newspaper publishers and the still rare authors who made a living from their writing. The educated often knew Europe and western political theory quite well. Regardless of their education and their positions, however, they remained first and foremost exponents of noble views, and it was to the nobility that they addressed their writings.

The boundaries of the literature of the Four-Year Diet or of political literature in general are difficult to draw. During this period even basic administrative publications, such as the Diet Marshal's announcements informing those at home of the proceedings of the Diet, were of a political nature. They attempted to convince the nobles of the correctness of decisions taken by the deputies rather than to simply present basic facts. Even the laws themselves were not free of publicistic elements. Foremost among these was the most famous, the Constitution of 3 May, which in its provisions contained not only concrete systemic solutions but also explanations for the need to apply them and even general considerations concerning the social role of the different social classes and the origin of sovereignty in the state.[6] Since not even the Government Statute, as the Constitution of 3 May was called, was devoid of publicistic elements, it is not surprising that practically all forms of literature took on political overtones. Not only political writings but also drama and poetry dealt with the most important problems connected with reform of the Republic. Political concepts were popularized from the stage,[7] and poetry described current events and their protagonists and provided commentaries on parliamentary debates. One extensive political treatise even presented its reform program in rather decent verse.[8] The expression of political views was not even avoided in scholarly works or textbooks (especially on law and history) and hence in works which would appear by their very nature to be neutral and objective.

A full study of such a varied and immense body of literature is not possible here and discussion is limited to political writing in its most typical form, the principal goal of which was to present the reader with a system of views and to convince him of its value. Even with such a narrowing of focus the volume of material is impressive. Without a more thorough bibliographical investigation

an estimate of the number of works in this category is difficult, but it is clear
that it reaches into the thousands. The flood of printed material was so great
that it attracted the attention of contemporaries, one of whom jibed that all
the expended quills could provide a mattress for exhausted authors.[9] The variety
was no less great.

This material included both the carefully published treatise with wider
political ambitions and the one page leaflet, often simply a scrap of printed
paper. Often authors used the latter form to publish parliamentary speeches.
As mentioned, speech making in the Diet and dietines had a long tradition in
Poland and once the importance of the printed word was appreciated it became
yet another characteristic form of political expression in Polish political life.
The leaflets also represented the most current commentaries on questions
discussed by the Diet since they were published almost simultaneously with
the parliamentary debates or even earlier when the author had the foresight to
send it to the printers. The publication of whole collections of speeches–this
time at the publisher's expense–attest to the wide interest in these writings.
The largest series was printed in Wilno between 1788 and 1790 and consisted
of twelve volumes.[10]

The most typical form of political literature fitting into the above-mentioned
limits were rather short pamphlets, usually several pages to several dozen pages
in length but seldom more than a hundred. Such works assumed various forms,
such as a letter written by a citizen in the provinces to a deputy in Warsaw or
a letter from a deputy to a friend in the countryside. Sometimes letters were
addressed to famous political figures, the best example of which are the *Listy
Anonima* (Anonymous letters) to Marshal Małachowski by Kołłątaj. They
could also be the fictitious correspondence between a father and his deputy
son or a discussion of the most fundamental problems of the Republic by two
individuals living in the distant provinces. Even those in the world beyond
were interested in the Polish government as can be seen from *Dwóch
nieboszczyków...* (Two dead men...)[11] and several other works representing
dialogues by the deceased. Apart from these fictional dialogues, letters or even
wills, there began to appear works which directly addressed the reader from
Warsaw or from the provincial outskirts; and these formed the majority. *Głosy*
(Speeches), *Uwagi* (Considerations), and *Myśli* (Thoughts), as they were
eagerly entitled, were most often printed in Warsaw but also appeared in Wilno,
Cracow and other towns scattered throughout the country.

Although the social status of authors can easily be determined, the
identification of specific surnames presents great difficulties since one
intentional characteristic of these publicist works was their anonymity. Most

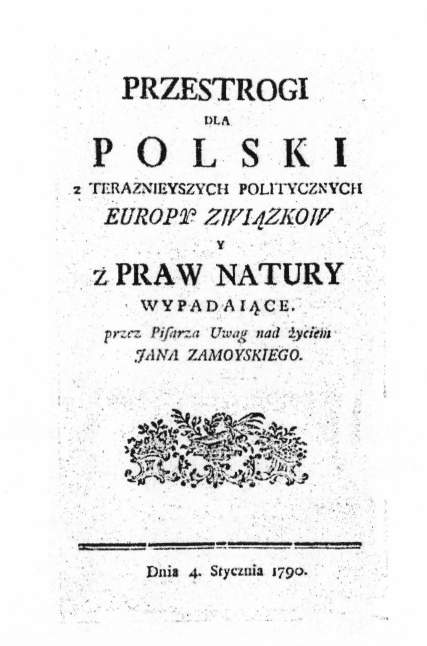

PRZESTROGI

DLA

POLSKI

z TERAZNIEYSZYCH POLITYCZNYCH

EUROPY ZWIĄZKOW

Y

ż PRAW NATURY

WYPADAIĄCE.

przez Pifarza Uwag nad życiem

JANA ZAMOYSKIEGO.

Dnia 4. Stycznia 1790.

Stanisław Staszic, *Przestrogi dla Polski z teraźnieyszych politycznych Europy związków y z praw natury wypadaiące*.... (Warnings for Poland emerging from the current European political alliances and from natural law) n.p. 1790. Title page. (Biblioteka Narodowa, Warszawa).

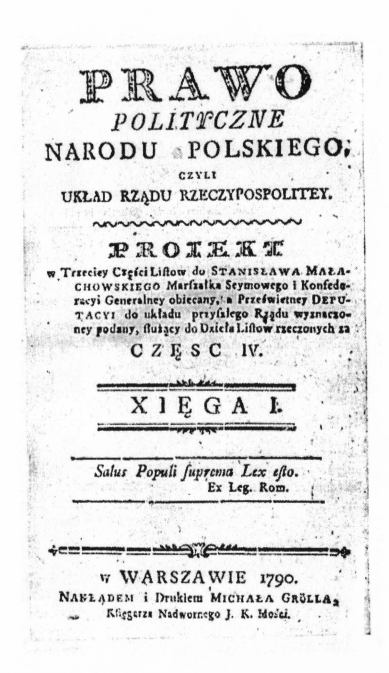

PRAWO

POLITYCZNE
NARODU POLSKIEGO;

CZYLI

UKŁAD RZĄDU RZECZYPOSPOLITEY.

PROIEKT

w Trzeciey Częśći Liſtow do STANISŁAWA MAŁA-
CHOWSKIEGO Marſzałka Seymowego i Konfederacyi Generalney obiecany, a Prześwietney DEPU-
TACYI do układu przyſłego Rządu wyznaczo-
ney podany, ſłużący do Dzieła Liſtow rzeczonych za

CZĘSC IV.

XIĘGA I.

Salus Populi ſuprema Lex eſto.
Ex Leg. Rom.

W WARSZAWIE 1790.
NAKŁADEM i Drukiem MICHAŁA GRÖLLA,
Kſięgarza Nadwornego J. K. Mośći.

Hugo Kołłątaj, *Prawo polityczne narodu polskiego* (Political law of the Polish nation).
W Warszawie. M. Gröll, 1790. Title page. (Biblioteka Narodowa, Warszawa).

titles of this kind were published without the author's name and often without the place of publication or the date. This applies not only to brief leaflets on current events which as a rule appeared without a name (parliamentary speeches being the exception), but also to serious treatises by authors such as Staszic and Kołłątaj. Such a state of affairs was not limited to Poland, but its causes were not always the same as in absolute monarchies. Seldom in Poland was fear of reprisal for overly bold pronouncements the motivating factor for anonymity since no one was threatened by such consequences. Authors who hid their identities were guided by other considerations. Sometimes an author with a known name did not want to influence the assessment of his work by virtue of his fame. One of the anonymous authors in the years preceding the Four-Year Diet stated that his work "was sent without my name, with no other intention than that, freed from prejudice, your mind would consider the work itself and not its author."[12] Often the concealment of a name had another purpose. Given the distrust of the capital, those who usually wrote in Warsaw presented themselves as a "citizen of the province" or a "nobleman from the land." False places of publication sometimes were used to confirm this fiction, suggesting that the work was printed in some distant place in the provinces. Magnates also masked as petty nobles amidst the surge of anti-magnate sentiment. In one of his works, Seweryn Rzewuski presented himself as a citizen of the Podlasie voivodeship.[13] Anonymity could also have another purpose: an author would issue several or maybe even dozens of works under various names to create the impression that his position was supported by many different individuals. Most typical of this kind of political writing is again Seweryn Rzewuski, who issued over twenty works attacking the concept of a hereditary monarchy, though he signed only six of them.[14] Others did the same but on a smaller scale. Ignacy Potocki, one of the joint authors of the Constitution of 3 May, published several brochures defending the new law.

Begun by contemporaries, attempts to identify authors have only been partially successful. Generally the authors of longer works are known, though some are still disputed. The best example of this is the nearly century-old discussion over the authorship of *Myśli polityczne* (Political thoughts), a treatise of undoubted quality published in 1789 and one of the few advocating a monarchist program.[15] Unidentified remain many authors who produced brief brochures, grasping the pen to add their voices to debates on a matter dear to them, and never to be heard of again.

These political works were actually the only commentaries produced on current events. In comparison to the veritable flood of these publications, discussions about political matters in the regular press was paltry. During the years 1788-1792 there was only one Polish language periodical on political matters: *Pamiętnik Historyczno-Polityczny,* edited from1782 by Piotr Świtkowski. It was joined after the convening of the Diet by *Journal Hebdomadaire de la Diète,* published in French by Jan Potocki. Both contained lengthy political analyses and commentaries that were omitted by the press. This situation changed in 1791 with the appearance of the newspaper *Gazeta Narodowa i Obca,* edited by parliamentary activists (I. Potocki, J.U. Niemcewicz and J. Mostowski), which clearly held the political line of the founders and defenders of the Constitution of 3 May.

Journalistic style, its language and manner of presenting a variety of topics, was on a rather high level. As a rule longer works were better since they were usually written by persons who could present their views in a calm and measured manner, often in refined language. This was the specific goal of Kołłątaj, whose works were characterized by clarity of argument and language. This was also true for the books published by the principal opponent of reform and defender of "golden freedom," Hetman Seweryn Rzewuski. There were, it is true, exceptions. The treatises by Leonard Olizar, a provincial politician who opposed all reforms, were so muddled and thick that the reader probably had to put more effort into reading them than the author did writing them.[16] But such works were already an anachronism in which probably only a few were interested. Shorter works were more varied than were longer treatises. Among them were very weak, obscure and stylistically inferior works as well as truly excellent pieces from the literary point of view. In the first group one can point to the inconsistent and unclear writings full of exaggerated republican phraseology by the young defender of royal elections and republican freedom, Wojciech Turski,[17] or those of a leading opponent of the Constitution of 3 May, Jan Suchorzewski.[18] In the other category were *Rozważania o wolności* (Reflections on freedom) by Jan Potocki,[19] the future author of the most famous Polish novel of the period, *Rękopis znaleziony w Saragossie*(Manuscript found at Saragossa), and the venomously ironic and irrefutably logical writings of Franciszek Salezy Jezierski.[20] The majority of authors usually presented their positions fairly clearly but there are lacunae in their arguments or a complete lack of a substantive argument as when, in the heat of the discussion, the writer concentrated on criticizing his opponents. Much space was devoted to this kind of criticism since the writings that appeared during the Four-Year Diet were usually polemical in nature. This was a period of intensified political conflict over governmental models for the state. This fact accounts for the vehemence of public debates which, it should be added, reflected the tone of statements made in the Diet. Criticism of an opponent's position always accompanied the presentation of the writer's own point of view, and this applied even to fundamentally programmatic works such as those by Staszic and Kołłątaj, to name only the most prominent. Greater distance or objectivity can be detected in the more subdued considerations of political and systemic problems in the years leading up to the Four-Year Diet. But no matter how much the author may have been politically involved, and sometimes this partisanship was intense, the works from 1788-92 as a rule aimed at a broader analysis of the Polish system and at prescribing a formula for its correction. This characteristic distinguished it from earlier literature. At moments of intense political struggle, political literature was dominated by works referring to current events and persons, and often exhibited qualities of a lampoon. If mention was made of legal systemic matters, it was in a most general manner, using universally known slogans. Such were the writings of the Bar Confederation in the not too distant past (1768-1772). In less than twenty years political writing not only joined the battle over the shape of the Republic, but it occupied a prominent place. Sometimes the level of political culture of the authors was surprisingly high, as when they freely moved through intricate systemic problems or, when writing about specific matters, they were able to connect them to the overall situation in Poland, or they delved into theoretical considerations. They readily backed their arguments by using examples from Polish history as well as those from foreign countries. Moreover, as Władysław Konopczyński observed, this was a literature so colorful that it is difficult to compare it with anything else in Europe.[21] But the difference was not limited to its colorfulness. Though the main topic of interest was, as in the West, the state, this subject was treated in a completely different manner. In Western Europe, especially France, political literature had a theoretical quality, operating on the level of abstract models, and generalizations had only distant objectives. Polish authors, on the contrary, thought in more practical terms about their state. Considerations of ideal systems and broad theories of state were rare in Polish political writings. Two factors are crucial here. The first is the circumstances in which Poland found itself. The dramatic events of the early 1770s, the governmental crisis caused by the partition, and a heightened sense of danger were not conducive to abstract theory. As participants in the debate about saving the Republic, writers on the period of the Four-Year Diet had as their goal specific, and not theoretical, considerations. In Western Europe, political literature was produced by people who did not have direct influence upon the government--the exception being England[22] --and hence they had no reason to expect that their work would have an effect on the system except, perhaps, in the distant future. Their main goal was to show society that other, better systems were possible. In Poland, the nobility, which produced most of the writers, felt a sense of responsibility for the state, though at times this took the rather odd form of defending the "golden freedom" in its most anarchistic aspect. They had a deep conviction that both the form of government and politics in Poland depended on their will.[23] Publicists wrote with a clear awareness of their political role and an expectation that their writings would have an effect on the government. It was their conscious civic duty to be involved. At the same time the absence of forbidden topics obviated any need for allegory or camouflage. Consequently there are few descriptions of imaginary systems or governments so removed that they could easily be molded at will by the author. Concrete problems in the Polish government which demanded immediate solutions were discussed, not issues in the distant future. This applied not only to leaflets but also to serious treatises containing full reform programs; alongside theoretical considerations there were always particular solutions which their authors thought could be implemented without delay. This sense of responsibility for the state also caused some authors to develop, along with very specific matters, comprehensive visions of what they deemed to be necessary changes in the Polish government.

The form of government was the primary subject of political discussions. This included above all the question of governmental authority, its relationship to the nation, understood either as the nobility or, as was increasingly the case, all the citizens, and the organization of and relations between legislative and executive powers. However, all topics which either were raised in parliamentary debates or interested the wider public, were included in political discussions. Be it foreign policy or the alliance with Prussia, the organization of parliamentary courts, taxes or the prosecution of the traitor Poniński, the army, education, the role of the clergy, freedom of the press or paper money, there was always one author or more often several authors who had an opinion to voice. To create order in this apparent chaos, several great debates may be isolated from this flood of print. This is possible because even though public debate continued throughout the Four-Year Diet, its intensity and subject matter changed. The first great polemical battle began before the opening of the Diet and was continued during its first months. The work that began this discussion was undoubtedly *Uwagi nad życiem Jana Zamoyskiego* (Remarks on the life of Jan Zamoyski) published by Staszic in March 1787.[24] This preparatory period lasted until the end of 1788. Titles of leaflets suggest the most important questions at that time: "What needs to be passed by this Diet?"[25]   "What will happen to us?" "What should be our first concern?"[26] An awareness of the growing external danger and of the importance of decisions to be taken by the upcoming Diet as well as the conviction that change was

Julian Ursyn Niémcewicz, copperplate by A. Bozza. (Muzeum Narodowe w Warszawie). Reprinted from: *Polska jej dzieje i kultura*, v.2 (Warszawa, 1930).

Julian Ursyn Niemcewicz, *Powrót posła* (Return of the deputy) Warszawa, M. Gröll, 1790. Title page.

necessary in the structure of government were all very strongly evident. Authors attempted to present comprehensive reform programs.[27] The two outstanding political treatises of the Four-Year Diet, and the most extensive, Staszic's *Uwagi* and Kołłątaj's *Listy Anonima*, arose from a concern for the continued existence of the Republic.[28] Both writers provided critical analyses of the existing situation and attempted to present the most comprehensive vision possible for political and social reforms. Their goals converged despite great differences of form and certain differences in their programs. They postulated the creation of an efficient governmental apparatus primarily through reform of the Diet and the local dietines: elimination of the *liberum veto*, extension of terms, a "standing Diet" or even a continuous Diet. In addition, they offered suggestions for the improvement of the executive branch which, still in the good Polish tradition, would remain answerable to the legislature, and they argued for the introduction of a hereditary monarchy, though Staszic did this contrary to his own convictions. These were clearly republican programs despite this last provision. According to both authors, even a hereditary monarch would be deprived of real power; at the most he would supervise the executive bodies ("oversee authority" according to Kołłątaj). A crucial point in both programs was the enfranchisement of townspeople and their admission to the Diet. In Staszic's view they would join the nobility in the same chamber; for Kołłątaj, townspeople would form a separate chamber, "the Commons" following the English model. This would help to replace the nation of noblemen with a unitary "nation of property owners." In time even peasants would be admitted, though initial discussion only discussed granting them personal freedom.

This, of course, is an oversimplification of the two programs, which covered the spheres of political, social and, to some extent, economic life in the Republic. The variety of issues treated in these works is shown by the number of polemics they evoked. This is particularly evident in the series of articles prompted by Staszic's *Uwagi*. Apart from works discussing major questions, such as the form of the government, reform of the Diet or succession, they also agreed or disagreed with Staszic on matters such as education, the army, taxes, role of the clergy, etc. Directly or indirectly, this single book spawned over twenty substantive works or leaflets, which were sometimes issued in collected volumes by publishers.[29]

Though quite lively, discussions prior to the convening of the Diet did not equal either in extent or ferocity the dogged publicistic battles during the Four-Year Diet concerning succession. This debate raged from the end of 1789 through 1790, though the topic remained current throughout the entire Diet. The choice between a hereditary and an elected monarchy became the subject of fierce political battles within and outside of the Diet.[30] The heated discussion in Warsaw enveloped the provincial nobility, which according to a decision taken by the Diet in early fall, 1790 was to be asked about their opinion on this matter. This did not occur, however. The local dietines in November only voiced their opinions on the issue of the candidacy of the Elector of Saxony for the Polish throne, but by this time the entire nobility was interested in the matter. The ferocity of the over one hundred published polemics, unusual even for those politicized times, is understandable since in essence this debate touched on matters fundamental to noble writers and their readers: Polish freedom. Defenders of the election regarded the selection of the king by the citizenry as one of the fundamental rights guaranteeing a free political system in the Republic, which they continued to identify with the nobility. Relinquishment of this right, in their opinion, would necessarily cause the Republic to be replaced by a monarchy, which they identified with despotism and bondage. Spokesmen favoring a hereditary monarchy understood freedom more as the right of the nation to choose its own direction, and in their opinion a hereditary throne accepted by the nation would not compromise this freedom, especially since the king would not have much power. Such a step might even help to safeguard freedom by avoiding stormy interregna, by providing for a continuity of government, and by improving Poland's position in monarchical Europe. Works published at this time often supplemented a discussion of the strengths and weaknesses of both systems with a presentation of broader reform programs deemed necessary for the government. Once again the two greatest authors, Staszic and Kołłątaj, joined the debate.[31] Adam Wawrzyniec Rzewuski backed the concept of republican reform together with the preservation of the practice of "free election."[32] The most radical republicans even proposed the abolition of the monarchy.[33] Almost every author who reached for a pen felt the need to comment on this issue. The loudest controversy, however, was caused by the demagogic, though expertly edited, work by Hetman Seweryn Rzewuski, *O sukcesyi tronu w Polszcze rzecz krótka* (A short essay on the succession to the throne in Poland).[34] Kołłątaj, Franciszek Salezy Jezierski, the old Bishop Adam Krasiński and many others issued replies. These were in turn challenged by adherents of Rzewuski and by Rzewuski himself, which evoked still new replies; in this way a whole series of polemics developed with escalating ferocity which finally led to personal attacks.[35]

Foreign models were also utilized in the heat of the debate. Most often these were used by proponents of a hereditary monarchy. The English system was particularly favored. It was at once the system best known by Polish authors and the one causing the greatest controversy. There was hardly a single publication that failed to mention the English system and there were some works which were devoted exclusively to England.[36] Both interest and debate were caused by the position that England was proof of the possibility of a hereditary monarchy in a free country. Opponents of a hereditary system questioned this freedom. Both sides showed a good, even detailed knowledge of the English government. Republicans used the United States to show that a large state could exist without a monarchy. Those in favor of succession countered by pointing to the extensive powers of the American president (greater than those of the Polish king), the different geographic position of the distant and newly born democracy, and sometimes to the different social base of its government.[37] The discussion about hereditary monarchy began to wane by the end of 1790, though several pieces on the topic appeared in early 1791. The end came with the Constitution of 3 May, which evoked a new wave of public debate. The new polemics differed from the previous ones above all by abandoning the realm of theory which was then to be put into practice. Programs were replaced by concrete practice which simultaneously bore the weight of the law. Perhaps this explains the absence of outstanding works such as those produced earlier by Staszic, Kołłątaj or Rzewuski. The goal of the public debate ceased to be the determination of the proper direction for repair of the Republic; it was replaced by a fierce discussion of whether or not what had been done actually was a solution. The problem of freedom returned, this time in the form of the question of whether the Constitution of 3 May destroyed freedom or safeguarded it. The majority of the pamphlets defended the Constitution, presenting the reader with its benefits. Partly this was the result of an organized propaganda effort by the framers of the Constitution, some of whom reached for the pen,[38] and partly this came from the personal conviction of individual authors. Though more difficult to verify, the same seems also to have been the case with the writings opposing the Constitution. Only a few pieces are known to have been inspired by future Targowicians. To these belong the most effective attack on the Constitution, *Uwagi* (Observations) by Dyzma Bończa Tomaszewski.[39]

Worthy of notice in this discussion are the persuasive arguments comparing the Constitution to other similar acts. These were used by defenders of the Constitution, who proudly underlined the fact that the Polish Constitution was one of the three written constitutions, the second after the American. The unwritten English constitution was also included. These fundamental laws were presented by the *Kalendarzyk polityczny na rok przestępny 1792* (Little political calendar for the leap year 1792), beginning with the oldest constitution, the English (its non-legal status was not differentiated) and continuously with

SEWERYNA RZEWUSKIEGO

HETMANA

POLNEGO KORONNEGO

O

SUKCESSYI

TRONU W POLSZCZE

RZECZ KRÓTKA.

W Amſterdamie 1789 Ru.

Seweryn Rzewuski, *O sukcessyi tronu w Polszcze rzecz krótka* (A short essay on the succession to the throne in Poland). (Amsterdam, 1789) Dresden 1790. Title page. (Biblioteka Narodowa, Warszawa).

ZASZCZYT
WOLNOSCI
POLSKIEY
ANGIELSKIEY WYROWNYWAIĄCY.

Z

UWAGAMI DO TEGO STOSOWNEMI

i OPISANIEM RZĄDU

ANGIELSKIEGO.

w WARSZAWIE,

u P. Dufour Konsyl: Nadwor: Druk: J. K. Mci
i Rzpltey, Dyrektora Druk: Korp: Kad:

M. DCC. LXXXIX.

Ignacy Łobarzewski. *Zaszczyt wolności polskiey angielskiey wyrownywający...* (The distinction of Polish freedom equaling that of the English). Warszawa, P. Dufour, 1789. Title page. (Biblioteka Narodowa, Warszawa).

the American, the Polish and the French: "We compare our Government Statute with the constitutions of free nations. In this group there are four constitutions: the English, which served as a model for others; the American, which sprung from it; the Polish, which benefitted from both; and, finally, the French, which had all three as models."[40] The supporters of the Constitution rather willingly pointed to the ties with the other three constitutions. They also invoked its framers, though more so those of the American Constitution than the French, which they regarded as the work not of individuals but of the National Assembly. Perhaps the most famous individuals in the political writings of the day were Franklin and Washington, whose names even appeared in the sermon by Father Michał Karpowicz at the dietine in Preny.[41] The publishers of the *Gazeta Narodowa i Obca* effectively took advantage of the warm feelings expressed for these two Founding Fathers by reprinting a letter from Benjamin Franklin to the Convention stating that despite many reservations he signed the Constitution in the interests of national unity.[42] The defenders of the Constitution of 3 May used the same slogan.

In the end, public discussion on the Constitution died out when in February 1792 the dietines gave their support to the Constitution.[43] The debate over the Constitution was the last great public political struggle of the Four-Year Diet. There were, however, other important topics that were discussed throughout the entire Diet. The most important of them, those concerning the rights for townspeople and the peasant question, were already mentioned in discussion on Staszic and Kołłątaj. Social questions evoked less interest than problems dealing with the political system and neither equaled the intensity of those which touched on constitutional problems.

The issue of extending personal freedom to the peasants and, in general, their place in a state where nobles held a privileged position were presented with some hesitation. The published material dealing with this topic is notable not because of its volume or propagandistic value, but because of its intrinsic importance. As shown by Władysław Konopczyński, in most discussions on this topic "there was a large gap between accusations which were full of pathos and practical solutions for the future."[44] Indeed, reform programs usually paled in comparison with the often dramatic descriptions of peasant poverty. Franciszek Salezy Jezierski offered the most explicit commentaries on the lot of the serfs but he did not offer any solutions since this was not the purpose of the *Katechizm...* (Catechism...).[45] Apart from parenthetical mention in discussions of other issues or in larger works - especially those of Staszic - a few dozen brief leaflets analyzed, from various perspectives, the question of personal freedom for the peasant, their relationship to the landowner and relevant laws and obligations.[46] Undoubtedly the best work on the topic was Józef

Pawlikowski's *O poddanych polskich* (Concerning Polish serfs), published anonymously.[47] It did not limit itself to a simple presentation of the peasant question but offered specific proposals: the conferment of personal freedom, the handing over to them of land either as leased or absolute property according to precise rental agreements with the landlord, and finally, abolition of manorial courts. Pawlikowski's book provided some public discussion,[48] but this discussion stood on the fringes of the main currents of political debate.[49] Characteristically, Pawlikowski only minimally directed his proposals for peasant reform at the state. Pawlikowski, like other authors, did not so much call for decisions from a superior governmental body as he did for the nobles themselves to improve the situation of peasants on their estates. For some of the authors and the majority of their readers, peasant matters were the private concern of landowners, and any form of action from above would be considered interference and a violation of property rights. Arguments were tailored to this viewpoint. Thus, apart from general discussions of the natural right of the individual to self-determination, there appeared and even dominated more practical arguments about the cost of serfdom to the nobility and the profits for the individual landowner and the country as a whole that would accrue from emancipation and the conversion to lease holdings. Western economic theory, be it physiocratic or cameralist, was readily used to argue that development of agriculture, population, and national power would come with a solution of the peasant question. Opponents of change in the lord-peasant relationship sometimes wrote that peasants were unfit for the demands of freedom, but more often they simply stated that no one had the right to interfere with the private affairs of the nobility. The matter was so delicate that even those authors and politicians who recognized the necessity of social reform expressed themselves very carefully, not wishing to alienate the middle nobility, whose support was crucial for the more immediately important political reforms. Typical was Kołłątaj, who recognized the importance of the peasant question, but who postponed its resolution to the time when, following political reforms, Poland would be strong enough for unpopular social reforms.

The burgher question provoked greater interest and more heated debate. Not only did it concern the issue of conferring civil rights on townspeople - on this issue there was general, unqualified consensus - but it also concerned an extension to them of political rights, circumscribed though they might be. Such a step would break the noble monopoly on political power and hence the question, "Does perfecting our political system require the admittance of plebeians into the legislative process?"[50] evoked strong emotions. This was also the only public debate in which non-noble authors approached the nobility demanding their rights, sometimes quite sharply. Not only did famous thinkers demand acceptance of townspeople in the Diet in the name of modernity but so did the townspeople themselves. In part this action was organized; the municipal government of Warsaw already in 1789 financed the publication of works and brochures defending the bourgeois position.[51] In arguing for access to offices and to military commissions, for personal inviolability and inclusion in lawmaking, townspeople referred back to their ancient rights which, owing to the powerful cult of the past, was a weighty argument for the nobility. The end of 1788 saw the preparation of *Wiadomość o pierwiastkowej miast zasadzie w Polszcze* (Remarks on the ancient principles for towns in Poland).[52] The famous *Memoriał* (Memorandum) presented to the King and the Diet by the cities in late 1789 also used historical arguments.[53] Later the cities used the same arguments in a publication for the special Commission established by the Diet: *Zbiór praw, dowodów i uwag z treści tychże wynikających dla objaśnienia zaszczytów stanowi miejskiemu ex iuribus municipalibus służących* (Collection of laws, proofs and observations serving to explain municipal privileges resulting ex iuribus municipalibus).[54]

Apart from these semi-official works, there were more propagandistic ones. At the forefront of bourgeois authors was Jan Baudouin de Courtenay with his spirited and sometimes passionate small books. He used the most factual arguments in favor of civil and political rights for the townspeople. Not restricting himself to historical argumentation, de Courtenay referred to the more modern concepts of person and citizen for which the privileges of a single estate at the expense of others were a contradiction. The best proof of his talent at disputation was his reply to the aggressive and hostile speech by the castellan Jacek Jezierski which de Courtenay entitled, *Bezstronne zastanowienia się nad mową J. W. Jezierskiego kasztelana łukowskiego mianą na sejmie dnia 15 grudnia 1789 przeciwko mieszczanom* (Impartial reflections on the speech given in the Diet against townspeople by the castellan of Łuków, His Honor Jezierski on December 15, 1789).[55] Others, not always bourgeois writers, demanded the right of townspeople to help determine their own fate and that of the country of which they were citizens. The nobility was also shown that republican systems of which they approved, such as Switzerland, Holland and the United States, admitted members of the lower classes into the government. The most dramatic appeal for bourgeois rights appeared in the letter-testament addressed to the Marshal of the Diet, Stanisław Małachowski, by the President of Warsaw, Jan Dekert, shortly before his death.[56] It threatened the Polish nobility with a fate similar to that of the French nobility should it ignore bourgeois demands.

The leading activists in the Diet joined bourgeois writers in the defense of the rights of this estate, pointing out not only the injustice of the present situation but also the benefits to the Republic from the development of cities.[57] The most active was Kołłątaj who cooperated with bourgeois activists and who was co-author of the Memorandum of the Cities. He took part both in political battles to pass reforms on the cities and in public debates on the same topic. In the latter, he was assisted by a group of authors, with Franciszek Salezy Jezierski at the fore, known as "Kołłątaj's Forge." In their writings, they argued in favor of a law for the full participation of the bourgeoisie in economics and public life and, to influence their noble readers, they wrote about the benefits that would accrue to the country and to the nobility itself.

Individuals who, like Jacek Jezierski, opposed extending rights to the townspeople demonstrated poorer writing skills and used weaker arguments. Their attack was primarily against the admittance of bourgeois representatives to the Parliament, a step that would infringe on the nobles' sovereignty and, as they warned, could become a tool of royal despotism.

Discussion of the bourgeois question died out in April 1791 with the passage of the Law on Cities, which conferred on townspeople full civil but only very limited political rights.

Though the topics discussed above had the most interest to writers during the Four-Year Diet, it should be emphasized once again that such public debates constituted only a fragment of the great discussion over the shape of the Republic which began many years prior to the Four-Year Diet and which reached its peak at that time. It might be worthwhile to mention again the use of foreign models in the debate. Their use shows both a solid knowledge among Polish authors of other political systems and their skill in utilizing these examples in the propaganda battles. "Europe" was always present in the public debates of this time. Particularly well known at this time were systems of government and their specific organization in so-called free states where people took part in making laws, that is, in those countries with representative bodies. The governments of such countries like England, Holland, Switzerland, the United States and the Italian republics were regarded as, in some sense, similar to Poland's and therefore available as models. Though the might of absolute monarchies was held in awe, there was no question of emulating them, since in those countries there was no freedom. As mentioned previously, the best known example of a free state was England. Though the others did not evoke the same emotion, two did exert a strong attraction--Switzerland and the United States. Foreign examples were used by everyone from the most outstanding authors to the most mediocre ones, and predominated in the latter since such citation tended to hide a lack of their own ideas concerning the Polish political system. Foreign examples offered weighty arguments, and the fierce debates about them attested to their importance.

Positions in the public debate in and outside of the Four-Year Diet, for all their variety and often contradictory nature, nonetheless had one common characteristic. They all believed in a republican system, whether they foresaw the preservation of the monarchy, or, more rarely, its abolition. They revealed most of all a deep and universal conviction that sovereignty resided in the people, the source of all authority. Consequently, the most prominent role was accorded to the elected legislative body to which executive authority was to be subordinated. Programs designed to strengthen the executive branch or even to hand it over to the king were the rare exception. It should be remembered that Polish publicists, regardless of how far their proposals departed from obligatory laws or practice, wished only to repair the existing governmental system of the Republic, not to destroy it. Perhaps this is why no foreign theory or political system was accepted totally. They borrowed, sometimes verbatim, what would fit into the Polish situation or into their own arguments, but "the main principles of the reformed system were drawn...from their own political traditions."[58] Polish political writers believed that their writings would play an important role in the formation of public attitudes, that they would "teach the art of governing." The fact that publicistic activity supplemented their political activism demonstrates how strongly they were convinced of the social power of this type of literature. Such was the case not only with Kołłątaj and Ignacy Potocki, but also with Seweryn Rzewuski and Szczęsny Potocki. Numerous reprints show that they were right in believing that this type of literature was read; the frequently fierce polemics indicate that they aroused keen interest. It was precisely this public discussion which changed the understanding of the idea of a free republic. It prepared the nobility to accept the May revolution and the changes in the governmental system, including the introduction of a hereditary monarchy.

Notes

1. "Unofficial literature in manuscript form almost totally took the place of official publications through the entire reign of August II and, to a large extent, during that of August III," in Juliusz Nowak-Dłużewski, "Staropolska literatura polityczna, jej charakter i postulaty wydawnicze" (Old Polish political literature, its character and publishing aims), *Przegląd Humanistyczny 2 (1958): 42;* Władysław Konopczyński, *Polscy pisarze polityczni XVIII wieku (do Sejmu Czteroletniego)* (Polish political writers of the 18th century up to the Four-Year Diet) (Warszawa: PWN, 1966), p 269.

2. See Bernard Krakowski, "Nad zagadkami Sejmu Czteroletniego" (Concerning puzzles of the Four-Year Diet), *Zeszyty Naukowe Wydziału Humanistycznego Uniwersytetu Gdańskiego*. Prace historyczno-literackie 3 (1974).

3. Bogusław Leśnodorski, ed. *Kuźnica Kołłątajowska. Wybór źródeł* (Kołłątaj's Forge: selected sources) (Wrocław: Ossolineum, 1949), p. 73.

4. Roman Pilat, *O literaturze politycznej Sejmu Czteroletniego* (On the political literature of the Four-Year Diet) (Kraków, 1872),p. 5. To date this is the most extensive work on the subject since the second part of "Polscy pisarze polityczni XVIII wieku" (Polish political writers of the 18th century) by Władysław Konopczyński which covers the writers of the Four-Year Diet and remains unpublished, Jagiellonian Library, BJ no. 52/61.

5. Based on an examination of all the Enlightenment writers born after 1730, barely 28% were townspeople. In respect to all political writers this percentage was much lower. See, Elżbieta Aleksandrowska, "Pisarze - generacje i rodowód społeczny" (Writers: generations and social origins), in *Słownik literatury polskiego Oświecenia* (Wrocław: Ossolineum, 1991), p. 405; concerning the reading public see, among others, Zbigniew Goliński, "Publicystyka" (Political literature) in *Słownik*, p. 492.

6. See for example, article 5, "All power in civil society should derive from the will of the people," or the opening of article 4, "The agricultural class of people, the most numerous in the nation, consequently forming the most considerable part of its force, from whose hands flows the source of our riches, we receive under the protection of national law and government." Quoted from: *New Constitution of the Government of Poland, established by the Revolution, the Third of May,* (London, 1791).

7. The two most famous examples are works by Julian Ursyn Niemcewicz, *Powrót posła* (Return of the Deputy) (1790) publicizing the policies of the "Patriotic Party" and *Kazimierz Wielki* (Casimir the Great) (1792) written as part of the celebration of the first anniversary of the Constitution of 3 May.

8. *Głos obywatela dobrze swej ojczyźnie życzącego do Narodu Polskiego, z dobrem publicznym przeciwko prywatnemu i wszelkiej niesłuszności dla krótszego w nim rzeczy zebranych wyrazu rymem ułożony* (The voice of a citizen wishing his fatherland well to the Polish Nation, to the public good against private and all injustice [and] written in rhyme to more briefly express the subjects included) (Kalisz, 1788).

9. [Franciszek Salezy Jezierski], *Ktoś piszący z Warszawy dnia 11 lutego 1790 r.* (Someone writing from Warsaw on February 11, 1790), n.p. and n.d., pp. 17ff; see also, *Listy do przyjaciela* (Letters to a friend), n.p. (1789), pp. 1ff and [Franciszek Jaxa Makulski], *Czamarka i sarafan w czasie sejmu patriotycznego w Polskę wprowadzone* (Old style Polish overcoat and sarafan introduced into Poland during the patriotic Diet) (Warszawa, 1791), p. 11.

10. *Zbiór mów i pism niektórych w czasie sejmu stanów skonfederowanych* (Collection of selected speeches and writings during the Diet of the confederated states), vols. 1-12 (Wilno, 1788-1790).

11. *Dwóch nieboszczyków. Dekert z ministrem o miastach* (Two dead men: Dekert with a minister about towns), n.p. [1791].

12. [Franciszek Bieliński], *Sposób edukacji w XV listach opisany, które do Komisyi Edukacji Narodowej od bezimiennego autora przesłane* (Educational method described in 15 letters and sent to the Commission for National Education by an anonymous author), n.p. (1775), p. 15.

13. *O polepszeniu sposobu elekcji królów polskich. Myśli obywatela ... 1788 roku* (On improving the method of electing Polish kings: Thoughts of a citizen ... [from] 1788), n.p., n.d.

14. Zofia Zielińska, *Republikanizm spod znaku buławy. Publicystyka Seweryna Rzewuskiego z lat 1788-1790* (Republicanism from under the banner of the hetman's mace: The polemical literature of Seweryn Rzewuski from 1788-1790) (Warszawa: University of Warsaw, 1988).

15. Emanuel Rostworowski, "Myśli polityczne Józefa Pawlikowskiego" (The political thoughts of Józef Pawlikowski), in *Legendy i fakty XVIII w.* (Warszawa: PWN, 1963), pp. 198ff.

16. The baroque title of the largest of Olizar's works indicates their style: *Co uważać ma Rzeczpospolita Polska w prawodawstwie, tak przed dopuszczeniem jako i po dopuszczeniu składu rządu angielskiego, stanu politycznego różnice i podobieństwa między sobą tych dwóch wolnych państw stosując....* (What the Polish Republic should be attentive to in legislation both before the inauguration and after the acceptance of the English form of government, comparing the differences and similarities in the type of the political state of these two free states) [Studenica, 1791].

17. Wojciech Turski, *Myśli o królach, o sukcesyi, o przeszłym i przyszłym rządzie* (Thoughts concerning kings, succession, past and present governments) (Warszawa, 1790); and *Odpowiedź na dzieło Ks. Hugona Kołłątaja referendarza W. Ks. Litewskiego. Uwagi nad pismem etc.* (Reply to the work by Hugo Kołłątaj referendary of the Grand Duchy of Lithuania. Observations on the work, etc.) (Warszawa, 1790).

18. Jan Suchorzewski, *Odezwa do narodu wraz z protestacją dla śladu gwałtu i przemocy, do której w całym prawie sejmie zbliżano, a w dniu trzecim maja 1791 dokonano* (Appeal to the nation accompanied by a protest against the signs of coercion and violence towards which almost the entire Diet tended and which were accomplished on May 3, 1791), n.p. [1791].

19. [Jan Potocki], *Essay d'aphorismes sur la liberté* [Warszawa, 1791]; Emanuel Rostworowski, "Dwa pisma polityczne Jana Potockiego" (Two political treatises by Jan Potocki) in *Wiek XVIII. Polska i świat* (Warszawa: PIW, 1974), pp. 85ff.

20. [F.S. Jezierski], *O bezkrólewiach w Polszcze i o wybieraniu królów...* (Concerning interregna in Poland and the election of kings...) (Warszawa, 1790); and *Katechizm o tajemnicach rządu polskiego...* (A catechism of the secrets of the Polish government...) [Warszawa, 1790] and others.

21. Konopczyński, "Polscy pisarze polityczni XVIII wieku," MS. Jagiellonian Library, BJ, no. 52/61 p. 444.

22. Paul Hazard, *European Thought in the Eighteenth Century from Montesquieu to Lessing* (New Haven: Yale University Press, 1954), pp. 156, 173.

23. Typical was the wording used by one of the deputies to the 1784 Diet: "...magistratury [urzędy] nam się sprawują, my samemu Bogu" (State offices are beholden to us, we are beholden only to God) in a speech by Szymon Zabiełło, October 27, 1784, in *Zbiór mów w czasie sejmu 6 niedzielnego roku 1784 mianych w Grodnie* (Collected speeches from the six week Diet in Grodno in 1784) (Wilno [1785]), p. 432.

24. Stanisław Staszic, *Uwagi nad życiem Jana Zamoyskiego kanclerza i hetmana wielkiego do dzisiejszego stanu Rzeczypospolitej polskiej przystosowane* (Remarks on the life of Jan Zamoyski, Chancellor and Great Hetman, applied to the current state of the Polish Commonwealth) (n.p. 1787), reprinted by Stefan Czarnowski (Kraków, 1926).

25. *Co na tym sejmie koniecznie ustanowić potrzeba*, n.p. n.d.

26. Full title: *Do sejmu. Co się z nami stanie? Co nam we wszystkich działaniach na pierwszej uwadze mieć należy*, n.p. n.d.

27. The more interesting works which appeared at this time were Stanisław Potocki, *Myśli o ogólnej poprawie rządu krajowego* (Thoughts on a general improvement of the country's government), n.p. (1788), French edition (1789), reprinted by Łukasz Kądziela in *Kołłątaj i inni. Z publicystyki doby Sejmu Czteroletniego* (Kołłątaj and others: From the political literature of the time of the Four-Year Diet) (Warszawa: Wyd. Szkolne i Pedagogiczne, 1991); anonymous, *Głos obywatela dobrze swej ojczyźnie życzącego...* (A voice of a citizen wishing his fatherland well) (Kalisz, 1788); *Myśli patriotyczno-polityczne do stanów Rzeczpospolitej Polskiej na sejm 1788 roku zgromadzonych, przez obywatela o wolności samowładztwo Rzeczpospolitej swojej gorliwego* (Patriotic political thoughts to the states of the Polish Commonwealth gathered in the 1788 Diet from a citizen concerned about freedom and the independence of his Commonwealth), n.p. n.d.

28. The full title of the first part, which appeared prior to the opening of the Diet, was *Do Stanisława Małachowskiego referendarza koronnego o przyszłym sejmie Anonima listów kilka* (Several letters by an anonymous author to Stanisław Małachowski, crown referendary, about the upcoming Diet); the next was entitled, *Do...marszałka sejmowego i konfederacji generalnej Anonima listów kilka* (To ... the Marshal of the Diet and the general confederation, several letters from an anonymous author), n.p. (1788), reprinted by Bogusław Leśnodorski and Helena Wereszycka in *Listy Anonima i Prawo polityczne narodu polskiego* (Warszawa: PWN, 1954).

29. Michał Gröll did this by publishing eight short works under the common title, *Zbiór pism do których były powodem Uwagi nad życiem Jana Zamoyskiego* (A collection of works which were prompted by the Remarks on the Life of Jan Zamoyski)

(Warszawa, 1788); a list of these works is provided in Wilhelm Hahn, *Stanisław Staszic, życie i dzieło* (Stanisław Staszic: life and work) (Lublin, 1926), pp. 36ff.

30. Zofia Zielińska, *"O sukcesyi tronu w Polszcze" 1787-1790* (On the succession to the throne in Poland 1787-1790) (Warszawa: PWN, 1991).

31. Stanisław Staszic, *Przestrogi dla Polski z teraźniejszych politycznych Europy związków i z praw natury wypadające, przez pisarza Uwag nad życiem Jana Zamoyskiego* (Warnings for Poland emerging from the current European political alliances and from natural law, by the author of Remarks on the life of Jan Zamoyski), n.p. (1790), reprinted by Stefan Czarnowski (Kraków, 1926); Hugo Kołłątaj, *Prawo polityczne narodu polskiego* (Political law of the Polish nation) (Warszawa, 1790), reprinted by Bogusław Leśnodorski and Helena Wereszycka (Warszawa: PWN, 1954) and *Ostatnia przestroga dla Polski* (Last warning for Poland) (Warszawa, 1790), reprinted by Kądziela in *Kołłątaj i inni.*

32. Adam Wawrzyniec Rzewuski, *O formie rządu republikańskiego myśli* (Thoughts about the form of a republican government) (Warszawa, 1790).

33. [Gabriel Taszycki], *Projekt bezkrólewia wiecznego* (Project for a permanent interregnum), n.p. (1790).

34. This was published in January 1790 in Dresden with Amsterdam incorrectly given as the place of publication; several printings followed.

35. For a full discussion of these polemics see Zielińska, *Republikanizm spod znaku buławy*; see also Zielińska, "Publicystyka pro- i antysukcesyjna w początkach Sejmu Czteroletniego" (Pro- and anti-succession literature at the beginning of the Four-Year Diet) in *Sejm Czteroletni i jego tradycje*, ed. Jerzy Kowecki (Warszawa: PWN, 1991).

36. [Ignacy Łobarzewski], *Zaszczyt wolności polskiej angielskiej wyrównywający ....* (The distinction of Polish freedom equaling that of the English) Warszawa, 1789; Leonard Wołczkiewicz Olizar, *Uwagi nad rządem angielskim i inne dla wolnego narodu użyteczne* (Observations on the English government and other matters useful to a free nation) n.p. (1791).

37. Anna Grześkowiak-Krwawicz, "Obce wzory ustrojowe w dyskusjach publicystycznych Sejmu Czteroletniego" (Foreign systemic models in the public debates during the Four-Year Diet) in *Sejm Czteroletni i jego tradycje*, p. 86.

38. Such was the case with Ignacy Potocki, who anonymously published three works: *Na usprawiedliwienie się Jaśnie Wielmożnego Imci pana Dłuskiego podkomorzego i posła województwa lubelskiego z manifestu przeciwko Ustawie 3 Maja roku 1791 ... odpowiedź* (For the justification of His Honorable Sir Dłuski chamberlain and deputy from Lublin, in (his) protest against the 3 May 1791 Statute ... a reply), n.p. [1791]; *Na pismo, któremu napis "O Konstytucji 3 Maja 1791"... odpowiedź* (A reply to a piece entitled, "About the Constitution of 3 May 1791," n.p. [1791]; *Do obywatelów po odbytych sejmikach* (To the citizenry after the completed dietines), n.p. [1792]. Reprinted by Anna Grześkowiak-Krwawicz in *Za i przeciw Ustawie Rządowej.*

Antologia. (For or against the Government Statute. An anthology). (Warszawa: IBL, 1992).

39. Dyzma Bończa Tomaszewski, *Nad Konstytucją i rewolucją dnia 3 Maja uwagi* (Observations on the Constitution and the Revolution of May 3rd), n.p. [1791]; Antoni Trębicki disputed this in, *Odpowiedź autorowi prawdziwemu "Uwag"...* (Reply to the true author of "Observations"), n.p. [1792]. Reprinted by Grześkowiak-Krwawicz in *Za i przeciw.*

40. *Kalendarzyk polityczny...* (The little political calendar) (Warszawa [1791]).

41. Michał Karpowicz, *Kazanie na pierwszym zafundowaniu powiatu prenskiego ... 14 lutego 1792 roku* (A sermon on the occasion of the founding of the first dietine in the Prenski district ... February 14, 1792) (Warszawa, 1792).

42. *Gazeta Narodowa i Obca,* 46, June 8, 1791.

43. See Grześkowiak-Krwawicz, "Walka publicystyczna o Konstytucję 3 Maja" (The publicistic battle over the Constitution of 3 May) in *Sejm Czteroletni i jego tradycje.*

44. Konopczyński, "Polscy pisarze ....," MS. Jagiellonian Library, BJ., no. 52/61, p. 291.

45. "Question: Is the peasant-farmer in Poland not a person? Answer: Definitely he is not. Question: How can this be if he has a soul and a body and by nature is an individual like a nobleman? Answer: The peasant in Poland has only the attributes of a soul and a body, but his personage is not a person but rather the property of the nobleman who being the sole lord over the peasant, can sell, buy or use him for his own profit, just as cattle is sold with estates and inventories." Franciszek Salezy Jezierski, *Katechizm o tajemnicach rządu polskiego....*

46. See Janusz Woliński, Jerzy Michalski, Emanuel Rostworowski, eds., *Materiały do dziejów Sejmu Czteroletniego* (hereafter MDSC) (Sources related to the history of the Four-Year Diet) (Wrocław: Ossolineum, 1959) vol 1.

47. [Józef Pawlikowski], *O poddanych polskich* (On Polish serfs) (Kraków, 1788) reprinted in MDSC, vol. 1.

48. It consisted of three brief pieces: [Dawid Pilchowski], *Odpowiedź na pytanie izaliż nieczułość w dawnych wiekach ... czyli dodatek do książki o poddanych polskich* (Reply to the question (was there) an absence of sensitivity in ages past ... or an addendum to the book on Polish serfs), n.p. (1789). This work disputes some of Pawlikowski's opinions but agrees with the book's main arguments; Ignacy Grabowski, *Dopytanie się u przodków czułości ku poddanym* (An inquiry concerning our ancestors' sensitivity towards serfs) n.p. [1789]. This work opposed rights for peasants; and, anonymous, *Uwagi praktyczne o poddanych polskich, względem ich wolności i niewoli* (Practical observations about Polish serfs concerning their freedom and bondage) (Warsaw, 1790). All three are reprinted in MDSC, vol. 1.

49. Konopczyński, "Polscy pisarze..." (MS. Jagiellonian Library, BJ. 52/61, p. 311.

50. Maurycy Franciszek Karp, *Pytanie i odpowiedź... czy do doskonałości konstytucji politycznej państwa naszego koniecznie potrzeba, aby gmin miał uczastek w prawodawstwie...* n.p., n.d. reprinted in MDSC, vol. 1.

51. Władysław Smoleński, *Mieszczaństwo warszawskie w końcu wieku XVIII* (Warsaw townspeople at the end of the 18th century), 2nd ed. (Warszawa: PIW, 1976), pp. 144ff.

52. Michał Świniarski, *Wiadomość o pierwiastkowej miast zasadzie w Polszcze, ich szczególnych przywilejach i wolnościach oraz o przyczynach upadku tychże miast* (Remarks on the ancient principles for towns in Poland, their specific privileges and freedoms, as well as the causes of their decline), Warszawa: (1789) reprinted in MDSC. vol. 2.

53. Krystyna Zienkowska, *Sławetni i urodzeni. Ruch polityczny mieszczaństwa w dobie Sejmu Czteroletniego* (City dwellers and the well born: the political movement of the townspeople in the age of the Four-Year Diet) (Warszawa: PWN, 1976), pp. 66ff and passim.

54. The publication appeared from January to April 1790, in 7 issues, reprinted in MDSC, vol. 3; see Krystyna Zienkowska, *Sławetni...*pp. 75ff.

55. N.p., n.d., reprinted in MDSC. vol. 2; compare Konopczyński, "Polscy pisarze....," MS. Jagiellonian Library, BJ, no. 52/61, p. 264 and Zienkowska, *Sławetni...*p. 81.

56. *List ... prezydenta miasta Warszawy do J.W. Małachowskiego marszałka sejmowego i konfederacji koronnej, die 3 octobris 1790 w wilię śmierci tegoż Dekerta pisany* (Letter ... from the president of Warsaw to His Honor Małachowski, Marshal of the Diet and the Crown Confederation, written on October 3, 1790, the eve of the said Dekert's death), n.p., n.d., reprinted in MDSC, vol. 3.

57. Zienkowska, *Sławetni...*, passim.

58. Edward Giergielewicz, *Atmosfera ideologiczna Sejmu Czteroletniego* (The ideological atmosphere of the Four-Year Diet) (Warszawa, 1939).

Translated by Janusz Duzinkiewicz

MONITOR

na Rok 1765.

Liczbę LXXVIII.
połarkuſzowych kartek
w ſobie
ZAWIERAIĄCY

Diſcite iuſtiam moniti, & non temnere
Divos
Virg.

w WARSZAWIE
w Drukarni Mitzlerowſkiey.

Title page of the journal *Monitor,* which was launched in 1765 by King Stanisław August and for the next twenty years became the leading periodical of the camp of reform and cultural renewal. Modelled after Addisson's *Spectator,* it often included translations from it and from the French *Encyclopédie* as well as Polish poetry, essays and polemics on political, social and literary issues. (Biblioteka Uniwersytecka w Warszawie).

9

The Art of the Possible

Adam Zamoyski

Homo Polonicus of 1791 was as different in attitude and demeanor from his counterpart of fifty years before as it is possible to be. The 1741 version was steeped in Sarmatian values. He was pious, if only superficially religious; he was distrustful of anything beyond the ken of his upbringing; he was ignorant in almost every field; above all he was utterly complacent, a complacency he justified by a half-baked belief in "Divine Providence." His descendant in 1791 had rejected religious devotionalism, had abandoned his parochial viewpoint, was eager to learn and question, boasted a reasonable degree of education and general knowledge, and was, above all, highly aware of the need for action in an uncertain world.

The outward manifestations of this transformation have been meticulously charted, yet its underlying causes are hardly addressed. The question of what made it possible is usually dispatched with general reference to improvements in education and above all the influence of the Enlightenment. But such explanations are deeply unsatisfactory. To make a perilously sweeping generalization, the "new ideas" of the Enlightenment were largely irrelevant in Poland. This is not to say that they did not penetrate the country. Quite the contrary. The works of the *philosophes* circulated widely both in the original and, from the 1760s, in Polish language editions. The playwright Franciszek Bohomolec describes the library of a typical Warsaw freethinker in the 1760s as containing books "which had been condemned by public decree to be burnt not only in Catholic states, but even in Geneva and Holland."[1]

The key elements of French Enlightenment thought were the destruction of established religion and of all hierarchy based on it, and the concept of the "rights" of the individual and by extension of the nation. Both of these are substantially absent from the Polish political and social revival of the second half of the eighteenth century, whose leaders clung, to the very end, to the belief in *"Fide, Rege et Lege."* (The Jacobin tendencies that emerged after 1792 affected only a minority, and were in any case prompted by political strategy rather than ideological conviction.)

In effect, what we see in eighteenth-century Poland is not this kind of Enlightenment, but renaissance. Change was brought about not through the dissemination of new ideas, but by teaching people to open their eyes and their minds to those that had always been there. The whole reform movement, from Stanisław Leszczyński's *Głos wolny*, through Stanisław Konarski's *O skutecznym rad sposobie* to Andrzej Zamoyski's *Zbiór praw* and Hugo Kołłątaj's *Listy Anonima,* was based on the concept of repairing the system, not altering or overthrowing it. There was nothing revolutionary about it - how many elements of the political and social ideology of the 1780s Pole were not held by his forefather in 1580? There is nothing peculiar about this, when one reflects that those who made the American Revolution were inspired more by the spirit of the "Glorious Revolution" of 1688 than by anything Voltaire had written.

Improvements to the educational system and the lively political literature of the time played an important part in this process of opening hearts and minds. Equally, and in some cases more, important was the part played by literature and the arts. They had a far wider reach, taking in, through the theatre and the visual arts, people who could not even read. And by their indirect but many-sided influence on all the senses, they were able to predispose people to accept notions that they might stubbornly reject in the form of the written word or the stated opinion.

The literature of the Saxon period fell broadly into two forms, both of them discarded as early as the seventeenth century in countries such as France: the devotional and the classical-courtly. It was inherently pointless. On the rare occasions when writers did address real issues such as the condition of the country they did so in a passive, almost religious manner. They lamented the state of powerlessness the *ojczyzna* (motherland) had fallen into just as they might compose reflections on the Sorrowful Mysteries of the Blessed Virgin. It was a devotional ritual that could be fulfilled before going off to a good lunch—there was never the slightest inference that anyone should actually do anything about the situation, let alone any suggestion as to how. The only exception to this was the woman poet Elżbieta Drużbacka (1695-1765), some of whose works did contain a moral didactic streak, even if it was couched in seventeenth-century Elysian terms.

This began to change dramatically during the 1740s and 1750s. The public theatre in the Saxony Garden in Warsaw, which had hitherto staged mainly ballets and silly comic intermezzos, began to present actual plays, by Molière, Regnard, Goldoni and even Diderot. But their influence was restricted by the location and the foreign languages in which they were staged. Of far greater import were the plays that began to be staged in the Jesuit and Piarist schools, and also in the country residences of the aristocracy. These included the major tragedies of Corneille and Racine, as well as more recent ones by Voltaire, in new and comprehensible translations. They were also supplied by native authors, such as Stanisław Konarski (1700-73), whose *Tragedia Epaminondy* (The Tragedy of Epaminonda) received its premiere at the Piarist College in Warsaw in 1756, and the Hetman Wacław Rzewuski (1706-79), whose two tragedies in the manner of Racine and two comedies in the style of Molière were published two years later. By far the greatest impact here was made by the Jesuit Franciszek Bohomolec (1720-84), whose *Komedie konwiktowe*, a collection of twenty five comedies written for performance in the Jesuit schools, were published at yearly intervals between 1755 and 1760. Twelve more comedies (among the best from his pen) followed in the years 1766-1784 written this time for the public stage established by Stanisław August.

In 1765, shortly after ascending the throne, Stanisław August brought into being a company of Polish actors - in effect a national theatre - to supplement the French and Italian troupes working in Warsaw. The company succumbed financially in 1767, but it was revived seven years later, and from then on continued to supply the Warsaw public with the latest in Polish and foreign drama. The plays of Bohomolec, Adam Kazimierz Czartoryski (1734-1823) but first of all by Franciszek Zabłocki (1754-1821), who pillaged world literature ancient and modern in search of plots for over 50 comedies that he wrote, provided its staple repertoire. They did not pretend to high art. Apart from a straightforward moral didacticism, their principal aim was to satirize stupidity, prejudice, superstition and ignorance on the one hand, and to ridicule excessive modish aping of foreign (usually French) fashions on the other.

This fight against the forces of obscurantism was waged assiduously through other media. Bohomolec himself opened up a new front when he accepted the editorship of the periodical *Monitor*, founded by the King in 1765. This twice-weekly journal was clearly inspired by Addison's *Spectator*. It often lifted copy straight from its English model, and also padded itself out with excerpts from the writings of the French *philosophes*. But the meat of every issue was a variety of Polish verse and essays. Among Bohomolec's collaborators were the Jesuit satirist Gracjan Piotrowski (1725-85) and, most important of all, the Prince-Bishop of Warmia, Ignacy Krasicki (1735-1801), possibly the greatest talent of the age.[2]

Krasicki is an interesting personality in the context of his time, and he illustrates admirably the point made at the beginning of this piece. Born into an ancient and titled (though recently somewhat distressed) family, he was directed into a clerical career, that well-worn refuge of the younger sons of the nobility. He became a friend of Stanisław Poniatowski in the late 1750s and owed his promotion to the latter when he became king. In 1767 he was made Bishop of Warmia, one of the prince-bishoprics in which the incumbent was the temporal as well as the spiritual ruler of his province. In 1772 this was detached from Poland by the First Partition, and he became a vassal of Frederick of Prussia. Though deeply patriotic, he was far too urbane to sulk, and he graciously accepted his new duty of entertaining Frederick at Sanssouci, where he was a greatly sought-after guest.

Ostensibly a typical Enlightenment figure enjoying good food and drink, beautiful things and refined company, and wearing his sacerdotal duties very lightly, Krasicki was in fact anything but. His first major work to be published was *Myszeidos Pieśni X* (The Mousiad) (1775), a mock-heroic poem about a war between cats and mice. This was followed three years later by *Monachomachia, albo Wojna mnichów* (Monachomachia, or The war of the monks), a Homeric epic about a quarrel between different orders of monks in a small provincial town. In 1779 he published *Satyry* (Satires) and *Bajki i przypowieści* (Fables and tales), the latter a retelling of fables culled from authors ranging from Aesop to La Fontaine. He wrote the first Polish novel, *Mikołaja Doświadczyńskiego przypadki (1776)* (*The adventures of Mr. Nicholas Wisdom*) (1992), whose inspirational pedigree includes Defoe, Swift, Rousseau and most obviously Voltaire's *Candide*, and the second, *Pan Podstoli* (The Steward) (1778), as well as a number of satirical plays, highly derivative of Molière's work. All these works carry on the struggle against what Krasicki called *dzikość* (wildness), meaning the compendium of ignorance, prejudice and complacency that had atrophied Polish society. But they do not promote any positive program, social or political.

Only the two novels and his *Listy* (Letters) have any didactic purpose, and what they convey is hardly the sort of message one might expect from a child of the Enlightenment. *"Ojców naszych prostota, cnota starodawna, Ta, która wzniosła naród, ta synom przykładem; Ich się nauk trzymajmy, idźmy bitym*

Ignacy Krasicki, painting by Per Krafft (Muzeum Narodowe w Warszawie).

śladem" (Let the simplicity of our fathers and their old-fashioned virtue, which made our nation, be an example to the sons; let us follow their example, and tread the path they trod), he writes in one poem.[3] This amounts to a rejection of one of the cornerstones of the Enlightenment namely the spirit of enquiry. Even more astonishingly, the self-indulgent prelate who ridiculed the bigoted clergy, wrote gallant poetic fragments to pretty ladies and joked about fasting and abstinence, earnestly tells his readers that it is better to have too much faith in God than too little, and that without religion there can be no virtue. No son of Rousseau, and no revolutionary, Krasicki was a man of profound wisdom whose principal care was to confound stupidity.[4]

Alongside this purely satirical onslaught on the forces of darkness in society, which was conducted at the simplest level and with weapons of the widest reach – the stage and the periodical – ran a second campaign: to make the language precise and pure, and to retrieve and dust off all that was best in Polish literature. The second half of the seventeenth century and the beginning of the eighteenth had seen the triumph of baroque forms of expression, peppered with allusions to antiquity and with words or whole phrases of Latin woven into the language. The result was a kind of declamatory nonsense that sometimes sounded good but obscured any meaning that might occasionally have been intended.

The writers of the second half of the century, many of them products of the reformed Piarist and Jesuit schooling system, reveal a gift for simplicity and clarity of expression. By their example, they taught people in general not to fear to state things plainly. The poet Franciszek Ksawery Dmochowski (1762-1808) applied himself to the subject directly, and in 1788 published his *Sztuka rymotwórcza* (The art of versification), a paraphrase of Boileau's *Art poétique*. He also used the writings of his Polish contemporaries to illustrate the point.

This linguistic revival was backed up by the publication, from the late 1750s onwards, of new editions of Polish classic texts from earlier centuries. The works of the great Renaissance poet Jan Kochanowski (1530-84), which had lain largely forgotten since his death, were published anew in the 1760s, enriching not only the stock of fine literature available in Polish, but also the intellectual life of the readers with his profound and wise understanding of life. Another classic that was resurrected (in 1792), not only for its stylistic virtues, was the Jesuit Piotr Skarga's (1536-1612) *Kazania sejmowe* (Parliamentary sermons), a series of homilies addressed to the Polish Parliament exhorting it to reform itself and look to the welfare of the Commonwealth before it was too late.

The works of these and other writers, as well as the great number of translations of English and French novels and plays published in the 1770s and 1780s, had far-reaching effects on the articulate sections of the population, an effect readily ascertainable from the violent reactions and arguments they gave rise to all over the country. Those who felt affronted or shocked were, by the very nature of satire, made to appear ridiculous to the more receptive, and particularly to the younger generation, who began to abandon old prejudices and shibboleths despite the strictures and curses of their parents. The stage works in particular not only convinced all but the most recalcitrant, they also taught the spirit of debate and the presentation of arguments, which was to help the younger generations to take an active and constructive part in political life.

In the 1780s, the poets and playwrights became more evidently involved in the political arguments of the day. Even an older man like Adam Naruszewicz (1733-96), titular Bishop of Smoleńsk and close friend of the King, became actively engaged. Known as "the Polish Horace" he had made his mark writing elegant odes and satires, but after the First Partition he applied himself assiduously to a task that fitted into the King's programme of political education and propaganda, namely to writing a modern history of Poland, *Historia narodu polskiego od początku chrześcijaństwa* (History of the Polish nation from the time of its Christianization), the first volume of which came out in 1780. Five more volumes followed, published annually, but the work remained unfinished, taking the reader up to the dynastic union of Poland with Lithuania in 1386. Its impact was nevertheless enormous. Previous histories of Poland had been semi-mythical fairy-tales designed to make the reader immeasurably proud of being Polish and treating the nation as God's chosen, and therefore under the protection of Divine Providence. Such a view of history discouraged active patriotism and re-evaluation. Naruszewicz's work was based on documentary sources and achieved a high degree of accuracy. If it did have a subjective message, it was that Poland had prospered under strong monarchy which guaranteed greater rights to the burghers and the peasants. This was the King's argument, and it was also the view taken by those who supported the Constitution of 3 May.

More directly political were poets such as Tomasz Kajetan Węgierski (1756-1787), a restless spirit and a poet of considerable talent who specialized in political lampoons. But it was the stage that saw the most political statements being made. Józef Wybicki (1747-1822), the distinguished political thinker and author of *Listy patriotyczne* (Patriotic letters), lacked any serious dramatic talent, but this did not stop him from writing four plays, the most important of which, *Kmiotek* (The serf), was the first to bring peasants on to the stage as central characters and to present their case in an affecting and indisputable way. But the lead was taken by Wojciech Bogusławski (1757-1829), an immensely prolific individual who translated dozens of foreign plays and wrote many of his own, usually directing them and acting in them. His *Henryk VI na łowach* (Henry VI at the hunt), staged while the Great Sejm was sitting, was openly polemical. Even more strictly programmatic was *Powrót posła* (The Deputy's homecoming), staged in 1791 by Julian Ursyn Niemcewicz (1758-1841), which directly lobbied in favor of the Constitution.

But even the least political of poets could be said to have had an effect on the psyche of Polish society. Stanisław Trembecki (1739-1812), possibly the most poetically gifted of all the writers of his day, was a rationalist and a sybarite, who had danced and dueled his way round Paris, meeting most of the luminaries of the Enlightenment before returning to Poland. He was not remotely interested in politics or even the cause of reform, despite the fact that he was a close friend of the King to whom it meant so much. Nor was Franciszek Karpiński (1741-1825), a sentimentalist with a gentle, bucolic style. Nor indeed was Franciszek Dionizy Kniaźnin (1750-1807), the titles of whose published collections of poems - *Erotyki* (1779), *Wiersze* (1783), and *Poezje* (1787-89) (Love Poems, Verses, Poems) - speak for themselves.[5] These poets nevertheless played their part in the transformation, by enriching and refining the language, by awakening the love of beauty, and above all by encouraging a new sensibility which by definition excluded the muddy-boots parochialism of the Saxon era and prepared the ground for arguably the most important leap of the imagination required of Polish society in the run-up to the reforms of the Great Diet and the Constitution - the capacity to think of the peasants as human beings.

The arguments of men like Wybicki, Staszic or Kołłątaj (all of whom at various stages despaired of ever turning the lower orders into real citizens) were one thing. The reality was quite another. And it was literature and the arts that could dress up that reality in a manner that spoke to the hearts rather than just to the minds of people.

Wybicki's play *Kmiotek* affectingly highlighted the love between two young peasants and the obstacles that stood in the way of their happiness. It also suggested a community of feeling, if not interest, between them and the "good" noble landowner. Bogusławski's *Cud mniemany, czyli Krakowiacy i Górale* (The imaginary miracle, or Krakovians and Highlanders), written in 1794,

King Stanisław August, copperplate acc. to the painting by Giovanni Battista Lampi the Elder. (Biblioteka Uniwersytecka w Warszawie, Gabinet Rycin).

The National Theatre in Warsaw, watercolor by Zygmunt Vogel (Muzeum Narodowe w Warszawie).

showed that the peasants could be not only charming, but politically useful as well.[6] It paved the way for Kościuszko's use of them in his army.

This play, for which Bogusławski's friend Jan Stefani (1746-1829) wrote the music, is actually on the borderline of opera. This is no coincidence, as music had begun to play a greater role in Polish life. It had also begun to reveal a "political" edge. While it had long been customary for composers all over Europe to write music supposedly inspired by folk airs or purporting to use folk rhythms, nobody had attempted or meant to bring the real idiom of the peasants into the concert-hall or the drawing-room. But towards the end of the century a group of Polish composers had discovered something altogether more meaningful in folk music. Stefani and his colleagues Jan Wański (1762-18??), Maciej Kamieński (1734-1821), Jan Dawid Holland (1746-1825), Józef Elsner (1769-1854) and Feliks Janiewicz (1762-1848) wrote conventional concertos, symphonies and operas in which not only folk themes but an often exuberant, even rebellious, popular spirit can be detected.[7]

To make too much of such phenomena can appear specious, but at the same time it has to be borne in mind that when dealing with the change of heart of a whole society, many of whose members were only semi-educated, subliminal influences can be far more significant than logic or argument. Breaking through prejudice is rarely achieved by words alone.

Most of what is true of literature in terms of changing attitudes is true of the arts at the time as well. From the middle of the century Poland was increasingly permeable to outside influences, and the growing prosperity of the late 1770s and the 1780s spread the reach of the arts wider. The arts themselves changed from being mere accoutrement, whether in religious ritual or family hierarchy, into an expression of a set of values and the panoply of a new consciousness. The role played by the King, Stanisław August, in this respect was seminal.

The most formative influence on the King's outlook had been his youthful travels, which had developed his artistic taste and awoken a passion for collecting. Long before anyone even dreamt of the possibility of his becoming king, he was obsessed with the idea of restoring Poland to greatness, and the development of his taste as well as his whole view of the value and function of art followed this aim very closely. So much so that it is difficult to isolate his artistic program from his political one at times. He had a very strong appreciation of the power of the arts, and harnessed them in a determined and almost cynical way to the promotion of his aims. These aims were largely personal to begin with, and Polish historians of the nineteenth and early twentieth centuries saw Stanisław August's profligacy in artistic matters as reprehensibly frivolous. While much of his patronage was indeed inspired by the desire for personal gratification or glorification, most of it adhered to a programme which had the interests of the Polish state and the Polish nation at heart. As well as contributing to the climate that made 1791 possible, his artistic patronage left behind a heritage that was of crucial importance in keeping the nation alive as a concept through the dark night of the century of partition.

Stanisław August believed that Polish state structures and Polish society's concept of the state, never strong, had disintegrated. He therefore intended to reinvigorate the Diet, increase the powers of the crown, and break the oligarchy of autonomous magnates. He saw that Poland's economic and military potential was lamentably under-exploited, rendering the country powerless to resist foreign pressure. He therefore intended to develop the one and build up the other, by encouraging industry and making the country self-sufficient. He was aware that Poland's human potential was hardly realized. He therefore intended to educate and create opportunities for Poles to develop their minds and their talents. He wanted to create a new type of Polish citizen, drawn from the lesser gentry and the middle classes, who would serve the state rather than himself or his tribe. Finally, Stanisław August was keenly aware that Poland's position in the world had become weak. He therefore wanted to re-establish the country's presence on the international map. He harnessed the potential of art to all four of these aims.[8]

Unlike so many of his subjects, Stanisław August had no court, few servants, and no establishment on the morrow of his election in 1764. The nature of the Polish monarchy was an increment of centuries of precedent, of powers curtailed, of influence circumscribed and of ill-defined prerogatives. The amount of effective power he wielded therefore depended less on written law than on how far his skill and intelligence allowed him to shift these hazy boundaries in his own favor. His travels had taken him to Vienna, Versailles, London, Dresden, Berlin and St. Petersburg, and in each place he had studied the court and its workings. This had taught him much about how courts generated power and upheld or even created the fiction of majesty, and how they had over the centuries turned regional potentates into courtiers and eventually servants of the state. He therefore set about creating a glittering court structure, which involved everything from new uniforms for his guards to music for courtly entertainments (Stanisław August had no ear for music, but he spent lavishly, particularly on ballets, which had a clear allegorical function). He set great store by ritual and pageantry.

He began by projecting an image of himself that would enhance his royalty. He summoned the Roman-born painter and pupil of Batoni, Marcello

Project for rebuilding the Castle by Dominik Merlini, 1776 (Biblioteka Uniwersytecka w Warszawie, Gabinet Rycin).

Bacciarelli (1731-1818), from Vienna, and made him superintendent of his artistic works.[9] He also recruited the services of the Swedish portraitist Per Krafft, the Swiss Anton Graff, two Frenchmen settled in Warsaw, Jean Pillement and Louis Marteau, the Polish-born miniaturists Vincent de Lesseur and Józef Kosiński (1753-1821), the pastellist Aleksander Kucharski (1741-1819) and the painter-decorator Jan Bogumił Plersch (d.1817). In the first instance, he put them to work on dozens of royal portraits, which were to bring the image of the king to his subjects.

The image itself was something of a problem, since he came from an unexalted background, with no intrinsic credentials to rule. He therefore fixed on the concept of Providence providing him with his monarchical credentials. He was to be the wise prince given to a people by Higher Powers. He hedged his bets as to the nature of these powers, by hinting, in the subtlest ways, at the similarity between his birth - of an unknown but honest father and a mother who was of the blood of kings - and that of Christ. At the same time, he dwelt at length on the astrological premises attending it - in the middle of Capricorn in a year when Saturn was in the ascendant - which gave rise to horoscopes and prophesies that he was destined for great things. These themes pervade everything, from the allegorical ballets to the painted ceilings of the Royal Castle at Warsaw.

Stanisław August's greatest need on ascending the throne was a new palace. The Royal Castle at Warsaw was an architectural warren, spreading out from a medieval core transformed in the mannerist style in the 1590s and neglected for over a century. It interlocked with the sprawling old city, which hemmed it in on three sides. But what he could do to it was restricted by the fact that it was also, as the Palace of Westminster had once been, the seat of the government as well as the royal residence, since the Parliament met there. Officially, it was "the seat of the King and the Commonwealth."

His response to this problem shows clearly how far artistic considerations were subject with him to political considerations. Within weeks of his election, he bought the derelict castle of Ujazdów just outside Warsaw, which he saw as his future Versailles or Caserta. He needed such a residence to proclaim his personal grandeur as monarch in juxtaposition to his position within the constitutional framework. And for this purpose he drew on his experience of the court of Dresden in particular, favoring an exuberant rococo style - a fitting environment for the king at rest. Lack of funds led him to abandon the project soon after, but not until a rich crop of projects and drawings had been brought forth.[10]

In the meantime, he applied himself to refurbishing the Royal Castle, which was to symbolize the king at work and which, by its architecture, was to project that view of the king's position within the constitution which he hoped to assume. He took the Sun-King Louis XIV as his paradigm, and pitched for the monumentalism and the configuration of French classical architecture of the seventeenth century. But he also looked further into the past for testimonials, and he wrote off to the king of Naples for plans and drawings of Herculaneum, which was then being excavated. He would underpin his reign with the twin pillars of *grand siècle* monarchy and classical mythology.

He put to work two home-grown architects, Jakub Fontana (1710-73)[11] and Efraim Schroeger (1727-83), and a French one, Victor Louis (1731-1800). Stanisław August described Louis, the still unknown architect who would come into his own with the Palais-Royal, as "a noble, prolific and wise genius."[12]

The results of this planning are breathtakingly ambitious. They include seven projects for the rebuilding of the Castle, five by Fontana, one by Schroeger, and one by Louis. All envisage a monumental structure, with facades imposing by their regularity, and enhanced by grand forecourts approached by converging avenues. This would have demanded the demolition of part of Warsaw's old town. They all alluded to the Louvre, to Versailles, and even St Paul's Cathedral in London, fusing the baroque with the classical in a statement that was cosmopolitan and strongly monarchical.

Much the same is true of the interiors, projected by Louis, who included a typical *appartement de parade*, centered on a state bedroom with raised bed behind a balustrade, designed for the levee. The ceiling was to depict Hercules wedding Hebe and being received into Olympus, an allusion to the deification that Stanisław August wished to insinuate as having taken place on his election. His personal contribution to these plans is very marked principally because they were so much a part of his attempts, during the first years of his reign, to recreate authority centered around the throne.

None of the building work could be put in hand for lack of funds, and the only results of this activity was that Stanisław August redecorated a couple of rooms and ordered the paneling, furniture, sconces and tapestry for several others. Although he predictably ordered some objects, including a set of magnificent torches, from the renowned Philippe Caffieri, he entrusted the majority to a young artist, Jean Louis Prieur, who exactly caught the King's own predilection for introducing Hellenistic elements into an otherwise regal Louis XIV style.

Only four years after his accession, the Confederation of Bar plunged the country into chaos and put paid to his original idea of recreating a strong monarchy. Yet not for a moment did Stanisław August forget about his artistic plans. He inveigled Bernardo Belotto-Canaletto (1722-1780) to come and settle in Warsaw,[13] and found time to take an interest in how the young artists

- Franciszek Smuglewicz (1745-1807), Aleksander Kucharski (1741-1819) and others he had sent to study abroad - were progressing with their work. He also continued to collect pictures and objects, and commission works abroad.

The only architectural project he managed to complete during the four yeas of civil war was the Marble Chamber of the Castle. Here the architect Fontana and the painter Bacciarelli created a sort of pantheon to the memory of Poland's greatest rulers. Their portraits are set into the green and black marble covering the walls, with Stanisław August's own portrait over the mantelpiece, facing an ornate clock, flanked by allegories of Justice and Peace. The room has no private or court function. It is a public room, with the atmosphere of a chapel, and it says much about the growing importance of the idea of the state. It also proclaims Stanisław August's constitutional pedigree, his right to rule, and the three elements on which he now based his policy–time, justice and peace.

After the First Partition, a chastened Stanisław August set about rebuilding the position of the Crown. Times and conditions had changed, and he now abandoned Louis XIV as a model, along with his first flush of monarchical ambition. With it went the cosmopolitanism of his youth, to be replaced by a more philosophical, Voltairian view of monarchy, embodied in the much-favored and less demanding model of Henri IV. Pragmatism was the order of the day. Stanisław August therefore strove to project a lower-key, more paternalistic image of himself. At the same time he stuck to his idea of his predestination, and kept trying to build up the prestige of the Crown in the political arena.

Five new projects, four of them by Dominik Merlini (1730-97), a native of Valsolda who had settled in Poland,[14] and one by Schroeger, were produced between 1776 and 1779. Comparison between these and the earlier projects eloquently demonstrates the change in the King's thinking. Gone are all references to the Louvre and Versailles, gone are the avenues and approaches. Schroeger's project turns the Castle into a sort of Capitol, with the Senate chamber as a focal point, and a courtyard that resembles a forum rather than a *cour d'honneur.* Hercules gives way to God the Father, and deities of Fame and Glory to great Polish kings from the past. Mythology was replaced by the Bible, Louis XIV and cosmopolitanism by Polish traditions. These were more organic, more baroque, but they also contained a strong tendency towards emulation of the political cultures of Greece and Rome. Thus a new mixture, almost a new style, was born.

Again, the projects for the actual rebuilding of the Castle remained on paper, but over the next ten years the interiors were entirely remodeled.[15] The

Coat of arms of the Commonwealth and the King with personifications of Peace and Justice by François Boucher (Biblioteka Uniwersytecka w Warszawie, Gabinet Rycin). It served as a model for several sculptural compositions at the castle.

Royal Apartments were redecorated between 1774 and 1777, followed in 1780-86 by the Apartments of State. In the Royal Apartments, Stanisław August stressed the legitimacy of his position as king. His bedroom, completed by Dominik Merlini, was paneled in Yew (Saturn's tree), and decorated with frescoes suggesting the biblical nature of his status. The room is more redolent of a very grand gentleman's bedroom than of a king's–there was no question of holding a ritual *levee* in it. The old throne room was redecorated by Merlini, with frescoes by Bacciarelli and Plersch, and sculptures by Giacomo Monaldi, again stressing his position: there were busts of Catherine of Russia, Elizabeth I of England, Henri IV of France and Poland's Jan III (Sobieski), portraits of Stanisław August's parents, and scenes portraying his assumed virtues of courage, justice, self-sacrifice and wisdom.

Previously the Senator's Antechambers, redecorated by Dominik Merlini and renamed as the Canaletto Chamber, was dominated by the theme of

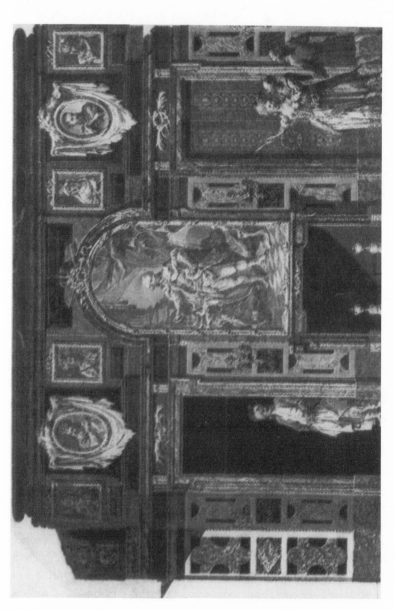

The north wall of the Marble Room decorated in 1769-1771 by Jakub Fontana with cooperation of Marcello Bacciarelli and André Le Brun, watercolor by Jan Ch. Kamsetzer, around 1784 (Biblioteka Uniwersytecka w Warszawie, Gabinet Rycin).

Stanisław August's election, a painting by Bernardo Belotto-Canaletto occupies the central position in the Chamber. The fourteen other paintings by Belotto-Canaletto that effectively panel the room are seemingly random views of Warsaw, but closer analysis reveals that they too have a theme. One shows the Palace of the Commonwealth, another the Arsenal, the two major public buildings in the capital; four more depict churches founded by preceding elected monarchs; the rest feature palaces of people who had held the highest temporal post in the Senate, the Castellany of Cracow, which Stanisław August's father had also held.

These subliminal suggestions turn into stronger statements in the Apartments of State. The Ballroom, to which the King devoted much time and thought, was opened in 1781. The ceiling represented Jove turning chaos into order, and the room is completed by two statues by André Le Brun, one of Apollo, modeled on Stanisław August himself, the other of Minerva, in which a likeness to Catherine is discernible. In the same year he began work on the Knights' Hall. The chamber, by Dominik Merlini and Jan Christian Kamsetzer, is a hall of fame, in which Stanisław August represented all those in Polish history he approved of. Apart from the figures represented, there was a huge clock supported by a statue of Saturn, flanked by Fame and Eternity. The same kind of messages appear in every interior: the Conference Cabinet which included portraits of contemporary brother-monarchs, or the Great Throne Room, a sacral interior in which a clock donated by the Pope reinforces his legitimacy, while statues of Pompey and Caesar, Scipio and Hannibal allude to the crushing of rebellion by legitimate authority, thus giving his view of his own position following the Confederation of Bar.

As the Castle grew more and more functionally constitutional in nature, so Stanisław August turned again to the idea of a residence away from it. But now all ideas of a Versailles or Caserta were thrown to the winds. In 1784 he gave the castle of Ujazdów to the army for a barracks, and concentrated on the park, which he laid out in the English style. In it he built a small palace, an Italianate villa and a couple of hermitages. He added a theatre, an orangery, a pavilion for dinners, and a number of kiosks and summer-houses. They were all designed by Merlini, in an extraordinary mixture of styles: some classical, some Italian, some Chinese, some Turkish. In the center of the park, surrounded by a lake, stood a seventeenth-century bath-house, *Łazienki* built for Stanisław Herakliusz Lubomirski by the architect Tylman van Gameren. Stanisław August rebuilt this, retaining only the shell-incrusted and stuccoed bathing chamber of the original. The rebuilding took over a decade, since the King kept changing his mind and adding new elements. It is in the neo-classical style, elegant and restrained in the northern facade, and warmer and more Italian in the southern elevation. The palace is small, reflecting a fresh, more Voltairian view of monarchy, and blends the frugality of a private gentleman's residence with a courtly lay-out in miniature. He was not king there, but he remained royal.[16]

"I shall not cease to work and build while there is breath in me," Stanisław August wrote to his friend Adam Naruszewicz, "in order to plant and graft good seed in our motherland, although I have long since realized that it is my destiny that it will not be me who gathers the fruit."[17] New ideas and plans were continually being dictated by shifts in his view of his role or by a political point he wished to make.

In the late 1780s, his plans reflect the concept of a presidential citizen-king, and the style grows increasingly neo-classical and civic, projecting an image of the king that is more stoical and determinedly patriotic. He also spent more time on buildings of a public nature. He commissioned a Temple of Providence from Jakub Kubicki (1758-1833) to commemorate the passing of the Constitution of 3 May 1791. At *Łazienki* in 1790 he built the amphitheatre, with a stage on a small island, which had seating for 1,000 people. Two years later, he built the Rotunda, which was to be a Pantheon to Poland's greatest kings.

As the country's future grew dimmer, he strove to erect architectural and artistic testimony to its past glory - by putting up statues to Jan Sobieski or getting his medallist Johann Philip Holzhaeusser to strike medals commemorating great events. He also strove to justify his own behavior, or at least his attitude. One of the last works he completed, the ballroom of Łazienki, a magnificent example of Stanisław August's taste and Kamsetzer's genius, depicts Apollo and Hercules, with Daphne and Dejanira representing their undoing. The final statement, in the main hall, is the depiction of the King as Solomon. He was saying that he had always acted wisely and well, but that he had been crushed by higher forces.

The vast stock of building, of architectural drawings and projects for interiors and furnishings left behind by Stanisław August is probably unique in its volume and richness. It is also unique in that it is almost entirely devoted to political purposes. But it only accounts for part of his artistic patronage.

Stanisław August's second great aim was to develop Poland, to cultivate his garden. The ceiling of the Throne Room shows Saturn reigning over the arts, agriculture and trade, and this was not an idle picture. The King set up factories and encouraged others to do so. His factories manufactured things as disparate as decorative ceramics, palace furniture and rifles for the army, but both their architecture and their produce were vetted in design terms, for he believed passionately that art was the mother of good design, and that good design was the basis of quality. In other words, that art was a lever for industry.

To this effect, he built up a collection of some 8,000 coins and medals, and one of the most important collections of prints and engravings in Europe, numbering over 30,000 plates, which, moreover, were bound up or shelved according to subject, so they could serve more easily for study. He also formed a collection of instruments, a cabinet de physique, and one of antiquities, curios, even examples of molding and friezes, and specially commissioned copies of famous pieces of sculpture from antiquity. "My prints and my medals are, in comparison with matters of greater import, nothing more than a pleasant distraction, but I also think of their useful side, and I would like them to become useful to others," he wrote to August Moszyński whom he sent abroad in search of objects.[18] They were to form the nucleus of a *Museum Polonicum*, for which he drew up plans in 1775, whose purpose was avowedly didactic.

The same was true of his picture-collecting. He had permanent agents in Rome, Naples, Paris and the Hague, and corresponded with others who could supply art. He issued specific instructions to them as to what he wanted, and liked to have every painting described fully before he considered acquiring it. He collected living artists such as Boucher, Casanova, Van Loo, Vien, Mengs, Lampi, Batoni, Piranesi, Kauffmann, Füger and David, Dutch and Flemish Old Masters, and he was particularly fond of Italian baroque painters such as Salvatore Rosa, Guido Reni, Bassano, Luca Giordano and others. He built up a quality collection of some 3,000 paintings, and while he derived the utmost pleasure from their presence in his private apartments, their ultimate destination was other. As early as 1766 he had asked Marcello Bacciarelli to draw up plans for a Royal Academy of Fine Arts. As usual, funds prevented him from acting on these plans, but he kept collecting in order to be ready if and when the opportunity arose. In one respect, the academy did actually come into existence.

Stanisław August had turned three great chambers under the State Apartments of the Castle into a studio in which the artists engaged on rebuilding the Castle worked. As well as his principal artists, a string of sculptors, plasterers and cabinet-makers labored there, under his close supervision, and making frequent use of his collections. The studio also accepted young artists as apprentices and opened its doors to students who wished to draw from life or make use of the royal collections.[19]

The material development of the country evinced this at every level. Stanisław August had the whole country mapped, and, because he paid such attention to the aesthetic and design aspects, the results were magnificent.

The Łazienki palace watercolor by Zygmunt Vogel (Muzeum Narodowe w Warszawie). Photo H. Romanowski.

The coinage of the realm which the King minted was probably the most beautifully designed in Europe. Every customs-house, guard-post, town hall, house of correction or barracks built was a small gem of good design and elegance. Every bridge and posting-station was subjected to the treatment. Johann Georg Forster, the Polish-born naturalist who sailed around the southern Pacific with Captain James Cook in 1772 and later became famous as a German political thinker, was astounded to find such elegance, and in one posting-station, he found prints of the ruins at Ephesus adorning the walls.[20] The same went for factories and farm-buildings. Stanisław August commissioned architects such as Jakub Kubicki and Stanisław Zawadzki (1743-1806) to produce projects for hotels, for public baths, for breweries, for cattle-sheds, for peasant cottages and small manor-houses.

Although the King's patronage was by far the most extensive and the most vigorous, it by no means overshadows the contribution of several other great patrons and a large number of more humble clients. In most cases, they did not even emulate the King's style or consciously follow his example. This is not surprising in the case of the two foremost patrons. Izabela Czartoryska taught herself everything about art, beginning with the relatively undemanding area of pleasure-gardens. The elysium she created in the 1760s at Powązki outside Warsaw gave work to a number of artists, most notably to the French painter Jean-Pierre Norblin de la Gourdaine (1745-1830), whom she had brought back from a trip to Paris. He in turn helped to teach a young Pole of talent whom Izabela Czartoryska's husband had spotted, Aleksander Orłowski (1777-1832), who was to become an outstanding artist, and also the engraver Michał Płoński (1778-1812). The Czartoryski court in Warsaw and later at their country seat of Puławy was a home to a number of poets, to painters such as Jan Rustem (1762-1835) and the architect Piotr Aigner (1746-1841), all of whom received liberal patronage.

Izabela Czartoryska's sister-in-law Elżbieta Lubomirska, was a woman of more refined taste. At Mokotów, just outside Warsaw, she commissioned an Italianate villa from Szymon Bogumił Zug (1733-1807), and she later transformed her country seat at Łańcut, using Aigner as her principal architect. She commissioned painting and sculpture in large quantities from Polish and foreign artists, and supported struggling young painters.[21]

Other patrons worth mentioning are Helena Radziwiłł, who rebuilt her country seat at Nieborów and created a unique Romantic landscape garden nearby at Arkadia; the King's brother Michał Poniatowski; his nephew Stanisław Poniatowski; as well as a number of bourgeois clients, such as the impresario Carlo Tomatis and the banker Piotr Ferguson Tepper.

It may appear perverse to mention patrons and clients before artists, but there is good reason for it. The first half of the eighteenth century had seen some remarkable buildings go up in Poland, such as the Saxony Palace, the Brühl Palace and the Visitation Sisters Church in Warsaw, and the Branicki Palace at Białystok. It had also seen large-scale commissioning of paintings and furniture from the very best artists in Paris, not to mention Meissen porcelain and other luxuries. But this had been for the most part mindless spending by a few grandees seeking to impress, and it did not give rise to important ensembles. Nor did it in any way encourage Polish artists or artisans. Nor, finally, did it affect wider spheres of Polish society.

The patronage of the second half of the century, beginning with that of the King, was an entirely different matter. It was based on genuine artistic appreciation and it had a purpose. For some, like the King, this purpose was, as we have seen, partly political. For others it was utilitarian. For others still it was a social or artistic statement. An increasingly insignificant fraction of the spending was on purely frivolous amusement. It is worth noting that while he was reforming the Jagiellon University in Cracow, Hugo Kołłątaj toyed with plans for a *"kolegium kunsztów wyzwolonych"* and wanted to write a book on art history.

Thinking patrons, like exacting clients, are good for the artist, and the patrons and clients of the 1770s and 1780s in Poland were increasingly demanding and educated. Many actually collaborated with their architects. The King himself was always interfering constructively. Stanisław Potocki actually conducted a dig in Italy and took Aigner there before collaborating with him on a number of projects. Stanisław Poniatowski, the King's nephew, worked closely with his architect Jan Lindsay while building the first Gothic house in Poland, at Korsuń. The degree of artistic education of people such as Stanisław August or Elżbieta Lubomirska meant that fine artists were spotted and used, while even mediocre artists could be made to produce works of quality when guided by a sure hand. The King successfully brought off the ultimate achievement of the patron–of harnessing a number of artists together and guiding them towards creating a common masterpiece.

His example was certainly widely followed. But he was not copied literally. The spread of education and of the new sensibility, as well as the growing wealth of the middle-rank *szlachta* and the emergence of a new bourgeoisie swelled the number of clients inordinately, imposing the necessity of making use of native artists and craftsmen to an unprecedented degree. This in turn gave rise to wide variations of taste and a number of different "styles" flourished concurrently.

King Stanisław August with an hourglass, copperplate acc. to the painting by Marcello Bacciarelli 1793 (Biblioteka Narodowa, Warszawa).

The King fostered a very characteristic style of architecture inspired by a number of influences ranging from antiquity through French *grand siècle* classicism and Dresden rococo to Italian palladianism. It was very sculptural and baroque in taste, although it was in essence neo-classical. Its prime exponents were Merlini and Kamsetzer, and while they also worked for others, including bourgeois clients such as Carlo Tomatis (at the palace *Królikarnia*), this style did not spread far beyond the capital. Foremost among its provincial emulators were Szymon Bogumił Zug, Hilary Szpilowski (1753-1827) and the Gdańsk-born Jan Ferdynand Nax (1736-1810), whose beautiful country residences at Opole Lubelskie, Nałęczów, Kurozwęki and Szczekociny show a greater French influence. By the 1780s, this style had been surpassed by the Palladian classicism of Stanisław Zawadzki, the purer neoclassicism of Jakub Kubicki and the severe antique style of Wawrzyniec Gucewicz (1753-98), all of them in some measure pupils of Stanisław August and recipients of travel bursaries from him.

The King had favored a more severe neo-classicism for public buildings or buildings with a civic connection, and he had used Zawadzki to build barracks for the guards and the artillery in Warsaw. Zawadzki had also designed military buildings for Poznań and an observatory for the university in Cracow before going on to build the lovely Palladian country houses for which he is best known. Much the same is true of Kubicki, but Gucewicz never really left the public domain, and his great monuments are the civic buildings of Wilno primarily the Cathedral.

While men such as Fontana and Schroeger were competent enough, there had been no great architects in Poland in the 1750s. By the 1780s, however, there were a dozen who can rightly be described as belonging to the first class of European architecture. Behind them stood dozens of others, undistinguished perhaps, but quite capable of designing functional and attractive buildings. Most of the better ones had worked for the King, been guided by him or at least been sent on travels by him. Kamsetzer, for instance, was sent on three separate trips by his royal patron, to places as different as England, Italy, Greece and Asia Minor. Some also traveled by courtesy of other patrons. The result was that this body of architects represented a huge fount of knowledge and experience, which permitted them to forge a specific and identifiable strain of neo-classical architecture that was widely copied throughout central and Eastern Europe and most of Russia over the next half-century. They also brought forth younger generations, ensuring a continuous and remarkably rich architectural tradition in Poland throughout the nineteenth century.

Much the same is true of the other arts. The half-dozen jobbing painters working in Poland at the beginning of Stanisław August's reign were as nothing to the bevy of outstandingly talented artists such as Kazimierz Wojniakowski (1772-1812), Michał Płoński and Aleksander Orłowski, not to mention the large numbers of good second-rank painters such as Michał Stachowicz (1768-1825), Józef Peszka (1767-1831) and Anna Rajecka (1760-1832), let alone the dozens of competent portrait-painters and decorators working around the country. They too were to give birth to a fine school of painting in the following century. The same process can be seen in the realm of music, where Elsner's pupil Fryderyk Chopin was to play such a role.[22]

It could indeed be said that the Polish nation found its way back on to the cultural map of Europe just at the moment when Poland itself was being wiped off it. This is no coincidence. One of Stanisław August's preoccupations had always been to reclaim for Poland a place among the civilized nations of Europe. Quite apart from his own proclivities for it, he was also deeply aware of the fact that by the eighteenth century art had become for civilized Europe what Christianity had been for Christendom - the greatest expression of its sense of community. Hence his continuous drive to lock into the artistic life of the Continent.

But the real thrust of his artistic policy nevertheless remained socially and politically didactic. He believed that by creating a refined environment, he could affect the behavior, political as well as social, of his subjects. By ennobling artists, both Polish and foreign, he raised their status and removed the stigma of the tradesman from them. He also used art, just as he did with respect to economic matters, as a purely educational element. When two bright young men had graduated from the Cadet Corps in 1769, Tadeusz Kościuszko and Józef Orłowski, he sent them to study at the *Académie Royale de Peinture* in Paris for a couple of years.

His hopes were fully borne out by reality. By the early 1780s the artistic flowering in Poland had reached a point where it had become self-perpetuating, with ever greater numbers of artists coming forward to satisfy an increasingly discriminating society. The process worked outwards and downwards. Outwards because it took in not only Warsaw and other major cities, but also hundreds of small provincial towns and country houses. Downwards because it produced in all the larger towns a flourishing artisanate of cabinet-makers, clock-makers and silversmiths.

Collecting had become more and more widespread, with not only the King but also his brother Michał Poniatowski, Tomasz Czapski, Joachim Chreptowicz, August Moszyński, Antoni Tyzenhaus and many others building up significant collections of antiquities, and Izabela Czartoryska, Elżbieta Lubomirska and Stanisław Poniatowski collecting works of art. This trend, which was followed albeit at a humbler level by most of the wealthier *szlachta* and the rising bourgeoisie, hugely increased the stock of art in Poland, which in turn helped in the formation of homegrown artists.

The fact is that by the mid 1780s an artistic and intellectual environment of great brilliance and sophistication had come into being in Poland. A young person growing up in it would have been exposed to a broad and brilliant array of literature and drama, to opera and music, to works of art and fine architecture. Aside from deepening his sensibility, this would have had a number of other important effects on him. Most of the literature and the art to which he would have been exposed were of a didactic nature, preaching a very strong morality of sentiment and civic virtue. Much of it had a subliminal political or patriotic message, and communicated a sense of history. Much of the architecture in particular proclaimed the existence of the state and its reformed institutions in a bold, almost austere neoclassicism that came to embody the idea of patriotic virtue for generations. In other words, young people in Poland as a whole, and in Warsaw in particular, were surrounded with the environment and wherewithal of a real education. And all the elements pointed towards the values that lie at the heart of the Constitution of 1791.

Notes

(Notes supplemented by the editorial staff)

1. Quoted in Franciszek Bohomolec, *Komedie konwiktowe* (Boarding school comedies), Jan Kott ed. (Warszawa: PIW, 1959), p.20.

2. On the Polish literature and culture in general during the Enlightenment see: Mieczysław Klimowicz, *Oświecenie* (The Enlightenment) (Warszawa: PWN, 1975); Wacław Borowy, *O poezji polskiej w wieku XVIII* (On Polish poetry in the 18th century) (Kraków: PAU 1948); Tadeusz Mikulski, *Ze studiów nad Oświeceniem* (Studies on the Enlightenment) (Warszawa: PIW, 1956); Zdzisław Libera, *Problemy polskiego Oświecenia* (Problems concerning the Polish Enlightenment) (Warszawa: PIW, 1969); *Wiek oświecony* (The enlightened age) (Warszawa: PIW, 1986); *Problemy literatury polskiego Oświecenia* (Problems concerning the Polish literature in the period of the Enlightenment), ed. Zbigniew Goliński (Wrocław: Ossolineum, vol. 1, 1973, vol. 2, 1977); *Problemy kultury literackiej polskiego Oświecenia* (Problems of literary culture in the Polish Enlightenment) ed. Teresa Kostkiewiczowa (Wrocław: Ossolineum, 1978); *Teatr Narodowy w dobie Oświecenia* (The National Theatre in the age of Enlightenment) eds. Ewa Heise, Karyna Wierzbicka-Michalska (Wrocław: Ossolineum, 1967); Karyna Wierzbicka-Michalska, *Teatr w Polsce w XVIII wieku* (The theatre in Poland in the 18th century) (Warszawa: PWN, 1977); Warszawa w wieku Oświecenia (Warsaw in the age of the Enlightenment) ed. Andrzej Zahorski (Wrocław: Ossolinem, 1986); Zdzisław Libera, *Życie literackie w Warszawie*

w czasach Stanisława Augusta (The literary life in Warsaw during the reign of Stanisław August) (Warszawa: PIW, 1971).

3. Ignacy Krasicki, "O obowiązkach obywatela" (On the obligations of a citizen) in *Pisma poetyckie*, ed. Zbigniew Goliński (Warszawa: PIW, 1976), vol 2, p.293.

4. Paul Cazin, *Le Prince-Évêque de Varmie, Ignace Krasicki* (Paris: Bibliotheque Polonoise, 1940); Roman Wołoszyński, *Ignacy Krasicki. Utopia i rzeczywistość* (Ignacy Krasicki. Utopia and reality) (Wrocław: Ossolineum 1970).

5. Claude Backvis, *Un grand poète polonais du XVIII siècle: Stanislas Trembecki* (Paris, 1937); Edmund Rabowicz, *Stanisław Trembecki w świetle nowych źródeł* (Stanisław Trembecki in the light of new sources) (Wrocław: Ossolineum, 1965).

6. Zbigniew Raszewski, *Bogusławski* (Warszawa: PIW 1972).

7. Ludwik Bernacki, *Teatr, dramat i muzyka za Stanisława Augusta* (The theatre, drama and music of Stanisław August's era) (Lwów: 1925); Alina Nowak-Romanowicz: "Muzyka polskiego Oświecenia i wczesnego Romantyzmu" (The music of the Polish Enlightenment and early Romanticism) in *Z dziejów polskiej kultury muzycznej* (Kraków: Polskie Wydawnictwo Muzyczne, 1966) vol. 2, pp. 9-101; Jan Prosnak, *Kultura muzyczna Warszawy XVIII wieku* (Musical culture in Warsaw at the 18th century) (Kraków: 1955).

8. Jean Fabre, *Stanislas-Auguste Poniatowski et L'Europe des Lumières* (Paris: Les Belles Lettres, 1952); Emanuel Rostworowski, *Ostatni Król Rzeczypospolitej* (The last King of the Commonwealth) (Warszawa: Wiedza Powszechna, 1968); Andrzej Zahorski, *Spór o Stanisława Augusta* (The controversy concerning Stanisław August) (Warszawa: PIW, 1988); Adam Zamoyski, *The last king of Poland* (London: Jonathan Cape, 1992).

9. Alina Chyczewska, *Marcello Bacciarelli* (Wrocław: Ossolineum 1973).

10. Marek Kwiatkowski, *Stanisław August Król-Architekt* (Stanisław August the King-Architect) (Wrocław: Ossolineum, 1983).

11. Aldona Bartczakowa, *Jakub Fontana architekt warszawski XVIII wieku* (Jakub Fontana Warsaw architect of the 18th century) (Warszawa: PWN, 1970).

12. Stanisław August to Madame Geoffrin, 15 IX 1765, in *Correspondence inédite du roi Stanisław Auguste et de Madame Geoffrin*, Charles de Muoy, ed. (Paris 1875); Stanisław Lorentz, "Prace architekta Victora Louisa dla Zamku Królewskiego" (The works of Victor Louis for the Royal Castle) *Biuletyn Historii Sztuki* 13, 4 (1951): 39-74.

13. K. Fournier-Sarlovèze, *Les peintres de Stanislas-Auguste II le roi de Pologne*, (Paris: 1907); Paweł Ettinger, "Bellotto v Varshave" (Bellotto in Warsaw) *Starye Gody* 10-12 (1914): 9-23; Stanisław Lorentz, Stefan Kozakiewicz, *Bellotto a Varsavia*, (Venezia: Alfieri, 1955); *Drezno i Warszawa w twórczości Bernarda Bellotta Canaletta* (Dresden and Warsaw in the works of Bernardo Bellotto Canaletto) (Warszawa: Muzeum Narodowe, 1964); . Kozakiewicz, *Bernardo Bellotto* (Greenwich: New York

Graphic Society, 1972) 2 vols.; Mieczysław Wallis, *Canaletto malarz Warszawy* (Canaletto painter of Warsaw) (Warszawa: Auriga, 7 ed. 1983).

14. Władysław Tatarkiewicz, *Dominik Merlini* (Warszawa: Budownictwo i Architektura, 1955).

15. Andrzej Rottermund, *Zamek Warszawski w epoce Oświecenia* (The Warsaw Castle in the epoch of Enlightenment) (Warszawa: Zamek Królewski, 1989).

16. Władysław Tatarkiewicz, *Łazienki Warszawskie* (The Warsaw *Łazienki*) (Warszawa: Arkady, 1957); Marek Kwiatkowski, *Łazienki Warszawskie* (The Warsaw *Łazienki*) (Warsaw: PWN, 1972).

17. Stanisław August to Adam Naruszewicz, quoted in Andrzej Rottermund, *Zamek Warszawski w epoce Oświecenia,* p. 212.

18. Tadeusz Mańkowski, *Mecenat artystyczny Stanisława Augusta* (Stanisław August's patronage of the arts) (Warszawa: PWN, 1976), p. 23.

19. Tadeusz Mańkowski, *Galeria Stanisława Augusta* (Stanisław August's art-gallery) (Lwów: 1932) 2 vols.; *Rzeźby zbioru Stanisława Augusta* (Sculptures in Stanisław August's collection) (Kraków: 1948); Adam Więcek, *Dzieje sztuki medalierskiej w Polsce* (The history of medal engraving in Poland) (Kraków: Wydawnictwo Literackie, 1972); Teresa Kossecka, *Gabinet Rycin króla Stanisława Augusta* (King Stanisław August's collection of engravings) (Warszawa: Zamek Królewski, 1995); Wacław Olszewicz, "Biblioteka królewska na Zamku Warszawskim" (The Royal library in the Warsaw Castle) *Roczniki Biblioteczne* 3-4 (1969): 557-569.

20. Wacław Zawadzki, ed., *Polska Stanisławowska w oczach cudzoziemców* (Poland of Stanisław August epoch in the eyes of foreigners) (Warszawa: PIW, 1963), vol. 2, p. 71.

21. Zygmunt Batowski, *Norblin* (Lwów: 1911); Władysław Tatarkiewicz, *Aleksander Orłowski* (Warszawa: 1926); Tadeusz Stefan Jaroszewski, *Christian Piotr Aigner architekt Warszawskiego klasycyzmu* (Christian Piotr Aigner architect of Warsaw Neo-classicism) (Warszawa: PWN, 1970); Marek Kwiatkowski *Szymon Bogumił Zug architekt polskiego Oświecenia* (Szymon Bogumił Zug architect of the Polish Enlightenment) (Warszawa: PWN, 1971).

22. Władysław Tatarkiewicz, *Rządy artystyczne Stanisława Augusta* (Stanisław August's rule concerning the arts) (Warszawa: 1919); *Klasycyzm. Studia nad sztuką polską XVIII i XIX wieku* (Neo-classicism. Studies on Polish art of the 18th and 19th centuries) ed. Władysław Tatarkiewicz (Wrocław: Ossolineum, 1968).

10

The Impact of the American Constitution
on Polish Political Opinion in the Late Eighteenth Century

Zofia Libiszowska

"In this century we had two outstanding republican governments - the English and the American....our constitution, which we are to establish today, surpasses both of them; it guarantees liberty, security and all freedoms."[1]

So said Stanisław Małachowski, Marshal of the Polish Diet, in his inaugural speech at the Diet's May 3rd, 1791 session. His remarks indicate that those who prepared the draft of the Polish Constitution took the American political system into consideration. The watchwords he used, "liberty," "security," "freedom," sound very much like those of the American Declaration of Independence and of the French Declaration of the Rights of Man and Citizen, although the French Revolution was not mentioned by Małachowski for political reasons.

The Constitution of the United States, which itself contained English and French political ideas, provided inspiration and example for the *Assemblée Nationale* and for the Polish Diet. When the constitutional era began, Poland was at the forefront of institutional and national change. The great Polish reform was the last endeavor to reinforce and modernize the state as well as the last chance for Poland to recapture her sovereignty, limited, even before the First Partition (1772), by a Russian protectorate.

How much was known in eighteenth-century Poland about the newly established American political system?[2] America's war for independence met with great interest and approval in Poland. The new political structure, which emerged after the victory at Yorktown, provoked a variety of comments in Polish political circles.[3]

The Articles of Confederation were reprinted in the Polish press and appeared in political writings as well. The draft of the Constitution proposed by the Philadelphia Convention was published in *Gazeta Warszawska* and reprinted in *Gazety Wileńskie* late in 1787. A Polish historian and writer, Franciszek Siarczyński, editor of the collection *Traktaty między mocarstwami europeyskiemi* (Treaties between European Powers) included the Articles of Confederation, with a long introduction, and the Treaty of Paris of 1783, with a short history of the American war in successive volumes. In the collection's last volume, printed in 1790, he published the New Constitution of the United States.[4]

Polish readers could also find the American Constitution in an appendix to Philip Mazzei's *Recherches historiques et politiques sur les États Unis de l'Amerique Septentrionale* (Paris, 1788, 4 vol.). Mazzei, a veteran of the American revolution and a friend of Jefferson, was an agent for the Polish court in Paris from 1788. An attempt was made, but not realized, to translate his work, admired by King Stanisław August Poniatowski, into Polish. Another participant in the revolutionary war, Lewis Littlepage, the first American to settle in Poland, was engaged as secretary to the Polish King in 1784.[5] One of the Polish King's secretaries, Scipione Piattoli, an Italian, and friend of Mazzei, was also well acquainted with Jefferson and well informed about the American Constitution. The Polish aristocrat, Jan Potocki, a great traveler, scientist and novelist, intended to write a history of the American War of Independence. Many articles on the American social and economic situation and on the political system were printed by Piotr Świtkowski in a monthly review, *Pamiętnik Historyczno-Polityczny.*[6] American news was to be found in the Polish press, especially in *Gazeta Warszawska* and *Gazeta Narodowa i Obca*, the organ of the "Patriotic Party."

The Polish court and some politicians owned works such as Jefferson's *Notes on the State of Virginia*, John Dickinson's *Letters From a Farmer in Pennsylvania*, Thomas Paine's *The Rights of Man* and Joel Barlow's *The Vision of Columbus*. King Stanisław August's correspondence with Mazzei shows that the King read *The Federalist*.[7] There is no doubt that American events and the new American system of government excited interest and hope in Poland on the eve of the Four-Year Diet.

During the first two years of the Great Diet, which opened in October 1788, two antagonistic political parties emerged: the so-called "Old

Republicans," guardians of "golden liberty," and the party of reform which, following the American and French examples, took the name "Patriots." Neither party had a majority in the Diet, and therefore both of them appealed to the public for support. The "Patriots," who were backed by the representatives of townsfolk in the Diet, also gained the support of the people of Warsaw. Patriot ideology was founded on the principles of the Enlightenment as expressed by Montesquieu and the Physiocrats. The conservatives were compelled to use the same language. They used a specific interpretation of the word "liberty." They also cited the American example in order to deprecate the English hereditary monarchy, which was a model for "Patriots" and the King himself.

In December 1789, when the Diet approved the Principles to Reform the Government, the situation seemed analogous to that of the American Congress before the adoption of the Constitution, and Poland appeared on the verge of constitutional reform. In the spirit of change, Piotr Świtkowski, the editor of *Pamiętnik Historyczno-Polityczny,* published an article entitled "Zasady Nowej Konstytucji i formy rządu zjednoczonej Ameryki Północnej" (The principles of the New Constitution and the form of government in the United States of North America.)[8] His intention to influence the Diet was obvious. The American solution, he argued, was much more progressive than other available political models, given its emphasis on equality of rights and duties and on the abolition of every form of privilege.

The crucial problem in Polish governmental reform was the monarchy. Should it be elective or hereditary? Would the king lose all his powers and prerogatives? Would the country have a permanent Diet and regional dietines of the nobility? Or would there be a hereditary monarchy with the king as chief executive?

Late in 1789, a war of pamphlets started between the two opposite parties in the Diet. The first attack came from Field Hetman Seweryn Rzewuski, a leader of the "Old Republicans." Rzewuski criticized the English constitutional monarchy. England was a kingdom without freedom. The Americans had no choice but to fight against it. Once free, they rejected the idea of a king, and formed a federal republic. "A hereditary monarchy," he concluded, "cannot be reconciled with freedom."[9] Rzewuski reasoned that federalism should be introduced in Poland to strengthen traditional republicanism.

Recalling Polish traditions and ancient noble liberties Rzewuski emotionally encouraged the Poles to follow the American example:

Franklin and Washington, those souls full of justice, those great souls,
to whom America owes her freedom and the whole world pays honor

and show its admiration, and whose example the Poles should follow, have shown mankind that in a Republic a free people...has no need of kings for its happiness.

This pamphlet was a great success, and a second edition soon appeared. Stanisław August, in a letter to Mazzei, expressed his anxiety about its undesirable effects in promoting the "Old Republican" cause.[10]

Some anonymous writers supported Rzewuski, invoking the same argument, that an elective system is the cornerstone of freedom, and that the proof of it was "the newly founded Republic in America."[11] Hereditary monarchy meant despotism and the loss of freedom as was evident from the oppression of American colonies.[12] These authors argued that Franklin and Washington demonstrated what the true spirit of English liberty was when they escaped the fictitious liberty of life under a hereditary monarchy to establish real liberty and freedom in the United States of America.[13] The English hereditary monarchy, as they presented it, was the source of wars and injustice; it was nothing but despotism.[14]

The most important response to Rzewuski's pamphlet came from Hugo Kołłątaj, the main ideologist of the "Patriots." Kołłątaj accused Rzewuski of perverting the ideas of the American leaders. He wrote that he would not be opposed, if the author of the pamphlet and its readers, "inspired by the spirit of Franklin and Washington ... and having become thoroughly acquainted with the rights of man, had thought about safeguarding the liberties of the Polish nation....so that the safety of the nation and the people's freedom should be the purpose of their designs, as was the case with Franklin and Washington." Kołłątaj asked Rzewuski, "Of whose freedom does he perorate, the nobility's or the common people's?" He insisted that Rzewuski "does not think in the same way as Franklin and Washington did, neither does he speak as a man; he speaks as a lord."[15] Then he explained his position and his own point of view on the American experiment as a model for all of humanity. "I myself also know Franklin's language, and I see what is likely to happen in the whole enlightened world." Is it possible, however, for Poland to follow the example of the United States? Their republic is protected from all sides by the ocean, by marshes and deserts, whereas Poland has the most powerful despots as neighbors. Their two and a half million people live in a country that can maintain for up to 30 million; here in Poland there is a dense population and a covetous fight for land. How is it possible to govern the Commonwealth without a king, demanded Kołłątaj. The federal form of government proposed by Rzewuski would unavoidably lead to the partition of the country.

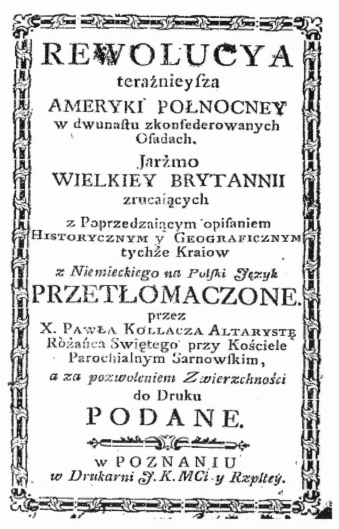

REWOLUCYA
teraźnieyſza
AMERYKI POŁNOCNEY
w dwunaſtu zkonfederowanych
Oſadach.

Jarżmo
WIELKIEY BRYTANNII
zrucaiących

z Poprzedzaiącym opiſaniem
HISTORYCZNYM y GEOGRAFICZNYM
tychże Kraiow

z Niemieckiego na Polſki Język
PRZETŁOMACZONE.
przez
X. PAWŁA KOLLACZA ALTARYSTĘ
Rożańca Swiętego przy Kościele
Parochialnym Sarnowſkim,

a za pozwoleniem Zwierzchności

do Druku
PODANE.

w POZNANIU
w Drukarni J.K. MCi y Rzpltey.

Rewolucya teraźnieysza Ameryki Północney w dwunastu zkonfederowanych Osadach. Jarzmo Wielkiey Brytannii zrucaiących z poprzedzaiącym opisaniem historycznym y geograficznym tychże Kraiów z Niemieckiego na Polski Język przetłomaczone przez X. Pawła Kollacza... (The present revolution of North America confederated in twelve states throwing off the yoke of Great Britain, preceded by a historical and geographical description of these states, translated into Polish from German by Father Paweł Kollacz) w Poznaniu w Drukarni J.K. Mci y Rzplitey (1778). Title page. Translation from an unidentified German original about the American War for Independence and including information about the geography, economy and history of North America (Biblioteka Narodowa, Warszawa).

HISTORYA

POLITYCZNA

REWOLUCYI

AMERYKANSKIEY

TERAZNIEYSZEY

przez

Sławnego Rainala.

w Francuzkim napisana ięzyku,

a teraz

na Polſki przełożona.

Za pozwóleniem Zwierzchnoſci.

w WARSZAWIE 1783.

Nakładem i Drukiem MICHAŁA GRÖLLA,
Kſięgarza Nadwornego J. K. Mci.
w Marywilu Nro 24.

Historya Polityczna Rewolucyi Amerykanskiey Teraźnieyszey przez Sławnego Rainala
w Francuzkim napisana ięzyku, a teraz na Polski przełożona. (The political history of
the present American Revolution, written in French by the famous Raynal and now
translated into Polish) w Warszawie, Michał Gröll, 1783. Title page. The translation
by Franciszek Siarczyński of Guillaume T.F. Raynal, *Revolution de l'Amerique*,
Londres, 1781. Reprinted from Zofia Libiszowska, *Opinia polska wobec Rewolucji
Amerykańskiej w XVIII wieku* (Łódź, Ossolineum, 1962).

Emphasizing that he is an enthusiastic supporter of American liberty and its founders, Kołłątaj explained, nonetheless, that foreign examples should be adapted to local conditions and circumstances. "The system of Franklin carries different consequences for each nation...The system of Franklin is concerned with the freedom of man and not with the means by which men everywhere try to recover their rights."[16] According to Kołłątaj, Franklin and Washington started their reform with the assertion that "in America there are no subjects, or class divisions; in America all men are equal."

Similar arguments about America's unique situation are found in many other replies to Rzewuski. They emphasize the geographical situation of America, its political system and the security of its frontiers. The strongest argument against the "Old Republican" position was that a republic cannot exist among despotic monarchies. "Wherever there is even a single despotic state, there it is hardly possible to preserve a republican government in the neighboring nations," warned Stanisław Staszic.[17] Ignacy Potocki, in spite of his conviction, stated, not without regret that "Given the present state of affairs, Poland is unfit to be a true republic... Poland, considering her territory, national organization and customs, cannot be a common republic (*une république simple*) nor a confederation. Therefore, all proposals of imitating ancient or modern republics should be forgotten; neither Lycurgus, nor Franklin can meet her needs. Poland can only be a limited monarchy *(une monarchie limitée)*."[18]

For its supporters, like Potocki and Staszic, a hereditary monarchy was perceived as necessary for Poland as it faced the danger of powerful despotic neighbors. In court circles it was seen above all, as a means of strengthening the executive within a system of separation of powers, in conformity with "the new theory of government" as Stanisław August called it.[19]

It is worthwhile at this point to examine the contents of a pamphlet entitled *Krótka rada względem napisania dobrej konstytucji* (Brief advice concerning the writing of a good constitution),[20] published in 1790. Its author, Kajetan Kwiatkowski, argued that in Poland the king should be the head of the executive branch. He explained:

> Though a nation has no king, nevertheless the legislative power and the executive power must be separate. Then executive authority shall rest with the magistrates and the legislative authority with the representatives of the nation. Such is the situation of the thirteen American provinces...where each province has its own magistrates, its own courts of justice and its own revenue and military offices, and all of them together have their parliament and their president, who is different from

the king of England only in name, but not in authority, and has executive power and the power of establishing laws over the whole territory.[21]

Again and again the example of America was used in various discussions. At the close of 1790, a year of stormy polemics, Jan Potocki, editor of *Le Journal Hebdomadaire de la Diète*, reflects,

> For us, who have the experience of past events and the education of an enlightened age, justice and truth are restored to their old rights, and the words addressed by Washington to the citizens of the United States eight years ago can be applied to our present situation. We have arrived at a time when the rights of man are better understood and more clearly defined than at any time before.[22]

It was beyond the ability of the representatives assembled in the Diet to solve these problems and to finish their work within the limit of two years. The 1790 election reinforced the position of the supporters of the King and the "Patriotic Party." The Republicans remained the only dangerous opponents to constitutional reform.

The project for the reform of dietines, prepared by the "Patriots" with the approval of the King, provoked a new protest by Hetman Rzewuski. Defending the landless nobility, whom the reform deprived of the vote, Rzewuski again used the American example. In America, he wrote:

> a tenant has *vocem activam* (the right to vote) in assemblies. The land he tills is not his own, but the opinion he holds is his own. He is a tenant on the soil, but a citizen in an assembly, and it often happens in debates that those who pay rent and those who receive it, hold opposite opinions.[23]

Rzewuski defended gentry republicanism because the landless nobility traditionally voted in support of the great landlords who were their patrons. Despite objections by Rzewuski and others Parliament passed the law that deprived the landless nobility of their political rights.

In the debates of the Diet and in journalistic discussions the question of the rights of burghers came to the fore. The image of the American revolution and of a society without discrimination (estates, and their privileges) played an important part in these exchanges. Piotr Świtkowski raised the issue of rights for the urban population in his article about the United States, in which he explained the conception of American liberty and equality. His allusion to Polish affairs is obvious. "Do not let us blunder by pretending that a great nation can be free and have one class of people hold the reins of government and control the rest of the nation."[24] In America, he claimed, not noble birth but personal merit assured the esteem and social advancement.

BENYAMIN FRANKLIN

Benjamin Franklin, copperplate, included in the article "Beniamin Franklin, czyli
niektóre o nim i zasługach jego wiadomości" (Benjamin Franklin, Information about
him and his accomplishments) in *Pamiętnik Historyczno-Polityczny*, January 1784.
Reprinted from Zofia Libiszowska, *Opinia polska...*

The anonymous author of the well-known pamphlet *Dwóch nieboszczyków...* (Two dead men), dealt with the problem of political and social equality for townsmen. "People!" he begged, "I am addressing you once and again. Oh! how gravely you are mistaken if you think that you should respect noble birth alone and not intelligence, merit, ability, and virtue. Let William Tell and George Washington bear witness to it."[25]

Similarly, another anonymous author concluded that "the recent revolution in America gave George Washington, a then unknown Virginian, the name of a great general and founder of liberty, and the whole world remembers this name with respect."[26] The loudest voice in favor of equal rights was that of Julian Ursyn Niemcewicz, who declared:

> Very often ordinary men saved their motherland and made it famous. None of us knows who the father of Washington was, or whom Franklin counted as grandfather....but everybody knows and future generations shall remember that Washington and Franklin liberated America.[27]

The question of rights for townspeople also had its economic side. America not only set an example, but, as a land of promise, was a rival to the old continent. Farseeing politicians warned that foreigners, instead of settling in Polish towns "ought to seek refuge in the free States of America beyond the seas where neither burgher nor craftsman is held in contempt."[28] Kołłątaj, demanding political rights for townspeople, argued that such freedom would have happy consequences for Polish cities. "We should encourage the friends of freedom from distant countries, who seeing no better shelter from oppression go beyond the sea to the land of Franklin and Washington."[29] Jacek Jezierski, industrialist and political writer argued "when they hear in foreign countries that we bestow freedom and justice not only upon cities, but upon everybody, they will come to Poland.... as to a new-found America."[30]

The Law on Cities of April 18, 1791, was a kind of agreement or even alliance between the nobility and the burghers. It was celebrated in town halls as well as in churches where the names of Washington and Franklin were often invoked.

The peasant question suggested fewer American comparisons. In the great mass of publications on that problem, only a few authors made use of American examples. Frequently, Polish peasants were compared to Negro slaves rather than to American farmers. Nevertheless, the problems of slavery and of indigenous Indians in America did not eclipse Polish statesmens' faith that the new state pointed the way to universal liberty.

In the debates concerning the form of the Polish government and the social system, arguments referring to the American Revolution were mostly

KONFEDERACYA

C Z Y L I

N O W A K O N S T Y T U C Y A

Stanów Ziednoczonych Amerykań-

skich, w Roku 1789.

Konstytucye Rządowe, luboby z naydoy-
źrzalszą rozwagą i przezornością ułożone,
nie mogą przecie w pierwiastkach swoich mieć
tey trwałości i powagi, która iest skutkiem po-
wziętego ku nim szacunku i nałogu, a zatym
i czasu. Dziwować się więc nie można, iż
Rzeczpospolita Amerykańska dźwigniona na zasadach niedobrze ieszcze osiadłych i umocowa-
nych, zachwiania się doznała. Wprowadzony
z niepodległością Rząd nowy, niechęć dawnych
Przyiaciół Anglii, przyiętych na iey łono, prze-
waga wkorzenionych przesądów, narażały ią
na burze, które wstrząsaiąc gmachem całym,
osłabiały iego fundamenta. Jedną z naycel-
nieyszych zawad do ziednoczenia sił zdólnych
ku zapobieżeniu szkodliwym skutkom niezgody,
był niedostatek zupełności władzy w Zgroma-
dze-

"Konfederacya czyli Nowa Konstytucya Stanów Ziednoczonych Amerykańskich, w
Roku 1789." (The Confederation. The New Constitution of the United States of
America, in the year 1789) in Franciszek Siarczyński ed. *Traktaty między mocarstwami
europeyskiemi*, vol. 6, Warszawa, 1790. The first page of Siarczyński's introduction
to the translation of the Constitution of the United States (Biblioteka Uniwersytecka
w Warszawie). In 1789 the first United States Congress amended the Constitution
which was ratified and the first president was elected.

kiey wagi robota, obwieszczona została Stanom Ziednoczonym dnia 17, Września, Roku 1787, pod tytułem:

AKT KONFEDERACYI, AMERYKI ZIE-DNOCZONEY.

My Naród Stanów Ziednoczo-nych, końcem doskonalszego umocnie-nia Związku, urządzenia Sprawie-dliwości, utwierdzenia spokoyności wewnętrzney, opatrzenia powsze-chnego beśpieczeństwa, pomnożenia szczęśliwości publiczney, i zapewnie-nia błogosławieństw Wolności Nam samym i Potomkom naszym, rozka-zuiemy i stanowiemy ninieyszą Kon-ftytucyą dla Stanów Ziednoczonych Ameryki.

A R T Y K U Ł I.

§. I. Cała Władza Prawodawcza, określo-na ninieyszą Konwencyą powierza się Kongres-sowi Stanów Ziednoczonych, który z Senatu i Jzby Reprezentantów ekładać się będzie.

§. II.

used as rhetorical ornaments, and the American example was not seen as applicable to Poland. Nevertheless, such references influenced the climate of the discussion and awakened the social and political consciousness of Poles, even if they did not offer actual models and solutions suited to Polish problems.[31]

Świtkowski discussed the Polish Constitution in a series of articles, comparing it with that of the United States. He explained to the readers of *Pamiętnik Historyczno-Polityczny* that the system adopted by the United States for the election of officials in the legislative and executive brances could be used only in countries not threatened from the outside. Polish conditions, on the other hand, made it necessary to strengthen the executive and to introduce hereditary monarchy.[32]

In the atmosphere of lively and heated discussion aroused by the proposed constitution, *Gazeta Narodowa i Obca* published a eulogy to the American Constitution written by Benjamin Franklin in a letter to Congress in 1788. Franklin pointed out that no law could be perfect and satisfy all requirements, as it was only a human work, but he praised the Constitution's indisputable merits, declaring: "I endorse this Constitution as, truly, I wonder if any other could be better for us."[33] Franklin's words were quoted to support the 1791 Constitution and to convince those who doubted its merits.[34]

American news published by the Polish press during the Four-Year Diet featured the remarkable prosperity of the union. Readers learned about the accession to the federal union of formerly recalcitrant states, about the development of trade and the growth of export, about finance, banking and the stable value of paper money. An interesting case was the news about America published in *Gazeta Narodowa i Obca* in May 1791 written in the form of letters from Philadelphia and Boston and clearly intended as an argument in the fight against the intrigues of the Polish political opposition:

> While Europe has fallen prey to cabinet intrigues, foreign wars and domestic discussions, and some people...praise the fortunate change of their fates while others travel to foreign courts to lay charges against their own country which has dared to become wisely self-governed and independent, the states of the United America are enjoying the blessings of tranquility and candor.[35]

Gazeta Narodowa i Obca also reported the proceedings of the Congress and President Washington's public pronouncements. His speech opening the first Congress was reprinted in two consecutive issues. In *Pamiętnik Historyczno-Polityczny* Świtkowski wrote that "at a time when some people make bold to maintain that free nations can neither wisely govern their state nor be happy, it is most profitable to observe that country which not long ago began its political existence under the banner of liberty."[36] In that same issue he published Washington's report to Congress. *Gazette de Varsovie* pursued a similar course. Informing its readers of the economic development of North America, it emphasized *"voilà les fruits de la liberté, voilà ce que produit un Gouvernement sagement organisé et doué d'énergie."*[37] At the moment that the work of the Four-Year Diet was imperilled by Rzewuski, *Gazeta Narodowa i Obca* quoted the words that the First Citizen of the United States addressed to his countrymen: "preserve, protect and defend the Constitution that you have given yourselves. The country shall find in it security and peace, the weak shall find protection and the brave a curb."[38]

During the festivities celebrating the proclamation of the Constitution of 3 May, and later on its first anniversary, special attention was paid to its connection with and relation to American models associated with Franklin and Washington. During a solemn session at Wilno University, professor of law Hieronim Stroynowski delivered an oration on the Constitution, in which he quoted a long passage from President Washington's speech previously printed in Polish newspapers. He spoke of Washington as "a great hero, enlightened legislator and expert politician, successfully controlling the helm of the free state."[39] In like manner, Franklin and Washington were mentioned among the champions of liberty during the celebration of the first anniversary of the Constitution of 3 May held at Cracow University.

The American Constitution represented a great and important break with the past. It foreshadowed a world where respect for general human values would be the measure of a successful government. It is not surprising that in Poland every political camp referred to it, in spite of different political programs.

The Constitution of the United States is now over 200 years old. It became the cornerstone of American democracy and part of the American national heritage. The Polish Constitution of 3 May lasted only one year. But it fixed in the minds of Poles a belief in the similarity between two constitutions that grew out of the struggle for independence and the rights of man. At every turning point in modern Polish history and during today's reconstruction of democracy in Poland, Polish statesmen have turned to these common constitutional roots, proving true Stanisław August's words written to Philip Mazzei: "I believe more and more that Washington and those in his country who think as he does will become humanity's best political mentors."[40]

Notes

1. *Gazeta Narodowa i Obca,* no. 37, 7 May 7 1791; see also Franciszek Siarczyński, *Dzień Trzeci Maja 1791* (The day of 3 May 1791) (Kraków, 1891), pp. 41-42.

2. Zofia Libiszowska, *Opinia polska wobec Rewolucji Amerykańskiej w XVIII w.* (Polish Opinion of the American Revolution in the 18th c.), (Łódź-Wrocław: Ossolineum, 1962); "Problematyka amerykańska w publicystyce Sejmu Czteroletniego" (America in the political writings of the Four-Year Diet), *Zeszyty Naukowe* UŁ 1, 45 (1966): 67-92. An important selection of pamphlets and articles appeared in the collection, *Materiały do dziejów Sejmu Czteroletniego* (Sources related to the history of the Four-Year Diet), eds. Jerzy Michalski, Emanuel Rostworowski, Janusz Woliński, vols. 1-5, together with Artur Eisenbach vol. 6 (Wrocław: Ossolineum, 1955-69), referred to hereafter as MDSC.

3. Libiszowska, *Opinia polska,* p. 116; see also "Stany Zjednoczone pod rządem Artykułów Konfederacji" (The United States of America under the Articles of Confederation) in *Konstytucja USA 1787-1987. Historia i Współczesność,* ed. Jerzy Wróblewski (Warszawa: PWN, 1987), pp. 52-77.

4. Franciszek Siarczyński, ed., *Traktaty między mocarstwami europeyskiemi* (Treaties between the European Powers) (Warszawa, 1773-1790), 6 vols. The Articles of Confederation, vol. 4, pp. 292-306, The Treaty of Paris, vol. 5, pp. 235-295, and The New Constitution vol. 6, pp. 220-253.

5. Curtis C. Davis, *The King's Chevalier* (New York: Bobbs-Merrill, 1961). About the suspicious role he played in his service to the King, see: Miecislaus Haiman, *Kościuszko: Leader and Exile* (New York: Polish Institute of Arts and Sciences in America, 1946), p. 25.

6. American topics are to be found in *Pamiętnik Historyczno-Polityczny,* Jan. 1790, pp. 42-49, Feb. pp. 1-19, 35-49, 68-80, Mar. pp. 179-202, Apr, pp. 276-331, Oct. pp. 1180-1193, Nov. pp. 1328-1342, Feb. 1791, pp. 138-153, and Apr. pp. 171-374.

7. The Polish King to Mazzei, 20 January 1790, MS. Ossolineum no. 9751, p. 16; a great part of the correspondence between the King and Mazzei was edited in Italy: *Lettere di Filippo Mazzei alla corte di Polonia (1788-1792),* ed. Raffaele Ciampini (Bologna: N. Zanichelli, 1937); a larger collection of letters was published in 1982, *Lettres de Philippe Mazzei et du Roi Stanislas-Auguste de Pologne,* vol. 1, from July 1788 to August 1789, eds. Jerzy Michalski, Monika Senkowska-Gluck, with Italian cooperation (Roma, 1982). For an English translation of this correspondence, see: Philip Mazzei, *Selected Writings and Correspondence,* vol. 2, 1788-1791. *Agent for the King of Poland During the French Revolution,* ed. Margherita Marchione (Prato: Cassa di Risparmi e Depositi di Prato, 1983).

8. Piotr Świtkowski, "Zasady Nowej Konstytucji i formy Rządu Zjednoczonej Ameryki Północnej" (The Principles of the new constitution and the form of government in the United States of North America), *Pamiętnik Historyczno-Polityczny,* January 1790.

9. Seweryn Rzewuski, *O sukcesyi tronu w Polszcze rzecz krótka* (A short essay on the succession to the throne in Poland) n.p., n.d. (1789). See Zofia Zielińska, *Republikanizm spod znaku buławy. Publicystyka Seweryna Rzewuskiego z lat 1788-1790* (Republicanism under a hetman's mace: political writings of Seweryn Rzewuski, 1788-1790) (Warszawa, 1988); *"O sukcesyi tronu w Polszcze 1787-1790"* (On the succession to the throne in Poland 1787-1790) (Warszawa: PWN, 1991).

10. Stanisław August to Mazzei, 27 January 1790, MS. Ossolineum no. 9751, p. 16. Mazzei, *Selected Writings,* p. 260.

11. (Seweryn Rzewuski), *Myśli nad różnemi pismy popierającymi sukcesyą tronu* (Thoughts on various writings supporting the succession to the throne), n. p., n. d. (1790).

12. *List z Warszawy do przyjaciela na wieś o projektach Nowey formy Rządu* (A letter from Warsaw to a friend in the country on proposals for a new form of government), 9 August 1790, n. p.

13. (Seweryn Rzewuski), *Uwagi dla utrzymania wolnej elekcyi króla polskiego do Polaków, w Warszawie roku 1789* (Remarks to Poles about the preservation of the free elections of the Polish king).

14. (Seweryn Rzewuski), *Wiadomość chronologiczna, w którym czasie, które państwo wolność utraciło pod rządem monarchów sukcesyjnych* (Chronological information concerning when and which states lost freedom under hereditary monarchs) (Warszawa, n. d. (1790)). Zofia Zielińska in her work *Republikanizm...* , convincingly argues that Rzewuski himself was the author of most of those pamphlets.

15. Hugo Kołłątaj, *Uwagi nad pismem... "Seweryna Rzewuskiego...o sukcesyi tronu w Polszcze rzecz krótka"* (Remarks about the work ... "Seweryn Rzewuski's...a short essay on the succession to the throne in Poland") (Warszawa, 1790), p. 66.

16. Kołłątaj, *Uwagi..,.* pp. 71-77.

17. Stanisław Staszic, *Przestrogi dla Polski* (Warnings for Poland), in *Pisma filozoficzne i społeczne,* ed. Bogdan Suchodolski (Warszawa: PWN, 1954), vol. 1, p. 192.

18. Ignacy Potocki to Eliasz Aloe, 7 August 1790. MS. Potocki Papers, no. 277 vol. 303, AGAD Archives, Warszawa. See Emanuel Rostworowski, *Legendy i fakty XVIII w.* (Legends and facts of the 18th c.) (Warszawa: PWN, 1963), p. 323.

19. (Mikołaj Wolski), *Zdanie o królu polskim 1792 roku* (An opinion of the Polish king in 1792) in *Rocznik Towarzystwa Historyczno-Literackiego,* Paryż 1867, pp. 10-28. See also about Stanisław August as the author of this pamphlet, Rostworowski *Legendy,* pp. 488-506.

20. Kajetan Kwiatkowski, *Krótka rada względem napisania dobrej konstytucyi* (Brief advice concerning the writing of a good constitution), n.p., 1790.

21. Kwiatkowski, *Krótka rada...*, p. 28.

22. *Journal Hebdomadaire de la Diète*, no. 51, 26 December 1790.

23. Seweryn Rzewuski, *Uwagi nad prawem, które by szlachcie bez posessyi activitatem na sejmikach odbierało* (Remarks on the law which would deprive the landless gentry of *activitatem* in the dietines), n.p., n.d. (1790).

24. "Stan prawdziwy wolnej Ameryki Północnej" (The real state of free North America), *Pamiętnik Historyczno-Polityczny*, April 1789.

25. *Dwóch nieboszczyków, Dekert z ministrem o miastach* (Two dead men, Dekert with a minister about towns) (1791) in MDSC, vol. 4, p. 57.

26. *Dusza krajów, czyli o poddanych polskich...* (The soul of the country or on the Polish peasantry...) (1789) in MDSC, vol. 1, p. 545.

27. *Gazeta Narodowa i Obca, no. 27,* 9 March 1791. A portions of Niemcewicz's speech was quoted by *The Newport Mercury* on 30 July 1790; see Miecislaus Haiman, *The Fall of Poland in Contemporary American Opinion* (Chicago: Polish Roman Catholic Union of America, 1935), p. 35.

28. *Usprawiedliwienie dysydentów mieszczan...* (A justification of the dissenter burghers...), in MDSC, vol 2, p. 90.

29. Hugo Kołłątaj, "Odezwa do deputacji Konstytucyjnej" (An appeal to the constitutional deputation), in *Listy Anonima i Prawo polityczne narodu polskiego,* eds. Bogusław Leśnodorski and Helena Wereszycka. (Warszawa: PWN, 1954), vol 2, p. 180.

30. Jacek Jezierski, *Miasta bez prawa* (Warszawa: Gröll, n.d. {1791}) (Cities without law), in MDSC, vol 4, p. 51.

31. A comparison between the American and Polish constitutions has became the subject of special studies: Joseph Kasparek-Obst, *The Constitutions of Poland and of the United States. Kinships and Genealogy* (Miami, Florida: The American Institute of Polish Culture, 1980); *European and American Constitutionalism in the Eighteenth Century,* ed. Michał Rozbicki (Warsaw: The American Studies Center, 1990); *Constitutionalism and Human Rights: America, Poland, and France,* eds. Kenneth W. Thompson and Rett R. Ludwikowski (Lanham: University Press of America, 1991).

32. Piotr Świtkowski, "Dalsze myśli i uwagi względem Konstytucji 3 Maja" (Further thoughts and remarks about the Constitution of 3 May), *Pamiętnik Historyczno-Polityczny*, August 1791.

33. *Gazeta Narodowa i Obca,* no. 46, 8 June 1791.

34. (Ignacy Potocki), *Na pismo, któremu napis "O Konstytucji 3 Maja 1791."... odpowiedź* (Response to the publication entitled "On the Constitution of 3 May

1791") (1791). See Władysław Smoleński, *Ostatni rok Sejmu Wielkiego* (The last year of the Great Diet) (Kraków, 1897), p. 77.

35. *Gazeta Narodowa i Obca,* no. 63, 6 July 1791.

36. "Stan Ameryki Północnej" (The state of North America), *Pamiętnik Historyczno-Polityczny,* December 1791, pp. 1128-1142.

37. *Gazette de Varsovie,* no. 19, 25 June 1792.

38. *Gazeta Narodowa i Obca,* no. 4, 14 January 1791.

39. Hieronim Stroynowski, *Mowa o Konstytucyi Rządu ustanowionej dnia trzeciego i piątego maja 1791 . . . czytana...dnia 1 lipca 1791* (Oration on the Constitution adopted on the third and fifth of May 1791...given...1 July 1791), see Smoleński, *Ostatni rok,* p. 11.

40. Stanisław August to Philip Mazzei, 17 April 1790, MS. Ossolineum, no. 9751, p. 29. Mazzei, *Selected Writings,* p. 327.

w *WARSZAWIE,*

w Drukarni Uprzywiejowaney Michała Grölla, Kfięgarza Nadw. J. K. Mci.

11

The Meaning of the Constitution of 3 May

Jerzy Michalski

B egun in 1764 by the Czartoryskis and Stanisław August, the attempt to introduce political reforms in Poland brought only partial success. It encountered resistance from the conservative noble community and, most importantly, the disapproval of the St. Petersburg and Berlin courts.[1] Ossified by Catherine II's 1768 guarantee, the political system of the Republic preserved the basic elements of "golden freedom" with the *liberum veto* at the forefront.[2]

This political system which ensured the weakness desired by Poland's neighbors was maintained after the First Partition.[3] The weakness of the semi-sovereign state in which the Russian ambassador exercised almost gubernatorial powers was not only the result of foreign prohibitions and orders. However, the aversion of noble society towards taxes caused the 30,000 man army legislated by the 1773-1775 Diet to total barely above ten thousand. In 1780 the Diet, not without foreign influence, rejected Andrzej Zamoyski's codification project which was supported by the King and which contained favorable modifications in the legal status of the peasants and townspeople.[4] Created after the First Partition at the 1773-1775 Diet and reorganized and strengthened through the efforts of the King during the 1776 Diet, the Permanent Council (*Rada Nieustająca*) - in effect the first central executive organ in Polish history - in general was not accepted by the nobility since it was imposed by Russia.[5] In addition, the deeply rooted "republican" ideology of the nobility caused it to regard the Council as a threat to its freedom.[6] This aversion was fostered by the antiroyal propaganda of the magnate opposition which was joined by the Czartoryskis who had become alienated from Stanisław August.[7] Thrown into disorder by the demagoguery of the magnate opposition and fettered by the principle of mandatory unanimity, the Diets of 1778-1786 were legislatively unproductive.[8] Political life was dominated by an atmosphere of sterility and demoralizing dependence on foreign control.

His attempts at reform decidedly restrained by Catherine II after 1776, the King[9] based his hopes for a better future either on possible changes in the international situation, or on the influence of Enlightenment ideology, especially on the outlook of the young generation of Poles educated in the schools of the Commission for National Education.[10] The process of change in the mentality and in the attitudes of society actually did gain in strength after the First Partition. Disseminated by a reformed school system, political publications and the *belles lettres*, the scope of Enlightenment ideas grew significantly. Civic mindedness increased and patriotic feelings came to life as a reaction to the tragedy of the partition and the loss of sovereignty.

The outbreak of the Russo-Turkish War in 1787 brought changes in the international situation, changes which most politically aware Poles recognized as positive. In its early phase the war went poorly for Russia; Austria, which in 1788 entered on Russia's side, suffered defeats. Sweden attacked Russia in the summer of 1788. Stanisław August maintained a pro-Russian stance and, to safeguard against Prussian expansionism that could demand territorial concessions from Poland as a condition for Russian and Austrian acquisitions at Turkey's expense, he sought a formal Russo-Polish alliance which would guarantee the Republic's territorial integrity. The King expected that by offering the participation of a small Polish contingent on Russia's side, he would receive Catherine's approval for expanding the treasury and the army and for, at least, secondary political reforms.[11]

The antiroyal opposition of magnates put forward its own alliance plan intended as a means of seizing power in the Republic.[12] Catherine II wished for peace in Poland. She believed that this goal could be achieved by maintaining a balance between the King and the opposition without, however, meeting any of their demands. She therefore did not agree either to the modification of the political system as proposed by the King or to the abolition of the Permanent Council as the opposition wished. Since an alliance could be drawn only at a confederated Diet (at which legislation could be passed by majority voting) the empress agreed to it this time. She also permitted the possibility of passing new taxes for enlarging the army.[13]

Catherine, however, underestimated the strength of the ferment that had gripped the Poles in the midst of developing war and unfolding political events. The idea of joining the war on the Austro-Russian side was universally dismissed; on the contrary, sympathies lay with the Turks and the Swedes. As patriotic fervor rose, the desire to emerge from impotence and dependence provided the impetus for expanding the army, a notion supported by both the royal party and the opposition.[14]

But this atmosphere was not sufficient in itself to bring about changes in the political system were it not for the decision by Prussia to challenge Russia's protectorate over Poland. This was both to counter Russia's violation of its treaty with Prussia in favor of rival Austria and to facilitate additional annexations at Poland's expense.

The leaders of the magnate opposition, having realized that the Russian court would not meet their demands, decided to look for support to Prussia whose anti-Russian policies they took to be permanent.[15] The Diet, which would go down in history as the Four-Year Diet, convened on October 6, 1788 and the following day it was confederated under the leadership of Stanisław Małachowski[16] of the Crown confederacy and Kazimierz Nestor Sapieha of the Lithuanian confederacy.[17] Members of the Diet and broader public opinion were greatly impressed by the declaration of the Prussian court received in October, objecting to the proposed Polish-Russian alliance, offering assurances of friendship and holding out the possibility of closer ties with the Republic. The declaration was viewed as a blow to Russia's hegemony and an opportunity for Poland to pursue an independent foreign policy.[18] Amidst unprecedented enthusiasm, on October 20th, the Diet approved by acclamation the levy of a 100,000 man army.[19]

The opposition, which adopted the name "Patriotic Party," strengthened by Prussian backing and in particular by the popularity of emancipation slogans, secured a majority in the Diet and enjoyed the support of popular opinion. Through a series of resolutions the Diet stripped the Permanent Council (in actuality, the King) of its power over the army and diplomacy; finally, in January 1789, it abolished the Council itself.[20] Having decided to remain in permanent session, the Diet became a governing Parliament uniting legislative and executive powers.[21]

Stanisław August who warned of the terrible consequences of breaking with Russia, found himself in the minority and became the object of criticism which at times was quite intense. He rejected, however, the call by Ambassador Stackelberg to withdraw from the Diet with his supporters and to form a new confederation under the protection of the Russian army. He remained convinced that the Diet would bring positive change to Poland and he attempted to work loyally with the Diet under the slogan, "the King with the Nation, the Nation with the King." For a long time, however, the leaders of the "Patriotic Party" did not trust him. Catherine II, absorbed by the war, decided against immediate counteraction and the restoration by force of her protectorate. For the time being, she likewise did not consider concluding an agreement with Prussia for a further partitioning of Poland.

Rashly perceived by Poles as permanent, the sudden and easy recovery of independence and the overthrow of "the horrendous dependency" as the preceding period was called, evoked a confidence in Poland's strength and liberated new energies in its society. Starting with the publication by Stanisław Staszic in 1787 of *Uwagi nad życiem Jana Zamoyskiego* (Remarks on the life of Jan Zamoyski),[22] published anonymously, political literature and the press developed on a previously unknown scale and included an unusually broad thematical range. Among such publications the works of Hugo Kołłątaj or those inspired by him, played a prominent role, especially the lengthy treatise, *Do Stanisława Małachowskiego...Anonima listów kilka* (To Stanisław Małachowski...several letters by an anonymous author),[23] which included a program of action for the Parliament. The political literature of the time at once reflected, disseminated and strengthened the conviction that the present moment created an unusual opportunity for Poles to freely establish internal order, to oversee the affairs of state and to do so in their own (variously understood) interests.

The Diet was deluged with bills drafted by deputies or offered from outside. Initially the parliamentary debates failed to bear legislative fruit because of a lack of procedural rules and the slow acquisition of political experience by deputies who, convinced of their importance, were intoxicated by their own verbosity. Only in the spring of 1789 were new taxes passed to increase the army to 100,000 as decreed earlier. Soon the projected size of the army was reduced to 60,000, but despite the doubling of the state budget, tax revenues still proved inadequate. The levying of taxes, however, attested to a major rise in patriotic feelings, since they also affected noble estates, a step that previously had been categorically rejected.

Not until September 7, 1789 did the Diet choose eleven of its members to serve on a Deputation "to draft proposals concerning the form of government" with the purpose of preparing a project for a new political system. Kołłątaj delineated far-reaching tasks for the Deputation in his appeal "*Do prześwietnej*

The Royal Castle in Warsaw, the central part of the painting: The General View of Warsaw as seen from Praga by Bernardo Belotto Canaletto, 1770 (Muzeum Narodowe w Warszawie). Photo. H. Romanowski.

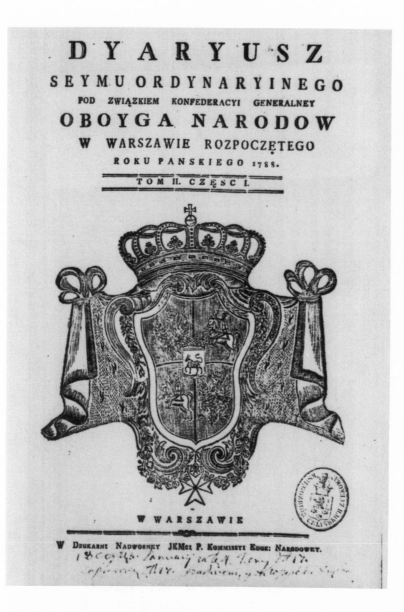

DYARYUSZ
SEYMU ORDYNARYINEGO
POD ZWIĄZKIEM KONFEDERACYI GENERALNEY
OBOYGA NARODOW
W WARSZAWIE ROZPOCZĘTEGO
ROKU PANSKIEGO 1788.

TOM II. CZĘSCI.

W WARSZAWIE

W Drukarni Nadworney JKMci P. Kommissyi Eduk: Narodowey.

Dyaryusz Seymu Ordynaryinego pod związkiem Konfederacyi Generalney Oboyga Narodów w Warszawie rozpoczętego roku Pańskiego 1788 (The Diary of the Ordinary Diet sitting as a General Confederacy of the Two Nations in Warsaw commenced in the year of Our Lord 1788) w Warszawie, w Drukarni Nadwornej JKMci P. Kommissyi Eduk. Narodowey. Title page (Biblioteka Uniwersytecka w Warszawie). The Diary was written by the Diet secretary Jan Łuszczewski.

Deputacji dla ułożenia rządu polskiego" (To the most illustrious Deputation for designing the Polish government) and expressed the hope that the "constitution of our government" which it would draft "would be a glorious epoch-making event at the close of the eighteenth century."[24] With optimism typical of Enlightenment ideologists, he believed that its principles would not be guided by "hypocrisy and prejudice" but by a reason which had discerned the immutable laws of nature. This was to be accomplished by the reconstruction of the social foundations of the state, that is by breaking with the noble monopoly on political rights and extending them to the townspeople; by ending the noble monopoly of power over the serfs by codifying and permanently safeguarding the legal status of peasants, and extending to them state protection.

As Kołłątaj published his appeal, the burgher's movement was coming to life in Poland - an event unprecedented in Polish history.[25] Its appearance was one of the most significant manifestations of growing social activity caused by the awareness of restored independence and by hopes for parliamentary action. The initiative for a united appeal of all Polish cities for change in the legal standing and the social status of the urban estate, or, as was often contended, the recovery of old rights and privileges, originated with the government of Old Warsaw and specifically with its president, the wealthy merchant, Jan Dekert.[26]

The Marshal of the Diet, Stanisław Małachowski, was the patron of the burgher's movement and its main proponent was Hugo Kołłątaj.[27] In response to a written summons from the city government of Old Warsaw, delegates of nearly two hundred cities and rural towns converged on the capital in November 1789. The delegates passed an act which united the cities and declared their solidarity in having their demands approved by the Diet. On December 2nd, the delegates presented the King with a Memorandum written by Kołłątaj.[28] They demanded broad parliamentary representation for towns; participation of their deputies in executive bodies; removing towns from under the authority of the noble magistrates (*starosta*) (whose power in smaller towns was similar to a lord's power over serfs); the right to purchase landed property; near parity with the nobility in access to church positions, civil offices, and military ranks as well as the extension over them of the *neminem captivabimus* privilege.

In all their declarations, the townspeople professed their love for the fatherland, trust in the King and the Diet, and respect for the nobility. They also argued that it was in the nobility's own best interest to attend to the economic rejuvenation of the cities (which would result from meeting their demands) and to enlarge the number of people devoted to Polish freedom by including townspeople.

Nonetheless, the very fact that the meeting of delegates had occurred without the government's permission and that an act of union was passed which was suspected to be an attempt to create a separate confederation of townspeople, caused apprehension and even outrage among deputies. Many saw in this an imitation of the French Revolution's model while others suspected machinations by the King or perhaps magnates who wished to bring into the Diet their clients in the guise of city deputies. The cities' Memorandum, therefore, did not receive a reading in the Diet. Nor was it sent to the Deputation for the Reform of Government; instead a separate parliamentary Deputation for Royal Cities was created to consider the cities' demands, and to keep in contact with plenipotentiaries chosen at the meeting of delegates. In May 1790, this Deputation drafted an appropriate parliamentary bill which, however, drastically reduced municipal representation in the Diet.[29] The bill did not reach the floor and the entire matter of municipal reform was left unfinished for a long time.

Kołłątaj's hope that the Deputation for the Reform of Government and the Diet would address the most fundamental social problem in the Commonwealth, the condition of the peasantry, proved to be illusory.[30] The Diet was dominated by the landed nobility which regarded reform of serfdom as undermining the foundation of its material existence. The preservation of the landed nobility's dominant position in the state was also the fundamental principle of the massive bill, numbering 658 articles, the Project to Reform the Government, submitted by the Deputation to the Diet in August 2, 1790.[31] Its main author, the guiding force of the Deputation and main leader of the "Patriotic Party," was Ignacy Potocki.[32]

The republican ideology voiced by Potocki and expressed in the Project possessed a certain Enlightenment polish and reflected contemporary anti-absolutism in European thought, but it lay securely within traditional noble republicanism. According to the Project, legislative power would lie directly in the hands of the entire nobility gathered at the dietines and not in the Diet. The Diet, meeting in the capital by the king's side would, according to noble republicans, necessarily be influenced by him. For this reason the most important matters would be decided by a majority of the binding instructions drafted by the dietines and not by a majority of the deputies themselves. The Project reflected traditional distrust of executive authority which itself was to be divided into the so-called Great Commissions, collegial bodies chosen by and directly subordinated to the Diet.

Selected by the Diet, the twelve-person Guardians of the Laws (*Straż Praw*) would be denied almost all authority and, true to its name, it could only stand by to ascertain that individual executive organs did not break the law. It was meant to be a "supervisory" authority and not a central executive organ guiding the operations of the Commissions. The role of the King was reduced to practically nothing. "In this reform of the governmental system" observed Stanisław August characterizing the Project, "the tendency is towards democracy for the nobility--in fact an aristocracy with respect to townspeople and peasants--which seeks to gain the upper hand at the local dietines not only over the king but the Diet as well. If this should happen, then God have mercy on Poland."[33]

The republicanism of the Project, however, had one great blemish: it introduced a hereditary monarchy. The leaders of the "Patriotic Party" saw in this a safeguard against the upheavals of interregna and they calculated that calling the favorite candidate to the hereditary throne, Frederick Augustus, the Elector of Saxony, would strengthen Poland's international position. Since the Elector had only a daughter, Ignacy Potocki wished that through her the Polish throne would go to a Hohenzollern and in this way solidify the Polish-Prussian alliance signed in March 1790.[34] The dietines which chose new deputies in November 1790 - the Diet having renewed its own term for another two years with the stipulation that a second, new set of deputies be elected - accepted the choice of the Elector as Stanisław August's successor. At the same time only five dietines voiced approval for a hereditary monarchy, against which extreme republicans had launched a violent campaign seeing in it the death of Polish freedoms.[35]

The instructions of the November dietines showed the conservatism of the nobility in the provinces; especially unpleasant for Ignacy Potocki, as a member of the Commission for National Education, was the demand that the school system be turned over to the religious orders and that educational funds go to the army. The contradiction between the republican concept of delegating legislative authority to the local dietines and the possibility of truly reforming and modernizing the Republic became manifestly apparent. This convinced Ignacy Potocki of the need to abandon a large part of the republican program, at least for the time-being. Two years of a ruling Diet had shown that the joining of legislative and executive functions hurts both. Public opinion as well as the deputies and senators themselves increasingly became convinced that Poland needed strong executive authority.

Beginning with the second half of 1789 Stanisław August, who despite reservations became reconciled with the pro-Prussian orientation, increasingly found common ground with the leaders of the "Patriotic Party" in positive legislative work and earned a growing trust among the deputies as well as greater authority in public opinion. As one of the most active supporters of the "Patriotic Party," Julian Ursyn Niemcewicz, recalled several years later, the King became "the leader of all well-reasoning people."[36] The restoration on September 13, 1790, of the King's power to appoint ministers and senators was an expression of this respect. When the Project to Reform the Government encountered problems in the Diet with its first articles - it was estimated that at the current pace the passage of the entire Project would take three years - Ignacy Potocki decided against forcing through his work and on December 4, 1790, turned to the King. In a meeting lasting several hours and covering all the important matters concerning the state, he asked him to produce a draft for the future constitution. It was decided that after final agreement by several privied individuals this draft would be presented to the Diet for immediate passage in its entirety.[37]

Shortly after this conversation, Stanisław August dictated his basic ideas concerning the reform of the Polish political system to his trusted secretary, Scipione Piattoli.[38] This Italian with old ties to Poland and to Poles possessed great secretarial and editorial skills and for some time had served as an intermediary between the King and Ignacy Potocki. Piattoli edited Stanisław August's thoughts into a developed project and presented two successive drafts to Potocki and perhaps to Marshal Małachowski and his advisor Kołłątaj. Taking into account their observations and reservations, Piattoli drew up a new version which he gave the King to translate into Polish since all the versions had been written in French. Stanisław August dictated to one of his trusted associates, the deputy from Cracow, Aleksander Linowski, the text entitled, *Reforma Konstytucji* (The reform of the Constitution) which, however, was not a translation but returned to his original conception. Stanisław August's program, reflected in various degrees in the different drafts of the future constitution, was conceived in the spirit of a constitutional monarchy. The executive branch would belong to the hereditary king and to ministers appointed or recalled by him (in contrast to previous lifelong tenures). The ministers would head appropriate commissions common to the Crown and the Grand Duchy of Lithuania and would be answerable to the Diet which could oust them on a two-thirds majority vote. The Diet would be "ever-ready," that is, it could be convened anytime during its two year term, it would pass measures by a majority vote, and it would consist of two nearly equal chambers having almost equal legislative power: the Chamber of Deputies, which would also include eighteen municipal representatives, and the Senate. The power to nominate the senators would belong to the king who would also have the right to initiate legislation in the Diet. Instructions from dietines to their

Stanisław Małachowski, Marshal of the Diet and the Crown Confederacy by Józef Peszka 1790 (Muzeum Narodowe w Warszawie). Photo H. Romanowski.

Kazimierz Nestor Sapieha, Marshal of the Lithuanian Confederacy by Józef Peszka, ca. 1791 (Muzeum Narodowe w Warszawie). Photo A. Pietrzak.

deputies would not be binding. The right to participate in the dietines would be limited to the literate gentry which owned landed property. The King's program accepted the demands from cities for legal equality with the nobility. It also postulated that the peasants would no longer be bound to the land and that retiring peasant soldiers would not be subject to manorial dues.

During March 1791, The Reform of the Constitution was corrected and expanded by Potocki, Małachowski and Kołłątaj. At Małachowski's request Kołłątaj compiled a compromise edition, *Prawa konstytucyjne* (Constitutional Laws), which was quite close to the final text of the Constitution of 3 May. Kołłątaj kept Stanisław August's overall concept but he deleted or modified many of his specific proposals. He limited the proposed involvement of the king and the Senate in the legislature and increased the Diet's influence over the executive branch. He increased the number of city deputies to over forty and provided for easier access to ennoblement for people "with special accomplishments in the army, in scholarship, in industry and the crafts and in exceptional, socially useful, inventions." However, he gave up on substantive reforms concerning the state of the peasants, limiting them to the very general formula of being placed under "the protection of national law and government." The Constitutional Laws were accepted by the King, Ignacy Potocki and Stanisław Małachowski. A somewhat wider group of individuals was admitted into the final revision process but discussions conducted with their participation did not yield significant changes.[39]

During the secret work on the proposed constitution the Diet, which from mid- December 1790 operated with double representation in the Chamber of Deputies, approved a couple of statutes that significantly improved the legislative process. On March 24, 1791, the Diet passed the Law on the Dietines according to which their activity was strictly regulated and landless nobles were excluded since they were considered to be passive tools of the magnates.[40] At the same time the Law on the Cities which was being considered in the Deputation for Royal Cities was brought to the floor. It became apparent, however, that the proposal to extend to the cities even limited representation in the Diet encountered the strong opposition of a large portion of the deputies. The King and the leaders of the "Patriotic Party" decided to make concessions. Approved unanimously by the Diet on April 18, 1791, the law entitled "Our Royal Free Cities in the Dominions of the Commonwealth"[41] (supplemented in June by the law "Administration of Free Cities of the Commonwealth in the Crown and in Grand Duchy of Lithuania")[42] did not admit townspeople into the legislative process. Only to a very limited degree did they receive access to the executive through municipal plenipotentiaries elected by twenty-four (originally twenty-one) "district assemblies" consisting of the representatives of all the formerly royal and now free cities. These plenipotentiaries were to sit on the Treasury Commission, the Police Commission and in the highest courts for towns, the Crown and Lithuanian Assessorial (Appellate) courts. Municipal commissioners were also admitted into the organs of local self-government, the so-called Commissions of Order. In all these organs they had a binding vote in matters concerning towns and trade and an advisory voice in all others. As negligible compensation for not allowing municipal plenipotentiaries participation in the legislative process they received the right to present the towns' demands in the Diet.

Despite its very limited extension of political rights, the Law of April 18 was accepted enthusiastically by townspeople since it met their most essential demands. It freed the cities from the authority of the noble magistrates, placed the *jurydyki* (parts of the urban agglomeration which were the property of the nobility or clergy) under the judicial and administrative authority of the cities and required that all owners of real estate in the towns pay city taxes. The cities obtained a more standardized and democratic form of self-government than previously. Abolished were lifelong terms for municipal offices and the system of co-optation which had together formed the foundation of the urban oligarchy. Significantly, permanent forms of organization bound the towns together in municipal districts into which the Commonwealth was divided. Each district had a city Court of Appeals. Biennially each town (in the larger towns, each borough) would hold a town meeting to elect deputies to the district meetings and to draft lists of proposals to be submitted there. The district meetings would elect appellate judges, city commissioners to the Commissions of Order and plenipotentiaries, as well as draft a list of proposals to be submitted by the plenipotentiaries to the Diet.

Townspeople received the *neminem captivabimus* privilege and access to military ranks (which had been closed to them by the 1786 Diet; the remaining exception was the national cavalry), to civil service and to positions as lawyers, prelates and canons at collegiate churches as well as the right to buy noble estates. The nobles in turn would no longer lose their status by accepting municipal citizenship (which permitted them to hold municipal offices and to represent the cities at the Diet), or by practicing a trade or craft. Generous opportunities for ennoblement of townspeople were created. The right to ennoblement was accorded automatically to city plenipotentiaries, military officers down to the rank of captain, and to purchasers of villages whose assessed taxes were of at least 200 złoty (this means that the value of the village was about forty thousand złoty). In addition to this, each Diet was to ennoble thirty burghers, first and foremost from among the city commissioners serving in the Commissions of Order, and persons demonstrating outstanding economic activity or military service.

The Law of April 18 was the most significant legislation of social reform of the Four-Year Diet and of all preceding legislation in the old Commonwealth. The implemented changes were admittedly more restricted than those accomplished in contemporary France but the power of the Polish and the French Third Estates were not comparable. The reform, though impelled by the action of the townspeople themselves, had a quality of being projected from above. It resulted from the realization by the privileged class that lifting the cities from their century-long decay was in the interest of the state and its own economic interests. An important characteristic of the reform was the preservation and expansion of municipal self-government at a time when reforms in neighboring absolutist monarchies followed strict bureaucratic subordination of the cities to the state and the termination of traditional organs of self-government. The Law of April 18 which soon was made a fundamental part of the Constitution of 3 May contributed to the growth of social and civic activity on the part of broad circles of townspeople in the Commonwealth and brought them closer to the program for national independence represented by the Four-Year Diet.

While the Law on the Dietines and the Law on the Cities were adopted through the normal legislative process, it was decided that the draft constitution prepared in secret would be passed in a single day through an almost *coup d'état*. It was realized that the strengthening of royal authority and especially the hereditary monarchy would meet with strong resistance from a part of the Diet and with disapproval from abroad. Contrary to Stanisław August's advice, there was no attempt to obtain approval for the draft constitution from the allied Prussians or from the Elector of Saxony despite the fact that the constitution handed over the hereditary Polish throne to him and his daughter. This was a continuation of a foreign policy based on illusions but it was in the end necessary for the adoption of the constitution.[43] The political program of the "Patriotic Party" would have been compromised in the eyes of the majority by the disclosure of disapproval from Prussia which opposed the introduction of a hereditary throne and by any clear-cut rejection by the Elector who, in fact, desired the Polish crown but who would make its acceptance dependent on the approval of Prussia, Austria and Russia. It was decided to present the foreign powers with a *fait accompli* in the hope that they would acquiesce to it when they saw that Poland itself accepted the new system. Moreover, it was believed that this system would strengthen Poland's international position.

The decision was made to introduce the draft constitution to the Diet immediately following the Easter holiday when many of the members would still be absent and those whose support was assured would have been recalled to the capital. Towards the end of April the shroud of secrecy was broken. Consequently the introduction of the draft, which had been planned for the 5th, was advanced two days. On May 2nd in Warsaw, at the Radziwiłł Palace where deputies supporting the reform programs of the King and the leaders of the "Patriotic Party" had been meeting for some time, the project entitled Government Statute *(Ustawa Rządowa)* was read aloud after which at the home of Marshal Małachowski, he and 83 deputies and senators signed a pledge to support the draft with "utmost determination."[44]

On May 3rd army units commanded by Prince Józef Poniatowski were concentrated around the Royal Castle where the Diet met.[45] The galleries were filled with spectators of whom an overwhelming majority were enthusiastic about the draft constitution. Crowds of townspeople gathered in front of the Castle and in its courtyard. To produce the desired impression, the session began with the reading of specially selected and even partially concocted fragments of reports from Polish diplomats attesting to the danger of a new partition. This was to justify the unusual remedies being taken by the Diet.

Called on by Ignacy Potocki to indicate a means of saving the country, the King declared that he saw it in the bill, the Government Statute. By acclamation the draft was read and an attempt was made to pass it immediately by acclamation. Though in the minority, opponents put up resistance. Some acted out of a sense of legal process since each new bill required a three-day deliberation period. Others strongly defended the principle of elective monarchy to which Stanisław August had sworn in his *pacta conventa* and for which a large majority of the dietines had voted the previous year. The King asked the Diet to release him from his oath and Marshal Małachowski cut through legalistic scruples by declaring that the present day was a day of "revolution" thus "all formalities must cease."

After nearly seven hours of dispute it proved possible to ask the King by acclamation to take an oath to the Government Statue. After swearing on the Bible and amidst general jubilation, the King was accompanied by a large majority of the members of the Diet present to St. John's Church where together with all those in attendance he took a second oath to the Constitution. The *Te Deum* was sung and street demonstrations in honor of the new Government Statute lasted far into the evening.

The small number of opponents did not protest energetically. Some honestly came to terms with the new system, others did so only in appearance, and still

Ignacy Potocki, Grand Marshal of Lithuania since April 1791, the main leader of the "Patriotic Party," by Mateusz Tokarski, ca. 1786 (Muzeum Narodowe w Warszawie). Photo H. Romanowski.

Dyaryusz Seymu Ordynaryinego pod związkiem Konfederacyi Generalney Oboyga Narodów w podwóynym posłów składzie zgomadzonego w Warszawie od dnia 16 grudnia, roku 1790 (The Diary of the Ordinary Diet sitting as a General Confederacy of Two Nations meeting in double numbers of deputies in Warsaw from 16 December 1790). W Warszawie, M. Gröll. Title page with the vignette, an allegory of Freedom, engraved by Karol Gröll acc. to a drawing by Franciszek Smuglewicz. (Biblioteka Uniwersytecka w Warszawie). The Diary was written by the Diet secretary Antoni Siarczyński others left the Diet. On May 5th the Diet unanimously completed the formalities left unfinished with the approval by acclamation of the Government Statute. It passed the Declaration of the States Assembled (*Deklaracja Stanów Zgromadzonych*) which annulled "all present and past laws" (including laws adopted by the Four-Year Diet that were in disagreement with the Statute) and which recognized as a component part of the Statute any future laws which appeared only in bare outline form in the present Statute.[46]

The Government Statute which entered history as the Constitution of 3 May (*Konstytucja 3 Maja*) had a framework quality though some matters were definitely decided.[47] The Constitution of 3 May broke with the anarchic elements of the political system of the Commonwealth, not with the system itself. It preserved the state institutions, but sought to adapt them to effective functioning in conditions of "orderly freedom." The Constitution recognized the principle of national sovereignty by declaring that "all authority in civil society should derive from the will of the people." The text of the Constitution does not presume that the nation must be understood in accordance with Polish tradition to mean the nobility exclusively. On the contrary Articles II, III and IV entitled, "The Landowning Nobility," "Towns and Townspeople" and "Peasants and Villagers" clearly suggest that all these strata comprise the Polish nation. This is explicitly stated in the article on the peasants which states, "this agricultural class of people is the most numerous in the nation and consequently forms the most sizeable part of its force..." Article XI entitled, "The National Armed Forces" states that "the nation owes it to itself to provide for its own defense and territorial integrity. Therefore, all citizens are defenders of the nation's territorial integrity and liberties." This departed from the myth that the burden of defending the fatherland fell only on the nobility, justifying in this way its privileges and monopoly on political rights. Among the general guarantees for the inviolability of the nobility's freedoms and property, the Constitution does not guarantee it a monopoly of political rights or authority over enserfed peasants.

This, however, was in the realm of theory and phraseology. In its concrete norms the Constitution upheld the estates system and the nobility's monopoly of legislative power. The most important social reform was the incorporation into the Constitution (as stated in Article III) of the April Law, "Our Royal Towns Free in the Lands of the Commonwealth," which abolished legal discrimination against townspeople and raised their status as citizens. The admission of property owning burgher representatives into the executive bodies, the expected numerous ennoblement of the urban elite on the one hand and the withdrawal of political rights from the landless nobility on the other, opened the way to replacing enfranchisement by birth with enfranchisement through property qualifications. It is generally known that such qualifications were the basis for political rights in most nineteenth-century European countries.

Taking political realities into account, the framers of the Constitution refrained from introducing tangible reforms which would alleviate the condition of the peasantry. Article IV, "Peasants and Villagers," did not contain any of the concrete reforms intended in Stanisław August's drafts such as the freedom to move from one lord to another and for military veterans' freedom and guaranteed usufructuary tenure of farms for which they would pay rent rather than manorial dues. But the inclusion of this article in the Government Statute symbolized a break with a system that had hitherto seen an almost complete separation from the state of this, the most numerous, social stratum. The "protection of national law and government," declared in this article, would have to acquire reality in specific laws which could only with difficulty be extracted from a Diet dominated by the nobles. The only moderately specific provision was the statement that all future voluntary agreements between a hereditary landowner and peasants would be binding acts protected by law and, therefore, safeguarded from unilateral cancellation or change. All this was very limited even when compared to Austrian reforms in Galicia but it portended a departure from the centuries-old total separation of the peasantry from the state and their unrestricted submission to the patrimonial authority of landowners.

The Constitution did, however, introduce radical changes in the political system. It embodied the concept of constitutional monarchy (despite the tint of republicanism in some of the formulations) and the principle of a separation of powers: legislative, executive and judicial. Legislative authority finally obtained a permanent basis for substantive and productive work by the abolition of the *liberum veto* (which had in the past applied to unconfederated Diets) and by the limitation of sessions to six weeks every two years. Legislative power was to be exercised by a bicameral Parliament and at the same time the sovereign character of the elected Chamber of Deputies was emphasized. "The Chamber of Deputies as a manifestation and repository of supreme national authority, shall be the temple of legislation." In concrete terms this meant that the final decision on more important legislative matters belonged solely to the Chamber of Deputies with the Senate having only a limited suspensory veto. This was a novelty in the Polish system.

The Diet was elected for a two year term and in addition to regular sessions it could be convened at any moment as a "ready" Diet when circumstances required. The Constitution singled out "general laws" which applied to the state system itself and civil and criminal laws as well as "permanent taxes" and "parliamentary resolutions" which covered all other matters such as, for instance, taxes levied for a set period of time, loans incurred by the state, treaty ratification, declarations of war, peace treaties, and control over executive bodies.

"General laws" would be passed by the Chamber of Deputies by a simple majority and the Senate, also by a simple majority could either confirm the law or suspend the bill until the following Diet. A second approval by the Chamber of Deputies would be final. "Parliamentary resolutions" were to be passed by a simple majority of both chambers counted together. The king had the primary power to introduce "general laws" and "parliamentary resolutions." The instructions from the local dietines would no longer be binding on the deputies. Deputies were to vote according to their own convictions.

The Constitution did not set apart any sacred "cardinal," unchangeable, laws nor any laws requiring a specific legislative procedure. Yet, the Government Statute itself could be changed only every twenty-five years by a special constitutional Parliament. The Diet was to elect members of the four so-called Great Commissions: of Education, Police, Treasury and Army. The Constitution not only preserved the criminal answerability of ministers in cases where they broke the law, in which instance a simple majority of the combined chambers could bring them before the Parliament's Court, but it also covered political matters, in which case a two-thirds majority in secret ballot of the combined chambers would require the king to remove a minister. The Constitution left to future legislation the determination of quorums in both the Chamber of Deputies and the Senate (a practice previously unknown in the Polish Parliament).

"The most perfect government" stated the Constitution "cannot exist or last without an effectual executive power.... Experience has taught us that the neglecting of this essential part of government has overwhelmed Poland with disasters." The Constitution placed this power in the hands of a hereditary monarch who operated with the help of a council called the Guardians of the Laws consisting of *ex officio,* the Primate "as head of the Polish clergy" and president of the Commission for National Education, and five ministers of Police, Treasury, Army, the Seal (Justice) and Foreign Affairs, chosen by the king.[48] The term of each minister in this Council lasted two years and the king did not have the power to remove them during this period. Only the Parliament had this power. A significant restraint on the king lay in the provision that the members of the Guardians of the Laws had to be drawn from among the sixteen traditional, lifelong ministers: the chancellors, the marshals, the treasurers and the hetmans. The single, but important, departure from the principle of lifelong tenure for ministers was their new political accountability.[49] Henceforth they would not only be held criminally answerable before the Parliamentary Court for breaking the law, but a no confidence vote of two thirds of both chambers would remove them. A decision of the king would be decisive for the Guardians of the Laws, but, in accord with the principles of a constitutional monarchy, no resolution would be binding without the countersignature of one of the ministers, who in turn, was answerable to the Parliament. As for the king, as the Constitution stated, "since no act can proceed immediately from him, he cannot be in any matter responsible to the nation." In the event that none of the ministers would countersign and the king persisted in his decision, the matter would be decided by a specially convened, "permanently ready Diet."

An additional element in the Diet's control over the Guardians was the inclusion of the Marshal of the Diet as an observer. He would be able to call the "permanently ready Diet" in case the king opposed convening it. The Guardians of the Laws had the power to issue binding orders to the Great Commissions as well as to the organs of local self-government, the so-called Commissions of Order. Contrary to Stanisław August's plans, the ministers - as members of the Guardians - had under their power particular departments, but they did not head the appropriate Great Commissions. The exception was the Primate who headed the Commission for National Education, but he was deprived of the right to countersign the king's decisions. On the other hand, also exceptional was the position of the Minister of Foreign Affairs and of the Minister of the Seal, since after the 3rd of May, following the principle of separation of powers, no Great Commissions for these purposes existed.

For contemporaries the most radical reform introduced by the Constitution of 3 May was the abolition of free elections to the Polish throne. The throne was made hereditary. The Constitution designated the Elector of Saxony, Frederick Augustus, the grandson of August III, to be Stanisław August's successor. Should he have no male heir, and this seemed certain, the Polish crown would be inherited by his ten year old daughter, Maria Augusta Nepomucena and her future husband. Since the younger brother of the Elector would succeed in Saxony, the Polish-Saxon personal union would be only temporary. According to Ignacy Potocki and some of the parliamentary leaders, the future marriage of the Polish Infanta was to create the possibility of a strengthened alliance with Prussia.

After May 3, a constitutional camp was established, consisting of former "Patriots" and royal supporters. The Association of Friends of the Constitution (*Zgromadzenie Przyjaciół Konstytucji Rządowej*) was organized in the second

King Stanisław August by Giovanni Battista Lampi the Elder, between 1787-1791 (Fundacja XX Czartoryskich, Muzeum Narodowe w Krakowie).

Hugo Kołłątaj, Vice-Chancellor of the Crown from May 1791 by Józef Peszka, 1791
(Muzeum Narodowe w Warszawie). Photo H. Romanowski.

Assekuracya, the first page of the Pledge to support the draft of the Constitution signed by Małachowski and 83 deputies and senators on May 2 1791. Reprinted from Bronisław Dembiński, *Polska na przełomie* (Lwów, 1913).

The proclamation of the Constitution of 3 May, Gouache by Jean Pierre Norblin (Polska Akademia Nauk, Biblioteka Kórnicka). Photo Z. Nowakowski.

half of May 1791 to provide this group with some organizational structure. It included 139 ministers, senators and deputies and 74 persons from outside the Parliament, including several leading activists in the burgher movement.[50] Skillful agitation and propaganda won support for the new system from the masses of provincial nobility despite the frightening visions painted by future leaders of the so-called Targowica Confederation that the abolition of the elected monarchy would mean the end of freedom. The dietines which met in February 1792 did not protest against the hereditary throne. Instead they sent delegations to the king with thanks for the Constitution and the majority of dietines took an oath to it.[51]

Thus, though drafted in secrecy by a small group of leaders and adopted in a "revolutionary" manner, the Constitution of 3 May was recognized as an act accepted by the nation of its own free will and not as reform dictated from above as nearly all of the reforms since 1764 had been considered. This social acceptance of the Constitution was, however, the result of a long process of change in political concepts and civic attitudes among the Poles. The beginning of this process can be traced to the Saxon period. It grew during Stanisław August's reign when the "light" of the eighteenth-century dissipated the old "prejudices" and reached a particular intensity during the Four-Year Diet.

The Constitution of 3 May produced a profound echo abroad. The courts at St. Petersburg and Berlin saw it as a dangerous source of increased power for the Polish state. Among enlightened opinion throughout Europe which had viewed Poland's old form of government as a relic of "feudal" anarchy, the Constitution met with almost universal approval. It was judged very positively in England. In revolutionary France, it was praised in moderate circles while radical elements criticized the insufficiency of social reform and the strengthened position of the monarchy.[52]

After May 3, the legislative process in the Parliament was greatly enlivened and made effective, producing in one year more than had been accomplished in the previous three years.[53] Among the laws passed were those regulating the Diet, the central executive organs, and the relations between the Grand Duchy of Lithuania and the Crown.[54] There were also laws reforming the judiciary and settling matters with religious minorities in the spirit of tolerance. Serious progress was made in the codification of civil and criminal law and the reform of the latter according to more humanitarian principles. A bill was prepared with the aim of abolishing the legal and customary barriers separating Jews from the rest of the population.[55] Some of the specific laws altered somewhat the letter and spirit of the Constitution by limiting royal powers and the activities of the executive. This was due to the conscious reference by some leaders of the constitutional camp to the earlier ideas included in the Project to Reform the Government as well as their efforts to win the widest possible approval for the new system from the nobility. For this reason the social solidarity and noble paternalism of this system were emphasized while the influence of the French Revolution spreading especially among the younger generation of Poles was renounced.

On the other hand, many activists in the constitutional camp were advocates of continued transformations of social and economic relations. Townspeople themselves demanded the widening of rights already gained and their extension to cities owned by the Church. There was a project to create a city militia to strengthen the country's defenses. Kołłątaj, who shortly after the 3rd of May became the Crown Vice-Chancellor and who was emerging as Stanisław August's primary advisor and minister, expressed the opinion that after the "political constitution" there should be an "economic constitution" to create conditions conducive to the economic growth of the country and regulating the status of the peasants as well as a "moral constitution" to mold "the character of Poles" in the spirit of Enlightenment.[56]

None of this could easily be accomplished, yet the awareness that a society which had overcome anarchy and had emancipated itself from foreign domination and was experiencing a great moment of rebirth, allowed for an optimistic view of the future. The Constitution of 3 May was already envisioned by those contemporary to it as the beginning of a great social turning-point. Later this vision would obscure what in 1791 had seemed most important, for example, a hereditary throne, and other issues which would shortly thereafter cease to be relevant. Thanks to this vision, for future generations living in bondage, the lost state was not simply a former Republic exclusively for nobles, but a state embracing the entire nation.

But there was a second reason why the 3rd of May was honored in the period of foreign domination. Catherine II's intervention destroyed the work of the Four-Year Diet. The time had come to pay for an unrealistic and a very dangerous foreign policy and for the failure to mobilize one's own strength according to the risk taken. For that matter, the latter could not have been accomplished at that historical stage. The war against Russia,[57] which started on May 18, 1792 with the invasion of Russian troops supporting the so-called Confederation of Targowica (in reality formed in St. Petersburg by three Polish magnates under the dictate of Catherine II),[58] was a war to defend the right of Poles to decide their own fate, and to defend the political system which was appropriate to the interests and aspirations of the society; it was not a civil war. Targowica never received genuine domestic support and was considered

King Stanisław August swearing the Oath to the Constitution. Drawing by Gustaw Taubert, etching by Johann F. Bolt, 1791 (Muzeum Narodowe w Warszawie). Photo S. Sobkowicz.

The first page of the manuscript of the Constitution of 3 May, prepared in the Diet chancellery, signed by both Marshals and the Diet's Constitutional Deputation and registered May 5 in Warsaw City Court in order to give it legal validity (Archiwum Główne Akt Dawnych, Warszawa). Reprinted from *Ustawa Rządowa, Konstytucja 3 Maja 1791*. Faksymile rękopisu z Archiwum Głównego Akt Dawnych w Warszawie w dwusetną rocznicę uchwalenia (Wrocław: Ossolineum, 1991).

at the time, and subsequently, as treason. Patriotic opinion did not acquiesce to the surrender to Russia on July 23, 1792 by the King and the majority of his advisors after receiving an ultimatum from Catherine II.[59] Public opinion was also influenced by protest resignations of officers, headed by Prince Józef Poniatowski and Tadeusz Kościuszko, who did not want to serve under the command of Targowica. The Constitution of 3 May became a symbol of true patriotism and uncompromising aspiration for independence.[60]

Notes by Łukasz Kądziela with assistance from the author

1. Władysław T. Kisielewski, *Reforma książąt Czartoryskich na sejmie konwokacyjnym roku 1764* (The Czartoryski's reform of the Convocation Diet 1764) (Sambor: 1880); Richard Roeppel, *Das Interregum. Wahl und Kronung v. Stanisław August Poniatowski* (Posen: 1892); Szymon Askenazy, *Die letzte polnische Konigswahl* (Goettingen: 1894); W. Mejbaum, *O tron Stanisława Augusta* (Concerning the throne of Stanisław August) (Lwów: 1914); Jerzy Michalski, "Plan Czartoryskich naprawy Rzeczypospolitej" (The Czartoryski plan for reform of the Commonwealth) *Kwartalnik Historyczny,* 63: 4/5 (1956): 29-43; Michalski, "Reforma sądownictwa na sejmie konwokacyjnym" (Judiciary reform at the Convocation Diet) in *Między wielką polityką a szlacheckim partykularzem. Studia z dziejów nowożytnej Polski i Europy ku czci Profesora Jacka Staszewskiego* (Toruń: 1993), pp. 295-313.

2. Władysław Konopczyński, *Liberum veto. Studium historyczno-porównawcze* (Liberum veto. A historico-comparative study) (Kraków: 1918); *Le Liberum Veto. Étude sur le développement du principe majoritaire* (Paris: 1930); Zbigniew Radwański, *Prawa kardynalne w Polsce* (Cardinal laws in Poland) (Poznań: 1952). Compare: Aleksander Kraushar, *Książe Repnin i Polska (1764-1768)* (Prince Repnin and Poland (1764-1768), 2 vols. (Kraków: 1897) and George T. Łukowski, *The Szlachta and the Confederacy of Radom 1764-1767/68.* 21 (Romae: Institutum Historicum Polonicum Romae, 1977).

3. Herbert Kaplan, *The First Partition of Poland* (New York: Columbia University Press, 1962); Tadeusz Cegielski, *Das alte Reich und die erste Teilung Polens 1768-1774* (Stuttgart-Warszawa: 1988); Władysław Konopczyński, "England and the First Partition of Poland" *Journal of Central European Affairs.* 8 (1948): 1-18; David B. Horn, *British Public Opinion and the First Partition of Poland* (Edinburgh: Oliver and Boyd, 1945).

4. Ewa Borkowska-Bagieńska, *"Zbiór praw sądowych" Andrzeja Zamoyskiego* (Collection of judicial laws by Andrzej Zamoyski) (Poznań: Wyd. Univ. im A. Mickiewicza: 1986).

5. Władysław Konopczyński, *Geneza i ustanowienie Rady Nieustającej* (The genesis and the establishment of the Permanent Council) (Kraków: 1917); Aleksander Czaja, *Miedzy tronem, buławą a dworem petersburskim. Z dziejów Rady Nieustającej 1786-1789)* (Between the throne, the Marshal's baton and the Petersburg court. The history of the Permanent Council, 1786-1789) (Warszawa: PWN, 1986).

6. Emanuel Rostworowski, "Republicanisme Sarmate et les Lumieres," *Studies on Voltaire and the Eighteenth Century*, 24/27 (1963): 1417-1438; "Republikanizm polski i anglosaski w XVIII wieku" (Polish and English republicanism in the 18th century) *Miesięcznik Literacki*, 8 (1976); Jerzy Michalski, "Quelques problèmes du courant républicain dans la pensée politique polonaise au XVIIIe siècle" *L'uomo e l'ambiente nel medioevo. La letteratura politica nell'eta dell'illuminismo. Atti del Convegno di studi polacco-italiano* (Nieborów 29 settembre - 2 ottobre 1981) a cura di Cosimo Damiano Fonseca (Lecce: 1986), pp. 199-215.

7. Jerzy Michalski, "Propaganda konserwatywna w walce z reformą w początkach panowania Stanisława Augusta" (The struggle of conservative propaganda with reform at the beginning of Stanisław August's reign), *Przegląd Historyczny*, 43, 3-4 (1952): 536-562; "Do dziejów stronnictwa austriackiego i polskiej polityki Austrii po I rozbiorze" (Remarks concerning the history of the Austrian party in Poland and Austrian policy toward Poland after the First Partition) in *Z dziejów wojny i polityki. Księga pamiątkowa ku uczczeniu siedemdziesiątej rocznicy urodzin prof. dra Janusza Wolińskiego* (Warszawa: 1964), pp. 139-146; "Le Mouvement antiroyal sous le regne de Stanislas-Auguste Poniatowski. De la contestation vers un programme positif" in *La Belgique - la Pologne et la Revolution francaise 1780-1830. Des reformes prerevolutionnaires aux revolutions nationales*, eds. Teresa Wysokinska and Stephane Pirard, (Bruxelles: Centre International Lelewel, 1991), pp. 13-32.

8. Jerzy Michalski, Sejm w czasach panowania Stanisława Augusta (The Diet during the reign of Stanisław August) in *Historia sejmu polskiego*, vol. 1, ed. Jerzy Michalski (Warszawa: PWN, 1984), pp. 373-381.

9. Emanuel Rostworowski, *Ostatni król Rzeczypospolitej. Geneza i upadek Konstytucji 3 maja* (The last king of the Commonwealth. The genesis and fall of the Constitution of 3 May) (Warszawa: Wiedza Powszechna, 1966); Jean Fabre, *Stanislas-Auguste Poniatowski et l'Europe des Lumieres.* (Paris: Le Belles Lettres,1952) (2 ed. Paris: 1984); R.N. Bain, *The Last King of Poland and his Contemporaries* (New York: 1909) (reprinted 1971); Adam Zamoyski, *The Last King of Poland* (London: Jonathan Cape, 1992).

10. Ambroise Jobert, *La Commission d'Éducation Nationale en Pologne (1773-1794). Son oeuvre d'instruction civique* (Paris: Librairie Droz, 1941); Renata Dutkowa, *Komisja Edukacji Narodowej* (The Commission for National Education) (Wrocław: Ossolineum, 1973).

11. Emanuel Rostworowski, *Sprawa aukcji wojska na tle sytuacji politycznej przed Sejmem Czteroletnim* (The problem of increasing the army and the political situation

before the Four-Year Diet) (Warszawa: PWN, 1957), pp. 177-184, 198-202; *Ostatni król* ..., pp. 129-133, 138-141.

12. Rostworowski, *Sprawa aukcji...*, pp. 184-200; *Ostatni król...*, pp. 133-138.

13. Jerzy Michalski, Zmierzch prokonsulatu Stackelberga (The decline of Stackelberg's proconsulate) in *Sejm Czteroletni i jego tradycje*, ed. Jerzy Kowecki (Warszawa: PWN, 1991), pp. 22-30.

14. Jerzy Michalski, "Sejmiki poselskie 1788 roku" (The deputies dietines of 1788) *Przegląd Historyczny*, 60 (1960): 65-66, 468-478; Emanuel Rostworowski, *Sprawa aukcji...*, pp. 109-116.

15. Jerzy Michalski, "Opozycja magnacka i jej cele w początkach Sejmu Czteroletniego" (Magnate opposition and its aims at the beginning of the Four-Year Diet) in *Sejm Czteroletni i jego tradycje*, pp. 50-62.

16. Edmund Machalski, *Stanisław Małachowski, marszałek Sejmu Czteroletniego* (Stanisław Małachowski, Marshal of the Four-Year Diet) (Poznań: 1936).

17. The most indispensable is still the work of Walerian Kalinka, *Sejm Czteroletni* (The Four-Year Diet) (Kraków: 1880) 2 vols. Last edition, Warszawa: Volumen, 1991. Quotations from this edition.

18. Kalinka, *Sejm Czteroletni*, vol. 1, pp. 142-145; Bronisław Dembiński, *Polska na przełomie* (Poland at the turning point) (Lwow: 1913); Szymon Askenazy, *Przymierze polsko-pruskie* (Polish-Prussian Alliance), 3rd. ed. (Warszawa: 1918); Robert H. Lord, *The Second Partition of Poland. A study in Diplomatic History* (Cambridge: Harvard Univ. Press, 1915) (2nd edition: New York: AMS Press, 1969), Chapters 4,5; Józef Dutkiewicz "Prusy a Polska w dobie Sejmu Czteroletniego" (Prussia and Poland during the Fourt-Year Diet), in *Cztery lata nadziei. 200 rocznica Sejmu Wielkiego*, ed. H. Kocój (Katowice: Uniwersytet Śląski, 1988), pp. 25-53.

19. Kalinka, *Sejm Czteroletni*, vol. 1, pp. 148-152; Leonard Ratajczyk, Wojsko i obronność Rzeczypospolitej 1788-1792 (The army and defense in the Commonwealth 1788-1792), (Warszawa: MON, 1975), p. 21 ff.

20. Kalinka, *Sejm Czteroletni*, vol. 1, pp. 284-290; Aleksander Czaja, *Między tronem...*, pp. 309-358.

21. Jerzy Michalski "Kilka uwag o koncepcji sejmu rządzącego w XVIIIv." (Remarks on the idea of a ruling diet in the 18th century) *Śląski Kwartalnik Historyczny Sobótka*, 37, 3-4 (1982): 241-248.

22. Stanisław Staszic, *Uwagi nad życiem Jana Zamoyskiego* (Remarks on the life of Jan Zamoyski), ed. Stefan Czarnowski (Kraków: 1926).

23. Hugo Kołłątaj, *Listy Anonima i Prawo polityczne narodu polskiego* (Anonymous letters and Political laws of the Polish nation), eds. Bogusław Leśnodorski and Helena Wereszycka (Warszawa: PWN 1954), 2 vols.; See also Rostworowski, *Sprawa aukcji...*, pp. 240-266; Andrzej Walicki, *The Enlightenment and the Birth of Modern*

Nationhood. Polish Political Thought from Noble Republicanism to Tadeusz Kościuszko (Notre Dame: Univ. of Notre Dame Press, 1989), chapters 3,4.

24. See: Hugo Kołłątaj, *Wybór pism politycznych* (Selected political writings), ed. Bogusław Leśnodorski (Wrocław: Ossolineum, 1951), pp. 157-176.

25. Władysław Smoleński, *Mieszczaństwo warszawskie w końcu wieku* XVIII (The Warsaw burghers at the end of the 18th century) (Warszawa: 1917) (2nd ed. Warszawa: 1976); Krystyna Zienkowska, *Slawetni i urodzeni. Ruch polityczny mieszczaństwa w dobie Sejmu Czteroletniego* (City dwellers and the well born. The political movement of the townspeople in the time of the Four-Year Diet) (Warszawa: PWN, 1976).

26. Władysław Smoleński, *Jan Dekert prezydent Starej Warszawy i sprawa miejska podczas Sejmu Wielkiego* (Jan Dekert, president of Old Warsaw and the burgher question during the Great Diet) (Warszawa: 1912); Krystyna Zienkowska, *Jan Dekert* (Warszawa: 1982).

27. Maria Pasztor, *Hugo Kołłątaj na Sejmie Wielkim w latach 1791-1792* (Hugo Kołłątaj at the Great Diet in the years 1791-1792) (Warszawa: Wyd. Sejmowe, 1991).

28. Published in: *Materiały do Dziejów Sejmu Czteroletniego* (Sources related to the history of the Four-Year Diet), hereafter MDSC, eds. Jerzy Michalski, Emanuel Rostworowski, Janusz Woliński, vol. 2 (Wrocław: Ossolineum, 1959), pp. 259-268, 305-320, 339-357.

29. See MDSC, vol. 3 (Wrocław: 1960), pp. 215-225.

30. See MDSC, vol. 1 (Wrocław: 1955).

31. Kalinka, *Sejm Czteroletni,* vol. 2, pp. 366-373; Bogusław Leśnodorski, *Dzieło Sejmu Czteroletniego 1788-1792* (The work of the Four-Year Diet 1788-1792) (Wrocław: Ossolineum, 1951), pp. 153-165; Emanuel Rostworowski, "Marzenie dobrego obywatela czyli królewski projekt konstytucji" ("The dream of a good citizen or the royal project of the Constitution"), in *Legendy i fakty XVIII wieku* (Warszawa: PWN, 1963), pp. 319-328.

32. Kazimierz M. Morawski, *Ignacy Potocki* (Kraków: 1911).

33. Letter from Stanisław August to Augustyn Deboli, Warszawa 22/01/1791, quoted from Emanuel Rostworowski, "Marzenie...," p. 365.

34. Compare note 18.

35. Zofia Zielińska, "*O sukcesyi tronu w Polszcze 1787-1790*" (On the succession to the throne in Poland 1787-1790) (Warszawa: PWN, 1991), Chapters 10, 11.

36. Julian Ursyn Niemcewicz, *Pamiętniki czasów moich* (Memoirs of my time), ed. Jan Dihm (Warszawa: 1957), vol. 1.

37. Rostworowski, "Marzenie...," pp. 346-347, 354 ff.

38. A. d'Ancona, *Scipione Piattoli e la Polonia con un'appendico di documenti* (Firenze: 1915); G. Bozzolato, *Polonia e Russia alla fine del XVIII secolo (Un*

avventuriero onorato: Scipione Piattoli) (Padova: 1964); See: Emanuel Rostworowski, "Scipione Piattoli e la Dieta dei Quatro Anni," *Rivista Storica Italiana,* 38, 4, (1966): 922-931.

39. The various stages concerning the preparation of the Constitution of 3 May were reconstructed by Emanuel Rostworowski in "Marzenie...." pp. 354-364 and in *Ostatni król...,* pp. 206-232.

40. Text in: *Volumina legum,* vol. 9 (Kraków: 1889), pp. 233-240; Kalinka, *Sejm Czteroletni,* vol. 2, pp. 438-445.

41. For the Polish text see: *Konstytucja 3 maja 1791* (The Constitution of 3 May 1791), ed. Jerzy Kowecki (Warszawa: PWN, 1991) pp. 123-135, and also in: *Volumina legum,* vol. 9, pp. 215-219. The English translation is included in: *New Constitution of the Government of Poland, established by the Revolution, the Third of May, 1791* (London: 1791), second editon, pp. 91-110.

42. *Volumina legum,* vol. 9, pp. 291-297.

43. Compare note 18 and Zielińska, *O sukcesji...*

44. A copy of the Pledge (Asekuracja) is included in Dembiński, *Polska na przełomie* p. 486; Jerzy Kowecki, "Klub Radziwiłłowski w Warszawie w 1791 roku" (Radziwiłł Club in Warsaw in 1791) *Wiek Oświecenia, 6* (Warszawa, 1989): pp. 85-124.

45. Kalinka, *Sejm Czteroletni,* vol. 2, pp. 506-519; Jan Dihm, *Trzeci Maj,* (The Third of May) (Kraków: 1932).

46. For the Polish text of the Constitution and the Declaration of the Assembled Estates see: *Konstytucja 3 Maja 1791....,* ed. Jerzy Kowecki, pp. 93-119; The English translations are included in: *New Constitution of the Government of Poland ..* pp. 3-42 and in *Polish Democratic Thought from the Renaissance to the Great Emigration: Essays and Documents,* eds. M.P. Biskupski and James S. Pula (New York: Columbia Univ. Press,1990), pp. 168-177.

47. For a recent analysis of the Constitution see: Zbigniew Szcząska, "Pierwsza Ustawa Zasadnicza Rzeczypospolitej" (The first Fundamental Statute of the Commonwealth) in *Konstytucje Polskie. Studia monograficzne z dziejów polskiego konstytucjonalizmu,* ed. Marian Kallas (Warszawa: PWN, 1990), vol. 1, pp. 46-87. See also: Bogusław Leśnodorski, *Dzieło...,* pp. 217-375 and Jerzy Michalski, *Konstytucja 3 Maja* (Warszawa: Zamek Krolewski, 1985), pp. 52-56.

48. Józef Wojakowski, *Straż Praw* (Guardians of the Laws) (Warszawa: Univ. Warszawski, 1982).

49. See Zbigniew Szcząska "Odpowiedzialność rządu w Polsce w latach 1775-1792," (The responsibility of the government in Poland in 1775-1792); *Czasopismo Prawno-Historyczne,* 27, 1 (1975): 97-106.

50. Adam Skałkowski, "Towarzystwo Przyjaciół Konstytucji 3 Maja," *(The* Association of the friends of the Constitution of 3 May), *Pamiętnik Biblioteki Kórnickiej,* 2, (1930): 5-38.

51. See W. Szczygielski, *Referendum majowe. Sejmiki lutowe* 1792 *roku* (May referendum. February dietines, 1792) (Łódź: Univ. Łódzki,1994).

52. Marceli Handelsman, "La Constitution polonaise du 3 mai 1791 et l'opinion francaise," *Revolution francaise*, 11 (1910); Fabre, *Stanislas-Auguste Poniatowski...*, pp. 533-541; Zofia Libiszowska, *Misja polska w Londynie w latach 1769-1795* (Polish diplomacy in London 1769-1795) (Wrocław: Ossolineum,1967); *Życie polskie w Londynie w XVIII wieku* (Polish life in London in the 18th century) (Warszawa: Pax, 1972), chapter 5,6.

53. See Władysław Smoleński, *Ostatni rok Sejmu Wielkiego* (Last year of the Great Diet) (Kraków: 1896).

54. See Jerzy Malec, "Problem stosunku Polski do Litwy w dobie Sejmu Wielkiego," (Problem of the attitude of Poland toward Lithuania during the Great Diet) *Czasopismo Prawno-Historyczne,* 34, 1 (1982): 31-50; Jerzy Michalski, "Zagadnienie unii polsko-litewskiej w czasach panowania Stanisława Augusta" (The problem of the Polish-Lithuanian Union during the reign of Stanisław August), *Zapiski Historyczne,* 51,1, (1986): 97-131.

55. Jerzy Michalski, "Sejmowe projekty reformy położenia ludności żydowskiej w Polsce w latach 1789-1792" (The Diet's proposals concerning reforms in the situation of the Jewish population in Poland during the years 1789-1792), in *Lud żydowski w narodzie polskim,* ed, Jerzy Michalski (Warszawa: Instytut Historii PAN, 1994), pp. 20-44; MDSC vol. 6, eds. Artur Eisenbach, Jerzy Michalski, Emanuel Rostworowski, Janusz Woliński (Wrocław: Ossolineum, 1969), pp. 491-515.

56. Emanuel Rostworowski, "Sprawa milicji mieszczańskich w ostatnim roku Sejmu Czteroletniego" (Burgher militias in the last year of the Four-Year Diet) *Przegląd Historyczny,* 46, 4 (1955): 561 -584.

57. Jan Dihm, *Sprawa Konstytucji Ekonomicznej z 1791 r. (Na tle wewnętrznej i zagranicznej sytuacji Polski)* (The problem of the Economic Constitution of 1791. [Against the background of the internal and external situation in Poland]) (Wrocław: Ossolineum 1959); Emanuel Rostworowski, "W sprawie Konstytucji Ekonomicznej 1791 r." (Concerning the Economic Constitution of 1791) *Przegląd Historyczny,* 51, 4 (1960): 727-755; "Jeszcze o Michale Ossowskim i jego Konstytucji Ekonomicznej" (More about Michał Ossowski and his Economic Constitution) *Przegląd Historyczny,* 53, 1 (1962): 175-189.

58. T. Soplica (A. Wolański) *Wojna polsko-rosyjska 1792* r. (The Polish-Russian War of 1792) (Kraków: 1920-1922),

59. Władysław Smoleński, *Konfederacya targowicka* (The Confederation of Targowica) (Kraków: 1903).

60. Smoleński, *Konfederacya..,* pp. 199-231.

Translated by Janusz Duzinkiewicz

12

The Fundamental Principles Concerning the Political System of the 3 May, 1791 Government Statute

Zbigniew Szcząska

The Constitution of 3 May was an attempt at peaceful, evolutionary reform of the political and economic systems with the aim of maintaining the independence of the Commonwealth of Two Nations. Hugo Kołłątaj, one of the authors of the Constitution, wrote in *Listy Anonima* (Anonymous Letters), published in 1788 before the opening of the Diet: "We would like to expect that in enforcing its strength and in reforming the government the genius of the nation would appear even more noble if it could...perfect the model of a free government through a gentle revolution without pressure or terror."[1]

The socio-political system created by the Constitution was based on the legal norms included in the Constitution and on the laws passed later which enacted these norms. Some of the laws modified the solutions accepted by the Constitution (for example, the Law on the Diet). Not all the legal acts connected with the Constitution were enacted. Further steps were planned: in addition to the political constitution, Kołłątaj spoke of an economic and a moral constitution. Work on the codification of law was begun. New solutions were forged in the battle of ideas and conceptions. The accepted formulations were the result of numerous compromises, some of which could have been the basis for further changes and reforms. The system created by the Constitution of 3 May, therefore, was not closed and permanent. It was more a process than a structure.[2]

The Constitution expressed a social and political compromise of the nobles and burghers. While the estate system was maintained, the townspeople obtained numerous civil and political rights. The Government Statute was also a compromise between republicanism and a constitutional monarchy. A hereditary throne and a division of powers appear alongside parliamentary sovereignty and the extensive limitation of executive power. In both the social and the political spheres the 3 May system was dynamic and subject to an evolution that was not always unidirectional. The practical application of the Government Statute was short-lived, however. The Parliament suspended its debates on May 29, 1792, because of the Russo-Polish war.

Approved on May 3, 1791, under the title of the Government Statute, it passed into history as the Constitution of 3 May. In eighteenth-century terminology the term "government" was understood as the political system, the organization of state authority. The term "constitution" had two meanings: first, the traditional sense in which it referred to each parliamentary resolution and second, the new meaning that was only beginning to break ground, in which the constitution meant the basic statutes regulating the foundations of the political system.[3]

On the whole, the Constitution of 3 May consisted of new ideas, though it still contained feudal and estate elements. Linked to the American model of a constitution as the basic statute setting the norms for the foundation of the political system, the Government Statute drew many ideas from French constitutional thought. The principles of the separation of powers and national sovereignty, which had been accepted as the basis of the new system under the French Declaration of the Rights of Man and Citizen (August 26, 1789), were also accepted by the Polish constitution. The influence of English constitutionalism (although without a written constitution) on the Polish political system was evident as well. The immune monarch who "could not act by himself" (Article VII of the Constitution of 3 May) being restrained by the mandatory countersignature of a politically and constitutionally answerable minister, was similar to the English king, who "can do no wrong" and for whom his advisors, the ministers, were accountable. The English ministers had to take into account the wishes of the Parliament not only because of the threat of the medieval "impeachment" (trial in the House of Lords initiated by charges from the House of Commons) but also because of the newly evolving informal mechanism of political answerability requiring the resignation of ministers who did not have support from a majority in the House of Commons.

The Constitution of 3 May contributed much to the development of modern constitutionalism, formulating *expressis verbis* the parliamentary principle of

The Castle Square as seen from Krakowskie Przedmieście Street. A fragment from a painting by Bernardo Belotto Canaletto 1774. (Muzeum Narodowe w Warszawie).

XI.

Siła Zbroyna Narodowa.

Narod winien iest sobie samemu obronę od napaści, i dla przestrzegania całości swoiey. Wszyscy przeto Obywatele są obrońcami całości i Swobod Narodowych. Woysko nic innego nie iest, tylko wyciągnięta siła obronna i porządna z ogólney siły Narodu. Naród winien Woysku swemu nadgrodę i poważenie za to, iż się poświęca iedynie dla iego obrony. Woysko winno Narodowi strzeżenie granic i spokoyności powszechney, słowem: winno bydź iego naysilnieyszą tarczą. Aby przeznaczenia tego dopełniło niemylnie, powinno zostawać ciągle pod posłuszeństwem Władzy wykonawczey, stosownie do opisów Prawa, powinno wykonać przysięgę na wierność Narodowi i Królowi, i na obronę Konstytucyi Narodowey. Użytym bydź więc Woysko Narodowe może na ogólną Kraiu obronę, na strzeżenie Fortec i granic, lub na pomoc Prawu, gdyby kto Exekucyi Jego nie był posłusznym.

Stanisław Nałęcz Małachowski Ref: W. K. Seymowy i Konfederacyi Prowincyi Koronnych Marszałek.

Kazimierz Xiąże Sapieha Generał Art: Litt: Marszałek Konfederacyi W. Xa Littgo.

Jozef Korwin Kossakowski Biskup Inflantski i Kurlandzki, N. Koadjutor Biskupstwa Wileńskiego iako Deputowany. Antoni Xiąże Jabłonowski Kasztelan Krakowski Deputat z Senatu z Maśey Polski. Symeon Kazimierz Szydłowski Kasztelan Żarnowski Deputowany z Senatu z Prowincyi Małopolskiey mp. Franciszek Antoni na Kwilczu Kwilecki Kasztelan Kaliski Deputowany do Konstytucyi z Senatu z Prowincyi Małopolskiey. Kazimierz Konst: Plater Kasztelan Generału Trockiego Deputowany do Kon: z Senatu W. X. Litt: mp. Waleryan Stroynowski Podkomorzy Buski Poseł Wołyński z Małopolski Deputat do Konstytucyi. Stanisław Kostka Potocki Poseł Lubelski Dep: do Kon: z Prow: Małopolskiuy mp. Jan Nepomucen Zboiński Poseł Ziem: Dobrzyń: Deput: do Konst: z Prowincyi Wielkop: mp. Tomasz Nowowieski Łowczy i Poseł Ziemi Wyszogrod: Deputowany do Konstytucyi P. W. Jozef Radzicki Podkomorzy i Poseł Ziemi Zakroczymskiey Deputowany do Konstytucyi z Prowincyi Wielkopolskiey mp. Jzf Zabiełło Poseł z Xięstwa Zmadzkiego Deputowany do Konstytucyi. Jacek Puttkamer Poseł Wctwa Mińskiego Deputowany do Konstytucyi z Prowincyi W. X. Litt. Post Cujns Constitutionis in Acta præsentia ingrossationem, Originale Ejusdem Eidem Offerenti prævia Officii sui quietatione est extraditum.

HERMAN mp.

Legi Moraczewski.

Sub eodem Actu.

AD Officium & Acta præsentia Castrentia Capitanealia Varsaviensia personaliter veniens Magnificus Antonius Siarczyński Sacræ Regiæ Majestatis, & Comitiorum Ordinsrorium Generalium ac Confæderationis Generalis Regni Secretarius, Eidem Officio & Actis Ejus, Constitutionem Infra exaretam obtulit, ad Ingrossandumque in Acta præsentia porrexit tenoris talis ══

Deklaracya Stanów Zgromadzonych.

Wszystkie Prawa dawne i teraźnieysze, przeciwne ninieyszey Konstytucyi, lub któremukolwiek iey Artykułowi, znosiemy; a opisy szczególne do Artykułów i każdey Materyi w ninieyszey Konstytucyi zamkniętych potrzebne, iako dokładniey wyszczególniaiące obowiązki i układ Rządu, za część składaiącą też Konstytucyą deklaruiemy. Władzy wykonawczey zalecamy, aby Straż swe obowiązki natychmiast pod okiem Seymu rozpoczęła, i ciągle utrzymywała. BOGU i Oyczyznie uroczyście przysięgamy na posłuszeństwo, na obronę wszystkiemi

B 2
stkiemi

The last but one page of the first edition of the Constitution of 3 May which includes the last Article of the Constitution, the names of the signatories: the Marshals and members of the Diet Constitutional Deputation, the information in Latin that the secretary of the Diet, Antoni Siarczyński, registered the Constitution in the Warsaw court and finally the first paragraph of the Declaration of the States Assembled. Reprinted from: *Konstytucja 3 Maja Podobizna pierwodruku* (Warszawa: PIW, 1991).

ministerial responsibility that through everyday practice in eighteenth-century England became the basis of the slowly emerging system of parliamentary government. This principle was adopted neither in the French Constitution of September 1791 nor in the American Constitution of 1787, which relied on the older English practice of judicial accountability of ministers.[4]

The Constitution begins with a preamble justifying the necessity for reform with concern for the continued independence of the state:

> Persuaded that our common fate depends entirely upon establishing and rendering perfect a national constitution; convinced by a long train of experience of many defects in our government, and willing to profit by the present circumstances of Europe, and by the favorable moment which has restored us to ourselves; free from the disgraceful shackles of foreign influence; prizing more than life, and every personal consideration, the political existence, external independence, and internal liberty of the nation, whose care is entrusted to us; desirous, moreover, to deserve the blessing and gratitude, not only of our contemporaries, but also of future generations; for the sake of public good, for securing our liberty, and maintaining our kingdom and our possessions; in order to exert our natural rights with zeal and firmness, we do solemnly establish the present Constitution, which we declare wholly inviolable in every part, till such period as shall be prescribed by law....[5]

The body of the text is divided into eleven general Articles: I. The Dominant National Religion; II. The Landed Nobility; III. Cities and Citizens; IV. Peasants and Villagers; V. Form of Government, or the Definition of Public Powers; VI. The Diet, or the Legislative Power; VII. The King, or Executive Power; VIII. Judicial Power; IX. Regency; X. Education of King's Children; XI. National Force, or the Army. The logical and transparent structure of the Government Statute should be emphasized. Its first section is dedicated to the social system with three Articles (II-IV) corresponding to the existing estates in Poland: nobility, townspeople and peasants. The second section, dedicated to the political system outlined in Article V, describes the tripartite division of powers into the legislative (Article VI), the executive (Article VII), and the judiciary (Article VIII); only the large volume of problems contained in Article VII necessitated a separation of the issues mentioned in this Article of the regency, education of the heir and the armed forces into separate Articles IX, X and XI.

Article III acknowledges as the integral part of the Constitution the Law "Our Royal Cities" passed by the Diet on April 18th. Closely tied to the Government Statute are the "Law on the Dietines" (March 25, 1791), attested to by the decisive language of Article VI of the Constitution ("The law concerning the dietines... as established by the present Diet, shall be regarded as a most essential foundation of civil liberty"), the "Declaration of the States Assembled" adopted May 5, 1791, which nullified all laws contrary to the Constitution, and the "Mutual Guarantee of the Two Nations" accepted by the Diet October 20, 1791, which had the character of a fundamental statute and maintained the federal character of the Commonwealth.[6]

The Polish Government Statute from May 3, 1791, was intended to initiate a rebuilding of every level of the state. The Declaration of the States Assembled (May 5, 1791) established that:

> All laws and statutes, old and new, contrary to the present Constitution, or to any part thereof, are hereby abolished; and the detailed description of the Articles and of every matter in this Constitution necessary for the more accurate specification of the obligations and character of the government, is acknowledged to be a component of the present Constitution.

On the same day, the Diet passed a resolution authorizing its Constitutional Deputation "to correct governmental laws in accord with the newly adopted Constitution." Later, in January 1792, the Diet called into being a committee to "edit the laws of the present Diet" by putting in order according to subject all the laws and statutes of the Diet, eliminating all contradictions and excluding all overturned statutes.[7]

Immediately after passing the Constitution the Diet began to work at high speed, producing an impressive number of laws: the Law on Diet (May 16); the Law on Diet Courts (May 17); the Law on Special Constitutional Diet (May 27); the Statute on Pardons (May 30); the Statutes on the Guardian of the Laws (*Straż Praw*) (June 1); the Statute on the Police Commission (June 17); the Internal Organization of the Commonwealth's Free Towns in the Crown and the Grand Duchy of Lithuania (June 27); the Organization of Municipal Courts and Assessorial (Appellate) Courts (October 3); the Statute on the Treasury Commission (October 27); the Reorganization of Voivodeships, Lands and Districts with Constitutionally Designated Dietine Venues (November 2); the Statute on Noble Courts (January 3, 1792); On the Crown and Grand Duchy Tribunal Courts (January 19); On the Permanent Settlement of Royal Lands (April 24); and, finally, The Statute of the Military Commission (May 18, 1792).[8]

In contrast to the French Constitution of September 3, 1791, and the constitutions of American states such as Virginia, the Government Statute did not include a bill of rights. Despite the upholding of the division of society into estates, the Government Statute and other laws passed by the Four-Year Diet created a corpus of civil laws, freedoms, as well as obligations, that were common to both the nobility and the townspeople. At times they reached even further and included all social groups. Article I of the Constitution declares freedom of religious faith and practice. Without exception all faiths are placed under the protection of the government. It was stipulated, nonetheless, that the Roman Catholic Faith was the national and dominant religion and conversion to any other persuasion from the dominant one was prohibited under pain of apostasy.

Article II of the Constitution and the Law on Cities guaranteed landowning nobles and propertied townspeople inviolability of person. The constitutional guarantee also covered noble and townspeople property. The Statute on the Police Commission prohibited the Commission from altering "traditional rights to personal freedom and property safeguarded by laws of the Commonwealth for all citizens and immigrants." (Art. III, part 1).

According to the Law on the Guardians of the Laws each decision undertaken by that body would be unconstitutional if "it infringes on personal freedom, freedom of speech (oral, written, and in print), and the right to private property." (Art. IV, part 4) Article IX of the Statute on Diet Courts proclaimed that "whatever the citizen of a free nation should say, write, print, do or intend to do in a manner described by law, which is not forbidden by law, can never be considered under the shameful name of plot." The Police Commission should then "keep watch that according to the provisions and conditions of the law, freedom of the spoken and the written word should remain secure and unhindered."(Art. IV part 5).

Article XIII of the Law on Diet Courts established that not only the noble but "whoever offers sufficient guarantees should be free from imprisonment or arrest without the verdict of a court." Article XXV of the same Law anticipates that:

> only the person who is judged to be the guilty party, whose act is specified in the law (by the principle *nullum crimen sine lege*) or determined as the perpetrator, should be sentenced only to a punishment dictated by law (*nulla poena sine lege*).

The cited provisions were a kind of Polish bill of rights whose equivalent is found in the French Declaration of the Rights of Man and Citizen from 1789 and the first ten amendments to the American Constitution adopted in 1791. They guaranteed the inviolability of person and property, freedom of religion, of the spoken and written word and the proper administration of justice. Their evolution pointed to the extension of these guarantees to other social groups.

Consequently, the Police Commission's resolution of June 24, 1792, replied to a memorandum of the Jewish community by determining that:

since the protection of the government was extended to all inhabitants of the country by the Constitution of 3 May, the Commission does not have any reason to exclude the Jews but does extend the same *Neminem captivabimus nisi iure victim* law to the Jewish people (except in *recens crimens*).[9]

In the regulations of the Law on Diet Courts and the Police Commission, citizen refers to the inhabitants of the country. Similarly in Article IV and, most importantly, in Article XI (National Force, or the Army) of the Constitution, nation or citizens refer to all the inhabitants of the country. The road to a non-estate understanding of nation could have developed from a sense of common civil obligations towards the country. The main obligation, formulated in Article XI of the Constitution, was defense of the state:

therefore all citizens are natural defenders of their country and its liberties.

The army is only an extract of defensive regular force from the general mass of national strength.

An important common obligation of all inhabitants of the country was obedience of the laws since "the happiness of the nation depends on just laws, but the good effects of laws flow only from their execution" (Article VII of the Constitution). These formulations show a willingness to delineate both the rights and the duties of people and citizens and thus indicate an attempt to gradually depart from estate divisions.

Recognized by Article III of the Government Statute as part of the Constitution, the Law on Cities of April 18, 1791, changed the status of the townspeople,[10] but there were few changes in the status of peasants. The authors of the Government Statute did not want to arouse the protests of the nobility. Nonetheless, Article IV of the Constitution which placed the entire "farming people under the protection of national law and government"[11] offered the possibility of further changes and reforms (as in Kołłątaj's project for an economic constitution). Article IV also encouraged landowners to contract agreements with their serfs specifying manorial obligations. The law was meant to guarantee that both sides keep their agreements. Personal freedom was guaranteed for all serfs returning to the country and for any foreigner wishing to settle in Poland. The stipulation in Article IV of the Constitution placing the peasantry under the protection of law and the government made possible the future passage of concrete measures. The abolition or restriction of serfdom was certainly planned. The realization of this idea was to occur through gradual reform. The decision to sell the royal demesne was such a reform. On December

STANISŁAW NAŁĘCZ MAŁACHOWSKI REFERENDARZ WIELKI KORONNY SEYMOWY
Y KONFEDERACYI KORONNEY,
NESTOR KAZIMIERZ XIĄŻE SAPIEHA GENERAŁ ARTYLLERYI i KONFEDERACYI
WIELKIEGO XIĘSTWA LITEWKIEGO.

MARSZAŁKOWIE

Proclamation of May 7, 1791 by Stanisław Małachowski Marshal of the Diet and Crown Confederacy and Kazimierz Nestor Sapieha Marshal of the Lithuanian Confederacy announcing the passage of the Constitution of 3 May (Biblioteka Narodowa, Warszawa).

GAZETA NARODOWA Y OBCA.

Sine ira & studio, quorum causas procul habeo.

C. Tacit.

Z WARSZAWY W SOBOTĘ DNIA 7. MAIA ROKU 1791.

Sessya Seymowa, na którey narod, po długim oczekiwaniu, uyrzał nakoniec pożądaną nstawę całkowitego rządu, a w niey zabespieczone trwałe swe szczęście, wolność, i niepodległość, iest takiey wagi, iż ią, iak można naydokładniey, wiadomości publiczney podaiemy.—*Dnia 3. Maia P. Marszałek Seymowy:* „Obrot „kolei pomyślney, z niepomyślnemi przeplatany bywa; do-„strzegamy, iak potężne piocarstwa, do upadku, a słabe do po-„dźwignienia się przychodzą.—Polska sława, naywidocznieyszym „przykładem stało się. Wyobrażamy ią sobie, przed trzema wie-„kami, świetną, i wyrownywaiącą innych Państw potędze; zo-„stała potym własnych błędow i obcych zaborow smutną ofiarą; „kray padł łupem, obywatele wzgardą okryci, własność ich na „wygodzie obcey służyła.—Niech Nieba odwracaią od nas klęski, „które nam i teraz grożą!—Deputacya interessów zagranicznych „doniesie wam PP. Stany wypadki teraźnieysze w okolicznościach „politycznych, do którey odwołuie się.—„

P. Sołtyk Krakowski: „Nayokropnieyszy, naysmutnieyszy „odgłos po całey Stolicy rozszerzył się; drętwieją usta do wymo-„wienia: co za nieszczęścia przygotowane dla naszey Oyczyzny! „doświadczenie, powinno w nas wzbudzić tę gorliwość do iey ra-„towania, która w sercu wolnego polaka głęboko iest wyryta— „Nie iest tobie N. Królu taiemnicą, co zawieraią w sobie wiado-„mości, które odebrała Deputacya zagraniczna; oprocz tych, „ia miałem z wielu mieysc od przyiacioł, i krewnych, za ga-„nicą bawiących, doniesienia, że nam grożą nowym rozbiorem kra-„ia.—Przychodzi ostatnia chwila silnego zaradzenia oyczyznie; „proszę z mieysca mego, żeby wiadomości, iakie na deputacya „były nam doniesione; w ten czas przydzie nam czas zapał, „gdzie okażemy, czy oyczyznę szczerze kochamy. Że zaś mieli-„śmy przykład przytomności arbitrów tam, gdzie o iedne Mia-„sto *Gdańsk* chodziło; tym bardziey tu, gdzie idzie o kray cały, „upraszam i zaklinam, aby wszyscy arbitrowie przytomni byli.—„

Król Imć. „Wzywany dopiero słyszanym obywatelskim głosem, winienem „dać to świadectwo; że ta takie wiadomości w deputacyi zagraniczney, które kapi-„talnie interessuią całość i bespieczeństwo oyczyzny.—Proszę WPana Mci Pana „Marszałka Seymowy, abyś dzielnością swoią to sprawił, iżby bez przerwania „Deputacya te wiadomości przywiodła.—„

P. Suchorzewski Kaliski. po długim domaganiu się o głos, koniecznie przed czytaniem depeszów, i krążeniem leżących po „ározod Izby; gdy mu głos dany został, to wyraził.—„Już to od kilku „dni szerzy się zaczęła wieść: że do tey Izbymaią wchodzić projekta „straszne na wolność, dla których ukutecznienia, przedsięwzię-„to wystawienie depesz zagranicznych, na pozorną wrożących „nam dywizyą Kraiu. Nie dość na tym, że widoki nieszczęścia „Kraiowego chcą nam wystawić, a tym przygotuńie nas do proje-„ktu, szkodliwego wolności: ale ieszcze rozsiana iest wieść, „iakoby była zmowa na nas przeciwiących się temu proiektowi: „żeby zabić, a swoie zrobić. Dla tego iż długo „żem wołały; ale ieżeli będzie łożem despotyzmu, gardzę nią, „i oświadczam że nieprzyiacielem Polski; ratować iey, przez „włożenie na wolnych kaydan, nie myślę.—Wtem i dowodzić będę, „że chciano mieszczan przeciwko opieraiącym się temu projektowi „oburzyć, wmawiaiąc, iakobyśmy nie kontenci byli z ich pra-„wa, i chcieli ich wrócić do dawnego stanu. Winienem powie-„dzieć przytomney publiczności, którą widzę w znaczney części „mieszczan wspoł-braci, i wspolbliźnich naszych złożoną; że iak „przyłożyliśmy się do ich uszczęśliwienia, tak one utrzymywać „chcemy; i ktoby chciał naruszyć ich przywileie, każdego Pola-„ka będzie miał przeciwko sobie nieprzyiacielem; iakiż nieroz-„szerzyć tych przywileiów, to zapewne zmnieyszyć ich nie my-„ślemy, bo związek z niemi silnieyszem nas robi. Jest ieszcze „anekdota, o którey zamienić musze. Upraszam P. Marszałka W. „Lit: i P. Stanisława Lubelskiego, Potockich, aby doniesli, zkąd „ta wieść, którą ich żony uprzedzone, iakoby oni na Sessyi zgi-

„nąć mieli, mdlały. Żona P. Stanisława, troskliwa o życie mę-„ża, znaydowała się w słabości. Proszę Stanów, o złożenie tym „końcem Sądu Seymowego; ia będę z moiey strony dowodził, „a wzaiemnie upraszam, aby PP. *Potoccy,* Autorow, dybiących na „ich życie, dochodzili.—Co do czytania depesz, idę za powsze-„chnym żądaniem.„

P. Matuszewic imieniem Deputacyi zagraniczney, czyta doniesienia: tych ważność, ogromność, nieszcześć, Rzplty gro-„żących, wszystkich umysły, nayżywszą przeięły trwogą == Tak „przez względy polityczne, iako też przez boiaźń nie naruszeuia „Ministrów naszych, u dworów zagranicznych rezyduiących, ga-„zeta Narodowa nie może się rozciągać nad szczegułami ich rapor-„tów; tyle tylko donosi, że zewsząd były przestrogi: iż bliskość „pokoiu, pewnieysza niż kiedykolwiek; że się lękać potrzeba, a-„żeby obce mocarstwa, strat i kosztów swoich rozbiorem Polski „nadgrodzić sobie nie chciały; że się skryte czynią układy; że „dwory stale nam nieprzyiazne, okazuią iak nayżywszą chęć, aże-„by w Polszcze, ani Rząd dobry, ani exekucya dzielna nigdy nie „stanęły;że żadnych do uskutecznienia tego nieopuszczaią środków; „że się cieszą, kiedy seym nie czynny, w cale zaś nie smakuią, „kiedy część iska rządu spiesznym posunie krokiem; że nako-„niec Elektor *Saski* powiedział Ministrowi Polskiemu w *Dreźnie,* „iż, iak żywo po powodzeń Rzplty interessuie się, tak poty o los „iey lękać się przestanie, poki nie uyrzy ustanowionego w niey „rządu trwałego i bespiecznego.

P. Potocki Marszałek W. Lit: „Tak mniemam, że po zdaney „Sprawie od Deputacyi do interessów zagranicznych, Wasza Krole-„wska Mść Pan moy Mił: Wy prześwietne Rzpltey Stany, z całą „przytomną powszechnością przekonani iesteście; że rzecz między „nami nie o żadne prywatne, ale o Oyczyzny zabowstwo toczy „się. Daruycie Prześwietne Rzpltey Stany, iż przez ustanowanie „głosu zacnego Posła, zapytany, co mniemam o rozsianey wieści, „iakoby wymierzone na mnie zabowstwo bydź miało? Powiem co „cznie: znam Narod Polski, moich wspołziomkom, znam szla-„chetność ich duszy; przeto żadeń odgłos o podłym i zdradzie-„ckim postępku, przystępu do moiey myśli niema. Z drugiey „strony na śmierć, bez trwogi patrzę; a gdyby ta w osobie mo-„iey potrzebną bydź miała Oyczyznie; śmierci pragnę. Jeżeli „kiedy, to w dniu dzisieyszym przytomne nam bydź powinny sło-„wa Lwa Sapiehy, który przykładem Rzymian, zostawiąc nie-„chęci w przysionku rad publicznych świątyni, nie raz w życiu „swoim doradzał. Obrzeżeni, iak koniecznie, iak nagle ratować „Oyczyznę przychodzi; dążmy do zgody, dążmy nayprostszą dro-„gą, która do tego doprowadza celu. Ровność, w którey od „urodzenia żyiemy, rozciągamy nie tylko do Prawa, nie nawet „do mniemania, iż ieden drugiemu w chęciach ku Oyczyznie u-„stępować nie winien. Pod tą szlachetną myślą ukrywaią się „każdey Rzpltey ułomnościludzkie, posądzenia, emulacye, nie „smaki, namiętności. Trudno więc mniemać, aby przy naywiększey „cnocie obywatel ieden, łatwo zyskał prędką, powszechną i nie „ograniczoną wiarę w materyi poprawy i odmianie Rządu. Lecz „Prześwietne Rzplty Skonfederowane Stany! sam skład Rzpltey „podaim Nam sposób, iak sobie w poprawie i odmianie Rządu „postępować winnismy. Mamy wyższego nad rowność Króla w „Rzpltey Naszey; mamy go wyższego nad innych osobistemi ro-„zumu i nauki przymiotami; mamy wyższego cnotami. Dozwa-„laiąc bowiem na mianowanie następcy za życia swego, oka-„zał, iż interes Oyczyzny nad swoy i swoich przekłada. Two-„iego światła, twoiey cnoty wzywam Nayiaśnieyszy Panie, „abyś nam odkrył (o czym innym nie wiemy, bo z zdol-„wieniu i szczęściu Narodu) widoki twoie ku ratunkowi Oy-„czyzny. Ty do tey usługi pierwsze masz Prawo, chęć i zdol-„ność nie wątpliwą. *Radźmy o dobru Rzpltey; a potym będzieli wola*

Nn

19, 1791, the Diet passed "The Principles for Organizing the Permanent Sale of Royal Lands." It was not until April 24, 1792, that "The Permanent Settlement of Royal Lands" was adopted.[12] The legal regulation of the status of peasants received extensive treatment in this statute.[13] Peasants on royal lands passing into private hands received recognition of permanent rights to the land they received, the right to sell that land and the freedom to leave the village. Landless peasants unfettered by any contracts were recognized as "free from all manorial obligations." The level of peasant obligations, rents, or corvee were to be determined by auditors preparing the sale of the royal lands and this was to be accomplished in "such a way that the economic needs of both the peasants and the manor would be accommodated." In this way, peasants obtained personal freedom and usufructuary rights to the land with the requirement of observing the owner's authority in the form of rent or work obligations. Proponents of peasant reform on private lands looked to the reform of royal lands for a similar resolution of the peasant question.[14] In the draft of the Stanisław August Code, regulations were proposed dealing with both landowner and peasant contracts, guaranteeing their free negotiation and conclusions, and assuring judicial protection of their execution.[15]

The Constitution maintained the dominance of the nobility in political life by confirming all their existing rights and privileges (Article II, "Landed Nobility"). But in accordance with the new concept of the primary importance of landed property (represented by Hugo Kołłątaj), the Law on Dietines (March 24, 1791) disenfranchised the landless gentry (*gołota*). The regulations stripping a large portion of the nobility of their political rights were adopted only after a fierce battle. The debate over the Law on Dietines lasted from January 10 to March 24, 1791. By excluding the landless nobles and renters of estates, the Diet's majority sought to weaken the dominance of the magnates who used landless nobles in their struggle for power.[16]

In accord with Rousseau's doctrine, Article V of the Government Statute accepted the principle of sovereignty of the nation as the basis for the political system, as well as Montesquieu's concept of division of state power into the legislature, the executive and the judiciary. The separation of powers was not, however, consistently followed. The Diet, or the legislative power gained the dominant position (Article V of the Constitution). As before, this parliament consisted of the Chamber of Deputies and the Senate. The role of the Chamber of Deputies was greatly enhanced since it was considered "the manifestation and repository of supreme national authority" and "the temple of legislation." The Chamber was to include 204 deputies (68 from each province [Great Poland, Little Poland and Lithuania]) elected by local noble dietines comprised of landed nobility. The Chamber of Deputies was also to include 24 municipal plenipotentiaries, with a consultative voice, elected by district town meetings of property owning burghers from royal towns. The Law on Diet described the position of the Diet, developing the provisions of the Constitution.[17] The Diet was to be "ever ready to meet." This meant that after the regular session, deputies maintained their mandates for two years and could be called into special session should the need arise. The *liberum veto* was abolished. All matters were to be decided by a majority vote. Electoral instructions were no longer binding and deputies would from then on be representatives of the entire nation. The Government Statute also forbade the creation of confederations.

Only landowning nobles twenty-three years or older received the right to vote at the local dietines. Passive participation was extended to landowners over eighteen. Candidates for the office of deputy had to have previous experience in public service.

The Senate was to include 132 senators nominated by the king for life. The Law on Diet provided that the number of secular senators equal half the number of deputies, that is, there would be 102 voivodes and castellans. In addition, there were 14 archbishops and bishops (including the Archbishop of Kiev, the Uniate Metropolitan), and 16 ministers. According to the Law on Diet, voivodes and castellans would become elective after the death of Stanisław August.

The Diet had a very wide jurisdiction. It covered the power to decide the character of the political system, lawmaking, final ratification of international agreements, declaration of war, conclusion of peace, determination of taxes and government expenditures, election of the executive branch (the Great Commissions), control over them (the Guardians of the Laws and the Commissions) and the settling of disputes between the King, the Guardians of the Laws, and the Commissions. The power to initiate legislation was awarded by the Constitution and executive acts to the king, the dietines, the provincial diets and each of the deputies. Senators were excluded. Decisions would be made by majority votes in the Chamber of Deputies. Should a bill pass the Chamber of Deputies after debate, the Senate could only issue the Chamber "its observations on the bill along with advice on its revision." A second passage through the Chamber of Deputies would make the bill law.

The Law on Diet regulated in detail the course and procedures of debates. The work of the Chamber of Deputies was led by its elected Marshal, after which the two houses went into joint session. Article IX of The Law on Diet defined the rules for this election. The first reading of legislative bills and the review of the executive branch were conducted in the joined houses. After the separation of the houses actual legislative work was begun.

After their first reading in joint session the Diet Deputation, also called the Constitutional Deputation, examined the bills. (The Deputation was one of the permanent Diet committees elected during the Diet's provincial meetings and consisted of one senator and three deputies from each province, Wielkopolska, Małopolska and Lithuania.) The Marshal participated in the work of the Diet Deputation. This committee was to take care that no bill violated the Government Statute.

The houses joined again towards the end of the debates. At that time, bills which had been passed were read for the third time. Should errors be detected, the texts would be compared with the originals signed by the Marshal and the Diet Deputation. After the reading of the newly passed statutes, they would be signed by the Marshal and the Diet Deputation provided there was no doubt about their consistency with the originals. Parliamentary debates ended with a ceremonious farewell to the king by the Marshal and the kissing of the king's hand by the senators and deputies.

A large role in the debates was played by the provincial sessions. These sessions convened during times free from Diet debate. These sessions involved all the senators and deputies of a given province (Wielkopolska, Małopolska and Lithuania). They were chaired by the highest ranking senator from the province. The provincial sessions chose the members of the Diet Deputation. Heads of the so-called Great Commissions and the municipal plenipotentiaries, who would serve on two of these Commissions (the Treasury and the Police) and on the appellate court for towns in Poland and in Lithuania, were also elected at the provincial sessions. The provincial sessions presented the postulates of their provinces and benefitted from the right to initiate legislation for the plenary sessions of the Diet.

The Government Statute fundamentally changed the position of the monarch. The king no longer was a separate estate in the Diet nor could he exercise a legislative veto; the monarch only remained the leader of the Senate with only one vote.[18] According to Article VII of the Constitution, executive power belonged to the king and the newly established institution of the Guardians of the Laws. The monarchy was to be hereditary from that time on and following the death of Stanisław August it was to pass to the Saxon Wettin dynasty.[19] On the English model, the king possessed immunity for his actions but the countersigning ministers were held responsible for the monarch. The king chaired the Guardians of the Laws which consisted of the Primate as head of the clergy and president of the Commission for National Education and five ministers: Treasury, Army, Police, Foreign Affairs and the Seal (Justice). The Diet Marshal also participated in the work of the Guardians of the Laws.[20] Decisions of the Guardians of the Laws were made by the king and countersigned by the ministers. Subordinated to the Guardians of the Laws and required to execute decisions made by the king in council were governmental agencies: the Education, Treasury, Army and Police Great Commissions. Only the Ministers of Foreign Affairs and of the Seal acted in their own capacity as a result of the non-existence of parallel elected Great Commissions. The king chose the members of the Guardians of the Laws from among the sixteen lifelong ministers and these could serve two year terms with a possibility of renewal. The ministers in the Guardians of the Laws were constitutionally accountable to the Diet; upon demand by the joined houses they could be brought before the Diet's court for violations of the law - and they had to vacate their positions in the event of a two-thirds no confidence vote of the joined houses.

The Constitution of 3 May did not introduce a cabinet system. There was no prime minister, which is understandable considering the late development of this position in other countries. The Guardians of the Laws were "the king's council" in which the king worked with the ministers. This system of the king in the Guardians of the Laws resembled somewhat the system of presidential rule in the American Constitution of 1787, though in the later case the ministers were not politically accountable.[21] Just as the "government" belonged to the king and the Guardians of the Laws, the "administration" (except for foreign affairs and justice) belonged to the great Commissions (Education, Treasury, Army and Police) as well as the local administrative commissions and city self-governments.

The composition and responsibilities of the Great Commissions were defined in separate statutes: Police Commission, Treasury Commission and the Military Commission.[22] The Great Commissions were required to cooperate in matters of common interest, such as the Police and the Treasury Commissions in road and canal construction. The Great Commissions, in their own jurisdiction, conveyed the recommendations and orders of the voivodeship, land and district civil-military administrative commissions. Elected for two year terms by the local dietines, these self-governing local administrative organs were among the most important reforms of the Four-Year Diet.

The Government Statute determined that the judiciary should be composed of independent courts. Article VIII of the Constitution maintained the estates

An allegory of the Constitution of 3 May on the title page of: Antoni Siarczyński
Dzień Trzeci Maja 1791, etching by Karol Gröll, w Warszawie, M. Gröll (1791)
(Biblioteka Narodowa, Warszawa).

Medal commemorating the Constitution of 3 May with the inscription on the reverse:
"Terrore libera ex perhonorifico comitiorum decreto d.111 may MDCCXCI" (Free
from fear by the glorious resolution of 3 May 1791) Medalier Johann G. Holtzhey.
(Muzeum Narodowe w Warszawie).

courts: land courts and tribunals for the nobility, municipal courts for townspeople and referendary courts for peasants. Also planned was a high Diet Court to decide cases of treason. Specific supplementary statutes to the Constitution regulated the organization and functioning of these courts. The social character of the courts was maintained to a high degree, especially with respect to noble courts. The local dietines were to elect judges to the noble courts and deputies to the tribunals. Social representation was used in the municipal courts, specifically in respect to the district appellate courts. On the British example, in criminal cases on the appellate level a jury was introduced consisting of eleven jurors.[23]

According to the statute from May 17, 1791, the Diet Court was to be primarily a state tribunal for judging the constitutionality of actions taken by the executive branch, that is, by ministers and commissioners. In addition, the court had jurisdiction over violations of state interests and security. Procedures in this court were modernized in the spirit of the Enlightenment. As mentioned, the statute accepted the principle *nullum crimen, nulla poena sine lege*. The accused was assumed innocent until proven guilty. All uncertainties with respect to the law or to the evidence were to be handled in the accused's favor. As experts, referendaries joined the 36 members of the Diet Court chosen by lot from among the senators and the deputies.[24]

After the adoption of the Statute on the Diet Court on May 17, on the 27th of the month it chose the members of this court of highest instance. The Guardians of the Laws began its vigorous and extensive activity.[25] Following the passage of the Statute on the Police Commission, also in June, the members of this collegiate body were chosen and immediately went to work. In August, the district meetings of the towns were held and elected members of the district appellate courts and municipal plenipotentiaries to the Diet. The plenipotentiaries were elected in September 1791 into the Police Commission, the Treasury and the Crown and Lithuanian Assessorial Courts by provincial sessions of the Diet. Dietines held on February 14, 1792, elected, among other officials, deputies to the tribunals of Małopolska, Wielkopolska and Lithuania. These dietines demonstrated the support of the provincial nobility for the Constitution. Nearly all the dietines took an oath to the Constitution or passed resolutions thanking the King.[26]

In the face of the growing threat of a Russian invasion, the Diet passed a resolution on April 16, 1792, concerning the Republic's defense readiness. The King obtained the right to command the military forces of the Republic for the national defense. The Treasury Commission was empowered to obtain a foreign loan for 30 million *zloty* for the needs of the army. On April 21 the resolution known as the "Temporary Declaration" was passed in which the Diet ordered the expansion of the army to 100,000 men. At the same time the King was given the right to choose, remove, and transfer corps commanders, and to levy recruits from all estates.[27] The final version of the statute "Permanent Settlement of Royal Lands" was passed on April 24. Income from the sale of *starostwa* was to be used for military needs. On May 3, 1792, an anniversary of the Constitution was solemnly celebrated in Warsaw.

On May 18, the Diet adopted the statute on the Army Commission. The same day, the Russian Ambassador Jakov Bulgakov handed the foreign minister, Joachim Chreptowicz, a declaration announcing the entry of the Russian army into Polish territory. On May 22, the Diet did hand over command of the army to the King.[28] On May 24, the Diet passed a statute for an extraordinary Diet Court to prosecute defectors.[29] On May 29, the Diet suspended its activities for the duration of the war.[30] At this point the Diet had not completed its work on all the laws filling in the constitutional framework. For example, bills had not yet been passed concerning the educational commission. Also left uncompleted was the work of the Crown and Lithuanian codification commissions preparing the Stanisław August Code as well as the work of the commission editing the laws of the current Diet.

The Constitution of 3 May was a legal monument of the Enlightenment era. The framers of the Constitution considered it neither flawless nor complete. The Government Statute was intended to initiate further reforms and transformations whose main goal was the preservation of the state's independence.

The political reality which took shape after the adoption of the Constitution of 3 May lasted only one year. Nevertheless, the work of the Four-Year Diet and particularly its main achievement, the Constitution, became, in the perception of the contemporary and later generations of Poles, "the last will of the dying Fatherland,[31] the great testament of the laudable ideas in the fight to reform and guarantee the independence of the Commonwealth."[32]

In 1918 when Poland's independence was restored, the Diet passed the law of April 29, 1919, adopting 3 May as a national holiday. After many years of interruption the tradition of the Constitution of 3 May was recalled in 1990. The Polish Republic regaining its sovereignty passed the law of April 6, 1990, pronouncing again the day of 3 May as a national holiday.

Notes

1. Hugo Kołłątaj, *Listy Anonima i Prawo polityczne narodu polskiego.* (Anonymous letters and Political law of the Polish nation), eds. Bogusław Leśnodorski and Helena Wereszycka, 2 vols. (Warszawa: PWN, 1954), vol. 1, p. 254.

2. Bogusław Leśnodorski, "Państwo polskie na przełomie dwu stuleci" (The Polish state at the turn of two centuries) in *Polska w epoce Oświecenia. Państwo. Społeczeństwo. Kultura* (Warszawa: Wiedza Powszechna, 1971), p. 422.

3. Stanisław Dubisz, "Komentarz stylistyczny do tekstu Ustawy Rządowej z dnia 3 Maja 1791 r." (Stylistic commentary to the text of the Government Statute of 3 May 1791) in *Epoka Konstytucji 3 Maja* (Warszawa: Wydawn. Epoka, 1983), p. 76; Bogusław Leśnodorski, *Dzieło Sejmu Czteroletniego (1788-1792): Studium historyczno-prawne* (The work of the Four-Year Diet, 1788-1792. A historical-legal study) (Wrocław: Ossolineum, 1951), pp. 379-380.

4. See Zbigniew Szcząska, "Odpowiedzialność prawna ministrów w państwach konstytucyjnych XVIII-XIX w." (Legal responsibility of ministers in the constitutional states of the 18th and 19th century) in *Wiek XVIII Polska i świat* (Warszawa: PWN, 1974), pp. 339-354.

5. See *New Constitution of the Government of Poland Established by the Revolution of the Third of May, 1791*, 2nd. ed. (London, 1791), reprinted in 1991 by the Royal Castle in Warsaw, pp. 1-2. This translation is used throughout this article, with alterations in cases when it differs from the Polish original.

6. "Prawo o sejmikach" (Law concerning dietines) in *Volumina legum* (Kraków, 1889), vol. 9 pp. 233-241. Referred to hereafter as *VL*; "Zaręczenie" (Mutual guarantee), *VL* vol. 9 p. 316. English translations included in *New Constitution...*: "Law Concerning Dietines", pp. 43-89; "Law Concerning Towns", pp. 91-110; "Declaration of the States Assembled", pp. 39-42.

7. "Powołanie deputacji redakcyjnej" (Appointment of the editorial deputation), *VL*, vol. 9, p. 401.

8. All these statutes are published in *VL*, vol. 9.

9. Władysław Smoleński, *Ostatni rok Sejmu Wielkiego* (The last year of the Great Diet) (Kraków, 1896), p. 405.

10. See Krystyna Zienkowska, *Sławetni i urodzeni. Ruch polityczny mieszczaństwa w dobie Sejmu Czteroletniego* (The city dwellers and the well-born. The political movement of the townspeople at the time of the Four-Year Diet) (Warszawa: PWN, 1976).

11. See Jan Dihm, *Sprawa Konstytucji Ekonomicznej z 1791 r. (Na tle wewnętrznej i zagranicznej sytuacji Polski)* (The problem of the Economic Constitution of 1791.

[Against the background of the internal and external situation in Poland]) (Wrocław: Ossolineum, 1959); Emanuel Rostworowski, "W sprawie Konstytucji Ekonomicznej 1791 r." (About the Economic Constitution of 1791) *Przegląd Historyczny 51 (1960)*, Rostworowski, "Jeszcze o Michale Ossowskim i jego Konstytucji Ekonomicznej" (More about Michał Ossowski and his Economic Constitution), *Przegląd Historyczny* 53 (1962).

12. *VL*, vol. 9, pp. 368-369 and 437.

13. Andrzej Stroynowski, "Reforma królewszczyzn na Sejmie Czteroletnim" (Reform of royal lands at the Four-Year Diet), *Zeszyty Naukowe Uniwersytetu Łódzkiego. Nauki humanistyczno-społeczne. Folia Historica* 1, 69 (1979).

14. See, for example, the anonymous pamphlet, *Zastanowienie się nad całego kraju włościanami z uwag nad projektem jmci księdza Ossowskiego...* (Reflections on the peasantry of the entire state from the remarks on the project of the priest Ossowski...), reprinted in *Materiały do dziejów Sejmu Czteroletniego*, eds. Janusz Woliński, Jerzy Michalski and Emanuel Rostworowski (Wrocław: Ossolineum, 1955), vol. 1, pp. 599-614.

15. *Kodeks Stanisława Augusta. Zbiór dokumentów* (Code of Stanisław August. A collection of documents), ed. Stanisław Borowski (Warszawa, 1938), pp. 66, 80, 116.

16. See Jerzy Jedlicki, *Klejnot i bariery społeczne; przeobrażenia szlachectwa polskiego w schyłkowym okresie feudalizmu* (The crest and social barriers; transformation of Polish nobility in the period of the decline of feudalism) (Warszawa: PWN, 1988), pp. 162-176; Adam Lityński, *Sejmiki ziemskie 1764-1793 Dzieje reformy* (Local dietines 1764-1793: The history of their reform) (Katowice: Wydawn. Uniwersytetu Śląskiego, 1988), pp. 118-124. According to calculations completed by Tadeusz Korzon, the nobility of the Republic in 1791 consisted of 725,000 individuals of whom 318,000 were landed and 407,000 landless. The landed nobility, therefore, constituted only 43.9% of the entire nobility. Tadeusz Korzon, *Wewnętrzne dzieje Polski za Stanisława Augusta (1764-1794)* (Internal history of Poland during the reign of Stanisław August, 1764-1794) 4 vols. (Kraków, 1882-86), vol. 1, p. 320.

17. "Prawo o sejmie" (Law on Diet), *VL*, vol. 9, p. 251; see Ryszard Łaszewski, *Sejm polski w latach 1764-1793: Studium historyczno-prawne* (The Polish Diet in the years 1764-1793: Historical-legal study) (Warszawa-Poznań: PWN, 1973); Jerzy Michalski, "Sejm w czasach panowania Stanisława Augusta" (The Diet during the reign of Stanisław August) in *Historia sejmu polskiego*, ed. Jerzy Michalski (Warszawa: PWN, 1984), vol. 1. pp. 350-415.

18. Ryszard Łaszewski, *Sejm polski ...*, p. 30.

19. See Henryk Kocój, *O sukcesję saską: Sprawa następstwa tronu polskiego w czasach Sejmu Czteroletniego* (The Saxon succession: The problem of succession to the Polish throne in the time of the Four-Year Diet) (Warszawa: Pax, 1972).

20. The Statute on the Guardians of the Laws, *VL*, vol. 9, pp. 266-270; see Józef Wojakowski, *Straż Praw* (Guardians of the Laws) (Warszawa: Uniwersytet Warszawski, 1982).

21. Bogusław Leśnodorski, *Dzieło...*, p. 319.

22. "Komisja Policji" (Police Commission), *VL*, vol. 9, pp. 277-287; "Komisja Skarbowa" (Treasury Commission), *VL*, vol. 9, pp. 319-326; "Komisja Wojskowa" (Military Commission), *VL*, vol. 9, pp. 457-464. Concerning the organization and activities of the Police Commission, see Andrzej Zahorski, *Centralne instytucje policyjne w Polsce w dobie rozbiorów* (The main police institutions in Poland during the partitions) (Warszawa: PWN, 1959). For treasury reform, tax legislation and administration of the Treasury, see Marian M. Drozdowski, *Podstawy finansowe działalności państwowej w Polsce 1764-1793* (The financial basis of the state administration in Poland 1764-1793) (Warszawa: PWN, 1975) and Grażyna Bałtruszajtys, *Sądownictwo Komisji Skarbowej w sprawach handlowych i przemysłowych 1764-1794* (The jurisdiction of the Treasury Commission concerning commerce and industry 1764-1794) (Warszawa: Uniwersytet Warszawski, 1977). For the expansion of the army and its organization, see Leonard Ratajczyk, *Wojsko i obronność Rzeczypospolitej 1788-1792* (The army and the means of defense of the Commonwealth 1788-1792) (Warszawa: MON, 1975).

23. For the noble court system in Wielkopolska, see Jacek Sobczak, *Wielkopolskie sądy ziemiańskie* (The noble courts of Wielkopolska) (Warszawa: PWN, 1977). Concerning municipal courts, see Zbigniew Szcząska, "Sądy przysięgłych w systemie sądownictwa miejskiego Rzeczypospolitej" (Jury courts in the system of the municipal judiciary of the Commonwealth), *Czasopismo Prawno-Historyczne* 28, 1 (1976): 123-129.

24. *VL*, vol. 9. pp. 243-249. For the organization, jurisdiction and procedures of the court according to the statute of May 17, 1791 see Zbigniew Szcząska, "Sąd sejmowy w Polsce od końca XVI do końca XVIII w." (The Diet court in Poland from the end of the 16th to the end of the 18th century) *Czasopismo Prawno-Historyczne* 20, 1 (1968): 116-122.

25. Józef Wojakowski, *Straż Praw*, p. 95ff. See also Jerzy Łojek, *Geneza i obalenie Konstytucji 3 Maja* (Origin and overthrow of the Constitution of 3 May) (Lublin: Wydawnictwo Lubelskie, 1986), pp. 163ff.

26. For the election of Diet judges see Zbigniew Szcząska, "Odpowiedzialność rządu w Polsce w latach 1775-1792" (Liability of the Government in Poland in the years 1775-1792), *Czasopismo Prawno-Historyczne* 27, 1 (1975): 97. On the choice of Police commissioners, appellate judges and municipal plenipotentiaries, see Władysław Smoleński, *Ostatni rok Sejmu Wielkiego...* pp. 43, 111-117. The debates of the February dietines are presented in Władysław Smoleński, *Ostatni Rok Sejmu Wielkiego...*, pp. 294-295. See also Jacek Sobczak, "Reforma sejmików na Sejmie

Czteroletnim i jej realizacja w Wielkopolsce" (Reform of the dietines at the Four-Year Diet and its realization in Wielkopolska), *Roczniki Historyczne* 46 (1980): 88ff and Adam Lityński, *Sejmiki ziemskie*, pp. 132-139.

27. *VL.* vol. 9, pp. 421, 423; Władysław Smoleński, *Ostatni rok Sejmu Wielkiego*, pp. 350, 364.

28. *VL*, vol. 9, p. 447.

29. *VL*, vol. 9, pp. 452-453; Zbigniew Szcząska, "Sąd sejmowy...," p. 122.

30. *VL*, vol. 9, pp. 469-479.

31. Hugo Kołłątaj (Ignacy Potocki, Fr. K. Dmochowski), *O ustanowieniu i upadku Konstytucji polskiej 3 maja 1791 roku* (On the enactment and the fall of the Polish Constitution of 3 May 1791), in 2 vols. (Metz), Kraków: 1793), vol. 2, p. 303.

32. Bogusław Leśnodorski, *Dzieło...*, pp. 449-468; Andrzej Zahorski, "Geneza i tradycja Konstytucji 3 Maja" (Genesis and tradition of the Constitution of 3 May) in *Epoka Konstytucji 3 Maja* (Warszawa: Wydawn. Epoka, 1983), p. 28.

Translated by Janusz Duzinkiewicz

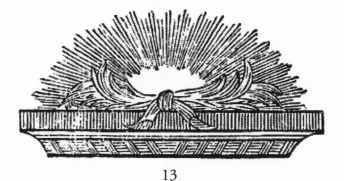

13

Main Principles of the First American, Polish and French Constitutions Compared

Rett R. Ludwikowski

A study of the first written constitutions in the world--the American Constitution of 1787, the Polish Constitution of May 1791, and the French Constitution of September 1791 immediately reveals a number of problems. The three countries which adopted written constitutions at the end of the eighteenth century differed in various ways. It has been often argued that the political systems during the period when the constitutions were being written in these countries manifested more differences than similarities. On the other hand, their constitutions were adopted at approximately the same time; moreover, before any other country completed a constitutional work, France adopted the next four constitutions (1793, 1795, 1799, amended in 1802, and 1804) and Poland was granted another constitution in 1807 (The Constitution of the Duchy of Warsaw). Was the impulse to create a constitution in America, France and Poland fairly coincidental and due exclusively to local causes? Do the first constitutional texts bear any structural and linguistic similarities? This paper is dedicated to the consideration of these questions. Some points of comparison are striking from the outset.

The Preamble to the American Constitution appeals to "the People of the United States." In comparison, the Polish Constitution begins with the words, "In the name of God, one in the Holy Trinity." For a person interested in studying the political culture of both countries, the first words of these foremost political documents are significant.

The American Constitution refers to religious matters in Article VI which declares that "no religious Test shall ever be required as a Qualification to any Office or public Trust under the United States." The First Amendment states clearly that "Congress shall make no law respecting an establishment of religion, or prohibiting the free exercise thereof."[1] The Polish Constitution did not only begin with an appeal to God, but Article I declared that "The Holy Roman-Catholic Faith, with all its privileges and immunities, shall be the dominant national religion. The changing of it for any other persuasion is forbidden under the penalties of apostasy."[2] This clear-cut difference between the two constitutions fades away in light of a more profound study of religious attitudes in America and Poland. As Thomas M. Cooley pointed out:

> It was never intended by the [American] Constitution that the government should be prohibited from recognizing religion, or that religious worship should never be provided for in cases where a proper recognition of Divine Providence in the working of government might seem to require it, and where it might be done without drawing any invidious distinctions between different religious beliefs, organizations or sects.[3]

The Polish Constitution drew the distinctions between Roman Catholicism and "other persuasions," but it also confirmed "to all persuasions and religions, freedom and liberty, according to the laws of the country."[4] Deviation from Catholicism was recognized as apostasy. On the other hand, the Constitution offered toleration and protection to those who were born non-Catholics. Almost since the beginning of its existence, Poland was within the Catholic cultural sphere and Catholicism had gained an unquestionable supremacy. On the other hand, Poland was always very proud of its religious tolerance. The Counter-Reformation strengthened the predominance of the Catholic Church, but the persecution of Protestants in Poland was never as strong as in Spain or Italy, where Protestantism was thoroughly suppressed. Poland preserved its tradition of religious tolerance and did not experience either mass executions or religious wars; it remained a Catholic country, primarily because of the peasants' and the nobility's, the two largest segments of the population, strong attachment to Catholicism. In the eighteenth century, because Poland was surrounded by Protestant, Muslim and Orthodox Christian nations, the protection of the primacy of the Catholic Church seemed to be an important national dogma. In America, with its "multiplicity of sects,"[5] the enforcement of religious conformity clearly contradicted the right to a free exercise of religion. As Carl B. Swisher wrote:

> Religious dissenters constituted important elements in the population of certain colonies – and religious dissent in those days usually signified traits of nonconformity and strength of will likely to resist regimentation by a government three thousand miles across the sea.[6]

In any case, it was a centralized, state-supported religion such as the Anglican Church in England that the Americans feared. American reality required not merely tolerance; religious liberty amounted to religious tolerance. However, it is noteworthy that despite this difference, the framers of both constitutions emphasized the significance of religious belief and incorporated this recognition into the constitution.[7] An air of genuine atheism can be found rather in the French revolutionary acts which emphasized not only the significance of religious liberty but were drafted in the spirit of Voltairian secular rationalism.

The preamble to the American Constitution states that the people of the United States ordained and established the Constitution. In comparison, the Polish Constitution was adopted and declared entirely sacred and imprescriptible by the King and the estates confederated in the Diet. The King in the Diet was to represent the Polish nation. In a manner similar to the Polish Constitution, the French Act of 1791 appealed to the National Assembly which "wished to establish the French Constitution upon the principles it has just recognized." These principles were deemed to be declared by the Declaration of the Rights of Man and Citizen, which was incorporated into the Constitution. The original text of the Declaration referred also to "the representatives of the French people, organized in the National Assembly."

The wording of the preambles to these foremost political documents was recognized as very telling. It was often argued that contrary to the American Constitution which was established "by the people," the Polish and French acts were adopted by the people's representatives. The Polish Diet and the French National Constituent Assembly had an exclusive *pouvoir constituant* and "the people" did not have a direct access to the constitutional works nor the possibility to approve or to disapprove of the final product. Robert R. Palmer wrote: "The Constituent Assembly (in France), on finishing its work in 1791, did not submit the new Constitution to any form of popular ratification, such as had occurred for the federal and some of the state constitutions in America."[8] This apparently clear-cut difference should not be exaggerated and, in fact, an analysis of the process of adoption and provisions on the amendment of the constitutions shows more similarities than was traditionally admitted.

A careful analysis of the constitutional processes will reveal a difference in the conceptualization of the role of constituent assemblies in America, France and Poland. The conviction that a constitution should be drafted not by regular legislative bodies but by special conventions to whom the people delegated constituent power was well grounded in America and France. The French Constituent Assembly and the American Constitutional Convention were each called to adopt a Constitution. The geopolitical situation of Poland and especially Russian protection of the Polish "golden freedom" worked against the heralding of constitutional reforms. The Polish Diet (1788-1792), later called the Four-Year Diet, was formed as a Confederation Diet. It was, however, a fairly common practice employed in the late eighteenth century to call diets in the form of confederations to prevent the use of *liberum veto*. The Diet extended its work to two sessions (1788-1790 and 1790-1792) and doubled its body in 1790, but otherwise it was conceived as a regular legislative assembly.

Differences in the people's direct contribution to the process of the drafting Constitutions have been either overlooked or exaggerated. Such differences should be viewed against the background of carefully examined local circumstances.

In America, a draft of the Constitution was produced by the Constitutional Convention and signed by thirty-nine of the fifty-five delegates. It was submitted to the Congress which referred it to conventions in several states. Through the ratification process, the draft was subject to nation-wide discussion s by the people. In France the National Constituent Assembly submitted the Constitution to the King on September 3 and the King signed it into law on September 14. The Polish King participated in the constitutional debate of May 3, 1791 and he was one of the main framers of the constitutional text. He promptly took an oath to the Constitution and two days later (May 5), the Diet majority passed a resolution that all protests against the Constitution were invalid.

Although it has to be admitted that the first European Constitutions were not submitted to popular ratification one has to balance this fact against the considerable direct contribution of the people to the constitution-making process in France and Poland. The average attendance at the meetings of the Philadelphia Convention was only about thirty and its debates were held behind closed doors.[9] The public was not familiar with the issues and controversies among the members of the Convention. The people were not given a chance to participate in the constitutional debate before the ratification process. In Poland in 1790 the body of deputies to the Diet was doubled and numbered over 500 representatives and senators.[10] It is a fact that the session of May 3

CONSTITUTION

OF

THE

UNITED STATES,

As recommended to CONGRESS

THE 17th OF SEPTEMBER, 1787.

BY

THE

Federal Convention.

PORTSMOUTH: NEW-HAMPSHIRE,
PRINTED BY JOHN MELCHER, 1787.

The Constitution of the United States, as recommended to Congress the 17th of September, 1787 by the Federal Convention. Portsmouth; New-Hampshire, Printed by John Melcher, 1787. (Indiana University Lilly Library).Title page of one of the editions of the Constitution of the United States printed for distribution in New Hampshire prior to that state's convention, which ratified the Constitution June 21, 1788. By this vote a majority of states ratifying the Constitution was achieved and the Constitution was put into effect.

was attended by only one hundred eighty two deputies and senators but the adoption of the Constitution was preceded by the twenty months of work by the Diet appointed Constitutional Deputation and the Deputation for Towns. The final draft of the Constitution was prepared in the course of secret consultations by the King and his closest counselors, but the basic principles of the forthcoming constitution were popularized by widely read political writers led by Hugo Kołłątaj, Stanisław Staszic, Józef Pawlikowski, Franciszek Dmochowski, Antoni Trębicki and others. Emanuel Rostworowski wrote:

> A compact patriotic and royal party was formed around the Constitution under the slogan of: "The King with the People, the People with the King." Kołłątaj, who was appointed Vice-Chancellor, was playing an increasingly important part in the Constitutional party. He organized a political club, called The Assembly of Friends of the Constitution, which enrolled both deputies and political leaders from outside the Diet. At the meetings of the Club, laws were drafted and parliamentary tactics worked out. Members of the Club serving as Diet deputies were bound to solidarity. The Assembly had a press organ of its own entitled *Gazeta Narodowa i Obca*. It was Poland's first political party to be organized on modern lines. The burghers all over the country were enthusiastic about the Constitution. The reservations of the provincial gentry were gradually overcome, as can be seen from the resolutions of the dietines.[11]

The French Assembly numbered over eleven hundred deputies and, as in Poland, constitutional principles were discussed in every house and club in Paris; "there was no privacy in the chamber, the galleries hooted and applauded as they chose."[12] There was a general consensus in France that to subject the Constitution to further public debate in the thousands of local electoral assemblies would mean "anarchy and dissolution."[13] As a result, the Constitution was not sent to the local constituencies but its principles were publicly discussed throughout the period of work of the National Constituent Assembly (28 June 1789 – 3 September 1791). Thus, even without a ratification process, the people's contribution to the making of the first European Constitutions has to be recognized.

One can, however, note a difference in the process of amending constitutional provisions. Commenting on the American approach to constitutional revision Madison wrote:

> As the people are the only legitimate fountain of power, and it is from them that the constitutional charter, under which the several branches of government hold their power, is derived, it seems strictly consonant to the republican theory to recur to the same original authority, not

only whenever it may be necessary to enlarge, diminish, or new-model the powers of government, but also whenever any one of the departments may commit encroachments on the chartered authorities of the others.[14]

The United States Constitution provided that the initiation of the amending process required a vote of two-thirds of both houses of the Congress or the application of the legislatures of two-thirds of the States. The amendments were to be ratified either by the legislatures or by special conventions of three-fourths of the States.[15]

The Polish Constitution resolved that the regular Diets have *pouvoir législatif*, but that the Constitution could be amended only by the extraordinary Diets equipped with the special *pouvoir constituant*. These special Diets were to be called every 25 years and the date of the next extraordinary Diet was set precisely for October 1, 1816.[16]

The French Constitution of 1791, like the American Constitution, declared that only "the nation has the imprescriptible right to change its Constitution" (Title VII). France, however, did not have a federate form of governmental organization, hence the referral of important decisions to *assemblées primaires* seemed unnecessary. The central legislative assembly was deemed to represent the nation. "What is a nation?" Sieyès wrote, "a body of associates living under a common law and represented by the same legislature."[17]

To amend Constitutions the future National Legislature was expected to turn into an "Assembly of Revision." This Assembly was to be composed of the regular members of the national legislative assembly augmented by one third of the delegates who were to be elected in the departments. The initiative to change the Constitution had to be supported by three consecutive national legislatures. Their decree for the convocation of the Assembly of Revision was not to be subject to the sanction of the King and the Constitution did not provide for any further ratification of the amendments.

People established constitutions and people were the addressees of constitutional rights, but not all the people equally. The American and French Constitutions were portrayed as democratic in contrast to the non-democratic Polish Constitution of 3 May, 1791, but the term "democratic" as used in reference to both Constitutions requires explanation.

Beginning with the very moment that the Constitution was adopted, the American political system was proclaimed the most democratic in the world. The French Constitution retained a monarchy but its populist character has not been questioned. The French Constitution was adopted in the name of the "third estate" which Sieyès claimed to be "a complete nation."[18] The French Constitution of 1791 declared that "all powers emanate from the nation."[19]

The framers of the American Constitution claimed that the document rested on the solid foundation of the consent of the people.

The Polish Constitution was adopted four months before the French and provided an apparently similar declaration. It proclaimed that "all power in civil society should be derived from the will of the people."[20] However, Poland was recognized as the Commonwealth of the Nobles and the Constitution did not undermine the monopoly of the nobility's political power. It declared that the nobility will take precedence in "private and public life" and guaranteed all its liberties. The Polish Act introduced the burghers into the political arena, but they could only work actively in the Diet Commissions and had *vocem activam* in matters concerning towns and commerce and were "consulted" *(vocem consultivam)* in other matters. The Polish Constitution was antiaristocratic in the sense that it abolished the ranks and degrees of nobility, but it did not abolish the hereditary nobility as did the French and American Constitutions.[21] Democracy in Poland was traditionally understood as "democracy among nobility." On the one hand, the Polish Constitution was "non-democratic" in the sense that it limited the group of addressees of political rights to a single social estate; on the other hand, it has to be admitted that, in comparison with West-European nations, the Polish nobility was a particularly numerous social group; it constituted ten percent of the whole population.

Although the framers of the American and French Constitutions opposed an "elitist" concept of nation and did not disenfranchise any single group of property owners, they did not, in fact, put voters and citizens on the same footing. "Democracy" in both the United States and Western Europe did not mean universal suffrage. "Democracy" wrote Conyers Read,

> was also termed 'pure,' 'perfect,' or 'simple' democracy, in order to keep it distinct from a democratic but representative regime. Jefferson called it a 'republic' or a 'pure republic' and called 'government democratical but representative' the parliamentary regime based on universal suffrage. Madison gave 'democracy' the common meaning and termed the representative system 'republic', thus the United States was a republic and not a 'democracy'.[22]

In America, as in Poland, "people" were divided between active voters and passive non-voters, and in theory, it was assumed that voters represent the interests of all the people.[23] Although the qualifications for voters werre left to the states and varied substantially, it can be assumed that about one-fifth of the adult white males in America possessed no vote.[24]

The French Constitution associated the principles of royalism, and antiaristocratism with a representative government. "Individual wills are the

USTAWA RZĄDOWA.

PRAWO UCHWALONE.

Dnia 3 Maia, Roku 1791.

w WARSZAWIE,

u P. Dufour Konſyl: Nadw: J. K. Mci
i Dyrektora Druk: Korp: Kad:

The title page of one of the first editions of the Polish Constitution of 3 May 1791 published after its adoption by the Diet. *Ustawa Rządowa. Prawo Uchwalone. Dnia 3 Maia, Roku 1791. w Warszawie u P. Dufour.../1791/* (Biblioteka Narodowa, Warszawa).

sole elements of the general will," wrote Sieyès, and in the period of the
Constituent Assembly his opinion prevailed.[25] The French Constitution
proclaimed that the French political system was representative and that a body
of the associated individuals was to be represented by the national legislature
and the King. Representatives were not to be bound by the instructions of
their constituencies. Sieyès wrote: "Since they are the only depositaries of general
will, they have no need to consult their constituents."[26]

The individuals who were the subject of constitutional rights, however,
were divided, as in the United States, into "passive citizens" without a vote,
and "active citizens," who had the right to vote. "Active citizens" did not elect
deputies to the national assembly directly. They voted for "electors," who, in
fact, were the only ones who were granted full political citizenship. To be an
"active citizen" it was necessary to be a Frenchman of at least twenty-five years
of age, domiciled in the electoral district and paying a direct tax equal at least
to the value of three days' labor. An "active citizen" could be chosen as elector
if he owned a property equal to 200 days' labor or was a tenant of a dwelling
equal to the value of 150 days' labor.[27] It had been determined by the
Constituent Assembly that on May 27, 1791 there were 4,298,360 "active
citizens" in the population of between 25,000,000 and 26,000,000. "I would
judge," Robert R. Palmer wrote, "that a quarter of adult males may have been
excluded from the vote by reason of poverty... One is led to conclude, if the
total of men over 25 was about 6,500,000, that almost seventy of them in a
hundred had the vote, about fifty in a hundred could serve as electors, and one
in a hundred could qualify as a national deputy, before August 1791."[28]

The constitutional systems of the countries which adopted the first
constitutions showed a constant tendency to extend voting rights; it took,
however, over a century for them to reach universal suffrage. In fact, it has to
be admitted that it was Poland which first (of the three countries) equated
voters and adult citizens through the enfranchisement of women in 1918.
The Nineteenth Amendment enfranchised women in the United States in
1920; the same right was granted by France in 1944.

The most impressive similarity of the three first constitutions was always
seen in the adoption of the principle of the division of power. The framework
for the application of this principle was set forth by Articles I, II, and III of the
American Constitution, Article V of the Polish Constitution, and Title III of
the French Constitution. It has been often pointed out that the doctrine of the
division of powers was applied differently by each of these constitutions.

America completed her struggle for independence before the adoption of
the Constitution and the liberty of her citizens did not seem to be in dangered
of being abused by the executive power. Division of power in America was

intended to protect the system established by the Constitution from domination by any single power. The Constitution put emphasis on the separation of powers and worked out an elaborate system of protective checks and balances. In fact, neither Locke nor Montesquieu believed that the powers should be equal and have no influence or even control over the acts of each other.[29] The powers in the English model were neither equal nor well separated.

In Poland, the Constitution was adopted by the nobility and their liberties did not require any further protection. The Polish concept of the division of powers was to balance the excessive freedom of the big magnates and to strengthen the authority of the king. The critics of the Polish Constitution argued frequently that, despite the declaration that the highest authority was vested in the three powers, the whole concept of the distribution, separation and balances of the main "branches" of government was not accomplished. The Constitution departed from the originally considered "checks and balances" and invested the Diet with far greater power.

In France, division of powers meant an imposition of efficient restraints on executive power and protection of citizens from the absolutism of monarchs. On the other hand, the King already existed as a reality which could not be disregarded.[30] The Constitution of 1791 offered a settlement by compromise. It confirmed that the person of the hereditary monarch is inviolable and sacred; he was, however, bound by law and proclaimed to be just a representative of the nation.

The French monarch was not as impotent as the Polish king but far less powerful than the American President. The form of government was declared as monarchical and executive power was delegated to the king, and exercised under his authority by ministers and other responsible agents. Contrary to the Polish Constitution which limited the king's selection of ministers and allowed the Diet to vote them down, the French Constitution left the choice and dismissal of ministers solely to the king. As distinct from the Polish ministers, who had guaranteed seats in the Senate, the French ministers, like the officers of American executive departments, could not combine executive and legislative functions. On the other hand, Polish and French ministers had to countersign the king's resolutions which otherwise were not executable.

The American and French Constitutions vested in the head of the executive the power to veto the decisions of the legislature. The Polish Constitution vested this right in the Senate in which the king had only one vote and a second vote in the case of a draw. The Polish Senate's veto could be overruled by the Diet in a second ballot at the subsequent session. The President of the United States has a veto unless two thirds of both houses overrule him. In France there was a good deal of discussion whether the king should have an "absolute veto" or a "suspensive veto" with a right to appeal to the people in successive elections. After the King's announcement through Necker that he supported the idea of a "suspensive veto," the Assembly voted down the "absolute veto" by 673 to 325.[31] The Constitution provided that "when the two legislatures following the one in which the decree was introduced have again successively presented the same decree in the same terms, the King shall be deemed to have given his sanction" despite a former refusal.[32]

The French king, like the Polish monarch and the American president was the supreme head of the army and navy, and, as in the American and Polish systems, the right to declare war was vested in the legislative body. The French Constitution provided that in case of imminent or actual hostilities, the king shall immediately notify the legislative body and cease hostilities upon the decision of the Assembly. The American and the French Constitutions gave to the heads of government the right to "maintain political relations abroad" with the power to make treaties with the "advice and consent of two thirds of the Senate," in America and "subject to ratification by the legislative body" in France.[33] The Polish Constitution emphasized more strongly the control of the legislature over the area of foreign relations. The Polish king was not allowed "to conclude definitively any treaty, or any diplomatic act;" and was "only allowed to carry on negotiations with foreign Courts, and facilitate temporary occurrences, always with reference to the Diet."[34] On the other hand, the Polish monarch was offered a legislative initiative which he exercised together with his ministers (Guardians of the Laws); the French king did not have direct initiative, he could only "invite the legislative body to take a matter under consideration."[35]

Unlike the American Congress and the Polish Diet, the French Assembly became a single house. The lack of federal organization and the fear, as Sieyès argued, that a senate of fifty men could stop an assembly of five hundred defeated the bicameral principle.[36]

The French Assembly also voted in favor of the Sieyès' proposal that the deputies represent the entire nation and that they could not receive a mandate from their constituencies.[37] Similar instructions, which normally were given to the deputies by the Polish dietines, were abolished by the Constitution of 3 May, 1791. Legislative functions were concentrated in the French National Assembly and the functions of the primary and electoral assemblies were limited to election.

The American and the French Constitutions are more specific than the Polish in placing limitations on the judicial branch. The U.S. Constitution does this by setting out (Article III, Sec. 2) specific matters to which the jurisdiction of the courts is limited. In the United States, these limitations are

CONSTITUTION

FRANÇAISE,

PRÉSENTÉE AU ROI

PAR

L'ASSEMBLÉE NATIONALE,

Le 3 septembre 1791.

A DIJON,

DE L'IMPRIMERIE DE P. CAUSSE.

M. DCC. XCI.

The title page of one of the editions of the French Constitution presented to the King by the National Assembly September 3, 1791 and approved by the King September 13. *Constitution Française, présentée au Roi par l'Assamblée Nationale, le 3 September 1791.* A Dijon, de l'Imprimerie de P. Causse. M.DCC.XCI. (Indiana University, Lilly Library).

not terribly significant these days. The federal judiciary is exceptionally powerful, although federal courts are still courts of limited jurisdiction. The United States Supreme Court expanded its power by assuming powers of judicial review of Congressional enactments even though the Constitution did not expressly provide for such judicial review. The French Constitution is much more explicit on this point and goes the other way; judicial review of National Assembly measures is prohibited: "The courts may not interfere with the exercise of the legislative power, suspend the execution of laws, encroach upon administrative functions, or summon administrators before them for reasons connected with their duties." (Chapter V, Art. 3).

All three first Constitutions declared that the judiciary constituted a separate branch which was distinct from the other powers. Actually, the textual similarities of the Polish and the French Acts with regard to the independence of the judiciary are quite striking; both Constitutions proclaim that judicial power may not be employed by the legislative body or the king but only by the elective magistrates.[38] Chapter V, 1. The French Constitution incorporated the essentials of the Decree Reorganizing the Judiciary of August 16, 1790. It placed at the top of the French judicial system a single Court of Cassation which upon the recognition of a violation of the rules of a proceeding or the law, could quash the judgment and remand the case to the lower courts. A National High Court was established as a court for crimes against the security of the State.[39]

In Poland, the various special courts for the nobility were replaced by landowners' courts *(ziemiańskie sądy)*, and by appellate provincial courts, staffed by judges elected for four years by the dietines. Townspeople were subject to the jurisdiction of the town courts and appellate, assessors' courts, while the peasants were subject to the jurisdiction of the landlords, and, in the king's dominions, to the special referendars' court. The most grave crimes "against the nation" were to be heard by the Diet Court composed of its members.

The French Constitution contains one provision that many have found sorely lacking in the U.S. document. The 1791 French Constitution – functioning perhaps a century and a half ahead of its time – guarantees "Public instruction free of charge in those branches of education which are indispensable to all men... and the establishments thereof shall be apportioned gradually, in accordance with the division of the kingdom." The Polish Constitution refers to the Commission for National Education, Europe's first Ministry of Education, which was established in Poland in 1773. The President of the Commission was given a permanent seat in the Guardians of the Laws, appended to the king for supervision of the integrity and the execution of the laws. The U.S. Constitution is totally silent on any right to education.

In sum, there are far more similarities than differences in the United States, Polish and French Constitutions. It is obvious that all three Constitutions were influenced by ideas of the separation of powers, of checks and balances, of a certain supremacy of the legislative brance (in that political power flows from the people and the people are represented primarily through the legislative branch), and of limitations on the power of the executive and the courts. Even with all the differences in tone and content, carefull study reveals that the textual similarities of the first Constitutions are by no means incidental and that a comparable set of factors stimulated the creation of all three constitutional works.

The Polish Constitution was favorably commented in the French Assembly. The provincial Societies of Friends of the French Constitution sent their congratulations to Poland. But the Polish Constitution was also criticized by the political radicals who raised the issue that Poles did not solve any of their urgent social problems.[40] In Poland, after an initial period of enthusiasm for the French revolutionary achievements, commentators split into two distinct groups: those coupling and those separating the French and the Polish reforms. The first group praised the French Revolution for spreading the ideas of liberty and fraternity. The others set the prudent and moderate Polish reforms against French anarchy and violence. The reaction against French Jacobinism in the nineteenth century and an inclination toward pointing to the "antidemocratic" character of the Polish Constitution of 3 May by contemporary socialist commentators, contributed to the presentation of the French and Polish Constitutions as antipodes of constitutional thought.

The revolutionary events leading to the adoption of the Polish Constitution were followed closely in the United States and reported by the daily press. Particularly lengthy articles were published in the *Pennsylvania Gazette* of July 27, 1791, which gave a full account of the events of May 3 in Poland and a synopsis of eleven sections of the new Constitution.[41]

The French Constitution of 1791 also received favorable attention in America. The House praised the Constitution for its "wisdom and magnanimity," while the Senate withheld the term "magnanimity" from its statement and simply acknowledged the fact of its adoption.[42] This symbolic gesture appeared to begin the process of polarized positions taken by commentators on the French events who in the next years were to split distinctly into two groups: those coupling and those separating the American and the French Revolutions. The first group, led by Paine and Jefferson, assumed and emphasized that the French uprising was an "afterglow" of the American struggle for liberty and had "produced incalculable blessings to [France]" and promoted the "interests of thousands."[43] The second faction, which assembled around Hamilton, "preferred to believe that the Revolution in Europe was the outbreak of an unruly and ignorant populace."[44] They believed that the French Revolution, particularly in its Jacobinian stage, lacked legality and could endanger the achievement of the American struggle for freedom. Hamiltonians were terrified by the changing teams of French leaders, the general defiance of authority, symptoms of anarchy and violence, and the lack of security of property. In their minds the French Revolution discredited democracy.[45]

Although the French Constitution of 1793 was widely criticized by American statesmen, the public was still enthusiastic, mostly due to the activity of democratic clubs and societies which approved wholeheartedly all that was happening in France. They were able to sway for some time a large part of the public opinion in favor of the French Revolution. In fact, the activity of the societies intensified a critical reaction of the leaders in Washington and helped the Federalists neutralize pro-French enthusiasm.

A careful study of the development of constitutional movements in the beginning of the constitutional era, shows that the completion of the process to form constitutions was the result of a combination of factors; some were the product of local circumstances, while others were present in more than one country and as such warrant a comparative analysis. For example, it was observed that the formation of the constitutions in America, Poland and France was stimulated by traumatic political events (the American struggle for independence, the First Partition of Poland, the beginning of the French Revolution) which stemmed from unique national factors. On the other hand, the process of creating the first constitutions was completed by countries which had comparable, remarkable constitutional traditions. Two centuries of colonial experience as well as several centuries of British experience provided the framework for the United States Constitution. In Poland, the process of limiting the king's power began as early as the fourteenth century and this country's emergence as a constitutional monarchy preceded by several centuries the period of written constitutions. Although France experienced a long period of absolutism, it had a significant tradition of attempts to establish restraints on the arbitrary power of her monarchs. While long and mature constitutional traditions constituted a part not only of Anglo-American, Polish and French history, it can be argued that such traditions played a leading role in determining the nature and the character of these first three constitutions.

Moreover, even a rough analysis of the first written constitutional acts shows that opinions about the incidental character of similarities requires careful verification. A sounder examination reveals an intensive interflow of ideas among the countries under consideration. It also shows remarkable similarities among the countries under consideration. It also shows remarkable similarities in the intellectual background of the framers of the constitutions and textual similarities in the constitutional texts. All these factors warrant a comparative analysis of the first written constitutions.

Notes

1. Thomas M. Cooley, *The General Principles of Constitutional Law in the United States of America* (Boston: Little Brown Co., 1880). The reference to the establishment of religion "meant the setting up or recognition of a state church, or at least the conferring upon one church special favors and advantages which are denied to others," p. 205.

2. *Konstytucja 3 Maja 1791* published under the title Ustawa Rządowa was translated into English as *New Constitution of the Government of Poland, Established by the Revolution, Third of May, 1791* (London: J. Debrett, 1791) and reprinted in 1991 by the Royal Castle in Warsaw and also by the Embassy of the Republic of Poland in Washington, Art. 1, p. 5 (hereafter cited as the Polish Constitution of 1791).

3. T. Cooley, *The General Principles...* pp. 205-6.

4. The Polish Constitution of 1791, Art. 1, p.6.

5. See *The Federalist Papers* by Alexander Hamilton, James Madison, John Jay, ed. Clinton Rossiter (New York: New American Library, 1961), no. 51 (J. Madison), p. 358, (hereafter cited as Federalist).

6. Carl Brent Swisher, *American Constitutional Development* (Boston: Houghton Mifflin Co., 1943), p. 8.

7. Justice William O. Douglas opinion in the case Zorah V. Clauson in *United States Reports* (Washington: United States Government Printing Office, 1952), vol. 343, pp. 313-14. We are a religious people whose institutions presuppose a Supreme Being. We guarantee the freedom to worship as one chooses. We make room for as wide a variety of beliefs and creeds as the spiritual needs of man deem necessary. We sponsor an attitude on the part of government that shows no partiality to any one group and that lets each flourish according to the zeal of its adherents and the appeal of its dogma. When the state encourages religious instruction or cooperates with religious authorities by adjusting the schedule of public events to sectarian needs, it follows the best of our traditions. For it then respects the religious nature of our people and accommodates the public service to their spiritual needs. To hold that it may not, would be to find in the Constitution a requirement that the government show a callous indifference to religious groups. That would be preferring those who believe in no religion over those who do believe. Government may not finance religious groups nor undertake religious instruction nor blend secular and sectarian education nor use secular institutions to force one or some religion on any person. But we find no constitutional requirement which makes it necessary for government to be hostile

to religion and to throw its weight against efforts to widen the effective scope of religious influence.

8. Robert R. Palmer, *The Age of Democratic Revolution* (Princeton: Princeton University Press, 1959), vol. 1, p. 501.

9. Swisher, *American Constitutional Development*, pp. 30, 41.

10. See *Dzieje Polski* (History of Poland), ed. Jerzy Topolski (Warszawa: PWN, 1977), p. 386.

11. Aleksander Gieysztor, Stefan Kieniewicz, Emanuel Rostworowski, Janusz Tazbir, Henryk Wereszycki, *History of Poland* (Warszawa: PWN, 1979), p. 318.

12. Palmer, *The Age of Democratic Revolution...*, p. 494.

13. Palmer, *The Age of Democratic Revolution...*, p. 496.

14. *Federalist*, pp. 313-314.

15. The United States Constitution, Art. 5.

16. Bogusław Leśnodorski, *Dzieło Sejmu Czteroletniego (1788-1792)* (The Work of the Four-Year Diet 1788-1792) (Wrocław: Ossolineum, 1951), pp. 282-283.

17. Emmanuel Joseph, abbé Sieyès, "What is the Third Estate?" in *A Documentary Survey of the French Revolution*, ed. John Hale Stewart (New York: Macmillan, 1951), p. 44.

18. Sieyès, "What is the Third Estate?" p. 43.

19. The French Constitution of 1791, Title III, 2.

20. The Polish Constitution of 1791, Art. 5, p. 12.

21. The Polish Constitution of 1791, Art. 2; The United States Constitution, Art. 1, Sec. IX, 8; The French Constitution of 1791, Preamble; See also Decree Abolishing Hereditary Nobility and Titles of June 19, 1790.

22. Conyers Read, *The Constitution Reconsidered* (New York: Columbia University Press, 1938), p. 106.

23. Edward S. Corwin, *The Constitution and What it Means Today?* (Princeton: Princeton University Press, 1954), p. 1.

24. Charles Warren, *The Making of the Federal Convention of 1787* (New York: Barnes & Noble, 1966), p. 40.

25. Sieyès, "What is the Third Estate?" p. 50.

26. Sieyès, "What is the Third Estate?" p. 54.

27. The French Constitution of 1791, Title III, Chapter I, Sec. II.7.

28. Palmer, *The Age of Democratic Revolution*, pp. 523-526.

29. E.C.S. Wade, A.W. Bradley, *Constitutional Law* (London: Longman, 1970), p. 25.

30. Jean Joseph Mounier, *Considérations sur les gouvernements et principalement sur celui qui convient à la France* (Paris: 1789), pp. 37-38.

31. Palmer, *The Age of Democratic Revolution*, p. 497.

32. The French Constitution of 1791, Title III, Chapter III, Sec. III. 2.

33. The American Constitution, Art. II, Sec. 2; The French Constitution of 1791, Title III, Chapter IV, Sec. III.3.

34. The Polish Constitution of 1791, Art. VII. p.21.

35. The French Constitution of 1791, Title III, Chapter III, Sec. I.1.

36. Palmer, *The Age of Democratic Revolution*, p. 496.

37. The French Constitution of 1791, Title III, Chapter I. Sec. III. 7.

38. The Polish Constitution of 1791, Art. VIII, p. 31; the French Constitution of 1791, Title III,

39. The French Constitution of 1791, Title III, Chapter V, 1.

40. See Leśnodorski, *Dzieło Sejmu Czteroletniego*, p. 447.

41. Bożena Sarnecka-Crouch, "LC Opens Exhibit," *Library of Congress Information Bulletin*, 50, 9, May 6 (1991): 164.

42. Charles D. Hazen, *Contemporary American Opinion of the French Revolution* (Baltimore: Johns Hopkins Press, 1897), pp. 150-151.

43. See Alpheno T. Mason, *Free Government in the Making* 3rd ed. (New York: Oxford University Press, 1977), p. 420; Dumas Malone, *Jefferson and the Rights of Man* (Boston: Little Brown, 1951), pp. 355-56; Gilbert Lycan, *Alexander Hamilton and American Foreign Policy* (Norman: University of Oklahoma Press, 1970), p. 132.

44. Palmer, *The Age of Democratic Revolution...*, (Princeton: Princeton University Press, 1964) vol. 2, p. 525.

45. Richard B. Morris, *The Emerging Nations and The American Revolution* (New York: Harper & Row, 1970), pp. 58, 71; see also John C. Miller, *Alexander Hamilton Portrait in Paradox* (New York: Harper & Row, 1959), p. 451.

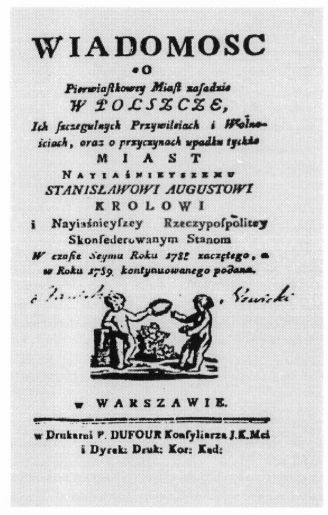

(Michał Świniarski *Wiadomość o pierwiastkowey miast zasadzie w Polszcze, ich szczególnych przywileiach i wolnościach oraz o przyczynach upadku tychże miast* (Information about the ancient principles for towns in Poland, their specific privileges and freedoms, as well as the causes of their decline), w Warszawie, F. Dufour, (1789). Title page. Reprinted from *Miasta polskie w tysiącleciu*, (Wrocław: Ossolineum, 1965). Published at the expense of the Warsaw municipality, dedicated to the King and the Diet in session, written in the name of all Crown and Lithuanian Royal Cities and using historical arguments, *Wiadomość* for the first time formulated a kind of political program demanding the expansion of rights for the burghers. Representatives of the Warsaw municipality presented copies of *Wiadomość* to the King, Senators and Deputies.

14

Reforms Relating to the Third Estate

Krystyna Zienkowska

The population in eighteenth-century Polish Commonwealth cities, Christians, Jews, and those of other faiths, made up 16 percent of the nation's total population, a rather large number for Europe of that time. One must, however, take into account that at the least 60 percent of Christian city-dwellers were actually small farmers who generally owned wooden houses and a piece of farmland, some meadow land, or a garden plot. Others were farmer-craftsmen, those who farmed while practicing a craft, sometimes only during the off season. Of course, the situation was entirely different in substantial cities, including Warsaw with its 100,000 inhabitants, where there were merchant's confraternities and crafstmen's guilds.

About 80 percent of Poland's cities, towns and settlements were the private property of the gentry or belonged to the church. Two-thirds of the country's urban population, Christian and Jewish, lived in these private towns.[1] Jews accounted for about 42 percent of the population of the towns owned by noblemen; they were forbidden residence in most church-owned towns. Though the urban population was free in theory, in private towns the owners or church administrators acted in both judicial and executive capacities. The rights of residents of private towns depended on specific, and at time arbitrary, agreements, contracts, and general relations between the owner, his representatives, and the residents.

It appears that the position of the Jews in some private towns was in some ways better than that of the other inhabitants since they were engaged in small trade and craft production and did not have to perform service in-kind. Though town owners often interfered in the work of local Jewish councils (*kahal*), they nevertheless allowed the councils to exercise direct power over the daily life, customs and religion of their communities.[2] The Christian population usually had its own magistrates, but town owners or ecclesiastical administrators prepared regulations for town life that frequently ordered the daily existence of the townspeople in detail. These rules went beyond specifying the dues to be paid in work and kind; they set the hours for work, prayer, and rest, the form of children's education, and even the kinds of clothes suitable for townspeople.

In royal, or so-called free cities, the home of about one-third of the urban population, the status of Christian residents was incomparably better than in private towns. These cities had relatively autonomous self-government with rights and privileges given and confirmed by successive monarchs. They had their own autonomous appellate courts of the highest judicial instance, the so-called *assesoria*, which were, in theory, independent, composed only of noblemen. The residents of royal cities were in this sense completely free.

City laws in royal cities provided that only citizens of the city, i.e., those individuals who accepted the law of the city and took an appropriate oath, could engage in trade and crafts. Jews were not allowed to become citizens and, until 1776, non-Catholic Christians, so-called dissenters, were also barred, as were serfs. If a nobleman agreed to become a citizen of a royal city he lost his status as a noble and his noble privileges. There were, then, barriers on both sides of urban citizenship, against those lower in the social hierarchy imposed by the city laws, and against those higher in the hierarchy, imposed by the laws of the nobility. In highly developed cities the citizens were mostly merchants and craftsmen who were full members of confraternities and guilds. Small rural towns with royal charters included propertied burghers, farmers and farmer-craftsmen among their citizens.

In actual practice many of the rights of free cities were only good on paper; they were arbitrarily violated by the gentry and restricted by legal means. The diets during the first decades of Stanisław August's reign limited the powers of city governments, especially in the areas of finance and courts, while supporting the authority of royal appointed officials (*starosta*), who held lifetime grants to royal lands, and so to the cities within those grants. Regional and central government bodies that had jurisdiction over the cities multiplied, but their work was uncoordinated. These included the Commissions of Good Order

Warsaw, Krakowskie Przedmieście street. Painting by Bernardo Belotto Canaletto (Muzeum Narodowe w Warszawie).

Jan Dekert, President of Old Warsaw. Painting by Ksawery Kaniewski (Muzeum Historyczne w Warszawie). Photo W. Wolny.

(Boni Ordinis) established in 1765, and the Department of Police of the Permanent Council (*Rada Nieustająca*) organized after the First Partition. Urban citizens, those with the greatest stake in the work of these agencies, did not have the right to serve in them.

The Four-Year Diet of 1788-1792 did not begin its work with reforms, but with an overthrow of the existing government and its institutions. The abolition of the Permanent Council on 19 January 1789 marked the rapid destruction of Russia's protectorate of more than two decades over Poland. The atmosphere in the Diet was one of exaltation over political freedom regained, and conflicting interests made their voices heard. There were political arguments, demagogic speeches, ideological ferment. It was a time that encouraged bold political thinking and acts. Out of all of this the future parties of the Four-Year Diet started to be organized. In the interval between the past and the unknown future, an idea took shape not very popular among the gentry: that the destruction, or at least restriction of the noble monopoly on legislative and executive power was a necessary condition of modernization and the preservation of true national sovereignty.

Hugo Kołłątaj, acting outside the Diet, along with a radical group of Diet deputies and of the Warsaw urban elite, led by Jan Dekert, President of Old Warsaw magistrate, and supported unofficially by the Marshal of the Diet, Stanisław Małachowski called a meeting of delegates from royal cities for November, 1789. An Association of Towns, a kind of urban confederation, was formed alongside the confederated Diet in session.[3] In December the plenipotentiaries from the royal cities presented the King and the Diet a Memorandum with a series of somewhat radical demands they called "petitions" and with new plans for reforms, which they termed "the restoration of past rights." But which groups of the urban estate could aspire to political partnership with the nobility? The Polish republican system that functioned, albeit poorly, throughout the eighteenth century operated in an estate society with strong social barriers. Formally, the laws of the Commonwealth acknowledged three "third estates" or "urban estates." These were: the Christian residents of private secular and ecclesiastical towns (about 60 percent of Christian townspeople); Christian residents of royal cities (about 40 percent); Jews, who as a specific religious and ethnic group had their own legal status, chiefly residents of secular private towns (only some 20 percent of urban Jews lived in royal cities).

Contemporary reformers felt it was obvious that interference in the legal status of the population of private cities must end in the failure of any attempted reforms. The gentry considered the judicial and administrative power that they held over the residents of the towns they owned a basic property right. Therefore, although the delegates to the urban confederation spoke in the name of the entire urban population, "a people a million strong," the actual reform plans they sent to the King and Diet in the fall of 1789 concerned only the royal cities.

No representatives from the private cities or of the communal Jewish authorities were among the plenipotentiaries. And, although there is no reference to the exclusion of non-Christians in the plans for reforms, the reforms were, without a doubt, intended solely for the Christian city dwellers. Silence on the Jewish issue was rather a tactical political measure than simply an oversight. Even if we overlook the conflicts between the townspeople of both faiths and take the hypothetical case that both "third estates" presented a joint reform package that included political reforms, which were, and were meant to be, the main part of any reform, it is certain that the Diet would have rejected such a package. The differences in culture, customs, and religion between the Jews and the gentry were even greater than those between the gentry and the Christians burghers. The rich Catholic and dissenting urban elites were not much different in language, education, culture, and behavior from middle, or even wealthy noblemen. If the Christian urban estate was not considered to be worthy to send its delegates to the Diet of the Commonwealth how can we even assume that this would be possible for the unassimilated urban Jews?[4]

Another, and hardly a secondary issue, was the antagonism of the Warsaw burghers towards both the Jews who lived illegally in Warsaw and those who came into the city legally during the regular meetings of the Diet. The Diet had already lasted not the usual six weeks, but over a year by the fall of 1789 and, according to Warsaw craftsmen and small merchants, the competition of Jewish businessmen was driving them into ruin and bankruptcy. Warsaw's Christian craftsmen and merchants expressed their discontent in numerous petitions to the magistrate of Old Warsaw. By March and April of 1790, there were open demonstrations of anger and outbursts of violence. In May, a riot broke out in which the rioters fought with the Crown-Marshal's Guards, who were responsible for keeping peace in the city.[5] The Warsaw notables who led the urban movement, members of the city administration, and of the merchant's confraternities also had their own complaints against the Jews. In the early days of the Four-Year Diet, in the fall of 1788, representatives of the Warsaw Jewish community turned directly to the Diet, omitting the Warsaw municipal authorities, with a petition for legal permanent residence and free practice of

The first page of one of the two original texts of The Law on Cities prepared at the Diet chancellery and signed by both Marshals and members of the Diet Constitutional Deputation. Reprinted from *Ustawa Rządowa, Konstytucja 3 Maja 1791. Faksymile rękopisu z Archiwum Akt Dawnych w Warszawie, w dwusetną rocznicę uchwalenia* (Wrocław: Ossolineum, 1991)

PRAWO

Pod Tytułem:

MIASTA NASZE KRÓLEWSKIE

WOLNE W PAŃSTWACH

RZECZYPOSPOLITEY

UCHWALONE

Dnia 18. Kwietnia, Roku 1791.

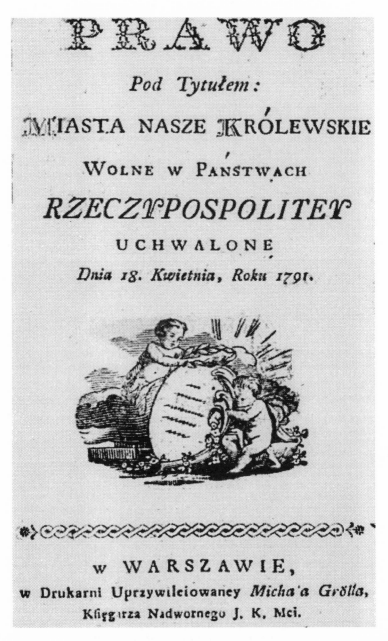

w WARSZAWIE,

w Drukarni Uprzywileiowaney *Michała Grölla*,
Księgarza Nadwornego J. K. Mci.

---

*Prawo pod tytułem: Miasta Nasze Królewskie Wolne w Państwach Rzeczypospolitej
Uchwalone* Dnia 18 Kwietnia, Roku 1791 (The Law entitled: Our Royal Free Cities
in the Dominions of the Commonwealth passed 18 April 1791), w Warszawie, M.
Gröll (1791). Title page. (Biblioteka Uniwersytecka w Warszawie).

their trades in Warsaw. A polemical memorandum rejecting these demands was soon published by the city magistrate.[6]

The plenipotentaries of the royal cities assembled in Warsaw during the fall of 1789 in their Memorandum first of all insisted on the right to participate in legislative and executive bodies, freedom from the authority of the permanent royal officials--in other words, a general broadening of urban self-government--and a partnership with the gentry. Among the numerous demands were: creation of a separate house of the Diet for the burghers, or the right to elect one-third of the members of the Diet, who would have full voting rights and would serve according to instructions from their communities, as did noble delegates; admission of members of the urban estate to government agencies in numbers equal to those of the gentry and with votes equal to theirs, especially the Police Commission, Commission of the Treasury, the provincial Civilian-Military Commissions, and the high court of appeals for free cities; the right to advance to the highest offices of the church, the military, and the educational system, and to hold official positions in judicial and financial bodies; the freedom to buy land with the right of passing it on to one's heirs. It is worth noting the points that called for an end to the penalties on noblemen who entered the urban estate and for equality of property rights in gentry-burgher marriages. They bear witness to burgher desires that the rights and privileges of both estates be made equal. A final point of interest is the broad way in which the urban reform proposals extended the right of *neminem captivabimus nisi jure victum*, long enjoyed by the Polish gentry, to the urban estate. It was to include not only the Commonwealth's city dwellers, but "sojourners, so that whoever sets foot on Polish soil will be safe in his person and his property."[7] The great majority of the urban representatives accepted these reform propositions enthusiastically and spread the news of them among the urban communities, whose response was likewise positive.[8]

Hugo Kołłątaj, the oldest supporter of the urban movement, prepared a manuscript note entitled *"Informacja względem interesu miast"* (Information concerning urban matters) for the Marshal of the Diet, Stanisław Małachowski, in December, 1789. Already at that time, Kołłątaj saw that Poland's situation was dangerous and uncertain not only because of the unpredictability of foreign developments but also because of its domestic problems. These extraordinary circumstances demanded rapid and decisive reforms. Next to the reorganization of the armed forces and the system of taxation, Kołłątaj saw that establishing a new form of government was fundamental to achieving the necessary changes, but that it was a task that the slow moving Diet was unable to perform. Can, he asked:

an excellent constitution be written when the noble estate alone exercises
full powers of legislation and execution? The cities have submitted their
Memorandum; its substance is the regaining of legislative and executive
power, in which they call for the right to own landed property, and ask
for the freedom for noblemen to become members of the urban estate
without losing their status as nobles, and that permanent royal officials
not interfere in their rights, their elections, or their collection of taxes.
That is the substance of the matter. The rest means nothing and, in my
opinion, what means the most in the enumerated points is legislative
and executive power.[9]

It is difficult not to agree with Kołłątaj that participation in the Parliament
and government by the burghers could have had a fundamental influence on
the process of modernization in the Commonwealth and that if Poland had
more time, that influence could have brought about substantial changes in
the social order and the abolition of the estate-based society more rapidly than
later occurred. It soon became apparent that the urban demands were utopian
and did not take political realities into account. But perhaps they were
consciously exaggerated to accustom public opinion to a new way of thinking
and in the hope of gaining something by first asking for too much.

The reform proposals that generated the greatest opposition among gentry
politicians and in the public opinion of the day, in and out of the Diet, were
plans for a political partnership between the burghers and gentry estates. That
opposition resulted in the narrowing down of the towns' demands concerning
this partnership in the law, "Our Royal Free Cities in the Dominions of the
Commonwealth," enacted 18 April 1791. Instead of the proposed 66 delegates
to the Diet the cities were to elect 24 plenipotentaries, who had advisory votes
on issues concerning the cities or commerce. These same plenipotentaries were
to sit in the Commissions of Police and the Treasury with full voting rights
only on matters involving the cities or business. They also sat in the city appellate
courts. Theoretically, their right to participate in the sessions of the Diet was
gained ex officio by sitting on these government commissions.

The Law on Cities granted the burghers most of the demands they had
made in 1789, including the right of *neminem captivabimus,* but in a restricted
form extended only "to persons established in cities." Although the privileges
of the Law on Cities applied to royal cities, nevertheless, paragraph 6 of section
I of the Law opened the possibility that private towns also could obtain the
rights of free towns.

It shall be permitted to any hereditary land proprietor to build and erect
towns on his estate, composed either of freemen, or of his own

PIESN

NA TRZECI DZIEN MAIA.

Wyżſzym nad Nieba wznioſły Maieſtatem,
O Ty! co raczyſz zawiadować Swiatem,
I Dobrodzieyſtwy , czym ieſteś, obiawić,
          Pozwól ſię ſławić.

Lud Twoy, lud Braci z nękan niegdyś marnie,
Wesoł do Twego Kościoła ſię garnie;
Przyim na ofiarę Opatrzności Swięta
          Stargane pęta.

Day użyć, coś dał, w pokoiu i zgodzie,
Day Ducha Rady i męſtwa w Narodzie,
Podległość Rządną, w ſwobodzie wſtrzymałość,
          w Działaniu trwałość.

Niech Łaſki Twoiey będzie uczeſtnikiem
Król, Radny, Rycerz, Mieſzczanin z Rolnikiém,
Dotąd gdy więkſzą ſzczęśliwiąc swobodą
          Tyś sam nadgrodą.

Ignacy Krasicki, *Pieśń na Trzeci Dzień Maja* (A Song for the Third Day of May): (Michał Gröll, Warszawa, 1792). (Biblioteka Z.N. im. Ossolińskich, Wrocław). The song was sung in Warsaw during the festivities commemorating the first anniversary of the Constitution.

emancipated villagers, and to grant them a particular charter. But such towns cannot be ranked among the free ones until the proprietor grants them in perpetuity a sufficient territory, and applies to us for the *diploma confirmationis,* wherein the original charter is to be inserted.[10]

The conditions then for a private town to join the rank of free towns was the renouncement by the owner of the ownership of the land (including all the traditional obligations of the inhabitants toward the owner) which would constitute a kind of "enfranchisement." There existed also a possibility that the town's inhabitants could buy out the land from the owner. In both cases this would be a long and complicated process.[11] The Law of 18 April allowed all those burghers whose political or government careers, or whose wealth, brought them into the social world of the nobility to be given noble rights. Ennoblement was not reserved only for those at the top of the urban social hierarchy. Nobility was to be conferred on every member of the burgher estate who: served two years as a Diet plenipotentiary; earned high military rank; received a high level appointment in administrative or judicial service; or obtained landed estates, a village, or town, of a certain value with the right of inheritance. In addition each Diet could grant nobility to up to thirty townspeople who had distinguished themselves in some other type of public service or in business as the owners of production shops or as "merchants dealing in Polish goods."

The Law on Cities was passed unanimously. In Article III of the Constitution of 3 May entitled Cities and Citizens, the nobility had to be assured that the Law became a part of the Constitution "as a law that provides to the Polish gentry, for the security of their freedom, and to the integrity of the common fatherland, new, true and effective force." Behind these carefully chosen formulations are two suggestions: that the Law did not impair noble freedoms; and that the fatherland is a common one shared by the nobility and the burghers. It is important to note that the Law was unclear in the legal sense. Section I paragraph 8 says that: "All citizens of towns either nobles or burghers by birth who are willing to carry on trade in retail and having their freeholds therein or after they obtain it of whichever dignity profession or craft they are must accede and be subject to the municipal laws" a provision that left the Law open to a broad interpretation. The royal cities also had Jewish residents who owned property and had businesses. It is only in paragraph 10 of section I, which specifies to whom cities "cannot refuse the right of citizenship and the inscribing in the town book," that adherence to Christianity appears. This time the clause excluding Jews was clearly written.

Thus the restrictiveness of the new Law was twofold. Its confessional provisions meant that it excluded the entire Jewish population, and its territorial focus excluded its application, with some possibilities of its softening to about 60 percent of urban Christians living in private cities. The principle of the applicability of the Law based on the criterion of ownership or domicile - whether noble or royal - was an approach to law based purely on estate, a fact which, in part, justified the exclusion of Jews from consideration under the new Law since they constituted a special estate-the Jewish nation, a separate community. Most Jews lived in private cities. Those that lived in royal cities mainly settled in areas owned by magnates and noblemen, so-called *jurydyki*, holdings within city limits that had been removed from city administration, often illegally. It is worth remembering that the legislators who framed the Law on Cities were guided not only by more or less precise legal formulas, but also by certain "obvious elements" of urban life. One such "obvious element" was the conviction that a reform of the legal status of Jews should include the entire Jewish population and be achieved through separate legal provisions. That conviction was shared by most of the population, deputies to the Diet, and Jewish communal authorities.

It is clear that legal limitations based on religious affiliation were a more sensitive subject than limitations based on territorial divisions even though the religious issue was not necessarily treated as one of discrimination or persecution.

Business competition between Jews and Christian urban inhabitants, though very important was not the only cause of their mutual antagonism. The lower levels of the urban population, craftsmen and small merchants, sellers in the market places, and street vendors felt the competition most strongly. On the other hand, members of the urban elite, caught as they were between the pressures put on them by the lower strata of townspeople, particularly in Warsaw, and their desire to build the consciousness of the burghers as a social group in a stormy period of political and intellectual ferment so that it might become capable of ruling the country in partnership with the nobility, wanted to maintain a clear distance between themselves and the Jews and to underscore the alien aspects of Jewish cultural traditions.

In its own mind and in the minds of other social groups the Jewish population was a separate and cohesive ethnic-religious-cultural entity. Among the Jews, however, maintenance of separateness in relationship to other groups and keeping up social distance was mainly in the interests of the Jewish communal authorities. The religious and secular leaders wanted to keep full and detailed control over daily religious and cultural life, over taxes and dues, over education and contact with Christians, over customs and rituals that kept the Jews apart from the outside world. This "savagery of customs," of which many members of the Jewish Enlightenment accused traditional Jewish culture, stood guard over the interests of the Jewish elite which did not want to lose its power, influence, or relatively high incomes. Of course, in many cases what was simultaneously at work was a deep faith in the idea that the Jews were a messianic chosen people who must keep their age-old identity unchanged. The lower strata of urban Jewry were disciplined by the communal authorities using arbitrary methods. A powerful weapon was excommunication, which resulted in the exclusion both from the religious and secular communities.

All too often the unity of culture and world view that contemporary observers perceived among the Jews of the eighteenth-century Commonwealth is still accepted as a self-evident fact. However, such external features as the Jews' separateness in language, dress, and customs were not necessarily signs of a unified moral outlook, world view, or political attitude.

In the second half of the eighteenth century, there was a deep crisis under way in the minds of the Jewish population of the Commonwealth most visible among the new non-conformist Jewish elite groups. However, the most popular new currents of thought that spread widely particularly among the impoverished Jewish population were derived from the messianic and cabalistic traditions. At least a four-fold crisis deeply divided the Jews of Poland and Lithuania. In the first part of the century, in the southern part of the Commonwealth, a mystical movement, Hasidism (from the Hebrew word *hasid,* pious), developed and won large numbers of followers. Another mystical cabalistic sect, different in its origins and character, took its name, Frankism, from its founder Jakub Frank. Part of the Frankists later converted to Catholicism. They were granted noble status and melted into Christian Polish society.[12] Though on a much smaller scale than in western Europe, and on a scale much smaller than Hasidism or Frankism, the Commonwealth also experienced the Jewish Enlightenment, the *Haskalah,* whose members favored assimilation and modernization and sharply criticized traditional Jewish culture and the conservative Jewish religious and secular communal authorities.[13] The last of these movements, and the most influential, was the preservationist, whose representatives wanted to maintain the Jewish culture of the day, distinct customs, and religious and institutional unity.

It is not, therefore, surprising that under these conditions any reform of the legal status of Jews faced numerous problems. There was obvious reluctance on the part of the Christian burghers to Jews obtaining equal rights in the cities, because the Christians believed that they were the only legitimate urban estate. Opposition to equalization of rights also dated back to 1789 when the opposition in the Diet used the Jewish reform issue to block the reform of cities (and sometimes also the reforming of the state). Added to these issues was the antagonism between the urban Jews and Christians and between the Christian townspeople and the nobility.[14] Noblemen opposed the administrative and judicial emancipation of Jewish communities living on their estates and in their towns.[15] Fragmentation and disagreements within the Jewish communities, the least known of all the factors affecting the reform of Jewish legal status, confused the situation further since internal quarrels made it impossible for the communities to agree on and to negotiate a single draft project for reform with the gentry legislators.[16] It seems that all future studies of the position, convictions, and ideas of the Jewish population of the Commonwealth at the end of the eighteenth century and of plans to reform its legal status during the Four-Year Diet must be linked, despite the serious difficulties involved, with an analysis of the period's religious and cultural currents and of the internal enmities that were breaking down that community.

The reasons that the Diet undertook a reform of the legal status of the Commonwealth's Jews along with its reforms concerning the status of other groups and why it undertook to reorganize the country's system of government are fairly obvious. Important were the basic ideas of the Enlightenment, though they were sometimes contradictory, calling for tolerance while promoting the creation of a unified culture and social integration. Financial issues were another reason. These included the search for new and higher taxes, repayment of Jewish communal, *kahal*, debts contracted with noblemen, and also, according to the plans of the King's secretary, Scipione Piattoli, sums needed by the treasury and the repayment of royal debts. Jerzy Michalski has recently drawn attention to an inherent contradiction in fiscal policy between the idea of equalizing taxation on Jews and other groups and the many plans to increase taxes on Jews in particular to benefit the national and royal coffers.[17] Another reason to undertake reform of Jewish status was one on which both those for and against Jewish emancipation agreed: that the status of a relatively large population, 8-10 percent of the Commonwealth, must somehow be "arranged."

Polish legislators were not pioneers in the area of Jewish reforms. Austrian laws regulating the status of Jews, those introduced in Galicia after the First Partition and the later edicts of Joseph II, were most certainly a starting point for Polish reformers. Maria-Theresa supposedly had a superstitious fear of Jews. She was terrified by the news that in her newly acquired city of Brody lived thousands of unassimilated Jews.[18] In fact, the annexation of Galicia

URZĄDZENIE LUDU ŻYDOWSKIEGO
W CAŁYM NARODZIE POLSKIM.

Proiekt od Deputacyi Podany. Chcąc liczny Lud Żydowski uczynić Ludem prawdziwie pożytecznym Państwu Rzeczypospolitey, w ktorey ma siedlisko swoie, My Król za zgodą Stanow zgromadzonych, nie przestaiąc na Prawach częściami o Istności Ludu tego decyduiących, ogolne Urządzenie, ktoreby Jego obyczaie, los i użyteczność wydoskonalić mogło, w ninieyszych stanowiemy Artykulach.

ARTYKUŁ I.

Co do Religii.

1mo. Podług Ducha Rządu Polskiego zupełną wolność Religii i Jey Obrządkow Zydom zabespieczamy.

2do. Wszelkiego Urągania, wyśmiewania a tym bardziey prześladowania Zydow, z powodu Jch Religii, zakazuiemy.

3tio. We wszystkich Pismach i Aktach Publicznych, tytuł, Niewiernych Zydom dawny, znosiemy, pod nieważnością odtąd tychże Aktow: a na to mieysce nazywać Jch Ludem Staro zakonnym rozkazuiemy.

4to. Nikt nie będzie mocen w dni Jch Święte wyciągać z nich iakowey posługi, lub powinności, ktoreby Jch Religii przepisom przeciwnemi były, oprocz przypadkow, potrzeby publiczney, to iest pożaru Ognia, wylewu Wod, powietrza i tym podobnych nieszczęść publicznych.

5to. Ktobykolwiek porwał i ochrzcił gwałtownie Osobę z Ludu Zydowskiego, lub do takowego uczynku przyłożył się, ten iako gwałtownik karany będzie. W czym Prawo ninieysze stosuiemy do Bulli Papieskiey Benedykta

A

The first page of: *Urządzenie Ludu Żydowskiego w całym Narodzie Polskim* (The arrangement concerning the status of the Jewish people within the Polish Nation). (Biblioteka Uniwersytecka w Warszawie). The text of the proposal was accepted by the Diet's Deputation and introduced to the Diet on 29 May 1792 by Hugo Kołłątaj.

increased the Jewish population of the Habsburg monarchy by about 50 percent![19] Galicia, for that reason, became the target of a "civilizing campaign," not free of repressive measures, aimed especially at the poorest parts of the Jewish community.

Just as the edicts of the Austrian government in Galicia sought to assimilate and Germanize the Jews and to achieve cultural conversion, and voluntary religious conversion by offering new converts special privileges, so the first, and to some degree later, Polish draft reforms were designed to effect the assimilation and Polonization of the Jewish communities. That was the tenor of the draft reforms prepared by Mateusz Butrymowicz in the fall and winter of 1789 and to a certain degree of the plan of the first Diet Deputation for the reform of Jewish status drawn up in August, 1790.[20] As in Austria, these proposals met with the opposition of all those Jewish groups that wanted to preserve traditional customs and culture and of those who guarded Jewish cultural separatism.

The actions taken by the Austrian and Polish reformers differed in a fundamental way. In Galicia reforms were introduced from above using repressive decrees. In Poland these repressive ideas remained on paper and after hearing out the interested parties, the reformers discarded most of them. The specific feature of the second stage of the debate on Jewish reform, prepared by Piattoli within Stanisław August's circle and by members of the "Patriotic Party" after the Constitution of 3 May, was the inclusion in these debates of Jewish plenipotentiaries.[21] Following the example of the urban plenipotentiaries of 1789, representatives of Jewish communities were called to Warsaw in the fall of 1791. Whether it was done on the King's initiative, Piattoli's, or on that of the Jews of Warsaw, it was done with the knowledge and approval of Stanisław August. According to the authors of the circular of 27 September 1791 "from the Jews resident in Warsaw" to communities in the Commonwealth, the King ordered them ("We have...an order signed by the King's hand and sealed with his ring") to assemble ten plenipotentiaries authorized by the synagogues from each province, thirty in all, in Warsaw on 3 November. The circular was signed by ten Jews "the leaders of the congregations in the royal city of Warsaw...who reside here."[22] According to the information of an urban delegate, a burgher from Cracow, at the end of November 120 Jewish delegates arrived in Warsaw from the communities in Poland and Lithuania.[23] Late in the fall, Piattoli began to hold meetings to consider various plans and gain support for reform. The work constantly met with new difficulties. Piattoli believed that these problems had three basic sources: the character, ideas, customs, suspicions, and fears of the Jews themselves; problems caused by the cities and towns; opposition by the owners of towns to any new laws that would limit their power over the people living on their property. Piattoli wrote an interesting description of the attitudes of the plenipotentiaries of the Jewish communities and of the ideas that inspired the reformers. To gain the trust of the plenipotentiaries, writes Piattoli, the reformers tried to show the utmost respect for the Jewish religion, a faith, that had in Poland such zealous and educated followers that Jews from all of Europe recruited their clergymen and teachers there. The reformers tried to write drafts that were simple and unambiguous statements of the rights and obligations of Jewish communities so that the benefits of reform were obvious and their permanence certain. Piattoli further wrote that the reformers had to resolve to act firmly to destroy the roots of Jewish oppression by freeing Jews from the abuses of the secular and religious Jewish authorities while simultaneously protecting them from the arbitrariness of the nobles and their employees.[24] Those goals were to be served by a radical reform of the organization and administration of the Jewish population. The reforms were also intended to modernize the education, life, and work of Jews. Schools were to be put under the authority of the Commission for National Education and the doors to Christian schools and training workshops opened to Jews.[25] In common with Jewish legislation in other European countries, there was also a plan to encourage Jews to settle down as farmers. The goal was to remove as many Jews as possible from the urban estate. According to contemporary belief it was trade, and especially small trade, that corrupted a person's character while work on the land ennobled one. And, yet, at the beginning of his note, Piattoli specifically defined Poland as a rural country that needed reform because it needed capital and workers to practice skilled trades and work in factories.[26] But what means of force or persuasion could be used to draw Jews away from small trade and turn them into skilled craftsmen when it was precisely in the skilled crafts that, in popular opinion, competition was sharpest and farming as a livelihood was tied to fears of enserfment? Not all of the ideas in Piattoli's note found their way into the final version of the reform plan. The final draft excluded, for example, the clauses opening Christian schools and craft guilds to Jews.

That stage of the reform process, which can be called "Piattoli's reform," lasted nearly a year. Starting in January, 1792, Piattoli worked on the reform together with the Diet's Deputation as augmented by the cooptation of new members including three city plenipotentaries. The importance of work on the Jewish reform had to be strengthened by the personal prestige of Hugo Kołłątaj, already Vice-Chancellor of the Crown, who became chairman of the Deputation despite his many other responsibilities. It was certainly his initiative that brought city plenipotentaries already sitting in the Diet into the Deputation. Kołłątaj fully understood the benefits that would come from "arranging the status of the Jews:" patriotic, facilitating the implementation of the ideas of Enlightenment, humanitarian, financial, administrative, and those advantages that would rescue Stanisław August from debts. His chief concern was, however, urban reform to which he wanted to give the broadest possible interpretation and about the vital importance of which he wanted to plant an understanding in popular thought. With that priority the first consideration was to avoid any flagrant violations of the real or imagined interests of the Christian townsfolk. In light of the threat and then the actuality of conflict with Russia, the Polish legislators did not want to antagonize noble owners of towns and villages or urban Jewish communities that did not want swift or radical change. Jewish leaders wanted, above all, to ensure religious freedom, the freedom to do business in the cities and villages, a government guarantee of autonomy for Jewish communal government and courts, and a guarantee of Jewish rights and privileges. In the end, there was a compromise reached between the parties involved. Whether we can call it a successful compromise is another matter. At the end of May, probably 20 May 1792, a majority of the Diet Deputation voted to accept the second version of "The Arrangement Concerning the Status of the Jewish People within the Polish Nation."

Although work on various versions of the reform proposals went on from the fall of 1789 to May 1792,[27] albeit with interruptions, the Arrangement gives the impression that it was written hurriedly and that changes were made ad hoc.[28] The Arrangement is long, twisted, unclear in places, illogical in places, and it is hard to interpret and to find the true intentions of its authors. It is hard to say how much of this lack of clarity was the result of inadequate legal precision on the part of the authors, how much was intentional obscurity meant to allow the Arrangement to be interpreted in a variety of ways, and how much was a consequence of talks between the interested parties that continued until the last minute. True, the matter was an especially difficult one in which complicated economic, ideological, religious, and political factors all played a role. There were two issues at stake: reform of the internal affairs of the Jewish communities; and statutory redefinition of the rights and obligations of Jews in relation to the government and to other subjects of the Commonwealth.

The most important and most general provisions of the Arrangement were: the Jewish population remained a kind of separate estate, as some reformers and most Jewish delegates felt was necessary in order to preserve its distinctiveness; but organized in a different way. The Jewish population was divided into five classes according to a combined reckoning of the type and

שירה חדשה

סבתו ההדרים · למלך גדול חכמה ובינה
חסיד וטוב לכל · ברוב תמלה ותגערה
מושל וחכם · וחכם כוסלי תבונה

סטאניסלאיים אינוסטוס

מלך אהב מישרים · נגיד עמים וטרים · במדינת
פלאני' ואנגלי' · ונשיא ליטא ופאדרי'
ה' ידים מעלתו וחדיו ועל מסלתו יאריך יסזובבוה

אמן

כן יתברה ה' בחסדי : אמן !

נעשה

בפקורת גבירי נבתרי ישראל עם סגולה ·
בעיר מלוכה ווארישי הגדולה עמר אהדטי
בני תגולה . לשור בקיל המולה ' להפארת
יים יא תשעלה' לידח זו הסמולה , יום
גמו'ל להד'ס מאי' לשרוז בתחלה . הוא
יום חדמו קמת סמלדרי המזולה'
תבון לו ולחרותו נצח סלה :

נרפם בקריה מלך רב ווארשי נודע בשערים
בשנה מלך מוסל בשרים : לפ'ק

HYMN

PRZY OBCHODZIE UROCZYSTOSCI

DNIA 3. MAIA 1791. ROKU.

NA PAMIĄTKĘ NOWEY RZĄDOWEY USTA-WY NA SEYMIE ROKU 1791.

OD

NAYIASN: RZEPLTEY STANOW UCHWALONEY.

Spiewany w Warszawie i w innych Rzeczypospolitey Miastach , od wszystkich Narodu Żydowskiego Zgromadzeń, na obznowe ich czułości powszechną radość dzwigny.

OFIAROWANY

OD

Deputowanych Zgromadzenia Żydowskiego Warszaw:

w WARSZAWIE

w Drukarni PIOTRA DUFOUR Konsyliarza Nadwornego
J. K. Mci i Dyrektora Drukarni Korpusu Kadetaw.

The title pages of: *Hymn przy Obchodzie Uroczystości, Dnia 3 Maya 1792 Roku.* (Hymn for the celebration of 3 May 1792) "Sung in Warsaw and in other cities of the Commonwealth by all communities of the Jewish people...presented by the Deputies of the Jewish Warsaw Community." W Warszawie, Piotr Dufour (1792). (Biblioteka Narodowa, Warszawa). The Hymn was published in Polish, Hebrew, French and German.

value of their real property holdings, their occupation, income, and position in the community; wherever there were ten or more Jewish families of the two highest classes they were to be organized into a small administrative unit called a settlement, meant to substitute for the *kahal*, which the Arrangement abolished. The settlements were to have "leaders and officials, schools, prayer houses, cemeteries, work houses for the poor...and finally offices, records of their proceedings, and seals." All the settlement officials, whose functions and responsibilities the Arrangement gives in great detail, were to be elected by majority vote at meetings of the settlement. The settlement was to be the basic element of Jewish self-government. It would carry out religious functions, be a court of first instance, an educational authority (for lower level schools), and take on fiscal and executive responsibilities. Following the example of the courts established in the free royal cities, though differing from them in many details, Jewish district courts were established, made up of three clergymen, a clerk, and alternate members of the court. One such court was mandated for each great province of the Commonwealth, Małopolska, Wielkopolska, and Lithuania. The members of the court were to be elected by delegates from the settlements at special district assemblies (another similarity to the district assemblies of the free cities).[29] The responsibilities of the district judges, also called district officials in the Arrangement, went beyond purely judicial affairs, they were also to keep law and order in the settlements of their district. The highest organ of Jewish self-government was to be the so-called provincial syndicate composed of six syndics, two from every great province, elected by general provincial assemblies. The syndics were the highest supervisory officials that oversaw the other organs of Jewish self-government. They were also to represent the Jewish population to the governmental bodies since they "were elected not only for the good of the Jewish people, but also for the benefit of the highest authorities." In special cases, the syndics alone had the power to excommunicate a person. To judge from the text they were only to take such action if it was demanded by the state authorities.

No less important than the establishment of Jewish self-government were the civil rights given Jews, though these were not always completely worked out in the Arrangement and so their extent could be either broadly or narrowly interpreted. The draft Arrangement asserted that Jews would everywhere enjoy the rights of "property and personal freedom." Jews were allowed to settle and live anywhere in the Commonwealth and on all private and ecclesiastical lands. They may establish residence based on existing and future agreements with landowners. In free cities they must have permission of the city authorities and may settle there on the basis of existing and future agreements which are to be monitored by the Commission of Police while all disagreements about

Jews settling in free cities were to be resolved by the highest city courts, the *assesoria*. There was, we can see, a contradiction between the declaration giving Jews the freedom to settle anywhere and the exercise of that freedom which depended on the good will of other social groups, in particular the owners of landed estates and the magistrates of free cities.

It is very interesting that the draft of the Arrangement weakened two of the fundamental taboos of social life in the eighteenth-century Commonwealth, albeit in an indirect way. While it affirmed the nobility's numerous powers over the Jews living on their estates, the Arrangement also allowed the Commission of Police a position of authority over Jewish settlements in matters concerning their organization and operation on private lands for "the maintenance of identical rights as concerns the Jews." In the free cities where Jews had the right to reside, or in those cities that agreed to allow it, Jews were permitted to obtain municipal citizenship, but without the right to participate actively or passively in elections.

The draft of the Arrangement gave the Jewish population full freedom to practice all trades and crafts and to set up any type of enterprise. It allowed acquisition of houses and lots, with full rights of ownership, and to build or found workshops and factories wherever Jews had the right to live. However, this was not full freedom—in the case that agreements with the cities expired, the privileges provided for in the Arrangement could be questioned causing many problems. Jews, in the Arrangement, were not given the right to own heritable landed estates, though they could lease such lands in perpetuity or for a designated period. The Arrangement exempted Jews who emigrated to the Commonwealth with enough capital to establish workshops or factories from public taxes for ten years, thus opening the borders to affluent Jews.

The Arrangement's main provisions on religious tolerance were: guaranteed freedom of religion and respect for religious rites. The term "infidel" in reference to Jews, was eliminated and in public documents the estimable "Old Testament believer" *(starozakonny)* was to be used. Clearly prohibited were attempts at Christian proselytizing of Jews before the age of twelve, a point which took its authority from a bull of Pope Benedict XIV. Jewish clerics were allowed freedom of dress. It is important to emphasize that religious tolerance was the least controversial issue in the discussions on Jewish rights and the wording on this matter is similar in all proposals.

To a minor degree the goal of the Arrangement was rapid assimilation imposed from above. The Arrangement declared that in order that the dress of Jews not differ from the dress of other inhabitants of the country, for their own good, in five years men, and in ten years women who had not yet turned sixty would be required to dress in "the manner of the various classes of people in the country," that is, according to their social position or their duties within the society at large. But a change in clothes is not assimilation. It is only abandonment of the outward signs of separateness. More could be achieved by the supervision of Jewish schools by the Commission for National Education, which was to prepare a secular curriculum for them. Two languages were to be used in official papers: Polish and Hebrew.

All of the new rights and privileges were intended for Jews who could obtain certification of their free status. In practice this meant they must prove that they had an established domicile, were a part of a particular community, and had appropriate financial resources. Another innovation was the assignment of surnames that could not be changed on penalty of losing one's free status and being degraded to the status of a vagrant. As a result, a population that up to this time was fluid and whose members were hard to identify individually by other social groups was to submit to the identification of its members, a step that also allowed their census. These were unavoidable prerequisites for the country's modernization. By establishing a registry of the nobility, the introduction of double books in the free cities, one for property owners and one for those without property, and a census of the Jewish population, new forms of government administration were gradually introduced.

The authors of the Arrangement draft wanted to defend the Jewish community from the financial, moral, and physical abuses heretofore practiced against it both by the Polish and by the Jewish religious and secular authorities. That is the substance of the declaration that "just as no resident of free Polish land cannot be other than under the authority of the government, so we take the Jewish people in general and in each of its individuals under the protection of the law and the care of the government." Nonetheless, the Arrangement did not attempt to equalize the rights and responsibilities of all Jews, but rather assigned rights and privileges according to wealth and social status.[30] Much like the statute for the townspeople of free cities, the Arrangement encouraged people to seek ways to better themselves, to achieve social mobility, to be entrepreneurial in commerce and production.

The draft of the "The Arrangement Concerning the Status of the Jewish People within the Polish Nation" was submitted by Kołłątaj to the Diet only on 29 May, which, as it turned out, was the last day it met, therefore, the Arrangement never became law, but remained a proposed reform. The Arrangement, apparently in agreement with the desires of most of the Jewish plenipotentiaries, and perhaps also consonant with the wishes of the representatives of the townspeople, did not anticipate rapid forced assimilation from above. The "Jewish nation" was to remain a separate ethnic-religious group and also a separate estate with its own administration, organization, and customs. Polish legislators chose the tolerant variant of the two tendencies in Enlightenment thought: acceptance of religious and cultural differences.

Notes

1. These and following figures are based on the calculations by Emanuel Rostworowski. Emanuel Rostworowski, "Miasta i mieszczanie w ustroju Trzeciego Maja" (Towns and townspeople in the 3 May form of government) in *Sejm Czteroletni i jego tradycje,* ed. Jerzy Kowecki (Warszawa: PWN, 1991), pp. 138-151.

2. See Jakub Goldberg, "Pierwszy ruch polityczny wśród Żydów polskich. Plenipotenci żydowscy w dobie Sejmu Czteroletniego" (First political movement among Polish Jews. Jewish plenipotentiaries during the Four-Year Diet) in *Lud żydowski w narodzie polskim. Materiały sesji naukowej w Warszawie 15-16 wrzesień 1992,* ed. Jerzy Michalski (Warszawa: Instytut Historii PAN, 1994), p. 57.

3. Krystyna Zienkowska, *Sławetni i urodzeni. Ruch polityczny mieszczaństwa w dobie Sejmu Czteroletniego* (The city dwellers and the well born. The political movement of the townspeople in the time of the Four-Year Diet) (Warszawa: PWN, 1976).

4. See Krystyna Zienkowska, "Stereotyp Żyda w publicystyce polskiej w drugiej połowie XVIII wieku" (The stereotype of the Jew in Polish political literature in the second half of the 18th century) in Michalski ed., *Lud żydowski.*.

5. "The Warsaw riot, referred to first as a "tumult" and later more frequently as a "bunt" (revolt), represents a rather isolated episode in eighteenth-century Poland, and as such would probably not merit further attention from historians. However, I believe that facts revealed in certain previously unknown historical records predating 1790 justify a more detailed look at these events. They show that the Warsaw riot was, in essence, a link in a long chain of alliances and conflicts which involved three sides: the nobles, the Christian townspeople, and the Jews. Krystyna Zienkowska, "The Jews Have Killed a Tailor. The Socio-political Background of a Riot in Warsaw in 1790" *Polin,* 3 (1983):78.

6. There is much indirect evidence that there was an informal, but organized, group of Jews in Warsaw that acted together, sometimes on a large scale. We can assume that it was a call issued by this group that brought some *kahal* and synagogue representatives from around the country to Warsaw at the end of 1791. See: Jakub Goldberg. "Pierwszy ruch polityczny...," passim. In the fall of 1788, three hundred Warsaw Jews petitioned the Diet to allow them permanent residence in Warsaw and permission to freely carry on business and practice trades in the city. In return they offered to pay, above and beyond other taxes, three hundred ducats yearly and make a one time payment to the treasury for military needs. The response of the magistrate of Old Warsaw was a harsh polemical letter published in January 1789 "Ekspozycja

praw miasta Warszawy względem Żydów oraz odpowiedź na żądaną przez nich w tymże mieście lokacyą" (An exposition of the laws of Warsaw concerning Jews and a reply to their demand of residence in the city) reprinted in *Materiały do dziejów Sejmu Czteroletniego*, hereafter MDSC, ed. Jerzy Michalski, Emanuel Rostworowski, Janusz Woliński, vols. 1-5, and with Artur Eisenbach, vol. 6 (Wrocław: Ossolineum, 1955-1969), vol. 2, no. 7. The reply, composed by the Jewish petitioners, or perhaps in their name by Kazimierz Chromiński, was "Wyłuszczenie praw wolnego mieszkania i handlu Żydom w Warszawie pozwalających, z odpowiedzią na pisma magistratu warszawskiego przeciw Żydom r. 1789 wydane" (An explanation of the laws permitting Jews the right of free residence and commerce in Warsaw, with a reply to the letter of the magistrate of Warsaw against the Jews published in 1789), MDSC, vol. 6, no. 3. The Jewish reply showed an exclusive reliance on the support of certain deputies to the Diet. And, in fact, February 1789 saw the first printed draft of a plan to reform the status of Jews written by the deputy from Pińsk, Mateusz Butrymowicz, "Sposób uformowania Żydów polskich w pożytecznych krajowi obywatelów" (A means to shape Polish Jews into useful citizens of the country) MDSC, vol. 6, no. 7.

7. See "Projekt. Miasta nasze Koronne i Wielkiego Księstwa Litewskiego" (Proposal. Our towns of the Crown and the Grand Duchy of Lithuania) [1 December 1789], MDSC, vol. 2, no. 64, p. 359; Zienkowska, *Sławetni...*, passim.

8. See Zienkowska, *Sławetni...*, passim.

9. (Hugo Kołłątaj), "Informacja względem interesu miast" (Information concerning urban matters) [December 1789], MDSC, vol. 2, no. 65, pp. 361-365.

10. *New Constitution of the Government of Poland Established by the Revolution of the Third of May, 1791* (London: 1791). Second edition, pp. 92-93.

11. For the many attempts to obtain the rights of free towns by towns owned by the gentry and the church see: Zienkowska, *Sławetni...* pp. 212ff.

12. Czesław Miłosz, *The History of Polish Literature* (Berkeley: Univ. of California Press, 1983), pp. 163-166; Jan Doktór, *Jakub Frank i jego nauka na tle kryzysu religijnej tradycji osiemnastowiecznego żydowsta polskiego* (Jakub Frank and his teaching on the background of the crisis in the religious tradition among eighteenth-century Polish Jews) (Warszawa: PAN, 1991); Aleksander Kraushar, *Frank i frankiści polscy, 1726-1816* (Frank and the Polish Frankists, 1726-1816) (Kraków, 1895).

13. The most outstanding representative of this group was the philosopher Salomon Majmon, the author, among other works, of one of the rare Jewish memoirs of the period. See also J. Calmanson vel Kalmanson, *Uwagi nad ninieyszym stanem Żydów polskich i ich wydoskonaleniem. Z francuskiego przez J. C.* (Warszawa, 1797); Jacob Katz, *Out of the Ghetto. The Social Background of Jewish Emancipation 1770-1870* (Cambridge, MA: Harvard Univ. Press, 1973).

14. See Zienkowska, "Obywatele czy mieszkańcy? Nieudana próba reformy statusu Żydów polskich w czasie Sejmu Czteroletniego," (Citizens or inhabitants?

Unsuccessful attempts to reform the status of the Polish Jews at the Four-Year Diet); in Kowecki, ed., *Sejm Czteroletni*, pp. 152-166.

15. The opinions of Kajetan Hryniewiecki, Lublin voivode, best characterize this group's interests. See MDSC, vol. 6, no. 17, 70 and the editors' comments.

16. Alongside the religious and ideological crises, this period saw quarrels between different groups of Jews with a variety of causes. Gershon David Hundert proposed a new interpretation to explain the increase in the number of outbreaks of disorder in Jewish communities in many cities in the second half of the eighteenth century (for example Leszno, Miedzybórz, Opatów, as well as Kraków, Lublin, and Vitebsk). Hundert challenges the thesis that the so-called craftsmen's revolts against the Jewish communal authorities by the poor and by unemployed young Jews were part of a struggle to democratize the life of the Jewish communities. Instead he suggests that the causes were a sudden increase in the natural growth rate of the population, unemployment, and a poor economic situation. To these factors we might add a rise in the business activity of certain groups of Christian townspeople that caused increased competition in the urban marketplaces and the influx of large numbers of poor Jews from Galicia and Prussia after the First Partition searching for work and homes. The disorders, writes Hundert, "were more likely instances of struggle within the upper strata of Jewish society in which poorer, less powerful people were manipulated by one side or the other." Gershon David Hundert, "Population and Society in Eighteenth-Century Poland," in Michalski ed., *Lud żydowski*; Gershon David Hundert, *The Jews in a Polish Private Town. The Case of Opatów in the Eighteenth Century* (Baltimore: John Hopkins Univ. Press, 1992).

17. Jerzy Michalski, "Sejmowe projekty reformy położenia ludności żydowskiej w Polsce w latach 1789-1792," (The Diet's proposals concerning reform in the situation of the Jewish population in Poland during the years 1789-1792) in Michalski ed., *Lud żydowski*, p. 40.

18. The empress wrote: "The city is built of wood, everything is wooden, even the surface of the roadway. Forty-four thousand Jews live in the city. I admit that this is something horrible, shocking. And this city will belong to us." As cited in François Fejto, *Joseph II. Porträt eines aufgeklärten Despoten* (München: M. Seitz, 1987).

19. Stanisław Grodziski, "Stanowisko prawne Żydow w Galicji: reformy Marii Teresy i Józefa II (1772-1790)" (The legal status of Jews in Galicja. The reforms of Maria-Theresa and Joseph II (1772-1790) in Michalski ed., *Lud żydowski*, passim. See also Stanisław Grodziski, *Historia ustroju społeczno-politycznego Galicji 1772-1848* (The history of the socio-political system of Galicia, 1772-1848) (Wrocław: Ossolineum, 1971), pp. 99-110.

20. Jerzy Michalski presents a systematic discussion of the substance, the intentions and changes in reform plans drawn up in the years 1789-1792. Jerzy Michalski, "Sejmowe projekty..." passim. See also Artur Eisenbach *The Emancipation of the Jews in Poland 1780-1870*, ed. by Antony Polonsky, trans. Janina Dorosz (Oxford: Institute for Polish-Jewish Studies, 1991), pp. 21-112.

21. Goldberg, "Pierwszy ruch polityczny..." in Michalski ed., *Lud żydowski*, passim.

22. "Przetłumaczenie listu cyrkularnego, czyli uniwersału, od Żydow bawiących się w Warszawie do braci w Israelu zamieszkanych w Polszcze i w Wielkim Księstwie Litewskim...przez Kalmansona, tłomacza JKMci i Komisyi Policyi," (The translation of the circular letter or proclamation from Jews, inhabitants of Warsaw to their brother Israelites residing in the Kingdom of Poland and in Grand Duchy of Lithuania...by Kalmanson, translator to His Royal Majesty and the Police Commission) [Warsaw, 27 September, 1791], MDSC, vol. 6, no. 48; Jakub Goldberg, "Pierwszy ruch polityczny..." in Michalski ed., *Lud żydowski*.

23. Goldberg, "Pierwszy ruch polityczny..." in Michalski ed., *Lud żydowski*, p. 46.

24. Many politically active Jews, especially from Enlightenment circles, saw the arbitrariness of the Jewish communal authorities as one of the sources of Jewish poverty and ignorance. "Three are the causes for the bondage of Jews in Poland: first are the rabbis; second is the kahal, the Jewish leaders; and third the Jewish courts" wrote Salomon Polonus. Salomon Polonus, "Projekt względem reformy Żydów," (The project of reforms concerning Jews) [Wilno, 1792], MDSC, vol. 6, no. 79, p. 432.

25. [Scipione Piatoli], "Mémoire" [January, 1792?] MDSC, vol. 6, no. 73.

26. Proposals to employ poor Jews in work houses or in future industry were numerous.

27. See Michalski, "Sejmowe projekty..." in Michalski ed., *Lud żydowski*, passim.

28. "Urządzenie ludu żydowskiego w całym narodzie polskim," (The arrangement concerning the status of the Jewish people within the Polish nation) [version A, after 23 January 1792; version B, 29 May 1792], MDSC, vol. 6, no. 96. Here I discuss only the second version, B, accepted by a majority vote of the Deputation, probably on 20 May, according to the editors of MDSC, and introduced in the Diet on 29 May by Hugo Kołłątaj.

29. See the statute entitled "Urządzenie miast wolnych Rzeczypospolitej w Koronie i Wielkim Księstwie Litewskim" (The arrangement concerning free cities of the Commonwealth in the Crown and the Grand Duchy of Lithuania) [Warszawa, 30 June 1791]. Also the draft entitled "Urządzenie wewnętrzne miast wolnych w Koronie i Wielkim Księstwie Litewskim," (Internal arrangement of free cities in the Crown and the Grand Duchy of Lithuania) MDSC, vol. 4, no. 197. See also Krystyna Zienkowska, *Sławetni...*, p. 179 ff.

30. For example, Jews belonging to the first three classes and able to post a bond could neither be arrested nor their property confiscated before a sentence was issued by a court. Michalski, "Sejmowe projekty..." in Michalski ed., *Lud żydowski*, p. 38.

Translated by George Makowski

Draft design by Jakub Kubicki of the Church of Divine Providence (Biblioteka Uniwersytecka w Warszawie, Gabinet rycin). In accordance with the decree in the Declaration of the States Assembled "that a church shall be erected and consecrated to Divine Providence in memory..." of the Constitution, on the first anniversary of the Constitution the King laid the foundation stone of the church. The church was never built but the site on which the church was to stand became a venerated place.

15

The Constitution of 3 May and the Mutual Guarantee of the Two Nations

Juliusz Bardach

The Great Diet (1788-1791), undertaking the reform of the Polish-Lithuanian Commonwealth, had also to express its attitude towards the problems of links uniting the Kingdom of Poland (usually called the Crown) and the Grand Duchy of Lithuania. Beginning with the Union of Lublin (1569), the created Commonwealth of the Two Nations was a dual state embracing the Polish Crown and the Grand Duchy of Lithuania, which included Byelorussian and Ukrainian lands.

The Union of Lublin, agreed upon after a long and dramatic dispute, was a compromise. This compromise linked the strengthening of the union between the Crown and the Grand Duchy to the preservation of the political autonomy of its components. The lasting character of the Union was assured by the oneness of the supreme authority, the king and the grand duke elected at the same election, as well as a joint parliament, while the subjectivity of the Commonwealth's components was assured by the doubled central authorities, separate treasury, army, judiciary and different legal systems. The III Lithuanian Statute elaborated by the Lithuanians themselves, and confirmed by King Zygmunt III at the Coronation Diet, was in force in that country since 1588. It represented not only the codification of court procedures, but also contained provisions concerning the rights of social strata and the political system of the Grand Duchy. The Lithuanians and Byelorussians considered the III Statute a legal expression of Lithuanian statehood.[1]

357

The several centuries of the Crown and Grand Duchy coexistence brought, in spite of numerous controversies and conflicts, both "political nations" (i.e., the magnates and nobility) closer together. However, the cultural Polonization of the Lithuanian upper classes during the seventeenth and eighteenth centuries did not cause their identification with the Polish nobility.[2] A two-tier national consciousness began to emerge in the "political nations" of the Grand Duchy during the eighteenth century. Briefly, it consisted in the fact that the Lithuanians considered themselves different from the inhabitants of the Kingdom of Poland, but recognized themselves also as Poles. We should not give these notions the meaning we attach to them today. Even during the nineteenth century the word "Lithuanian" meant a person who lived in the Grand Duchy regardless of whether he or she was ethnically and culturally Lithuanian, Byelorussian, or Polish, while the word "Pole" meant a citizen of the Commonwealth of the Two Nations irrespective of whether he or she came from the Crown or the Grand Duchy.[3]

The Lithuanian and Byelorussian nobility, although Polonized, defended the separate character of the "Lithuanian Province" (a name used in parallel with the Grand Duchy during the eighteenth century) referring to the document of the Union of Lublin as a basis of a formal equality of the two nations. The feeling of a political Lithuanian separateness was combined with the recognition of the supremacy of the bonds of the federal Commonwealth. However, it opposed trends towards a centralization of the state.

Tendencies towards the unification and centralization of the state clearly appeared during the Enlightenment when the problem of streamlining the functioning of the state mechanism came to the fore. Stanisław August Poniatowski, who became King and Grand Duke in 1764, an educated monarch and an advocate of modern forms of government, considered the state dual of the Commonwealth an anachronism and gave expression to his views frequently. He made an early attempt to unify the central authorities of the Commonwealth, initiating preparations of a law on the consolidation of the union of the Grand Duchy of Lithuania and the Crown in 1766. However, the opposition of the Lithuanians and the Czartoryski family caused him to withdraw. He did not altogether abandon his efforts, however, and made an attempt to codify and unify the Commonwealth's laws. This initiative was also a failure. The draft Code of Laws, prepared by a commission headed by the former Chancellor, Andrzej Zamoyski, was voted down by the Diet in 1780, also as a result of the opposition of the Lithuanian nobility. The King, however, was still thinking about strengthening ties between the Crown and

Lithuania. The constitutional reform undertaken by the Great Diet in 1788 seemed a good occasion for this.[4]

The radical reformist movement also pointed to the need for the centralization of the state in parallel with the king's unification drive. Its ideologist and spokesman, Hugo Kołłątaj, postulated the unification of the administration and of the laws of the Crown and the Grand Duchy.[5] Warsaw was to be the seat of all central authorities. "If we want to be lastingly free," wrote Kołłątaj, "we must remember that we should unite and not divide, we should have one capital of our freedom, one army, one treasury and other authorities common for both nations."[6]

The draft legislation proposed by the reformers during the confederated Great Diet did not go that far. Although they aimed at strengthening the links between the Crown and Lithuania, they left the dualism intact for the sake of tradition and political reality, reasons based on the *sacrosanctae vinculae unionis*. The structure of the Diet itself, composed of the Crown and Lithuanian confederations headed by separate marshals, called for moderation in this field. The Court Marshal of Lithuania, Ignacy Potocki, *spiritus movens* of the Deputation for the Reform of Government wrote in the proposal presented to the King May 27, 1790, in Article I of *Tableau des lois fondamentales de la nouvelle Constitution* as follows: "The Commonwealth--Poland and the Grand Duchy of Lithuania--will always constitute a federal state (*un État confédéré*) according to the Act of Union which is confirmed *(ratifié)* in the present constitution to the full extent."[7] Also the first chapter of the ample draft of the Project to Reform the Government, presented by the Deputation on August 5, 1790, and dealing with Cardinal Laws, commenced with a determination of mutual relations between the Crown and the Grand Duchy: "The Crown provinces and the Grand Duchy of Lithuania," we read in Article I, "linked by the Union forever, as well as other lands constituting the single body of the Commonwealth, will be linked inseparably to this body. This right we solemnly recognize as cardinal."[8] The fact that this provision was placed under Article 1 of the large draft consisting of 658 articles testifies to the importance attached to it. Similarly, two of the leading Articles (IV and V) of the Deputation's project, legally confirmed on January 8, 1791, and entitled Perpetual Cardinal Laws, referred to the "perpetual union . . . of the two states of which the Commonwealth is composed and will be composed in the future."[9]

On the other hand, drafts dictated or inspired by the King clearly aimed at a unitary and centralized state. The first draft prepared by Father Scipione

Piattoli, the King's private secretary, on December 20, 1790, reads as follows in that part of Article I which deals with mutual relations between the Crown and the Grand Duchy: "The two nations, Polish and Lithuanian, will constitute only one nation from now on," and therefore, "all dualities, differences and alternative offices, ranks and titles" are abolished. A leaning towards unification was clear. However, under pressure from dualists (for whom the existence of double ministerial posts, in the Crown and in Lithuania, was not unimportant), the new version of January 1791 reads: "The two nations, Polish and Lithuanian, will jointly form the Commonwealth according to the Act of Union which is confirmed by the present constitution."[10] The traditional model was thus revived.

The following months, however, brought an essential and significant change. The next abbreviated version prepared by Piattoli does not mention mutual relations between the Crown and Lithuania at all. It can hardly be assumed that a problem so important for a dualistic state, one which played a leading role in all previous constitutional drafts, disappeared all at once from the field of vision of the lawmakers. Such omission as Emanuel Rostworowski pointed out, can only be explained by the sensitive nature of this matter.[11]

The conformity of views between the King and Hugo Kołłątaj (soon to be the Vice-Chancellor of the Crown) are reflected in the fact that the problem of relations between Poland and Lithuania was not discussed at all, neither in the King's version of the Constitution from the beginning of March 1791, known under the title The Reform of the Constitution, nor in Kołłątaj's succeeding draft of March 25 (which was already very close to the final version of the Constitution) entitled The Constitutional Laws, which had a longer title, The Final Laws Constituting the First Chapter of the Political Constitution of the Polish Nation.[12] In a later speech Kołłątaj would develop the idea that following the political constitution a moral and an economic constitution, and the codification of laws would follow as the next steps in the reform of the state. There is no doubt that for both the enlightened King, who always dreamed about "an English style of government," and the enlightened republicans, who focused their attention on the United States, and later,on revolutionary, but still monarchical France, "the Constitution of 3 May did not conclude the task of restructuring the Commonwealth, but opened broad, new perspectives."[13] Given such an approach, certain problems, even some very important but controversial ones, were omitted, or merely suggested in "the First Chapter." They were to be addressed later, their formulation depending on the internal political situation of the Commonwealth and on the international situation.

This explains why the Government Statute of 3 May, the official name of the Constitution of 3 May 1791, not only disregarded the problem of mutual relations between the Crown and Lithuania, but also did not use the popular expression "the Commonwealth of the Two Nations," a term which usually denoted the dualistic state. The term "Commonwealth" appeared only once, in Article IV, dealing with the status of peasants. Neither are the two components of the Commonwealth mentioned. Rather, such expressions as "the Homeland" or "Poland" are used.

Considering these changes in terminology, Bogusław Leśnodorski concluded that the Constitution did not formulate an official name for the state.[14] It seems that the intention of the Government Statute was to create a uniform state in place of the existing federation. However, keeping in mind the possibility of protests from Lithuanians the authors did not word it explicitly. The terminological juggling was probably necessary to pave the way for the centralization and unification of the state through detailed regulations that were to follow. Recognizing this intent, Stanisław Kutrzeba and other historians stressed that "the Constitution [of 3 May] abolished the Union and merged the two existing states linked by a factual union into one."[15]

This view became widespread and began to be presented in history and legal history handbooks. Is it, however, well founded, especially if one considers the Constitution of 3 May not as a separate document, but together with other laws which, taken together, formed a Commonwealth reformed by the Great Diet?

An attempt at such a complex approach was made soon after World War I by Władysław Smoleński in his inaugural lecture opening the 1919-1920 academic year at the University of Warsaw.[16] His remarks went almost unnoticed at the time. Only Rostworowski, and later Jerzy Malec and Jerzy Michalski, in the eighties, made independently attempts at such an analysis, arriving at a revision of the prevailing opinion.[17]

The final draft of the Constitution was prepared secretly by a tight group of conspirators and was presented even to the supporters of reform only on 2 May, the day before the session that itself was called in a manner intended to take the opposition by surprise. Contemporaries, therefore, and later historians often termed the passage of the Constitution a *coup d'état,* and the group preparing the historical document conspirators.[18]

The Great Diet sat as a confederacy. The Crown confederacy was headed by the Crown Referendary, Stanisław Nałęcz-Małachowski, and the Lithuanian by the General of the Lithuanian artillery, Prince Kazimierz Nestor Sapieha. Both marshals of the confederacies signed the Constitution of 3 May since both signatures were necessary to make the document valid. This validity, however, was not easy to achieve due to the fact that Sapieha, although a Freemason and the Grand Master of the Polish National Lodge of The Great East[19] from January 1789, remained in the political orbit of his uncle, the Great Hetman of the Crown, Franciszek Branicki, a declared adversary of the reform. His mother, Elżbieta Sapieha, neé Branicki, was also against the reform. It is not strange, therefore, that the Constitution was prepared secretly and Sapieha was not a party to that secret.

Sapieha's brothers in the Lodge were active in the semi-secret Radziwiłł Club uniting the "Patriots." The name of the Club stemmed from the palace where it used to gather.[20] On the eve of May 3 there was a meeting at the Radziwiłł palace at which the text of the Constitution was read and later that night supporters of the Constitution gathered at Marshal Małachowski's house where they signed a document entitled *Assekuracya.* In the document, they pledged to support the draft of the Constitution. In addition to Małachowski's signature there were 83 signatures of senators and deputies, but only one senator was from the Grand Duchy. Sapieha's signature was not on it.

This is the reason why Sapieha stated when the draft of the Constitution was read at the session of 3 May, that he was hearing the text for the first time and found things there he could not accept.[21] He proposed, therefore, a second reading and a discussion, steps which are generally understood as a compromise in which the main reforms would be preserved, but only after the introduction of some changes. This procedure was opposed, however, by Stanisław August and Hugo Kołłątaj and there were important reasons for it.

According to the count made by historians,[22] there were 182 deputies and senators present (about one third of the total number) of whom more than seventy were opposed to the draft. There were also many who were undecided. The King and the activists from the reform camp pressed Sapieha to accept the draft in the face of dangers to the Commonwealth and in the name of a general concord. Finally, the Marshal of the Lithuanian Confederacy gave in, signing and swearing loyalty to the Constitution. His action was significant in terms of neutralizing the Lithuanian opposition. Some of the leading speakers of this opposition, such as Tadeusz Korsak, became supporters of the Constitution. After the Constitution had been passed and the deputies and senators had sworn their allegiance to it, the number of opponents who submitted their "no" for the record decreased to 26 deputies and one senator. There were only two Lithuanians among them.[23]

The acceptance of the Constitution as a whole by a great majority of Lithuanian deputies did not mean, however, that they accepted the model of a

ZARĘCZENIE WZAIEMNE
OBOYGA NARODOW.

Prawo Dnia 20. Miesiąca Października
Roku 1791. uchwalone.

KU WIECZNEY PAMIĘCI SPRAWY NIZEY OPISANEY.

MY STANISLAW AUGUST
z Bożey Łaski i Woli Narodu,
KROL POLSKI,
WIELKI XIĄŻĘ LITEWSKI, RUSKI, PRUSKI, MAZOWIE-
CKI, ZMUDZKI, KIIOWSKI, WOLYNSKI, PODOLSKI, PO-
DLASKI, INFLANTSKI, SMOLENSKI, SIEWIERSKI
Y CZERNIECHOWSKI.

za Zgodą
PANOW RAD SENATU
TAK DUCHOWNYCH, IAKO Y SWIECKICH;
oraz
POSŁOW ZIEMSKICH KORONY
POLSKIEY, Y WIELKIEGO XIĘSTWA LITEWSKIEGO.

Bacząc uftawicznie na powinność Naszą ku
wfpolney Oyczyźnie fwey Rzepltey Polfkiey,
którey wfzyftkę ozdobę, pożytek pofpolity, a
naywięcey umocnienie od niebefpieczeńftwa tak
wewnętrznego, iako i zewnętrznego, opatrzyć
powinniśmy; maiąc przytym przed oczyma

A

Zaręczenie Wzajemne Oboyga Narodów. Prawo dnia 20, miesiąca października roku 1791 uchwalone, (Mutual Guarantee of Two Nations. Law passed on October 20, 1791). The first page. (Indiana University, Lilly Library).

KOMMISSYA SKARBOWA

RZECZYPOSPOLITEY

OBOYGA NARODOW

Prawo Dnia 27. Miesiąca Października 1791
Roku uchwalone.

I.

Mieysce Kommissyi.

Kommissya Skarbowa Oboyga Narodów, odbywać się ma w Mieście Rezydencyi Krolewskiey.

II.

Skład Kommissyi.

1mo, Kommissya Skarbowa Oboyga Narodów, składać się ma z Podskarbich, y z szesnastu Kommissarzów, iako to: 1. Dwóch Senatorów, to iest: ieden z Korony alter-

---

Kommissya Skarbowa Rzeczypospolitey Oboyga Narodów. Prawo dnia 27 miesiąca października 1791 roku uchwalone. (The Treasury Commission of the Commonwealth of Two Nations. Law passed on October 27, 1791). The first page. (Indiana University, Lilly Library).

unitary state. The Lithuanian senators and deputies accepted the May Constitution to enable the reform of the political system in the Commonwealth. They did not intend, however, to resign the political autonomy of the Grand Duchy. They made use of the fact that the authors of the Constitution of 3 May avoided involving themselves in that problem, leaving it to be solved in detailed regulations. The Lithuanian parliamentary representation chose to defend the rights of Lithuania through the proper formulation of laws, which would supplement the Constitution of 3 May, and which, according to the Diet's May 5 resolution, should also have the character of constitutional laws.

These activities were based on instructions received from the dietines of the Grand Duchy which, electing the second group of deputies in November 1790, formulated a number of postulates for their representatives. We know of six sets of instructions by dietines in Wilno, Troki, Kowno, Wilkomierz, Grodno and Lida.[24] They all deal with various aspects of relations between the Crown and the Grand Duchy and they do so from the point of view of expected reforms in the political system of the Commonwealth. Generally, these instructions concerned:

1. Preserving the Union as a base of mutual relations;

2. Preserving the system of alternate sessions of the Diet, i.e., that every third session be held in Grodno under the marshallship of a Lithuanian (the Wilno dietine wanted these sessions to be moved to Wilno, the historical capital of Lithuania);

3. Preserving a separate Lithuanian Treasury Commission, or at least separate treasury courts in Lithuania;

4. Maintaining the III Lithuanian Statute in force; and

5. Eliminating various infringements on Lithuanian rights.

The intention of protecting the rights of Lithuania in the Diet was already expressed in Sapieha's speech made on May 3, before he had sworn to the Constitution, when he said: "Mistakes in government laws can easily be corrected...by the nation's self-government." The King responded immediately with a conciliatory speech in which he addressed the Marshal's remarks and explained that with the exception of those items specifically decided by the Constitution, namely the hereditary throne and the King's Council, the Guardians of the Laws *(Straż Praw)*, "other points would be discussed and decided in detailed resolutions of sessions which were to follow."[25] Already two days later in the "Declaration of the States Assembled" of May 5 the terminology relating to the Polish-Lithuanian Union was restored. According to the Declaration the oath of allegiance to the Constitution should be taken "by the whole national army quartered in the states of the Polish Crown and the Grand Duchy of Lithuania," and later the term "Both Nations" was used.

As a result, the Lithuanian party secured that, in spite of Hugo Kołłątaj's suggestions, the procedure of holding every third session of the Diet in Grodno, (as well as Lithuanian provincial sessions during which senators and deputies of the Grand Duchy discussed draft laws concerning Lithuania and coordinated their position before plenary sessions) was upheld in the Law on Diet of May 16, 1791. Another concession in favor of Lithuania, and a form of recognition of the constructive attitude of Sapieha, was the fact that Sapieha had been nominated by the Diet on May 18, as a member of the Guardians of the Laws with powers equal to those of a marshal of the Diet.[26] This was contrary to the Constitution which had spelled out the composition of the Guardians of the Laws in detail. However, the legal aspects were waived in order to re-establish cooperation between the representatives of the Crown and Lithuania.

Further agreements concerned the organization of central collective authorities--the Great Commissions. The starting point was favorable for centralistic aspirations. The National Education Commission (established in 1773) and the Military Commission (1788) were already in place. After the Constitution was passed, work on the creation of two new Commissions--Police and Treasury--was started. When the Commission of Police was established on June 17, 1791, certain Lithuanian deputies demanded the creation of a separate Commission for Lithuania. There were, however, also supporters of a common commission among them. A common commission was also opted for by the King and supported by Sapieha, and therefore a common commission was agreed upon, but one third of its members were to originate from the Grand Duchy. Also an official name of the commission was chosen. It was to be called the Commission of Police of the Two Nations. The two latter decisions were concessions in Lithuania's favor.

According to Article VIII of the Constitution of 3 May, a committee was to be appointed, "to form a civil and criminal code of laws." But the Lithuanian deputies asked to appoint a separate codification committee for the Grand Duchy of Lithuania.[27] Speaking on the Duchy's behalf, Sapieha stipulated "in the name of the Lithuanian province, that she having separate laws..., it should also have a separate committee to write its laws."[28]

This matter was raised in the Diet on June 28 when the Vice-Chancellor of the Crown, Hugo Kołłątaj delivered the above mentioned programmatic speech, containing proposals for further reforms, which taken together would create a basis for the foundation of a new form of government. He proposed to complete the political Constitution of 3 May with "an economic constitution, and further, with a moral constitution," a regulated system of education, and finally, a codified civil and criminal law. Having unification in mind, Kołłątaj suggested that the Lithuanian Statute be the point of departure for the work of codification. His aim, together with his high expression of praise for the Statute, was to favorably dispose the Lithuanian deputies to this proposal:

> When speaking of the Lithuanian Statute, I speak of a work which one can not even mention without reverence. It must be considered as the most excellent work on law in all of Europe, with the exception of minor shortcomings, such as excessive punishments, a fault of former times which did not have as their teacher the Marquis Beccaria.[9]

The Lithuanians, however, remained unconvinced. Sapieha demanded the appointment of a separate committee for the Grand Duchy, and presented a draft resolution which had been adopted at a session of the Lithuanian provincial Diet. On this occasion, he evoked the tradition of his family, remembering Vice-Chancellor (later Chancellor) Lew Sapieha, who was active in the preparation of the III Lithuanian Statute, and later, its publisher:

> The glorious memory of my ancestor, Lew Sapieha, will serve as a stimulus, at least in part, to follow in his footsteps. His work, the Lithuanian Statutes, have become sacred to Lithuania. The Lithuanian Statutes require a few changes under present circumstances, but our province wants to preserve the fundamentals of the Statutes.[30]

As a result, the Diet, on the basis of two separate acts, appointed two committees. The Crown committee would accept the Statute of Łaski (the collection of Polish laws from 1506) and the Lithuanian Statute as a point of departure, but the Lithuanian committee accepted only the Lithuanian Statute. Both committees in their work were to take into consideration, when necessary, laws both domestic and foreign, and also the principles of natural law. Both acts which appointed the two committees conclude with the statement: "This collection of civil and criminal law, when it becomes law, will bear the name, the Stanisław August Code."[31] A problem still under consideration was whether the outcome of the work of the two committees would lead to complete unification or if it would only approximate one system of law. It should be noted that in the acts which brought the two committees into being, was a provision that the codification proposal would first be agreed to at the Lithuanian provincial session, and only later presented to the Diet. This provision shows that only those norms would become law in Lithuania which gained the agreement of the deputies of the Grand Duchy. Taking into consideration that such agreement did not have to be consistent with the point of view taken by the deputies of the Crown, it can be assumed that the work of codification would result not in unification, but rather in two close systems of law achieved, among others, by accepting the Lithuanian Statute as one of the bases for the codification of law in the Crown. Józef Weyssenhoff, the leading member of the Lithuanian codification committee, in the preserved draft of his proposal for the future code, referred to Montesquieu, Beccaria, and Franklin. The influence of humanitarian ideas of the Enlightenment is clear in both proposals:Weyssenhoff's and Józef Szymanowski's, his counterpart in the Crown committee. Nevertheless, there existed some differences between them, particularly those concerning criminal law. Weyssenhoff was for the abolition of the death penalty, and against punishment by fine, as it would hurt innocent family members. He was also against banishment and the deprivation of citizenship, and considered higher birth, education, and wealth as aggravating circumstances. Weyssenhoff's ideas were more humanitarian and modern in comparison with Szymanowski's.[32] From the above, it can be concluded that despite the fact that the Constitution provided for the appointment of one committee to form a civil and criminal code of law, ensuing acts and practice of the law preserved the separateness of the Grand Duchy's law.

The principal discussion took place in October 1791 when the problem of establishing the most important commission--the Commission of the Treasury--came up. The Lithuanian deputies categorically demanded a separate Treasury Commission for the Grand Duchy. Defending this standpoint, Sapieha stated: "Privileges of nations are not a property of their representatives, or even of the whole present generation. We have no right to renounce them. We inherited them from our ancestors and we should pass them to our descendants intact."[33] Lithuanian deputies active in the Association of Friends of the Constitution, a formal party created after 3 May on the basis of the Radziwiłł Club, and especially Dominik Gieysztor, a deputy from Troki, obtained the acceptance of this influential party for the formation of a separate Treasury Commission for Lithuania.[34] The King also expressed his acceptance:

Our first consideration should be the satisfaction of the whole Lithuanian province and the strengthening of its confidence in us; we should act in such a way that we will remove any reason for discord and mutual sadness. This kind of conduct will defend and become the strongest protection of our unity. This is the reason that I am persistently asking all of you who prefer a unified treasury to be inclined, as brothers, to the demands of the Lithuanian province, and leave this to the future, when the Lithuanian citizens themselves will become convinced about the need for the unification of the treasuries.[35]

Trying to save the idea of a joint treasury, Stanisław Potocki, a deputy from Lublin, proposed a compromise. His idea was to create a singleTreasury Commission in which Lithuanians would constitute half of its members. Such a step would bring about a considerable strengthening of the Lithuanians' position in this organ.

The Lithuanians, however, made their acceptance of a common Treasury Commission conditional on the passage of a law in the Diet confirming the political rights of the Grand Duchy and its equality with the Crown. On October 20, 1791, Sapieha presented to the Diet a draft resolution prepared by the provincial Lithuanian session entitled the Mutual Guarantee of the Two Nations. Initially, it encountered opposition from some of the Crown deputies. It was, however, neutralized by the King who was ready for concessions in order to broaden the social base of the reformed political system. Also, apprehension that the St. Petersburg court, hostile to the constitutional reform, could take advantage of the controversy, induced him to accept the proposal of the Lithuanian party. Stanisław August appealed therefore to the deputies at the October 20, session to pass the resolution unanimously: "In this moment that would be inscribed in the annals of history as the most happy and illustrious, the union so much desired, which could not be severed by any human power, will reach its final stage." The King asked for the passage of the resolution which would strengthen the unity of "the whole Polish and Lithuanian nation . . . [and] will leave no space for traps and insidious intentions."[36] As a result, the Diet passed the Mutual Guarantee unanimously.[37] Its decision embraced equal representation of the Grand Duchy in the central authorities and the preservation of certain institutional differences, namely:

1. It guaranteed Lithuania the same number of representatives in the Military and Treasury Commissions as the Crown. This was to become a rule concerning all central authorities created in the future. Only the ratio in the Commission of Police remained unchanged--two thirds and one third, according to the "free will" of the Grand Duchy.

2. It obliged the Grand Duchy to maintain the same number of ministers and high officials as the Crown with the same titles and competencies.

3. Representatives of Lithuania and the Crown would head the Military and Treasury Commissions alternately during equal periods of time.

4. The treasury funds derived from the Lithuanian public income were to remain in Lithuania.

5. Court cases between Lithuanian citizens and the Treasury were to be tried by a separate Treasury Court for the Grand Duchy.

The above points were preceded by a preamble that stressed the dual character of the state based on the Union and presented the effected changes as a further step towards the realization of its aims:

... having in mind the laudable and desirable relationship and association between our Two Nations, which was by the Act of Union created forever by our ancestors, and many times confirmed by the common agreement of the Polish Crown and the Grand Duchy of Lithuania, and maintained until today, thanks to the friendship and steadfastness of both parties, we proclaim that as we have one Law on Government for our whole State, serving the Polish Crown and the Grand Duchy of Lithuania, we express our desire to have under the rule of this Government our Army united, and treasuries included in one National Treasury, but under the following conditions...

These conditions were discussed above.

The Mutual Guarantee was considered an act of the same importance as the provisions of the Union of Lublin. It was stressed that this would become a part of the *pacta conventa* sworn by the king and his successors when assuming the throne. One senses the intention of the document as one reads the concluding sentences:

All matters here decided and guaranteed, We the King, with the consent of the Confederated States, considering them to be necessary and useful for the Two Nations, the Polish Crown and the Grand Duchy of Lithuania, as for the one common and undivided Commonwealth, We acknowledge to be the articles of the Act of Union between these Nations, by this Act We guarantee, confirm, and strengthen the durability and inviolability of these articles, with the same conditions, confirmation, and strength as in the Act of Union between the Polish Crown and the Grand Duchy of Lithuania. And We the King consider all of this as an article of the *pacta conventa,* We wish that it would be placed with the *pacta conventa* to be sworn to by our successors.

The legal system sanctioned by the Great Diet was set up with an awareness of the hierarchy of the political system norms. *Pacta conventa* similar to the earlier *Pacta Henriciana* (Henrician Articles), were of the foremost importance. Once formulated by the Diet in consultation with the Elector of Saxony, who was to become the next king commencing a new dynasty, and sworn to by him and by every new king assumng the throne, they were to constitute a permanent and inviolable element of the reformed political system. They could not be amended by the special extraordinary sessions of the Diet which were to revise the Constitution every twenty-five years.[38] In the hierarchy of basic laws, they were, therefore, placed higher than the Constitution of 3 May, formally at least. Here, one can see an attempt to compensate the Lithuanians for the fact that the problem of the Union had been disregarded in the Government Statute. The particular importance of the Mutual Guarantee was stressed also by its solemn form and archaic language.[39]

The Guarantee was an important addendum to the Constitution, going in a direction different than that intended by the King and Kołłątaj, but following first drafts by the Deputation for the Reform of Government and Ignacy Potocki, its chairman. It also satisfied the wishes of the "political nation" of the Grand Duchy.

It should be recognized that the Mutual Guarantee was the supreme achievement of the Lithuanian representation at the Great Diet. After the Constitution of 3 May was passed, it succeeded in sanctioning the federal character of the Commonwealth based on the principle of equal rights of the Crown and Lithuania after agreeing to the formation of common central organs.[40] Taking into consideration the fact that the Grand Duchy was usually considered one of the three provinces of the Commonwealth during the eighteenth century, it becomes obvious that the Mutual Guarantee considerably strengthened the position of the Duchy. It stressed its equal status in relation to the Crown, since half the members of the central committees were to come from Lithuania.[41]

Although the Mutual Guarantee of the Two Nations was a success for the Lithuanian party, the achieved compromise strengthened the position of the whole reform camp. The historical importance of the act was obvious. After the Mutual Guarantee was passed, Lithuanian senators and deputies gave a grand party to commemorate the anniversary of Stanisław August's coronation, attended by the King, the Marshal of the Crown confederacy, state dignitaries and the diplomatic corps. A commemorative medal was also issued which was recorded by Nikolai Kostomarov.[42] The medal had a Latin inscription which, unfortunately, we know only in a Russian translation. It read: "The Closest Union Completed during Stanislaus Augustus Initially Commenced during [the reign of] Sigismundus Augustus." This medal cannot be found in Polish collections.

A week later, after the adoption of the Mutual Guarantee on October 27, a bill was passed entitled "The Treasury Commission of the Commonwealth of the Two Nations." A half-year later, on May 18, 1792, the bill on the Military Commission of the Two Nations was amended. In agreement with the Mutual Guarantee half of its members would be from the Grand Duchy, and its presidency would alternate between the Crown and Lithuania.[43] Furthermore, the law "The Plan of Provinces, Lands, Counties, and Cities, Including Places Where, According to the Constitution, Dietines Will Take Place in the Provinces of the Crown and the Grand Duchy of Lithuania" should be considered as a fulfillment of Lithuanian demands. According to this law, in the Republic's three provinces: Great Poland, Little Poland, and Lithuania, an equal number of 68 deputies were to be elected. As a result, Lithuania gained 14 deputies, Great Poland only 2, and Little Poland 11.[44] Consequently, this Law was advantageous for Lithuania.

After the fall of the 3 May Constitution, Hugo Kołłątaj evaluated the role of the Mutual Guarantee in the collective work, *O ustanowieniu i upadku Konstytucji polskiej 3 Maja 1791 roku* (On the Enactment and Fall of the Polish Constitution of 3 May 1791) in the following way:

> The noble, or rather brotherly sacrifice of the Crown province facilitated everything. The holy vows of the union between Lithuania and the Crown were renewed. The memorable resolution was passed on the grounds that all government agendas were to be composed half of Lithuanian and half of Crown citizens, although Lithuania did not constitute even a third part of the population, or wealth in comparison with the Crown.[45]

Kołłątaj, a proponent of a complete integration of the Commonwealth, evaluated the Mutual Guarantee from the perspective of time as the renovation of the Union of Lublin, and he gave credit for the achievement of compromise to the concessions made by the representatives of the Crown.

Just as the acceptance of the Constitution of 3 May by Lithuanian senators and deputies was a concession in favor of the Polish party made for the sake of the supreme interest of the whole Commonwealth, the Mutual Guarantee of the Two Nations was a concession in favor of Lithuanians. It was achieved within the framework of the Union not by the creation of significant changes in the basis of the federation, but through strengthening it by common organs created according to the principle of equal rights. This, in turn, strengthened the bond between the "political nations" of the Crown and the Grand Duchy.

This notion was expressed by the Marshal of the Lithuanian confederacy, Kazimierz Nestor Sapieha, who said when he presented the draft of the Mutual Guarantee: "To the reign of Zygmunt August the nations owe the Union. To the reign of Stanisław August they will be indebted for even a stronger bond with the stamp of sovereignty."[46]

The Mutual Guarantee has been underestimated by historians for a long time. Stanisław Kutrzeba, for example, whose opinion has already been mentioned, concluded that the Mutual Guarantee was an "addendum to the

Constitution" liquidating the two-channel military and treasury administration. The remaining differences were, according to Kutrzeba, "relics of the former division without any particular importance."[47] This evaluation was repeated by Władysław Konopczyński, Bogusław Leśnodorski and finally by Jerzy Łojek, according to whom the Mutual Guarantee was just an insignificant amendment to the Constitution.[48] Władysław Smoleński by contrast, as already noted, in emphasizing the importance of the "historical session of the Diet," that adopted the Mutual Guarantee, perceived this law as the crowning achievement of a process, the apogee of which was the Union of Lublin. He then placed the law of October 20, 1791 prominently in the history of the Union tradition.[49]

A turn in the evaluation of the Mutual Guarantee found its expression in the work of Emanuel Rostworowski. Referring to Smoleński's opinion, he perceived the Mutual Guarantee as a compromise achieved with difficulty, far from the maximalism of the early proposal that aimed toward integration.[50]

Jerzy Malec, who presented the Mutual Guarantee in a broader context, argued that this law expressed agreement with the notion of a centralized executive power, and at the same time preserved the separateness of the Lithuanian province and its law. The price for this agreement was an acceptance of the Grand Duchy "not as one of three provinces, but as an equal partner in the rights of the Union. It is with good reason that the Mutual Guarantee was termed a renewal of the Act of Union."[51]

Jerzy Michalski also stressed that the Mutual Guarantee originated as a way of solving the dispute concerning the Commission of the Treasury; then a broader meaning was attached to it, and was then perceived as a new act of Union, which finally regulated the mutual relations of the two nations.[52] This point of view has made its way into recent works. According to Zbigniew Szcząska, the Mutual Guarantee retained–despite strivings toward centralization–the federal character of the Polish-Lithuanian State.[53]

Both the Constitution of 3 May and the Mutual Guarantee of the Two Nations were created by the Great Diet, and both were intended to assure the welfare and the future of the Commonwealth. The political wit and cautiousness of the Polish and Lithuanian deputies should be highly valued. They were able to combine the requirements of the reformed organization of the state with the tradition of the Union and the preservation of the political autonomy of the Grand Duchy of Lithuania. It should be added that in a critical time in Polish history Sapieha opposed the capitulation to Russia and condemned the Confederation of Targowica, and that the Lithuanian deputy Tadeusz Korsak, and many others from Lithuania, fought with heroism and gave their lives in defense of the Polish-Lithuanian state during the Kościuszko Insurrection. It can be assumed that the fact that the Lithuanian nation survived, preserving a sense of its individuality and tradition of statehood, and that it was able to regain its independence in 1918 was partly the achievement of those who acted effectively during the Great Diet in the name of preserving the separateness and rights of the Grand Duchy within the framework of the Commonwealth of the Two Nations.

Notes

1. Juliusz Bardach, "Statuty litewskie w ich kręgu prawno-kulturowym" (The Lithuanian Statutes in their legal and cultural context) in *O dawnej i niedawnej Litwie* (Poznań: Uniwersytet Adama Mickiewicza, 1988), p. 45ff.

2. Jerzy Malec, "*Coaequatio iurium* stanów Wielkiego Księstwa Litewskiego z Koroną Polską z 1697 r." *(Coaequatio iurium* of the estates of the Grand Duchy of Lithuania with the Polish Crown in 1697), *Acta Baltico-Slavica* 12 (1979): 203-214.

3. Władysław Wielhorski, "Stosunki narodowościowe, wyznaniowe i językowe w W. Ks. Litewskim" (Relations in the Grand Duchy of Lithuania concerning nationality, religion, and language) in *Dzieje ziem Wielkiego Księstwa Litewskiego,* Alma Mater Vilnensis (London: 1953), vol. 3, pp. 215-242; Juliusz Bardach, "0 świadomości narodowej Polaków na Litwie i Białorusi w XIX-XX wieku" (On the national consciousness of Poles in Lithuania and Byelorussia in the XIX and XX centuries) in *O dawnej i niedawnej Litwie...,* pp. 201-211.

4. Concerning this problem see Emanuel Rostworowski, "Marzenie dobrego obywatela, czyli królewski projekt konstytucji" (The dream of a good citizen or the royal constitutional proposal) in *Legendy i fakty XVIII wieku* (Warszawa: PWN, 1963), pp. 407ff, 439-441, 451-453; Jerzy Malec, "Próby ściślejszego zespolenia Litwy z Koroną w latach 1764-1786" (Attempts to bring Lithuania and the Crown closer, 1764-1786) *Lituano-Slavica Posnaniensia,* Studia Historica 2 (1987): 176-184, and "Problem stosunku Polski do Litwy w dobie Sejmu Wielkiego (1788-1792)" (The problem of the attitude of Poland toward Lithuania during the Great Diet, 1788-1792), *Czasopismo Prawno-Historyczne* 34, 1 (1982): 31-48; Jerzy Michalski, "Zagadnienie unii polsko-litewskiej w czasie panowania Stanisława Augusta" (The problem of the Polish-Lithuanian Union during the reign of Stanisław August), *Zapiski historyczne* 51, 1 (1986): 97-130.

5. Hugo Kołłątaj, *Listy Anonima i Prawo polityczne narodu polskiego* (Anonymous Letters and the Political Law of the Polish Nation), eds. Bogusław Leśnodorski and Helena Wereszycka (Warszawa: PWN, 1954), vol. 1, pp. 220, 370-371; vol. 2, pp. 10-11, 245-246.

6. Hugo Kołłątaj, *O Sejmie,* Biblioteka Ossolińskich, Ms. 1778/111. Cited in Maria Pasztor, *Hugo Kołłątaj na Sejmie Wielkim 1791-1792* (Hugo Kołłątaj at the Four-Year Diet, 1791-1792) (Warszawa: Wyd. Sejmowe, 1991), p. 155.

7. Rostworowski, *Legendy i fakty,* p. 451.

8. Malec, "Problem stosunku," p. 37.

9. *Volumina legum* (hereafter referred to as *VL*) (Kraków: 1889). vol. 9. pp. 203-204.

10. Rostworowski, *Legendy i fakty,* pp. 451-452.

11. Rostworowski, *Legendy i fakty,* pp. 451-452.

12. Rostworowski, *Legendy i fakty,* p. 405.

13. Rostworowski, "Naprawa Rzeczypospolitej (W 190 rocznicę Konstytucji Trzeciego Maja)" (The reforms of the Republic (on the 190th anniversary of the Constitution of 3 May) in *Popioły i korzenie. Szkice historyczne i rodzinne* (Kraków: 1985), pp. 135-137.

14. Bogusław Leśnodorski, *Dzielo Sejmu Czteroletniego* (The work of the Four-Year Diet) (Wrocław: Ossolineum, 1951) vol. 1, pp. 199, 240, 390; Bogusław Leśnodorski, ed., *Historia państwa i prawa polskiego (The history of the Polish state and Polish law)* (Warszawa: PWN, 1966), vol. 2, "Od połowy XV wieku do 1795," p. 532.

15. Stanisław Kutrzeba, "Unia Polski z Litwą" (The Union of Poland with Lithuania) in *Polska i Litwa w dziejowym stosunku* (Kraków: 1914), p. 657; Stanisław Kutrzeba, ed., *Historia ustroju Polski* (The history of the Polish form of government) (Warszawa: 1949), vol. 8, "Korona," p. 380.

16. Władysław Smoleński, *Studia historyczne* (Warszawa: 1925), p. 73ff.

17. See note 4.

18. Adam Mieczysław Skałkowski, "Towarzystwo Przyjaciół Konstytucji 3 Maja" (The association of the friends of the Constitution of 3 May) in *Pamiętnik Biblioteki Kórnickiej,* 3 (1930): 16; Emanuel Rostworowski, *Ostatni król Rzeczpospolitej. Geneza i upadek Konstytucji 3 Maja* (The last king of the Commonwealth: the genesis and fall of the Constitution of 3 May) (Warszawa: Wiedza Powszechna, 1966), p.231; Krystyna Zienkowska, *Spisek 3 Maja* (The plot of 3 May) (Warszawa: PWN, 1991).

19. Ludwik Hass, *Wolnomularstwo w Europie środkowo-wschodniej w XVIII w.* (Freemasonry in Central-Eastern Europe in the XVIII century) (Wrocław: Ossolineum, 1982), p. 208.

20. Jerzy Kowecki, "Klub Radziwiłłowski w Warszawie w 1791 roku" (The Radziwiłł club in Warsaw in 1791) *Wiek Oświecenia,* 6, (1989): 85-123.

21. Kazimierz Bartoszewicz, *Konstytucja 3 Maja. Kronika dni kwietniowych i majowych w roku 1791* (The Constitution of 3 May: A chronicle of events in April and May in the year 1791) (Warszawa: 1906. Reprinted 1989), pp. 108-110.

22. Władysław Smoleński, *Ostatni rok Sejmu Wielkiego* (The last year of the Great Diet) (Kraków: 1897), pp. 49-50.

23. Andrzej Stroynowski, "Reprezentanci Wielkiego Księstwa Litewskiego w czasie uchwalania Konstytucji 3 Maja" (The deputies of the Grand Duchy of Lithuania during the adoption of the Constitution of 3 May) in *Trzeciego Maja w tradycji i kulturze polskiej* (Łódź: Wydawnictwo Łódzkie, 1989), pp. 5-16.

24. The instructions are preserved in copies made by a Lithuanian historian, Adolfas Sapoka, from the court records kept in the State Archives in Vilnius, which form a part of the Central Library of the Lithuanian Academy of Sciences. Adolfas Sapoka unit, f. 233.125 and f. 233.126.

25. Bartoszewicz, *Konstytucja 3 Maja,* pp. 108-10.

26. *VL*, vol. 9, pp. 250, 253.

27. Stanisław Borowski, *Kodeks Stanisława Augusta. Zbiór dokumentów* (The Stanisław August Code: A collection of documents) (Warszawa: 1938), p. 9.

28. Adam Lityński, "Nieznane materiały do projektu Kodeksu Stanisława Augusta" (Previously unknown documents concerning the proposal of the Stanisław August Code) *Czasopismo Prawno-Historyczne* 30, 2 (1978): 226.

29. Borowski, *Kodeks,* pp. 17-18; Smoleński, *Ostatni rok, pp.* 354-58. Kołłątaj, cautioning against haste in the work on the codification of the law, referred to the example of the "13 American provinces" which, though they had such eminent law makers as Franklin and Adams, nevertheless assigned a five-year period for the preparation of the code of law.

30. Lityński, "Nieznane materiały," p. 227.

31. *VL*, vol. 9, pp. 289-90; Michalski, "Zagadnienie unii," p. 125.

32. Zbigniew Zdrójkowski, "Nieznane litewskie prospekty karne Józefa Weyssenhoffa z 1792 r." (Previously unknown Lithuanian drafts of criminal law by Józef Weyssenhoff) *Czasopismo Prawno-Historyczne* 10, 1 (1958): 91-123; Adam Lityński, "Prawo karne w projekcie Kodeksu Stanisława Augusta" (Criminal law in the proposal for the Stanisław August Code) *Przegląd Prawa i Administracji* 5 (1974): 177-88.

33. Nikolai Kostomarov, *Poslednije gody Reãipospolitej* (The last years of the Commonwealth) (St. Petersburg, 1886), vol.1, p. 536.

34. Skałkowski, "Towarzystwo Przyjaciół Konstytucji," p. 16.

35. Smoleński, *Ostatni rok,* p. 126.

36. Smoleński, *Ostatni rok,* p. 127; Michalski, "Unia polsko-litewska," p. 121.

37. *Zaręczenie Wzajemne Oboyga Narodów* (Mutual Guarantee of the Two Nations) Prawo Dnia 20 Miesiąca Października Roku 1791 uchwalone, *VL,* vol. 9, p. 316; Malec, "Problemy stosunku..," pp. 45-47.

38. Leśnodorski, *Dzieło Sejmu,* pp. 363-66; Rostworowski, *Legendy i fakty,* pp. 457-58; *VL,* vol. 9, p. 242.

39. Michalski, "Zagadnienie," p. 121.

40. Witold Kamieniecki, *Litwa a Konstytucja 3 Maja* (Lithuania and the Constitution of 3 May) (Warszawa: 1977), p. 22.

41. Malec, "Problem stosunku," p. 47.

42. Kostomarow, *Poslednije gody,* p. 537.

43. *VL,* vol. 9, 457.

44. *VL,* vol. 9, pp. 326-38; Leśnodorski, *Dzieło Sejmu,* p. 248; Jerzy Michalski, "Sejm w czasach panowania Stanisława Augusta" (The Diet during the reign of Stanislaw August) in *Historia Sejmu polskiego* vol. 1, ed. Jerzy Michalski (Warszawa: PWN, 1984), pp. 411-12.

45. Hugo Kołłątaj, *O ustanowieniu i upadku Konstytucji polskiej 3 Maja 1791 roku* (On the enactment and the fall of the Constitution of 3 May 1791) (Paryż: Księgarnia Luxemburgska, 1868), vol. 5 p.5.

46. Michalski, "Unia polsko-litewska," p. 120; Malec, "Problem stosunku," p. 45.

47. Stanisław Kutrzeba, "Unia Polski z Litwą," p. 657.

48. Władysław Konopczyński, *Dzieje Polski nowożytnej* (The history of modern Poland) (Warszawa: PAX, 1986) vol. 2, p. 238; Leśnodorski, *Dzieło Sejmu,* pp. 241-242; Jerzy Łojek, *Konstytucja Trzeciego Maja* (The Constitution of 3 May) (Lublin: Wydaw. Lubelskie, 1981), p. 34. The opinions of Lithuanian historians on this matter differ. A negative evaluation of the Mutual Guarantee is presented in the works of J. Żmuidzinas, *Commonwealth polono-lituanien ou l'Union de Lublin (1569)* (Paris-La Hayne-New York, 1978), p. 221; S. Vansevičius, "Lituvos valstybingumo problema po Liublino unijos (1569)," in *Teisiniu Institutu Raida Lietuvoje XVI-XIX* (Vilnius: 1981), p. 54. The importance of the confirmation in the Mutual Guarantee of the Union by the Four-Year Diet is presented in *Lietuvos Istorija,* ed. Adolfas Sapoka (Kaunas, 1936, reprint 1989), and also by Sapoka in *Lietuviskoji Enciklopedija* (Kaunas, 1937), vol 4, p. 686, where he wrote: "Consequently on 20 October 1791, the Lithuanian deputies achieved the aim for which Lithuania had striven for over 200 years" (that is, from the Union of Lublin).

49. Smoleński, *Studia historyczne,* pp. 73-74.

50. Rostworowski, *Legendy i fakty,* p. 452.

51. Malec, "Problem stosunku," pp. 48-49.

52. Michalski, "Zagadnienie Unii," p. 121.

53. Zbigniew Szcząska, "Pierwsza ustawa zasadnicza Rzeczpospolitej" (The first fundamental law of the Commonwealth) in *Konstytucje Polski. Studia monograficzne z dziejów polskiego konstytucjonalizmu,* vol. 1, ed. Marian Kallas (Warszawa: PWN, 1990) p. 58.

An allegory of the Constitution of 3 May by Friedrich T. M. John, 1791. (Biblioteka Narodowa, Warszawa).

16

Local Government Reform during the Four-Year Diet

Łukasz Kądziela

The Four-Year Diet undertook a series of initiatives aimed at modernizing Polish local government that were simultaneous with its better known central government reforms. While the local reforms are not well known, and, in fact, were not all successful, they are still an important part of the Diet's reforms and they deserve our attention. In addition, they provide an example of how various political ideas interacted in the Diet, which can better our understanding of Poland's "gentle revolution." Advances in research on local reforms make a reassessment of the accepted historiography on this subject worthwhile. Recent literature does not answer all questions about changes in local government during the Four-Year Diet, but it suggests a modification of generally held opinions.[1]

The problem that faced the Diet was how to divide the Republic into workable territorial units. Administrative divisions evolved over centuries and included provinces *(województwa)* of unequal size, containing different numbers of counties *(powiaty)* of various sizes, in each province. Some regions, for example Mazowsze and Podlasie, included a third level of division, the lands *(ziemie)*, a relic from former local princedoms, some of which contained several counties. This unsymmetrical administrative division made government difficult because it complicated tax assessment and gentry representation in the Diet, in the latter case because of the connection between administrative units and the distribution of dietines. These difficulties disposed many legislators towards reform. Further, Western European ideas concerning these matters constituted an additional impulse toward the reorganization of the country's administrative division.[2]

There was an awareness of the need for reform before the Four-Year Diet. In a 1785 article, Stanisław Siestrzeńcewicz, Archbishop of Mogilev, proposed a reorganization of territorial divisions modeled on the Russian provincial system.[3] At the beginning of the Diet's deliberations, Hugo Kołłątaj also suggested a reform of governmental units, as did Jan Ferdynand Nax in 1790, though Nax's plan lacked detail. Siestrzeńcewicz wanted to make the provinces equal in size and population. Kołłątaj preferred making the number of counties equal in all provinces. He explained his choice in political terms; such a reform would ensure each province equal representation in the Diet. He opposed establishing provinces on the basis of equal population, arguing that the population in less settled areas would grow when their residents received personal and property rights.[4] Thus, the debate, known from Western Europe, over "arithmetical" or "geometrical" administrative division of the state started also in Poland.

Early in the Four-Year Diet, work on the national budget revealed a need to increase tax revenues, which added to the pressure for local reform. Debate on the national budget concerned both tax assessments and how the tax burden should be distributed among the Republic's great provinces: Wielkopolska, Małopolska, and the Grand Duchy of Lithuania. Provincial tax levels were the subject of numerous complaints introduced in the Diet by delegates from Małopolska since the sums each great province paid were set at the Diet of 1773-1775, which oversaw the First Partition, when many Małopolska delegates were absent for political reasons.[5] Whether Małopolska was treated fairly or not is impossible to know today without research on that particular question, in any case, a Małopolska delegate from Bracław, Fryderyk Moszyński, presented a report to the Diet on 9 March 1789 that described the population, size, tax obligations, and Diet representation of the three great provinces.[6] Moszyński showed that Wielkopolska together with Mazowsze had smaller populations, covered a lesser area, and paid lower taxes, but had the largest representation in the Diet. If we pass over the economic concerns that were most important to Moszyński, it is clear that his data could be used to support any one of the plans for local redistricting. In addition, he drew a connection between tax levels and representation in the Diet.

Despite numerous reasons in favor of a complete reform of the Polish system of administrative divisions, the Four-Year Diet failed to take such measures. Territorial reorganization's chief opponents were the mass of conservative gentry and may have included certain leaders of the "Patriotic Party."[7] Those reforms that the Diet did introduce fit the needs of the parliamentary system rather than those of improved local government. The Diet ruled that the three great provinces would have equal representation in the Diet, each with sixty-eight delegates, and set the number of delegates elected by each dietine at two. These changes in the number of delegates elected to the Diet required that new venues be set for dietines, which in turn meant that the division of counties in each province must be reorganized to fit the new election laws. Local redistricting affected a variety of special interests and their backers lobbied in their defense. Lengthy negotiations over the inclusion of particular parishes in one county or another ensued delaying a final Diet decision on redistricting until 24 October 1791. Equalization of the number of delegates to the Diet from each great province gave Lithuania fourteen new seats, Małopolska eleven, and Wielkopolska two.[8] The most important point considered in territorial reform was the balance of representation among the great provinces, which can, in part, be explained by the antagonism that arose between the constituent parts of the Republic during the debate over representation in the Diet. At the same time, however, the new law upheld the traditional distribution of dietines other than those that elected delegates to the central diets. The result, in many counties in the Kingdom of Poland itself, was a mosaic of gentry gatherings held in different places depending on their function. This hindered the development of commonly acknowledged administrative centers in the counties and provinces.

The members of the Four-Year Diet neither carried out a fundamental reform of Polish local government nor enacted Kołłątaj's relatively modest program in its entirety. The Diet's legislation rationalized territorial divisions in the provinces, but was guided by the needs of the parliamentary system with its traditional underpinnings, not by the demands of modern government. A year later, in 1792, when Szczęsny Potocki, leader of the Targowica Confederation, turned to the idea of dividing the Republic "geometrically" in his legislative plans,[9] the opposition he encountered showed a general attachment to the traditional organization of the Republic and a mistrust of the all-encompassing systems proposed by contemporary theoretical works as solutions to national problems.[10]

The system of local government established by the Four-Year Diet like many of the Diet's laws, grew out of the needs of the moment. Increasing abuses in military recruitment warned the delegates that they must set up local institutions that would both satisfy the army's needs and guarantee civilians safety. The circumstances of the new institutions' birth determined their name: Civilian-Military Commissions of Order. The Diet passed separate laws establishing these Commissions for Lithuania on 17 November and Poland on 24 November 1789.[11] The Commissions began their work following the local economic dietines held in February 1790.

Numerous earlier reform plans proposed local commissions strictly subordinate to the central government of the Republic.[12] This was in line with the practice of absolutism in the neighboring monarchies and with the political theories of the time. The laws on the Civilian-Military Commissions of Order, however, were passed by the ruling Diet (*sejm rządzący*)[13] at a time when the old system of government had been destroyed, republican sentiments dominated the Diet and public opinion, and opposition to all central authority was high. Therefore, the legislation on the Commissions did not speak about subordinating the Commissions of Order to the Central Military Commission or Treasury Commission, but about "cooperating" with them. The Commissions of Order belong to the early acts of the Four-Year Diet; the Diet's later reforms, the most important of which was the Constitution of 3 May 1791 belong to a different period. But, because the autonomy of the Commissions of Order fit the Polish model of constitutional monarchy with its powerful Diet, and their work was generally beneficial, the constitutionalists decided to keep the Commissions as part of the new system of government adopted in 1791. The 1791 Law on dietines made minor changes in the original statute on the Commissions. The Four-Year Diet never passed legislation regulating the relationship of the Commissions to the highest executive authority established by the Constitution of 3 May, the Guardians of the Laws (*Straż Praw*). Time ran out before the Diet could complete the new system of local government.

The Civilian-Military Commissions of Order were established in individual counties, lands, or provinces. Thus, their jurisdictions were neither regular in size, including various territorial units, nor did the number of Commissions correspond to the number of dietines in a given area. In general, there were fewer Commissions than dietines, and fewer dietines than counties, though there were local variations in this pattern. More importantly, the Commissions were considered equal to each other without regard for the area of their jurisdiction and the Commissions operated at a single level; there was no system of Commissions of first and second instance, for example, county and provincial commissions.[14]

In the Kingdom, the Commissions of Order had sixteen gentry members and three members of the diocesan clergy from one of the Catholic rites, Roman or Eastern. Later, the 1791 Law on Cities added three members of urban estate who were to be elected by the city electoral assemblies (*miejskie zgromadzenia wydziałowe).* The Law on Cities tried to unify the estates and, therefore, allowed members of the gentry, so long as they owned urban property, to sit on the Commissions as city representatives alongside born burghers.

Commissioners were elected every two years by the so-called electoral dietines. To ensure continuity in the Commissions' work, six commissioners kept their seats through each election. The commissioners served without pay, which may be seen as a victory of traditional republican views on the subject of pay for public service. In accordance with republican ideas of promotion in state service through a series of ranks, service as a Commission member became a necessary step for promotion to Diet delegate, member of a tribunal (*deputat trybunału),* member of a ruling commission (a ministerial level post), or receipt of a royal order. The chairman of a Commission of Order was a senator, if a senator sat on the Commission. Otherwise, the chair went to the highest ranking noble royal official *(urzędnik ziemski).* Their statute ordered that the Commissions meet daily, but the quorum was set at three. The commissioners were to fix an attendance schedule. Once they set the schedule, attendance was mandatory and absences could be punished by loss of rights to hold office for three years. The law provided each Commission a chancellery and archive to help in its work.

The Commission statute for Lithuania differed in two main respects from the Kingdom's law. Commissions had fifteen members and included ex officio senators and high ranking officials, though the ex officio members could not outnumber those elected. This aspect of the law shows the characteristic influence of the magnates and richer gentry on local affairs in Lithuania in contrast to the Kingdom, where the middle gentry controlled local government.[15]

According to their statute, the Civilian-Military Commissions of Order combined activity in the areas of civilian-military relations and government fiscal affairs. The Commissions resolved issues concerning the quartering of military units within their jurisdictions. In cooperation with the central Military Commission, the Commissions of Order could place military units in all manors of landed estates, except heritable gentry lands. (Thus the Commissions of Order could quarter troops in royal, church, and other estates.) In return, they could ask those units to help them keep order. Cities could avoid quartering of troops in private homes by building a barracks at municipal expense. In addition, the Commissions were to help local military commanders with recruiting. A set of special regulations governed cooperation between the army and local Commissions on recruiting and aimed at preventing recruiting abuses, stopping desertion, and halting crime committed by deserters. The

Commissions' responsibilities also included establishing and maintaining army supply depots, organizing military transport for food and ill soldiers, and preparing camps for large units in the event of troop concentrations or transit of large units. Further, the Commissions had judicial power in cases of conflict between civilians and the military.

Civilian oversight of military activities was meant to end widespread abuses by army units stationed in the countryside. While the Commission of Order statute spoke of full cooperation of military authorities with the commissioners, it gave civilian commissioners the upper hand in the relationship. The preference for civilian power is evident in the severe penalties for military violation of the three mile limit on the use of locally requisitioned transport, in the make up of Commission courts, which included only one high military officer, and in the assignment of two commissioners to supervise military encampments, providing food and shelter for the army and protecting the civilian population from military abuses.

Other parts of the tasks given to the Commissions of Order were less practical, but showed the ideas prevalent in the Four-Year Diet on dividing the Republic into new territorial units. The Commissions of Order were to collect annual census information about the number of subjects of all estates and religions in their jurisdictions and about changes in the population. The Christian clergy was to report on the Christian population and estate owners and urban magistrates on the numbers of Tatars, Karaims, Jews, and others. Collected data from the counties, lands, and provinces went to the central Treasury Commission, which reported to the Diet on the nation's population. The Police Commission also recorded this data.[16] The census clauses of the Commission of Order statute were very important to the Republic's leaders, who did not accurately know the country's population and used a number of very different population estimates in their work, confusing each other and historians.

The Commissions of Order were charged to collect taxes into their own coffers and then disburse those funds to the military according to rates fixed by the Military Commission. If needed, Commissions could ask the army to help collect back taxes and even impound recalcitrant taxpayers' property, putting it under Treasury Commission administration. By leaving tax money in the hands of the Commissions with their decentralized treasuries, which were more numerous than the local offices of the Treasury Commission, the only previous local fiscal institutions, the Commission of Order reform cut the distance between the taxpayer and the treasury and limited the need for cash shipments around the country.

OBIASNIENIE I EXPLIKACYA PRZYŁĄCZONYCH TABELL PODATKOW, INTRAT I SZACUNKU DOBR KORONY I LITWY.

TABELLA PIERWSZA
Okazuiąca Generalne Intraty i Maßę fortuny Kraiowey, tudzież Ofiary Dziefiątego Dwudziestego i Pięćdziesiątego Procentu.

STAROSTWA CZYLI DOBRA KROLEWSKIE.

1mo. Pierwfza Kathegorya na iedney Stronie zawiera w fobie Podatek od połowy Intraty, czyli 50. Procentu, wzięty z nowey Luftracyi Intrat Dóbr Królewfkich. Do którego włączona ieft Intrata z Licytacyi wynikła, i z Expektatyw wzmiankowanych Staroftw.

2do. Cała Intrata Dóbr tychże Królewfkich z powyżfzego Procentu ułożona, do czego włączona ieft druga połowa Intraty przez Poffefforow participowana dla uftanowienia całey Intraty wyżey wfpomnionych Dóbr.

3tio. Szacunek tychże Dóbr w Kapitale, uftanowiony, z całości Intraty wynikaiący, rachowany po pięć od fta, albo dwadzieściu Tyfięcy za Tyfiąc.

4to. Dymy Miaft i Wfiow podług nowey Taryffy z Korony i Litwy wyciągnięte.

5to. Szacunek Dymu w Kapitale wypadaiący z exdywizyi Summ za Szacunek Dóbr uftanowionych przez Liczbę Dymow każdego w fzczególności Woiewodztwa wynaleziony.

6to. Intrata z Dymu z powyżfzego Szacunku onychże wynikła, rachowana po pięć od Sta.

7mo. Podatek z Dymu, ieft Dziefiąta Część Intraty iednego Dymu, albo Dziefięć od Sta.

8vo. Każda Prowincya ieft podzielona na Woiewodztwa, dla okazania wiele Podatku na Dym w każdym refpective Woiewodztwie wypada i ofobno ieft za fummowana. Gdzie trzeba uważać, że tylko pierwfze Cztery Kolumny znofzone bydź mogą. Bo inne trzy Kolumny niemogą bydź znieffione, ponieważ każda w fzczególności Summa przez exdywizyą zrobiona ieft.

DOBRA ZIEMSKIE.

1mo. Pierwfza Kathegorya na drugiey ftronie zawiera w fobie Podatek Dziefiątego grofza z Dóbr Ziemfkich, czyli Dziefięć Procentu Ofiary.

2do. Cała Intrata wypadaiąca przez rozmnożenie Podatku przez Dziefięć ieft uformowana. Ponieważ Właściciele Dóbr takich Dziefięć Procentu opłacaią.

3tio. Szacunek Dóbr w Kapitale wyprowadzony z całości Intrat, rachowany na pięć Procentu, i formuiący Kapita i wartość każdych Dóbr, w każdym fzczególnie Woiewodztwie.

4to. Dalfza Progreffya albo Rachunek Dóbr Ziemfkich, ieft podobnyż iak Dóbr Królewfkich, iako fię wyżey opifało tak co do fzacunku Dymu iako i Intraty i Podatku z niego.

UWAGI I EXPLIKACYE NAD REKAPITULACYĄ GENERALNĄ.

Jedna Strona okazuie zaraz różne Podatki gatunkami Summatim w każdey Prowincyi, to ieft też fame Pięćdziefiąt Procentu, z Dóbr Królewfkich, Dwadzieścia i Dziefięć Procentu z Dóbr Duchownych. Dziefięć zaś Procentu z Dóbr Ziemfkich, z liczbą Dymow i podzieleniem Summ na Podatek z iednego Komina. Aby za iednym oka rzuceniem widzieć można, wiele Podatku Pięćdziefiątego, Dwudzieftego i Dziefiątego Procentu każda z tych trzech Prowincyi oddzielnie przynofi.— Druga Strona wyftawia zaraz Podatki Prowincyami, iako Intratę, Szacunek cały Dóbr w Kapitale, tak w fzczególności każdey Prowincyi, iako też w ogólności całego Króleftwa. Również Liczba Dymów, z fzacunkiem tegoż dymu, z niego Intraty, i Podatku któren on opłaca, rachowany w teyże famey Proporcyi iak w powyżfzey Tabelli. Podatki które Dobra Duchowne płacą, a Dziefięć i Dwadzieścia Procentu nie będąc fegregowane wyraźnie w Taryffach Prowincyi Koronnych wpifane zoftały razem Prowincyami, ale w Litwie gdzie te Podatki Duchowne rozdzielnie rachowane po Dwadzieścia i po Dziefięć pro Cento tym dokładnieyfzy formuią Rachunek. Do tegoż ogólnego rachunku dołożono Podatek Miafta Warfzawy płacącego ryczałtem Złt: 400.000. fię rachowane iako Dwadzieścia Procentu od Intraty, albo od 2,000.000.— Naftępuią po nich Intraty Ekonomii Królewfkich w Koronie i w Litwie, z których kładzie fię Intraty plus minus 2.000.000, które równie a Pięć pro cento determinuią Szacunek a Kapitale tychże Ekonomii. Co zaś do ocenienia Intraty i Maiątku Poddanych, iako Pofindaczow w większey Części Gruntów w Kraiu, dla wynalezienia pewney Proporcyi wzięto pro Bafi wytrącenie czwartey części z całkowitości Dymow na Dymy Szlacheckie i Duchowne. Z czego wypada, iż ciż Poddani iako pofiadaiący refztę (opłacaiąc iuż część tego przez robociznę Ofypy i Czynfze które iuż w rachowane w Intratę Dóbr Panow fwoich) wypłacaią w teyże famey Proporcyi na całkowitość Podatku Prowincye wynofzącego Złt: 8,013.236. gr: 20. trzy czwarte części in circa teyże Summy, to ieft 6,009.927. Złt. 15 gr: iako Podatek od dwudzieftu Procentu ich Intraty. Taż Intrata rachowana po pięć od Sta formuie Maffe całkowitą i ocenienie w Kapitale Dóbr przez Poddanych pofiadanych. Potrzebna tu iefzcze wiadomość, iż dla tym dokładnieyfzey exdywizyi gdy naymnieyfza Część denara w rozrzuceniu na Dymy, tak w exdywizyi, iak multyplikacyi znaczne czyni Summy, gdzie krocie i milliony fię rachuią, podzielono Denar, których Ofmnaście grofz miedziany fkłada, na Ofm Cząftek, przez co w tymże grofzu 144. części zawiernią fię, co tym doftatecznieyfzą pewność w zrobionych Rachunkach i podziałach ftanowi. A każda ofmka Deuara w tychże Tabellach wfkazuie, iż takich 77.760. ieden Czerwony Złoty zawiera.

TABELLA DRUGA.
Okazuiąca Summaryufz wfzelkich dochodow Rzeczypofpolitey.

W TEY NAŚTĘPUIĄCE POTRZEBNE UWAGI I OBIASNIENIA.

1mo. Podymne z Dóbr Ziemfkich i Duchownych i Put-podymne z Miaft i Wfiow Królewfkich wzięte iako inne wfzyfikie Podatki w Rubrykach fię znayduiące. z Taryff w Kommiffyach Skarbowych znayduiących fię.

2do. Miedzy Podatkami Dziefiątego i Dwudzieftego Procentu od Duchownych które złączono znayduią fię i Podatki z Dóbr Exiezuickich wraz z fuperatą od tychże podług nowego Prawa.

)2(3tio.

The Commissions of Order had the task of reporting to the central Treasury Commission about the economic condition of their territories. They were to promote agriculture, trade, crafts, industry, and see to the development of transportation. The powers of the Commissions, however, were not commensurate with their broad mandate. The gentry limited the Commissions to a strictly advisory role in agricultural matters by its jealously guarded control over village life.[17] In agriculture, Commission activities were limited to sending parishes plans for model farms, and providing aid in cases of famine, crop failure, and livestock plagues. As to the merchantry, the Commissions were to direct those wronged by treasury officials, for example by collection of excess customs duties, to the Treasury Commission courts or to release impounded goods to their owners if the commissioners judged such a course was appropriate.

Commissions of Order were legally responsible for the maintenance of local roads and for carrying out the orders of the central Treasury Commission for the upkeep of highways in their areas. The Commission statute placed special emphasis on maintaining the navigability of rivers and canals. Legislation on the Commissions of Order made them responsible for reporting to the Treasury Commission about ways to use mineral resources, to establish or revitalize mines and factories with the goal of supplying the military from domestic sources. Generally, the role of the Commissions in economic matters was one of information gathering and reporting. The unwillingness of the Treasury Commission to compromise its place as the state's main economic agency and the Republic's need to mobilize its resources in quantities larger than those available in any single local jurisdiction limited the Commissions' economic work. The informational function of the Commissions of Order was also apparent in their responsibility to report to the central government on vacant leases and crown estates (*starostwa*) as well as on any new villages or settlements so that the latter might be included in the tax rolls. Contemporary surveys of crown lands *(lustracje)* and registers, which were irregularly updated, every few years, or sometimes only every few decades, did not show the actual state of affairs in the Republic. One of the most important expectations of the new Commissions was that they would help end such inconsistencies.

There were two other areas where the power of the Commissions of Order was somewhat greater. In education, they were to supervise the endowments assigned to support schools and, in Lithuania, to report their findings to the Commission for National Education. Also Commissions of Order had to see that parish priests, who had enough property to pay the land tax, maintained elementary school teachers in their parishes at their own cost so that the poor gentry and other subjects in the Kingdom, or any subjects in Lithuania could obtain basic schooling. Parish priests who fell into this category were obliged to report to the Commissions about the help they gave the schools. Social welfare responsibilities of the Commissions included establishment of hospitals at their own cost and watching over the provisions that landlords made for "people used up tilling their soil."[18] In a variety of matters: sanitation, health, freedom of the press, inspection of weights and measures and the quality of craft production, and organizing flood and fire control activities, the Commissions reported to the Police Commission. Legislation on the Police Commission defined the responsibilities of the Commissions of Order to the Police Commission.[19]

The long catalog of tasks given to the Commissions of Order was the result of a strengthening conviction that a state's power was related to the resilience of its executive institutions. The practical experience in government gained from 1775-1788, frequently underemphasized, when the generally criticized Permanent Council (*Rada Nieustająca*) became the Republic's actual executive, contributed to these feelings.[20] Modern points of view on the work of local administration developed under the influence of political literature of 1776-1787 which spread modern ideas and showed growing cameralist influences.[21] It is that literature that was the source of the ideas of progress, public service, humanitarianism, and concern for the state's economic development found in the statute on the Commissions of Order. However, the statute also contained elements that threatened their effective operation: collegial decision making and non-professional membership, relics of traditional republican thinking about government.[22]

The Commissions of Order had two functions; they were at once organs of local self-government and the central government's local agents. The joining of these two types of responsibility in a single body was analogous to the "middle way" taken by the Four-Year Diet in other reforms, where the ongoing influence of the legislative on the executive was ensured by including legislators in executive bodies; the Marshal of the Diet in the Guardians of the Laws and deputies and senators in the executive commissions. However, the Commissions of Order had broad powers because of their legal mandate and because their local competition had been eliminated. The Castle Administrators *(starostowie grodowi)* lost their executive power to the Commissions and the economic dietines were limited to suggesting plans to the Commissions for forwarding to the Diet, while retaining some power over tax collection, and thus some influence on the Commissions. The drive toward centralized government cost both the Commissions of Order and the economic dietines their autonomy since the Diets became the main judicial authority, even in local matters. As court for the whole Republic the Diet would have been overloaded with trivial affairs, but delegates to the Four-Year Diet, remembering the ascendancy of the local dietines under the Saxon kings, were inclined to face that kind of difficulty to establish the power of central state institutions.

Historians have given high marks to those few Commissions of Order that have been studied.[23] Although the collegial organization of the Commissions led to frequent waste of time, they carried out their basic tasks. The Commission courts were notable for their swift proceedings as compared to the contemporary criminal, and especially civil courts. Judicial speed resulted from expedients such as uninterrupted proceedings *(ciągłość orzekania)*, no court charges, and the sure execution of the courts' decisions by the army if necessary.[24] Justice, as dispensed by the Commissions of Order, was possible because they held both executive and judicial power, albeit the union of these powers in a single institution was improper. In the area of primary education, the Commissions first worked to increase the number of parish schools.[25] In a number of counties and provinces, the Commissions served as the chief governing bodies under the political supervision of the Commission of Police's twenty-four inspectors.[26] The value that contemporaries put on the Commissions' work is evident in a petition to emperor Paul I of Russia, after the Third Partition of Poland, asking him to reestablish the Commissions, which had operated "with such benefit to the provinces."[27]

Keeping population records, one of the most important duties of the Commissions of Order, was understood as the continuous updating of information gathered by the census decreed on 27 June 1789. There was, however, no specific body of instructions to the Commissions for registering people. The provisions for counting the population were part of the statute on enumerating households for tax purposes. Such a combined approach to maintaining accurate census data could show the desire to take advantage of the tax registration process to count the population.[28] Discussions held in the Diet show that population records were also to serve military recruiting needs. The 1789 census lasted nine months, which was in line with census practices in other countries. But, the count was not comprehensive because it excluded the gentry, who opposed any attempt to count them, and the clergy. Census takers used two forms, one for urban dwellers and one for rural residents. In each case, the individual's sex, age (under or over fifteen years old), and social-economic status was to be recorded. The same method was used to tally information about Jews and Karaims. The census decree's order that data be gathered in a standard and comparable manner was, nonetheless, not carried

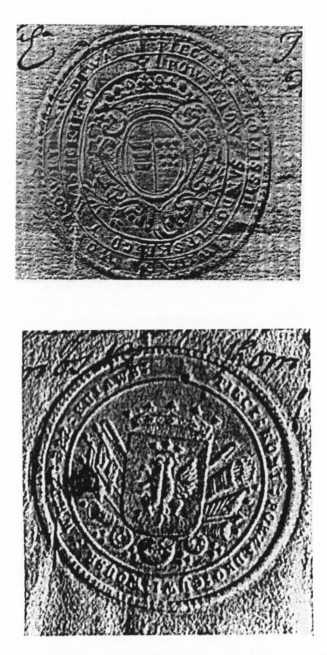

Voivodeship seals of Civilian Military Commissions of Order, 1792. (Muzeum Narodowe w Warszawie). Photo A. Skarżyńska, W. Jerke. Reprinted from Stefan Krzysztof Kuczyński, *Polskie herby ziemskie* (Warszawa: PWN, 1993).

out. The Commissions of Order frequently did not receive the census forms and instructions for their use directly and many Commissions interpreted the same parts of the instructions differently. Most of all, the census suffered from incomplete information gathering, for example, failure to record individuals' names in entire villages or even several villages in an area and the census' connection to the enumeration of households for tax purposes. Further, completion of the census forms was the responsibility of the landlords who owned many villages, that is those persons with the best reason to conceal the true state of their holdings from the government. Problems with the census have led historical demographers to suggest a number of ways to correct its findings to more accurately show Poland's late eighteenth-century population.[29]

The 1789 census covered the entire Republic. Unfortunately, few census materials survived the Second World War.[30] Fryderyk Moszyński, the census' initiator, prepared the collected data for publication and printed the census results in mid-1790.[31] Despite the many criticisms that may be applied to Moszyński's presentation of the census findings, it shows that the most enlightened delegates to the Four-Year Diet had a sense of the need to gather information on the Republic's demographic potential and fixes Poland's place among the European states that carried out national censuses already in the eighteenth century.

Though the 1789 census did not include the gentry, the Four-Year Diet tried to gather data also on this estate. The size of the Polish Republic's gentry population has central meaning for modern debates about the country's social structure, a debate in which conclusions are presented categorically though without adequate factual backing.[32]

The legislators of the Four-Year Diet took away the poor gentry's political rights by interpreting property qualifications for political participation in a way which remains controversial to the present day.[33] Having done so, they faced the task of legitimizing the position of the richer gentry. Hugo Kołłątaj proposed introduction of gentry registers in each province patterned in part on Austrian practice.[34] Moszyński modified Kołłątaj's plan, edited the Diet's law on gentry registers, and directed their subsequent printing and distribution. The statute on gentry registers had a difficult time in the Diet as did the Law on dietines, to which it was linked. The debates lasted for weeks until on 25 March 1791, the statute on gentry registers passed unanimously, a day after the Law on dietines.[35] The statute on gentry registers gave the Commissions of Order a new responsibility. They were to prepare a register for each dietine in their jurisdictions, often more than one for each Commission. The registers were to list, parish by parish, all the citizens who paid enough taxes to satisfy the conditions for enjoying political rights. There were also provisions for updating register entries before every dietine and for registering the property qualifications of gentrymen who held land in areas covered by more than one register. The legislation on gentry registers, meant to make dietines more efficient, had other effects as well. Gentry registers allowed the richer gentry to be counted. Entries in the registers could be used to prove membership in the noble estate. The body of information contained in the registers could serve to illustrate patterns of gentry landholding, an irreplaceable source for both contemporary statesmen and modern historians.

The law required that the registers be completed by the last day of June 1791. Some Commissions of Order held gentry assemblies before that date to compile the registers.[36] In October 1791, the Diet discussed gentry registers again because of problems encountered with their compilation and, in December, the Commissions of Order reworked the registers according to new instructions received in the meantime from the Treasury Commission.[37] It appears that a significant number of registers were compiled since the first dietines held under the new law, which restricted participation to the richer gentry on the basis of information recorded in the registers, met in February 1792. However, historians have not found a single gentry register of this kind. We may hope that the ongoing search for them will be successful and that, when found, the registers will give us a better idea of how the Commissions of Order enrolled the gentry and of the reality of eighteenth-century social life. It seems clear that the idea of compiling gentry registers was part of the same trend toward organizing, systematizing, and describing social life as the other measures taken by the Four-Year Diet described above.

What was the source of encouragement for these administrative measures? Older Polish literature maintained that the method used was native. This opinion was grounded in the conviction that cameralism regarding state administration could not be copied in Poland because of the Republic's unique political structure.[38] In a police state, after all, the directives that controlled the state's executive activity were not laws, but instructions to the state's agents, which proceeded from the absolute power of the monarch. Not until the beginning of the nineteenth century was executive action explained in terms of law, and did administrative law become part of the liberal idea of the state. Proponents of the Polish origins of late eighteenth-century ideas for reforming the Republic argued that the power of the Diet over the king prevented the development of absolutism and so of a police state. It was the incongruence of cameralist state administrative ideas with the Polish Republic's political structure which made their adoption in Poland impossible. The growth of

Polish administrative law was, from its beginning, closer to the next step of political evolution, the state of law.[39]

Recent authors take a less categorical stance. They argue that cameralist doctrines based on ideas of "making the subjects happy," which contributed to the growth of administration eager to satisfy social needs, could easily be accepted in eighteenth-century Poland. That is, so long as it did not forward the cause of absolutism and the state did not interfere unduly in the life of the individual.[40] Newer studies indicate that the works of Nicholas de la Mare, Johann Heinrich Justi, and Josef Sonnenfels were available in Poland in the eighteenth century, which, together with contacts made during Poles' travel and study abroad, brought those authors' ideas to Poland. Some Polish writers showed the visible influences of a cameralism which emphasized police and executive power. This voice was strongest in the years 1776-1790 when Remigiusz Ładowski, Józef Wybicki, and Jan Ferdynand Nax wrote the most important works advocating this aspect of cameralism.[41] In 1792 a selection of passages from de la Mare's *Traité de la police* was published in Poland as a handbook for executive officials.[42] However, the majority of Polish publications do not show a strong cameralist influence and late eighteenth-century Polish political literature is not dominated by one particular influence, but is a mosaic of different ideas.[43]

It is possible to notice a similar state of affairs in the practical implementation of administrative measures in government reform. Cameralist influence was more apparent in policies intended to satisfy particular social needs than in the organization of government institutions where traditional native elements predominated. The combination of Polish and foreign currents of thought was characteristic of the entire system of government built by the Four-Year Diet.

Notes

1. I have limited my notes to recent publications. Nonetheless, the pioneer works by T. Korzon and W. Kalinka are indispensable: Tadeusz Korzon, *Wewnętrzne dzieje Polski za Stanisława Augusta (1764-1794)* (The history of Poland's internal affairs in the reign of Stanisław August), 2nd ed. 6 vols. (Kraków: 1897) and Walerian Kalinka, *Sejm Czteroletni* (The Four-Year Diet), 4th ed. 2 vols. (Kraków, 1895).

2. See Pierre Legendre, *Histoire de l'Administration de 1750 à nos jours* (Paris: Presses Universitaires de France, 1968), pp. 110-116.

3. Jerzy Malec, *Polska myśl administracyjna XVIII wieku* (Polish administrative thought in the 18th century) (Kraków: Uniwersytet Jagielloński, 1986), p. 60.

4. Hugo Kołłątaj, *Listy Anonima i Prawo polityczne narodu polskiego* (Anonymous letters and Political law of the Polish nation), eds. Bogusław Leśnodorski & Helena Wereszycka (Warszawa: PWN, 1954), vol. 1, pp. 324-325; Malec, *Polska myśl administracyjna...*, pp. 76-77.

5. Roman Rybarski, *Skarbowość Polski w dobie rozbiorów* (Financial matters of Poland in the period of partitions) (Kraków: 1937), pp. 236-237.

6. Stanisław Konferowicz, *Fryderyk Józef Moszyński statystyk doby Sejmu Czteroletniego* (Fryderyk Józef Moszyński, a statistician of the Four-Year Diet era) (Warszawa: Szkoła Główna Planowania i Statystki 1961), p. 64b.

7. Ignacy Potocki sneered at the "political arithmetic" as practiced by Moszyński.

8. Bogusław Leśnodorski, *Dzieło Sejmu Czteroletniego (1788-1792). Studium historyczno-prawne* (The work of the Four-Year Diet 1788-1792. A study in legal history) (Wrocław: Ossolineum, 1951), pp. 248-249; Ryszard Łaszewski, "Sejmiki przedsejmowe w Polsce Stanisławowskiej. Problemy organizacji i porządku obrad" (Local electoral dietines in the reign of Stanisław August. Their organization and agendas), *Acta Universitatis Nicolai Copernici,* Nauki Humanistyczno-Społeczne 83, Prawo, 15. (1977): 108 ff.; Jerzy Michalski, "Sejm w czasach panowania Stanisława Augusta" (The Diet in the reign of Stanisław August) in *Historia sejmu polskiego,* ed. Jerzy Michalski (Warszawa: PWN, 1984), vol. 1, pp. 411-412; Adam Lityński, *Sejmiki ziemskie 1764-1793. Dzieje reformy* (Local dietines 1764-1793. History of their reform). (Katowice: Wyd. Uniwersytetu Śląskiego, 1988), pp. 107-108. The text of the law is in *Volumina legum* (Kraków, 1889), vol. 9, pp. 326-338.

9. See Jan Wąsicki, *Konfederacja targowicka i ostatni sejm Rzeczypospolitej z 1793 roku. (Studium historyczno-prawne)* (The Confederation of Targowica and the last Polish Diet of 1793. A study in legal history) (Poznań: Poznańskie Towarzystwo Przyjaciół Nauk, 1952), pp. 45-51; Emanuel Rostworowski, "Potocki, Stanisław Szczęsny," in *Polski Słownik Biograficzny* (Wrocław, 1985),vol. 28 pp. 196-197.

10. Łukasz Kądziela, "Prymas Michał Poniatowski wobec Targowicy" (Primate Michał Poniatowski's attitude towards the Confederation of Targowica), *Przegląd Historyczny* 84, 4 (1994).

11. Kalinka, *Sejm Czteroletni,* vol. 1, pp. 642-644. Texts of Laws in *Volumina legum.* vol. 9, pp. 136-142, 146-156.

12. These are discussed in Malec, *Polska myśl administracyjna...*, pp. 89-93.

13. See Jerzy Michalski, "Kilka uwag o koncepcji sejmu rządzącego w XVIII w." (Some remarks on the concept of the ruling diet in the 18th century), *Śląski Kwartalnik Historyczny Sobótka, 37,* 3-4 (1982): 241-248.

14. In Wielkopolska, there was usually one Commission of Order for each province. However, in Mazowsze, as many Commissions were set up as there were lands, the former local princedoms. Leśnodorski, *Dzieło Sejmu Czteroletniego..*, pp. 335-336.

15. Leśnodorski, *Dzieło Sejmu Czteroletniego...*, pp. 339-340.

394 Łukasz Kądziela

16. Andrzej Zahorski, *Centralne instytucje policyjne w Polsce w dobie rozbiorów* (Central police institutions in Poland during the partitions) (Warszawa: PWN, 1959), p. 91. The Commissions' statute used F. Moszyński's earlier legislative projects as a source for its provisions on gathering census data. See also Konferowicz, *Fryderyk Józef Moszyński...*, pt. 1, pp. 119-122.

17. This explains the failure of the attempt to establish a rural police force in the Republic, like that in Austria, and in accordance with the recommendations of the cameralists on this subject. See Malec, *Polska myśl administracyjna...*, pp. 93-98.

18. Leśnodorski, *Dzieło Sejmu Czteroletniego..*, pp. 337-339.

19. Zahorski, *Centralne instytucje policyjne*, pp. 91-92.

20. Aleksander Czaja, *Między tronem, buławą a dworem petersburskim. Z dziejów Rady Nieustającej 1786-1789* (Between the throne, the hetman's mace and the Petersburg court. The history of the Permanent Council, 1786-1789) (Warszawa: PWN, 1988), pp. 96-130.

21. Malec, *Polska myśl administracyjna*, pp. 49-58.

22. Leśnodorski, *Dzieło Sejmu Czteroletniego...*, p. 339.

23. Tadeusz Korzon, "Komisye porządkowe cywilno-wojskowe wojewódzkie i powiatowe w latach 1790-1792," (Civilian-Military Commissions of Order in provinces and counties 1790-1792), *Ateneum*, 25 (1882): 427-455. Korzon worked with the records from Radziejowice, Rawa Mazowiecka and Czersk and with the summary records from the Łuck and Chełm Commissions. Wiesław Szaj, "Organizacja i działalność administracyjna wielkopolskich komisji cywilno-wojskowych 1789-1792" (Organization and administration of Wielkopolska Civilian-Military Commissions 1789-1792), *Studia i Materiały do Dziejów Wielkopolski i Pomorza* 23 (1976): 85-102. Szaj worked with the records of the Commissions of Order from the regions of Wieluń, Ostrzeszów, Poznań, Kalisz, Kruszwica and Radziejów.

24. Wiesław Szaj, "Sądownictwo cywilno-wojskowe w okresie Sejmu Czteroletniego" (Civilian and military judiciary during the Four-Year Diet) *Studia i Materiały do Historii Wojskowości 27* (1984): 169-175.

25. Tadeusz Mizia, "Komisje porządkowe cywilno-wojskowe a szkolnictwo parafialne w okresie Sejmu Czteroletniego" (Civilian-Military Commissions of Order and parish schools during the Four-Year Diet) *Rozprawy z Dziejów Oświaty,* 6 (1963): 40-92; Barbara Sobolowa, "Wielkopolskie komisje porządkowe cywilno-wojskowe a szkolnictwo parafialne" (Civilian-Military Commissions of Order and parish schools in Wielkopolska) *Rozprawy z Dziejów Oświaty,* 16 (1973): 7-20.

26. Zahorski, *Centralne instytucje policyjne...*, pp. 130-131.

27. Korzon, "Komisye porządkowe..." pp. 432-433.

28. Karol Buczek, *Mapa województwa krakowskiego z doby Sejmu Czteroletniego (1788-1792). Źródła i metody* (A map of the Kraków province at the time of the

Four-Year Diet. Sources and the Methods) (Kraków, 1930), pp. 27-28; Konferowicz, *Fryderyk Józef Moszyński...*, pt. I, pp. 116-119; Władysław Rusiński, "Struktura osadnictwa i zaludnienia powiatu kaliskiego w 1789 r." (Settlement patterns and the population of Kalisz county in 1789), *Rocznik Kaliski,* 3 (1970): 53-55; Irena Gieysztorowa, "Badania nad historią zaludnienia Polski" (Studies in the demographic history of Poland) *Kwartalnik Historii Kultury Materialnej,* 11, 3-4 (1963): 523-558; Irena Gieysztorowa, *Wstęp do demografii staropolskiej* (An introduction to the demography of old Poland) (Warszawa: PWN, 1976), pp. 110-112. See *Volumina legum,* vol. 9, pp. 101-102.

29. Rusiński, "Struktura osadnictwa...," p. 82, suggests adding 10 percent to the recorded population in the county (*powiat*) of Kalisz which he studied. Gieysztorowa, *Wstęp...*, p. 115, compared the nineteenth century census figures with the census of 1789 and concluded that, in central Poland, the only area for which the comparison can be made, it recorded less than half of the actual population.

30. In addition to the works cited above see: J. Milczarek, "Dawny powiat szadkowski w świetle spisu ludności z 1789 r." (Former Szadkow county as described by the 1789 census) *Łódzkie Studia Etnograficzne,* 6 (1964): 163-169, and Zenon Guldon and Kazimierz Wajda. *Źródła statystyczne do dziejów Pomorza Wschodniego i Kujaw od 16 do początków 20 w.* (Statistical sources about East Pomerania and Kujawy from the 16th to the beginning of the 20th century) (Toruń, 1970), pp. 59, ff.

31. For Moszyński's results see Gieysztorowa, *Wstep do demografii...*, p. 114.

32. For another opinion on this subject see Emanuel Rostworowski, "Ilu było w Rzeczypospolitej obywateli szlachty?" (How many noble citizens were there in the Republic?) *Kwartalnik Historyczny* 94, 3, (1987): 3-39.

33. *Volumina legum,* vol. 9, p. 234. Prawo o sejmikach, Art. 4. (The law on local dietines, Art. 4).

34. Kołłątaj, *Listy Anonima...,* vol. 1, pp. 327-328.

35. Lityński, "Sejmiki ziemskie...," p. 106. *Volumina legum,* vol. 9, pp. 240-241.

36. Korzon, "*Komisye porządkowe...,*" pp. 447.

37. Lityński, "Sejmiki ziemskie..." p. 107, footnote 167.

38. See George S. Langrod, "La science de l'Administration publique (Esquisse historique)" in *Studi in onore di Silvio Lessona* (Bologna: Zanichelli, 1963), vol. 1, pp. 490-497. For extensive bibliography see Hans Maier, *Die ältere deutsche Staats und Verwaltungslehre,* 2nd ed. (München: Deutsche Taschenbuch, 1980). In Polish still irreplaceable is the work of Józef Bogdan Oczapowski, *Policyści zeszłego wieku i nowożytna nauka administracyi. Przyczynki do dziejów tej nauki* (Cameralists of the past century and the modern science of administration) (Warszawa, 1882).

39. Jerzy Starościak, "O administracji polskiej w XVIII wieku" (On Polish administration in the 18th century) *Państwo i Prawo,* 7, 5-6 (1952): 723-724.

40. Bogusław Leśnodorski, "Administracja w państwie burżuazyjnym. Czynniki rozwoju" (Administration in the bourgeoise state: factors of development) *Państwo i Prawo,* 26, 3-4 (1971): 531-532. Malec, *Polska myśl administracyjna...,* p. 103.

41. (Remigiusz Ładowski), *Krótkie zebranie trzech praw początkowych, to jest: prawa natury, politycznego i narodów z różnych autorów wyjęte...* (A short collection of three primary laws, that is the law of nature, political law and the law of nations, quoted from different authors...) (Lwów, 1780). See Władysław Sobociński, "Polnische version 'des Wohlfahrtsstaates' vom ende des 18. Jahrhunderts (System des politischen Rechts von 1780)" *Archiwun Iuridicum Cracoviense,* 10 (1977); Malec, *Polska myśl administracyjna...,* p. 105; Józef Wybicki, *Myśli polityczne o wolności cywilnej* (Political thoughts on civil liberty) (Wrocław: Ossolineum, 1984).

42. *Początkowe prawidła policji ogólnej w kraju* (Basic rules of police powers in the state) vol. 1 (Warszawa, 1792).

43. Malec, *Polska myśl administracyjna...,* pp. 103-107; "La science de la police et son influence sur la reforme de l'administration publique au siècle des Lumières en Pologne" in *Wissenschaft und Recht der Verwaltung seit dem Ancien Regime,* E.V. Heyen ed., Ius Commune-Sonderhefte, vol. 21 (Frankfurt am Main, 1984), pp. 59-69.

Translated by George Makowski

17

The Reform of Criminal Law during the Four-Year Diet

Adam Lityński

Thehe happiness of the nation depends on just laws...." This quote from Article VII in the Polish Constitution of 3 May 1791 conveys the conviction, present during the Enlightenment, of the primary and redeeming role of law for societies, nations and states. The philosophers of this Age of Light were absolutely certain that perfect law guarantees human happiness and also that the combined happiness of all the citizens results in the happiness of nations and states. Therefore, the welfare of the country depends upon ideal and perfect laws. By the reign of Stanisław August, these ideas already had a relatively long history in Europe, reaching as far back as the seventeenth century. These concepts also took root in Poland. During the Enlightenment, the exaggerated belief that law is one of the most important factors in the success and welfare of the state, the society and the nation was greatly stressed. The perfection of government and the success of the country was considered as dependent on the maintenance of justice: "Kingdoms stand upon justice, through injustice they fall," declared one of the deputies at the forum of the Great Diet.[1] Józef Konstanty Bogusławski, professor of Wilno University, in a treatise imbued with humanitarian spirit, expressed the prevailing view that "the imperfection of legislation is the source of the violation of the law and, as such, is the true cause of the misfortune and fall of nations."[2] If good laws guide human actions and grant people happiness, imperfect laws are the source of infractions and the downfall of nations. Poland's unfortunate internal situation and its fall from power on the international front were seen as clearly connected with the state of law and justice. Man is not born virtuous. Virtue comes from education, and excellent legislation is the result of education. It is no accident that Hugo Kołłątaj's "moral constitution" was to include both education and the codification of judicial law.

The certainty in the omnipotence of law is not by accident associated with the changes that occurred in the great historical era of the Enlightenment. This belief, known among philosophers and lawyers as a legal world view, was the result of a search to replace the extant theological world view with a new outlook and a new authority. In this new system, the supremacy of law replaced the omnipotence of supernatural forces. Acceptance of the absolute power of the ideal law was accompanied by the belief that such a law could be created. On the basis of these beliefs, many West European philosophers demanded the absolute destruction of the entire existing legal system in favor of a new law, created *ex nihilo*. Voltaire was not the only one to suggest "if you want good laws, burn the ones you have and write new ones."

European reformist trends coincided in the West with a powerful humanitarian movement in criminal law. The humanitarian movement found its philosophical justification in the doctrine of natural law. The ideas and principles formulated by the advocates of this movement led to the most significant turning point in the history of criminal law. Not only can the validity of these ideas be clearly demonstrated by their continued acceptance in the present day, but many of the postulates of the humanitarian school must still be recognized. The directions of change, formulated ideas, principles of law and reformist postulates introduced by the humanitarian school of criminal law had great impact on Polish thinkers, Polish concepts and the paths of Polish reform.[3]

As the Four-Year Diet assembled, the ideas and postulates of the humanitarian school had already diffused throughout the intellectual elite of Poland. In fact, the ideas were generally accepted by persons of different political leanings and social outlooks. Italian and French thinkers received the greatest attention. Western treatises were known in Poland, in their original form or in French translation, from the late 1760s and early 1770s. Concurrently, the most notable of these works were translated into Polish, namely: *Dei delitti e delle pene* of Cesare Beccaria in 1772, *De l'ésprit de lois* of Charles de Montesquieu in 1777, *Commentaries in the Law of England* of William Blackstone in 1786 and *Della scienza della legislatione* of Gaetano Filangieri in 1791-93. The translator of Blackstone's work was Teodor Ostrowski, one of the outstanding Polish jurists of the time. Ostrowski did not confine himself to mere translation of this work but provided it with extensive commentary

PIERWSZA CZĘSC
PRAWA ZIEMSKIEGO,

z strony opisánia person Sądowych/ y záśie-
dzienia ich vrzędu.

SĘDZIA ZIEMSKI.

Ieden Sędzia niech będzie w kázdéy
ziemi.

Z wielkości Sędzi / iákosmy te-
go doználi w spráwách o iednéy rzeczy ro-
zmáitym obyczáiem/ y róznie skázowano
częstokroć: dla tego chcąc pewną liczbę
postánowić Sędzi / y zábieżeć róznośći
pszerzeczonéy/ vstáwiamy : áby ieden w
Krákowskiéy / á drugi w Sędomirskiéy
Aa a   ziemi

Sąd ziemski (Land noble court), woodcut in Stanisław Sarnicki, *Statuta y metrika przywileiów koronnych*, Kraków 1594. (Biblioteka Sejmowa, Warszawa).

comparing Polish and English laws. He also added valuable remarks relating to the need for the reform of Polish law and the direction that this reform should take. Ostrowski demanded that penalties be milder and capital punishment considerably limited. He suggested that the latter be replaced by imprisonment combined with labor. Ostrowski also emphasized the prophylactic activity of the state. In his opinion social welfare and the propagation of education play a particular role in crime prevention.[4] He was by no means isolated in his views. Józef Konstanty Bogusławski also vividly emphasized the importance of public education as a factor in crime prevention.

The need to conduct a conscious criminal policy particularly of a prophylactic type by means of public education and improvement in the standard of living was advocated by many representatives of the age. Sebastian Czochron was one of the more outstanding among them. A professor at Cracow University, an advocate of physiocracy, he was the author of several treatises including *Dysertacya o prawodawctwie kryminalnym* (1788) (A dissertation on criminal law). He adopted the view that criminal law should take into account the psychology of man and steer the actions of an individual in such a way that his happiness would coincide with the happiness of all. He proclaimed the maxims typical for humanitarians of the age, demanding that capital punishment be confined to the most extreme cases and that, generally, it be replaced by imprisonment. He also advocated the abolishment of public execution and a general humanizing of the penal system. According to Czochron, the preservation of the proportion between the crime and the penalty should be the guiding light of the mitigating reform. For him, the inevitability of punishment and the speed of the proceedings were more important than the severity of the penalty. Czochron also criticized the abuses of preliminary detention.[5] Similar views were shared by Tomasz Kuźmirski, the most radical thinker among Polish jurists. He condemned the feudal penal system, and his theories complied with the basic ideas of the humanitarians, and particularly with those of Beccaria, from whom he borrowed a great deal.[6]

It seems that the democratic tradition of the Polish political and legal culture would make it particularly receptive to trends toward moderating the system of criminal law. In the mid-eighteenth century, humanitarian demands for the correction of the criminal law codes coincided with a growing acceptance of the need for general reform of the State, which would also include the reform of criminal laws. Thus, the contemporary European ideas found fertile ground in Poland and gave added incentive to native efforts.

By the 1780s, no one would voice general disagreement with the ideas of the humanitarians. Perhaps the reason for this attitude was the particularly mild character of Polish land law,[7] both substantive criminal law as well as criminal procedure. Indeed, the land law in Poland varied greatly from laws covering the gentry in both West and East European countries. Poland differed in this area just as its political system differed from most European countries; for criminal law is a product of the political system, a reflection of its character. As a result, Polish problems concerning criminal law varied to a great extent from those of most other European countries. West European humanitarian thought was an outgrowth of a critical attitude toward feudal criminal laws in absolute monarchies. Enlightened thinkers greatly opposed the cruelty of these laws. However, in the Polish Republic of nobles, criminal law was unusually mild in nature. Much of this mildness can be ascribed to the antiquated nature of the law: a system of composition, of monetary restitution for injuries incurred had been maintained since the Middle Ages (e.g. *główszczyzna* or head-money, *nawiązka* or indemnity)[8]. Although this system reduced the use of corporal punishment, it nevertheless bore witness to the obsolescent nature of a system that continued to rely upon the solutions of the Middle Ages.

Safeguards of the person and possessions stemming from noble privileges formed an important system of protection, particularly procedural, with the privilege of personal inviolability *(neminem captivabimus nisi iure victum,* 1425-1433) at its head. Polish legal proceedings for the noble estate had never allowed torture and, in 1776 torture was banned unconditionally, absolutely, and without allowance for the substitution of other methods in the legal systems of the remaining estates (burgher and peasant). In the context of the inquisitional nature of legal proceedings in the rest of Europe (with the imprisonment of suspects, tortures and deprivation of the right to a defense), the Polish legal process appears to be a system guaranteeing the rights of the defendant. However, as in substantive law, these guarantees in procedural law were in part due to the maintenance of elements of outmoded private law.[9] Centuries earlier, Europe had shifted to a more effective system of public law in criminal procedures. Consequently there was something paradoxical in this mildness resulting from an antiquated legal system: by virtue of its obsolete nature it actually coincided with the new postulates of humanitarian law. Such a paradox could only be unraveled by the modernization of the entire legal system. However, this could not simply be any modernization, but rather one rooted in the ideals of the humanitarian school.

The land law of the noble estate was not the only legal system in Poland. There were two other, contemporaneous systems, which differed greatly from Polish land law. The first of these, town law, was quite similar to the brutal laws of Poland's western neighbors. The second, the peasant law, was very similar to the town law. Such diversity, reflecting the strict differences defining each estate, was in direct conflict with one of the primary claims of the Enlightenment: the principle of equality in criminal law.

It is with good cause that the eighteenth century is known in legal history as the century of codification.[10] One of the primary goals of the humanitarians was the codification of laws. Among the goals of such criminal law codification was the elimination of uncertainty and lack of definition within the law, so as to eliminate any possible judicial arbitrariness which might result. The model for the necessary change was drawn from Montesquieu's theory of the tri-partite division of power: it is not the judge, but the legislator who determines what constitutes a crime and outlines the appropriate punishment for it. In Poland this demand for the codification of laws found particularly favorable conditions. Unlike the law in most other European countries, the law of the Polish nobility remained largely uncodified since the time of Kazimierz the Great's statutes in the first part of the fourteenth century. There had only been two partially successful attempts at a compilation of the laws: the collection of Jan Łaski in 1506 and the fragmentary *Formula processus* in 1523. The great number of source materials, and the fact that it was widely dispersed, was painfully evident in the daily practice of the law and it met with sharp criticism during the Enlightenment. Even simple attempts to compile the enormous quantity of judicial rules and regulations, such as Antoni Trębicki's collection prepared just before the convocation of the Great Diet with the intention of simplifying the work of the future codifiers, met with interest and approval. The Grand Duchy of Lithuania, which already had an excellent code of judicial laws dating from 1588, was in an entirely different situation.[11]

The difficulty resulting from the wide dispersion of sources, their sheer quantity, as well as their obsolescence was, indeed, enormous. As a result, Polish political leaders decided that codification must be their primary step in the reform of the overall legal system, not just of criminal laws. This issue appeared repeatedly in several programs of reform since 1764, even before humanitarian ideas took root in Poland. The era's new trends completely coincided with the direction of Polish needs and ideas, even if they were the result of rather different situations. The 1778 attempt at the codification of judicial laws by Andrzej Zamoyski *Zbiór praw sądowych* (Collection of judicial laws) was not the result of new trends.[12] Rather, it was an attempt to bring Polish substantive criminal law and criminal proceedings to the level that other European countries attained by the mid-eighteenth century. Concerning substantive criminal law, the Code was still behind new trends of the Enlightenment, in which criminal procedure already included some new ideas.

O

PRZESTĘPSTWACH

Y

KARACH

W Y K Ł A D.

Z FRANCUSKIEGO
NA JĘZYK POLSKI.

- - - *Adfit*

Regula, peccatis quæ pœnas irroget æquas.

Horat. Sat. III. L. I.

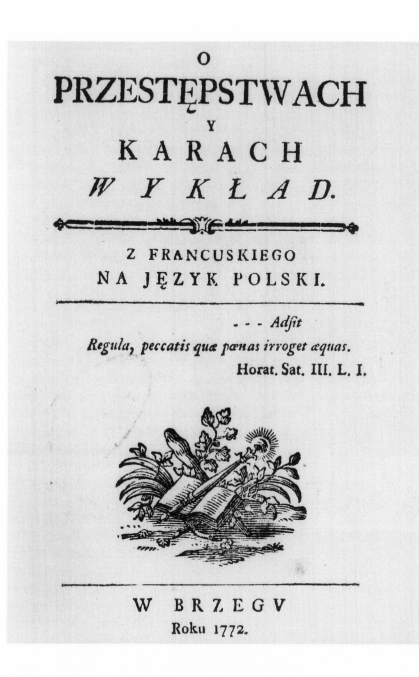

W BRZEGV
Roku 1772.

(Cesare Beccaria) *O przestępstwach y karach wykład.* Z francuskiego na język polski,
w Brzegu 1772. Title page. A translation by Teodor Waga of Beccaria's work *Dei
delitti e delle pene* (Biblioteka Uniwersytecka w Warszawie).

PRAWO
KRYMINALNE
ANGIELSKIE

PRZEZ

WILHELMA BLAKSTONA

ZEBRANE

A PRZEZ X. T. OSTROWSKIEGO S.

WYTŁÓMACZONE

I UWAGAMI DO PRAWA POLSKIEGO
STOSOWNEMI POMNOŻONE.

TOM I.

w WARSZAWIE R. 1786.
w Drukarni J. K. Mci i Rzeczypospolitey
u XX. *Scholarum Piarum.*

Za pozwoleniem Zwierzchnofci.

(William Blackstone) *Prawo kryminalne angielskie* przez Wilhelma Blakstona zebrane a przez, X. Teodora Ostrowskiego. S.P. wytłómaczone i uwagami do prawa polskiego stosownemi pomnożone. W Warszawie, R. 1786, w drukarni J.K.Mci i Rzeczypospolitej u XX. Scholarum Piarum. Title page of vol. 1 of Willliam Blackstone's work *Commentaries in the Law of England* with a comparison between English and Polish law provided by the translator. (Biblioteka XX Czartoryskich, Kraków).

The public nature of the proceedings was reinforced, thus removing the most serious drawback of the former accusatory proceedings. The rights of the accused to counsel and the principle that guilt must be fully proven were reaffirmed and further extended. The Code strove to have a universal character, with laws applicable to all, irrespective of social affiliation. However, the principle of equality before the law was not fully projected. Finally, the Code also included far-reaching recommendations for important political and social reforms which influenced future debates on these matters during the Four-Year Diet.

Codification usually inaugurates legal reform or change, often at the most fundamental level. To achieve the much needed depth of change in Poland the elimination of the strict division among the estates and, at the same time, the elimination of the several various legal systems was required. In addition, a shift from private to public law was required in the character of criminal law and process. Such change would require the abandonment of the system of monetary restitutions and the procedure of private claims. Essentially, these were the tasks before the deputies, as they assembled for the Four-Year Diet.

During the first two years of the Four-Year Diet, the proponents of penal legislation did not have a clear program. All of the initial measures taken in this area were rather chaotic. The provisions of criminal law were not established with the intention of reforming criminal law, but rather were intended to guarantee the realization of changes in the form of government. Therefore, as a rule, the resulting regulations were individual and disjointed rather than part of a coherent whole.

One larger group of criminal regulations, included in the Law on the Military Commission (established 15 December 1788), had precisely such a disjointed character.[13] These provisions were designed largely to protect both representative institutions and courts from attacks by the Commission, and to protect the Commission itself from foreign corruption. These provisions of criminal law for the Military Commission were clearly the result of a general distrust of this institution. They expressed the fear of a possible "violence against the freedom of the nation" or of an attempt by the Commission to seize power from democratic institutions governing public life: i.e. the Diet, dietines, tribunals and other courts, and free elections. Thus, these laws were an attempt to protect the country and its democratic system, as well as to strengthen at least one fundamental civil right, personal inviolability. This law, then, was one more among the many in the history of Polish penal legislation to address more immediate purposes.

Beyond the Law on the Military Commission and certain insignificant, scattered regulations, the problems of judicial and, especially, criminal law were addressed in the Principles to Reform the Government,[14] dated 17 December 1789. Although the Principles did not address the idea of legal codification, it did, nevertheless, announce two important reforms. The first was the separation of the legislative and judicial bodies of government. The second was to establish a law on the parliamentary court, which would include "a description of all matters pertaining to that court, and a description of the legal procedure applicable." These important elements of the Principles became the foundation for a special Law on Diet Courts, which was passed shortly after the Constitution of 3 May. This Law included both the elements of partial codification and anticipated the exhaustive preparation of a unified code. This law was also designed to protect the state, its government, all the governing bodies, and its internal security. It is significant that the penal norms that protected the nation, government and, the rights of the citizens come to the fore in this law.

The second half of the sessions of the Great Diet began with an interesting discussion concerning the deputies' oath not to accept any foreign salary. Despite many objections, the Diet finally passed a law declaring such action criminal.[15] The law was significantly named a "declaration" since it made evident, or rather re-emphasized, a pre-existing regulation: the acceptance of foreign salaries was punishable by sanctions of the highest degree. This "declaration" applied specifically to the senators and deputies.

The Unalterable Cardinal Laws (published in January 1791, though decided earlier) principally address the factors determining the sovereignty of the Republic. Here too were laws guaranteeing citizens' civil and political rights: i.e., the right to personal inviolability *(neminem captivabimus)* as well as the right to "cast a free vote" in the diets and dietines. Before the enactment of the Constitution, the right of personal inviolability was extended also to the burghers.[16]

The Law on Dietines, also passed prior to the Constitution on 28 April 1791, contained an extensive chapter of criminal regulations concerning challenges to the security of the dietines or their participants, as well as adherence to the rules and ethical standards (corruption, among others) in the deliberations of the dietines. It is worth noting that the Law on Dietines was the first among several statutes comprising a new "form of government." The issue of legal protection of the diets was similarly ensured in the Law on Diets, 16 May 1791.[17]

The statutes mentioned above were the only ones in the legislation of the Four-Year Diet to include provisions of criminal law of higher importance. Prior to May 1791 criminal legislation was largely dominated by norms designed to secure the state and citizens' rights. What was not in evidence, however, was any plan to put judicial law in some order, much less codify it. A vague intention of such codification was presented only during the preparation of the Constitution. The need to forge codes of civil law and penal procedure was consistently outlined in the king's constitutional draft.[18] However, it is difficult even there to point to a "program" since the matter was confined to only one sentence, which was later included in Article VIII of the Constitution.

The Law on Diet Courts is the only significant penal enactment of the Four-Year Diet. It was passed 17 May 1791[19] as part of the aforementioned Principles to Reform the Government. This broad and innovative law was concerned not only with the structure of the court, but also with criminal procedure and, to a lesser degree, substantive criminal law. Included among others was a new systematization of political crimes. (The statute addressed only political crimes, since only these crimes were adjudicated by the Diet courts.) Treason was treated as a crime against the nation, while an insult to the king's majesty was a crime against the government of the Republic. Both legal changes fully reflected the postulates of the representatives of the humanitarian school concerning the need to transform certain typically feudal concepts of crime. This Law clearly incorporated the principles of *nullum crimen, nulla poena sine lege*, and eliminated all remnants of collective responsibility in the form of infamy for the entire family of a perpetrator of a most serious crime. The fact that all provisions of the Law were to be applied to the accused regardless of social status was an indication of new social awareness and of changes leading toward the liquidation of class distinctions. It is worth emphasizing the significant changes in the legislative technique. A conscious and well considered approach to the technical problems of the construction of laws is evident here. Where needed, the legislator provided legal definitions for terms used. Legal procedure was also regularized in a modern manner. Elements of public law, new to Polish law, were linked to the right of the accused to a defense, which was already well established in Poland. The right to counsel for the defendant was also maintained. The court was even obliged to appoint counsel, if the accused so requested. The principle of the openness of proceedings protected the rights of the accused. The principle *in dubio pro reo* (deciding cases where doubt existed in favor of the accused) accompanied the principle of the presumption of the accused's innocence, for which the humanitarians had strived so hard. A strong emphasis was placed on the principle of personal inviolability before sentencing (*neminem captivabimus*), which had already been applied to the landed gentry for centuries. Now however, this principle was to be applied to every accused regardless of his social status, which was another sign of a new consciousness in ideas about both judicial law and social issues. Thus, personal inviolability, which hitherto had been the jealously and closely guarded privilege of the nobility, became a principle of legal procedure. This was the transformation from class privilege to universal principle in court proceedings.

The Law on Diet Courts and the principles and solutions formulated therein had a limited application, however, since they only applied to the relatively few cases which were decided in the Diet courts. Nevertheless, they were an expression of a new direction in thinking and, as such, foreshadowed further changes in penal law.

Several of the later laws, passed after May 1791, contained only single, and usually procedural, provisions of penal law. As usual, these too were meant to ensure the security and just functioning of the courts, as well as to protect the rights of the accused to a defense and to insure his personal inviolability. Nonetheless, it would seem that one can observe two repeating elements emerging from the chaos of the penal legislation of the Four-Year Diet: the protection of the state and the protection of the individual and citizen.[20]

Article VIII of the Constitution of 3 May included an outline for the foreseen creation and implementation of a code of judiciary law, which was planned to be named after the King as the Code of Stanisław August. This outline is but one example of the existing idea to supplement the Constitution. Hugo Kołłątaj's vision of two further constitutions, one "economic" and one "moral," illustrates the notion of supplementing the political constitution. A code of judicial law was to follow the moral constitution. Moral statutes were to be the "principles" of good civil and penal laws, suggested Kołłątaj in his famous speech of 28 June 1791. In this speech Kołłątaj also demanded the convocation of a codification commission for the purpose of establishing the Code of Stanisław August.

From the available information about the relationship between moral statutes and civil and penal laws, it is evident that for Kołłątaj, moral statutes were the basis for a type of religious, patriotic, and civic education. These moral enactments were to "mold the character of a Pole," while the code of judicial law was to prevent any perversion of that character.[21] In this way the moral statutes were to be the very "principles" of the code. The code, in turn, was to be a safeguard, sanction, and protector of virtue for the moral statutes.

At the same time, Kołłątaj expressed the view that a code of civil and criminal laws was necessary for the happiness of the nation. Only good laws could lead the Republic away from its "old disorder." The moral statutes forming the character of the Pole were to make him "the perpetual defender of freedom." Thus, Kołłątaj reasoned, freedom was founded in personal security and the preservation of personal possessions. In this way, Kołłątaj presented both theoretical and practical goals to which the codifiers were to aspire: the assurance of happiness through the creation of a perfect code based upon moral principles; and, in practical terms, the fixing of the freedom of every citizen through the safeguarding of the inviolability of person and property. These were two assignments presented to the future codification commission and to the future code.

There was still one more point in Kołłątaj's instructions: a criticism of the present state of law along with practical suggestions for the codification commission. Both of the above elements are present in Kołłątaj's speech of 28 June, along with one further issue: Kołłątaj's fear that the codification of the law would be too radical for conservatives and even moderates. This must explain why Kołłątaj insisted that the new code couldn't be "styled as some novelty and ruin the provisions of the forefathers." Rather, it will be only a compilation of the old laws and the enactment of those that had been neglected.[22]

Kołłątaj's practical suggestions and criticism of the actual state of affairs emphasized the scattered nature of the laws and the intermingling of the various branches of law. To further prove his point of view, Kołłątaj suggested that the Łaski Statute (1506) and Lithuanian Statute (1588) should serve as examples, "in which only the order and method need to be improved, without any change in the text of the laws themselves, if they were in no way contrary to natural justice." The stipulation for natural justice indicates Kołłątaj's true intentions for the planned code. His mention of the need to mitigate punishments in accordance with the teachings of Beccaria, of the need to consider the "laws of foreign countries" and the laws of the free people of the American states, all further demonstrate his intentions. It seems, however, that Kołłątaj saw the possibility for the utilization of old laws through their correction. This is best illustrated by his positive attitude toward Antoni Trębicki's very simple compilation of the laws.

Contrary to the wishes of Kołłątaj, whose aim was the complete unification of Polish and Lithuanian laws, the Lithuanians, not wishing to part with their already excellent Statute, showed clearly separatist tendencies. As a result, on 28 June 1791, the Diet convened not one, but two separate codification commissions: one for Poland, and one for the Duchy of Lithuania. Kołłątaj was chosen to head the Polish commission. The other leaders of the Polish commission included: the poet, lawyer, and later minister of justice in the Kościuszko Uprising government, Józef Szymanowski; professor of Cracow University Józef Januszkiewicz; politician, political writer, playwright, and later author of the Polish anthem, Józef Wybicki and Franciszek Barss, the renowned lawyer and defender of the burghers' rights. The leaders of the Lithuanian commission included: the rector of Wilno University, Hieronim Stroynowski; the radical politician, deputy Józef Weyssenhoff; and finally, Antoni Trębicki, author of the just published compilation of Polish laws. In the field of criminal law, the proposals of Szymanowski and Weyssenhoff were the most notable. From the many available projects, some of which were even submitted from outside the commission, these two proposals distinguish themselves with up-to-date solutions. Legal codification, not unlike other reforms of the Four-Year Diet, including the Constitution, was carried out under the notion of compromise and "gentle revolution," a term which Kołłątaj had borrowed from Gaetano Filangieri's *"pacifica rivoluzione."* Unfortunately, all work on the Code of Stanisław August was interrupted by the Russian invasion. The preserved results of the commission's work, however, allow one to evaluate the committee's discussions as well as the drafts of the Code.[23]

Kołłątaj reasoned that civil, that is private, laws are established to "diligently guard the maintenance of justice among citizens." In the strict sense, civil law was to define "the obligations of one citizen toward another."[24] So stated, the idea of the equality of one citizen to another is emphasized. For the authors of the Code, private property had its basis and justification in natural law as well as in the social contract, and as a social contract was also perceived the Constitution of 3 May. Nevertheless, the division of citizens into estates was also in accordance with mankind's natural law.[25] Consequently, the relationship between lord and vassal was maintained in its feudal state. The law on obligations, however, gave a new definition to the labor law: labor was to be leased, i.e. manual labor was to be purchased. As a result of Poland's expanding economy, a new law on promissory notes was established by special statute in 1775 and was to be included in the Code of Stanisław August.

Equally notable was the very inclusion of the regulations of matrimonial law in the plans for the code. The basis of these regulations was founded in canon law, but formally, they were an independent part of secular law. The projected Code regulated every formal detail of marriage: its legality, separation, divorce and so on. These regulations were an effort at formal secularization of matrimonial law.

The proposals for the future Code, Szymanowski's for Poland and Weyssenhoff's for Lithuania, included the principle of equality in criminal law among their basic principles. This was to be a decisively new determination not only in its social ramifications, but also because it would cause the liquidation of the various systems of criminal law. From this point, the legislator would recognize only socially detrimental acts as criminal. The proposals emphasized that acts that were in no way socially harmful should not be prohibited. Szymanowski added that a crime was an act specifically prohibited by law. In this way the codifiers sought to realize in the Code one of the leading postulates of the Enlightenment for criminal law reform: the principle of *nullum crimen sine lege*. This principle was supported by the rule that a punishment for a committed offense could only be determined by law, that is, by the principle of *nulla poena sine lege*. So, customary law was completely excluded. Such actions were characteristic of the humanitarians, they strove for the removal of uncertainty and obscurity from the law.

The problem of punishment was central to the humanitarian movement of the Enlightenment. It was not as dramatically evident in Poland, mostly, as was mentioned earlier, because of the mild nature of Polish land law. The purpose of punishment, as stated in the proposals of Szymanowski and Weyssenhoff, was two-fold: first, the correction of the criminal, and second, the prevention of crime. In this way punishment became an instrument in the formation of people's attitudes and behavior as well as an instrument in the education of society. Punishment by the government was to preserve the law. The aim was to guarantee the happiness of society by inducing certain individual members to act in accordance with the principles of the laws of nature. Law was to assure prosperity and happiness.

The principle of the proportionality of punishment in relation to the crime, one of the leading principles of the humanitarian movement, was clearly formulated in both Szymanowski's Polish and Weyssenhoff's Lithuanian proposals. The magnitude of the penalty was to be dependent upon the injury to society incurred by the crime. At the same time, the proportionality of the penalty depended upon the degree of guilt (evil intent) of the perpetrator. All of these principles were reflected as much in the diversity of penalties, as in the rules of the meting out and execution of the punishments. In accordance with the ideals of European Enlightenment, the punishment must fit the crime.

Among the punishments proposed in the plans for codification, the most common were imprisonment and penalties affecting property. In the spirit of humanitarianism, it was decided that property fines should not leave the perpetrator destitute. The degree of the fine should be dependent not only upon the severity of the offense, but also upon the perpetrator's ability to pay. Here, Weyssenhoff went further in his humanitarian ideals than did Szymanowski, for he criticized the very concept of the wide application of pecuniary punishments. He indicated their negative side effects to the perpetrator's family and creditors, as well as the detrimental tendencies of the state treasury to abuse the application of such penalties for fiscal reasons. Both authors were absolutely opposed to a penalty of forfeiture of property. Therefore, this punishment was removed from the register of penalties on grounds very typical of the Enlightenment: this was a penalty that infringed upon the principle of individual responsibility because it affected to an equal degree the perpetrator as well as his family.

Imprisonment could result in the simple deprivation of liberty or could be combined with compulsory labor. Correctional labor was not an invention of the Enlightenment. However, the idea of correctional labor was supported by the humanitarians for a new reason: work resocializes the prisoner and at the same time is beneficial to society, which the perpetrator had harmed. The proposals emphasized that those responsible for the daily life of the prison must be ever mindful of the basic purpose of punishment, the rehabilitation of the criminal so that he may be returned to society morally healthy.

The death penalty, which was used in the pre-Enlightenment legal systems of Europe, was never widely applied in Poland. The traditional mildness of Polish land law was carried over to the Code of Stanisław August, though again with a new basis in contemporary ideals. In Szymanowski's proposal, capital punishment was applicable only in extreme cases. This sentence could only be imposed in those particular cases, where "preserving the criminal's life could pose a threat to society." The execution itself was to be carried out by very humanitarian means. By contrast, Weyssenhoff's more radical proposal for Lithuania called for the complete abolition of capital punishment. The author based his proposal on the conviction, in accordance with the principles of the social contract, that society has no right to take a human life.

In both proposals the circumstances influencing the degree of the penalty were divided into two categories: objective, taking into account the method, means, and time; and subjective, taking into account the guilt, motives, character, gender, age and recidivism of the perpetrator. The more radical Lithuanian plan interpreted higher birth, education and wealth as encumbering circumstances. The authors of these plans understood that:

the legislator cannot describe every instance, but rather should outline the general, theoretical rules, and the judge can later lessen or increase

the penalty prescribed by law according to the specific circumstances,
which either mitigate or aggravate the severity of the crime.

This solution, present in both codification projects, distinguished itself as
favorable to some of the European solutions, which attempted to enumerate
even the most minor circumstances and to regulate all possible sanctions. The
Law on Diet Courts and later Szymanowski's proposal for the Code both
contain a statutory command to differentiate between detainees awaiting trial
and sentenced prisoners. In both cases the same guiding principle is evident: a
detainee awaiting trial should be treated as if he were innocent, since that,
formally, is what he remains prior to sentencing. Clearly, pure humanitarianism
toward the individual deprived of liberty is not the only foundation for such
an outlook. The more important reason was the principle of the presumption
of innocence, which had been acknowledged as one of the leading principles
of procedure and also as one of the leading principles of legality in general.
This principle was further strengthened by the rule *in dubio pro reo.*

The presumption of innocence and *in dubio pro reo* appeared for the first
time in the Law on Diet Courts and then in the proposal for the Code. This
did not constitute any delay in the development of Polish law since only with
the Enlightenment European philosophers included both these principles
among their postulates for legal reform. There is no doubt, however, that in
the old Polish legal claims procedure, the maintenance of both of these
principles, and especially of the presumption of innocence to some extent,
became a necessity during the proceedings. The situation was exactly the
opposite in the inquisitional process of West European courts, where the
effective deprivation of the accused of the right to a defense essentially allowed
the prosecutor and judge to be one and the same. In Poland, the formulation
of the above-mentioned rules was not considered to be an immediate legal
need. The situation was different in the West, where the principle of the
presumption of innocence was raised to the rank of a natural and inalienable
right and therefore deemed worthy of its place in the Declaration of the Rights
of Man and Citizen.

The right to a defense, in its most general scope, as well as the right to
counsel for the defense (including an appointment by the court) and the right
to engage in procedural actions in preparation for a defense in judicial
proceedings had long and well-established traditions in Poland. It is, then,
entirely natural that these rights were maintained and even emphasized, not
only in the Law concerning Diet courts, but also in the projected Code of
Stanisław August. Polish legal solutions, even prior to the Great Diet, could

have served as models for other countries in terms of satisfying the requisites of humanitarian teachings. Among these model solutions was the principle of controlled judicial decisions in the due course of instances, that is the right to appeal a court decision, which was elevated to constitutional rank (Art. VIII, Constitution of 3 May). Also notable was the early and complete elimination of torture and all other methods of coercion in penal procedures.

In his project, Szymanowski maintained that even misleading questioning of the accused was intolerable. Szymanowski's project was the first to include an interdiction against swearing in the accused. Administering an oath binding the accused to tell the truth had already been criticized by Teodor Ostrowski, but at that time he had no allies. This issue only seems to be insignificant: what is important here is the humanitarian thought, which could perceive humanity even in the criminal and recognize that his natural fear of punishment leads him to lie, even if the punishment is justified. The leaders of the humanitarian school, i.e. Cesare Beccaria and Gaetano Filangieri, tried to solve such "contradictions of laws with the natural feelings of man"[26] in man's favor, even in the favor of the criminal-man and his "natural" feelings.

In short, in the proposed principles for the Code equality before the law and *nullum crimen, nulla poena sine lege* were included. The following were identified as the purposes of punishment: the correction of the offender, although not without the maintenance of general, as well as specific, preventive measures; the meting out of penalties proportioned to the offense; the utilitarianism of the punishment; the limiting of the scope of the system of penalties; a change in the order of penalties in accordance with new humanitarian trends; the liquidation of (in Weyssenhoff), or limitation to, a minimal usage of the death penalty; and the change in the nature of punishment from private law to public law punishment.

Weyssenhoff did not leave any proposed plan regarding the criminal process, or rather none has been found to date. By comparison, Szymanowski's proposal reflects a significant degree of acceptance of the solutions presented in the Law on Diet Courts from May 1791. The criminal procedure adopted in May 1791 closely resembled the mixed procedure[27] used in Poland today.

Szymanowski's and Weyssenhoff's proposals were accepted as the basis for further works on the Code, and although very modern, included some thoughts inherited from Polish law of the previous centuries.

The very long-standing privilege of personal inviolability *neminem captivabimus nisi iure victum* had already been in force in Poland for centuries when the Western humanitarians took up the battle for personal inviolability and that principle was being proclaimed by the French Declaration of the

Rights of Man and Citizen. While in Poland this fifteenth- century privilege had feudal limitations since it only concerned the landed nobility, the demands of the humanitarians categorically called for a general principle of equality before the law. The postulates of the philosophers and lawyers of the West were a result of their dramatic experiences with the brutality of justice not experienced by the proponents of reform in Poland. However, they knew from practical experience how the principle of personal inviolability diminishes the effectiveness of penal reprisals, especially toward the magnates. It is no surprise, then, that many deputies were calling for limiting the protective powers of the principle of personal inviolability even before the convocation of the codification commissions. The case of Adam Poniński is the best known example: though the facts of his treason were well proved, specific grounds for overturning the protection of personal inviolability were sought.[28]

Parallel to demands for an objective limiting of personal inviolability, demands for its subjective widening became evident. These demands concerned the burghers, who were covered by the principle of *neminem captivabimus* in the Law on Cities (18 April 1791), and the Jews, who were included under the protection of this privilege by the Police Commission in 1792. In due time, the reformers would demand that the privilege be extended to the peasants, who were supposed to become citizens. However, this was a demand to which the Diet would not agree. It was, of course, true that such reform was completely unrealistic for the second half of the eighteenth century, but only as long as the principle of personal inviolability remained a privilege, and a privilege of the nobility, and not a principle of legal procedure.[29]

This breach had already been achieved by the Law on Diet Courts. In accordance with Kołłątaj's ideas, this Law stated the universal principle of personal inviolability (with a guarantee) with respect to all those brought to trial by the terms of the Law. In the Szymanowski version of the proposed Code of Stanisław August, the principle of personal inviolability is stated for the first time as a general principle of criminal procedure and not as a privilege.[30] In so doing, Szymanowski formulated a universal principle of personal inviolability.

Attempts to keep up with the most advanced ideas on reform in Europe were evident in Poland. However, the specifically Polish historical experience and actual circumstances were rather different from those described in the ideas of the western philosopher-humanitarians. The Poles were trying to save the democratic state and, at the same time, utilize criminal law codes to attain their goal. The reformers foresaw the need to limit the objective power of personal inviolability in order to ensure the effective functioning of their criminal law. On the other hand, the transformation of the principle of personal inviolability from noble privilege to a universal principle of procedure is also visible.

If one were to compare the principles on which the Code was based with those principles proclaimed in the American Declaration of Independence and the French Declaration of the Rights of Man and Citizen, it would become evident that the Code states everything that the Americans and French pledged in their declarations with the exception of *lex retro non agit*. However, a closer analysis of the whole would reveal that even the rule of *lex retro non agit* was maintained in Szymanowski's project.

The philosophers of the Enlightenment wished to create a perfect code, one which was in conformity with an ideal code, the code of natural law, so as to bring happiness to humanity. The Polish thinkers of the Enlightenment shared in this goal, although it would seem that their practical attitude kept them closely focused on the complicated realities present in Poland. The American Declaration of Independence and the French Declaration of the Rights of Man and Citizen proclaimed that the rights of man were self-evident, natural, inalienable and sacrosanct. The general direction of the Polish reform of criminal law coincided with the epoch's tendencies toward the humanization of laws, the reconciliation of legal codes to the natural laws, modernization, and codification. This consistency clearly manifested itself, although the point of departure was different in Poland when compared with countries governed by absolutism. Some of the almost revolutionary innovations of the West, such as the widely recognized right to a defense and personal inviolability, among others, had long been acknowledged and respected principles of Polish land law. These principles only needed to be modified to conform with the Enlightenment idea of the equality of men.

The possibility of continuing the tradition of Polish land law, if only in part, was a particularly reassuring feature in Poland's political circumstances. The Polish nobility was conservative in its attitude toward tradition, the "true law of the forefathers," and it was suspicious of innovations. Generally speaking, the ability to establish a new legal system without having to resort to the utter destruction of the old system seems to have some merit.

An analysis of the legal reforms in Poland during the Four-Year Diet reveals two clearly new, significant innovations: equality before the law, and a re-evaluation of the aims of penalties and, as a consequence, of the system and catalogue of punishments. Both of these reforms were first introduced in the plans for the Code of Stanisław August, but there was no time to put the Code into practice. However, equality before the law was already introduced in part by the Law on Diet Courts, but of course only in cases applicable to this court.

The concurrence of the old principles and traditions of Polish law with the modern postulates of the Western philosophers of the Enlightenment who fought for the freedom of the individual and citizen, can be explained by the fact that the Polish-Lithuanian Commonwealth had realized much earlier the concept of the citizen, as well as the freedom of the individual. Namely, it was this freedom, known as "golden freedom," which was the treasure so highly prized by the Polish nobility. Freedom required many safeguards, including the realm of criminal law. Consequently, these safeguards, now known as the guarantees of the rights of the accused (defendant, suspect), had already been utilized by Poles long before the Declaration of Independence or the Declaration of the Rights of Man and Citizen. It was no accident that the state was a "Republic." However, it was exclusively a nobleman's republic, and the Enlightenment demanded that the discrepancy be corrected. The Great Diet in its final stages tried to achieve this goal.

The specific character of law and its reform during the reign of Stanisław August was not just the result of the tradition of Polish law and its moderate nature, though it stemmed from different sources than the postulates of the humanitarians. These differences were also the result of the political and international situation of the Commonwealth, on the brink of destruction by its neighboring absolutists' powers. Consequently, criminal law was utilized as a safeguard to the state and its political system, and the freedom of its citizens. Both the Law on Diet Courts and the penal regulations on the protection of diets and dietines were dedicated to this cause, to the protection of democratic representative institutions. On the whole, this was the essential component of all of the penal regulations ratified in the four-year session of the Great Diet.

There was another consequence to this dramatic situation of the state: if the state was to be saved, its political leaders could no longer afford the luxury of theoretical discussions. Instead, they had to search out those ideas that could realistically be put into practice. These circumstances are the main reason why practical aspects dominated concepts of reform in Polish laws.

The reforms included in the plans of the Code of Stanisław August could not be implemented. The work of the Code and the whole work of the Diet was interrupted by the Russian invasion. However, it is important to remember that during the Uprising of 1794, under the leadership of Tadeusz Kościuszko, an extensive and greatly humanitarian reform of penal law was enacted. This included reform of the legislation as well as administration of justice. The principle of equality before the law was invoked for the first time in Poland and Lithuania. The determining factor in criminal behavior was the harm caused to society. The innovative principles of *nullum crimen sine lege* and *nullum poena sine lege* were both strictly enforced. The proportionality of the punishment to the severity of the crime was emphasized; the burden of collective liability was dismissed; the importance of resocialization as a goal of punishment was raised. The death penalty was retained; however, it was applied very rarely, given the military and revolutionary nature of the times. Criminal procedure became a typically mixed process. It is noteworthy that during the process of an investigation and the administration of justice, the accused was treated very humanely. The organization of a completely new legal system was included, in the duties of Józef Szymanowski, the head of the department of justice. The introduction of laws and legal practices in the spirit of humanitarianism in such unfavorable conditions is one of the most fulfilling moments in the annals of European criminal law in the decisive Enlightenment period.[31] Without the many previous reforms in eighteenth-century Poland, this would have been impossible.

Notes

1. Jan Krasnodębski, *Mowa na sesji sejmowej (3 maja 1790)* (A speech at a session of the Diet) (n.p.).

2. Józef Konstanty Bogusławski, *O doskonałym prawodawctwie czyli o pożytkach wydoskonalonej edukacji narodowej* (On improved legislation, or on the usefulness of improved national education) (Warszawa, 1786), p. 47, see also p. 11, passim; Irena Malinowska-Kwiatkowska, "Humanitarian Concepts and Ideas in Polish Publications on Legal Questions before the Partitions," Adam Lityński, "The Struggle for Reform of Polish Criminal Law and Procedure in the Years 1776-1794" in *Humanitarian traditions of the Polish criminal procedure,* ed. Stanisław Waltoś, Zeszyty Naukowe Uniwersytetu Jagiellońskiego. Prace Prawnicze, no. 102, (Warszawa-Kraków: PWN, 1983); Adam Lityński, "Myśl humanitarna w Polsce czasów Oświecenia. Prawo karne materialne." (Humanitarian thought in Poland during the Enlightenment. Substantive criminal law) in *Z dziejów sądów i prawa.* Prace naukowe Uniwersytetu Śląskiego no. 1277 (Katowice, 1992), pp. 65-83.

3. Concerning the period preceding the Four-Year Diet, see Bogusław Leśnodorski, "Beccaria w Polsce XVIII wieku" (Beccaria in 18th-century Poland), *Nauka Polska,* 3 (1965): 45 ff.; Adam Lityński, "Problem kary śmierci w Polsce 1764-1794. Z badań nad historią polskiej myśli prawniczej" (Problems of the death penalty in Poland 1764-1794. Research concerning the history of Polish legal thought), *Czasopismo Prawno-Historyczne* 2 (1988): 269, passim, further sources and literature included.

4. Zbigniew Zdrójkowski, *Teodor Ostrowski (1750-1802) pisarz dawnego polskiego prawa sądowego* (Teodor Ostrowski writer of old Polish judicial law) (Warszawa: Wyd. Prawnicze, 1956) pp. 187, 189, 190-198, 279.

5. Zbigniew Zdrójkowski, "Prace naukowe Sebastiana Czochrona z dziedziny procesu i prawa karnego (1788-1790)" (Sebastian Czochron's studies on criminal procedure and criminal law) in *Miscellanea juridica złożone w darze Karolowi Koranyjemu w czterdziestolecie pracy naukowej* (Warszawa: PWN, 1961), p. 191 ff.

6. Zbigniew Zdrójkowski, "Tomasz Kuźmirski nieznany osiemnastowieczny polski prawnik humanitarysta i jego pisma..." (Tomasz Kuźmirski, an unknown 18th-century Polish jurist-humanitarian, and his writings), *Czasopismo Prawno-Historyczne* VII, 2 (1955): pp. 150 ff.

7. Polish land law *(prawo polskie ziemskie)*: each social estate had its own separate system of law. The most important was so-called Polish law, or land law, i.e., the law of the noble estate.

8. System of composition *(system kompozycyjny)*: from the Latin *compositio*, meaning an arrangement, agreement, accommodation. This system in criminal law has enjoyed a very long tradition: in the early Middle Ages a person wronged by a crime and the crime's perpetrator could come to an agreement. The perpetrator would pay a certain amount of money (an indemnity [*nawiązka*] for wounds, and head-money [*główszczyzna*] paid to the family of the victim for his head) to the injured party. This was called a penalty of accommodation, and as such was private in nature, although it was imposed by a state court.

9. Criminal procedure in Polish land law was a private-action process. This means that the state authorities essentially left to private persons the instituting of an inquiry of proceedings and investigation in court. Actually, there were no public institutions specialized in providing these services. The criminal procedure had the characteristics of private claims and was ruled largely by elements of private law, not public law.

10. Katarzyna Sójka-Zielińska, "Wiek XVIII - wiekiem kodyfikacji" (The 18th century - a century of codification) in *Wiek XVIII: Polska i świat*. Dedicated to Bogusław Leśnodorski. Andrzej Zahorski, ed. (Warszawa: PIW, 1974), p. 269.

11. See Juliusz Bardach, "Statuty litewskie w ich kręgu prawno-kulturowym" (The Lithuanian statutes in their legal and cultural context) in *O dawnej i niedawnej Litwie* (Poznań: Wyd. Uniw. im. A. Mickiewicza, 1988), p. 9 ff.

12. See Ewa Borkowska-Bagieńska, *Zbiór praw sądowych Andrzeja Zamoyskiego* (Collection of judicial laws by Andrzej Zamoyski) (Poznań: Wyd. Uniw. im. A. Mickiewicza, 1986), p. 237 ff.

13. *Volumina legum. Prawa, konstytucye y przywileie Królestwa Polskiego, Wielkiego Xięstwa Litewskiego y wszystkich Prowincyi należących* (The laws, constitutions and privileges of the Kingdom of Poland, the Grand Duchy of Lithuania and all Provinces) (Kraków, 1889), vol. 9, p. 58. Referred to hereafter as *VL*.

14. *VL,* vol. 9, p. 158.

15. *VL,* vol. 9, p. 203; see also Adam Lityński, *Sejmiki ziemskie 1764-1793. Dzieje reformy* (Local dietines 1764-1793. The history of their reform) (Katowice: Wyd. Uniw. Śląskiego, 1988), p. 89.

16. *VL,* vol. 9, pp. 203-204, 214, 216.

17. *VL,* vol 9, pp. 239, 265; Adam Lityński, *Przestępstwa polityczne w polskim prawie karnym XVI-XVIII wieku* (Political crimes in Polish criminal law in the 16th-18th centuries) (Katowice: Wyd. Uniw. Śląskiego, 1976), pp. 97-121; Lityński, *Sejmiki ziemskie,* pp. 106, 128.

18. Emanuel Rostworowski, "Marzenie dobrego obywatela czyli królewski projekt konstytucji" (The dream of a good citizen or the royal constitutional proposal) in *Legendy i fakty XVIII w.* (Warszawa: PWN, 1963), p. 448.

19. MS. Archiwum Główne Akt Dawnych w Warszawie, Akta Sejmu Czteroletniego, no. 19, pp. 224-234; see *Dziennik Czynności sejmu głównego ordynaryjnego warszawskiego pod związkiem konfederacji Obojga Narodów agitującego się 1791* (The daily report of the main ordinary Warsaw Diet constituted under the confederation of the Two Nations held in 1791), part IV, no page numeration, dietary session no. 427, 17 May 1791; *VL,* vol. 9, pp. 243-249.

20. Adam Lityński, "Tradycje i nowości w ustawodawstwie karnym Sejmu Czteroletniego (ze szczegółowym uwzględnieniem projektu Kodeksu Stanisława Augusta)" (Traditions and novelties in the criminal legislation of the Four-Year Diet with special emphasis on the proposal of the Stanisław August Code) in *Konstytucja 3 maja Prawo-polityka-symbol,* Anna Grześkowiak-Krwawicz, ed. (Warszawa: Polskie Tow. Historyczne, 1992).

21. *Kodeks Stanisława Augusta. Zbiór dokumentów* (Code of Stanisław August. A collection of documents), Stanisław Borowski, ed. (Warszawa, 1938), pp. 11, 14. Referred to hereafter as *KSA.*

22. *KSA,* pp 9-19; see also Hugo Kołłątaj, *Listy Anonima i Prawo polityczne narodu polskiego* (Anonymous letters and Political law of the Polish nation), Bogusław Leśnodorski and Helena Wereszycka, eds. (Warszawa: PWN, 1954), vol. 1, pp 355, 366, vol. 2, pp. 111, 215, 222, 253; *VL,* vol. 9, p. 289.

23. Adam Lityński, "Prawo karne w projekcie Kodeksu Stanisława Augusta" (Criminal law in the proposal of the Stanisław August Code), Acta Universitatis Wratislaviensis, 234, *Przegląd Prawa i Administracji,* V (1974): 177 ff.

24. *KSA,* pp. 11,17.

25. Alfred Ohanowicz, Zbigniew Radwański, "Ostatnia próba kodyfikacji prawa cywilnego w Rzeczypospolitej szlacheckiej. *Kodeks Stanisława Augusta.* " (The last attempt at the codification of civil law in the Commonwealth of nobles (The Code of Stanisław August)), *Państwo i Prawo* VII, 11 (1952): 675-676; see also Zbigniew

Radwański, Jan Wąsicki, "Najważniejsze zmiany w polskim prawie cywilnym w okresie Oświecenia" (Main changes in Polish law during the Enlightenment), *Czasopismo Prawno-Historyczne, 4* (1952): 56, 73.

26. Cesare Beccaria, *On Crimes and Punishments,* trans. David Young (Indianapolis: Hackett, 1986), p. 49. The first Polish translation of this work dates to 1772. There is a great volume of literature on the subject of Beccaria and the humanitarians, see Marcello T. Maestro, *Voltaire and Beccaria as Reformers of Criminal Law* (New York: Columbia University Press, 1942); *Cesare Beccaria and the Origins of Penal Reform* (Philadelphia: Tempa Univ. Press,1973).

27. Mixed procedure: a procedure originating from the combination of investigative elements with the elements of a complaint suit. First, the investigative elements dominate and then, in the second phase (before the court), the complaint elements. This type of procedure was developed at the turn of the eighteenth century. In Europe it mostly spread as a result of the French code concerning criminal proceedings of 1808. It is used in Poland to this day.

28. Adam Poniński, grand Under-Treasurer of the Crown, a traitor serving the countries responsible for the partition of Poland, Marshall of the Diet in 1773-75, during which the First Partition was ratified; tried in 1789-90 for treason by the Diet court and sentenced. Great efforts were taken to find extraordinary reasons to justify his temporary arrest, among which was the suggestion that the principle of *neminem captivabimus* binds the king and the municipal councils but not the Diet, which is the personification of the entire nation.

29. Marian Mikołajczyk, "Z badań nad zagadnieniem nietykalności osobistej w okresie Sejmu Czteroletniego" (Research concerning personal inviolability during the Four-Year Diet) in *W dwusetną rocznicę wolnego Sejmu. Ludzie - państwo - prawo czasów Sejmu Czteroletniego.* ed. Adam Lityński (Katowice: Wyd. Uniw. Śląskiego, 1988), pp. 146, 149, passim.; see also Lityński, "Podstawowe gwarancje praw oskarżonego w polskim procesie karnym po Konstytucji 3 maja" (Basic guarantees of the rights of the defendant in Polish criminal legal proceedings after the Constitution of 3 May) in *Pierwsza w Europie. 200 rocznica Konstytucji 3 maja 1791-1991,* ed. Henryk Kocój (Katowice: Wyd. Uniw. Śląskiego, 1989), p. 93, passim.

30. *KSA,* p. 207.

31. Adam Lityński, *Proces karny insurekcji 1794* (Legal proceedings of the 1794 Insurrection) (Wrocław: Wyd. Uniw. Śląskiego, 1983), passim.; *Sądy i prawo w powstaniu kościuszkowskim* (Courts and law during the Kościuszko uprising) (Wrocław: Ossolineum, 1988), *passim.*

Translated by Beata Pawlikowska

An allegory commemorating the first anniversary of the Constitution of 3 May 1791, aquatint by Friedrich T.M. John acc. to a drawing by Franciszek Smuglewicz 1791. (Muzeum Narodowe w Warszawie). Photo E. Gawryszewska.

18

Citizen, Nation, Constitution:
The Realization and Failure of the Constitution of 3 May, 1791
in Light of Mutual Polish-French Influence

Jörg K. Hoensch

In *De la Pologne* published in Paris in 1839, the radical democrat François V. Raspail put forward the view that the intellectual current of Ancient Roman legal thought that had been revived by humanism gained ideological significance for the French Enlightenment and the Revolution of 1789 only through Polish transmission. In this process he ascribed a key role to Jan Zamoyski, a statesman, military commander, learned humanist, and constitutional theorist, who, as author of the treatise *De Senatu Romano* and coauthor of *Dialectica Ciceronis* and as founder of the Academy of Zamość, had applied republican ideas derived from Roman constitutional history to the political life of Renaissance Poland.[1] Raspail attempted to derive Rousseau's *volonté générale* from Zamoyski's principle of *communis consensus* when he had him say to Henri de Valois: *"... nous sommes tous nobles égaux, nous ne formons tous qu'un seul corps; toutes nos volontés individuelles composent la volonté général"* (p. 52). Raspail asserted further that during their stay in Poland in 1573 Henri de Valois and his entourage were "infected" with the ideas of equality, liberty, and fraternity such that this influence remained active in France to 1789: *"la peste qu'il nous rapporta de Pologne gagna la royauté française en 1789"* (p. 53).

Although this genesis of the leading slogans of the French Revolution today seems questionable, the secret of the democratic structure of the Polish nation of nobles rested on Zamoyski's comparison of the nobility with the *civis Romanus* of the Roman republic. More essential, of course, was that the heritage of the formal equality of all nobles within the gentry republic was retained and enriched into the last years of the eighteenth century. Until 1791 there were no *de jure* differences of rank among the approximately 725,000 nobles of the "royal republic." The "equality" and "liberty" (*równość i wolność*) of all members of the sovereign nation of nobles remained such a self-evident legal principle that the many attempts of the *possessionati* to exclude the landless plebeian nobles from the active and passive electorate remained unsuccessful up to the Law on Dietines and the Constitution of 3 May 1791. Thus, the nation of nobles, despite some residual traits of feudal orders and despite its differentiated social strata, constituted neither a governing caste nor an aristocracy but rather a self-contained legal corporation. The equality and liberty of all nobles found their original moral-political substantiation in the idea of "brotherhood" (*braterstwo*), which rested on the higher ethical obligation which noble birth entailed in relation to other estates and an equal obligation within the nation of nobles. Thus, at least theoretically, a consistent *communis consensus* in political decisions had to be maintained among the *tota communitas* of the nation of nobles, which stood over the republic as guardian, protector, and sovereign. All these elements gave the nation of nobles, at least in its internal structure, a thoroughly democratic character. The poorest plebeian from the *gołota* could proudly claim the same civil and political rights as the magnates, who in status, possessions, and power, if not in noble rights, were the equal of the German imperial princes. So deeply were these principles anchored in the consciousness of the people of Poland that they became proverbial: "the nobleman on his estate is the equal of the voivode" (*szlachcic na zagrodzie równy wojewodzie*).

For a nation of nobles, which could regard only the commonality and equality of political rights as a binding criterion, the use of the title of "citizen" was not merely a natural decision but rather a proudly proclaimed and jealously guarded right. Only the nobleman could adorn himself with the rank of "citizen" (*obywatel*), for only this designation symbolized political rights and thereby his belonging to the sovereign nation. This never-forgotten, at most partially repressed, consciousness of noble citizenship received a powerful new stimulus in the middle of the eighteenth century from the Enlightenment, especially from the penetration of the *citoyen* concept of the Encyclopedists. Further, the Enlightenment fashion of reaching back to the forms of the Roman republic at the same time furthered reflection on the Poles' own Roman-republican traditions integrated during the Renaissance. As demonstrated in the work *Głos wolny wolność ubezpieczający²* of 1749 that has been attributed to the emigré King Stanisław Leszczyński³, the ideas of the Enlightenment that were new to Europe–those of "liberty," "equality," "democracy," and *res publica*–were long comprehended in the nation of nobles, albeit recently in a degenerate form. All the more ruthlessly could he attack the sickly political conditions of the Republic as he was able to preach the return to the old civic "virtues and talents," to the reformed "true" Republic.⁴ For him, accordingly, the question of the formation of the Polish nation, which the Enlightenment regarded as decisive, was already solved by the existence of citizenship.

A little later, in 1763, the Piarist Stanisław Konarski attempted to rouse the old civic pride by bluntly translating the ethically binding *civis Romanus sum* as "I am a Polish nobleman."⁵ In his *Uwagi nad życiem Jana Zamoyskiego*, of 1787, Stanisław Staszic praised the noble virtues because they had been considered Roman and republican since the times of the great Chancellor.⁶ With this work Staszic opened a lively discussion of Zamoyski and the principles he represented.⁷ Both the reformist and conservative factions of the Four-Year Diet–and here they outdid the contemporary French constitutional theorists–used the conceptual world of the ancient republic as the arsenal of their terminology. The senators were referred to as *patres conscripti*, the deputies as *tribuni plebis*; while Hugo Kołłątaj attributed the *corona civica (korona obywatelska)* to the civic sense of community,⁸ his opponent Seweryn Rzewuski posed as the "archtribune of the republic"⁹ and its old unrestricted liberties.¹⁰

The strength and broad appeal of the reform ideas discussed in Poland and the patriotism that sprang from them, the natural sensibility of a community of free citizens with equal rights, entered the cosmopolitan world of the Enlightenment after the Confederation of Bar of 1768. Rousseau's *Considérations*,¹¹ written under the influence of the Sarmatian-Roman concepts of the Bar Confederation, can well be regarded "as one of the first manifestoes of integral nationalism."¹² Regarding Poland, Rousseau stood rather alone in his positive, not always accurate, evaluation of the Polish political system. (King Stanisław August Poniatowski called the *Considérations* "the most beautiful political novel about Poland.)"¹³ Most contemporary foreign observers, under the influence of the ruthless self-criticism of the Poles, tended to regard degeneration and disease as the decisive criteria of the Polish Republic. Judgments such as that of James Madison that Poland combined "aristocracy and monarchy in their worst forms"¹⁴ accurately portrayed much of the praxis without reaching the essence of the Polish political system. Even Alphonse de Lamartine, who was deeply concerned about the Polish question, termed the nation of nobles an "aristocracy without a people" and revised his judgment only when Zygmunt Krasiński put to him the rhetorical question: "one million electors, each of whom can become a representative, a senator, or even king–is that an aristocracy without a nation?"[15] More justified was the critique directed at those aspects of the Polish polity in which the welfare state of Enlightened absolutism was clearly superior, such as in the promotion of the urban and peasant estates. Through the weakening of the king and the establishment of noble sovereignty that had made the king a "first oligarch," the non-noble estates were robbed of their natural protector, and thus disappeared the highest independent authority that alone could have hindered the identification of noble interests with those of the entire nation. The unsatisfactory political and social situation of the peasantry and urban population in comparison with those of France, Prussia, or the Habsburg Monarchy essentially resulted from the omnipotence of the Polish nobility.

The peculiar characteristic of the history of the Polish-Lithuanian Union from Krewa in 1385 to 1791 was the fact that the governing noble class proceeded after the Polish-Lithuanian Union of Lublin in 1569 from a purely personal, monarchical union to a real constitutional one, which had a solid foundation in a broad social union. This was a social union of the nobles of all historical-ethnic regions into the corporate body of the nation of nobles. Poland was the first state in Europe to raise the principles of religious, and beyond that national, or rather prenational, tolerance to a fundament of its political system. In the course of the eighteenth century, the governing estates developed into a Polish-speaking state-nation, which stretched over nine-tenths of the state's territory in 1791. The fusion of the higher estates into a national society united by language and culture resulted primarily from common rights, liberties, and privileges. The non-Polish nobility, as well as the townspeople, had already assimilated by 1648, at least in language. By 1791 the result was impressive: of the approximately 2.1 million nobles, bourgeois, and yeomen who played the central role in the establishment of civil society, over 80 percent were Polish speakers. The higher and more privileged the rank of an estate in the social hierarchy, the more complete was its linguistic and cultural Polonization.[16]

Around 1770 Baroque Sarmatism, which was the dominant Catholic and proto-national tendency until the Confederation of Bar, found a kind of connection with French rationalism, although, of course, it shared neither its original cosmopolitan tendency nor its anticlerical passion. The fruit of this synthesis of Catholic with secular and Enlightenment ideas was a powerful, deeply historically rooted state patriotism. The developing civil society drew on the most convinced carriers of patriotic ideas from the nobility, the middle

UWAGI
NAD RZĄDEM
POLSKIM
oraz nad Odmianą, czyli Reformą
onego projektowaną.

przez

J. JAKUBA RUSSO.

OBYWATELA GENEWENSKIEGO.

z Francuzkiego na Oyczyſty ięzyk przełożone,

Mieſiąca Grudnia dnia 20. R. 1788.

CZĘŚĆ I.

Cena w oprawie alla ruſtica zł. 1. gr. 22 ½

w WARSZAWIE, 1789.
Nakładem i Drukiem MICHAŁA GRÖLLA,
Kſięgarza Nadwornego J. K. Mci.

Uwagi nad rządem Polskim oraz nad Odmianą, czyli Reformą onego projektowaną
przez J. Jakuba Russo.... w Warszawie, M. Gröll, 1789. Title page of the Polish
translation of Jean Jacques Rousseau, *Considérations sur le Gouvernement de Pologne*
et sur sa réformation projetée. (Biblioteka Narodowa, Warszawa).

LA VOIX LIBRE

DU CITOYEN,

OU

OBSERVATIONS

SUR

LE GOUVERNEMENT

DE POLOGNE.

PREMIERE PARTIE.

M. DCC. LXIV.

(Stanisław Leszczyński), *La voix libre du citoyen, ou Observations sur le gouvernement de Pologne* n.p. 1764. (Indiana University Library). Previously published in 1749, 1753 and also in the many editions of the *Oeuvres du philosophe bienfaisant.*

classes, the yeomanry, and especially from the ethnically mixed provinces. The unity of the Polish cultural nation was taken for granted by the supporters of the reform of 1791. Thus Franciszek Salezy Jezierski could aptly define the concept of the nation for the Poles: "Nation–this is a union of people who have a common language, customs, and manners, a union that comprises common and general legislation for all citizens."[17] His reference to language in no way sprang from an early breath of Romantic sensibilities; he meant only the *lingua nationalis* as the idiom of civil society. Therefore, the united national existence of the *societas civilis* of the Poles remained vital in the national consciousness of its bearers. The most striking evidence of the unitary character of this nation was that it designated itself not as a "society" in a pluralistic sense but rather as a "community" (*towarzystwo*); the modern term *społeczeństwo* as a designation for the social formation replaced the older *towarzystwo* (actually, "association" in the sense of the *societas civilis*) only in the middle of the nineteenth century. Under these conditions it could not be doubted that the civil society of the Polish Republic toward the end of the eighteenth century formed that *nation une et indivisible* that so impressively demonstrated its unity after the final partition of the state territory.

No national consciousness was present among the non-Polish-speaking peoples of Poland before 1795; even the elementary preconditions of an independent national identity were lacking. For the nobility, on the other hand, the commitment to Polish as a native language, to Polish culture and history and thus to the Polish nation was self-evident, although the old differentiation between *gens* and *natio* was still in general use at the time of the partitions and the conventional formulation of *gente Ruthenus, natione Polonus* still enjoyed undisputed recognition. Language was thereby regarded not as the essential characteristic of nationality but only as an emblem of social rank; that Polish was the "lords' language" and Ruthenian, Lithuanian, and Latvian were "peasant languages," while Yiddish was the idiom of a large part of the urban population, was a natural occurrence for the thinking of the time. Polish thus became the *lingua nationalis;* the non-Polish languages were regarded as *linguae vulgares.* "Nation" (*naród*) could mean the entire Republic as well as the lands of the Polish Crown, on the one hand, and those of the Grand Duchy of Lithuania, on the other. In view of the diversity of ethnic, linguistic, religious, and estate structures and of the frequent changes of state territory, the uniting principle of the aggregate Polish nation consisted of a common history, which was politically and culturally represented by the Polish governing class. Thus, in the period of its decline, Poland must be defined, at least as an ideal type, as a "historic nation." At that time, the designation of "nation" became binding for the entire territory of Poland through the renewed union of Lithuania and the lands of the Crown of 20 October 1791, which reformed the Commonwealth of Two Nations *(Rzeczpospolita Obojga Narodów)* and especially strengthened the "united and indivisible Republic."

In spite of everything, from 1573 to 1789 Poland could claim to be the only territorial state in Europe in which the "nation" practiced a constitutionally established democracy. According to the ideas and social-political configurations common at that time, the republic was to be classified simply as a democracy as such, not merely as a democracy within the ruling class. It may be debated whether the republic bore the greatest democratic potency, the greatest ability to extend civic democracy to broader social spheres and eventually to the entire populace. In any event, for the era up to the beginning of the French Revolution, Krasiński was thoroughly justified when he wrote his friend Lamartine that the Polish constitution was "the most magnificent democracy that has ever been realized in Europe."[18] The civic-patriotic mentality not only remained active in Poland until the Constitution of 1791 but also was transferred through Rousseau to France up to the revolution, to Robespierre, and even to Fichte.[19] The Polish elements in their constitutional thinking, especially the connection between civil-political rights and patriotism, were not infrequently so self-evident to the heirs of the French revolutionaries of 1789 that they–as with Adolphe Thiers or F. V. Raspail–occasionally exaggerated this intellectual inheritance.

The Contents of the Patriotic Reform Movement

The discussions of reform that were undertaken in Poland in the mid-eighteenth century endeavored to grasp the problems of state and society in their totality and, along with historical analysis, to reveal ways to limit the "excess of liberty" (Leszczyński) and to terminate the general condition of anarchy and powerlessness.[20] The most important demands put forward were the abolition or at least restriction of the *liberum veto,* the modernization of the administration and the establishment of new central authorities, state support for trade and manufacture, the protection and opportunity for development of the cities and peasantry, and the foundation of an educational system open to a broad section of the public. After the shock of the First Partition of 1772, the establishment of the Permanent Council *(Rada Nieustająca,* 1775)[21] as the central organ of government and the founding of the Commission for National Education (*Komisja Edukacji Narodowej,* 1773)[22] created the prerequisites for the consolidation of the reform movement.

Especially the ideas of the French Enlightenment–transmitted in part by young Polish nobles, great numbers of whom became acquainted with West European conditions through their studies or through travel–were integrated and adapted to Polish conditions. At his court King Stanisław August Poniatowski sought to gather a circle of enlightened thinkers who agreed on the general tendency of the renewal but not on all specific questions and methods.[23] This initiative found resonance primarily among representatives of the middle and lower nobility, among whom many were clerics descended from the impoverished gentry. This circle was not as numerous or important as that of France, but it did boast an abundance of political talent.[24] The members of this circle belonged thoroughly–and here is also a certain parallel to the politicians of the French Revolution–to the relatively young generation that was born around the middle of the century.

Distinguished among them were Józef Wybicki, a deputy in the Diet, and especially Hugo Kołłątaj, who in 1788 gathered a circle of younger intellectuals in his "Forge" (*"Kuźnica Kołłątajowska"*);[25] not to mention Franciszek Salezy Jezierski, Franciszek Ksawery Dmochowski, Antoni Trębicki, and Jan Dembowski. Alongside these radicals of the lower nobility stood members of the townspeople such as the Warsaw city president Jan Dekert, who was actually of greater importance as a practical politician than as a constitutional theorist, and his associate, the lawyer and politician Franciszek Barss, but especially Stanisław Staszic, who had provided the opening contribution to the constitutional debate in his *Uwagi nad życiem Jana Zamoyskiego.*[26]

So penetrating was the general desire for reform of the political system at its root and branch that it had even seized the thoroughly noble officer corps. Tadeusz Kościuszko devoted himself to the idea of patriotic-democratic reform. As engineer-general in the American Revolutionary War and as fortifier of Saratoga and West Point, he had won great fame, and finally in 1789 he took a military post again as major-general in the Polish army and became a demigod for many younger officers.[27] Next to him and his moderate views, the brilliant officer Jakub Jasiński, who, like Kościuszko, came from the Cadets' Corps and who later gained national fame as the liberator of Wilno in 1794, was considered a burning adherent of the French Revolution.[28] The same could be said of the young Prince Józef Sułkowski–who later demonstrated his republican convictions as political confidant of Carnot in the French Army of Italy in 1796 and as Napoleon's adjutant. Thus, the reform movement was embraced by and ranged from the landed noble to the bourgeois, from the priest to the line officer, and from the royal official to the noble plebeian. Its members held diverging political convictions, and the desire for reform was most pervasive among the young. The schools of the Commision for National Education, the Cadets' Corps, the copious reform literature, and not least the bitter experience of the Confederation of Bar had borne fruit. Notwithstanding the plethora of political opinions, the young reformers were united by the fact that they based their ideas first on the native Polish constitutional tradition, strengthened by the spirit of the ancient republic, and on the views of natural rights and social theory of the French Enlightenment. It was hardly a coincidence that Russo (Rousseau) and Monteskiusz (Montesquieu) are among the few French surnames that have been polonized.[29] Alongside the French Revolution, the American debates of 1787-1789 preceding the ratification of the Constitution lent a further strong impulse.

The reform party in the mid-1780s advocated the immediate shaking off of the Russian protectorate established in 1768 as well as the enlargement and reorganization of the army, a financial and tax reform, modernization of the work of the dietines and the Diet, the introduction of a hereditary monarchy, political rights for urban citizens, the beginning of the liberation of the peasantry through the elimination of corvée, the integration of Jews into society, and, most important, the curtailment of the omnipotence of the magnate oligarchs. Political journalism had a long tradition in Poland; "public opinion" was more of a direct political force in the Republic of nobles than elsewhere. An impressive number of newspapers and journals appeared, an abundance of tracts, letters, satires, and pamphlets on relevant or potentially relevant questions, because the latter publications corresponded more to the reading habits of the provincial nobility. Alongside the *Monitor*, which appeared from 1763 to 1784 and patterned itself on the British *Spectator*, the most influential publications were the *Pamiętnik Historyczno-Polityczny* (1782-1792) published and edited by Piotr Świtkowski, the *Gazeta Narodowa i Obca*, shaped by Julian Ursyn Niemcewicz and Józef Weyssenhoff, and the *Pamiętnik Historyczno-Literacki i Ekonomiczny*. These organs presented the contents of important foreign reform writings–such as Camil Desmoulin's *La France libre* or Emmanuel Joseph Sieyès' *Qu-est-ce que le Tiers État?* (1789)--describing the course of the debates on the ratification of the American Constitution and the French constitutional discussions, and offering vivid descriptions of events in France. Especially during the Four-Year Diet political literature swelled to a vast flood of diverse writings–including series of discussions with theses, replies, and counter replies–with the goal of mobilizing the masses of passive or neutral people in the cause of reform. In this "Kołłątaj's Forge" acted as a modern propaganda center with specialists for the various levels and interest groups of the *szlachta* and townspeople and for regional special interests.

HISTOIRE
GÉNÉRALE
DE'
POLOGNE,

Par M. le Chevalier DE SOLIGNAC,
Secrétaire du Cabinet & des Comman-
demens du Roi de Pologne , Duc de
Lorraine & de Bar.

TOME PREMIER.

A PARIS,

Chez JEAN-THOMAS HERISSANT, rue
S. Jacques, à S. Paul & à S. Hilaire.

M. DCC. L.
Avec Approbation & Privilége du Roi.

Pierre J. De Solignac, *Histoire générale de Pologne* volume 1-3 à Paris 1750. The
author served as the secretary of Stanisław Leszczyński and of the Academy at Nancy
founded by Leszczyński. (Biblioteka Narodowa, Warszawa).

Relatively little was published by the camp of the conservative opposition, which—as the supporter of Russia—partly out of conviction, partly out of self-interest, and partly because of their unconditional commitment to the maintenance of the unrestricted liberty of the nobility, called on the "republican" heritage and rejected the stabilization and the strengthening of central state power and the reorganization of the parliamentary system. The Grand Hetman Franciszek Ksawery Branicki, the Field Hetman Seweryn Rzewuski, the Bishop of Livonia (in partibus) Józef Kossakowski, and General Stanisław Szczęsny Potocki led the "Republicans." Opposed to them stood the "Patriots," which included among the magnates the Marshal of the Diet Stanisław Małachowski, the brothers Ignacy and Stanisław Kostka Potocki, the Czartoryskis, and the Lithuanian Grand Hetman Michał Ogiński. The King and his followers—led by his brother, Primate Michał Poniatowski and Great Crown Chancellor Jacek Małachowski—long sought to assume an intermediary position, until at the end of 1790 he sided definitely with the "Patriots." In the battle of opinions the patriotic faction supported by Prussia quickly gained ground in view of the involvement of Russia in a difficult war with the Turkish Empire and in view of the enthusiasm that the program of the reformers found among the middle and lower nobility.

The great social and political importance of the first term of the Four-Year Diet[30] rested on the fact that its decisions on the alliance with Prussia (29 March 1790), on the expansion of the army to 100,000 men (20 October 1788), and especially on tax policy—and here the Polish awakening was not dissimilar to the contemporary French Revolution—aroused a powerful movement for general improvement of the political system among the middle and lower levels of the politically enfranchised population as well as among the city dwellers. The broad current of reform sentiment, which had been active for more than a generation and was artificially held back by the Russian guarantees and their defenders among the magnates, now surged forward. "That every nation is free and independent, that the nation has the right to establish the form of government that it holds to be best, that no foreign state has the authority to interfere with its constitution—this is the first and most important maxim of international law."[31] This thesis presents the point of view that human rights justify constitutional reform as encapsulated in the sentence: "A nation that does not have the right to govern itself is not a nation."[32]

Both camps, the patriotic as well as the republican, used the American and French debates as an arsenal for their arguments. Despite their essentially democratic convictions, the "Patriots" were in the paradoxical situation of having to curtail old, apparently self-evident liberties in order to strengthen the republic, and their republican opponents did not neglect to capitalize on this situation. This tactical reversal of fundamental positions came to the fore especially in the decisive questions of the replacement of the electoral monarchy by an inherited kingship and of the introduction of the principle of majority rule. Thus, Seweryn Rzewuski painted a frightening picture of the tyranny of hereditary monarchy, which would give rise to a renewed age of Tarquinius; he praised those great Americans "to whom America owes her freedom," who had certainly felt that "a hereditary monarchy cannot be reconciled with freedom."[33] Hugo Kołłątaj could only reply that Great Britain and the Netherlands were free under their kings and that France had not abolished monarchy "in its current revolution;" the Polish nation would deal with refractory kings "just as England had done with the Stuarts, the Netherlands with Joseph II, and France with Louis XVI."[34] When Rzewuski praised the *liberum veto* as "a mighty bulwark of our form of government" and feared that majority rule would produce a new bondage, "the right of the strongest," Kołłątaj could with more reason reply: "Did Franklin and Washington not have in mind the notion of general liberty when they began?" Moreover, it became clear in this discussion that the conservative "Republicans" could proclaim ultrademocratic slogans because, thanks to clientage, they served the interests of the oligarchy, while the essentially democratic "Patriots"–and this was indeed a unique situation in Europe at that time–wanted to curtail the existing democratic laws in order to raise the democracy of the nobility from the disfunction that had lasted for generations. If the "Patriots" were thereby in an outwardly less favorable position, their unconditional advocacy of the natural rights of the individual, of liberty and equality before the law, proved the purity of their intentions. "The rights of the individual are the foundation of all other rights among people," wrote Kołłątaj around 1790,[35] and Staszic added a clear jab at the magnate oligarchy: "Any association that is established between a few or a few thousand people, between a dozen or several dozen families, without the permission of the other people who are forced to live in this social formation is not a human society but rather a conspiracy against humanity."[36] Here the basic question of constitutional reform is revealed; the reform could not be limited to a strictly institutional change, but rather, to be truly successful, it must fundamentally reshape the class of politically enfranchised citizens.

The Constitution of 3 May 1791 and Its Reception

The political confrontation over the reform of noble voting rights rested on the principle, "Birth makes a man a noble, but only property makes him a citizen."[37] The emancipation of the urban population had taken a prominent place in the first term of the Four-Year Diet but was brought to legislative ripeness only in the second term that opened on 16 December 1790 after the doubling of the number of delegates. The parallel events of the French Revolution and the growing fear of revolution among the *szlachta* were skillfully used by the patriotic political writers to arouse readiness for at least modest concessions.[38] Meanwhile the international constellation, which had been favorable to the Republic since the middle of 1790, had severely deteriorated.[39] The further development of the revolution in France and new intentions in British policy provided the impetus for a disentanglement of the military-political complexities of Eastern Europe. The Reichenbach Convention of 27 July 1790, in which Joseph II's successor Leopold II accepted the Prussian conditions, prevented the outbreak of war between Prussia and Austria but at the same time, by settling conflicts between Berlin and Vienna, removed a crucial precondition of the Prussian-Polish alliance of 29 March 1790. This alliance lost appeal to King Frederick William II as he recognized in August-September that the Diet had no intention of ceding Gdańsk and Toruń in accordance with the "Great Plan" of his minister Hertzberg. The separate peace signed at Werela on 14 August 1790, under which King Gustav III of Sweden withdrew from the war with Russia, further strained the international position of the republic of nobles. Finally, after long negotiations with the Porte, Leopold signed the Treaty of Sistowa (24 August 1791); this treaty cleared the way for the Declaration of Pillnitz of 27 August 1791, in which the monarchs of Austria and Prussia joined for common surveillance of the French Revolution. From July 1789 Catherine II of Russia had been occupied with the plans of Prince Potemkin and his secretary Bezborodko for the "creation of a confederation" against the reform measures in Poland and had considered plans to provoke an uprising in Polish Ukraine. The Russian military success against the Sublime Porte raised the danger that Russia, after an advantageous peace treaty, could march experienced troops into Poland. Therefore, it was high time for the "Patriots" to bring the reform effort initiated in extensive legislation to a conclusion in order to crown their efforts by the codification of a general constitution:

> Persuaded that our common fate depends entirely upon the establishing
> and rendering perfect a national constitution... and willing to profit by

the present circumstances of Europe, and by the favorable moment which has restored us to ourselves...We do solemnly establish the present Constitution.[40]

The patriotic camp found itself in a favorable parliamentary position, because several leaders of the "Republicans"–among them Szczęsny Potocki[41] – had left the country due to their disappointment over the course of the proceedings, while the King, since the elections held for the second term in the fall of 1790, stood with the reformers. The solidarity of King and nation, the ideal of the French Gironde of 1790-1792, and the office of *Roi Citoyen*, which the founders of the French Constitution of 1791 had in mind, deeply moved Stanisław August at the time of the Polish constitutional discussions.[42] Knowledgeable about and friendly to the American Constitution (a bust of Washington adorned his study) in July 1788 he had already made the Florentine Philip Mazzei, the representative of Virginia in France and a confidant of Jefferson, his agent in Paris.[43] Through Mazzei, who from 1790 was co-founder of the Society of 1789–which included moderate Jacobins such as Lafayette, Sieyès, and Mirabeau and which offered honorary membership to Franklin, Washington and Stanisław August[44] –the King was familiar with all the personalities of the French Revolution from Condorcet to Robespierre and with all the intellectual currents of France. Although Stanisław August was certainly no "Jacobin," rather at most an advocate of constitutional monarchy, he nevertheless thoroughly approved of social reforms in the republic, and he was determined to defend "our revolution" and its *citoyens*. In the contest between the parties the King gained great personal influence, and through his loosely organized circle of friends, he was able to exert it in support of constitutional reform .

Thus to the King fell the decisive role of furthering the work of the Constitutional Deputation, which had begun its work in September 1789 and whose guiding spirit was the magnate leader of the "Patriots," Ignacy Potocki. The strong impact of American and French influence is also seen in the introductory declaration of human rights in the first draft of the Principles to Reform the Government proposed by Potocki on December 17:: "...the nation has the obligation to guarantee and to preserve the freedom, property and equality of every citizen..."[45] Thanks to the constructive suggestions of the King and the willingness to compromise of the leading reformers, the text of the constitution, which had been prepared in secret in spring 1791, gained the approval of the Diet on 3 May 1791–in a *coup d'état* according to its opponents.[46]

In view of its derivation from native constitutional traditions as well as from contemporary American and French ideas, the Constitution was of a moderate and mixed type.[47] If the electoral monarchy, the old symbol of the democracy of the nobility, was replaced by hereditary monarchy through the house of Wettin and thus a certain affinity shown for monarchical sovereignty, nevertheless "the definition of public powers" in the Constitution expressly declared that "all power in civil society should be derived from the will of the people." The preamble found a compromise in that it designated that the monarch rules "by the grace of God and the will of the Nation."[48] Further, no agreement was reached on whether the terms "citizen" and "nation" used in the Constitution were to be applied beyond the noble estate;[49] thus, at one point "nation" was understood as the old nation of the nobility (Article II), at another as the entire populace of the Republic, including even the enserfed peasants (Article IV).[50] In any event, the Constitution placed greater weight on the description of social along with strictly constitutional conditions, and therefore laws on noble rights and the royal cities were incorporated as integral parts (Article III, Article VI). On this social structure rested the triple division of public authority into the legislative, the executive, and the judicial, which according to the advice of Montesquieu was put into constitutional practice and which appeared for the first time in Europe (Article V).

The idea of popular sovereignty was firmly anchored in the Constitution, for the Chamber of Deputies, "being the manifestation and repository of supreme national authority," would be "the temple of legislation" and should determine the law; the Senate held only a suspensive veto (Article VI). For the final enactment of laws "the votes of both Houses shall be jointly computed, and the majority, as described by law, shall be considered as a decree and the will of the Nation. . . . The majority of votes shall decide everything, and everywhere; therefore we abolish, and utterly annihilate, *liberum veto* "(Article VI). Executive authority was entrusted to the king and behind him a state council of Guardians of the Laws (*Straż Praw*) consisting of the Primate of Poland, the five cabinet ministers responsible to the Diet, and two secretaries (Article VII). Finally, "as judicial power is incompatible with the legislative, nor can be administered by the king, therefore tribunals and magistratures ought to be established and elected" (Article VIII). The Constitution and all its institutions thus represented an example of a parliamentary monarchy based on a democratically organized nation of citizens, and it would assume a model character for modern constitutional history as the first codified Constitution in Europe and–after the American federal Constitution–the second in the world.

This exemplary character was eloquently expressed in the stormy acclamation that the Polish Constitution found in all European countries, from Portugal to Sweden and from the Netherlands to Italy.[51] In Amsterdam the citizenry had a commemorative medal struck for the Polish King; in London a society was formed to celebrate the anniversary of the Polish Constitution with yearly banquets; and in revolutionary Paris the popular sections celebrated the government of the great King and generous nobility in votes of thanks at their reunions of 1 and 4 June 1791. Among European constitutional theorists, above all Edmund Burke praised the Constitution in that he ascribed to himself a sort of philosophical protectorate over its drafting; also he sought to launch his attack on the French Revolution in the name of the Polish Constitution. Burke's opponent Mackintosh and his colleagues Henry Fox, Mallet du Pan, and Volney, Sieyès and Condorcet, but also the historian and economist Sismondi, all had approving or even admiring words for the creation of this Constitution. Even the very critical Thomas Paine had to at least acknowledge that the Polish Constitution provided an example of a reform based on internal strength On the other hand, in the German states, which were mostly under absolutist governments, the Constitution was little noticed. Nevertheless one should mention here the lecture, including remarks on its contents, held on 6 October 1791 at the Berlin Academy by Count Hertzberg and the account of Friedrich Schulz of Courland.[52] In the United States of America, where Kościuszko and Pułaski were still remembered, public opinion was particularly interested in the Polish Constitution because the ratification of the federal Constitution and the associated constitutional comparisons lay only two years in the past.[53]

Of course, nowhere did the news of the enactment of the Polish Constitution arouse greater enthusiasm than in France.[54] Even the Jacobin Club, in some Chapters of the Society of the Friends of the Constitution, endorsed the Republic and its King. In general, however, a naive and spontaneous enthusiasm, springing from the idea of a brotherhood of constitutional nations, predominated, especially among the Jacobins in the provinces. Letters of homage to Stanisław August were sent from a series of French cities from Lyon to Neu-Breisach in summer 1791, and an address by the Jacobins of Valognes celebrated the King for his "reason and philanthropy" and as a "benefactor of the human race."[55] In this way, the Polish Constitution was certainly essential to the final draft of the French revolutionary constitution of 3 and 14 September 1791, which in turn served as a model, in many respects, for subsequent constitutional monarchies in Europe.[56]

Within the Polish Republic the Constitution was significant primarily in that it thoroughly corresponded to the expressed political wishes of the majority of citizens. The weakening of the magnate oligarchy and its clientele, the strengthening of executive power, and legislation through majority rule appealed mainly to the middle nobility, the "knights," and to propertied urban citizens.

Thus, it was natural that the citizens of Warsaw, Wilno, Poznań, Lublin, and other large cities took a passionate interest in the creation of the Constitution and were willing to defend it with arms if necessary.[57] The electorates of the individual palatinates quickly accepted the Constitution in their dietines; that of Połock was the first (18 August 1791), and this, in light of the demonstrative arrival of Russian batteries north of the border along the Dvina River, was no coincidence.[58] On 4 February 1792 all the dietines assembled to elect the judges and officials as the Constitution had foreseen.[59] Despite the machinations of the "Republicans," the majority of the dietines confirmed the Constitution, while a minority contented themselves with dispatching delegations to thank the Diet and the King. By May 1792 nearly all the dietines had ratified the Constitution, and the supposed *coup d'état* of 3 May 1791 was thereby brilliantly justified.[60]

Despite some inconsistencies, the Constitution that had thus been ratified distinguished itself from all existing European constitutions in that it was the first to apply the term "nation" to all inhabitants of the Republic[61] wherein the chamber of deputies was no longer a congress of delegates but rather a representative of the entire nation. The statesmanlike wisdom of the fathers of the Constitution also revealed itself in the fact that, although they had set down the unchanging foundations of the Constitution (such as the principle of separation of powers), they provided for necessary modifications in the Constitution every quarter century in the interests of further social development. In view of its structure and its electorate the Constitution assumed a middle position between the contemporary constitutions of France, Great Britain, and the United States: in its deep historical roots it equaled the British; in its combination of monarchy and democratic natural rights principles, the French; and in its peculiar combination of unitary nation and federative territorial structure, as well as in terms of the relationship between electorate and populace, the union of states of the United States of America, especially the states south of the Mason-Dixon line. The common criterion of the social constitution of the Polish Republic and the southern states of North America was the existence of a democratically organized electorate consisting of landowners and propertied city-dwellers, which in turn rested on a broad stratum of unfree persons–in the Republic the enserfed peasants, in the southern United States the slaves.

After the elimination of the plebeian noble voters, roughly 160,000 citizens enjoyed full political rights, out of a total population of approximately 8.8 million inhabitants. The Polish Republic thus assumed a most honorable place among the constitutional states of the world at that time. In Europe Polish standards were exceeded only by the French Constitution of 1791, which was then in preparation. The latter recognized the electoral rights of 1.8 million active citizens out of a total population of roughly 25 million people in the Kingdom of France. Thus, the Four-Year Diet and the Constitution it passed became a significant, socially cohesive force, which nourished traditional state patriotism and, by undermining the oligarchy, called forth a natural interest in the success of the state and its unlimited sovereignty among broad strata of the propertied middle nobility and urban populace.

The Fall of the Reformed Republic

It was a dramatic coincidence in the history of the Polish Republic that the main cause of its fall was attributed to its achievement in establishing the first codified constitution in Europe. It was the strengthened internal coherence that the reforms of 1791-1792 bestowed on the structure of Polish society that supplied the most essential cause for the imminent fall of the Republic. The oligarchic factions, anarchist excesses, and a general communal disfunction, which discredited the republican idea in practice (and even seemed to reduce it to absurdity) was thoroughly acceptable to the neighboring powers of Prussia, Austria, and Russia. The customary "disorder" of the Polish polity was even excellently suited to demonstrate the apparent necessity of a strict, absolutist monarchy. Finally, the material achievements of, for instance, the Prussian state outwardly appeared much more impressive than the seemingly fruitless argument over the "cardinal rights" or the ponderousness of a parliament dependent on *communis consensus*. A reformed Republic, however, which would almost certainly be functional, placed the internal justification of absolute monarchy, even if Enlightened, in question.[62] Thus, the strong discomfort that Frederick William II and the more reformist Leopold II experienced in regard to the upheavals of 1791 was understandable. For Catherine II the loss of the Russian protectorate over the Republic was irksome; moreover, she must have been aware of the imminent danger posed by a functioning constitutional state on the western border of her empire, in view of the clear discrepancy between the fashionable, republican content of her speeches, on the one hand, and her despotic government, on the other.

The peace with Turkey of 9 January 1792 had hardly been settled when Catherine II marched her armies to the eastern border of Poland and negotiated the principles of the Second Partition with Prussia.[63] In the belief that the "pure" republic based on the laws decreed in 1768 could be restored, she placed the leaders of the Polish "Republicans" at her disposal and on 27 April 1792 established the notorious confederation that was later named for the Ukrainian border town of Targowica and falsely dated to 14 May.

The beginning of the invasion and thereby the end of the new Constitution were announced in the Empress' manifesto of 7/18 May 1792, which was typical of Catherine's grandiose Machiavellianism in its political insincerity and unscrupulousness. The woman of the Enlightenment, a supporter of liberty and natural rights and a correspondent of Voltaire, Grimm, Falconet, and d'Alembert, denied the Polish nation its freedom to establish a constitution for itself and took refuge in the state guarantee of 1768. The autocrat criticized the "despotism" of the new hereditary monarchy and simultaneously its democratic elements.[64] Above all, with perfect skill she made use of old Europe's fear of the French Revolution in that she introduced the useful notion that the reform was the work of the Jacobins. She wrote her friend Grimm on 9 May 1792: "the Jacobins of Warsaw are in regular correspondence with those of Paris, and you want me...to concern myself only with those of Paris? No, I will fight and defeat them in Poland."[65]

It was especially ironic that she made use of Szczęsny Potocki, the Marshal of the Confederation of Targowica and a fierce opponent of absolute monarchy, and of Seweryn Rzewuski, a politician who loved to invoke Franklin and Washington. The proclamation of the Targowicians was scarcely less politically hypocritical than that of their "principal." According to them, the Constitution had transformed the "republic into a monarchy," and in the cities of Poland "clubs on the Parisian model" had arisen. The extensive arsenal of contemporary republican phrases was exploited for the justification of the restoration of oligarchic liberty, and it was difficult to cover over the contradiction between accusations of royal despotism, on the one hand, and of Jacobinism, on the other.[66] It was scarcely conceivable that the Targowicians could believe that the Empress sought only the reestablishment of the former oligarchy and the Russian proconsulate.

Only an armed conflict carried out according to the rules of the old cabinet wars, which ended with the exhaustion of Polish resources, sealed the rapid fall of the new Constitution and, presently, the further dissection of the country.

Although nullified as state law, the Constitution of 3 May 1791 lived on in the hearts of the citizens and, beyond that, of all Poles. Not the internal weaknesses or instability of the reform movement but rather its liquidation by external force provided the cause of the fall of the Republic. The demise of Poland that was already underway was thus an indication not of its powerlessness but rather that the rediscovery of its internal strength had become frightening to the Russian Empire. Here lay the real reason that, of the three great social movements of 1787-1789 that introduced the "revolutionary decade" in Europe and America, only the French and American developed freely while the Polish movement seemed to disappear in political destruction. In this the forcible suppression of the reformed Polish Constitution provided a valuable, if unintentional, service in the birth of modern democracy in France.

The Confederation of Targowica constituted itself in St. Petersburg seven days after the declaration of war of 20 April 1792 that the French government issued to the German Emperor as King of Hungary and Bohemia and thereby implicitly to all of conservative Europe. The beginning of the offensive of the Duke of Brunswick against revolutionary France (25 July 1792) coincided almost to the day with Stanisław August's joining the camp of the Confederation of Targowica; and the bloody genesis of the French Republic, which stretched from the September murders to the opening of the Convention and the abolition of the monarchy (2-21 September 1792), marked for the Polish Republic the establishment of the Targowician state authority under the protection of Russian arms. In any event, the Russian Empire–for a full three years–was militarily engaged in the Republic, so that it could not intervene against France. In consideration of the enticements from St. Petersburg, Prussia also had decided to conduct the campaign in France at only half strength, since it was now seriously interested in the annexation of Gdańsk, Toruń and Great Poland.[67] By the time that the Duke of Brunswick set out from Coblenz, the military preparations for the march into Poland had begun.[68] Under the shadow of these preparations against Poland occurred, for Goethe at least, the "world historical" Battle of Valmy (20 September 1792), which brought about the withdrawal of the allied Prussians and Austrians. Thus, France owed the first great military reversal in the war of the coalition to a great degree to the Polish Republic. Here, there truly appeared to be a cunning historical wisdom at work, which used the demise of constitutional life in one country to prepare a home for it in another.

Thus, a motive presents itself for the virtually natural alliance between the French and Polish republics, which resulted not only in a foreign policy but also to a large degree in an internal affinity. The French republic recognized the advantages of this support but, as in 1791, limited its help for Poland to empty declarations of sympathy. Thus, on 26 August 1792 Kościuszko along with Washington was granted French citizenship for his service in "the protection of peoples against despots." This was demonstrated emphatically on 23 January 1793 as the agreement on the Second Partition was concluded between the courts of Berlin and St. Petersburg and as Prussia sent troops into Great Poland under the watchword of Catherine II that they had to stop "the spread of French democracy and the principles of the horrible reds who seek proselytes everywhere."[69] Thus was completed the defeat of the reform Constitution of 1791 and the second act of the final liquidation of Poland, which after 1795 left behind a "nation without a state" for 123 years.

Notes

1. Wacław Sobieski, *Trybun ludu szlacheckiego* (The tribune of the noble folk) (Warszawa: Gebethner i Wolff, 1905); Artur Śliwiński, *Jan Zamoyski–kanclerz i hetman wielki koronny* (Jan Zamoyski - Chancellor and Great Hetman of the Crown) (Warszawa: Trzaska, Evert i Michalski, 1947); Adam Andrzej Witusik, *O Zamoyskich, Zamościu i Akademii Zamoyskiej* (On the Zamoyskis, Zamość, and the Zamoyski Academy) (Lublin: Wydaw. Lubelskie, 1978).

2. (Stanisław Leszczyński), *Głos wolny wolność ubezpieczający* (The free voice that safeguards freedom) (Nancy, 1743). Also published in 1749 in French: *La voix libre du citoyen, ou Observations sur le gouvernement de Pologne* and reprinted many times in both languages.

3. In his essay "Czy Stanisław Leszczyński jest autorem *Głosu wolnego?*" (Is Stanisław Leszczyński the author of *Głos wolny?*) in *Legendy i fakty XVIII w.* (Warszawa: PWN, 1963),pp. 67-144, Emanuel Rostworowski argued that only the Lithuanian *starosta* Mateusz Białłozor could have been the author of *Głos wolny*. Compare the older view in M. K. Dziewanowski, "King Stanisław Leszczyński: Some Remarks and Question Marks," in *Jahrbücher für die Geschichte Osteuropas* 16 (1968): 104-116.

4. Leszczyński, *Głos wolny,* pp. 55-57.

5. Stanisław Konarski, *O skutecznym rad sposobie albo o utrzymywaniu ordynaryjnych seymów* (On effective counsel), in 4 volumes (Warszawa, 1760-63), vol. 2, p. 203; also published in German, *Von einem nützlichen Mittel zum Bestande der ordentlichen Reichstäge in Pohlen* (Warschau, 1762).

6. Stanisław Staszic, *Uwagi nad życiem Jana Zamoyskiego kanclerza i hetmana wielkiego koronnego do dzisiejszego stanu Rzeczypospolitej Polskiej przystosowane* (Remarks on the life of Jan Zamoyski, Chancellor and Great Hetman of the Crown, applied to the current state of the Polish Commonwealth) (Łuck?: 1785) (Warszawa:

1787); Stefan Czarnowski, ed., *Uwagi nad życiem Jana Zamoyskiego* (Wrocław: Ossolineum, 1952), pp. 223, 238, 315, 362, 364, et al.

7. Above all to be mentioned here are the anonymous remarks "Myśl na myśli" (Remarks about remarks) (1788), and Staszic's "Poprawy y przydatki" (Emendations and additions) (1788). But the discussion took place in numerous other writings that were not concerned solely with Zamoyski; compare here Władysław Smoleński, "Spór o Jana Zamoyskiego w publicystyce polskiej wieku XVIII" (The controversy over Jan Zamoyski in Polish political writings of the 18th century), in *Wybór pism* (Warszawa: Książka i Wiedza, 1954), pp. 202-10.

8. Hugo Kołłątaj, *Listy Anonima i Prawo polityczne narodu polskiego* (Anonymous letters and Political law of the Polish nation), in 2 volumes, edited by Bogusław Leśnodorski and Helena Wereszycka (Warszawa: PWN, 1954) vol. 2, pp. 37 ff; *Wybór pism politycznych* (Selected political writings) ed., Bogusław Leśnodorski (Wrocław: 1951). The original *Listy Anonima* of 1788 comprised three volumes, to which *Prawo polityczne* was added as a fourth in 1790.

9. As characterized by Walerian Kalinka, *Sejm Czteroletni* (The Four-Year Diet), in three volumes (Kraków: 1895-96), vol. 2, part 2, p. 514; also in German translation, Valerian Kalinka, *Der Vierjährige Polnische Reichstag 1788-1791,* in two volumes (Berlin: 1896-98).

10. Especially in the work *O sukcesyi tronu w Polszcze rzecz krótka* (A short essay on the succession to the throne in Poland) (1790); a contemporary German translation appeared as "Gedanken über die Erb-Thronfolge in Polen" in *Reichstags-Diarium* 4: pp. 108-28.

11. *Considérations sur le Gouvernement de Pologne et sur la reformation projetée en avril 1772* (Londres, 1782). It is fairly certain that this well-known work was written between November 1770 and January 1771 and that the final emendations were completed before 1 January 1772, that is, before the first rumors of the partition. One of the leaders of the Confederation of Bar, Michał Wielhorski, delivered essential materials to Rousseau, and further Rousseau may have been at least indirectly aware of the work of Konarski through the mediation of Stanisław Leszczyński, the Abbé G. F. Coyer, and Pyrrhys de Varilles, among others. Thanks to this Polish aid, the influence of Polish theorists on the *Considérations* may well have been rather great. On this, compare Jean Fabre, *Stanislas-Auguste Poniatowski et l'Europe des lumières* (Paris: Les Belles Lettres, 1952), pp. 108 f., 343 ff., 640, 656 f.

12. Fabre, *Stanislas-Auguste Poniatowski,* p. 108.

13. Fabre, *Stanislas-Auguste Poniatowski,* p. 344.

14. Alexander Hamilton, James Madison, and John Jay, *The Federalist,* edited by Benjamin F. Wright (Cambridge, MA: Belknap Press of Harvard Univ. Press, 1961), p. 152.

15. Zygmunt Krasiński, "Lettre à A. M. Lamartine," in *Pisma Zygmunta Krasińskiego* (The Works of Zygmunt Krasiński) (Kraków, 1912), vol. 7, p. 223.

16. Oscar Halecki, *Das Nationalitätenproblem im alten Polen* (Kraków, 1916), p. 69.

17. In his work *Niektóre wyrazy porządkiem abecadła zebrane* (Some terms collected in alphabetical order) (Warszawa, 1791), cited in Bogdan Suchodolski, ed., *Nauka polska w okresie oświecenia* (Polish scholarship in the age of Enlightenment) (Kraków: PWN, 1953), p. 584.

18. Krasiński, *Pisma,* p. 213.

19. This extended influence was traced with some certainty by Fabre, *Stanislas-Auguste Poniatowski,* pp. 180 f. On the intellectual influence of Rousseau on Fichte, see Iring Fetscher, *Rousseaus politische Philosophie. Zur Geschichte des demokratischen Freiheitsbegriffs* (Neuwied: Luchterhand, 1960).

20. Michael G. Müller, *Polen zwischen Preußen und Rußland. Souveränitätskrise und Reformpolitik 1736-1752* (Berlin: Colloquim, 1983); Zofia Zielińska, *Walka "familii" o reformę Rzeczypospolitej, 1743-1752* (The struggle of the "family" for reform of the Commonwealth, 1743-1752) (Warszawa, 1983); Jörg K. Hoensch, *Sozialverfassung und politische Reform. Polen im vorrevolutionären Zeitalter* (Köln, Wien, Böhlau, 1973); Kurt Georg Hausmannn, *Die politischen Begriffe und Wertungen in der polnischen Aufklärung. Zum Selbstverständnis der Polen in ihrer Reformpublizistik am Ende der Adelsrepublik (zweite Hälfte des 18. Jhs.)* (Phil. Diss., Göttingen, 1958); Hans Roos, *Der Fall der polnischen Nation und die Idee der Demokratie* (Habil.-Schrift Tübingen, 1961).

21. Daniel Stone, *Polish Politics and National Reform, 1775-1788* (New York: Boulder, Colorado U. Press: 1976).

22. Ambroise Jobert, *La Commision d'Éducation Nationale en Pologne (1773-1794). Son euvre d'instruction civique* (Paris: Librairie Droz, 1941); Renata Dutkowa, *Komisja Edukacji Narodowej* (The Commission for National Education) (Wrocław, Ossolineum, 1973); Łukasz Kurdybacha and Mieczysława Mitera-Dobrowolska, *Komisja Edukacji Narodowej* (Warszawa: PZWS, 1973); Bogdan Suchodolski, *Komisja Edukacji Narodowej* (Warszawa, 1973).

23. Emanuel Rostworowski, *Ostatni król Rzeczypospolitej. Geneza i upadek Konstytucji 3 maja* (The last king of the Commonwealth: The genesis and fall of the Constitution of 3 May) (Warszawa: Wiedza Powszechna, 1966); Andrzej Zahorski, *Stanisław August polityk* (Stanisław August as a politician) (Warszawa: Książka i Wiedza1966).

24. See Bogusław Leśnodorski, "Les facteurs intellectuels de la formation de la société Polonaise moderne au Siècle des Lumières," in *La Pologne au X Congrès International des Sciences Historiques à Rome* (Warszawa: PWN, 1955), pp. 167-216 including rich bibliographical references.

25. Władysław Smoleński, *Kuźnica Kołłątajowska* (Kołłątaj's Forge) (Kraków, 1885), with biographical references for all members; Bogusław Leśnodorski, ed., *Kuźnica Kołłątajowska. Wybór źródeł* (Kołłątaj's Forge: selected sources) (Wrocław: Ossolineum, 1949), with numerous selections from texts by Kołłątaj, Jezierski, Dmochowski, Kossakowski, Trębicki, Zabłocki, and others, as well as a number of pamphlets from the time of the uprising of 1794.

26. Hausmann cites the most important writings of the authors named, see pp. 198-203 (here the easily accessible new editions are also listed); also to be mentioned is the *Reichstags-Diarium* published by Michael Gröll, a printer and publisher of Warsaw and Dresden, which includes numerous pamphlets in contemporary German translation. The relevant secondary literature is also listed by Hausmann, pp. 203-208; see further Charles Dany, *Les idées politiques et l'esprit public en Pologne à la fin du XVIIIe siècle. La constitution du 3 Mai 1791* (Paris: 1901); Bogusław Leśnodorski, *Dzieło Sejmu Czteroletniego (1788-1792). Studium Historycznoprawne* (The work of the Four-Year Diet, 1788-1792: A historical-legal study) (Wrocław: Ossolineum, 1951), pp. 75-91.

27. On Kościuszko see especially Tadeusz Korzon, *Kościuszko–Biografia z dokumentów wysnuta* (Kościuszko: A biography deduced from documents) (Kraków: 1894); H. Monfort, *Le drame de la Pologne–Kościuszko* (Paris, 1945); Henryk Mościcki, *Kościuszko–Listy, odezwy, wspomnienia* (Kościuszko: Letters, addresses, reminiscences) (Warszawa: 1917); Miecislaus Haiman, *Kościuszko: Leader and Exile* (New York: 1946), and *Poland and the American Revolutionary War* (Chicago: Polish Roman Catholic Union, 1932).

28. On Jasiński see Emil Kipa, "Z młodych lat Jakuba Jasińskiego" (The Youth of Jakub Jasiński), in *Studia i szkice historyczne* (Wrocław: Ossolineum, 1959) pp. 3-29; H. Mościcki, *Generał Jasiński i powstanie kościuszkowskie* (General Jasiński and the Kościuszko Uprising) (Warszawa: 1917).

29. The intellectual influence of Rousseau and Montesquieu on Polish constitutional thought has been so often and so exhaustively treated that here only the standard works need to be mentioned: Władysław Smoleński, *Monteskiusz w Polsce w wieku XVIII* (Montesquieu in Poland in the 18th century) (Warszawa: 1925); Marian Szyjkowski, *Myśl Jana Jakuba Rousseau'a w Polsce XVIII w.* (The Thought of Jean Jacques Rousseau in Poland of the 18th century) (Kraków: 1913). Hausmann undertook a systematic presentation of Enlightened natural rights thought in Poland in his fundamental chapter, "Die Theorie der Gesellschaft," pp. 33-65.

30. Leśnodorski, *Dzieło Sejmu Czteroletniego;* Jerzy Łojek, *Geneza i obalenie Konstytucji 3 Maja* (The genesis and overthrow of the Constitution of 3 May) (Lublin: Wydaw. Lubelskie, 1986); Jerzy Kowecki, ed., *Sejm Czteroletni i jego tradycje* (The Four-Year Diet and its traditions) (Warszawa: PWN, 1991); among the older literature Kalinka's *Sejm Czteroletni* stands out.

31. Hugo Kołłątaj [Ignacy Potocki, Fr. K. Dmochowski], *O ustanowieniu i upadku Konstytucji polskiej 3 maja 1791 roku* (On the enactment and the fall of the Polish Constitution of 3 May 1791), in 2 volumes ((Metz), Kraków: 1793), taken from the Paris: 1868 edition), vol.1, p. 5; also in German translation by Samuel Bogumił Linde, *Vom Entstehen und Untergang der Polnischen Konstitution vom 3ten Mai 1791* (Leipzig: 1793).

32. Kołłątaj, *O ustanowieniu i upadku,* p. 5.

33. Seweryn Rzewuski, *O sukcesji tronu w Polszcze.*

34. Hugo Kołłątaj, *Uwagi nad pismem . . . Seweryna Rzewuskiego hetmana polnego koronnego o sukcessyi tronu w Polszcze rzecz krótka* (Remarks on Field Hetman of the Crown Seweryn Rzewuski's work, A short essay on the succession to the throne in Poland) (Warszawa: 1790); a German version appeared under the title ". . . Gedanken über die unter dem Titel: Severin Rzewuski ... erschienene Schrift...," in *Reichstags-Diarium* 4, pp. 150-77, 209-17.

35. In a work not published at that time, "O prawach i prawodawstwie" (On laws and legislation), in *Wybór pism politycznych,* p. 180 f.

36. Stanisław Staszic, *Przestrogi dla Polski* (Warnings for Poland) (Warszawa 1790), reprinted in *Pisma filozoficzne i społeczne* (Philosophical and social writings), in two volumes edited by Bogdan Suchodolski (Warszawa: Kraków: PWN, 1954), vol. 1, p. 207; German translation, *Warnungen für Polen* (Oliwa: 1794).

37. Kalinka, *Sejm Czteroletni,* vol. 1, part 2, p. 659.

38. Examples in Hausmann, *Die polnische Begriffe,* pp. 108 f. 124.

39. Kalinka, *Sejm Czteroletni,* and Łojek, *Geneza i obalenie,* describe the international situation in detail.

40. Cited from the preamble to the Constitution of 3 May 1791, *New Constitution of the Government of Poland Established by the Revolution of the Third of May, 1791* (London: 1791), pp. 2-3; K.H.L. Pölitz, *Die Constitutionen der europäischen Staaten seit den letzten 25 Jahren,* in 4 volumes (Leipzig and Altenburg: 1817-25), vol. 2, pp. 16-31.

41. After Szczęsny Potocki gave up his plans to emigrate to the U.S., he stayed in Paris from 30 March 1790; Szymon Askenazy, *Przymierze polsko-pruskie* (The Polish-Prussian Alliance) (Warszawa: 1918), pp. 257-68.

42. The decisive role of the King in the constitutional debates is described in detail by Emanuel Rostworowski, "Marzenie dobrego obywatela, czyli królewski projekt konstytucji" (The dream of a good citizen, or the royal project for a constitution), in *Legendy i fakty XVIII w.,* pp. 265-464.

43. The importance of Philip Mazzei for the transfer of ideas of the French Revolution to Poland has not been adequately evaluated in the literature; see the article by Witold Łukasiewicz in *Polski Słownik Biograficzny,* vol. 20 (1975): 322-24; R. C. Garlick,

Philip Mazzei, Friend of Jefferson: His Life and Letters (Baltimore: 1933); Howard R. Marraro, *Philip Mazzei, Virginia's Agent in Europe* (New York, 1935); Fabre provides a summary, *Stanislas-Auguste Poniatowski,* pp. 505-33; Szymon Askenazy, *Napoleon a Polska* (Napoleon and Poland), vol. 1, *Upadek Polski a Francja* (France and the Fall of Poland) (Warszawa and Kraków: 1918), pp. 163 ff. Philip Mazzei, *Selected Writings and Correspondence,* vol. 2, 1788-1791. *Agent for the King of Poland During the French Revolution.* Margherita Marchione ed. (Prato: Cassa di Risparmi e Deposito, 1983).

44. The King wrote on this to Mazzei, "Je me trouverai toujours très honoré de me voir en compagnie de Franklin et de Washington," Fabre, *Stanislas-Auguste Poniatowski,* p. 519; Mazzei, *Selected Writings,* p. 344.

45. Remnants of this declaration–which was understandably rejected by the "Republicans"–reached the Constitution in Article V, *New Constitution of the Government of Poland,* p. 12. See also Kołłątaj, *O ustanowieniu...,* vol. 2, p. 34; Leśnodorski, *Dzieło Sejmu Czteroletniego,* p. 149. Rostworowski; *Legendy...*p. 295.

46. Only 182 deputies, roughly one-third of the total, took part in the decisive session because the other deputies were still on Easter vacation. Because the Constitution was subsequently ratified by most of the dietines, however, doubts about the legality of its passage appear unwarranted; see Kalinka, *Sejm Czteroletni,* vol. 3.

47. Marceli Handelsman, *Konstytucja Trzeciego Maja roku 1791* (The Constitution of the Third of May 1791) (Warszawa: 1907), pp. 85-109; Leśnodorski, *Dzieło Sejmu Czteroletniego,* pp. 219-375; Jerzy Michalski, *Konstytucja 3 Maja* (Warszawa: Zamek Królewski, 1985).

48. This formulation, unique for its time, was later used in a similar way by the Napoleonic principate; significantly, it was never used by the German monarchies, even after the establishment of constitutional forms of government.

49. Both terms were discussed in the Diet but no agreement was reached; compare Handelsman, *Konstytucja 3 Maja,* pp. 58 ff.

50. Article IV expressly stated that the rural populace was "the most numerous in the nation, consequently forming the most considerable part of its force," *New Constitution of Poland,* p. 9.

51. Extensive citations from copious contemporary opinions were gathered as early as 1793 by Kołłątaj in *O ustanowieniu i upadku,* vol. 3, pp. 42-49; and by Joachim Lelewel in *Geschichte Polens* (Leipzig, 1847), pp. 319-27. For a more recent work, see Fabre's *Stanislas-Auguste Poniatowski,* pp. 526-33, which takes the older literature fully into consideration.

52. Ewald Friedrich Graf v. Hertzberg, "Abhandlung über äußere, innere und religiöse Staatsrevolutionen" in: *Staatsanzeigen* 17 (Göttingen 1792): 46. The first edition of Schulz's *Reise eines Liefländers von Riga nach Warschau ...* (Berlin, 1795/96). For the description of his stay in Warsaw (September 1791-June 1792), see the new

edition by Klaus Zernack, *Reise nach Warschau* (Frankfurt: Suhrkamp Verlag, 1982). See also: Hermann Vahle, "Die polnische Verfassung vom 3. Mai 1791 im zeitgenössischen deutschen Urteil," in: *Jahrbücher für Geschichte Osteuropas* 19 (1971): 347-370.

53. On this see the collection of several hundred comments from the contemporary United States by Miecislaus Haiman, *The Fall of Poland in Contemporary American Opinion* (Chicago: Polish Roman Catholic Union, 1935).

54. Marceli Handelsman, "Konstytucja 3 maja r. 1791 a społeczna opinia publiczna we Francji" (The Constitution of 3 May 1791 and public opinion in France), *Studia historyczne* (Warszawa, 1911), pp. 75-104; Fabre, *Stanislas-Auguste Poniatowski*, pp. 526-30. The reception of French events by "public opinion" in Poland was investigated by Helena Rzadkowska, *Stosunek polskiej opinii publicznej do Rewolucji Francuskiej* (The attitude of Polish public opinion to the French Revolution) (Warszawa: Książka, 1948).

55. Fabre, *Stanislas-Auguste Poniatowski*, p. 529.

56. This theme cannot be further pursued at present; see, among others, Charles E. Konic, *Comparaison des constitutions de la Pologne et de la France* (Lausanne, 1918); Henry B. Hill, "The Constitutions of Continental Europe, 1789-1813," *Journal of Modern History* 8, 1 (1936): 90 ff.

57. The citizens of the larger cities wished to form militias, for which Kołłątaj in particular made a stand; but even patriotic spokesmen such as Ignacy Potocki recoiled before such action because of the "French example." On this, Emanuel Rostworowski, "Sprawa milicji mieszczańskich w ostatnim roku Sejmu Czteroletniego" (The question of citizens' militias in the last year of the Four-Year Diet), *Przegląd Historyczny* 46 (1955): 561-84.

58. Bronisław Dembiński, *Ze źródeł do dziejów drugiego i trzeciego rozbioru Polski* (Sources on the history of the Second and Third Partitions of Poland) (Lwów, 1902), pp. 37 ff.

59. Kołłątaj, *O ustanowieniu i upadku,* vol. 3, pp. 48-54, vol. 4, p. 79.

60. Compare Handelsman, *Konstytucja 3 Maja,* pp. 104 ff.

61. In Article IV of the cardinal law of 1768 the nation was expressly identified with the noble estate; this definition was clearly nullified in Article IV of the new constitution, Handelsman, *Konstytucja 3 Maja,* pp. 84, 91. Tadeusz Łepkowski referred to the fundamental importance of this development in *Polska–narodziny nowoczesnego narodu 1764-1870* (Poland–the birth of a modern nation, 1764-1870) (Warszawa: PWN, 1967), p. 233 and passim.

62. Handelsman, *Konstytucja 3 Maja,* pp. 108 f.

63. The most extensive study of the Second Partition is that of Robert Howard Lord, *The Second Partition of Poland: A Study in Diplomatic History* (Cambridge:

Harvard Univ. Press, 1915). On the problem of the partitions and the current state of research and interpretation, see Michael G. Müller, *Die Teilungen Polens 1772, 1793, 1795* (München: C.H. Beck, 1984).

64. German text in F. von Smitt, *Suwarow und Polens Untergang, nach archivalischen Quellen,* part 2 (Leipzig and Heidelberg, 1858), pp. 40-51, 223-27. See also Władysław Smoleński, *Konfederacja Targowicka* (The Confederation of Targowica) (Kraków, 1903).

65. Cited in Askenazy, *Napoleon a Polska,* p. 195.

66. Bogusław Leśnodorski presents the entire issue of Polish Jacobinism, *Les Jacobins Polonais* (Paris, 1965).

67. Besides Askenazy, *Przymierze polsko-pruskie,* pp. 195 ff, see also Lord, *The Second Partition,* pp. 377 ff, on the Prussian fear of the odium of breaking the existing alliance.

68. General von Möllendorf presented a "Plan for the invasion of Poland" already on 1 July 1792, before the beginning of the offensive against France; on 8 November 1792, during the withdrawal from France, the mobilization order against the Republic was issued.

69. The German text of this proclamation is in R. Prümers, *Das Jahr 1793–Urkunden und Aktenstücke zur Geschichte der Organisation Südpreussens* (Posen, 1895), p. 21 (The declaration is dated already to 6 January 1793).

Translated by Philip Pajakowski

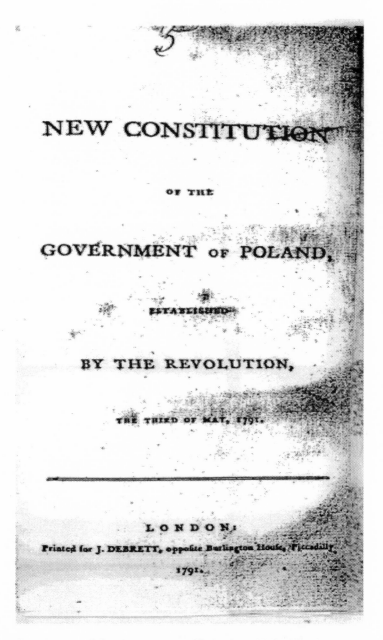

NEW CONSTITUTION

OF THE

GOVERNMENT OF POLAND,

ESTABLISHED

BY THE REVOLUTION,

THE THIRD OF MAY, 1791.

LONDON:

Printed for J. DEBRETT, opposite Burlington House, Piccadilly.

1791.

New Constitution of the Government of Poland established by the Revolution the Third of May 1791. The first edition. London: J. Debrett, 1791. Translated by Franciszek Bukaty the Polish Minister Resident in London, it also included the Declaration of the States Assembled. The title page. From the library of Thomas Jefferson (Library of Congress, Washington).

19

European and American Opinions of the Constitution of 3 May

Samuel Fiszman

The crowning achievement of the sessions of the Four-Year Diet, the Constitution of 3 May aroused lively interest, and the process of its creation was followed assiduously by the press in Europe and the United States. A large volume would be needed to contain the numerous statements, articles, reviews and even poems from the last decade of the 18th century that relate to the Constitution and reflect the intense debates of the time concerning the different paths leading to revolutionary reforms in the political and social sphere. It is fair to state on the basis of even inadequate research concerning this topic that it would be hard to find a serious newspaper or journal of the time in Europe or the United States which did not discuss, sometimes at length, the significance of the Polish Constitution, or one which did not include excerpts or often a complete translation of its articles.[1]

The *Nouvelles Extraordinaires de Divers Endroits*, universally called the *Gazette de Leyde*, played a leading role in reporting political news from Poland. As the most prominent international newspaper in the second part of the 18th century, with its extraordinarily large circulation and a reputation for its independence and impartiality, the *Gazette de Leyde* was the main source of information, not only for its readers, but also for other newspapers, about European political events both in Europe and in the United States. It was also an important and most objective source of news about the American revolution, and it published many materials received from John Adams and Thomas Jefferson. The latter had a high regard for the *Gazette* and called it "the only paper in Europe worth reading."[2]

Ideologically the *Gazette de Leyde* was clearly and consistently committed
to democracy. It sided with independence movements, political and social
reform and came out against absolutist regimes. Initally after the events of
July 14, 1789 it took a friendly position towards the reforms in France and
reprinted the text of *Declaration du droits de l'homme et du citoyen*, but the
rapid radicalization of the revolution caused a change in the *Gazette*'s attitude
and ever increasing reservations toward events in France.

The editors of the *Gazette,* Etienne Luzac (from 1738) and his nephew
Jean Luzac, who joined the editorial board in 1772 and after Etienne's death
in 1787 became the editor-in-chief until 1798, were able to provide rapid and
detailed information about events in Poland, due largely to the dispatches of
their correspondents in Poland, to the use of bulletins issued by the royal court
in Warsaw, and to the efforts of Augustyn Middleton who, starting in 1790,
was first the secretary and later the minister of the Commonwealth in the
Hague.

The first period during which the *Gazette* published news about Poland
relates to the years 1772-1775, the years of the First Partition and the stormy
discussions of the post-partition Diet. The second period embraced the years
of the Four-Year Diet, the Russian invasion, and the Kościuszko Insurrection.[3]

Often accompanied by editorial comments, and extensive reports, which
at times took up a significant part of an issue and often continued in the
Supplement to each issue, the *Gazette de Leyde* provided information about
the political situation in Poland, the long negotiations concerning the alliance
with Prussia, and it reported extensively on the proceedings of the sessions in
the Diet, pronouncements of the deputies and, especially, those of the King,
continually coming out on the side of the partisans of reform, the "Patriotic
Party," since the moderate nature of their ideas corresponded with the editor's
own convictions.

In 1789 the Polish burgher movement intensified its activities and became
formally organized when delegates from approximately two hundred royal
cities from Poland and Lithuania signed the Act of Union in Warsaw. The
movement, which strove for improvements in burgher rights, found particular
resonance among the middle class in Holland and in the rest of Europe. In its
Supplement of December 29, the *Gazette* wrote about the Memorandum,
which contained the burghers' demands, and which was presented on December
2 to the King, to the Marshals of the Diet, and to the Chancellors by the
delegates of cities assembled in Warsaw: "Les dix points, dont il est composé,
sont tous également remarquables et tendent directement à réintégrer les
Bourgeois dans leurs Droits de Citoyen." This was already the second version

of the Memorandum presented by the delegates who, clad in black costumes resembling those worn by French burghers, arrived at the royal castle in a solemn procession of carriages (hence the term "black procession"). The first Memorandum had been criticized by the King, who found in it expressions "borrowed from the contemporary French press."[4] Eventually even the second version was not considered to be fully satisfactory and a final, slightly different, version was prepared. In the January 1, 1790 issue, the *Gazette* placed a condensed text of the third version entitled Memorandum of the Cities of Poland and the Grand Duchy of Lithuania, which had been distrubuted to the King, and the Diet between December 8 and 10, 1789. The terms used in the commentary to these reports: *Tiers-état, Droits de Citoyen* immediately suggested a comparison with contemporary French terms referring to the Third Estate, while the phrase "*L'époque où nous sommes,...fertile en Révolution...*" placed the demands of the Polish cities in the broader context of the American and French revolutions.

The interest of the *Gazette de Leyde* in Polish affairs was roused not only by the burghers' quest for rights, but even more so by the work of the Diet on the reform of the State. In its edition of January 8, 1790, the paper contained information about the Principles to Reform the Government, the text of which was submitted to the Diet by the Marshal of Lithuania and the leader of the "Patriotic Party," Ignacy Potocki, on December 17, 1789. On January 12, the *Gazette* published the amended eight-point second version of the Principles together with a report on the furious discussion in the Diet over both the final version of the Principles and the Memorandum of the Cities, In this discussion, continued in the January 15 issue, essential differences were noted between the *partisans de l'oligarchie polonaise* and the champions of reforms whose ideas were in accord with the spirit of the times. The next stage in the reformation of the state, the new and extensive Project to Reform the Government, proposed on August 2, 1790, did not escape the notice of the paper. In the September 21 edition, the paper reports on controversy which was immediately stirred up by the Project with regard to the question of succession versus free elections to the throne, whereas the October 5 edition gave a generally positive characterization of the Project. However, the *Gazette* did not overlook the difficulties of quieting the voices of the opponents of reform in the Diet.

Les dernières Delibérations de la Diète ont été des plus intéressants puisque l'on y a posé les principes fondamentaux du Gouvernement de la République. Dans un travail, qui avait pour objet de lui donner une Constitution permanente, l'on aurait pu s'attendre à de grandes innovations proportionnées aux lumières de notre Siècle et au changement, survenu dans la plupart des systèmes politiques, depuis que la Pologne a reçu sa Forme actuelle. Mais, soit le nombre de difficultés insurmontables, qui se sont présentées, soit la force des préjugés Nationaux, l'on ne s'est guères écarté des anciennes Loix fondamentales.

The *Gazette de Leyde* filled its pages with extensive news about the work of the Diet with even greater frequency when the Diet in 1791, after protracted discussions on projected reforms, began to promulgate new laws. The news about the passage of the Law on Cities met with special approval from the editor, who wrote in the *Supplement* of May 3:

A l'époque si intèressante pour les Droits de l'Humanité, dont nous sommes témoins, nous regardons comme l'un de nos principaux devoirs d'éclairer le Public, par de fidèles rapports, sur les succès qu'ont les généreux Défenseurs de leurs Concitoyens et les Amis de la Liberté, dans les divers Pays de l'Europe...C'est donc avec la plus vive satisfaction, que nous nous voyons en état de communiquer à nos Lecteurs des détails authentiques sur le nouvel ordre de choses, qui va naître en Pologne.

This promise is fulfilled in the May 3 to May 17 issues in which the paper reported news from Warsaw about the circumstances surrounding the passage by the Diet on April 14 of the Principles to the Project on Cities; printed a translation of the 18 points of the Principles; and reported on the session of the Diet on April 18 when the final version of the Law on Cities was decided on.

In the May 3 issue, the *Gazette de Leyde*, announcing the passage by the Diet on April 14 of the Principles, deems it a manifestation of the Epoch of Human Rights, a victory by the Friends of Freedom and stresses the differences in approach in France and Poland both in terms of substance and in the manner of passage of these rights. In France this took place in conditions of turmoil and violent upheaval, whereas:

La Pologne seule aura la gloire de se regénérer sans troubles civils, sans convulsions, parce qu'elle le fait par degrés, et qu'elle ne s'expose point à risquer le tout pour le tout, en changeant tout-à-coup ses principes et la Forme de son Gouvernement.

Such a comparison in which the peaceful character and the moderate nature of Polish transformations is revealed, came to characterize accounts of Polish reforms on the pages of the *Gazette*.

With the greatest satisfaction the paper reports on the passage of the Law on Cities on April 18 in its May 6 issue:

La nouvelle Constitution de la Pologne, telle qu'elle a été agréée dans la Séance du 14 de ce mois, vient d'être sanctionnée et convertie en Loi.

N U M E R O XXXVII.

NOUVELLES EXTRAORDINAIRES

D E

DIVERS ENDROITS

du MARDI 10. Mai, 1791.

EXTRAIT d'une Lettre de VARSO-
VIE *du* 23. *Avril.*

IL est difficile de peindre l'enthousiasme, qui règne ici depuis que le
18. de ce mois les Etats assemblés
en Diète ont converti en Loi Con-
stitutionnelle les 18. Articles, pro-
posés le 14. par Mr. *Suchorzewski,*
pour rendre aux Villes leurs anciens
Droits & rétablir l'Ordre Bourgeois dans l'exer-
cice de toutes les Prérogatives, attachées à
l'état de Citoyen. Le Roi, comme il a été
le premier à seconder de son appui un Projet
aussi juste & aussi utile, est aussi le premier à
jouir de cette satisfaction intime, qui naît de
la conviction d'avoir fait un sacrifice au bien
public & préféré le salut de tous à la préémi-
nence du petit nombre. Ce sentiment éclata,
lorsque le 19. la Bourgeoisie de *Varsovie* en
Corps alla faire ses remercîmens à Sa Majesté.
Témoin de la reconnoissance, l'on peut même
me dire des transports de ces Citoyens, dont
la plûpart lui baisèrent la main, quelques-uns
lui embrassèrent les genoux, Elle ne put s'empê-
cher de dire, qu'*en ce moment Elle jouissoit de
tout le plaisir de la Royauté.* Cette parole,
adressée à l'un des Officiers de la Cour, fut
entendue; & la Salle d'Audience rétentit des
cris de *Vive le Roi!* Il semble, que le nouvel
ordre de choses ait fait disparoître tout orgueil
de rang, & que chacun s'empresse à fouler

aux piés les tristes préjugés de Noblesse, qui
bientôt ne seront considérés en *Pologne* que
comme des traces de l'ancienne barbarie. Non-
seulement le Prince *Adam Czartoriski* s'est
fait inscrire parmi les Bourgeois de *Varsovie*;
son exemple a été suivi par le Comte *Potocki*, Grand-Maréchal de *Lithuanie*; & le
Comte *Malachowski*, Maréchal de la Diète,
en faisant la même démarche, a témoigné,
qu'à l'expiration de sa Dignité actuelle il se
croiroit honoré d'être Bourguemaître de *Varsovie*. — Ce n'est pas seulement l'esprit d'é-
galité vraiment Républicaine, qui a tout-à-
coup gagné le dessus parmi les Représentans
de la Nation *Polonoise*; c'est encore celui de
la Tolérance Religieuse & Civile. En rédigeant
la nouvelle Constitution, l'on suggéra l'idée
de donner la préférence à la Religion *Catholique* pour les Magistratures & les autres Charges des Municipalités: Cette idée fut appuyée
par des recommandations étrangères. L'on
s'en étonna d'autant plus, parce que des Nations, qui ne sont pas elles-mêmes dans le sein
de la Religion *Catholique*, ne sçauroient avoir
aucun intérêt, qu'en *Pologne* leurs Frères *Pro-
testans* soient exclus des Postes honorables,
qui pourroient être la récompense de leur ver-
tu civique, sans différence de Religion: L'on
craignit les effets d'une Politique, faite pour
rallumer les anciennes querelles des *Dissi-
dens*, & en semant la zizanie dans l'intérieur

The page of the May 10, 1791, issue of *Gazette de Leyde* describing the enthusiasm
in Warsaw after the adoption of the Law on Cities. (Indiana University, Lilly
Library).

SUPPLEMENT AUX NOUVELLES EXTRAORDINAIRES
DE DIVERS ENDROITS
du NUMERO XL.
De L E Y D E, *le* 20. *Mai,* 1791.

EXTRAIT d'une Lettre de VARSOVIE *du* 4. *Mai.*

LA journée d'hier 3. Mai, qui a fait changer de face à la *Pologne*, fera trop remarquable dans fes Faftes, pour ne pas rapporter avec quelque détail les circonftances les plus immédiates, qui ont précédé, accompagné, & fuivi cette grande Révolution. A 3. heures du matin, un nombre affez confidérable de Patriotes, inftruits en fecret du but qu'on fe propofoit de remplir à la Séance du jour, fe rendirent chez le Roi: L'on y convint, en préfence de Sa Majefté, d'effectuër la Révolution dans la journée; & l'on en prit l'engagement folemnel. La Séance devant être publique, comme d'ufage, les Tribunes & Galeries des Spectateurs, dès que la Salle fut ouverte, furent fi remplies dans une demie-heure, que des milliers ne purent entrer & refférent devant la porte dans l'attente du grand évènement, qui alloit fe paffer. La délibération du jour devoit avoir les Finances pour objet: Mais ce ne furent point les Maréchaux, qui en firent l'ouverture comme d'ordinaire: Le Roi lui-même prit la parole: Sa Maj. dit en fubftance, "que, malgré toutes les affurances, il ne ceffoit de fe répan- dre un bruit fourd, & que de tous côtés l'on recevoit des avis, que les trois Puif- fances voifines pourroient enfin s'accorder & terminer la jaloufie, qui les divife, aux dépens des Poffeffions de la République; que l'unique moyen d'affurer à la *Pologne* fon intégrité & de la préferver d'une ruine, que lui préparoit la Politique étrangère, c'étoit de lui donner une Conftitution, qui affurât fon Indépendance dans l'Intérieur; que dans cette vuë Elle avoit fait rédiger le Projet d'une Conftitution, calquée principalement fur celles de l'*Angleterre* & de l'*Amérique-Unie*, en évitant néanmoins les défauts, qu'on pouvoit leur reprocher, & en fe prêtant, autant qu'il étoit poffible, aux circonftances particulières & locales du Pays." A l'appui des informations, relatives aux Puiffances Etrangères, il fut communiqué à la Diète quelques Dépêches des Miniftres de la République dans l'Etranger, qui annonçoient, combien ces Cours étoient oppofées? ce qu'il fut donné une nouvelle Conftitution à la *Pologne*, & combien il étoit probable, qu'un nouveau danger menaçoit fes Poffeffions. Comme le Roi avoit terminé fon Difcours, en demandant que la lecture de fon Projet fût faite fur le champ, & qu'on le convertit en Loi dans la jour- née même, le Plan, que S. M. avoit fait dreffer, fut lu: Il eft conçu avec autant de clarté que d'étenduë, treçant avec exactitude les limites des trois Pouvoirs, leurs devoirs, la manière de les établir, leur refponfabilité, les Droits de chaque Ordre de Citoyens, leurs relations réci- proques &c. (*Nous en avons rapporté les principaux Articles dans notre* Gazette *de ce jour.*) — Tel fut le commencement paifible de la Révolution: En voici les circonftances ultérieures."

"Lecture faite du Projet préfenté par le Roi, chacun eut la liberté de dire fon fentiment: Il fe prononça plufieurs Difcours, foit pour en faire l'éloge, foit pour le defapprouver, foit pour en demander un examen long & réfléchi: L'ardeur fe mêla naturellement bientôt à cette difcuf- fion: Il y eut des cris & un commencement de tumulte. Tous les Repréfentans des Provinces de l'*Ukraïne* & de *Podolie* fe déclarèrent contre la nouvelle Forme de Gouvernement qu'on leur of- froit. Mr. *Suchozewfki*, Norce de *Kalifch*, qui tout récemment s'eft diftingué d'une manière fi brillante en faveur de l'admiffion de la Bourgeoifie aux Droits de la Nobleffe, & qu'on peut re- garder comme l'un des principaux Auteurs de cet achèminement à la Révolution, s'oppofa au- jourd'hui avec non moins de zèle au complément de cette regénération de la Patrie: Le Patriotif- me, qui l'anime, fut alarmé fur-tout de l'Hérédité de la Couronne: Il s'avança & fe jetta à ge- noux fur les marches du Trône, en fuppliant, en conjurant le Roi, *de renoncer à fes vuës pour la Succeffion Héréditaire à la Royauté, puifqu'elle feroit le Tombeau de la Liberté* Polonoife. Plu- fieurs autres Nonces, qui étoient dans les mêmes fentimens, alléguèrent les Inftructions de leurs Provinces, qui *leur défendoient expreffément de confentir jamais à l'Hérédité du Trône.* On leur répondit de tous côtés, "qu'il ne s'agiffoit pas aujourd'hui d'une Légiflation en forme, mais d'une Révolution d'Etat, qui n'admettoit point des formalités, d'ailleurs impraticables dans la fituation préfente des chofes, & pour le fuccès de laquelle, fi l'on s'y oppofoit, la force fuppléeroit au manque de volonté des réfractaires." On infifta, qu'au moins le Projet fût pris *ad deliberandum,* comme toute autre Loi nouvelle; mais la très-grande pluralité s'y refufa: il faut (crièrent-ils) *paffer outre aujourd'hui! Nous ne defamparerons point d'ici que la chofe n'ait fon accompliffement:* L'Oppofition repartit: *Et nous ne defamparerons point qu'on n'y ait re-*

Ce fut avant-hier, 18 Avril, que le Comité pour le travail de la
Constitution présenta à la Diète in pleno le Projet, touchant les droits
des Villes et de la Bourgeoisie, couché dans toute son étendue; et il
passa unanimement, à la grande satisfaction de la Capitale et de tous les
bons Citoyens, qui en témoignèrent leur joye, non pas néanmoins par
des applaudissements, qu'on croit ici déroger à la dignité des
Représentants d'une grande Nation et plus convenir à un Théatre qu'à
une Assemblée Législative...Chacun sent le dégré de force et par
conséquent de véritable indépendance, que la Nation Polonaise va
acquérir par la réunion de toutes ses parties dans un seul Corps, que les
intérêts opposés de deux Ordres distincts ne partageront plus. Il en est
même parmi la haute Noblesse, qui se montrent supérieurs aux préjugés
et à l'amour-propre de leur naissance.

Praise for the stance taken by the Polish nobles, their voluntary agreement
to the conferment of rights on townspeople and their participation in the
reforms of the state became issues to which the paper was to return more than
once.

Describing in its issue of May 10 the enthusiasm with which the
townspeople had greeted the rights they had been granted, their gratitude to
the King for his assistance, and the enrollment of the Marshal of the Diet,
Stanisław Małachowski, into Warsaw's city register, the *Gazette de Leyde* notes:

Ce n'est pas seulement l'esprit d'égalité vraiment Républicaine, qui a
tout-à-coup gagné le dessus parmi les Représentans de la Nation
Polonaise; c'est encore celui de Tolérance Religiouse et Civile.

Looking at the Law on Cities from the perspective of a Protestant country
and recalling earlier arguments in the Diet about religious dissent, the
newspaper saw the passage of the Law as a manifestation of religious tolerance
and an affirmation of the fact that all Christians may become citizens of towns.
It further expressed its approbation by the assertion that "in this instance Poland
has emulated the splendid example of France."

But the *Gazette* devoted its greatest attention to the debates on and the
adoption of the Constitution of 3 May. Almost the whole issue of May 20 was
filled with dispatches from Poland about this event:

La journée d'hier a produit ici la Révolution la plus heureuse pour la
Pologne, en ce qu'elle n'a pas coûté une goutte de sang; qu'il n'y a pas
été employé un seul Soldat, ni aucune Arme, et que sans aucune violence
elle a été effectuée de manière, que tous les droits légitimes de la Liberté
sont assurés plus que jamais...

S'il y a dans ce siècle des Miracles, il s'en est opéré un en Pologne...toute
la Constitution Polonaise a été refondue, améliorée, fixée, passée et

décrétée dans un seul jour, dans une seule Séance; il ne reste que quelques Réglements à faire, qui en sont la suite naturelle. Ce qu'il y a de plus étonnant encore, c'est que cette Révolution, qui sera à jamais mémorable dans les Annales de la République et dans l'Histoire de l'Humanité, a été tout-à-fait inattendue, qu'elle s'est effectuée sans appareil Militaire, sans appui étranger, sans intrigues comme sans violence, par la sagesse du Roi, aidé d'un petit nombre de Ministres Patriotes et éclairés, et par un mouvement volontaire de la très grande pluralité des Représentants de la Nation, applaudie par l'unanimité des Habitants de Varsovie.

Reports from Warsaw about the day of May 3, together with a condensed, but not entirely accurate, version of the articles of the Constitution were printed in the same issue. They were accompanied by commentary from the publisher where the opinion is expressed that in terms of form, the Polish Constitution is to a significant degree a copy of the French Constitution (that is, the *Declaration du droits de l'homme et du citoyen*).

Telle est l'esquisse rapide de la nouvelle Constitution, qui va régénérer la Pologne...Ce que nous venons de dire suffit pour faire voir, que, quant à sa forme, elle est calquée en très grande partie sur la nouvelle Constitution Française. Et, si cette Constitution a pour ennemis tous les Partisans du Pouvoir arbitraire, répandus sur la surface de l'Europe...ce n'est pas une petite gloire pour la Nation Française, que son exemple ait sitôt servi à modéler une heureuse réforme chez d'autres Peuples.

However, in terms of its less extreme content and, especially, in the manner of its creation the Polish Constitution differs from its exemplar, in favor of the former, As distinct from the French, the Polish Constitution was prepared and sworn to by the King and the Diet, and it was welcomed by the nation. Such distinctions were, in fact, noted earlier in the pages of the *Gazette de Leyde* in its treatment of the Law on Cities. They became even more pronounced in reference to the Polish Constitution, and the *Gazette* emphasized its moderate and peaceful nature as opposed to the stormy events in France. It also pointed out that the democratization of the Polish governmental system was achieved as a result of the good will shown by a patriotic King, enlightened magnates and noble deputies.

The *Supplement* to the issue of May 20 and the *Gazette* of May 24 with its *Supplement* published more details on the events of May 3 and on the adoption of the Constitution, as well as a more detailed and corrected summary of its articles. This was continued in the issues of May, June and July. In the *Supplement* to the issue of June 21, the paper announced that it is starting to reprint the entire text of the Constitution from the French translation published in Warsaw by P. Dufour and added the following explanation:

Quoique nous ayons déjà donné le Précis de cette Constitution une
Pièce aussi essentielle, soit pour l'histoire de l'époque présente, soit pour
la connaissance du Droit Public, mérite, que nous l'insérions
successivement, mais en entier, dans nos Feuilles.

The last installment appeared in the issue of July 15.

In the remaining months of 1791 and in the first half of 1792, the *Gazette
de Leyde* provides extensive accounts of sessions in the Diet and of the new
laws passed there. The ceremony of welcoming the first city deputies in the
Diet was described in the August 4 issue. The October 21 issue contained
information on the speech given in the Diet by Stanisław Sołtyk, deputy from
Cracow and an active proponent of reform, on the occasion of the proclamation
of the French Constitution in September, Sołtyk called on the Diet:

pour rendre aux principes de la Révolution Française la justice, que
tout Ami de l'Humanité leur doit, mais qu'il est surtout du devoir de
tout vrai Polonais de ne leur point refuser, à raison de la conformité,
qu'il y a dans les principaux points entre la nouvelle Constitution
Polonaise et celle de France.

One should note that the French Constitution was immediately reprinted in
Warsaw, both in the original and in translation and that articles expressing
admiration for the French Constitution and noting the similarity to it of the
Polish Constitution appeared simultaneously in the press.[5] The avoidance of
any reference to such a connection and even an expressed denial of any similarity
in the official declarations by Stanisław August was, to a great extent, caused
by the necessity of not providing Poland's neighbors with arguments against
the Polish Constitution.

On November 11 the paper described the circumstances leading to the
preparation of the Law of Mutual Guarantee of Two Nations which regulated
the relations between the two basic components of the Republic, Poland and
Lithuania, and it published the relevant text. In the fall of 1791 the newspaper
gave special attention to the extended debates in the Diet concerning the sale
of royal demesnes which had previously been leased, usually for life, to the
royal officials *(starosta)*. Those in Poland who opposed this proposal argued
that it imitated similar resolutions by the French National Assembly. In the
Supplement of January 3, 1792, the paper noted with satisfaction that "Enfin
la longue discussion sur la vente des Starosties et des Biens Domaniaux de la
Couronne s'est terminée par la triumphe du Parti." The resolution of December
19 was in fact won with great difficulty by the "Patriotic Party," due particularly
to the efforts of Hugo Kołłątaj, the main ideologist behind the plan for broad
reforms. The paper returned to this resolution in its January 17, 20, and 27

issues where it published the text of the resolution, explained its goals, and cited the King's words from his address to the Diet that the rights of the peasants living on these estates "are guaranteed on the basis of ancient royal prerogatives." Such assurances were not accidental. The main purpose of selling the estates was to reorganize the treasury and to create funds for the army, but this occasion also provided the opportunity, consciously undertaken, to touch on the matter of guaranteeing the rights of the peasants and to provide "a precedent and model for a broader peasant reform."[6]

The *Supplement* of March 9, 1792, carried the news about the sessions of the dietines, which voiced their approval of the Constitution. The paper unfailingly continued to report on the work of the Diet and on the external situation of Poland until the time that the Diet terminated its deliberations on May 29 as a result of the Russian invasion.

Collected together, information about the Diet in the pages of the *Gazette de Leyde,* the texts of passed laws, the discussions, the addresses of the King, marshals and deputies, would form in large measure a diary of the Four-Year Diet's activities. Extensive also were its reports about prevailing attitudes, and about the popular support enjoyed by the Constitution, both in the circles of the nobility and among city dwellers. Less space was given to the isolated and generally condemned group of enemies of reforms, who were preparing "sous les auspices et avec le secours de la Russie, une contre-révolution en Pologne." Here the names of the future leaders of the infamous Targowica Confederacy were mentioned for the first time. Reports about the Diet and the internal situation of the Republic were interspersed with equally extensive information about Poland's international situation. Such information, collected in a single volume, would also form a kind of chronicle of events.

In all of these reports and in the editorial commentaries, the Constitution met with general applause in the *Gazette* which referred to it as a "grand événement," "grande Révolution," "hereuse Révolution," "memorable Révolution," "monument trop digne." During the dramatic weeks of war with the Russian invader, Jean Lusac in an editorial of June 29, 1792, expressed his admiration for the Polish revolution, contrasting it in even sharper terms than previously to the French revolution, which was taking on even more radical turn in this period. He writes that:

Si la fin du dix-huitième Siècle, dont nous sommes les témoins, formera dans l'Histoire une époque aussi intéressante qu'aucune de celles que nous offrent les Annales de l'Humanité, ce n'en est pas une des moindres singularités, qu'il existe à cette même époque deux Révolutions à la fois, entreprises pour la réforme du Gouvernement et pour l'établissement de la Liberté Nationale,...

The revolution and the manner of its realization, wrote Luzac, was exactly opposite in the two countries, since the unity of the nation is evident in Poland while anarchy and lawlessness came to rule in France. Given such a state of affairs, he argues, the Polish revolution provides a shining example which serves to negate the arguments of the enemies of humanity who would deny man's aspirations toward freedom:

> Il semble, que la Providence ait réservé la Révolution Polonaise pour réfuter les calomnies des Fauteurs du Despotisme, qui se servent de l'exemple de la Révolution Française en preuve de leur thèse, que "la vraie Liberté n'est par faite pour le Genre humain, et que les Souverains sont interessés à châtier sévérement tous les Peuples, qui oseraient y aspirer."

In the *Supplement* to the issue of 10 August 1792, Luzac once again affirmed his high regard for the Polish Constitution, so often given voice in the pages of the *Gazette de Leyde*. This time he wrote when the Constitution already ceased to have force as a result of external military intervention:

> La Pologne est en ce moment, après la France, le principal objet de l'attention publique dans toute l'Europe. Le dénouement des circonstances compliquées, qu'a amené la Révolution Française, s'approche. Celui de la Révolution Polonaise est déjà venu. Les principes généreux, sur lesquels celle-ci était fondée; l'excellence de la nouvelle Constitution prise en général; l'approbation presqu' universelle; la joie du People surtout en la recevant; le courage, avec lequel la brave armée Polonaise l'a défendue;–tous ces titres réunis lui eussent mérité une issue des plus favorables, et cependant sont sort est malheureux.

One can certainly agree with Jeremy D. Popkin's statement that:

> With the exception of the American Constitution, he had never committed his paper so enthusiastically to the celebration of such a movement... Luzac's paper ensured that Poland's fate did not go unnoticed...More than any other periodical at the time, the *Gazette de Leyde* publicized the valiant efforts at reform that culminated in the liberal constitution of May 1791, and thus preserved for posterity proof that Poland's fate was not wholly due to internal weaknesses and divisions. The *Gazette de Leyde*'s coverage was one link in the chain of publicity that kept sympathy for Polish independence alive in western Europe throughout the nineteenth century and made some contribution to the eventual reemergence of an independent Polish state after the First World War.[7]

According to the testimony of the time, as well as from a historical perspective, together with the *Gazette de Leyde* the most respected and most widely read newspaper in the last decade of the eighteenth century was the *Moniteur*, the full title of which was *Gazette Nationale, ou Le Moniteur Universel*.[8] Beginning with its first issues which appeared in November 1789, the *Moniteur* devoted a great deal of attention to news from Poland, both its external and internal situation. The very quantity of its information compares favorably and at times supplements that of the *Gazette de Leyde*, since the *Moniteur*, like the *Gazette*, had its own correspondents in Poland. One should also mention in this context the significance of the efforts to create contacts with the French press made by Philip Mazzei, a participant in the American Revolution and a friend and correspondent of Jefferson, who acted as the agent for Stanisław August in Paris. The manner in which the two newspapers interpreted news from Poland differed. The tone taken by the *Gazette de Leyde* concerning Polish reforms was consistently similar and at times identical to that of the "Patriotic Party" and the King. The attitude of the *Moniteur* to the reforms, together with approval, was tinged with criticism which grew sharper as the paper became more radical, reflecting the growning radicalism of the French Revolution.

The first matter which significantly engaged the attention of the *Moniteur*, as it had the *Gazette de Leyde*, was the burgher movement of 1789. Initiated in Warsaw and restricted at this time to royal cities, the movement sought to secure rights for the burgher class and had spread in the fall of that year to other royal cities in the Republic. In the December 3, 1789 issue, the *Moniteur* writes approvingly of opinions which had at this time arisen in the Diet concerning the rate of taxation which was to be levied on Warsaw and other large cities. It writes specifically of those in the Diet who had the audacity to assert:

qu'il serait peut-être nécessaire un jour d'être justes envers une classe nombreuse d'hommes utiles, qui n'ont point de Patrie dans le pays où ils ont pris naissance; dans un pays qu'ils servent de leur industrie, qu'ils soutiennent de leur labeur, et qui pourtant sont forcés de se dire habitants d'une République, sans en être citoyens.

In the following issues from December, the *Moniteur* reports on the meeting of delegates from royal cities and on the postulates they presented to the King. While the realization of these postulates is uncertain, the paper is convinced that the burghers must ultimately attain their rights, and hopes that "alors nous apprendrons s'il y aura bientôt en Europe un Peuple Polonais, et en Pologne une vraie République." In the December 23 issue the newspaper further deliberates on the situation of the burghers, and also the peasants, and asserts: "Donner une existence politique à un Peuple, c'est créer des hommes. Nous l'avons déjà dit en parlant de la Pologne; les habitants d'une République doivent en être les citoyens." Writing on December 25 about the December 2 manifestation of the delegates from royal cities and about their Memorandum of Cities, the paper notes that in Warsaw these events were identified with those in France: "On dit que la revolution de France éveille dans le Peuple de la République un véritable esprit de liberté." In the January 8 issue the paper summarized the postulates contained in the Memorandum of Cities and in the February 22, 26 and 28 issues it published a translation of the second edition of the Memorandum. Nor did the *Moniteur* fail to mention the project to reform the situation of the Jewish population which was proposed to the Diet on November 30 and December 5, 1789. The *Moniteur* wrote in its January 14, 1790 issue: "Il est probable que le dernier mémoire en faveur des Juifs, presenté à la diète, contient des principes d'humanité et de justice proportionnés aux progrès que font les lumières en Pologne."

In addition to the burgher question, the *Moniteur* devoted a great deal of space to the proposals for changing the political system in Poland. In the January 10 issue the newspaper placed, just as the *Gazette de Leyde* had done on January 12, its own translation of the Principles to Reform the Government, presented to the Diet on December 17, 1789. It concluded that this document could become the basis for a future constitution, but on the condition that it take into consideration the rights of the two estates, the burghers and the peasants.

In the course of 1790 news about Poland's internal and international situation received significant coverage in the *Moniteur,* especially the sessions on the Diet, reports on the deliberations concerning the Polish-Prussian alliance, addresses by the King, and, on numerous occasions, proceedings of lengthy discussions referring to the introduction of laws governing an orderly succession to the throne. The paper asserted with regret that the postulates forwarded by the burghers still had not been passed and that the Polish gentry considers itself to be the only class empowered to discharge legislative and executive duties. It felt that the present Diet had in fact made progress in some areas, that it had become, like the Estates General, a constitutional assembly, but that it was essentially composed of the nobility while the participants in the Estates General came from the Third Estate.

In the wealth of information about Poland in the first months of 1791 one notes approving comments relating to the comedy *Powrót posła* (The Return of the Deputy) by Julian Ursyn Niemcewicz. In the February 7 issue, the paper comments on the play's biting criticism of Sarmatian prejudicies, its advocacy of political reform, and its effect on current political debates, particularly those concerning the question of a hereditary throne. In the April 27 issue the *Moniteur* expresses its enchantment with the eloquent speech by Niemcewicz in the Diet where he argued for equal rights for the burgher class. The *Moniteur* cites his disagreement with the opinion that a nation is composed solely of those of noble birth and it poses the question: "Qui nous parle du père de Washington: qui s'informe des aïeux de Franklin: et cependant nous savons et la postérité saura que l'Amerique doit la liberté à ces deux hommes si justement fameux."

The postulates of the burghers finally became law and the paper welcomes the Law on Cities passed on April 18 in its issue of May 7, 1791:

La diète a terminé, dans la séance d'avant hier, jour devenu mémorable, un des points les plus importants de la constitution nouvelle, l'affaire des bourgeois, événement heureux pour la Pologne, lequel donne en un seul jour tant de citoyens à la republique. Les bourgeois des villes ont obtenu les articles constitutionnels qu'ils demandaient.

This statement is followed by a description of a long, intense debate at the session of the Diet which ended in the unanimous passage of the Law on Cities, and by a synopsis consisting of five points summarizing the privileges gained by the burghers. In connection with the reported discussions in the Diet concerning the rights of the burghers, the paper predicts a new destiny for Poland and contrasts events taking place at that time in Russia with those in Poland:

Ainsi l'on peut prévoir les nouvelles destinées de l'empire polonais. Tandis que...l'empire russe, se repaît de victoires, et donne des fêtes sur la tombe de trente mille turcs égorgés en un jour à Ismail, le Polonais discute les droits de l'homme et du citoyen, et manifeste son avancement dans l'art social, la premiere des sciences utiles et honorables pour l'espèce humaine.

The adoption of the Constitution of 3 May was received by the *Moniteur* with genuine enthusiasm. The *Supplement* from May 21 printed in its entirety the translation of the Constitution published by Dufour. In its May 22 issue the *Moniteur* published extensive information on the event:

La séance du 3 mai sera à jamais célèbre dans les fastes de la Pologne. La plus heureuse révolution s'est faite, pour ainsi dire, en ce seul jour mémorable. Dans une république de nobles, pays d'esclavage pour les autre hommes, la liberté a été rendue à tous, et les droits politiques aux habitants des villes, sans effusion de sang; il n'y a pas été commis une seule violence; il ne s'est pas présenté un seul soldat, et le peuple était sans armes.

There follows a description of how the text of the Constitution was prepared by "friends of the public weal," the role played by its creators, above all that of the King, details of the deliberations in the Diet, which led to the adoption of the Constitution by acclamation, and, finally by a discussion of the most important articles contained in the Constitution. The May 23 issue printed excerpts from numerous letters from Warsaw about the revolution which had taken place on May 3. The issue of May 26 published the proceedings from successive deliberations of the Diet devoted to the Constitution, while the May 30 issue contained a sizeable condensation of all eleven Articles of the Constitution, as well as the Declaration of the States Assembled from May 5, which nullified former laws contrary to the Constitution. In its June 2 issue the *Moniteur* placed a description of the celebrations in Warsaw on May 8 in honor of the King's birthday, a circumstance which provided a fitting occasion for the expression of the prevailing enthusiasm precipitated by the unique event of the 3 May revolution.

In the following months of 1791 and 1792 the *Moniteur* in almost every issue covered Poland's standing in the international arena, the situation in Poland, the proceedings of the Diet and the legislation passed there. Occasionally it printed texts in their entirety, such as the law of Mutual Guarantee in the November 16 issue, printed in a translation identical to that found in the *Gazette de Leyde*. Like the *Gazette de Leyde*, the *Moniteur* attached great importance to the long discussions concerning the matter of the sale of the royal demesne, stressing in the January 2 issue that in this respect Poland is following in the footsteps of France: "Le France s'en ressent et la Pologne va l'éprouver à son tour..." The newspaper wrote in its January 10 issue about the intelligent tactics of the designers which caused the Diet, on December 19, to pass the Principles for Organizing the Permanent Sale of Royal Lands, and on January 18 it provided further details concerning the vote on these Principles. A number of times the paper wrote about machinations by the enemies of the Constitution and compared them to the anti-revolutionary forces in France. With particular satisfaction it reported about the cooperation between the nobility and the burghers, about the election of burgher representatives to the Diet and their solemn reception by applause from the asembled deputies. On numerous occasions the paper discussed the role of Stanisław August, the *roi-citoyen*, as a promoter of reform. On the other hand, the paper praised the participation and the might of the Third Estate in the French revolution and contrasted it with the small role played by the burgher class in Polish reforms. Given the influence exerted by political clubs on events in France, the paper also exhibited a keen interest in the club which was formed in Warsaw called The Association of Friends of the Constitution.

As the situation in France took a more radical turn, the *Moniteur* adopted a more radical stance and, consequently, became more critical of the moderate Constitution of 3 May. In an article entitled *Réflexions sur la constitution polonaise*, which appeared on January 7, 1792, its author prefaced his remarks with the admission that:

> Il faut bien connaître l'état de dégradation où se trouvaient en Pologne les habitants des villes, pour apprécier les avantages que la nouvelle constitution leur a accordés. Sous ce rapport on doit convenir qu'on a beaucoup fait. C'est le premier pas vers les lumières, c'est-à-dire, vears la véritable prospérité de l'Empire...Stanislas-Auguste mérite sans dout les plus grands éloges, ainsi que les principaux de la noblesse, qui ont si efficacement concouru à la réforme des lois de l'Etat.

Nevertheless, later the article criticized not so much the Constitution as a whole, but its social program which did not grant freedom to the peasants, while the rights granted to the burghers related only to the royal cities, omitting private cities altogether. The author points out that the Constitution permits the gentry to grant freedom to their peasants (that is to exchange villein service for a rental charge) and to declare towns belonging to them as free. The alternative, he warns, is to risk civil war. In addition, the Law on Cities applied only to Christians; Jews and other non-Christians were excluded. The author concedes that the burghers gained a great many privileges since their representatives have become members of government commissions, the courts and the Diet, but he argues that their voice is of an advisory nature and restricted to matters concerning towns. It is true, he notes, that distinguished burghers will be granted nobility, but this is not a solution to the problem. The author concludes that the Polish nation is truly represented only by the nobility; the burghers still do not constitute a political force. Written from the point of view of achievements made in the realm of individual right by the French revolution, the article contains still another reproach, one often expressed in France, that in Poland "devenant un mode de dépréciation, par rapport à la célebre revolution française." It would appear that the article did not take into account the admiring statements (referred to above) about the French constitution found in the pages of the organs of the reform camp in Poland. The avoidance of offical statements comparing the two revolutions or showing the dependence of the Polish revolution on the French, did not intend to diminish the latter's importance. The lack or absence of such statements was, as has already been stated, the result of fears that such comparisons might be

AVIS A MM. LES SOUSCRIPTEURS.

MM. les souscripteurs du Moniteur sont prévenus que l'on ne recevra plus à l'avenir les souscriptions qu'au seul bureau de la rue des Poitevins, n.º 18. Les personnes qui ne voudront pas s'y transporter, sont priées de vouloir bien en donner avis, par la poste de Paris, à M. Aubry, directeur du bureau; qui enverra toucher chez elles le prix de l'abonnement pour trois, six, neuf mois, ou pour l'année entière, au choix de MM. les souscripteurs.

POLITIQUE.

POLOGNE.

Réflexions sur la constitution polonaise.

Il faut bien connaître l'état de dégradation, où se trouvaient en Pologne les habitans des villes, pour apprécier les avantages que la nouvelle constitution leur a accordés. Sous ce rapport on doit convenir qu'on a beaucoup fait. C'est le premier pas vers les lumières, c'est-à-dire, vers la véritable prospérité de l'Empire.

Autrefois les bourgeois des villes n'étaient pas libres, et l'on sait ce que c'est que de n'être pas libre en Pologne : il n'y avait point de vraie propriété pour eux, puisqu'ils ne pouvaient transmettre leurs biens à leurs héritiers. L'accès de presque toutes les places importantes ou lucratives leur était fermé : ils ne pouvaient être admis dans les tribunaux même inférieurs, ils étaient exclus des places d'avocats, des chaires publiques, et des canonicats gradués.

Stanislas-Auguste mérite sans doute les plus grands éloges, ainsi que les principaux de la noblesse, qui ont si efficacement concouru à la réforme des lois de l'État. Mais comme il ne s'agit point de peser les choses faites à la balance fautive d'un homme d'État, au lieu d'examiner en législateur ce qui reste à faire, il est bon et utile de préférer l'Europe à l'égard de la révolution de Pologne, de l'enthousiasme qui se distingue ni le présent de l'avenir, ni la réalité des illusions, enthousiasme qui, relativement à la Pologne, devenant un mode de dépréciation, par rapport à la célèbre révolution française, se communique particulièrement, et séduit d'abord tous les hommes nés pour la médiocrité dans leurs pensées comme dans leurs espérances.

Ensuite, on n'a rien fait pour garantir les droits du bourgeois contre les usurpations de la noblesse qui peut encore les tenir dans tel degré d'assoupissement qu'il lui plaît. Enfin, dans toutes les révolutions, (témoin la française) c'est dans l'exécution que se trouve la difficulté. En Pologne où tout le monde voulait être maître, où l'ordre était regardé comme le tombeau de la liberté, on pouvait délibérer de très-bonnes choses; mais le moyen de les exécuter! Comment une ville ou son magistrat parviendront-ils à contraindre un noble qui refuse obstinément de se soumettre au nouvel ordre des choses? La loi se fait, et voilà une source abondante de troubles, du moins au commencement. Toute la Pologne, la capitale même, retentissait des plaintes les plus amères sur l'état d'avilissement où la noblesse tenait ou s'efforçait de tenir les bourgeois, même les plus considérés. Après le 18 avril et le 3 mai, le bourgeois est resté, en Pologne, un zéro politique, et plusieurs Juifs ont déjà refusé de se faire bourgeois, d'après le nouveau système, persuadés qu'ils se trouveraient mieux dans la qualité de protégés.

Le bourgeois a maintenant la faculté d'acheter des biens nobles; mais alors il est soumis, à leur égard, aux tribunaux nobles. Il peut acheter pour lui et ses héritiers un village ou une ville entière, et alors il est anobli par la diete suivante. Dans l'armée, la cavalerie nationale exceptée, il peut monter par degrés jusqu'au grade d'officier, et certains grades lui donnent la noblesse ainsi qu'à sa postérité, sans qu'il soit obligé de payer les droits ordinaires. Il peut travailler dans différentes branches de l'administration, et dès qu'il est parvenu à certaines places, il devient noble; enfin chaque diete donnera la noblesse à trente bourgeois distingués par leurs services ou par leur mérite. Mais si quelques individus y gagnent, la classe entière y perd. On croirait difficilement que celui qui proposerait de faire chrétien, de tems en tems, les Juifs les plus distingués par leurs talens, par leur fortune ou par leur conduite, aussi résolu le problème de l'amélioration du sort de ce peuple.

Nous ajoutons, que la nation en Pologne n'est encore que la noblesse, et qu'il paraît que le tiers-état de France, du tems de Philippe-le-Bel, a été politiquement mieux partagé que ne l'est, à présent même, le bourgeois en Pologne.

Extrait d'une lettre de Varsovie, du 14 décembre,

exploited by the absolutist neighboring states, something that did, in fact, take place. The article was correct in perceiving the difficulties of bringing to fruition certain legislation, including that concerning social reforms. However, to answer some of the criticism in the brief period that the Constitution was in force, a number of private towns did in fact become free towns, and a proposal was submitted that cities belonging to the church would also be granted the same rights as the royal cities.[9] As far as the Jewish population is concerned, the Diet Deputation continued its work which had as its aim the regulation of the legal status of the Jews. Furthermore, the situation of the peasants, as was pointed out earlier, was also in the minds of the reformers, as is evident from their attempts to connect the resolution of the peasant problem with the decision to sell the royal demesnes. As can be seen from Hugo Kołłątaj's plans for the future, the co-author of the 3 May Constitution intended it not as a termination, but as the beginning of further social reforms.

In the first half of 1792 the *Moniteur* continued to devote a great deal of attention to events in Poland and to the deliberations in the Diet, but with the growing threat to Poland's independence, greater space was given to political news. In its May 28 issue the *Moniteur* published a detailed description of the ceremony in Warsaw organized to honor the first anniversary of the Constitution of 3 May. The *Moniteur* did not cease publishing detailed relations about the war with Russia, especially the Kościuszko Insurrection and, when Polish resistance was nearing its end, it wrote in the February 26, 1794 issue: "Ainsi a fini la plus juste des guerres, entreprise pour la cause la plus belle et la plus glorieuse qu'un peuple ait à défendre." The *Moniteur* has been called "the faithful mirror of the French Revolution," but it was also, in a significantly more modest way, for its contemporary and later readers, a mirror of the Polish revolution, of the dramatic battles in defense of its achievements, and of Poland's quest for independent existence.

Together with those of the *Moniteur*, there were other rapid and varied responses to the proclamation of the Constitution of 3 May in the French press, which had developed greatly in the revolutionary period and represented various parties, fractions and institutions. The special interest in the Polish constitution and at the same time the dissimilar and often ambivalent response of revolutionary France to the revolution in Poland was motivated by a number of factors. The memory of an old, close friendship which had joined Poland and France for centuries, memories of political and cultural ties, as well as very recent connections in the realm of political thought unquestionably played a role. Thanks to the rich political literature in 18th century France which touched on or was directly devoted to Polish affairs, France was not only well aware of such faults of the Polish political system as the all-powerful nobility and the bondage of the peasants. Due to Stanisław Leszczyński's *Voix Libre* published in France in several editions and due to the treatises devoted to Poland by Mably and, especially, by Rousseau, they were also aware of a very specific idea in Poland which proclaimed "a close bond between the concept of democracy and patriotism since love of country is a direct result of a republican political system." Jean Fabre notes that Garran de Coulon, himself a revolutionary activist, when he searched for antecedents to the young French revolution credited Poland with "le mérite d'avoir sauvegardé, en des siècles d'absolutisme, la liberté politique et comme l'image vivante de la démocratie." According to Fabre:

> Avant l'exemple américain, l'exemple polonais compte donc parmi ceux qui ont favorisé la cristallisation d'une certaine pensée politique française, celle qu'on trouve chez les lecteurs de Mably et de Rousseau, autour d'un idéal spécifiquement républicain.[10]

But, of course, the main reason for the admiration, and also a cause for argumentation, was the publication on May 3, 1791, of the Constitution in Poland, which occurred at the very moment when France, embroiled in debate, was nearing the moment of finishing its own Constitution.[11] At the meeting of the General Council of the Paris municipality on May 24, one of its members, the same Garran de Coulon mentioned above, proposed "that the municipality of the French capital send greetings to the municipality of Warsaw on the occasion of the successfully completed revolution, and that on June 3 a citizens' holiday be declared to honor the occasion."

> Il a exposé que les officiers municipaux de la ville de Paris qui avaient le plus contribué à la glorieuse révolution de France devaient voir avec la plus grande satisfaction que cet exemple fût imité à l'extrémité de l'Europe, que cet heureux événement donnait une nouvelle stabilité à notre ouvrage et rompait les projets de tous les monarques qui auraient l'intention de la détruire.[12]

Garran de Coulon's proposition did not receive the support of the majority, primarily due to the opposition of the Jacobin clubs. However, this did not prevent other clubs in Paris and the provinces from sending to Stanisław August a number of congratulatory messages.[13] Garran's proposition provoked a lively discussion in the newspapers and at the meetings of the Jacobin clubs, as well as in the sections of the Council of the Paris municipality. Opinions on Garran's proposal, both for and against, contain the same arguments as those presented in the press in its reactions to the Polish Constitution. *Logographe,* edited by Le Hodey, a most important paper at the beginning of the revolution, which started publishing in April 1791, having changed its name from *Journal des États Généraux*, reacted critically in its May 23 issue to the Polish Constitution, claiming it to be one which the French aristocracy could welcome. The paper saw it as the creation of a single caste which only by virtue of the degraded state in which the burghers of Poland and Lithuania found themselves, was forced to grant concessions to the burghers, but only in part. Nevertheless, the paper concluded:

> mais il n'était peut-étre ni possible, ni prudent de pousser plus loin ce premier essai. La diète a fait beaucoup, et quoiqu 'elle n'ait pas fait assez, il est toujours vrai que les amis de l'humanité lui doivent un juste tribut d'éloges; il sera toujours grand qu'investie de la toute-puissance et juge dans sa propre cause elle n'ait point attendu comme l'aristocratie française... et n'ait cédé qu'à l'ascendant irrésistible de la raison, de la justice, du patriotisme et des insinuations d'un monarque vertueux.[14]

Much more sharply worded statements concerning the Constitution appeared in the radical press and in the organs of revolutionary parties. The main figure among the Girondists was Jacques-Pierre Brissot. The organ of the Girondists, *Le patriote français,* in its May 23 issue restricted its comments to the opinion that the Polish revolution may possibly exert an influence on neighboring countries: "On ne peut nier que cette révolution qui va changer la Pologne ne doive changer la face des affaires de ce côté. Car la Pologne inoculera sans doute la liberté à tous ses voisins, ainsi que la France l'a fait."[15] A much more clearly unfavorable position was taken by Antoine-Joseph Gorsas, who, moving closer to the ideology of the Girondists, wrote in his journal *Le Courrier des 83 departements*:

> La Pologne est *libre*, elle vient d'opérer sans efforts, *sans la moindre effusion de sang* la plus belle et la plus glorieuse des révolutions. Tel est le cri public dans la capitale, [mais] ceux que les caresses perfides du despotisme n'ont jamais séduits ne voient dans la révolution polonaise qu'un moyen adroit de perpétuer l'esclavage.[16]

In the article "Révolution du 3 mai, à Varsovie" published in *Révolutions de Paris*, the organ of the Jacobins, edited by Louis Marie Prudhomme, the author linked the Polish revolution to the French:

> La nation polonaise, en ce moment, rend de solennelles actions de graces au ciel, en reconnaissance de la mémorable journée du 3 mai qui lui donne aussi une constiution, et la délivre du joug des Palatins. C'est au roi qu'elle en est redevable; c'est lui qui vient de porter un coup mortel au régime féodal, endoctriné, ajoute-t-on, par une correspondance avec des patriotes de Paris. Aussi est-ce à la révolution française qu'on fait

honneur de cet événement, qui n'est pas seulement à l'avantage du peuple polonais.

However, in the latter part of the article, the author cooled his initial enthusiasm and came to the conclusion that this Constitution was granted by a king and nobles in order to strengthen their own power. But the author was especially indignant at the emphasis given by the French press to the restraint shown by the Polish revolution and saw in this an attempt to diminish the achievements of the French revolution.[17]

The varied responses in the French revolutionary press to the Polish constitution presented here by way of example have one feature in common. They not only reflect attitudes towards the Polish constitution, but reflect simultaneously the writer's attitude towards the direction in which the French revolution was moving.

Opinions about the Polish constitution were not restricted to the pages of the press; they were also given voice in the French National Assembly where it received high praise. At the May 24 session of the Assembly General Jacques-François Menou expressed his admiration for the Polish nobility: "...la noblesse la plus orgueilleuse de l'Europe, qui venait, par un élan sublime d'amour pour la liberté et de respect pour les droits des peuples, d'adopter les principales bases de notre constitution."[18] Sièyes, Volney, Condorcet and other declared their goodwill for the Polish revolution. Deliberations about it can also be found in historical works. The first to ponder its significance was Louis-Philippe de Ségur:

> Jamais peut-être, dans aucune époque de son existence, cette nation infortunée ne développa plus de patriotisme, de sagesse et d'énergie qu'au moment qui précéda sa ruine. La diète, abjurant les préjugés sans détruire trop subitement les institutions antiques, et réformant les abus sans attaquer les propriétés, profitant des lumières de la philosophie sans manquer aux calculs de la politique, relevant le peuple opprimé sans sacrifier les classes supérieures, préparant graduellement à la liberté les hommes qu'un affranchissement trop rapide aurait portés à l'anarchie, proclama, le 3 mai 1791, la constitution qu'elle venoit de décréter, et qui fut reçue par tous les citoyens avec d'autant plus d'enthousiasme qu'elle sembloit assurer et la gloire et le bonheur des générations futures, sans coûter de larmes ni de sang à la génération qui existait.[19]

While in England a century-long tradition of political and cultural ties with the Polish Republic was not as developed as it was in France, the response evoked by the proclamation of the Constitution of 3 May was significant and widespread.[20] A certain role in such interest was played by the recent, but brief alliance between England, Prussia and Holland against Russia, an alliance which, had it not failed, would have inevitably involved Poland. Information about the revolutionary resolutions of the Diet appeared rather quickly in British journals. News came from the journals' own correspondents, from diplomatic reports of the foreign office, from occasional translations from the *Gazette de Leyde*, and from frequent reports given by the unfailingly active Minister of the Commonwealth Franciszek Bukaty, who, on instructions from Stanisław August, established close contacts with the editorial offices of newspapers. Already on May 24 Bukaty was able to apprise the King of the fact that the Constitution, which he had translated, was already in print and that it would soon be supplemented by the texts of the Law on Dietines and the Law on Cities, also in his translation. It was published by John Debrett and in terms of appearance had precisely the same look as the American and French Constitutions, also published by Debrett.

The passage of the Law on Cities created just as great an impression in the British press as it had in the *Gazette de Leyde* and the *Moniteur*. In its May 3 issue, the independent *Times,* which had a wide readership, hurried to register its approval of the discussions in the Diet concerning the rights of the burghers: "The Diet has just given very strong proof of its desire to improve the Constitution. The cause of the people has been most ably supported and has nearly triumphed over all former prejudices, in conformity to the first principles of civil society." Already in its May 11 edition the *Times* was able to provide information about the passage of the Law on Cities based on a note from Warsaw from April 20 entitled "Important particulars of the Revolution in Poland:"

> The new Constitution of Poland, as it was delineated in the sitting of the Diet, on the 14th instant, has been sanctioned and enacted into a Law. The day before yesterday, the Committee appointed to propose Constitutional Articles, presented to a full Diet, the plan which they had drawn relative to the Rights of the Citizens of the several towns, at full length. It passed unanimously, to the inexpressible joy of the inhabitants of the capital, and of all other good citizens.

Approved on April 14, the 18 points of the Principles to the Project on Cities, which became the basis of the Law on Cities passed on April 18, were published on May 16 in the *Times* in a condensed version. The article contains a brief commentary which emphasized, like the *Gazette de Leyde*, that the new law for the burghers embraces all Christians: "Every man who professes the Christian religion may be of whatever sect he pleases, and adopt whatever mode of worship which he shall prefer to others." The government sponsored *Courier de Londres*, which appeared twice weekly, reported in its May 10 and 11 issues, on the passage of the Law on Cities. Comparing it to the *Declaration de droits de l'homme et du citoyen,* the newspaper gave the Law on Cities its highest praise.

News of the passage of the Constitution of 3 May evoked real enthusiasm in England, a fact which was reflected both in the government and the oppositionist press. The Polish revival was perceived as an event of epoch making proportions. Special attention was given to its peaceable nature, a characteristic specifically underlined by the *Courier de Londres* in its edition of May 24 in much the same terms as those of the *Gazette de Leyde* on May 20. The *Courier* also included a condensed version of the articles of the Constitution in its May 27 issue, and continued with a description of events which took place in Warsaw on May 3rd.

The *Times*, which was the first to notify its readers about the passage of the Constitution in its May 20 issue, and in its next issues gave details surrounding the events of May 3, expressed the hope in its May 31 edition that: "The Revolution so happily begun will, according to all appearance, be completely consolidated, without violence or tumult." In its June 15 edition the *Times* published a summary of the eleven Articles of the Constitution, together with the main points of the Declaration of the States Assembled adopted on May 5, and provided the following commentary:

> Such is this excellent Constitution, dictated by equity, enlightened by understanding, and founded on the imprescriptible rights of man. If this new Constitution is maintained in its purity and retouched from time to time, as the beneficent Sovereign and illustrious State propose, the result will be, that the Polish nation after having vegetated so long in obscurity, groaning under the yoke of oppression, will become one of the happiest nations in the Universe.

The political literary monthly *The Gentleman's Magazine* already in its May issue included a short note about events in Poland:

> ... a most important Revolution took place in Poland, where the King has planned a new Constitution founded on that of England as improved in America, which the Diet adopted. But more of this when brought to maturity.

This promise was realized in the issue for June. In its section "Foreign Intelligence," the journal published a detailed report of the events which had lately taken place in Poland, and which had entirely changed the constitution of that Republic. The article describes the proceedings of the session in the

Diet on May 3 and includes a quotation from the Crown Marshal Stanisław Małachowski's speech (erroneously attributed to the King) that there has been prepared a plan of a Constitution, founded principally on those of England and the United States of America, but avoiding the faults and errors of both, and adapted it, as much as possible, to the local and particular circumstances of the country. Further, the article reports the reaction to the Constitution in the capital: "Cries of joy filled the streets; but this joy was the expression of a pure and calm patriotism." This is followed by information about the session of May 5 when the adoption of the Constitution was confirmed and the visit of Małachowski and the deputies to the Warsaw Town Hall "where they were solemnly received as citizens." The report also summarizes, not entirely correctly, the articles of the Constitution, underlines the role of the King, "who had been the chief author and promotor of it," and notes that not only the capital, but the whole country were filled with "utmost joy," and that: "Without the almost universal sentiment, so great a revolution could never have been effected with so little trouble." The *Supplement* to the *Gentleman's Magazine* for the year 1791 contains a somewhat shortened text of the Constitution of 3 May and the Declaration of the States Assembled, printed along with the French Constitution.

The universal approbation given the Polish revolution in England came from opposing sides which, nevertheless, had a single source, namely their relationship to the French revolution. British radical circles which sympathized with the French left, wanted to see in the Polish revolution ideas close to those of the French revolution, while the Tories and the moderate Whigs claimed that it represented a denial of the French revolution and that it was modeled on the British example. These differences found their expression both in the press and in a variety of public activities. At the manifestation in honor of the French revolution organized in London on June 14, 1791, toasts were raised in honor of three revolutions, the French, American and Polish, seen as outposts of a new order based on the natural rights of man. In Ireland, where ideas of revolution were joined to those of national independance, during a manifestation honoring the anniversary of the French revolution by a throng of many thousands, banners announced the common revolutionary goals of America, France and Poland. Under the slogan of the close relationship between the French and Polish revolutions a meeting took place in London in May, 1792, described in the *Morning Chronicle* and other papers, which honored the anniversary of the 3 May Constitution.

The nature of the Polish revolution was presented from a different position in the yearly, *The Annual Register, or A View of the History, Politics and*

CHAP. VI.

Situation of Poland at the Close of 1790. *Poland treated with Insolence by the Courts of Petersburg and Vienna. Sound Policy of an Alliance between Poland and Prussia. Unusual Condescendence of the Courts of Vienna and Petersburg. Awakened Spirit and Patriotism of the Polish Nation. Abolition of the permanent Council, and Establishment of a permanent Diet in Poland. Concessions to the Poles by the Russians and Austrians. Augmentation of the Military Strength of Poland. Situation of Northern and Eastern Europe at the Commencement of 1790. Sketch of a New Constitution favourable to the Liberty and Happiness of all Ranks. Excites Jealousy and Alarm in the Courts of Berlin and Petersburg. King of Prussia demands the Cession of Dantzick and Thorn. Character, Circumstances, and Conduct of the King of Poland. Patriotic Ardour of the Poles of all Ranks. Decrees of the Polish Diet in favour of the Commons. The Meeting of the Polish States changed into a Diet of Confederation; in which all Questions are to be decided by a Majority. The Diet opened by the King in Person. The Diet absolves the King from his Coronation Oath. Debates in the Diet. The King and the Diet accept, with the Solemnity of an Oath, the New Constitution.*

THE situation of Poland at the close of the year 1790, was become extremely critical. The Polish nation was full of resentment at the thraldom in which it had been held, ever since the dismemberment of the kingdom in 1773, by its three neighbouring powers, Russia, Austria, and Prussia; and had, from that fatal epocha, been watching with indefatigable diligence for an opportunity to break the fetters of this ignominious bondage; but near fifteen years elapsed before the least ray of hope appeared. It was not until the ambition of the two principal oppressors of Poland had involved them in a war with the Turkish empire, that the patriotic party in Poland, long silent and inactive through the consciousness of its inability to speak or to act to any effectual purpose, began at last to conceive that the period was come when an attempt might be made

with some confidence of success, to throw off the yoke of those oppressors.

The courts of Petersburg and Vienna had recently exhibited a striking proof of the contempt in which they held the Polish government. Without condescending to the usual formality established between separate states, of requesting permission, or even giving previous notice, they had stationed two large bodies of their respective troops on the Polish territory. Such an infringement of territorial rights, had been further aggravated by a proposal to assemble a diet, in order to enter into an alliance against the Porte with those two powers; whose intentions to expel the Turks from Europe, had raised no little alarm in this part of the world, particularly in Poland; which, for obvious reasons, could not view without the most serious concern, the depression of a power, of which

it

The Annual Register... for the year 1791. The first page of chapter six devoted to Poland (Indiana University Library).

Literature for the Year 1791. The Annual Register was assisted, starting with its first volume in 1758, by Edmund Burke and the imprint of his ideas is clearly visible in the issue of 1791, particularly when praise of the Polish revolution is contrasted with criticism of the French. This attitude is presented in the Preface of the Annual Register:

> The year 1791 seemed auspicious to human nature. In two of the greatest kingdoms in Europe, new constitutions were formed...The revolutions and the new constitutions in Poland and in France, are vast subjects of reflection in themselves, and as they are connected with the affairs of other nations. In themselves, though both of them intended to promote the welfare with the liberty of the nation, they were strongly contrasted by the different means through which the same ends were expected to be accomplished. The French legislators considered mankind under general views, and lost sight not only of individuals, but of particular classes in society...The Poles did not want talents for abstraction, nor the faculty of perceiving the symmetry and beauty of ideal systems; but they were too generous and good to suffer any general principles to break in upon the happiness of the different ranks of society. Liberty was dear to them, but humanity dearer.

Chapter six of the first part of the *Register*, devoted to the history of Europe, deals with the external and internal situation in Poland at the close of 1790 and the first half of 1791, including a detailed discussion of the circumstances that led to the preparation and adoption of the Constitution of 3 May and a general evaluation of its achievements:

> Poland had the honor, and seemed to have the felicity of attaining the end it proposed without the loss of a single life. Whether the constitution it embraced was the best that could be framed, has been a matter of doubt and dispute among politicians; but this was certain, that on a retrospect of the situation of the Poles, antecedently to this constitution, it wrought a most advantageous and desirable change in their circumstances, and was calculated, if foreign violence had not intervened, gradually to produce most of those national improvements and benefits that can only be expected from the progress of time.

The translation of the complete text of the Constitution of 3 May, together with the Declaration of the States Assembled, along with the French Constitution is published in the second part of the *Register*.

The contrast between the Polish and French revolutions formed one of the arguments in Edmund Burke's famous pamphlet published in 1791, *An Appeal from the New to the Old Whigs, in Consequences of Some Late Discussions in Parliament, Relative to the Reflections on the French Revolution*. The preceding pamphlet, *Reflections on the French Revolution*, mentioned in the title, was published a year earlier and produced a sharp debate in the House of Commons which brought about a break in the Whig party. *An Appeal....* forms another attack by Burke against the English devotees of the French Revolution and a defense of English parliamentarism. Depicting the internal situation in Poland before the reforms in the darkest of colors, Burke greets the manner in which the revolution was conducted and the resulting changes with the warmest approval:

> We have seen anarchy and servitude at once removed; a throne strengthened for the protection of the people, without trenching on their liberties; all foreign cabal banished, by changing the crown from elective to hereditary....Inhabitants of cities, before without privileges, placed in the consideration which belongs to that improved and connecting situation of social life. One of the most proud, numerous, and fierce bodies of nobility and gentry ever known in the world arranged only in the foremost rank of free and generous citizens. Not one man incurred loss or suffered degradation. All, from the king to the day laborer, were improved in their condition. Everything was kept in its place and order, but in that place and order everything was better. To add to this happy wonder, this unheard of conjunction of wisdom and fortune, not one drop of blood was spilled; no treachery; no outrage; no system of slander more cruel than the sword; no studied insults on religion, morals, or manners; no spoil, no confiscation; no citizen beggared; none imprisoned; none exiled; the whole was effected with a policy, a discretion, a unanimity and secrecy such as have never been before known on any occasion, but such wonderful conduct was reserved for this glorious conspiracy in favor of the true and genuine rights and interest of men.[21]

Burke emphasizes the rights granted the burghers, expresses his praise for the behavior of the nobles regarding this matter and concludes with the highest praise for the king. After this splendid rhetorical exposition there follows a comparison of the two revolutions as well as ironic commentary addressed to those who in place of congratulating the Polish revolution, express their enthusiasm for the French. Burke's severe view of the French revolution evoked sharp polemics. The most famous response to Burke's censure was Thomas Paine's *Rights of Man* in which the Polish revolution is also referred to, and in which Paine notes its exceptional nature, but incomparably more modestly than Burke. "Poland, though an elective monarchy, has had fewer wars than those which are hereditary; and it is the only Government that has made a voluntary essay, though but a small one, to reform the condition of the country."[22]

A summary of the events in Poland in 1791 can be found on the pages of the yearly, *The New Annual Register* or *General Repository of History, Politics and Literature, For the Year 1791* established in 1781 mainly due to the efforts of biographer Andrew Kippis. In Chapter V of *The New Annual* entitled "British and Foreign History," the Polish Revolution is included among the important events which took place in Europe in the year 1791. The author describes Poland's complicated and dangerous external political situation and states:

> Happily for Poland, she was at this crisis possessed of some men of the most eminent abilities, and apparently of the most exalted patriotism. The King had indeed been elected by the Russian interest, but he has shown that foreign obligations have not been able to eradicate from his breast an attachment to his country. During the session of the diet many excellent decrees had been passed in favor of general liberty, and calculated to attach the citizens to the interests of their country.

The article greatly praises the law passed on April 18, 1791, which recognized the rights of the burghers and describes in detail the session in the Diet on May 3 (in wording similar to the description in *The Gentleman's Magazine*), and formulates the following conclusion: "Thus without bloodshed, and even without tumult, was effected a revolution honorable to those who projected it, and promising to be essentially conducive to the happiness of the people." There follows a general summary of the Constitution which is viewed in favorable terms.

The situation in Poland aroused lively interest in the English press in 1792 and in years that followed. An example is provided by the *Courier de Londres* where reports on the work of the Diet in Warsaw and on the political situation in Poland appeared among the foreign news in almost every issue. Like the *Gazette de Leyde* and the *Moniteur,* the issue of January 17 contained information about the principles of the law concerning the sale of the royal demesnes, and included a translation of its articles. The issue of February 17 published, among others, news about the appointment of a committee responsible for the preparation of new statutes for the Jewish population in Poland. In the issue of March 2 the paper wrote about the treacherous activity directed against the Constitution by Szczęsny Potocki and Seweryn Rzewuski: "Il est glorieux pour la Pologne, de ne compter parmi ses nobles que deux ennemis de son immortelle constitution." In subsequent issues until June, the paper published reports about the sessions of the Diet and the growing danger of Russian intervention.

At the end of May 1792 the English press placed a description of the solemn celebrations of the anniversary of the Constitution in Warsaw. Soon afterwards the intervention of Russian troops provoked a campaign of protests from the *Times*, the *Courier de Londres*, the *Morning Chronicle* and others. The *Times* was the first in its May 13 issue to condemn this unprovoked attack on the Constitution, passed with the agreement of the nation. On June 31 the *Times* once again expressed its praise for the Polish revolution as "one of the most important events in history, and which reflects the highest honor on the whole nation."

After the defeat in the war with Russia in 1792 and the overthrow of the Constitution, *The New Annual Register for the year 1792* in Chapter V of the Section "British and Foreign History" began its report on events in Poland with the words: "In our last volume we announced to the public the establishment of a free, and apparently, well-poised constitution in Poland. In this we have the ungrateful task of recording its destruction...The spirit of humanity indignantly rises at such unprovoked and unprincipled attack upon the independence and the freedom of a nation." The article was pleased to inform the readers about a monetary subscription organized in England to help the cause of fighting Poland, which, however, turned out to be belated.

After the fall of the Kościuszko uprising and the Third Partition, the *Annual Register for the Year 1795* printed an extensive article devoted to Poland. The first part of the *Register*, devoted to the history of Europe, in chapter two provides "a summary view of the vicissitudes of [Poland's] history and government" in the last two years of its existence. The chapter ends with a reflectioin on the significance of the Constitution of 3 May:

> The new constitution of 1791 was still a greater proof of temper and moderation, and appears to be the happiest medium that had hitherto been adopted between monarchy and popular government. For moderation, equity, and sound political wisdom, it formed a contrast with the precipitation, violence, and impracticable complexity of the French revolution, or rather revolutions. In the former, the ground work of the constitution remained the same; respect was paid to the rights and privileges of all the orders of the subjects; and the reform begun, but not considered as finished, was to be carried on, as the way to perfection should be pointed out by times and circumstances.

The first sketchy news reaching America in July 1791, about the Polish Constitution adopted on May 3 in Warsaw immediately drew the attention of George Washington, who, in a letter of July 20, shared his opinion on the subject with his close friend David Humphreys, at that time the American minister in Lisbon:

> The example of France will undoubtedly have its effects on other kingdoms. Poland, by the public papers, appears to have made large and unexpected strides towards liberty, which, if true, reflects great honor on the present King, who seems to have been the principal promoter of the business.[23]

Humphreys in turn, in a letter dated August 1, wrote to his companion in arms in the American war of independence, Tadeusz Kościuszko, and included excerpts relating to Poland from Washington's letter as proof of the President's "very favorable "opinion on "the unexpected and happy revolution which has taken place in your country."[24] Washington's words to Humphreys, and the fact that they were relayed to Kościuszko have special significance. One of the reasons for the American interest in the changes taking place in Poland in 1791 was the memory of the Polish volunteers in the Revolutionary War, of Pułaski, who gave his life in defense of American independence, and of Kościuszko's service "to the land whose liberties you had been so instrumental in establishing," as Washington was to write later to Kościuszko in a letter of August 1797.[25]

The word "unexpected" used by Washington and Humphreys also has an explanation. In the heat of intense debates about a model for the new nation during the Constitutional Convention in 1787, the specific features of government in the far away Polish Republic were referred to a number of times in a critical manner. In addition, it was judged to be a government without balance by John Adams in A Defense of the Constitution of the Government of the United States, published in 1787.[26] Neither the aspirations of the Polish reformers in the 18th century nor the achievements of Polish social and political thought, which prepared the ground for the Constitution of 3 May, were known in America. Therefore, the "unexpected" Polish constitution, one which removed the faults of the system and introduced such major social and political reforms, was evaluated with even greater appreciation.[27]

But there was yet a third and most important reason for the weight given the Polish revolution, seen by Washington as resulting from the influence of the French revolution. The early transformations in France were understood as a continuation and a confirmation of the American revolution. To the enthusiasm in America for the French revolution was added a fascination with the Polish revolution; together with the American, it provided even greater justification for the hope that the ideas of freedom and democracy which lay at their basis would spread and take hold in other countries.

Perhaps the first from among illustrious American statesmen to react to the 3 May Constitution was Gouverneur Morris, the author of the later plan to reconstruct Poland, who was in Europe at the time. He notes (partially incorrectly) in his diary for May 22, 1791:

> The kingdom of Poland has formed a new Constitution which will I think change the political face of Europe by drawing that Kingdom out of Anarchy into Power. The leading features of the change are an hereditary monarchy, the affranchisement of the peasants and a share of the government given to the towns. These are the great means of destroying pernicious aristocracy.[28]

The American press drew its information of European events mainly from the British newspapers and the *Gazette de Leyde*. In addition, some news contained in reports sent in by American diplomatic representatives in European capitals filtered down to the newspapers. Due to the efforts of Jefferson, who at that time was the Secretary of State, the news from the *Gazette de Leyde*, including news about Poland, was translated and printed in the American press. For a brief time in 1790 Jefferson himself selected and translated excerpts from the *Gazette* for the *Gazette of the United States*, among others a condensed version of the postulates contained in the Memorandum of Cities. Printed in the April 24, 1790 issue, the postulates initially appeared in the January 1, 1790 issue of the *Gazette de Leyde*. Jefferson's efforts resulted in the fact that in 1791 excerpts from the *Gazette de Leyde* were also printed in the *General Advertiser*, and in 1792 in the *National Gazette*, the editor of which was Philip Freneau, the translator from the French to the office of the Secretary of State.[29]

News about the Law on Cities passed on April 18, 1791, reached American newspapers in July. Readers of the *Newport Mercury* were able to read the following dispatch on July 30:

> The 18th of April, the day before yesterday, will hereafter be a memorable day in the annals of Poland. In the session of that day a law was passed by the Diet relative to cities and their inhabitants, which restores them to their primitive rights, associates them with the legislative power, and will serve as a basis for still more extensive regulations, to reduce the different orders of citizens, to that relative quality, which constitutes the very soul of a solid and just constitution.[30]

The paper repeated the praise, expressed on numerous occasions in European opinion, for the role played by the Polish nobility in granting rights to the burghers:

> When the National Assembly of France reduced the nobility to an equality with the citizens, the greater number of its members consisted of the *Tiers Etat,* but when Poland raised her citizens to that equality the Diet consisted of nobility only.

William Short, who at that time was the Chargé d'Affaires in France, also noted such differences in a letter to Jefferson written on May 8, 1791, in Paris:

> The Diet of Poland have come to a determination to give the right of citizenship to the *Bourgeois* of the Republick. They have adopted the inverse system of France. Instead of taking the nobility from those who possessed it they have given it to those who had it not. The bourgeois have now the privileges of nobility, this being granted by an assembly of nobles almost unanimously and of their own accord is a strong proof of the progress of philosophy even in that region.[31]

In the same July 30 issue of the *Newport Mercury,* Niemcewicz's address to the session of the Diet on April 14 did not escape the attention of the paper, which quoted in a slightly altered version Niemcewicz's argument (already noted among others by the *Moniteur)* against the assertion that only the noble-born are entitled to have all the rights and honors: "None of us knows who were the ancestors or what was the religion of Washington and Franklin; but all of us know what important services these illustrious characters rendered to their country." A short discussion of the rights gained by the burghers can be found in the *Newport Mercury* which wrote on August 6: "Yesterday civil and religious prejudices were abandoned in the same moment, and the *Tiers Etat* admitted without distinction of birth or religion, to a participation of the legislative and executive powers." The newspaper expressed its admiration for the role played by Stanisław August in bringing about "the most difficult and most glorious reformation." It repeated the information contained in the *Times* and the *Gazette de Leyde* about the enthusiasm generated among the burghers by the fact that they were granted rights and about the acceptance of citizenship from the city of Warsaw by Marshal Małachowski and the deputies to the Diet.

Simultaneously with the news about the Law on Cities there appeared in the pages of the American press notes and articles about the adoption by the Diet of the new Constitution on May 3. Apparently the press materials from Europe on which the news about the Constitution was based arrived by the same ship. Soon after, copies of the translated Constitution published in

LONDON, May 19.

REVOLUTION in *POLAND.*

IN different foreign letters, we have already laid before our readers details of the events which have lately taken place in Poland, and which have entirely changed the Conftitution of that Republic. It cannot, however, prove unacceptable to our readers to have the whole proceedings laid before them in one connected view.

At three o'clock in the morning of May 3d, a number of patriots, who had preconcerted the great objects which they meant to accomplifh in the fitting of the Diet that day, affembled in the King's chamber. There, in the prefence of the King, they engaged to effectuate the Revolution that day, and they pledged themfelves to each other, by a folemn engagement, not to feparate until they had accomplifhed their end.

The affembly was opened at the ufual hour.— The galleries were crowded with fpectators, and the Houfe was furrounded with thoufands who could not gain admiffion. Inftead of the Marfhals, the King himfelf opened the feffion. He faid in fubftance, that "notwithftanding all af-
"furances to the contrary, there was an alarming
"rumour, confirmed by the advices daily receiv-
"ed, that the three neighbouring Powers would
"make up and terminate all their jealoufies and
"divifions at the expence of the poffeffions of
"the Republic; that the only method of affur-
"ing to Poland the integrity of its poffeffions, and
"of preferving it from the ruin which foreign
"politics were preparing for it, was to eftablifh
"a Conftitution, which fhould fecure its internal
"independence. That in this view there had
"been prepared a plan of a Conftitution, founded
"principally on thofe of England, and the Unit-
"ed States of America; but avoiding the faults
"and errors of both, and adapting it as much as
"poffible to the local and particular circumftan-
"ces of the country." In fupport of the information relative to the foreign powers, the King communicated to the Diet fome difpatches received from the Minifters of the Republic at foreign courts, ftating how eager they were to oppofe all fettlement of the Conftitution, and that every thing feemed to announce their hoftile defigns on Poland. The King defired that the plan, which he fubmitted to them, might be read, and that they fhould proceed forthwith to enact it into a law, if they approved of it. The plan was accordingly read, and a very long and important debate took place.

All the reprefentatives of the Provinces of Volhynia and Pudolia, declared themfelves againft the new form of conftitution.

M. Suchorzewfki, who fo recently diftinguifhed himfelf in fo brilliant a manner as an advocate for the people, and who is juftly regarded as the principal author of the movements that have

charge of 200 pieces of cannon. There were between thirty and forty Nuncios who did not follow the King to church. The King, with his fuite, returned to the Affembly Houfe, and adjourned tho Diet to the 5th of May, after charging the Marfhals to give the oath to all the Departments. The oppofing Nuncios, feeing that all refiftance was ufelefs, refolved to proteft againft the new Conftitution, by the publication of a Manifefto, after which they retired without noife to their own houfes. There was no attempt made to interrupt them, nor was any infult whatever offered to their perfons. Cries of joy filled the ftreets, but this joy was the expreffions of pure and calm patriotifm. Through the whole day there was not the fmalleft confufion, nor diforder, nor riot. At eleven o'clock the ftreets were fo perfectly calm, that one would fcarcely believe that it had been the epoch of a new order of things.

It is pretended, that on the eve of this memorable day, a certain foreign Minifter had endeavoured, by the dextrous application of 50,000 ducats, to avert the revolution: but all was forefeen and prevented. The bufinefs was executed in every point with as much addrefs as it was framed. On the 4th inft. eighteen Nuncios publifhed their Manifefto againft the proceedings of the day before; and Mr. Suchorzewfki returned the *Cordon bleu*, with which his Majefty had invefted him fifteen days before. On the 3d May, the poft was ftopped, and even foreign Minifters fubmitted to the general order; but on the 4th, expreffes were fent off in all directions.

The following is an authentic copy of an addrefs, prefented to W. WILBERFORCE, Efq. on Thurfday the 5th of laft month, by the Africans in and about London.

SIR,

WE are fenfible that the acknowledgments of a few humble natives of Africa, can add but little to the fatisfaction of a gentleman, who finds his generous exertions amply recompenfed in the confcioufnefs of worth; yet we have prefumed to gratify our own feelings at leaft, by prefenting this fmall tribute of thankfulnefs, as well on our own behalves as on that of our kindred in mifery and chains.

We are, fir, as you well know, though participating of perfonal freedom, yet in very low ftations, claiming however, and not unworthily we hope, to be confidered as fober, and diligent and juft: with faces of colour indeed, but unknown to the magiftrate, and with names not to be found in the lift of offenders of any kind; yet, lawly as we are, if, upon the queftion lately agitated in Parliament (involving the fate of our whole race) we were without the fenfibilities of admiration and gratitude and hope, we fhould in good truth not be men.

As concerning the event of this queftion, it may not, perhaps, become us to fpeak; yet ftrong and lively is our hope, that the principle explained, and the fenfations excited by you, can never be fatisfied till they have obtained their end.

London reached the American shore. As is evident from American library holdings these were for the most part the second edition since the first sold out rapidly. There is, however, a copy of the first edition in Jefferson's library, undoubtedly sent out as soon as it appeared. But Jefferson was already aware of the principles guiding the initial draft of the future Constitution because they had been sent to him by Scypione Piattoli in a letter dated March 9, 1790. These principles were in turn based on the draft of the Principles to Reform the Government, by Ignacy Potocki.[32] Piattoli, who had been in Poland since 1783 was in Paris between 1785 and 1789 where he became friends with Philip Mazzei and where he became acquainted with Jefferson. When he returned to Poland in 1789, Stanisław August employed him as his reader. Piattoli was also closely connected to Ignacy Potocki and undoubtedly served as an advisor in the elaboration of the Principles. Piattoli, an advocate of American democracy, played a significant role in reconciling various positions during 1790-1791, years when the text of the Constitution was being prepared.[33]

The first extensive report, based on an article in the *Gentleman's Magazine*, appeared in *Dunlap's American Daily Advertiser* on July 26, 1791. It reported on the stormy discussions in the Diet on May 3; the swearing in of the Constitution; the service in the Cathedral; the joy of the citizenry in the capital; and on the session in the Diet on May 5 when the text of the Constitution was signed. *Dunlap's* also contained a somewhat inaccurate condensation of the articles of the Constitution, which *Dunlap's* characterizes as: "...combining liberty with subordination, and subjecting the first citizen as well as the last to the law, secures to all the means of happiness, and gives to each citizen the true enjoyment of his rights." The paper quite naturally focused its attention on Marshal Małachowski's address to the Diet on May 3 (his words erroneously ascribed to the King), in which he stated that the Constitution was "founded principally on those of England and the United States of America." A similar statement was made by David Humphreys in a letter to Jefferson dated June 17, 1791: "Change in government of Poland 'certainly one of the wonderful events of this age.' It is said the King stated the new constitution to be modelled after English and American constitutions."[34] Many newspapers reprinted the full text of the Constitution published in London. The *Gazette of the United States* printed this text in succeeding issues starting with September 10.

A characteristic feature of the information about the Constitution found in the American press is a selection of texts, primarily from the British press, which highlight the role of the King in the preparation and passage of the

Constitution. *Dunlap's American Daily Advertiser* in the August 23, 1791, issue writes:

> In the history of mankind there are but very few instances to be found, where kings, unsolicited and unintimidated, have made a voluntary surrender of their power. There are many great sayings of great acts; but we read of none that deserves to be preferred to the late conduct of the King of Poland. The form of the new constitution of Poland, is not merely sanctioned by the King; but dictated, framed, and fashioned in the exalted superiority of his own mind, affords a new lesson to the world.

In its March 23, 1792, issue the *American Apollo* reprinted from William Coxe's *Travels into Poland, Russia, Sweden and Denmark* (1784) a very favorable characterization of the Polish King with the following footnote:

> It is worthy of special remark, that the two most accomplished and virtuous Princes now existing, the King of Poland and the President of the United States, were born in the same year, that both were raised to their stations by election, and not by hereditary claim; and that both have been active instruments of rescuing their country from confusion, and establishing just and free Constitutions of Government.

Given the prevailing enthusiasm in America for both the French and Polish revolutions, the American press, as distinct from the European, rarely pointed to sharp contrasts between them, restricting itself to comparing the different roles played by the nobility in the revolutionary changes brought about in both countries. These differences, pointed to in Edmund Burke's pamphlet *An Appeal from the New to the Old Whigs*, were noted again in the *Gazette of the United States* on July 18 and on August 29 it reprinted the entire section containing praise for the Polish revolution from this well-known pamphlet.

The American press continued its scrutiny of the Diet's activities, looking for "the completion of the most wonderful revolution;" it wrote about the laws concerning the Internal Organization of Cities and the law of Mutual Guarantee of the Polish and Lithuanian Nations; and about plans to regulate the legal status of the Jewish population. Summarizing the events of 1791, the *Columbian Sentinel* wrote on January 4, 1792:

> The year just expired has been pregnant with great and interesting events in Poland with propriety we may say, that a Nation of Freemen has, in the preceding year, been born in a day. Therein we have seen, a Revolution in government favourable to the people, planned, promulgated and put into execution by its King.

Admiration for the Polish revolution manifested itself not only in the press. It was also voiced during a variety of celebrations, among others those celebrating the French revolution. As an example one can cite the commencement at Harvard in 1792 where students debated "upon the comparative importance of the American, French and Polish revolutions to mankind," as reported by *Dunlap's American Daily Advertiser* on July 28, 1792. On the occasion of George Washington's 60th birthday, the *Gazette of the United States* printed on February 22, 1792, a poem by an anonymous poet which began:

Wak'd by the vernal breeze, see Poland, France,

With youth renew'd , and vig'rous health advance.

Poems in honor of the Constitution and Stanisław August were written by two poets and diplomats who belonged to the circle of writers known as the "Connecticut or Hartford Wits," David Humphreys and Joel Barlow. Humphreys enclosed his poem with the letter to Kościuszko (August 1, 1791) mentioned above:

To thee, thou Sage of higher, nobler sort,

Than e'er before adorned an earthly Court,

Parent of Millions! Paragon of Kings!

A Bard from new-found Worlds new laurels brings,

To thee, great Stanislaus!–Thy glorious name

Shall stand unrivaled on the rolls of fame–

Hail patriot King! And hail the Heav'n-born plan

Thy voice pronounc'd to fix the rights of man;

The godlike voice, that op'd the feudal graves,

Call'd to new life innumerable Slaves,

Nor call'd to life alone... Inspir'd by thee

Thy gen'rous Nobles made those Vassals free–

Hail blest example! Happy Poland hail!

No more... to lure thy foes... shall feuds prevail;

No more shall bord'ring Pow'rs, with lawless arms,

Divide thy confines and despoil thy farms;

No more shall Slav'ry sterilize thy soil,

But fruits, that prompt, shall pay the Peasant's toil;

While soothing Faction! rage, fair Concord reigns,

And crowns with bliss the plenty of the Plains;

While, Age succeeding Age, a patriot King!

Both Worlds admire and all the Muses sing.[35]

Barlow sent King Stanisław August Poniatowski the first version of his poem, entitled *The Vision of Columbus,* (now known under its later title, *Columbiad*) in which he praised Kościuszko, and received a letter dated May 25, 1791, in which the King wrote that he would "endeavor to have it translated into Polish." In his answer of February 20, 1792, Barlow wrote about the Constitution of 3 May: "The extraordinary and successful manner in which Your Majesty has lately given a constitution to your country has excited no small degree of my admiration; and I cannot forbear offering you my congratulations on a subject so interesting to mankind."

In the conclusion of his poem *The Conspiracy of Kings,* as in his letter to the King written the same year, Barlow expressed his admiration for the "sceptred sage" who "points the progressive march:"

In northern climes, where feudal shades of late
Chilled every heart and palsied every State,
Behold, illumin'd by th' instructive age,
That great phenomenon, a sceptred sage;
There Stanislaus unfolds his prudent plan,
Tears the strong bandage from the eyes of man,
Points the progressive march, and shapes the way
That leads a realm from darkness into day.[36]

Jefferson's judgment, expressed in 1816 in a letter to John Adams, that "A wound indeed was inflicted on the character of honor in the eighteenth century by the partition of Poland,"[37] is a good reflection of the prevalent public opinion in the United States in the years when the crime of the partitions was being perpetrated. American newspapers reacted to Poland's defense of its independence and its constitution against the Russian invader in numerous articles full of goodwill for Poland and sharp condemnation of the invader. Based on reports from London from July 3, *Dunlap's American Daily Advertiser* wrote on October 8 that Poland's neighbors are planning to divide among themselves Poland "which offended no other, which never meddled in foreign affairs, which in peace, and without spilling a drop of blood, or doing injury to its fellow citizens, had created a new Constitution, which merited the admiration of Europe..." The destruction of Polish democratic reforms was viewed broadly as an attack of despotism on the achievements of freedom by the *Columbian Sentinel* on November 7, 1792. Representing the views of politicians allied with Jefferson, the paper wrote that: "Notwithstanding the late excesses of the republican party in France, the cause of the French is still that of humanity – is still the cause of freedom." The article treats Poland, together with France, as an example of a country in Europe where the principles of the American revolution had become disseminated. "Poland--people, nobles, king, with one voice, framed a constitution, founded principally on the unalienable rights of the people, bearing, in many parts, a striking resemblance to our forms of government." Coming out against the victory of these principles was Catherine, "unwilling to see one link of the despotic chain broken." The article, written during the war between revolutionary France and Austria and Prussia, sees a threat coming from "Europe's despots fearing the further spreading of the sacred flame..." a threat not only to France, but also to America from where the flame emanates.

The ensuing battle of freedom with despotism, the Kościuszko Insurrection, received a great deal of attention in American newspapers which published the entire "Act of Insurrection" and other documents. They published detailed descriptions of battles and the uprising in Warsaw, Wilno and other parts of the country. They also quoted toasts in honor of the uprising and of Kościuszko given during a variety of celebrations in numerous American cities, as well as the texts of a number of poems dedicated to the uprising or describing the imprisonment of Kościuszko, his liberation and the triumphant reception in America of this "illustrious Defender of the Rights of Mankind."[38]

The examples cited here of opinion in Europe[39] and America about the renewal taking place in Poland in 1791 testify to the fact that the Polish revolution was recognized in its time as the next step after the American and French revolutions on the path of creating states and societies concerned with the rights of man. This was as Robert R. Palmer notes, "the two countries which along with America were then the most famous for revolution--Poland and France."[40] The conviction about the crucial and equiponderant significance of the three revolutions for the future of the world was widespread. Palmer cites the opinion of Peter Ochs, a member of the Council of Basel, who, enchanted by the French revolution, wrote in 1791: "The revolutions of America, France and Poland obviously belong in a chain of events that will regenerate the world."[41] The habit of mentioning them together in one breath lasted a long time. Noah Webster in the first edition (1828) of *The American Dictionary of the English Language* defines the term "revolution" as: "revolution in politics, a material or entire change in the constitution of government. Thus the revolution in England in 1688...so the revolution in Poland, the United States of America and in France consisted in a change of constitution." In the years 1791-1792, when they were in force simultaneously, the three constitutions were honored together on various occasions, especially in England and America, as visible realizations of the slogans of freedom and democracy. In actual fact, manifestations of revolutionary aspirations for change in the political system could be seen in those years in Holland, Belgium, Switzerland and Ireland, but only in three countries, significant in terms of territory and population, were the main ideas of the age of Enlightenment consolidated in fundamental laws of State, in constitutions which derived from the social contract and natural law. The three legal documents were viewed as having a common genesis and common goals: the establishment of democratic governments and the recogntion of individual rights. Attention was given not only to their common origins, but also to the connections existing between the constitutions. The ties which existed between the Polish, English and American constitutions were noted by Marshal Małachowski at the session of the Diet on May 3, and his words were quoted in all European and American press reports. Małachowski purposely omitted mention of the obvious connections to the French revolution taking place at that time, not wanting to provoke the despotic rulers of the three neighboring countries. Nevertheless, it was specifically these connections,[42] made in the form of comparisons and contrasts, that played a distinct role and assumed a remarkable feature in the western press. As Albert Sorel noted long ago: "La révolution de Pologne eut le rare privilége d'être admirée à la fois par les partisans de la Révolution française et par le plus irréconciliable de ses adversaires."[43]

As an example of the latter, Sorel cites the praise of Burke. In France as well, even the few critical voices were not lacking in admiration, and the extremist Gorsas had to admit that public opinion in Paris expressed its regard for the Polish constitution. Its deliberate preparation, its revolutionary promulgation during a single session of the Diet, its content full of visible compromises, the gradual realization of its founding assumptions and the open declaration of guaranteed changes in the future, all pointed to the distinct character of this model of a constitution and distinguished it from the other two.

English parliamentarism, reshaped by the "glorious revolution" of 1688, as well as the example of French Enlightenment thought (especially Montesquieu) lay at the foundations of the American Declaration of Independence, The Virginia Plan, and the Constitution of 1787. The *Declaration des droits de l'homme et du citoyen* of 1789 grew out of the French intellectual revolution, from the thought of Montesquieu, Voltaire and especially from Rousseau's *Contrat social*, but the American example as well as the English model, so highly regarded by Montesquieu and Voltaire, also played a very significant role. In the intertwined connections between London, Philadelphia and Paris one also finds Warsaw. In republican Poland, however, such connections manifested themselves differently than they did in monarchist France, since they were superimposed on a parliamentary tradition centuries in duration, one which, to be sure, had become deformed in the 18th century and petrified in this form as a result of foreign wardship, but a tradition which was, nevertheless, alive and continued to harbor voices hoping for reform. Therefore, when, as a result of Russia's entanglement in a war with Turkey, Poland gained, as it turned out for only four years, full sovereignty, the advocates of reform used a different model for introducing political and social changes than that used in France, one which saw changes accompanied not by a bloody outburst, but which took on the form of a truly benign revolution. Both Europe and America followed with the greatest attention this alternate possibility of realizing common aspirations for a just system, and public opinion on both continents expressed a real enthusiasm for this peaceful departure from an antiquated form of government and relations between estates. In the conclusion of an article cited above, *The Annual Register for the Year 1795* wrote about the exemplary nature of such a constitution: "On the whole, as the history of the old Polish constitution warns men of many things to be avoided, so the new constitution, though strangled at its birth, exhibits others worthy of imitation."

The image of the Polish Republic undergoing reform was recorded and preserved in the pages of the newspapers and journals of Europe and America, publications which were full of high regard for the direction of such reforms and for the efforts required to defend the independence of the renewed nation. An important role played by such publications is that they bore witness to and served to preserve the truth--which later was to be frequently undermined by historians of countries which participated in the partitions of Poland--about the real nature of the Constitution of 3 May, and about the important role it played along with the American and French Constitutions in initiating a constitutional era in world history. Finally, it told the truth about the condemnation by public opinion in Europe and America of the outrage committed by the partitions, and about the confirmation by this same public opinion of the right of the Polish nation to "political existence, external independence and internal liberty," as set forth in the preamble of the Constitution of 3 May.

Notes

1. See Zofia Libiszowska, "Odgłosy Konstytucji 3 Maja na Zachodzie" (Repercussions of the 3 May Constitution in the West) in Alina Barszczewska-Krupa ed. *Konstytucja*

3 Maja w tradycji i kulturze polskiej (Łódz: Wyd. Łódzkie, 1991) pp. 70-81; Samuel Fiszman *The Bicentennial of the Polish Constitution of 3 May 1791*. An Exhibition of Rare Publications (Bloomington: Indiana University Polish Studies Center, Lilly Library, 1991).

2. *The Papers of Thomas Jefferson*, Julian P. Boyd, ed. (Princeton: Princeton U. Press, 1961), vol. 19, p. 467.

3. See Jerzy Łojek, *Polska inspiracja prasowa w Holandii i Niemczech w czasach Stanisława Augusta* (Polish attempts to influence the press in Holland and Germany in the time of Stanisław August) (Warszawa: PWN, 1969); Jerzy Łojek, "International French Newspapers and their Role in Polish Affairs during the Second Half of the Eighteenth Century" *East Central Europe* 1,1 (1974): 54-64.

4. Janusz Woliński, Jerzy Michalski, Emanuel Rostworowski, eds. *Materiały do dziejów Sejmu Czteroletniego* (Sources related to the history of the Four-Year Diet) (Wrocław: Ossolineum, 1959), vol. 2, p. 322.

5. Helena Rzadkowska, *Stosunek polskiej opinii publicznej do rewolucji francuskiej* (The attitude of Polish public opinion toward the French revolution) (Warszawa: Książka, 1948), pp. 70-72.

6. Emanuel Rostworowski, *Ostatni król Rzeczypospolitej. Geneza i upadek Konstytucji 3 maja* (The last king of the Commonwealth. The genesis and fall of the Constitution of 3 May) (Warszawa: Wiedza Powszechna, 1966), p. 253.

7. Jeremy D. Popkin, *News and Politics in the Age of Revolution Jean Luzac's Gazette de Leyde* (Ithaca: Cornell U. Press, 1989), pp. 228, 257-8.

8. See Andrzej Zahorski, "*Moniteur* 1789-1795 w sprawach polskich" (*Moniteur* 1789-1795 on Polish affairs), *Przegląd Historyczny* 62, 1 (1966): 70-96.

9. Emanuel Rostworowski, "Miasta i mieszczanie w ustroju Trzeciego Maja" (Cities and burghers in the system of 3 May) in Jerzy Kowecki ed. *Sejm Czteroletni i jego tradycje* (Warszawa: PWN, 1991), p. 149.

10. Jean Fabre, *Stanislas-Auguste Poniatowski et l'Europe des Lumières* (Paris: Les Belles Lettres, 1952), pp. 87-88,

11. See Marceli Handelsman, "La Constitution Polonaise du 3 Mai 1791 et l'Opinion Française" *La Révolution Française* 58 (1910): 412-434; Julien Grossbart, "La Politique Polonaise de la Révolution Française jusqu'aux traités de Bâle," *Annales Historiques de la Révolution Française* 6: (1929), 34-55.

12. See Handelsman, *La Révolution*, pp. 429-34.

13. Fabre, *Stanislas-Auguste*...pp. 526-530.

14. See Handelsman, pp. 414-415.

15. See Handelsman, p. 422.

16. See Handelsman, p. 422.

17 *Revolution de Paris*, 23-28 May, 1791, pp. 311-316.

18. Albert Sorel, *L'Europe et la Revolution Française* (Paris: Libraire Plon, 1895) vol. 2, p. 214.

19. Louis-Philippe Comte de Ségur, *Histoire des principaux événements du règne de F. Guillaume II. Roi de Prusse, et Tableau politique de l'Europe, depuis 1786 jusqu'en 1796, ou l'an 4 de la République; Contenant un précis des révolutions de Brabant, de Hollande, de Pologne et de France* (Paris: 1800), vol. 2, pp. 195-201.

20. Zofia Libiszowska, *Życie polskie w Londynie w XVIII wieku* (Polish affairs in London in the 18th century) (Warszawa: Pax, 1972); "Polska reforma w opinii angielskiej" (Polish reform in English opinion) in Kowecki, ed. *Sejm Czteroletni...* pp. 63-74; see also Izabela Rusinowa, "Rozbiory Polski w opinii *The Annual Register*" (The partitions of Poland in the opinion of *The Annual Register*) in *Francja - Polska XVIII-XIX w.* (Warszawa: PWN, 1983), pp. 339-348.

21. Edmund Burke, *An Appeal from the New to the Old Whigs* (London: J. Dodsley, 1791), pp. 102-104.

22. Thomas Paine, *Rights of Man. Part the Second Combining Principle and Practice* (London: J.S. Jordan, 1792), p. 25.

23. *The Writings of George Washington*, ed. John C. Fitzpatrick (Washington: U.S. Government Printing Office, 1939), vol. 31, pp. 320-21.

24. Miecislaus Haiman, *The Fall of Poland in Contemporary American Opinion* (Chicago: Polish Roman Catholic Union of America, 1935), p. 53.

25. *The Writings of George Washington...* (1941), vol. 36, p. 22.

26. Adams includes a long quotation from the treatise *Voix Libre*, attributed to King Stanisław Leszczyński, one more proof of the popularity of this treatise in France. The quotation deals with the miserable state of the Polish peasant, but Adams failed to notice that this passage provides one of the arguments in what is a call for political and social reforms.

27. Haiman, *The Fall...*, pp. 5-13; Piotr S. Wandycz, *The United States and Poland* (Cambridge: Harvard U. Press; 1980), pp. 32-50; Piotr S. Wandycz, "The American Revolution and the Partitions of Poland" and Anna M. Cienciała, "The American Founding Fathers and Poland" in Jarosław Pelenski ed. *The American and European Revolutions, 1776-1848* (Iowa: University of Iowa Press, 1980), pp. 95-124; Janina W. Hoskins, "A Lesson which all our Countrymen Should Study. Jefferson Views Poland," *The Quarterly Journal of the Library of Congress* 33,1 (1976); 29-46.

28. *Gouverneur Morris: A Diary of the French Revolution*, Beatrix Davenport ed. (Boston: Houghton Mifflin, 1939), p. 188.

29. *The Papers of Thomas Jefferson*, vol. 16, pp. 246, 257-8.

30. Quotations from American newspapers are based on Haiman, *The Fall...*

31. *The Papers of Thomas Jefferson*, vol. 20, p. 385.

32. *The Papers of Thomas Jefferson*, vol. 16, pp. 214-219.

33. Rostworowski, *Ostatni król Rzeczypospolitej*, p. 180.

34. *The Papers of Thomas Jefferson*, vol. 20, p.556, as recorded in Jefferson's "Summary Journal of Letters."

35. Haiman, *The Fall..*, pp. 53-4.

36. *Columbian Centinal*, August 18, 1792, see Haiman, p. 59.

37. *The Writings of Thomas Jefferson*, ed. A.A. Lipscomb (Washington: T. Jefferson Memorial Association, 1904), vol. 14, p. 394.

38. Haiman, *The Fall...*, pp. 123, 360; Izabela Rusinowa, "The Kościuszko Insurrection through the Eyes of *The New York Herald*, 1794-1795" *Polish-American Studies* 1 (1976): 59-74.

39. For opinions on the Constitution of 3 May in the German states see: Hermann Vahle, "Die polnische Verfassung vom 3 Mai 1791 in zeitgenössischen deutschen Urteil." *Jahrbücher für Geschichte Osteuropas*, 19 (1971), 347-370.

40. Robert R. Palmer, *The Age of Democratic Revolution* (Princeton: Princeton U. Press, 1959), vol. 1, p. 407.

41. Palmer, *The Age...* vol. 1, p. 364.

42. See Henri Mazeaud, *Les Constitutions française et polonaise de 1791* (Paris: Institute de France, 1983), pp. 1-10.

43. Albert Sorel. *L'Europe...* vol. 2, p. 215.

Thomas Jefferson, steel engraving by Michał Sokolnicki acc. to a drawing by Tadeusz Kościuszko with the inscription: "Thomas Jefferson, A philosopher, a Patriote and a Friend. Dessiné par son ami Tadée Kościuszko et gravé par M. Sokolnicki" (Muzeum Narodowe w Warszawie).

20

The Kościuszko Insurrection:
Continuation and Radicalization of Change

Jerzy Kowecki

The armed intervention by Catherine II in 1792 (in which the Targowica Confederation played the role of figurehead), put an end to the efforts of Polish patriots during the Four-Year Diet of 1788-1792 to solidify the foundations of independence of the Commonwealth. The Constitution of 3 May, 1791, not only gave expression a year earlier to aspirations for independence, but also reached new heights in introducing reforms that would open the path for further changes.

After the surrender of the Polish army, triumphant Russia, by means of Targowica decrees, simply crossed out the achievements of the Four-Year Diet. Polish patriots, reconciled neither to the military surrender, nor to the overthrow of reform, nor, above all, to the loss of sovereignty, lost little time in forming a conspiracy, both in Poland and in emigration in Saxony, that was to prepare armed insurrection. Conspiratorial activity increased after the Second Partition.

The social and political program of the insurrection was deliberated among the conspirators at home and abroad.[1] A variety of positions emerged, determined by attitudes towards the Constitution of 3 May, towards the political system formed by the Four-Year Diet, towards social matters, especially towards peasant reforms, and towards making the uprising dependent on foreign assistance.

Regardless of how great the differences were dividing the supporters of opposing positions, they nevertheless agreed that the reforms of the Four-Year

Diet did not go far enough. As one might expect, from a formal point of view the validity of the Constitution of 3 May and other statutes of the Four-Year Diet was never questioned at a moment when an insurrection was undertaken against an invader who intervened in the Commonwealth with the aim of destroying the achievements of the Diet. The Constitution of 3 May at this time did not yet form a tradition. It represented, rather, a set of new laws which at the moment of the insurrection had barely existed three years, and at the beginning of the conspiracy two years. Its resolutions had at that time the advantage of obligatory norms. After all, its authors had resolved:

> Willing to prevent, on one hand, violent and frequent changes in the national constitution, yet, considering on the other, the necessity of perfecting it, after experiencing its effects on public prosperity, we determine the period of every twenty-five years for an Extraordinary Constitutional Diet, to be held purposely for the revision and such alterations of the constitution as may be found requisite.[2]

Nevertheless the binding nature of the legislation from 1788-1792 was not that apparent in rapidly changing events. It is also worth remembering that while the Constitution was supported by the entire country (which never means all its citizens), it was evaluated critically, and not only by what was to become the Targowica opposition. It was also criticized by such patriots who, while giving it overall support, regarded the new legislation as too conservative, especially in the area of social change. Such criticism referred to the Law on Cities, among others, passed on April 18, 1791.[3] Critics expressed their concern that the inhabitants of cities were not given fuller participation in power and that the doors leading to the Diet and government commissions were barely opened to them.[4] They questioned on the one hand the process of ennobling the city dwellers, considering that it removed from their midst their best, most dynamic leaders, and thereby enriched the noble class with these very qualities, and on the other hand they were critical of the "classification" of the nobility, that is, the removal of the poorest groups from political privileges and in practice from membership in the ruling class.[5]

Even among the authors of the Constitution there was no lack of assertions that only that which was possible had been done. The rest was left to "changes in the future," leaving more just and pertinent resolutions for later, when the situation would ripen to the point that more fundamental changes might be carried out. King Stanisław August wrote concerning this matter to his agent in France, Philip Mazzei on June 11, 1791:

> You cannot doubt that my self-esteem feels greatly flattered by the approbation with which our work is honored in France. That, however,

does not prevent my being very well aware of its considerable shortcomings. I do not blame myself for not introducing at one blow all the reforms we need. On the contrary, I believe that it was necessary not to do everything at once. But there are many faults in the things already done which could not be avoided without reducing the number of minds that had to be brought together.[6]

All such reservations and doubts multiplied among a significant number of the leading patriotic activists immediately after the collapse of the Great Diet's activities. Such an attitude was clearly evident both in the activities and manifestos of emigrants concentrated in Saxony, especially in their chief propagandistic work *O ustanowieniu i upadku Konstytucji polskiej 3-go Maja 1791 roku* (On the enactment and the fall of the Polish Constitution of 3 May 1791) as well as inside Poland in the arguments among the conspirators of the uprising. In both cases the relevancy of the Government Statute was put to the question.[7]

They now determined that more energetic steps and radical changes were needed and clearly stated: "The example of Poland proves how unsatisfactory moderately employed means are when enemies of humanity impose ever-present barriers against their freedom."[8]

They took a similar position in their contacts with the leaders of revolutionary France as they sought help for the planned insurrection in Poland as evidenced by the document handed by Tadeusz Kościuszko in Paris to the foreign minister Pierre-Henri Lebrun in the beginning of 1793.[9] Although these documents were written with the intention of gaining the favor of its recipients, the programmatic aims of the organizers of the insurrection are, nevertheless, quite clear.[10]

Their intentions were once again presented on February 2, 1794, to the French foreign minister by Pierre Parandier who was the intermediary in contacts with Poles and who sympathized with their cause. He gave assurances that the leaders of the intended insurrection were not interested in a restoration of a constitution for the nobility, "but in the eradication of the allies of Russia and Prussia, in breaking down the fetters of bondage, in restoring to the common people their freedoms, independence and rights of self-government." Furthermore, he signaled intentions which were soon to be given expression in the Act of Insurrection of March 24:

At the onset of the insurrection a revolutionary provisional government shall be installed, which will organize and direct the peoples' forces in a spirit of true revolution and institute for a truly free nation, a final constitution as determined by its desires. Such a pause will serve the function of preparing public opinion and directing it on a path toward a constitution of truly republican principles.[11]

Such matters evoked controversy among the conspirators at home. The leaders of the insurrection argued among themselves about "political principles according to which the revolution was to begin," as Józef Pawlikowski stated. A participant in the Warsaw conspiracy, its co-organizer and an activist in its radical wing, perhaps its most radical member, he described its deliberations and arguments in his memoirs. According to him, General Ignacy Działyński, who headed the tenth infantry regiment of the Crown armies (which was soon to gain fame as the Działyński regiment in the Warsaw insurrection), and who was a member of the right in the Warsaw conspiracy, "demanded" in the beginning stages of the conspiracy that the uprising commence "according to [the principles of] the Constitution of 3 May." On the other hand, other members of the conspiracy, still not very numerous in the spring and summer of 1793, judged that "the principles of the Constitution of 3 May are now unsatisfactory. We want to affect the entire nation and it is therefore necessary to provide all classes of people with equal freedoms." Such a position was professed by Kościuszko as well. According to his account, Pawlikowski, during a meeting with conspirators in October of that year in the foothills near Cracow, informed the future Supreme Commander "about the Warsaw conspirators' opinions, which were to direct our insurrection and to inquire about his thoughts on the subject." Kościuszko, taking Pawlikowski by the hand, responded with emotion: "I will not fight only for the nobility. I want freedom for the entire nation and only for them will I risk my life."[12]

The determination of some of the conspirators to carry out transformations in the structure of the government which would go beyond those of the Four-Year Diet is also apparent from Pawlikowski's own position in his account of the arguments at that time. Concerning the uprising's dependence on foreign, particularly French, help, Pawlikowski asserted that "we cannot depend" on this help, that it ought not to come before an uprising by the Poles and, besides, it is "by far more praiseworthy and useful if we liberate ourselves and not depend on others for help. We can then create for ourselves a Constitution and Laws which we judge to be worthy of the national genius."[13]

Prior to the insurrection, other centers of conspiracy in Poland gave evidence of similarly radicalized social and political programs when such views are compared to those from the years of the Four-Year Diet. This was manifested especially clearly in Wilno, second in strength after Warsaw in terms of its support for the uprising and headed by the poet and artillery colonel, Jakub Jasiński, considered to be the main Polish Jacobin. Maintaining tenuous ties

Tadeusz Kościuszko in the uniform of a Polish general major with the American Order of the Cincinnati and the Polish Cross of Virtuti Militari. Copperplate by Friedrich T.M. John acc. to Josef Grassi, 1794 (Biblioteka Narodowa, Warszawa).

Tadeusz Kościuszko taking the Oath on the Cracow Market Square, March 24, 1794, by Franciszek Smuglewicz 1797 acc. to an earlier gouache by Michał Stachowicz (Muzeum Narodowe w Poznaniu).

with Warsaw, the Wilno conspiracy followed the example of revolutionary France more closely, and it had a more radical character. There is no question that the Wilno program for the uprising, in significant measure under the influence of Jasiński, tied the struggle for independence to the social revolution much more closely and called for equality for all, regardless of class origin.[14]

The ultimate decision about the principles governing the system of authority and social principles on which the insurrection was to be based, and therefore, about the relationship to the statutes of the Four-Year Diet, was to find its way into the Act of Insurrection. According to the reliable testimony of Hugo Kołłątaj, Kościuszko himself decided what form the leadership of the insurrection was to take:

PRZYSIĘGA

Wykonana przez TADEUSZA KOSCIUSZKĘ Naywyższego Naczelnika Siły zbroyney Narodowey.

Ja TADEUSZ KOSCIUSZKO przysięgam w obliczu Boga całemu Narodowi Polskiemu, iż powierzoney mi władzy, na niczyi prywatny ucisk nieużyię, lecz iedynie iey dla obrony całości granic, odzyskania samowładności narodu, i ugruntowania powszechney wolności używać będę. Tak mi Panie Boże dopomoż i niewinna męka Syna iego.

(I, Tadeusz Kościuszko, swear in the sight of God to the whole Polish nation that I will use the power entrusted to me for the personal oppression of none, but will only use it for the defence of the integrity of the boundaries, the regaining of the independence of the nation, and the solid establishment of universal freedom. So help me God and the innocent Passion of His Son.) The text of Kościuszko's Oath, a contemporary print (Biblioteka Jagiellońska, Kraków). Translated by Monica M. Gardner.

> In order that the unfortunate events of the French revolution be avoided, we have agreed that the insurrection in Poland should be under the dictatorship of one individual invested with universal trust. The entire nation (and the army) saw Kościuszko as that individual. Consequently, as the one chosen, he stipulated that the insurrection, together with the revolutionary government, be under military control...[15]

In the Act of Insurrection proclaimed in Market Square in Cracow on March 24, 1794, its authors avoided a clear expression of their attitudes to the timeliness of the legislation passed by the Four-Year Diet. Until such a time that "the sacred aims of our uprising" are achieved, that is, "Poland is liberated from foreign soldiers, its borders are returned and fully guaranteed, all compulsion and lawlessness, both foreign and domestic, are eradicated, and freedom for the nation and independence for the Commonwealth are established," the leaders of the insurrection were suspending the binding force of its laws. They did not restore constitutionally-based institutions, nor the central administration, and in their place "so that courageous authority might direct the National Forces," they "elected and appointed Tadeusz Kościuszko as the Sole and Supreme Commander and governor of our entire military uprising," and they established the Supreme National Council.[16]

No mention was made of the office of the King and the person of Stanisław August Poniatowski, with the exception of a highly critical formulation in the politico-ideological preamble to the Declaration, was almost totally ignored. Such an act was tantamount to stripping the King of his powers which, for the duration of the insurrection, was placed in the hands of the Supreme Commander and the Supreme National Council, which was dependent on him.

The relatively mild criticism of the King no doubt came about due to an unwillingness to alienate his more moderate supporters. Depriving the King of political importance was clearly the result of the republicanism which dominated the views of the insurrection's leaders. At the same time, the King was saddled with the responsibility for the collapse of the reforms of the Great Diet and for the surrender in the Polish-Russian war of 1792. This fact prevented the possibility of entrusting him with even a shadow of power or of keeping even symbolic representative functions. Thus in the Declaration of Insurrection Stanisław August was tacitly permitted to formally remain on the throne, but he was stripped, also tacitly, of all royal prerogatives.

The Act of Insurrection gave assurances to the temporary and provisional nature of the new authority and its structure, stipulating that "it will not be able to promulgate any laws which would lead to the formation of a Constitution." The appointed authorities were to remain in power "until such time that Polish lands are liberated from any armed power resisting our uprising and until the integrity of their borders is guaranteed."

Such resolutions can be seen as an attempt by the leaders of the uprising not to prejudge the fate of the legislation of the Four-Year Diet and its normative power in the future. On the other hand, the resolution concerning this matter proclaimed that after the victory of the uprising "the nation, represented by its delegates," that is, the Diet, "will deliberate on its own coming happiness and on the happiness of future generations."[17] Such assertions suggest an intention of creating new legislation, including legislation relating to the work of the Four-Year Diet. This of course should not necessarily lead one to conclude that a total destruction of the system established by the Four-Year Diet was intended. Yet it is certain that there was a desire to further develop and deepen certain changes. A tendency in this direction came into view quite clearly almost the day after the adoption of the Constitution of 3 May, and it can be seen in the opinions and in the programs of the insurrection's leaders of the pre-uprising conspiratorial period.

This position that the decision concerning the form of the future government should be postponed was taken by Kościuszko on numerous occasions. He asserted that it was first necessary to regain freedom and only afterwards to think of the form government would take.[18] As early as September

24 in an address to the nation he gave assurances that after the liberation of the fatherland "the nation having gathered its representatives, will create the kind of government which it deems most satisfactory in assuring its security and happiness."[19]

In practice authorities on various levels for the most part did not turn to the legislation of the Four-Year Diet and referred to it infrequently in the course of the insurrection. There were, of course, different attitudes towards this problem, as well as others, which is understandable given not only the variety of political views, but, above all, problems of communication among the insurrectionists in vast areas of the Commonwealth. Thus there appeared, at the start of the uprising in the Grand Duchy of Lithuania, more radical slogans of "liberty, equality and independence" and the "recovery of civil liberty and equality"[20] at a time when the official slogan of the insurrection was "liberty, unity and independence." The first acts of insurrection in Lithuania were also more radical in their calls to follow the example of the French revolution. In the April 25 proclamation of the Wilno Supreme Council one already finds the assertion about the "valiant French nation" that "proffers its hand in friendship, demands our insurrection and to this end offers its help."[21]

Thus the insurrection of 1794 did not grant to the legislation of the Four-Year Diet the power of binding law but created its own system of law and government. However this does not mean that it opposed the Diet. In various areas one can easily see references to it as well as continuations, but continuations which, as a rule, greatly radicalized solutions achieved a mere two years beforehand. A full analysis of such continuations as well as oppositions would require voluminous study. Here it is only possible to refer to certain selected areas and to cite only selected examples.

In the realm of the political system, the leaders of the insurrection suspended institutions and central authority from the period of the Four-Year Diet (the king, the Guardians of the Law, governmental commissions, as well as the Diet itself, which was to convene only after the victorious termination of the battle), not to mention those from the Targowica and the Grodno periods which were, of course, totally rejected. They did, however, preserve the idea of territorial authority, which was put into effect through Commissions of Order. Nevertheless, the form and tasks of such commissions were altered, and the scope of their jurisdiction was extended, especially as it related to the needs of conducting the war. The composition of the commissions was also altered by increasing burgher membership – a fact connected with the further strengthening of the burgher element and an increase in their activity. In addition, local authority was increased by the addition of an institution of lowest rank, the office of a custodian, whose powers were in turn to promote above all the realization of radical peasant reforms.[22]

The Commissions of Good Order established in 1765 were composed only of the nobility. In spite of the fact that they had certain merit in reforming the administration of cities, they did not infringe on the nobility's discharge of authority, even as it related to matters concerning the burghers. In similar fashion, the Civilian and Military Commissions of Order created in 1789 and chosen in the dietines were composed of the nobility and the clergy. Only in 1792 was the decision made to admit to them members of the burgher class, and only three of them at that. This decision was not put into effect due to the invasion of the Russian army. In the course of the insurrection the composition of the Civilian and Military Commissions of Order was changed radically. They were now to consist of the representatives of the nobility and the burghers in equal numbers, and also include the clergy.

In reality such parity was often not attained and the burghers constituted a minority. Sometimes in practice the whole matter looked entirely different, especially in the beginning of the insurrection when, for example, patriotic fervor was simply not accompanied by information necessary to understand the principles of the system being introduced. For that matter these principles were only then in the process of formation and dissemination. In these matters the principal decisions were undertaken by Kościuszko already on April 30, in the publication *Organizacja Komisji porządkowych* (On the organization of Commissions of Order).

Final adjustments were made by the Supreme National Council on May 30, when it increased the number of Commission members, subordinating to itself the Commissions and introducing changes in their structure.[23] The first, the Cracow Commission of Order, constituted on March 25, consisted of sixteen commissioners and to a great extent followed the pattern from the times of the Four-Year Diet. But Kościuszko appointed to it seven representatives of the landed gentry, seven townsmen and two clergymen.[24] The Commission from Chełm and the Krasnostaw district, constituted on April 6, was composed of eleven landowners and eight townsmen.[25]

In the Mazovian Duchy the Provisional Council appointed a Commission of Order in the Warsaw Territories on April 20, and on April 30 appointed deputations of the Commission of Order to specific areas.[26] Although the Council cited the Cracow Act of Insurrection, it used the legislation of the Four-Year Diet as a model. Only its subsequent resolutions departed from a formal duplication of this model. This could attest to an initial ignorance of the Cracow model, but it was undoubtedly also an expression of conservative

A K T

POWSTANIA OBYWATELOW, MIESZKANCOW WOIEWODZTWA KRAKOWSKIEGO.

Wiadomy iest światu stan teraźnieyszy nieszczęśliwey Polski. Niegodziwość dwoch sąsiedzkich Mocarstw i zbrodnia Zdraycow Oyczyzny, pogrążyły ią w tę przepaść. Uwzięta na zniszczenie Imienia Polskiego, Katarzyna II, w zmowie z wiarołomnym Fryderykiem Gwilelmem, dokonała zamiárow nieprawości swoiey. Nie masz rodzaiu falszu, obłudy i podstępu, ktoremi by się te dwa rządy nie splamiły, dla dogodzenia swoiey zemście i chciwości. Ogłaszaiąc się bezwstydnieCarowa za gwarantkę całości, niepodległości i szczęścia Polski, rozrywała i dzieliła Jey Kraie, znieważała Jey niepodległość, trapiła bezustannie wszelkiego rodzaiu klęskami. Gdy zaś Polska zbrzydziwszy sobie jey obelżywe iarzmo, odzyskała Prawa samowładności swoiey, użyła przeciwko niey ztrayowOyczyzny, bezbożny ich spisek wsparła całą swą mocą zbrojną, a chytrze od obrony Kraju odwiodłszy Krola, ktoremu Seym prawy i Narod wszys·kie siły swie powierzył, wkrotce samychże zdraycow haniebnie zdradziła. Przez takie podstępy stawszy się Panią losow Polski, wezwała do lupow Fryderyka Gwilelma, nadgradzaiąc iego wiarołomstwo, w odstąpieniu nayuroczystszego z Rzeczypospolitą traktatu. Pod wymyslonemi pozorami, ktorych falsz i bezczelność samym tylko tyranom przystoi, w istocie zaś dogadzaiąc nienasyconey chciwości i chuci, rozpostarcia tyranii przez opanowanie przyległych Narodow ; zagarnęły te dwa spiknione na Polskę Mocarstwa, odwieczne i niezaprzeczone Dziedzictwa Rzeczypospolitey, otrzymały na zbrodniczym zieździe zatwierdzenie zaborow swoich, wymusiły przysięgi na poddaństwo i niewolą, wkładaiąc naysroższe na Obywatelow obowiązki, a sami żadnych procz arbitralney woli nie znaiąc; oznaczyły zuchwale, nowym i niesłychanym dotąd w Prawie Narodow ięzykiem, ilłność Rzeczypospolitey w rzędzie państw niższego stopnia; okazuiąc iawnie, że tak prawa iak granice państw udzielnych od ich upodobania zawisły, i że patrzą na pułnocną Europę, iak na łup przeznaczony dla ich drapieżnego despotyzmu.

Pozostała resata Polski, nie okupiła tak strasznemi klęskami polepszenia stanu swego. Ukrywaiąc Carowa niebespieczne Europeyskim Mocarstwom dalsze zamiary swoie, poświęciła ią tym czasem barbarzyńskiey i nieukoioney zemście. Depce w niey nayświętsze Prawa Wolności, bespieczeństwa, własności Osob i maiątkow Obywatelskich ; myśli i czucia poczciwego Polaka, nie znayduią schronienia przed iey podeyrzliwym prześladowaniem : mowie samey więzy narzuciła. Zdraycy tylko Oyczyzny maia od niey pobłażanie, aby się bezkarnie wszelkich dopuszczali zbrodni. Rozszarpali oni maiątek i dochody publiczne, wydarli obywatelska własność, podzielili między siebie Urzędy krajowe, iak gdyby łupy na pokonaney Oyczyznie zdobyte ; a przybrawszy sobie świętokradzko imię Narodowego rządu, wszystko gwoli obcey tyranii i na pierwsze iey skinienie, niewolniczo dopełniaią. Rada Nieustaiąca, twor obcego narzutu, prawą Narodu wolą zniesiona, a świeżo od zdraycow na nowo wskrzeszona, targa, na rozkaz Posła Moskiewskiego, te nawet granice władzy swoiey, ktore od tegoż Posła z podłością przieła, gdy ledwie co zniesione, lub uchwalone uftawy samowolnie podnosi, przerabia i niszczy. Słowem, Rząd mniemany Narodu, Wolność, bespieczeństwo i własność Obywatelow, zostaią w ręku niewolnikow-stu i Carowy, ktorey przemagaiące w kraju Woyska, są tarczą dla ich nieprawości.)ː(

Akt powstania obywatelów, mieszkańców woiewodztwa krakowskiego (The act of insurrection of citizens, inhabitants of the Cracow province). The first page of the Act of the Kościuszko Insurrection (Biblioteka Jagiellońska, Kraków).

Tadeusz Kościuszko in a peasant coat and a "liberty cap" with the American Order of the Cincinnati and the Polish Cross of Virtuti Militari on the background of rays of sunshine emerging from the clouds symbolizing the dawn of freedom, copperplate by G. Fiesinger acc. to a drawing by Gustaw Taubert based on a lost portrait by Josef Grassi (Muzeum Narodowe w Warszawie).

tendencies which dominated at this time among the leaders of the Warsaw uprising.

Various approaches in creating Commissions of Order can also be observed in the Grand Duchy of Lithuania. Thus the Commission of Order of the Kowno district was elected "to realize the aims of the Constitution of 1791."[27] The Commission of Order of the Wiłkomierz district was sworn in (only on May 3) and was composed of the same members as those of 1792.[28] Nevertheless in the course of the uprising the system of instituting Commissions of Order was in accordance with the instructions of the insurrection authorities.

The organization and the make-up of the army had to be subordinated to the needs of conducting a war, to the accepted social and political assumptions of the insurrection, and to material possibilities and limitations. This was given expressions by Kościuszko in a letter from May 12 to Franciszek Sapieha, the general of Lithuanian artillery forces, whom he was appointing a lieutenant-general. He wrote:

Our war has a specific character which has to be understood properly. Its success is based above all on kindling a universal fervor in all our inhabitants and on arming everyone in our land. To this end it is necessary to arouse a love of one's nation in those who until now didn't even know that they had a fatherland. To raise all at once an army of a hundred thousand live troops is difficult in our circumstances, but it will be easy to raise an army three times that number if that is honestly desired by the landed gentry and clergy who hold sway over the people. I know that military men, used to customary means of waging war, especially those from foreign services, will initially have difficulties in assuming command over such forces, but it will be necessary upon occasion to deviate from general rules.... It is, therefore, necessary that the infantry, given effective leadership, when joined with line troops, should always play a decisive role in gaining victory. For that reason it is necessary to tie the peasantry closer to the common goal.... The easing of villein service is an absolute necessity.

It is good to remember that these words were written after the publication on May 7 of the Połaniec Manifesto. Kościuszko went on to say: "Finally, be aware of the fact that our undertaking is great and that such deeds demand revolutionary ways and means, that is, those that are rapid and courageous."[29]

From the Four-Year Diet Kościuszko took over the program of a regular army numbering 100,000 and throughout the course of the uprising attempted to maintain this level. To reach this goal new recruits were called up and ordered to supplement existing detachments or to form new units which, after a necessary period of training, were incorporated into the units of regulars. On May 26, for example, he gave the order to the colonel of the Lublin district militia, Antoni Radzimiński, to form units from among those soldiers who were in the military for life, adding that: "Infantry battalions as well as regiments should be formed in the manner prescribed by the constitutional Diet."[30]

Nevertheless, significant modifications accompanied attempts to form the army of 100,000 indicated by the Diet. The proportion among different types of arms was changed to favor the infantry. Successful efforts were made in unusually difficult circumstances to expand the artillery. The organization and the structure of the cavalry was altered radically, whereby the difficulties of assignment by class were overcome. Finally, promotions for officers and non-commissioned officers were radically accelerated, resulting from the necessity of quickly increasing the size of the army and from the departure of the old cadres who did not side with the insurrection.[31]

In the question of promotions Kościuszko rejected the rule of primacy according to length of service, preferring instead such criteria as usefulness, ability, devotion to the uprising and real achievements. In a reply on April 25 to a report by Stanisław Mokronowski on the victorious Warsaw uprising, he appointed him to the rank of lieutenant-general and commandant of the armed forces of Warsaw and the Duchy of Mazovia; the active officers who participated in the battles of the 17th and 18th of this month received an advance of one grade, while non-commissioned officers who had distinguished themselves were raised to the rank of officer. He also gave assurances that "henceforth in considering the promotion of officers I will give greater weight to usefulness than to seniority," and that "any man from the ranks can become an officer if he merits it." Just as logically he gave the order that "lieutenant-general Mokronowski should immediately bestow the rank of officer on at least a few of those soldiers who behaved sensibly and exhibited courage."[32] As for himself, on April 13 he promoted two recruits from the peasantry, Bartosz Głowacki and Józef Świstacki, to the rank of ensign after they had distinguished themselves in the first battle of the uprising near Racławice.

Far too meager in comparison to enemy strength, the regular army needed support from improvised units, a "dissemination of zeal, a universal arming of the inhabitants of our lands," and the utilization of "revolutionary ways and means." Attempts to form such units were made already towards the end of the Four-Year Diet in the face of an impending defensive war against Russian intervention. But the resolutions of the Diet came too late, a step which was criticized both by Kościuszko in his *Opis Kampanii 1792 r.* (Description of the 1792 Campaign)[33] and by the authors of *O ustanowiemiu...* who made use of the Description and who, one must add, themselves shared in the responsibility for the tardiness. But in his call for a general uprising and for the formation of provincial and local militias Kościuszko took his examples for the most part from the revolutionary experience of the French and, above all, from the American experience, which he valued highly and in which he was personally involved via his participation in the War of Independence.[34]

As far as solutions of social problems in comparison to those that had faced the Four-Year Diet, the furthest reaching transformations during the insurrection concerned matters relating to the peasants. If one can speak here about some form of continuation, it is only in the sense of intentions which were barely sketched in the Constitution of 3 May and appeared in a slightly clearer form in contemporary political and other writing. One finds certain references to the Constitution of 3 May in the ideological justifications and in the preambles to Kościuszko's appeals and proclamations to the peasants. In one of the earliest, *Odezwa za familią włościan do walczenia z nieprzyjaciółmi, wezwanych* (An appeal to the family of peasantry called on to battle the enemy), published on April 19 in the Bosutowo camp, one finds the phrase, repeated in the Połaniec Manifesto of May 7:

> Let it be said that it is not only today that the peasantry receives the protection of the national government and that the oppressed have recourse to the Commission of Order in their province.[35]

Similarly, on May 6, Kościuszko wrote to the Cracow Provincial Commission of Order that "the peasants merit the protection of the government, as granted by our laws,"[36] by which he understood to mean the laws of the Great Diet. This was a reference to the phrase in the Constitution that "the protection of the government and national law" was to be extended to the peasant. In practice such protection meant at the time guarantees given by government authorities concerning the permanence of agreements between peasants and country squires (which were actively encouraged), as well as protection for new arrivals from abroad. The reforms of the insurrection, on the other hand, introduced comprehensive and profound changes. They abolished serfdom, strongly limited villein service, and declared the universal nature of such reforms, including government protection that extended to these entirely new relations in the countryside. More importantly, these reforms created centers and institutions responsible for their implementation.[37] Thus it is clear that the radicalism of publicized and realized changes in social relations in the countryside brought about by the 1794 insurrection ranged far from the first faltering steps taken by the Four-Year Diet. All that they had in common was the basic direction of such changes.

Insurrectionist propaganda, agitating the peasants to active participation in armed battle, besides emphasizing benefits guaranteed peasants by the uprising, also made reference to the benefits already granted country folk by the Constitution of 3 May, benefits that were generally magnified.[38] The anonymous author of *Głos za włościanami* (The voice in defense of peasants), his extreme radicalism bordering on utopianism in his demand that peasants participate in national offices, including the highest, asserted: "It was only the Constitution of 3 May which finally stated that it placed the peasant under the protection of the law, but the peasantry has not even tasted of this fruit."

It was undoubtedly the role of the townspeople in the conspiracy of the insurrection and especially their role in the Warsaw and Wilno uprisings on April 17 and 18 that brought about a significant increase in their civil rights, including participation in governance. Among the leaders of the insurrection, some of whom were co-authors of the Four-Year Diet there were supporters of such an increase already in the years 1788-1792. But at that time the nobility-dominated Diet was not predisposed to share its power. The townspeople were granted many of the privileges hitherto monopolized by the "noble-born." They were given broad powers of self-government in cities and the possibility of entering noble ranks, due to numerous acts of ennoblement carried out by the Diet. On the other hand, the townspeople were not allowed to participate in the government. Cities were only granted the right to elect 24 plenipotentiaries, but without executive authority as deputies. From their group the Diet appointed commissioners to the Treasury Commission, to the Police Commission, and to the Appellate Courts, where they were allowed an active voice only in matters concerning the cities and commerce. In the Diet they acted only as commissioners. Without a decisive voice they could only register the desiderata of the cities.

The attitudes towards townspeople changed radically at the beginning of the uprising. There could no longer be any talk of ennoblements; in their stead came the elimination of class barriers and the equalization of laws. This found expression in the factual elimination of restrictions in promotions for the townspeople, both in the holding of office and in military rank. Symbolic of this trend was the appointment by Kościuszko of the shoemaker Jan Kiliński to the rank of colonel for his contributions in the Warsaw uprising. There were quite a number of such promotions of townspeople where class membership played no role.

Similarly, from the very beginning of the insurrection limitations on participation in power which had earlier been imposed on townspeople were abandoned. Cities, of course, retained all the privileges that had been gained in the years 1791-92, above all self-rule. It was mentioned above that townspeople were granted parity with the nobility in the Commissions of Order. The more active townspeople, those who had achieved distinction, found themselves in the institutions of central power. Thus when the Provisional Council (which was, after all, a conservative body) was convened immediately after the expulsion of the Russians from Warsaw, it counted seven townspeople among its twenty-five members.

This ratio was less advantageous in the Supreme National Council appointed by Kościuszko. In its first composition it had absolutely no representatives from the cities among its eight members and to the group of thirty-two deputy councillors appointed by Kościuszko later there were only nine townsmen.

The diminished participation of the townspeople in the central apparatus of the uprising, from 28% in the Provisional Council to 22.5% in the Supreme National Council, is not an expression of Kościuszko's attitude towards the townspeople or his favoritism of the nobility. Nor does it reflect the views of Ignacy Potocki or especially those of Hugo Kołłątaj, who at that time must have had a genuine influence on the decisions of Kościuszko concerning personnel. Members from cities belonging to the central powers were recruited from among the patrician class, that is, from among conservative elements connected with the court. For the most part they belonged to the well-to-do class. Many had been granted nobility (mainly by the Four-Year Diet), or they were connected by marriage to the wealthy or at least the hereditary nobility.[39] The appointment as councillors of only members of the nobility and the designation of only a small number of townspeople as deputy councillors evoked the latter's opposition. The protest received the support of Kiliński and the banker Jędrzej Kapostas, both honored members of the pre-insurrection conspiracy.[40]

They gave voice to their protest either at the last meeting of the Provisional Council or the first of the Supreme National Council on May 28, and appealed to Kościuszko himself.[41] Kościuszko's reply on June 7 was characteristic:

Brothers and Fellow Citizens! —First let us expel the enemy and then let us establish a permanent foundation for our well-being. The government...is made up of...honest citizens and friends of the people and in appointing them I did not reflect on whether they were peasants, townspeople or the nobility.[42]

This phrase achieves symbolic proportions. Aside from its likely propagandistic intentions, it gives witness to tremendous, even revolutionary changes in consciousness, to changes in the approach to social issues that had occurred in the two years since the deliberations of the Great Diet had ended.

The highest representative of the powers conducting the uprising, its dictator, publicly declaring the nullity of the criteria of class. Although this novelty was only weakly reflected in the makeup of the government, nevertheless, it is worth mentioning that in other governmental offices, in the various deputations and commissions summoned in Warsaw, there were many townspeople, even though not many of them had been sufficiently prepared for the role of governing a country. Such a situation would have been unimaginable two years earlier.

A total change in the institutional system of the state, a change in the structure of the state, the removal of the king's influence on the administrative process, relatively radical social reforms (especially in peasant affairs and the political position of the townspeople), a departure from a class-oriented society (in particular in the relationship between the nobility and townspeople and military promotions of peasants, admittedly not yet very numerous), the demand that the nobility fight on equal footing and alongside the peasantry (for example, in a mass call to arms), the process of democratizing the composition of the army – this is but a partial list of events bearing witness to the road traversed by Poland from the years 1788-1792 to 1794.

This did not indicate a rejection or a negation of the achievements of the reformers in the Four-Year Diet, but a radical continuation of their work, even though it was acknowledged as insufficient in new circumstances (and even when, to use the formulation of the authors of *O ustanowieniu*, those "methods born of moderation" were undertaken).

There is yet another problem that it is impossible to resolve definitively because one can never be certain what course the historical process might have taken had it not been brutally interrupted. One cannot assert with total certainty what the government or society would have been like had the insurrection succeeded. We have even less foundation for making categorical assertions concerning the shape of the state and society that the leaders of a victorious insurrection might have desired. It appears certain that they did not want to return to the state of affairs of 1792. It is similarly difficult to predict what the composition of the diet – which was to be convened, as called for in the Act of Insurrection – would have looked like. And then what decisions would such a diet have undertaken? Would it return to the Government Statute of May 3? This seems likely, but what changes would it have introduced, since changes would have to be made? It is unthinkable that such changes would not be effected. It would have been impossible to reverse the changes which had taken place; to revoke rights and the position achieved by the townspeople; to return to the enserfment of the peasants, forcing them into villein service of former proportions. Such a regression could only be achieved by invaders with an alien apparatus of coercion.

The army and the mass participation of townspeople and peasants in the battle for Polish independence also played a great role in effecting changes in thinking, in transforming the social structure and in forming new notions about a modern nation from which the caste system was being forced out. Changes in the social make-up in the military were far reaching and affected not only the officer and non-commissioned officer cadres but can even be observed in the reorganization of the cavalry (hitherto dominated by the nobility) in a democratically guided spirit. Yet another result of the atmosphere created by a war of liberation and by insurrectionist propaganda was the perceived significance of large masses participating in a national movement. Together with published reforms this had to influence the psychology and mentality of the peasantry and to awaken an awareness of nationality in them. It produced an extremely vital link in the birth process of a modern nation as the nation reintegrated its plebeian classes. The year of 1794 produced a precedent and together with it a military prepared to continue the struggle for an independent Poland. It gave birth to tradition and to a legend that played a major integrative function in the nation in the next generations.

Although the Kościuszko uprising failed, it strengthened and intensified the achievements of the Polish Enlightenment by renewing the Republic and by modernizing the social structure of the nation and the mental outlook of Poles. Thanks to the fact that the first step was made by the Constitution of 3 May and "a space was left for further changes," thanks to the fact that the 1794 insurrection achieved these "changes," the nucleus of a modern nation with an awareness of community was so strong that Poles were capable of enduring the partitions. Their invaders were unable to divest them of their national character or to discourage them from repeated attempts at regaining their national independence.

Notes

1. For a more detailed presentation of my point of view on this matter see Jerzy Kowecki, *Pospolite ruszenie w insurekcji 1794* (Levy in mass during the Insurrection of 1794) (Warszawa: MON, 1963), pp. 47-77.

2. *New Constitution of the Government of Poland, Established by the Revolution, the Third of May, 1791*, 2nd ed. (London, 1791), Art. VI. The Diet, or the Legislative Power, pp. 18-19.

3. For example, see the article attributed to Piotr Świtkowski, "Nobilitacye liczne są li lub jak mają być z pożytkiem dla kraju?" (Are the ennoblements numerous or how

can they be useful for the country?), *Pamiętnik Historyczno-Polityczno-Ekonomiczny*, no. 9, November 1790, pp. 1299-1311, reprinted in *Materiały do dziejów Sejmu Czteroletniego*, eds. Janusz Woliński, Jerzy Michalski, Emanuel Rostworowski (Wrocław: Ossolineum, 1960), vol. 3, pp. 402-406; Franciszek Salezy Jezierski, *Głos naprędce do stanu miejskiego* (In a hurry to give voice to the burgher estate) n.p., n.d. (the end of 1790), reprinted in *Materiały...*, pp. 428-430; *Prawdziwy szlachcic do prawodawców* (A true nobleman's address to the lawmakers), n.p., n.d. (March 1790), reprinted in *Materiały...*, pp. 460-461.

4. Compare Krystyna Zienkowska, *Sławetni i urodzeni. Ruch polityczny mieszczaństwa w dobie Sejmu Czteroletniego* (City dwellers and the well-born: the political movement of the townspeople in the time of the Four-Year Diet) (Warszawa: PWN, 1976), pp. 157 ff. and passim.

5. Jerzy Jedlicki, *Klejnot i bariery społeczne. Przeobrażenia szlachectwa polskiego w schyłkowym okresie feudalizmu* (The crest and social barriers. Transformations of the Polish nobility in the period of the decline of feudalism) (Warszawa: PWN, 1968), pp. 126-132, 205-206; Zienkowska, *Sławetni i urodzeni*, pp. 142 ff; Jerzy Kowecki, "U początków nowoczesnego narodu" (The beginnings of a modern nation) in *Polska w epoce Oświecenia. Państwo - społeczeństwo - kultura* ed. Bogusław Leśnodorski (Warszawa: Wiedza Powszechna, 1971), pp. 120-124.

6. Philip Mazzei, *Selected Writings and Correspondence*, vol. 2, 1788-1791. *Agent for the King of Poland during the French Revolution*, ed. Margherita Marachione (Prato: Cassa di Risparmi e Depositi di Prato, 1983). p. 563.

7. Hugo Kołłątaj (Ignacy Potocki, Franciszek K. Dmochowski), *O ustanowieniu i upadku Konstytucji polskiej 3 Maja 1791 roku* (On the enactment and the fall of the Polish Constitution of 3 May 1791), 2 vols. ((Metz) Kraków: 1793), p. 14.

8. Kołłątaj, *O ustanowieniu...*, p. 246.

9. Władysław M. Kozłowski, "Nowy przyczynek do wyjaśnienia misji Kościuszki i próby nawiązania stosunków z Francją w r. 1793" (A new contribution to the explanation of Kościuszko's mission and attempts to establish relations with France in 1793), *Przewodnik Naukowy i Literacki* 34 (1906).

10. For more on this question see Kowecki, *Pospolite ruszenie...*, pp. 56-59; Marian Kukiel, "O Kościuszkę" (Concerning Kościuszko), *Teki Historyczne*, 1-2 (London 1949): 34; Bogusław Leśnodorski, *Polscy jakobini. Karta z dziejów insurekcji 1794 roku* (Polish Jacobins. A chapter from the history of the Insurrection of 1794) (Warszawa: Książka i Wiedza, 1960), pp. 150, 242, 336. Different opinions were expressed by Szymon Askenazy, *Napoleon a Polska* (Napoleon and Poland) (Warszawa-Kraków: 1918), vol. 1, p. 52; Adam Skałkowski, "Zagadnienia Kościuszkowskie" (Problems concerning Kościuszko), *Sprawozdania Poznańskiego Tow. Przyjaciół Nauk* (1948): 34.

11. Aleksander Kraushar, *Barss palestrant warszawski, jego misya polityczna we Francji (1793-1800)* (Barss, the Warsaw lawyer: his political mission in France 1793-1800) (Lwów: 1903), pp. 48-49.

12. Józef Pawlikowski, "Pamiętnik o przygotowaniach do insurekcji kościuszkowskiej" (A diary concerning preparations for the Kościuszko Insurrection), ed. Lucjan Siemieński, *Przegląd Polski* 10, 7 (1876): 76-77, 86. About divisions inside the conspiracy see: Wacław Tokarz, *Insurekcja warszawska 17 i 18 kwietnia 1794 r.* (The Warsaw insurrection on 17 and 18 April 1794) (Warszawa: Książka i Wiedza, 1950), p. 70; "Marsz Madalińkiego" (Madaliński march) in *Rozprawy i szkice* (Warszawa: PWN, 1959), vol. 2, pp. 90 ff; "Klub jakobinów w Warszawie" (The Jacobin club in Warsaw) vol. 1, pp. 175-178.

13. Pawlikowski, "Pamiętnik o przygotowaniach..", p. 70.

14. See Zdzisław Sułek, *Sprzysiężenie Jakuba Jasińskiego* (The conspiracy of Jakub Jasiński) (Warszawa: MON, 1982), pp. 60, 236-237.

15. "Memoryał Kołłątaja o przygotowaniach do powstania r. 1794, napisany dla Tomasza Wawrzeckiego" (Kołłątaj's memorial about the preparations for the uprising in 1794, written for Tomasz Wawrzecki) in Wacław Tokarz, *Ostatnie lata Hugona Kołłątaja* (1794-1812) (Kraków: 1905), vol. 2, pp. 238, 249.

16. "Akt powstania obywatełów, mieszkańców województwa krakowskiego" (Act of uprising by the citizens and inhabitants of the Cracow voivodeship) in *Zbiór wszystkich pism urzędowych od zapisania Aktu Powstania Narodowego w Krakowie i innych do niego się ściągających. Dzieło służące do napisania historyi Powstania Narodowego* (Kraków: 1794), vol. 1, pp. 8-9.

17. *Zbiór wszystkich pism...*, pp. 14-15.

18. See Tadeusz Kupczyński, *Kraków w powstaniu Kościuszkowskim* (Cracow in the Kościuszko uprising) (Kraków: 1912), pp. 106-107.

19. *Akty Powstania Kościuszki* (Acts of the Kościuszko Uprising), eds. Szymon Askenazy, Włodzimierz Dzwonkowski (Kraków: 1918), vol. 2, p. 185. Referred to hereafter as APK.

20. "Akt związku w Szawlach uczynionego przez wojskowych" (Act of Association by the military men in Szawle), in Leonid Żytkowicz, "Litwa i Korona w r. 1794," *Ateneum Wileńskie* 12 (1937): 50-52; and also 19-20, 25; "Akt Powstania Narodu Litewskiego z 24 IV" (Declaration of Uprising of the Lithuanian nation addressed 24 April), *Gazeta Narodowa Wileńska* no.2, 7 May 1794, pp. 5-6.

21. *Uniwersał do województw i powiatów Wielkiego Księstwa Litewskiego i miast wolnych* (Manifesto addressed to the voivodeships and counties of the Grand Duchy of Lithuania and to free cities), n.p., n.d.

22. Wojciech M. Bartel, "Dozory w insurekcji kościuszkowskiej" (Supervisory institutions in the Kościuszko insurrection) in *Ustrój władz cywilnych powstania kościuszkowskiego* (Wrocław: Ossolineum, 1959), pp. 190-213.

23. "Organizacja dla wszystkich ogólnie komisjów porządkowych" (General rules for all Commissions of Order) in APK, vol. 1, pp. 216-220.

24. Kupczyński, *Kraków w powstaniu..*, pp. 157-158.

25. *Uchwała obywateli ziemi chełmskiej i powiatu krasnostawskiego* (A resolution of the citizens of the Chełm district and Krasnostaw county), n.p., n.d.

26. APK, vol. 1, pp. 10, 83-87.

27. MS. Jagiellonian Library, BJ. no. 222409/111, 2. For a similar resolution, see Commission of Oszmiany county. MS. Kórnik Library, BK, no. 1090, k. 174.

28. MS. Kórnik Library, BK, no. 1090, k. 271-272.

29. *Pisma Tadeusza Kościuszki* (Works of Tadeusz Kościuszko), ed. Henryk Mościcki (Warszawa: Państwowe Zakłady Wyd. Szkolnych, 1947), pp. 114-115.

30. Zygmunt Luba Radzimiński, "Z papierów generała Antoniego Radzimińskiego" (Documents of general Antoni Radziminski), *Kwartalnik Historyczny*, 31 (1917): 267.

31. See Stanisław Herbert, "Żołnierze niepodległości" (Soldiers of independence), in *Polska w epoce Oświecenia*, pp. 402-407.

32. APK, vol. 1, pp. 92-93.

33. *Tadeusza Kościuszki dwie relacje o kampanii polsko-rosyjskiej 1792 roku* (Two accounts of the Polish-Russian campaign of 1792 by Tadeusz Kościuszko), ed. Piotr Bańkowski (Warszawa: PWN, 1964).

34. Kowecki, *Pospolite ruszenie...*, pp. 25-77.

35. APK, vol. 3, eds. W. Dzwonkowski, Emil Kipa, Roch Morcinek (Wrocław: Ossolineum, 1955), p. 16.

36. APK, vol. 3, p. 22.

37. Jerzy Kowecki, *Uniwersał Połaniecki i sprawa jego realizacji* (The Połaniec Manifesto and the problem of its implemtation) (Warszawa: PWN, 1957), pp. 52 passim.

38. See *Odezwa Rady Najwyższej Narodu Litewskiego do rolników i ludu wiejskiego*, 30 IV 1794 (Proclamation of the Supreme Council of the Lithuanian Nation to peasants and villagers), n.p., n.d. See also "Mowa X.J.G. Plebana W. Do ludu rolniczego swojej parafii" (Sermon of Father X.J.G., Vicar of W., to the villagers of his parish), *Gazeta Narodowa Wileńska*, 18 May 1794, Supplement, pp. 27-28.

39. Dzwonkowski, "Wstęp" (Introduction) in APK, vol. 1, pp. XXVIII-XXXI.

40. Dzwonkowski, "Wstęp," p. XXXII.

41. APK, vol. 2, p. 319.

42. *Pisma Tadeusza Kościuszki...*, p. 124

Translated by Jerzy Kolodziej and Mary Helen Ayres

21

The Influence of the Constitution of 3 May on Constitutional Life of the Second Republic (1918-1939: Reality and Myth

Andrzej Ajnenkiel

Esteemed Deputies!

As we gather today we are still under the sway of the recent national celebration commemorating that noble document which has such special significance for the present Diet.

Why has the Constitution of 3 May, in spite of all its shortcomings revealed in the criticism of subsequent generations, remained a source of pride throughout the whole century of enslavement and become a symbol of our rebirth?

Because the Constitution of 3 May was unique in the history of mankind. It marked the first time in history that a nation which had slipped into anarchy, bloodlessly rallied from its effects and became aware that golden freedom alone could not offer a foundation for the state. It realized that order - without which freedom could not long survive - was necessary too.

It was unique in contemporary Europe, elsewhere divided into the privileged classes and the common people, to see a nation whose advantaged classes offered up their privileges at the altar of the Motherland not only without great upheavals, but also without pressure from below.

Today, we are facing the same task the Four-Year Diet faced on the eve of 3 May. Today we are about to lay the foundation for the state edifice of this nation.... Let us be certain that in the judgement of posterity our generation stands up to the great moment providence has prepared for us today.[1]

The speech above, given by the Marshal of the legislative Diet, Wojciech Trąmpczyński, referred to the recent anniversary celebrations of the Constitution of 3 May established as a national holiday by a legislative act adopted on April 29, 1919. While the legislative act was adopted amid political struggles and sharp polemics, Trąmpczyński's speech, since it was the first major address in the Diet devoted entirely to the Constitution of 3 May, was received calmly. One should note here that the attention of the deputies in the Diet was focused on deliberations concerning the creation of a new constitution and that the anniversary of the Constitution of 3 May did not particulary stir the passions of either the Right or the Left.

The Constitution of 3 May lasted only one year. The Partitions of Poland had severed the continuity of the independent state and its legal institutions. Thus the Constitution had become a "noble document." It proved the Poles' ability to present a program for bold, and at the same time, reasonable transformations. These transformations stemmed from the traditions of the state and the nation's historic roots. The scope of changes it envisaged was broad and it entailed fervent appeals for the defense of the integrity and sovereignty of the state as well as the freedom of its citizens.

Few other developments in Poland's past matched the Constitution's importance for different political forces which—irrespective of profound disparities between them—saw it necessary to continue efforts aimed at bringing independence to Poland in the future. Hence the readiness of the whole political spectrum, from Conservatives, National Democrats, members of peasant parties, to Socialists, to refer to the Constitution of 3 May was apparent. The fact that the war of 1792 and the November Uprising of 1830-31 were referred to as the Polish-Russian wars over the Constitution indicates that it occupied a major place in the thought and propaganda of the Polish insurrectionist trend.

1917 saw the emergence of the Provisional Council of State in the Polish territory occupied by the Central Powers. Dependence on the occupying powers, as well as fear of voicing declarations which might be regarded as questioning Prussian and Austrian rule over territories of the old Polish Republic, caused the Council to make little reference to the provisions of the Constitution of 3 May. Such steps might have been seen as a challenge to the Central Powers.[2] As a matter of fact, the Regency Council which succeeded the Provisional Council adopted a similar stance.

Official documents and statements at the time of Poland's rebirth as an independent state in the fall of 1918, reveal the presence of two trends. On the one hand, they emphasize that Poland was implementing her never-extinguished right to sovereignty and independent statehood, so cruelly violated by the partitions, and on the other hand they stress - in keeping with the facts - that the state was actually being built anew.[3] These documents never make direct reference to the Constitution of 3 May. Given the circumstances, any such reference was bound to be seen as anachronistic and even as a manifestation of reactionary, monarchist tendencies. However, putting emphasis on Polish national liberation and democratic traditions sounded quite different. In such a context the Constitution of 3 May occupied a place of outstanding importance.

At this time, Piłsudski and his associates saw the introduction of democratic parliamentary elections as the most urgent task before them. The Head of State believed that elections would provide a stabilizing factor in the country, integrating the formerly divided Polish lands and that they would serve as a dam to the threat of a communist revolution strongly supported from the outside. Elections were also intended as a means of gaining international recognition for Poland, above all, from the allied powers. The establishment of a central authority able to pass the most indispensable legislative acts, including the constitution, was essential. At the same time the elections were seen as a way of verifying the actual influence of political parties in Poland.

Against the resistance of the Right, Piłsudski decided to hold elections as soon as possible. The elections to the Legislative Diet were held 76 days after Piłsudski's return to Warsaw and 64 days after he assumed the office of the Provisional Head of State. One should stress at this point that both his title (*Naczelnik Państwa*) and his powers corresponded most closly to those adopted during the Kościuszko Insurrection of 1794.

The election campaign in 1918 to 1919 was held in a very tense atmosphere. Party interests came to the foreground as was especially evident in the propaganda exercised by peasant parties. Ideological issues also played a considerable role in attempts to deal with the problems of national defense and the communist threat. Nationalist phobias emerged amid ethnic conflicts heightened by the war. These factors made it difficult to draw on the Constitution of 3 May which represented a very specific type of state ideology in which the notion of nation encompassed not only the nobility, not entirely homogenous in ethnic terms, but was also beginning to encompass all inhabitants of the state. In this respect the notion was closer to formulas applied in France at that time. There, the nation was seen in political terms as a collection of all citizens of the state. During the election campaign, forces active in rural areas made frequent references to the Constitution of 3 May in their political activity. They pointed out that the Constitution had put the state under an obligation to protect the peasants. This argument formed the core of the peasant movement's utilization of the political tradition.

The solemn Holy Mass held on 10 February 1919 at St. John's Cathedral in Warsaw before the first session of the Diet, represented a continuation of an old tradition in the Polish Diet and demonstrated an understanding of the role played by the Roman Catholic Church in the affairs of state. The Head of State, Prime Minister Ignacy Paderewski, and many deputies were present. After the mass, the first session of the Diet in the independent Second Republic was held. The eloquent opening speech was delivered by the Head of State. In speaking of the past, he referred to the Poles' struggle for independence, which had lasted for more than a century. He stressed the role of the Diet as the supreme organ of state authority. The legal system in the state, based on the constitution, was to provide the basis for all state activity, and at the same time act as the foundation of civil rights.

Even though Piłsudski repeatedly stressed that he was representing all citizens in the state, given his activities in the not so distant past, his speech was received as the voice of a man who was close to the Left. The speech delivered by Prince Ferdynand Radziwiłł, who chaired the meeting by virtue of his seniority, was quite different in tone and content. A member of one of the most prominent families in the Republic and a longtime Polish parliamentarian in German representative bodies, he pointed out the traditions of the Polish state before the partitions and its role as the bulwark of Europe's freedom. While he made no direct reference to the Constitution in his speech, its style was somewhat reminiscent of that used in the Constitution.

Similar to the decree establishing the office of the Provisional Head of State for Piłsudski, the Diet resolution of February 20, 1919 on "further entrusting the office of the Head of State to Józef Piłsudski" drew neither on the terminology nor the solutions employed in the Constitution of 3 May. Under the provisions of this resolution known as the Little Constitution, the Head of State was to be the supreme executive authority implementing the resolutions of the Diet in civilian and military matters, while the Diet defined itself as the supreme organ of state authority. Nevertheless, one can say that the identification of the Diet as the center of power resembled solutions adopted in the Constitution of 3 May. The Constitution of 3 May more clearly stressed the principle of a separation of powers. Actually, the period from 1919 to

1922, when the Little Constitution was in force, saw the establishment of a specific balance between the Diet and the Head of State.

As mentioned above, on April 29, 1919 the Constitution of 3 May became the cause of a conflict in the Diet when the Polish Socialist Party presented a motion--without a real chance of winning a majority–to recognize May 1 as a national holiday. When the motion fell through, the socialists declared that the voting demonstrated the reactionary views of the Diet's majority. Immediately afterwards, when centrist and rightist deputies proposed a motion that the anniversary of the Constitution of 3 May become a national holiday, the socialist deputies left the Chamber. They returned after the Chamber passed the resolution. For several years thereafter, Polish Socialist Party propaganda described celebrations of the 3 May anniversary as subversive acts aimed against the workers' May 1 holiday.

The draft of the new constitution made clear reference to the Constitution of 3 May. Internal Affairs Minister Stanisław Wojciechowski who headed the government's constitutional effort (he had been a founder of the Polish Socialist party and later a well-known activist in the cooperative movement) invited Władysław Wakar, a leading activist in the leftist Polish peasant party *Wyzwolenie* (Liberation), to participate in the drafting of the documents. Wakar wrote a draft entitled "Foundations of Order in the Polish Republic," which was patterned after the Constitution of 3 May in its style, structure, and legal rules interwoven with moral and political declarations. However, the political image of the state emerging from it was quite different. It was founded on local governing units enjoying extensive powers. The government was to be elected by groups representing different occupations and interests. The executive authority was to be held by the Supreme Head of the Republic vested with wide powers and elected in general elections for a term of six years. The government turned down Wakar's draft which subsequently became the basis of a bill bearing the same title and submitted to the Diet by the *Wyzwolenie* party.

Although he did not accept Wakar's draft, Minister Wojciechowski made extensive use of it in his work on the document "Constitutional Declaration by the Government." Quite significantly, the declaration was adopted by the Council of Ministers on May 3, 1919. Modeled on Wakar's draft, it resembled the Constitution of 3 May in its form and layout, and in its preamble it almost literally quoted a number of phrases from the opening of the 3 May document. However, the contents dealt with other matters. It only referred to the pre-partition tradition in connection with Piłsudski's federation ideas (shared by prime minister Paderewski and by Wojciechowski) when it announced its efforts to establish closer ties with nations which "had shared the misery of Poland." Wojciechowski stressed in his diary that in keeping with the trend present in the Constitution of 3 May, his aim was to strengthen the authority of the executive.

The declaration was presented to the Diet on May 6, 1919, i.e. the first meeting following May 3rd. It was introduced by the Marshal in the previously quoted speech. The main ideas of the draft were explained by Minister Wojciechowski. He pointed out that in its work on the bill, the government did not strive "to please a single line of political thought or a social trend." It tried to "profoundly comprehend the feelings of the broad masses of the nation and endow the Republic with the contents and form matching our native thought, not borrowed from foreign patterns. The continuity of Polish thought... being the result of the work, lives and experience of many generations and centuries... has to be preserved."[4]

The statement made by Wojciechowski indicated that the government was submitting a document which stemmed from its own considerations irrespective of the chances of obtaining a majority in support of it. The government also stressed its desire to base Poland's constitution on past traditions. One should add at this point that the reference was not a direct one. Apart from the wording, it referred to the tradition of ideas rather than to practical solutions.

The debates in the Chamber showed that neither the government's declaration nor the draft presented by the *Wyzwolenie* party had a chance of being adopted. Both texts met with sharp criticism. What is more, their form and content were ridiculed.

A proposal drawn up by the so called "Questionnaire" - a team of mostly conservative experts and politicians - proved somewhat more successful. Appointed by the government, the team came up with a draft that oscillated between solutions adopted by the United States and by the Third Republic in France. Although the government did not officially submit it for consideration by the Diet (it was given to them for informational purposes), some detailed solutions in the document were used in subsequent work on the constitution. Significantly, the preamble to the proposal included the following statement: "In the first session of the Diet in resurrected Poland we are forging a new link in the law and connecting it to the last link of the chain of laws severed after the Great Diet, by establishing the present Constitution of the Republic.[5]

Ultimately, work on the Constitution followed patterns employed in the Third French Republic. The role of the Parliament, and especially that of the Diet was strengthened. The power of the President of the Republic was curbed. That development stemmed from the Right's reluctance to see Piłsudski become

USTAWA Z DNIA 17 MARCA 1921 ROKU

KONSTYTUCJA
RZECZYPOSPOLITEJ
POLSKIEJ

W IMIE BOGA WSZECHMOGĄCEGO
MY, NARÓD POLSKI,
dziękując OPATRZNOŚCI za
wyzwolenie nas z półtorawiekowej
niewoli, wspominając z wdzięcznością męstwo i
wytrwałość ofiarnej walki pokoleń, które najlep
sze wysiłki swoje sprawie niepodległości bez
przerwy poświęcały, nawiązując do świetnej tra
dycyi wiekopomnej Konstytucyi 3-go Maja - dobro
całej zjednoczonej i niepodległej Matki - Ojczyzny
mając na oku, a pragnąc Jej być niepodległy,
potęgi i bezpieczeństwo oraz ład społeczny,
utwierdzić na wiekuistych zasadach prawa i
wolności pragnąc zarazem zapewnić rozwój
wszystkich Jej sił moralnych i materialnych dla
dobra całej odradzającej się ludzkości, wszystkim
obywatelom Rzeczypospolitej równość, a pracy
poszanowanie, należne prawa i szczególną opiekę
Państwa zabezpieczyć - tę oto Ustawę Konsty-
tucyjną na Sejmie Ustawodawczym Rzeczypospolitej Polskiej uchwalamy
i stanowimy

The first page of the Polish Constitution of 17 March 1921 including the reference to the "glorious tradition of the historic Constitution of 3 May" (Biblioteka Sejmowa, Warszawa).

the first President of the Republic. In general, no reference was made to the Constitution of 3 May during the deliberations. The sole exception was the call by conservatives that the attitude toward churches and religious denominations in Poland be based on Chapter One of the Constitution of 3 May which had declared that the Roman Catholic faith was the dominant religion in Poland. This proposal was not appreciated by the Right either. Arguments over the form the government of independent Poland lasted two years and finally ended with the passage of the Constitution on March 17, 1921. Following in the footsteps of the ceremony which took place 130 years earlier when the Constitution of 3 May was adopted, immediately after the passage of the new Constitution the Head of State, members of the government and the Diet proceeded to St. John Cathedral for a solemn mass. There Marshal Trąmpczyński paid homage to the creators of the 3 May Constitution by placing a wreath under the monument of the Marshal of the Four-Year Diet, Stanisław Małachowski The preamble to the Constitution of March 17, 1921, also known as the March Constitution, made a direct reference to the "glorious tradition of the historic Constitution of 3 May." But this reference too was limited in scope. The main point was to stress the continuity of Polish statehood in relation to pre-partition Poland and the continuity of Polish parliamentary institutions and constitutional traditions. The March Constitution's division of power into three branches of government and the clear-cut description of their powers, the concept of the people as the source of authority, and declarations protecting individual rights, set forth general standards already formulated in the Constitution of 3 May. These are standards of modern constitutionalism in which the Constitution of 3 May occupies a prominent place, notwithstanding its orientation towards differences between the estates. No wonder then that these standards, adequately expanded, found their way into the March Constitution. It must be stated, however, that while the Constitution of 3 May was pervaded with the idea of strengthening executive authority, improving the functioning of the state as a whole, and with the important policy of defending the state against external threats, such ideas found minimal expression in the March Constitution. One could risk the statement here that the victory in the war against the Bolsheviks and the favorable resolution of other frontier problems seemingly deminished the lawmakers' interest in problems of national security. Apparently, they failed to notice that passage of the March Constitution coincided with the end of the favorable resolution for Poland in international developments which the country enjoyed in the past few years.

Criticism of the March Constitution and its implementation began shortly after its adoption. The criticism launched by the center-right was in line with the premises of the Constitution of 3 May which adopted Montesquieu's principle of the separation of powers as its starting point. The postulate of strengthening the position of the president was in keeping with solutions adopted in the Constitution of 3 May. Differing from these solutions were the proposals to expand the powers of the Senate at the expense of the Diet as well as to curb the democratic principles in the electoral law.

The circles, which after the 1926 coup, formed the ideological nucleous of the Piłsudski camp, followed a different course in their political thinking. Members of this camp believed that given contemporary circumstances, the separation of powers formula was difficult to apply. They also opposed what they referred to as the "creditor's attitude towards the state," and viewed the Parliament and political parties from this perspective. They greatly valued the role of the individual and actions for the common welfare. It was in moral terms that they highly regarded the framers of the Constitution of 3 May perceiving them as fathering the idea of work for the good of the state. Although after the coup the Diet lost its status as the center of state authority, the Parliament remained a podium from which the voices of all political forces in Poland could be heard with little interference. The so-called August Amendment of 1926, imposed limits on the powers of the chambers. However, it did not mark a formal alteration of relations between the supreme organs of authority.

In 1928, after a great propaganda campaign, the ruling camp set to work on drafting a new Constitution. The necessity of defining a new role for the President in Poland came to the foreground, motivated by external threat and the domestic situation. The negative role of the Parliament was stressed and no mention was made of its achievements. The same attitude was assumed regarding political parties. Statements by political writers abounded, especially in reference to the Constitution of 3 May. The main thrust of their criticism was aimed against those pre-partition institutions which weakened the state. The Constitution was seen primarily as the work of a strong-willed political elite, which achieved the necessary solutions despite the passivity and resistance of the nobility at large. That stance served both to legitimatize the May 1926 coup and to justify the possible implementation of a new constitution.

It is only today, in a Poland which has regained her sovereignty and has built her democratic institutions from a perspective offered by the experience of living over fifty years in a totalitarian state, that conditions are ripe for a

more profound analysis of the 23 April 1935 Constitution and for discussing
its accurate solutions and weaknesses. Each of the general principles of the
1935 Constitution–i.e., the idea of strengthening the state, improving the
activity of its organs and the status of its citizens –was elaborated on in a
manner that differed from that found in the Constitution of 3 May. The process
of adopting the two constitutions also differed. In this respect, the claim that
in both cases we are dealing with a homogenous *coup d'état* carried out within
the Parliament by an active minority acting in defiance of the passive majority
sounds quite lame. Another difference should be noted--during the year that
it remained in force, the Constitution of 3 May became a tool which greatly
expanded the political ranks in Poland, that is those who identified themselves
with the state. On the contrary, the Constitution of 1935 tended to discourage
a portion of the population from taking an active part in the life of the state.
The opposition for its part organized a boycott of the 1935 elections which
were held on the basis of new electoral laws, compatible with the Constitution.
On the other hand one can hardly overestimate the role played by the 1935
Constitution in the recreation of state functions by the government in exile
after September, 1939. It formed the legal basis both for internal law and for
the government's recognition internationally as a lawful continuator of the
independent Polish state.

   In accordance with the resolution passed on April 29, 1919, the Constitution
of 3 may was a national holiday celebrated both by the government and church
and by the broad masses of the population in cities, towns and villages. The
increasing threat to the security of the state in the last years before World War
II brought about the situation that patriotic manifestations of national solidarity
came to the fore while the vehemence of opposing views was tempered. As
they had done so often before, the traditions of 3 May played the role of an
integrating factor.

Notes

1. *Sprawozdanie Stenograficzne z 33 posiedzenia Sejmu Ustawodawczego* 6 maja
1918 r. vol. 33, 3/4.

2. Hence, for example, the following quite enigmatic statement in the first manifesto
by the Regency Council of December 27, 1917: "We owe it to these factors from the
time of the Constitution of 3 May, the Duchy of Warsaw and the Congress Kingdom...
that throughout the one-hundred-year-long enslavement we did not lose the purity
of national spirit and now, when the hour of justice has come, we face the whole
world armed with the undeniable right to sovereign existence. We are appealing to

that creative force of the entire nation at the present moment." *Czas,* no. 499, December 28, 1917.

3. Both trends are evident in, among other documents, the Message by the Regency Council of October 7, 1918 (*Dziennik Praw Królestwa Polskiego,* no. 12, item 23, 1918) as well as in the wire by Józef Piłsudski, Commander of the Armed Forces, November 16, 1918, *Monitor Polski,* no. 206, November 18, 1918.

4. *Sprawozdanie stenograficzne z 33 posiedzenia Sejmu Ustawodawczego* z 6 V 1919 r., vol. 33, 5.

5. *Sejm Ustawodawczy,* no. 443, p. 1.

6. On the April Constitution see: Andrzej Ajnenkiel, *Polskie konstytucje* (Polish Constitutions), (Warszawa: Wydawnictwo Szkolne i Pedagogiczne, 1991), pp. 272-322; *Konstytucje Polski. Studia monograficzne z dziejów polskiego konstytucjonalizmu* (Polish Constitutions. Monographic Studies from the History of Polish Constitutionalism), ed. Marian Kallas (Warszawa: PWN, 1990), vol. 2, pp. 141-216. The attitudes adopted by different political camps toward the Constitution of 3 May in the interwar period, and the anniversary celebrations are described in detail in: *Sejm Czteroletni i jego tradycje* (The Four-Year Diet and its traditions), ed. Jerzy Kowecki (Warszawa: PWN, 1991), as well as in: *Konstytucja 3 Maja w tradycji i kulturze polskiej* (The Constitution of 3 May in Polish tradition and culture), ed. Alina Barszczewska-Krupa (Łódź: Wydawnictwo Łódzkie, 1991).

Leaflet commemorating the anniversary of the Constitution of 3 May issued in Piotrków in 1915. (Biblioteka Narodowa, Warszawa).

The central part of the Senate Chamber, reconstructed after WWII, at the Royal Castle in Warsaw, where the Constitution of 3 May 1791 was enacted and sworn in.

22

Two Revolutions: 1788-1792, 1980-1990

Piotr S. Wandycz

In the last two hundred years Poland went through two revolutions of a
very special kind. They were bloodless and marked by restraint, but their
nature was truly revolutionary in the sense of deep change they heralded
or brought about. Indeed Poland found herself in the international limelight,
and progressive public opinion hailed the developments as of greatest
importance. The first event culminated in the Constitution of 3 May, 1791.
Both friends and enemies called it a revolution and compared it to the American
and French Revolutions.[1] The second centered around the birth of the trade
union *Solidarność* which appeared as totally unprecedented. For the first time
the communists peacefully abandoned their monopoly of power to a movement
that grew out of a spontaneous workers' upheaval.

Is it possible to attempt a comparison between the eighteenth-century
Revolution and Solidarity? The two events occurred in totally divergent
historical contexts, had different aims and character. The first Revolution
brought about a constitutional act which survived for one year, but which
became an integral part of Polish history and legend. Already the reformers,
conscious of the importance of the 3 May document, declared the date a national
holiday and celebrated its first anniversary in 1792. Subsequent Polish
generations continued to revere 3 May. The Great Emigration commemorated
it annually.[2] After Poland recovered her independence, a decree issued on April
29, 1919, established 3 May as a national holiday. Eliminated by the
communists, 3 May was restored in 1989.

The Solidarity, outlawed under martial law after some sixteen months of existence, reemerged victorious, albeit in a changed form nearly eight years later. It is paradoxically both a part of the present and the past. Its story is too recent and it arouses too much passion to permit a detached and authoritative evaluation. Nevertheless, given the underlying perennial Polish problems and dilemmas, the temptation to compare these two momentous events is too great to resist. Such a comparison is bound to be incomplete, tentative, perhaps at times far-fetched. It will show contrasts as well as some parallels, but for all the pitfalls it may well be instructive.

To begin with the 3 May Revolution, did it represent a break with Poland's past? Did it seek to obliterate the native tradition in the name of European Enlightenment and modernization? Did it represent a "Europeanization" of Poland? While one can find divergent interpretations, the present consensus is that 3 May was essentially a reform of the existing system – a far-reaching and long-term reform – but not a denial of the Polish historical heritage and its constitutional "republican" model. Let us recall briefly the nature of this model and trace its degeneration to a point when a sweeping reform became imperative.

Crystallized by the fourteenth - sixteenth centuries the Polish* political system was based on the equilibrium between three factors: the King, the Senate, and the Chamber of Deputies.[3] This *forma mixta* was supposed to reflect a combination of the monarchic, the aristocratic and the democratic elements, although from a strictly socio-economic point of view the Polish society was composed of three estates: nobles, burghers and peasants. Politically, however, only the nobles (*szlachta*) constituted the nation. *Szlachta* was not simply an aristocracy and it did not constitute the wealthiest group in society. In fact, it ranged from poor landless freeman at the bottom of a socio-economic pyramid to a magnate controlling huge estates at the top. But taken as a whole it represented the political nation, or in other words active citizens. Since the *szlachta* amounted to some 8-10 percent of the total population, Poland had more voters than England before the 1832 Reform Bill or France under the Bourbon Restoration. The major difference was, of course, the criterion of active citizenship; in old Poland it was that of noble birth.

The official name of the state was *Rzeczpospolita,* in Latin *Respublica* which can best be translated as Commonwealth. The Polish nobleman, educated in classics, saw himself as a new *Civis Romanus,* and thought of the Commonwealth in terms of a Roman Republic. Indeed, as Robert Lord put it, the Commonwealth represented "the largest and the most ambitious experiment with a republican form of government that the world had seen since the days of the Romans."[4] A Polish historian remarked that it was "a political form of realization of *szlachta's* freedom."[5] Indeed, the key words of the Polish political dictionary were freedom *libertas,* and the law. "Our *libertas,* freedom and latitude of which we boast vis-à-vis other nations" wrote the Vice-Chancellor Piotr Myszkowski in the sixteenth century "does not consist in the expression of our will..., but in that we all serve the law."[6] A legal text of the period stated that "both the king and all the estates of the realm shall be subject to the law."[7]

The Polish constitutional system was praised by such great lawyers as Hugo Grotius, but it was difficult to operate. The perennial conflict between the monarchy and the noble nation, *maiestas* versus *libertas* was, of course, not a unique Polish phenomenon but common to most of Europe. Except for England, Holland or Switzerland, to cite the most obvious cases, it was resolved to the advantage of the ruler. In Poland the delicate equilibrium began to be disturbed by a threefold process: a weakening of the monarchic power of the elected kings; a weakening of political strength of the gentry manipulated by the magnates, and a growth of the might of the latter. The magnates profited most from economic developments and suffered least from the war damages of the fateful seventeenth century. They gained all that the kings had sought in vain: a sound financial base, a private army and a vast political clientele. Yet, they did not seek to establish a well-functioning oligarchic system based on the Senate. Instead they contributed to what a historian called a "decentralization of sovereignty" symbolized by the notorious *liberum veto.*

The political nation grew increasingly self-centered, xenophobic and believing in the unique virtue of the republican system clothed in a Sarmatian ideology. According to it, Europe needed the *Respublica* because it was its granary, its shield against the Eastern invaders, and its best political system. Increasingly the *szlachta* lived in a world of illusions. Having achieved what it regarded the best and freest form of government it refused to devise means to defend it. A standing army was opposed as a potential instrument of absolutism; the myth of 200,000 noble swords to defend freedom was utterly anarchronistic in the eighteenth century. The slogan of "no government" *nierządem Polska stoi* was elevated to a dogma.

The seventeenth-century wars accompanied by prolonged foreign occupation deepened the economic decline and plunged Poland into a state of chaos. In the early eighteenth century Tsar Peter the Great of Russia became an arbiter between the Saxon-born ruler and the noble nation. The country presented an increasingly sore picture. The election of kings was decided by foreign gold and foreign bayonets. The vain and powerful aristocracy appeared barbarian to West European observers. They also noted that the lot of the peasant was becoming worse and the status of the burghers was deteriorating. The state was treated as a "wayside inn" by foreign troops that freely traversed its territory. Even the Polish-Lithuanian dualism on which the Commonwealth was based - and which represented a successful example of a voluntary union of two countries - was becoming an element of weakness. The huge *Respublica* was unable to mobilize its power potential. This state of affairs was alarming a growing circle of reformers. "Poland is barely in the fifteenth century. All of Europe is finishing the eighteenth century," cried out in anguish one of the ideologies of reform Stanisław Staszic.[8] An impressive political literature which gained momentum as the eighteenth century progressed was diagnosing and denouncing the ills of the Commonwealth, political, social and economic. The ideas of the Enlightenment to mention only the concepts of natural right of man, social contract, the people as source of government, and the division of powers served as inspiration. In the famous quarrel between the "wig and the mustachio" the Polish westerners denigrated everything that was Polish, including language, dress and native tradition. They slavishly imitated French or English fashions. But as a native revival became evident in most fields economy, education, art and political thought, respect for national heritage grew. Thus, the Poland of King Stanisław August Poniatowski was hardly a passive recipient of Western Enlightenment. As the French historian Jean Fabre put it, "Under the ashes accumulated by the destitutions of the seventeenth century, and hardened by the Saxon negligence the centers of thought did not all die out. To rekindle the flame one needed just a breath of air, and it could come only from the West."[9]

Voltaire wrote that "for a state to be powerful, the people must either enjoy a freedom based on law or be led by a strong and unchallenged government."[10] Enlightened absolutism embodied the latter; the Polish reformers invoking the republican tradition turned to the first.[11] Prepared by and accompanied by an inspiring and high level polemical literature, the reformist movement centered its activities on the Great or Four-Year Diet (*Sejm*) which assembled in 1788. It proceeded first to dismantle the existing structures and then began to build a new constitutional model. Volumes have been devoted to the analysis of this process which we must sketch here in the briefest possible way. To begin with the international context, Europe in the 1780s was divided into two rival "systems:" one comprised Russia, Austria, France and Spain, the second England, Prussia, the Netherlands, Sweden and Turkey. Stanisław August sought initially to cooperate with the former, but his offer of joining Russia in her war against Turkey was turned down; Catherine did not want

Poland to strengthen her position. The King wanted to await the outcome of the Russo-Turkish war (joined by Austria), and complicated by the outbreak of the Swedish-Russian war in 1788. The two major Polish factions wanted action. The powerful Czartoryski *familia*, seconded by other magnates, advocated an alliance with Prussia and adherence to the English-sponsored anti-Russian front. The die-hard conservative party of Szczęsny Potocki, Branicki and Rzewuski continued to look up to St. Petersburg. The cautious Stanisław August was unable to resist the dynamic Diet "too strong a horse for his rider" as he put it.[12]

Indeed, the Diet dismantled the Permanent Council, hated as a Russian device for controlling Poland although it had had some reforms to its credit, and tried to govern the country through a number of commissions. At the same time it debated at great length the country's constitutional reform. The Diet's majority was anti-monarchic. The "false patriots," as they came to be called in distinction to the later emerging true patriots, clamored for republican solutions. Led by the above mentioned Szczęsny Potocki, Branicki and Rzewuski, they wished to preserve the old system and even extend it through further decentralization of authority (federalization) and possibly even the abolition of monarchy. While they constantly invoked the old slogans of "golden liberty" and *szlachta's* equality they aimed to increase the magnates' power. The true patriots although also led by magnates sought the opposite.

The patriotic leaders in the Diet such as Ignacy Potocki or Stanisław Małachowski were seconded by a lively pressure group which propagated the reformist ideas through political writings. Those of Hugo Kołłątaj, Staszic and Pawlikowski were the best known. Republicanism meant to them a system in which the monarch would become hereditary to ensure stability but he would reign and not rule. The real power would be in the Diet (not Senate) and the dietines. Their deputies would be chosen by an electorate from which the landless gentry – the traditional clientele of the magnates – would be excluded. This transition of the political nation from nobility to property owners was in keeping with West European trends. In Poland, however, one of the ways of associating the inferior estates with the political nation was to be through massive ennoblements.

For the first time the burghers representing over one hundred and forty royal towns became a pressure group on the Diet and a source of support for the reformers. The peasants were, of course, in no position to play any political role and while the reformers wanted to improve the lot of the serfs, they had to proceed with caution. This republican program of the patriots proved susceptible to changes which would bring it closer to the constitutional

monarchism of the English type which Stanisław August favored. By the end
of 1790 a compromise intervened and it was eventually embodied in the final
text of the constitution drafted by Kołłątaj. The document, let us repeat, was
not a rejection of the Polish constitutional past, but its radical reform. It also
took into account Montesquieu's principle of the division of powers, the
Constitution of the United States, and the French Declaration of the Rights
of Man and Citizen. In the words of the Marshal (speaker) of the Diet, Stanisław
Małachowski, the new Constitution surpassed the existing two glorious,
"republican" regimes, the English and the American. What were its salient
features?

The preamble provided the rationale:

Persuaded that our common fate depends entirely upon the establishing
and rendering perfect a national constitution; convinced by a long train
of experience of many defects in our government, and willing to profit
by the present circumstances of Europe... prizing more than life, and
every personal consideration, the political existence, external
independence, and internal liberty of the nation, whose care is entrusted
to us; desirous, moreover, to deserve the blessing and gratitude, not
only of our contemporaries, but also of future generations; for the sake
of the public good, for securing our liberty, and maintaining our
kingdom and our possessions; in order to exert our natural rights with
zeal and firmness, we do solemnly establish the present Constitution...

Article V affirmed that "All power in civil society should be derived from the
will of the people." In Article VII, we read that: "The happiness of the nation
depends on just laws, but the good effect of laws flows only from their execution.
Experience has taught us that neglecting this essential part of government has
overwhelmed Poland with disasters."[13]   Finally, in the words of Stanisław
August himself: "The true and only objective of a new form of government
was only that, insofar as it is humanly possible, all members of the Polish
nation would equally enjoy their share of freedom and the security of their
possessions."[14]

The Constitution of 3 May represented an interesting blend of constitutional
monarchism and Polish republicanism. It retained the division of the society
into estates but paved the way to a modern concept of the nation. To soften
the impact of reforms, to which the masses of the *szlachta* had to be won over,
socio-economic provisions were simply outlined, to be worked out in a separate
document.

The kingship became hereditary in order both to avoid the instability of
elections and to legitimize the Polish throne in the family of European

monarchs. The subjects could not refuse their allegiance to the ruler as in the past, but the monarch was no longer one of the three elements of government. He could call and dissolve the Diet but he lost the right of veto. His executive powers were diminished. He chose the ministers to sit in the Council called Guardians of the Laws *(Straż Praw)* but the latter were responsible legally and politically (a novelty by European standards) to the Diet, and they had to countersign royal decrees to make them binding. The Diet could recall a given minister, and it elected members of the commissions or collegiate ministries.

The Senate which was viewed as representing the magnates also lost some of its functions. It had no more legislative initiative and had only a limited veto. After the death of Stanisław August his successor could no longer freely name senators but would choose them from a list submitted by the dietines.

Under the Constitution the real power resided in the Diet in accordance with the republican model. The Diet would be henceforth elected by landowning *szlachta* who would not be bound by explicit instructions of their voters. It would also include a number of burgher representatives elected by property owners and watching mainly over the interests of towns. Naturally, the old *liberum veto* disappeared altogether.

The Constitution emphasized throughout the text the term "nation," beginning with the king, "by the Grace of God and the will of the Nation" and ending with the peasants as a class of people "the most numerous in the nation." It was the nation whether still equating the *szlachta* or in the long run embracing all inhabitants that was to be the sovereign to the detriment of the king and of the magnates. No drastic change in the position of the peasantry was possible at this point, and the Constitution spoke merely of contracts between landowners and peasants under the protection of the state. Not only conservative Polish nobles but even Jean-Jacques Rousseau in his *Considérations sur le gouvernement de Pologne* expressed his opinion that the peasantry had first to be educated before it could be fully emancipated.

The noble-burgher division was becoming blurred to the extent that the nobles could henceforth engage in trade, and if they resided in towns would fall under municipal jurisdiction. As for the burghers, they became beneficiaries of the *neminem captivabimus* provision – guarantee against arbitrary arrest. Kołłątaj envisaged an eventual merger of the burghers with the nobles through ennoblement. If realized it would have represented a specific Polish solution of the division into estates.

The 3 May document was to be complemented by two others: an economic and a moral (educational) constitution. This showed, as a German historian noted, that the reformers were attuned to the socio-economic realities, old criticism of Russian and Prussian historiography notwithstanding.[15] The economic constitution, which survived as an unfinished project, was to create, through state intervention, conditions for a freer flow of capital and goods. A peasant reform was to stimulate agricultural production and to create a labor market. A national bank extending low interest and long term credits was to introduce incentives for investments. A reform of the Church-owned estates was to regulate property relations.

While Catholicism was, according to the Constitution of 3 May, the "dominant national religion;" full toleration was extended to others. The Uniate Metropolitan received a seat in the Senate. A Jewish reform existed in a project stage.

The Constitution was adopted thanks to a determined minority which did exert some pressure on its opponents and took them by surprise (of which more later). But free discussion was allowed and decisions were taken by majority vote.[16] On May 5, the Constitution was endorsed even by the opponents which brought it further legitimization. In the course of the next twelve months the majority of the dietines were won over to the Constitution so that it was supported by the political nation as even its adversaries admitted. The fate of the 3 May Revolution depended, however, not on the Poles but on Poland's powerful neighbors, especially Catherine II, who made use of the Polish die-hard conservatives, Branicki, S. Potocki and Rzewuski who announced on May 14, 1792, in Targowica the creation of a Confederation. Both its place and the date were spurious: the document having been drawn up in St. Petersburg on April 27, and accepted there on Catherine's orders. The Targowica leaders also received Catherine's assurance that Poland would not be partitioned again, and called on her to intervene militarily to restore the old order. A Polish-Russian war began in 1792 in which the outnumbered troops of the Revolution (the 100,000 figure originally decreed by the Diet remained on paper) had little chance of winning the struggle. Still, the decision of the King supported by a majority in the Council to submit to Catherine and join the Targowica Confederation, which discredited Stanisław August, may have been a bad mistake. Here one is touching on one of the most hotly debated topics, the international context of the Polish Revolution.

The international constellation between 1788 and 1792, and especially the Prusso-Russian tension, had brought Poland a few years of freedom or maneuver albeit wrought with great dangers. Maneuvering with great finesse at home, Polish leadership did not prove equal to the diplomatic tasks. Was the alliance with Prussia a masterstroke or a major blunder? If the Poles wanted badly Berlin's support should they not have taken to heart Berlin's warnings?

The Prussians intimated that they would not defend a drastically reformed Commonwealth and they wanted territorial concessions: Gdańsk and Toruń. Unwilling to make any concessions the Poles founds themselves operating in a vacuum. Their situation grew worse when the anti-Russian course of Britain's policy suddenly collapsed. Could they have played better their hand in London?

In Vienna, Emperor Leopold and Chancellor Kaunitz were rather favorably disposed toward the changes in Poland and tried to persuade Russia that 3 May was likely to prevent the spreading of French revolutionary ideas. The court of Berlin was complimentary but in actual fact the events in Warsaw frightened its leaders. The old minister Hertzberg commented that the Poles, by adopting a constitution that was better than the English, and introducing a hereditary kingship were likely to become strong enough to threaten Prussia's security. With Berlin antagonistic, the key to the situation lay in St. Petersburg. On May 7, 1791, Stanisław August had felt that Branicki's acceptance of the offer to join the Council *(Straż)* was an indication "that Moscow will not declare war on us because of this revolution."[17] Historians disagree on whether Catherine was immediately determined to intervene militarily in Poland and was merely waiting for the end of the Turkish war, or was uncertain how to act. Was the view of Panin that Russia without the control over the Commonwealth "would lose one-third of her strength" and have her security threatened, still the prevailing opinion?[18] Or did the various groups and cliques fight for different options, and the decision to intervene was only taken in 1792?

Let us now turn from this brief survey of the 3 May Revolution to the recent times and the story of Solidarity. Coming into existence in 1980 at the Gdańsk shipyard, the Solidarity had its roots in developments that went back to the end of the Second World War. The communist system introduced in Poland in 1945 was a foreign transplant which the Polish organism eventually rejected. Being alien and unfree it went against the grain of the national character and heritage. But, as communism triumphed through fraud and terror over the populist-led Mikołajczyk opposition in 1946-7 it seemed destined to remain the determining factor in Poland for the foreseeable future. Internationally, the world division symbolized by Yalta had assigned Poland to the Soviet sphere; this also seemed to be more than a temporary arrangement. True, the Soviet handling of its bloc, the erection of the Iron Curtain, as Churchill called it, led to the Cold War between the West and the East. But whether American foreign policy operated under the sign of Containment or Liberation the chances of Poland and the so-called satellites recovering their freedom were slender.

Original illusions for some form of compromise under the communist regime were dispelled in the 1945-48 period, and for most Poles the choice was either collaboration, in one form or another, with the regime, inner emigration (meaning total withdrawal) or seeking freedom and political activity abroad. True, there were certain domains in which national energy and even enthusiasm could be channeled: rebuilding Warsaw and the devastated country, repopulating the Western Territories, spreading education and promoting some socio-economic reforms. With the advent of Stalinism, which brought trials, executions and terror, the main goal of a citizen of Poland was survival. This is why the change which came in 1956, during the "Polish October" was welcomed so enthusiastically. The objective of Party leaders such as Gomułka appeared to converge with popular and national aspirations. Only time was to show that the two were not identical. Two main ideological postures were the result of the "Polish October:" revisionism and what we may call, for want of a better word, Catholic positivism. The first postulated an evolution within the framework of Marxist ideology, a revision of practice rather than doctrine. Had not Gomułka himself spoken out against the "error and deformations" of the previous years? Had not one of his associates condemned "lunar economics"? The Catholic positivist position stood for limited involvement in politics – the Znak representation in the Diet – but without any ethical compromises. The group had not hesitated to pay the price for its refusal to print a eulogy of Stalin, namely the closing of its periodical *Tygodnik Powszechny,* and persisted in speaking the truth or remaining silent.

The fourteen years of Gomułka's rule gradually dispelled the illusions about the compromise between the nation and the Party. Witnessing a steady abandon of the ideals of the "Polish October," the period called into question the validity of revisionism. Was the communist system reformable at all? That was the issue. The year 1968 saw a domestic crisis in which the anti-intellectual and anti-Zionist (euphemism for anti-Jewish) campaign coincided with the participation of Polish troops in the invasion of Dubček's Czechoslovakia. Truncheons used against students in Warsaw and the tanks rumbling through Czechoslovak roads spelled the end of revisionism. A new workers' uprising caused (as that of Poznań in June 1956) by price increases rocked the Baltic ports in 1970. It was bloodily suppressed, but Gomułka had to go. It was characteristic of the prevailing situation that the shipyard workers fought alone, just as the intelligentsia had struggled in isolation two years earlier.

It took six years of Gierek's (Gomułka's successor) pragmatic and consumerist policies of building a "Second Poland" as he put it, to show that the plan did not work. All the unforeseen external difficulties apart, the

An envelope and a print commemorating the anniversary of the Constitution of 3 May illegally published by *Solidarność* 1985 and 1987. (Biblioteka Narodowa, Warszawa).

communist system absorbed a great deal of foreign credits, without bringing about a structural change for the better. Once again the workers protested and their 1976 riots were put down. But a significant change occurred. Jacek Kuroń's famous dictum: "do not burn Party's committees but create your own" found its expression in the emergence of the Committee for the Defense of Workers (KOR) followed later by other groups, for instance the Movement for Defense of the Rights of Man and Citizen (ROPCIO), a name with a historic ring to it. These new departures, particularly when KOR added to its name the letters KSS which stood for Committee for Social Self-Defense, meant that the dissidents were concentrating henceforth on building up civil society – the word acquired quickly a special meaning – outside of the state or the Party-ruled structures. In this respect the emphasis placed on human rights by the Helsinki Conference of 1975 and by the Carter Administration - in which Zbigniew Brzeziński favored an ideological offensive - proved of immense value to the anti-communist opposition. The latter insisted on the observance of the Helsinki provisions, and stressed the legality of its own activity. To prove that they operated within the law, the dissidents' names and addresses were prominently displayed in their publications.

Gierek, whose policy was tied to the existing international detente resorted to a relatively mild and selective harassment of the opposition. But if his regime appeared to have some neo-Stalinist features it was a Stalinism without terror, hence essentially ineffective and self-contradictory. Just as the revisionists have virtually disappeared from the scene – protesters would now sing the Polish anthem at their gathering rather than the "Internationale" – so the days of the Catholic positivism were also numbered. A neo-Znak group collaborating with the regime replaced the genuinely Catholic deputies in the Diet. These people lacked credibility as did that peculiar formation, PAX, which for a long time had sought to share power with the communists on the basis of a Marxist-Catholic ideology.

The position of the Catholic Church in communist Poland was special and unusual. Being the only organized independent force in the country the Church operated both as a transcendental force and a powerful institution with which Marxism-Leninism even if taken seriously could hardly compete. Cardinal Wyszyński, the Primate of Poland was a towering figure, and he knew how to combine iron will and determination with flexible tactics. Remaining at first in his shadow, and deliberately so, was the Metropolitan of Cracow and the second Polish cardinal Karol Wojtyła. His long-range impact on the Polish developments could hardly be overestimated.

During these years the traditionally anti-clerical democratic Left began a dialogue with the Church and its overtures were reciprocated. The books of Cywiński and Michnik marked the beginnings of this dialogue.[19] The common ground was the defense of freedom and human dignity endangered by the common enemy communism. The Church now spread its protective umbrella over the ideological, cultural, and artistic activities of the opposition. One could speak of a triple force the communists were now facing: the Church, the intelligentsia and the workers. The foundations of Solidarity were being laid. The election of Cardinal Wojtyła to the Holy See and his 1979 visit to Poland as Pope John Paul II marked another step in the evolution of the country. During the week of his stay communist Poland was but a shadow without substance; the millions of people who greeted the Pope and prayed with him crossed the barrier of fears. Characterizing the papal visit as a manifestation of "ideological pluralism" a sociologist tried to convince the Party that "Catholic masses" realized fully their political might and their alienation from the system. One can assume, he went on, that the Party "ceased to be a political alternative for the Poles."[20]

The story of Solidarity since its emergence as a trade union in the summer of 1980 until its destruction through the martial law of December 1981 has a large literature. All that can be attempted here is to recall the most important developments during these sixteen months and characterize the nature of the movement. The negotiations in the Lenin Shipyard in Gdańsk between the striking workers led by Lech Wałęsa and the governmental delegation resulted in an agreement advertized as having no victors or vanquished. Striking a patriotic tone, the governmental delegate spoke of an accord between Poles, hence fraternal and sincere. The reality was very different. The Gdańsk agreement permitted the creation of a free and self-governing trade union which in a short time comprised several million members, a huge and somewhat unmanageable organization. Unlike typical trade unions, *Solidarność*-because of the nature of the communist system - became much more than a representation of the workers for bargaining purposes. In order to become a genuine force outside the Party and independent of the Party, as well as a real spokesman and guarantor of a pluralistic civil society, Solidarity had to aim at a lasting transformation of the existing socio-economic and political system. Deliberately limiting its objectives so as to achieve a compromise with the Party and indirectly with the USSR, it did not seek to overthrow the Party's rule, but to limit its total nature. A historian of Solidarity called it a "mighty popular revolution, a bloodless revolution in which a defenseless society faced an armed power of a modern totalitarian state."[21] It was not only because of this obvious discrepancy between its own strength and that of the state, but also for reasons connected with its very ethos, that Solidarity eschewed violence and emphasized again and again the supremacy of dialogue over force. In its search for a basic renewal of the Polish society and state, it invoked the relevance of Christian ethics. Timothy Garton Ash called Solidarity a social crusade of national rebirth which constituted its strength and attraction. Another student of the movement spoke of it as a "broad front for all Polish citizens."[22]

Already the early demands of Solidarity during the Gdańsk negotiations went beyond narrow economic concerns of the workers. Solidarity postulated the curtailment of censorship, a certain pluralism in the mass media – for instance radio broadcast of the Sunday mass – the end of special privileges for the Party and security apparatus. Solidarity claimed the right to be consulted about crucial socio-economic decisions. The concept of "a self-limiting revolution" popularized by Staniszkis stemmed from the realization, well expressed by Adam Michnik, that Poland could not be governed either against the people or through the abolition of the communist rule. National independence and parliamentary democracy were, as he put it, far off goals, not an immediate objective.

If the notion of compromise was essential to Solidarity the nature of the compromise was differently perceived by individuals and groups within the movement. What is more the inimical attitude of the communist leadership and of the Soviet Union was pushing Solidarity toward a more radical stance. A series of confrontations that occurred was enlarging the domain of its activities and multiplying the points of friction. The difficulties encountered in registering Solidarity as a trade union focussed the attention on the legal system; the dramatic March 1981 clash in Bydgoszcz directed the attention to the militia; steady attacks by the government-controlled mass media made them a relevant issue for Solidarity. The movement had to fight for every concession and in the final analysis its only weapon was the strike. The union did not resort to a general strike after the Bydgoszcz incident, which to some leaders was a major mistake. Was Solidarity becoming too radical or not radical enough? While violence was avoided and Solidarity could boast that it harmed none of its adversaries, the situation in the country was becoming chaotic.

On December 13, 1981, General Jaruzelski who at this point united in his hands the functions of the first secretary, prime minister and commander-in-chief made the State Council impose martial law. This took everyone by surprise. Solidarity was outlawed; its leaders arrested and interned: a Military Council of National Salvation (WRON) assumed power. If Solidarity

Revolution could be termed mild, its suppression was also characterized by some restraint. Fewer people died than one could expect in this kind of a repressive action. But the nation was deeply humiliated and in the years to come found it difficult to forgive or to forget. Had Jaruzelski acted to avoid Soviet intervention or did he - like another controversial Polish statesman of the nineteenth century Margrave Wielopolski - feel that the movement must be broken because it was plunging the country into chaos? There undoubtedly were Soviet pressures and according to a later testimony by the Soviet foreign minister Sheverdnadze, there were people who favored intervention. But there was also apparently a growing realization in Moscow that an armed Soviet action would not resolve anything in the long run.[23] We shall never know which trend would have prevailed.

If Jaruzelski had expected that martial law would be followed by a normalization in which the government – the Party was increasingly pushed into the background – would gain legitimacy through limited reforms, he was mistaken. Attempts to enlarge the basis of the regime misfired; a Solidarity underground continued to operate; a deadlock ensued. In the long run the slogan "There is no Freedom without Solidarity" had to be recognized. With the Church acting as intermediary a round-table compromise was negotiated in the Spring of 1989. Solidarity was restored although it was no longer the same as of nine years ago, and elections were held to the newly created Senate and to a number of seats in the Diet – the result was a Solidarity landslide. Although the movement had at first no intention of assuming power, the formula of Adam Michnik: "Our premier – your president" was eventually accepted. A cabinet comprising some communists and their former allies and Solidarity leaders headed by Tadeusz Mazowiecki came into being. It was an unprecedented case of communists abandoning power without armed resistance.

This second phase of the 1980-1990 revolution differed considerably from the first. Seeking to alter drastically the economic as well as the political system, Solidarity began to build a pluralistic, free market society. But the newly won freedom had a bitter taste. Living conditions became harsh for many, a struggle for ideas became a struggle for power. This may have been an inevitable process, seen in many revolutions, but it harmed severely the Solidarity ethos and its image. What is more, Polish events merged in a sense in a total transformation of East Central Europe, the *annus mirabils* of 1989. A postcommunist trauma spread throughout the whole region bringing similar problems and a mixture of hope and depression.

Let us return now to the original question: can one compare the two revolutions separated by two hundred years and occurring in vastly different conditions? There are certainly some features which, if not analogous, permit drawing interesting parallels. As already noted the Constitution of 3 May and *Solidarność* were based on the notions of compromise and non-violence. The former embodied the monarcho-republican and a socially moderate model; the latter insisted on its self-limiting nature. In the 1989 phase of Solidarity a search for compromise was evident in the round-table negotiations and accord. Kołłątaj referred to 3 May as *pacifica rivoluzione*;[24] the Solidarity leaders emphasized that not one window was broken during the sixteen months of 1980-81. If moderation was dictated by pragmatic considerations of not antagonizing Russia – one can draw parallels between the appointment of Branicki to the Council (*Straż*) and of Kiszczak to the Mazowiecki cabinet – the Solidarity ethos played a conspicuous role in the pacific attitude. True, the Constitution of 3 May was passed by means that were revolutionary in the sense of stretching the rules and overawing the opponents by a display of strength. Małachowski justified it by saying that grave danger demanded drastic remedies.[25] Except for some radical verbosity in the last stages of Solidarity prior to the martial law, one cannot readily find comparable situations. One sees rather some contrasts as one examines subsequent events. There was popular retribution against the Targowica leaders during the Kościuszko Insurrection, while Jerzy Urban seen by many as the symbol of martial law has continue to thrive. But, here one enters a realm in which analogies tend to be far fetched or non-existent.

Both revolutions were influenced, although in different ways by contemporary Western trends. This is particularly striking in the case of the Constitution of 3 May which is very much a document of the Enlightenment albeit impregnated with native Polish concepts.[26] One of the characteristic features of the document is its didactic, almost propagandistic tone. The reformers were using the text to explain basic ideas of modern government. The inspiration of the French philosophers is obvious. To give a concrete example, Article IV, which deals with the peasantry, is couched in a language permeated with the French physiocratic concept that land is the source of riches and so is the work performed on it.[27] Perhaps the only analogies that come to mind are the conceptions of the value of work developed by Father Józef Tischner, the "bishop of Solidarity" and the Papal Encyclical *Laborem Exercens*.[28] In the 1980s Rome rather than Paris was the source of inspiration.

While the Catholic Church was ever present in Solidarity – the crosses and open Masses in the Gdańsk shipyard amazed Western observers – Freemasonry was very influential in the 1789 Revolution. Since this has been a much debated issue, exploited demagogically by some opponents of the Constitution, it seems worthwhile to recall Władysław Konopczyński's appraisal: "[Freemasonic] lodges cultivated humanitarianism and moderate rationalism, spreading West European education through Poland's arteries; and in this lies their undoubted merits."[29] The term "civil society," which figured so prominently in the political vocabulary of Solidarity, can be found in Article V of the Constitution although this is a translation of the Polish term *społeczność ludzka*. Still, one can argue that the republican civil society helped the nation to survive the age of partitions by contrasting social identity of the Poles with the foreign state. As we know, the concept of civil society was crucial in the development of "dissent" in the 1970s. The Helsinki declaration on human rights played here a very important role.

It is clear that both in the case of the 1791 Revolution and in the 1989 phase of Solidarity the notion of Poland "returning to Europe" was of great significance.[30] True, and it bears repeating, the reformers of 3 May as well as Mazowiecki in his address to the Council of Europe in Strasbourg, on January 30, 1990, emphasized that Poland did not have to return to Europe because it was part of Europe. But the two notions coexisted. The "return" meant really overcoming the long years of corruption and demoralization: the Saxon rule of six decades and the forty-five years of communist government. Is the Pole of the Saxon era and the *homo sovieticus* a comparable figure? In some ways, yes. There are other developments in which one may perceive similarities and contrasts. The emergence of the first modern political party – the Friends of the Constitution *(Klub Przyjaciół Konstytucji)* – may at first glance seem comparable to the Solidarity parliamentary representation (OKAP) which was called into life to support the Mazowiecki government. Still, the two were very different bodies. Was the project of selling the royal lands *(królewszczyzny)* to private individuals a forerunner of present-day reprivatization? One must be careful lest such search for analogies lead us astray.

The question of a return to Europe is linked with what may be the most important and fruitful area in which analogies and contrasts can be shown – the international context of the two revolutions. In the case of the 1791 Revolution the beginnings, as already pointed out, were favorable to Poland's emancipation from Russia. This was hardly the case in 1980 when the Brezhnev regime still subscribed to its doctrine of intervention in the countries of the Socialist Bloc. Did the May reformers and Solidarity seek to establish some form of dialogue with Russia, or were the two movements bound to be seen as provoking the Big Brother? One may argue that neither the diplomacy of

1788-92 nor that of 1980-81 was farsighted and adroit. Russia was bound to be antagonized by the demands to withdraw her troops from the territory of the Commonwealth, and by Solidarity's appeal to the workers of the Bloc to support Poland's struggle. But did this really change anything? Would an attempt by Solidarity to convince Moscow that their movement was no threat to Soviet security likely succeed? The situation changed drastically with the advent of Gorbachev and his realization that reform was the only solution for communist-ruled countries. The May 1791 reformers did not have the same chance, although some historians have argued that if the Poles had proceeded slowly and cautiously their cause may have been saved by the 1796 death of Catherine and the advent of the pro-Polish tsar Paul. This hypothesis like any similar argument based on "what-would-have-happened-if" theory is of limited value to the historian.[31]

In 1790 the Commonwealth counted on the Prussian alliance and cooperation with the West which proved illusory. Solidarity's expectations concerning American assistance were to some extent and in the long-run justified, if we think of policies of Carter and Reagan, the input of Zbigniew Brzeziński and the mediatory role of the U.S. ambassador to Warsaw, John R. Davis. But it was the combination of such moves as the American sanctions and Gorbachev's *glasnost* and *perestroika* that provided the room of maneuver that did not exist in 1792.

Could the Russian military intervention of 1792 have been avoided? Are there any analogies between Targowica and the martial law of Jaruzelski? It seems clear that Stanisław August hoped to avoid a war with Russia and believed that a solution could be found through negotiations. He refused to continue the struggle, admittedly hopeless in the long run but perhaps providing Warsaw with means of bargaining, and chose capitulation. He refused to give up hope that he could thus save the country. The price he paid – the tearing up of the Constitution and the adherence to the Targowica Confederation – tarnished his image in the eyes of the Poles. Even today the figure of Stanisław August arouses passions; and those who point to his many talents and accomplishments are confronted with those who regard any defense of the King as justification of treason.

General Jaruzelski avoided a Soviet intervention – assuming that such intervention was likely and there is no consensus[32] – through the imposition of martial law. The latter had long-range effects, particularly psychological. It is likely that the General, like the last King of Poland, is destined to remain a tragic and controversial figure in Polish history. Some analogies between him and Stanisław August, despite the fact that the two men offered a complete physical and mental contrast, suggest themselves. There is the Russian link early in their careers, and subsequent close ties with the Russian/Soviet establishments. Stanisław August was disliked and despised as a *homo novus* who owed his crown to Catherine II. He briefly gained popularity during the 3 May Revolution, and his rule was extolled for bringing Enlightenment to the country. His fall was all the harder. General Jaruzelski, seen as a military and not a Party man, and credited with having refused to use the army against the workers in 1970, aroused some expectations. Condemned by all in December 1981, he regained a certain respect for his role in the "soft landing" of 1989. The degree of his present popularity or lack thereof as reflected in opinion polls - is debatable. It is clear, however, that the intensity of hatred he arouses in some quarters is comparable to the antagonism felt by certain people toward the last King of Poland.

There may be room for attempting other analogies concerning Poland's "return to Europe," for instance the pro-Prussian stance in 1790 and the rapprochement with Germany in 1990. Be it as it may, a comparison of the European, indeed world dimension of the impact of the two Polish revolutions, offers undoubtedly many interesting parallels.

The deliberations of the Great Diet and the reforms it was voting attracted wide attention of the neighboring countries and of the West. In Hungary which in 1790 reached a crisis in reaction to Joseph II's Enlightened absolutism, the Polish example was invoked. Edmund Burke compared the Polish and French revolutions and he praised the former for its moderation, gradualism and foresight. Condorcet, Sieyès and a host of leading figures in France lauded Poland. *Gazette of the United States* of Philadelphia wrote about the "recent and important Revolution in favor of the rights of man ... begun without violence and tumult." Praises of this "most wonderful revolution" filled American journals and the poet Joel Barlow celebrated Stanisław August in a poem which ended with the words: "[the king] leads a realm from darkness into day." The Pope sent a congratulatory letter to Warsaw; the *London Critical Review* comparing Polish, French and American constitutions, opined that the Poles had "caught the spirit" from the Americans. Viennese salons applauded the constitution, and so did Danish and Dutch statesmen. Stanisław August was somewhat nonplussed by the praise, especially when coming from revolutionary France, and he tried to distance himself and the Polish Constitution from the suspicion of a "Jacobin" spirit. For the neighboring powers the Polish Revolution was a threat to monarchic absolutism. Neither Prussia, Russia nor Austria had elected parliamentary bodies comparable in power to the Polish Diet as envisaged by the Constitution of 3 May. None of them contemplated the kind of socio-economic reforms that Poland did. None had such self-government in towns and such possibilities for the burghers to acquire land and eventually move into the noble class. May 3, 1791, was revolutionary in its East Central European context.[33]

The highest accolade was to be bestowed by Karl Marx who wrote: "Despite its shortcomings, this constitution looms up against the background of Russo-Prusso-Austrian barbarism as the only work of liberty that Eastern Europe has ever accomplished independently. And it emerged exclusively from the privileged class, from the nobility. The history of the world has never seen another example of such noble behavior of the nobility."[34]

The successful strike in the Gdańsk shipyard in 1980 and the unfurling of the Solidarity banner impressed the outside world more than most other events in recent memory. Headlines such as *ex Oriente lux* which highlighted the unprecedented victory of the workers in a communist society, appeared in many Western newspapers.[35] The Solidarity ethos gained the ecstatic approval of an American journalist who wrote that this "was a movement that lived by breathing the openness it exhaled."[36] Poland during the first Solidarity interlude, commented a British historian, "showed that it is a repository of moral ideas and ancient values that can outlast any number of military or political catastrophes."[37] He tended to agree with a Polish view that "Solidarity was the product of the best features of the democratic traditions of the gentry."[38] A Czechoslovak historian living abroad, Milan Hauner, marveled that this was "the only spontaneous and genuine working-class revolution which had ever occurred in history, directed against the 'socialist' state governed by bureaucrats (in the name of but, in reality against the working class) and carried under the sign of the cross and with the blessing of the Pope."[39] Apart from the expected attacks coming from the neighboring communist states which feared the Solidarity virus, there were some misgivings also in the West. As the Polish Revolution reached a critical stage in late 1981, fears of chaos and international complications became more visible. Hence, there was an audible sigh of relief in certain West European quarters (especially the financial establishment) after Jaruzelski's martial law made "order reign in Warsaw" once again.

The defeat of Solidarity in 1981, its rebirth in 1989, and its assumption of power in Poland allows us to place the Polish Revolution in a broader perspective. For all its great achievements, Solidarity had also its weaknesses. Still, its role as a catalyst in the former Eastern Bloc has been conspicuous. In a broad sense, writes a student of this period, "the workers of the Baltic Coast opened a prison door that all the peoples of the East have come crowding through."[40] And a leading chronicler and analyst of East Central and Polish revolutions concludes: "No country did more for the cause of liberty in Europe in the 1980s, and no country paid a higher price."[41] This seems a fitting epitaph for Solidarity and a proper ending to this paper which tried to compare it with the event that occurred two hundred years ago.

Notes

*The term Polish and Poland is not used here in an ethnic sense. Eighteenth-century Poland was a multi-ethnic Polish-Lithuanian Commonwealth.

1. The term "revolution" appears, for instance both in the Russian propaganda tract, *Mémoire sur la révolution de Pologne* (St. Petersbourg, 1791), and in articles about the "Happy Revolution" in Poland, in West European and American journals.

2. See *Konstytucja 3 maja 1791 w tradycji Towarzystwa Historyczno-Literackiego w Paryżu w latach 1832-1861: obchody, mowy, relacje* (The Constitution of 3 May 1791 in the tradition of the Historical-Literary Society in Paris in the years 1832-1861: commemoration, addresses, reports) (Paris, 1991).

3. As a contemporary put it in "our country in some strange and unusual way a mixture of three forms of government had formed." Cited in Jaroslaw Pelenski, "Muscovite Russia and Poland-Lithuania 1450-1600: State and society—some comparisons in socio-political developments," in Jaroslaw Pelenski, ed., *State and Society in Europe XV-XVIII* (Warszawa: PWN, 1985), p. 113.

4. Charles H. Hoskins and Robert H. Lord, *Some Problems of the Peace Conference* (Cambridge, MA, Harvard University Press, 1920), p. 160.

5. Jan Kieniewicz in Michał Tymowski, Jan Kieniewicz, Jerzy Holzer, *Historia Polski* (The history of Poland) (Paris: Editions Spotkania, 1986), p. 151.

6. Cited in Bogusław Leśnodorski, *Konstytucja 3 maja jako dokument oświecenia* (The Constitution of 3 May as a document of the Enlightenment) (Warszawa: Czytelnik, 1946), p. 39.

7. Cited in Manfred Kridl, Władysław Malinowski and Józef Witlin, eds., *For Your Freedom and Ours: Polish Progressive Spirit through the Centuries* (New York: Frederick Ungar Publishing Company, 1943), p. 32.

8. Cited in Jerzy Michalski, "Sarmatyzm a europeizacja Polski w XVIII wieku" (Sarmatism and the europeanization of Poland in the 18th century) in *Swojskość i cudzoziemszczyzna w dziejach kultury polskiej* (Warszawa: PWN, 1973), p. 163. The author also quotes a poem "Oda do Polaków" dated 1792 which says:

Gdy się u obcych przemysł rozpościerał
Polak był istnym prostakiem
Z tym wszystkim mniemał w uprzedzeniu dumny

Że obcy nie wart, a on sam rozumny."

9. Jean Fabre, *Stanislas-Auguste Poniatowski et l'Europe des lumières* (Paris: Les Belles Lettres, 1952), p. 69.

10. Cited in Fritz R. Stern, ed., *The Varieties of History: From Voltaire to the Present* (New York: Meridian Books, 1956), p. 43.

11. As a foremost Polish historian put it: "Modernization of the state carried out in the eighteenth century not through reforms from above... but adopted in the hum of debate in a chamber of deputies was an unusual political experiment in this part of Europe." Emanuel Mateusz Rostworowski, *Popioły i korzenie: szkice historyczne i rodzinne* (Ashes and roots: Historical and familial essays) (Kraków: Znak, 1983), p. 134.

12. Cited in Rostworowski, *Popioły,* p. 163.

13. See *New Constitution of the Government of Poland, established by the Revolution the Third of May, 1791* (2nd. ed. London, 1791, reprinted in 1991 by the Royal Castle in Warsaw and by the Embassy of the Republic of Poland in Washington), respectively pp. 3-4 and 19.

14. Speech of May 3, 1792 cited in Emanuel Rostworowski, *Maj 1791 - Maj 1792. Rok monarchii konstytucyjnej* (May 1791-May 1792: One year of the constitutional monarchy) (Warszawa: Zamek Królewski w Warszawie, 1985), p. 17.

15. See Jörg K. Hoensch, *Sozialverfassung und politische Reform. Polen im vorrevolutionären Zeitalter* (Köln: Wien: Böhlau, 1973).

16. In the words of Władysław Konopczyński "A new system was granted to the country, as is usually the case, by a goal oriented minority; nevertheless, the rights of the majority were preserved...after a frank discussion, but not without the exertion of pressure, and a surprise for those participating in the voting," Konopczyński, *Dzieje Polski nowożytnej* (The history of modern Poland), 2nd ed. (London: B. Świderski, 1959), vol. 2, p. 383.

17. Letter to Bukaty, cited in Kazimierz Bartoszewicz, *Konstytucja 3 maja. Kronika dni kwietniowych i majowych w Warszawie w roku 1791* (The Constitution of 3 May: The chronicle of the April and May days in Warsaw, 1791, 3rd ed.: (Warszawa: Epoka, 1989), p. 168.

18. Cited in Robert H. Lord, *The Second Partition of Poland. A Study in Diplomatic History* (Cambridge Harvard Univ. Press, 1915), p. 47.

19. Respectively Bohdan Cywiński, *Rodowody niepokornych* (Genealogy of the unbowed) (Warszawa: Więź, 1971) and Adam Michnik, *The Church and the Left* (Chicago: The University of Chicago Press, 1993).

20. The sociologist Jan Szczepański cited in Jerzy Holzer, *"Solidarność" 1980-1981. Geneza i historia* (Solidarity 1980-1981. Its origin and history) (Paris: Instytut Literacki, 1984), pp. 62-63.

21. Holzer, *Solidarność*, p. 352.

22. Roman Laba in *The Roots of Solidarity: A Political Sociology of Poland's Working-Class Democratization* (Princeton: Princeton University Press, 1991).

23. See Adam Michnik - Sheverdnadze conversation reprinted from *Gazeta Wyborcza* by *Nowy Dziennik*, April 10, 1991.

24. See Hubert Izdebski, "Political and Legal Aspects of the Third May 1791 Constitution," in Michał Rozbicki, ed., *European and American Constitutionalism in the Eighteenth Century* (Warszawa: American Studies Center, Warsaw University, 1990), p. 106.

25. "W gwałtownym niebezpieczeństwie gwałtownego należy chwycić się lekarstwa." Cited in Emanuel Rostworowski: *Ostatni król Rzeczypospolitej* (Warszawa: Wiedza Powszechna, 1966), p. 235.

26. As a prominent German historian put it: "Neben gemässigt aufklärerischen Zügen hatte die Verfassung von 3 Mai somit besondere polnische Eigenheiten, die es schwierig, ja nahezu unmöglich machten, sie als Beispiel für die Nachbarn aufzufassen." Gotthold Rhode, *Geschichte Polens. Ein Überblick* (Darmstadt: Wissenschaftliche Buchgesellschaft, 1980) p. 321.

27. See comments in *Historia państwa i prawa Polski* (History of the Polish state and its laws), ed. Juliusz Bardach, vol.2 *Od Połowy XV wieku do 1795* (Warszawa: PWN, 1966), pp. 524-26.

28. See Józef Tischner, *Polski kształt dialogu* (The Polish form of the dialogue) (Paris: Editions Spotkania, 1981); *Polska jest ojczyzną* (Poland is the motherland) (Paris, 1985); *Etyka Solidarności* (The ethics of Solidarity) (Kraków: Znak, 1981).

29. Cited in Leśnodorski, *Konstytucja,* p. 68.

30. Prince Adam Czartoryski declared in 1835 that May 3 had erased old Polish errors and linked the Polish cause "with the fate of progress and European civilization forever." *Konstytucja 3 maja 1791 w tradycji Towarzystwa...* p. 43

31. See the chapter entitled "Co byłoby gdyby ..." (What would it be if ...?) in Rostworowski, *Maj 1791 - Maj 1792*, pp. 27-33.

32. See Michnik-Sheverdnadze conversation.

33. For citations and general appraisal see R.R. Palmer, *The Age of the Democratic Revolution* (Princeton: Princeton University Press, 1959), vol. 1, pp. 429-32.

34. Cited in Andrzej Walicki, *The Enlightenment and the Birth of Modern Nationhood: Polish Political Thought from Noble Republicanism to Tadeusz Kościuszko* (Notre Dame, IN: University of Notre Dame Press, 1989). p. 108. Slight linguistic changes by this author.

35. See for instance, Reed M. Smith, "The Treatment of the Polish Crisis in the American Press," *Polish Review,* 30, 1 (1985): 81-97.

36. Lawrence Weschler, *The Passion of Poland* (New York: Pantheon, 1984), p. 92.

37. Norman Davies, *The Heart of Europe: A Short History of Poland* (Oxford, New York: Oxford University Press, 1984), p. 462.

38. Wojciech Karpiński cited in Stanisław Gomułka and Antony Polonsky, eds. *Polish Paradoxes* (London: New York: Routledge, 1991), p. 3.

39. Hauner, "Prague Spring" in Norman Stone and Eduard Strouhal, eds., *Czechoslovakia Crossroads and Crises* (London: Macmillan, BBC, 1989), p. 208.

40. Laba, *Roots of Solidarity,* p. 182.

41. Timothy Garton Ash, "Poland After Solidarity," *The New York Review of Books.* June 13, 1991.

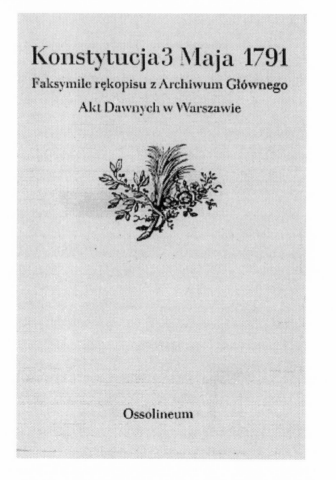

Faksimile edition of the manuscript of the Constitution of 3 May published in 1991 in commemoration of its 200th anniversary. Title page.

Index